南京大学历史学院资助

東學西問

张良仁 著

中国社会科学出版社

图书在版编目（CIP）数据

东学西问 / 张良仁著. —北京：中国社会科学出版社，2021.8
ISBN 978-7-5203-8988-4

Ⅰ.①东… Ⅱ.①张… Ⅲ.①考古学—文集 Ⅳ.①K87-53

中国版本图书馆 CIP 数据核字（2021）第 169914 号

出 版 人	赵剑英
责任编辑	郭 鹏　李金涛
责任校对	刘 俊
责任印制	李寡寡

出　　版	中国社会科学出版社
社　　址	北京鼓楼西大街甲 158 号
邮　　编	100720
网　　址	http://www.csspw.cn
发 行 部	010-84083685
门 市 部	010-84029450
经　　销	新华书店及其他书店
印刷装订	北京君升印刷有限公司
版　　次	2021 年 8 月第 1 版
印　　次	2021 年 8 月第 1 次印刷
开　　本	787×1092　1/16
印　　张	39
插　　页	7
字　　数	668 千字
定　　价	228.00 元

凡购买中国社会科学出版社图书，如有质量问题请与本社营销中心联系调换
电话：010-84083683
版权所有　侵权必究

彩图 1　A toilet-box from Tomb No. 3 at Mawangdui in Changsha city, Hunan province, early Western Han, diameter 24.1cm, height 16.9cm, in the Hunan Provincial Museum

(Extracted from Fu, Juyou, *Zhongguo Qiqi Quanji*, Fuzhou: Fujian Meishu, 1998, Vol. 3 pl. 78; reproduced with permission from the Fujian Meishu Chubanshe)

彩图 2　A toilet-box from Tomb No. 1 at Sanjiaoxu in Tianchang county, Anhui province, middle Western Han, diameter 9.9cm, height 9.5cm, in the Tianchang Museum

(Extracted from Fu, Juyou, 1998, *Zhongguo Qiqi Quanji*, Vol. 3, Fuzhou: Fujian Meishu, pl. 194; reproduced with permission from the Fujian Meishu Chubanshe)

彩图 3　A case from Longshenggang in Guangzhou City, Guangdong province, Eastern Han, diameter 8.2cm, height 12.5cm, in the Guangzhou Museum

(Extracted from Fu, Juyou, *Zhongguo Qiqi Quanji*, Fuzhou: Fujian Meishu, Vol. 3, 1998, pl. 298; reproduced with permission from the Fujian Meishu Chubanshe)

彩图 4　A platter from a tomb at Xinqiao in Qingzhen county, Guizhou province, Yuanshi year 4 (AD 4), diameter 27.2cm, height 4.1cm, in the Guizhou Provincial Museum

(From Fu, Juyou, *Zhongguo Qiqi Quanji*, Fuzhou: Fujian Meishu, 1998, Vol. 3, pl. 293; reproduced with permission from the Fujian Meishu Chubanshe.)

彩图 5　An ear-cup from a tomb at Yalongba in Qingzhen county, Guizhou province, Yuanshi year 3 (AD 3), diameter 16.6cm, height 3.8cm, in the Guizhou Provincial Museum.

(From Fu 1998a, pl. 292; reproduced with permission from the Fujian Meishu Chubanshe.) (A color version of this figure is available at journals.cambridge.org/ASI)

彩图 6　A jar from Tomb No. 101 at Yaozhuang, Hanjiang county, Jiangsu province, late Western Han, diameter 7.8cm, height 6.9cm, in the Yangzhou Museum

(Extracted from Fu, Juyou, *Zhongguo Qiqi Quanji*, Fuzhou: Fujian Meishu, Vol. 3, 1998, pl. 260; reproduced with permission from the Fujian Meishu Chubanshe)

彩图 7　罗汉像，藏于 Los Angeles County Museum of Art。画家不详，15 世纪上半叶。唐卡，纸质上施矿物颜料和金粉。尺寸为 64.77 × 53.98 厘米
（Los Angeles County Museum of Art，Photo © Museum Associates/ LACMA）

彩图 8 "弥勒在兜率天"壁画，江孜菩提塔。画家不详，1427—1440 年

[引自 Ricca, Franco, and Erberto Lo Bue, *The Great Stupa of Gyantse: A Complete Tibetan Pantheon of the fifteenth Century*, London: Serindia Publications, 1993, pl. 37（Ricca Franco 教授提供图片使用权）]

彩图 9 "觉密"壁画，江孜菩提塔东北四号龛。画家不详，1427—1440 年

（引自 Ricca, Franco, and Erberto Lo Bue, *The Great Stupa of Gyantse: A Complete Tibetan Pantheon of the fifteenth Century*, London: Serindia Publications, 1993, pl. 105, Ricca Franco 教授提供图片使用权）

彩图 10　杨洪（1381—1451）像，藏于 Freer Gallery of Art and Arthur M. Sackler Gallery, Smithsonian Institution, Washington, D. C.。画家不详，作于 1451 年前后。立轴，丝质，施墨和色。尺寸为 220.8×127.5 厘米

（Freer Gallery of Art and Arthur M. Sackler Gallery 提供照片和使用权）

彩图 11　"转法轮"壁画，白居寺。画家不详，15 世纪上半叶

［引自金维诺主编《中国壁画全集》第 34 卷，《藏传寺院壁画》第 4 册，彩页 84（金维诺教授提供图片使用权）］

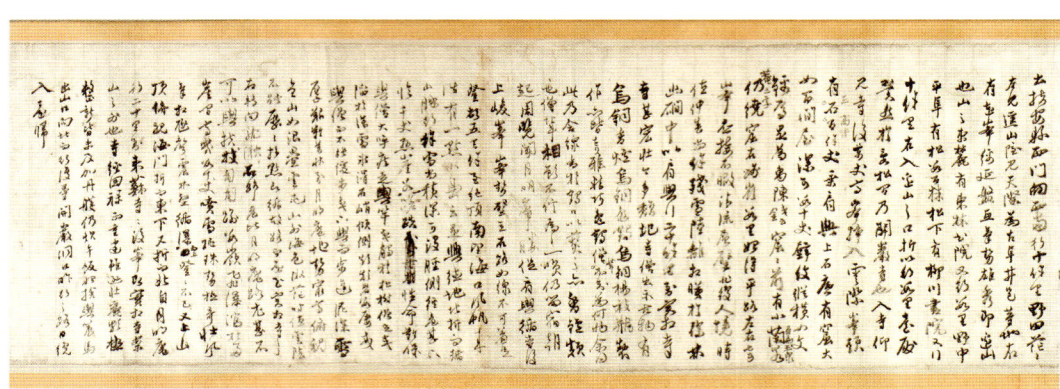

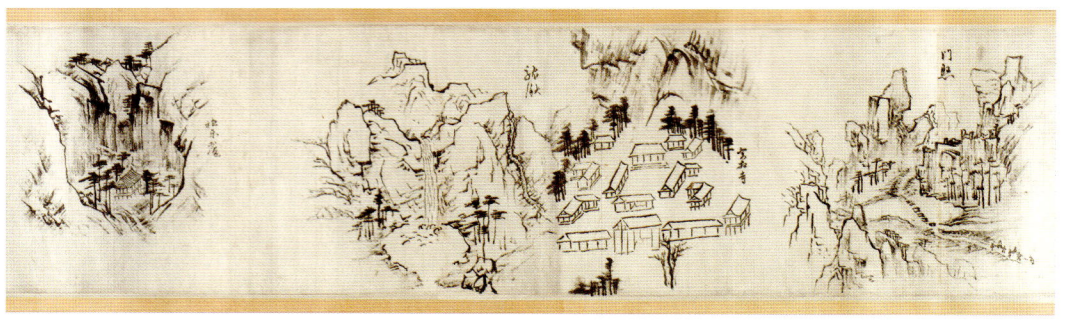

彩图 12　Kang Sehwang, *Scenes of Puan Prefecture*, handscroll, ca. 1770, **ink on paper**, 25.4 × 267.3 厘米

(Los Angeles County Museum of Art, Los Angeles. Photo © Museum Associates/ LACMA)

彩图 13　**Map of Puan Prefecture** 1747–1750

(*Haedong Chido*, Seoul: Seoul National University, Kyujanggak, Vol. 2, 1995, p. 22)

彩图 14　Kang Sehwang, "Yŏngt'ong-dong"

(From *Journey to Songdo*, ca. 1757, ink and light color on paper, 32.8×53.4cm, photo©The National Museum of Korea, Seoul)

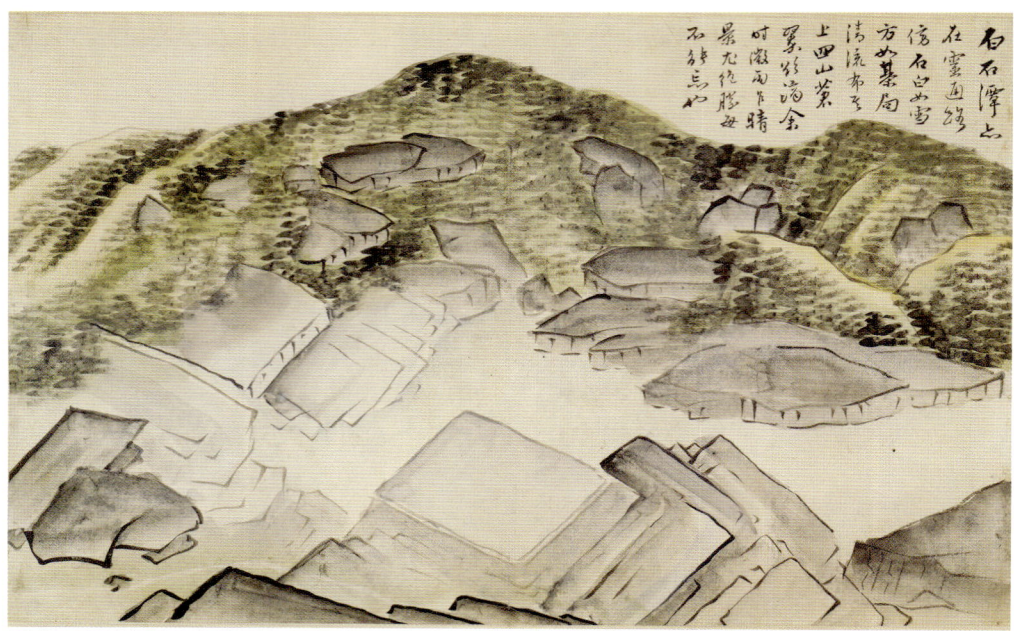

彩图 15　Kang Sehwang, "Paeksŏk-dam"

(From *Journey to Songdo*, ca. 1757, ink and light color on paper, 32.8×53.4cm, photo©The National Museum of Korea, Seoul)

彩图 16　Kang Sehwang, "Yizhaimiao"

(Album leaf from *Journey to China*, 1784, ink on paper, 26.5 x 22.5cm, photo ⓒ Sŏngbo Museum, Tongdosa)

彩图 17　阿拉木图附近的伊塞克（Issyk）塞克人墓地出土的金人，哈萨克斯坦的中央历史博物馆大厅展出（盖伯利尔摄）

彩图 18　新西伯利亚考古与民族研究所陈列的卡尔金冢复原像（张良仁摄）

彩图 19　纳德利土丘雪景（佚名摄）

彩图 20　伊斯兰时期的仿华青花陶（阿里·瓦赫达提摄）

自　　序

每一个人的成长之路都是独特的，我也是如此。我出生于浙江西部的农村，祖辈都是农民，没有家学渊源，自然没有做学问的基因，也没有当学者的志向。我小时候身体弱，干不了农活，父母的愿望就是我考上大学，跳出农门，学什么都可以。但是因缘巧合，我还是走上了研究之路。1987年考大学那年，因为分数不够，调剂进了考古系，学了闻所未闻的考古学。1991年大学毕业后进入中国社会科学院考古研究所工作，分到商周室，先后参加了陕西省长安县（现西安市长安区）沣西、河南省偃师县二里头的发掘工作。那些年经费短缺，所以发掘工作不多。1993年就进入中国社会科学院研究生院读硕士，师从殷玮璋教授，1996年获得了硕士学位，毕业后参加了偃师商城宫城的发掘工作。

照这样下去，我将是个商周考古方面的专家。可惜我骨子里是个不安分的人，想换个方向。当时在商周考古领域，大家写的大多是夏商文化分界、先周文化、偃师商城性质之类的论文，我自己的硕士论文的题目是"试论二里头文化的分期和性质"。关于这些选题前辈们已经写了不少，新意难寻，想找新选题又缺乏灵感，所以决定出国留学，并且改学外国考古。2000年，我很幸运地去了美国的加州大学洛杉矶分校留学，跟随罗泰（Lothar von Falkenhausen）教授。罗泰教授是个中国考古学家，但是他让我学俄罗斯考古。因此除了英语，我又学了俄语，开始跑俄罗斯。2007年我用俄罗斯乌拉尔山和中国安阳的考古资料完成了博士论文，获得了博士学位。

我的博士论文 Ancient Society and Metallurgy[①]的核心就是针对国内外

[①] Liangren Zhang, *Ancient Society and Metallurgy: A Comparative Study of Bronze Age Societies in Central Eurasia and North China*, Archaeopress, 2012.

◇❖◇ 自 序

考古学界关心的社会复杂化问题提出了一个新理论，用俄罗斯青铜时代和中国商代的考古资料加以验证。该书一方面以村落和宗族为单位来研究欧亚大陆社会复杂化进程，而不同于以往国外理论流派以个人（如部落、酋邦和国家首领）为中心的思路，另一方面一反西方人类学家热衷的和谐观念，将马克思主义的生产关系学说，也就是生产资料的分配方式，融入社会复杂化理论。该书将村落/宗族和生产关系学说融入到西方学术界的主流理论，也就是萨林斯—塞尔维斯的"游团—部落—酋邦—国家"四阶段说，结合西方民族学家收集的民族学材料，重新定义了四个阶段的特征。该书着重提出，宗族是古代社会政治、经济和文化活动的核心单位，社会复杂化也发生在宗族之间和宗族内部；在部落阶段，一个宗族或宗族联盟作为土地等生产资料的拥有者，通过征服其他宗族或宗族联盟，占有其土地，成为统治者和剥削者，因此进入酋邦阶段；酋邦增加了官僚机构以后，形成了国家。

在加州大学洛杉矶分校，我修了不少课程，打开了眼界。因为身在艺术史系，所以学了不少中国艺术史、日本艺术史、朝鲜艺术史、西藏艺术史和希腊考古方面的课程，写了一些课程论文，其中一部分已经发表。《关于洛杉矶县立博物馆收藏的一件唐卡的几个问题》[①] 讨论的是洛杉矶县立博物馆（LACMA）收藏的一幅罗汉唐卡。这幅唐卡非常特别，中央表现一位罗汉，周围表现的可能是他的本生故事；根据其绘画技法和配色，该文推测这幅唐卡可能是15世纪上半叶明代宫廷作坊的作品，用于馈赠来访的西藏高僧。*Wucheng and Shang: The Rise of a Bronze Age Civilization in Southern China*[②] 重新诠释了长江中游吴城文化的起源和发展历程，提出商朝移民在二里岗上层时期来到赣江流域建立了吴城，为商朝统治中心输送高岭土和铜料；吴城文化本来是商文化的派生文化，只是吸收了部分本地文化，但是后来商朝势力退出长江流域，吴城文化脱离了母文化独立发展，地方文化得到了加强。20世纪法国考古队在阿富汗的贝格拉姆城址发现了一些汉代漆片。这些漆片几位西方学者做过研究，大多定为东汉早期，尤其是公元1世纪前半叶。*Chinese*

---

① 张良仁：《关于洛杉矶县立博物馆收藏的一件唐卡的几个问题》，《艺术史研究》第11卷，2010年。

② Liangren Zhang, Wucheng and Shang: The Rise of a Bronze Age Civilization in Southern China, *Bulletin of Museum of Far Eastern Antiquities*, 78 (2010): 53-78.

*lacquers from Begram：date and provenance*①重新讨论了这些汉代漆片的年代和产地。该文利用20世纪初以来的朝鲜平壤乐浪郡贵族墓葬、蒙古国匈奴贵族墓葬和我国湖南省、贵州省等地汉代贵族墓葬出土的汉代纪年漆器，将其年代提前到西汉晚期和新莽时期，并将其定为蜀郡工官等皇家作坊和广陵国诸侯作坊的产品。这段时间贝格拉姆的历史我们不清楚，但是该城的贵族与我国西汉和新莽保持着政治和经济联系。

我前后修了三次伯格林德·琼曼（Burglind Jungmann）教授的朝鲜艺术史课程，为此写了三篇课程论文。2001年洛杉矶县立博物馆收了一幅奇特的朝鲜山水画。这是一幅横轴，上面画了五幅山水画草稿，画的是五处风景，还有一幅长篇游记《游禹金岩记》，但是没有署名。当时伯格林德·琼曼教授怀疑是朝鲜后期画家姜世晃的作品，我很快在他的文集《豹庵遗稿》中找到了这篇游记，说明是他的作品。20世纪90年代以来，学术界兴起了有关朝鲜后期"真景画"的讨论。姜世晃是19世纪的文人画家，也是"真景"山水画的实践者和倡导者。但是何为"真景"，学术界还有争议。有人认为真景画一反过去朝鲜画家表现中国的名山名水，着重表现本土的山水，而且一反传统的文人画法，采用了写实的欧洲透视画法。论文 *Kang Sehwang's Scenes of Puan Prefecture：describing actual landscape through literati ideals*②仔细分析了这幅横轴。五幅风景画描绘的是今韩国南部边山（今为风景区）的真实风景，但是采用了传统的文人画法，用了一些《芥子园画传》等画谱的模型；更引人注意的是，游记记录了作者游览各处风景的感官体验，绘声绘色，惊险刺激，明显受了我国明代公安派文学的影响。

中国历代绘画影响朝鲜很深，但是中国绘画作品和思想如何传播到朝鲜和日本我们并不十分清楚。第二篇论文探讨了这个问题。第二篇论文 *Artistic Activities of Korean Envoys in China*③讲的是明清时期朝鲜使团访华时的艺术活动。明清时期朝鲜王朝经常派使团访华，一个使团少则

---

① Liangren Zhang, Chinese lacquers from Begram：date and provenance, *International Journal of Asian Studies*, 8.1 (2011)：1-24.

② Liangren Zhang, Kang Sehwang's Scenes of Puan Prefecture：describing actual landscape through literati ideals, *Arts Asiatiques*, 65 (2011)：75-94.

③ Liangren Zhang, Artistic Activities of Korean Envoys in China,《史地》第3辑，社会科学出版社2019年版。

◇❖◇ 自　序

40人，多则几百人，其中有文人也有画家。在访华途中和在北京期间，他们经常光顾店铺，拜访文人，寻访画家。因此每次使团都会带回去不少作品、画谱和技艺，不断为朝鲜绘画输入新鲜血液。

2007年博士毕业后，我在南加州大学做了两年博士后，教了《东亚考古》和《中国艺术史》两门课。2009年应王巍所长的邀请，回到了原来工作的中国社会科学院考古研究所。但是因为北京的生活成本太高，难以维持，于是在2010年调到了西北大学。从那年起到2012年主持甘肃张掖西城驿遗址的发掘工作。在发掘时，引入了多学科研究理念，邀请了中国社会科学院考古研究所和北京科技大学的科技考古学家参与了此课题。迄今为止，一些初步成果已经发表。我自己研究了西城驿遗址出土的土坯建筑，发表了一篇论文 Ancient mud-brick architecture of northwest China。[1] 土坯建筑起源于近东，然后向中亚和南亚传播。西城驿遗址的土坯建筑颇为独特，它虽然吸收了中亚的土坯建筑技术，但是融入了中原传来的夯筑技术，是东西方建筑技术的结晶。

中国考古学20世纪50年代以后的发展史在国内外学术界少有人问津，基本上是个空白，为此从2011年起我前后发表了几篇论文。论文 The Chinese School of Archaeological[2] 讨论了我国考古学在理论方面的发展历程，着重讨论了历史唯物主义和辩证唯物主义以及类型学的本土化，以及中国文明"满天星斗"和"中国民族多元一体"说的形成过程。论文 New developments in Chinese archaeology[3] 讨论了2009年国家文物局出版的《田野考古工作规程》。此规程是对1984年版的大幅度修改，吸收了西方先进的理念和技术；由于国家文物局的大力推广，此规程大幅度提升了我国田野工作的水平，与世界接轨。其价值在国内外学术界还没有得到重视，此文乃是首次向国际学术界介绍此规程的论文。

近几年应《全球考古学大百科全书》（Encyclopedia of Global Archaeology）的邀请，我撰写了文章 Chinese Archaeology in the 21st Century。21世纪以来由于中国经济飞速发展，考古学在科技考古、大遗址保护、

---

[1] Liangren Zhang, Ancient mud-brick architecture of northwest China, *Paléorient*, Vol. 44.1, pp. 93–103, 2018.

[2] Liangren Zhang, The Chinese School of Archaeological, *Antiquity*, 87 (2013): 896–904.

[3] Liangren Zhang, New developments in Chinese archaeology, *Antiquity*, 88 (2014): The Project Gallery.

自　序

一带一路考古和水下考古方面突飞猛进，该文归纳了这些成就。

2011年7月，我申请的国家社科基金项目《新疆史前金属器研究》得以立项。在立项时我邀请了俄罗斯、新疆、北京的有关专家参加，本课题因而成为一个跨国家、跨机构的课题。2011年11月，我两次组织课题组成员考察了新疆伊犁、塔城、阿尔泰等博物馆收藏的金属器。后来我又联合德国学者申请了美国Wenner-Gren基金，进一步采集新疆东部的金属器和铜矿石样品。但是由于课题组成员工作繁忙，课题一直拖到2017年才结题。

2014年，由于种种原因，我调到了南京大学，并且启动了酝酿已久的俄罗斯和伊朗的考古发掘项目。在俄罗斯，我们与阿尔泰国立大学合作，在俄罗斯阿尔泰边疆区开展考古调查和发掘，解决跨区域的学术问题。俄罗斯阿尔泰边疆区位于中国新疆西北部，通过额尔齐斯河与中国新疆北部相连。现在已有证据表明，俄罗斯阿尔泰边疆区青铜时代的阿凡纳谢沃、安德罗诺沃、卡拉苏克文化的陶器见于中国新疆北部，而中国新疆北部的切木尔切克文化的陶器见于哈萨克斯坦东部和蒙古国西部。在早期铁器时代，俄罗斯阿尔泰山区早已发现的迈埃米尔和巴泽雷克文化的墓葬现在也发现于中国新疆北部。但是这条通道作为草原丝绸之路的价值远远没有得到重视。我们现在知道，中国西北部的冶金技术也来自欧亚草原，这些因素如何传播就成了国际学术界关注的重要问题。同时，欧亚草原和新疆也是民族迁徙频繁的区域，中国新疆的古代居民与欧亚草原如何互动又是一个重要的学术问题。中俄联合考古队前后四次发掘了青铜时代的卡勒望湖—1和苏联路—1遗址。在此过程中，开展多学科合作，采集兽骨、陶片、冶金样品，交专家分析，收集证据，来讨论上述问题。

在伊朗，我们与伊朗文化遗产与旅游研究所合作，在伊朗东北部发掘一座土丘遗址。伊朗东北部在古代属于呼罗珊，是丝绸之路的重要部分。居住在呼罗珊的粟特人和其他民族连续不断地来到中国，从事贸易，带来了西方的商品和技术（金银器、玻璃器），也从中国带去了丝绸、陶瓷和印刷术。但是，伊朗东北部的考古工作做得很少，一些基础问题（如年代学、农业起源和冶金起源）还没有解决，因此学术潜力很大。同时，这里的土丘遗址很有意思，它是几千年里人们反复居住生活的结果。因此发掘一座土丘遗址，可以获得从铜石并用时代到伊斯兰时期的建筑、墓葬、土坯、农作物、兽骨材料。可以说，一座土丘本身

自　序

就是一部历史书，读好它就能深入了解一个区域的历史。从中得到的遗迹和遗物可以探讨文化传播与古代人群的迁徙问题。

前几年开展的科研项目正在开花结果。"新疆史前金属器研究"课题产生了《吐鲁番史前考古》（《早期中国研究》第2辑，2016年）、《哈密史前考古》（《欧亚学刊》，2016年）、《西西伯利亚南部的青铜时代分期》（《考古学集刊》第20集，2017年）三篇论文。前两篇建立了吐鲁番和哈密地区史前时期的文化序列和文化联系，前者提出了吐鲁番盆地的早期居民为阿尔泰山脉来的游牧人群，后者提出哈密地区的最早居民来自河西走廊的四坝文化。第三篇论文系统整理了西西伯利亚的俄罗斯考古资料，讨论了西西伯利亚青铜时代文化的分期。

中国高校正在建设一流学科和一流大学，但是要实现这个目标，就需要培养具有研究能力的学生。中国的研究生教育还存在种种问题。有一些导师要么放羊，要么把学生当作学术民工使用，不怎么用心培养学生；还有一些导师有心培养学生，但不知道如何培养。学生不知如何选题，不知如何论证，也不知如何写作论文。归根结底就是缺乏学术研究和论文写作训练。为此我写了两篇文章《研究生怎样做研究》和《研究生怎样写论文》，开了一门训练课程《研究生论文写作》，分收集目录、阅读文献、寻找新问题、设计研究方案，以及学术训练几个方面训练研究生。其中新问题是重中之重，需要学生熟悉考古资料和研究成果，发现新问题。有了新问题，就可以设计研究方案，实施针对性的学术训练。经过这样一个完整的过程，学生的科研能力就可以得到很大的提升。

从1987年开始，我进入考古学已经30年了。由于自己的求学经历和研究兴趣，除了培养学生的研究能力，我现在把精力集中在中国新疆的古代冶金以及俄罗斯和伊朗的考古项目上，开设《世界考古》课程，培养世界考古人才。我以为，世界考古是我国考古学未来的发展方向，只有"走进世界"，才能"走出自己"；只有"认识世界"，才能"认识自己"。现在我国高校和科研机构正在走出去，到世界各国开展考古工作。但是世界考古在我国基础薄弱，需要积蓄力量，凝聚共识，才能生根发芽。我自知志大才疏，只有以此寻求同道，彼此呼应，共同前进。

张良仁
2020年11月

目　录

第一部分　中国考古学史

The Chinese School of Archaeology ……………………………………（3）
New Developments in Chinese Archaeology ……………………………（18）
Chinese Field Methods …………………………………………………（24）
Chinese Archaeology in the Twenty-First Century ……………………（32）
中国国际考古合作的现状和问题 ………………………………………（49）

第二部分　考古学理论

Wucheng and Shang: A New History of a Bronze Age
　　Civilization in Southern China …………………………………（71）
农业和文明起源 …………………………………………………………（101）
村落和社会进化 …………………………………………………………（110）

第三部分　中国西北和欧亚草原考古

哈密地区史前考古 ………………………………………………………（133）
吐鲁番地区早期铁器时代考古 …………………………………………（159）
关于吉尔赞喀勒墓地用火遗物的一点看法 ……………………………（197）
张掖市西城驿遗址的彩陶 ………………………………………………（212）
Ancient Mud-brick Architecture of Northwest China …………………（224）
Metal Trade in Bronze Age Central Eurasia ……………………………（241）

目 录

西西伯利亚南部的青铜时代分期 ……………………………………（264）
The Transmission of the Karasuk Metallurgy to the Northern
　　Zone of China ……………………………………………………（317）

第四部分　东亚艺术史

Artistic Activities of Korean Envoys in China ……………………（351）
Chinese Lacquerwares from Begram: Date and Provenance ………（382）
关于洛杉矶县立博物馆收藏的一件唐卡的几个问题 ………………（408）
Kang Sehwang's Scenes of Puan Prefecture-Describing
　　Actual Landscape Through Literati Ideals ………………………（421）

第五部分　欧亚考古见闻

俄罗斯考古见闻 ………………………………………………………（463）
在中哈萨克斯坦考古 …………………………………………………（473）
俄罗斯考古访问纪行 …………………………………………………（483）
英国访问纪行 …………………………………………………………（497）
中伊合作考古，续写丝路故事 ………………………………………（521）
一杯红茶一个馕　一把手铲方中忙
　　——南京大学赴伊朗考古记（一）………………………………（526）
玫瑰花的全部价值，只有夜莺才知道
　　——南京大学赴伊朗考古记（二）………………………………（531）
认识伊朗文化遗产
　　——苏西亚纳平原 ………………………………………………（538）
学者相聚大不里士　共话古代丝绸之路
　　——第三届丝绸之路考古与文保国际学术讨论会纪要 ………（554）

第六部分　书评

评韩建业《中国北方地区新石器时代文化研究》 …………………（563）

精烹细调　可以咀嚼
　　——读许宏《最早的中国》 ………………………………（574）
建德垂风　维城之基
　　——读罗泰教授《宗子维城》 …………………………（579）

第七部分　研究生培养

研究生怎样做研究？ ……………………………………………（597）
研究生怎样写论文？ ……………………………………………（606）

第 一 部 分
中国考古学史

The Chinese School of Archaeology*

Introduction

In 1959, at a meeting reviewing the "archaeological achievements of the past 10 years" in celebration of the tenth anniversary of the New China (1949 –   ), the leading archaeologist Yin Da (1906 – 1983), then director of the Institute of Archaeology of the Chinese Academy of Sciences (CAS), urged all the archaeologists in China "to cooperate fully, so that in the next three or five years, in the entire nation, we can build up a scientific and holistic system out of all cultural remains of all periods; that is to say, to build up a Marxist Chinese archaeological system."①

This call had two key words in it. One was "Chinese". Ever since the early twentieth century, growing national consciousness had drum-beaten Chinese archaeologists to search for Chinese cultural origins.② A particularly urgent matter for archaeologists of the 1950s was to dispel the notion of "the western origin of Chinese culture" that was current among foreign and native archaeologists during the Nationalist Era (1911 – 1949). To achieve this goal, it was imperative to undertake archaeological investigation systematically so as to prove the autochthonous origins and undisrupted development of Chinese

---

* The article was originally published in *Antiquity* 7, 2013, pp. 896 – 904. It is reprinted in this anthology with minor changes.

① Yin, D., Zuzhi qilai dajia dongshou bianxie "shinian kaogu", *Kaogu* 3, 1959, p. 123.

② Liu, L., X. Chen, China, in T. Murray ed., *Encyclopedia of Archaeology: History and Discoveries*, Vol. 1, Santa Barbara (CA): ABC CLIO, 2001, pp. 315 – 333.

civilisations. The second word, "Marxist", reflects a process of cutting the umbilical cord of the reborn archaeology of the "New China" from the "bourgeois archaeology" of the "Old China" and swaddling the discipline with the mantle of Marxist theories and models.

Archaeology as a modern discipline came to China as a result of foreigners' exploration—partly research-oriented, partly treasure-oriented—in the late nineteenth and early twentieth centuries.[1] As the Nationalist government curbed their activities from the late 1920s, native archaeologists, mostly western-trained, from a few isolated institutions (primarily the Cenozoic Research Laboratory of the Geological Survey of China, the Institute of History and Philology of Academic Sinica and the Society for Historical Studies of National Peking Academy), actively conducted research-oriented excavations at Anyang and other sites.[2] The political instability and economic feebleness of the time, however, restrained the discipline from desirable development. Although much progress was made in excavation techniques and typological analysis,[3] only a modest number of sites were excavated, and a small group of personnel trained.[4] Moreover, when the Communist Party took power in 1949, several major archaeologists followed the Nationalist regime to Taiwan, significantly curtailing the number of trained archaeologists left behind in mainland China.

---

[1] Chen, X., *Zhongguo Shiqian Kaoguxueshi Yanjiu* 1895 – 1949, Beijing: Sanlian Shudian, 1997, pp. 42 – 49; Liu, L., X. Chen, *The Archaeology of China: From the Late Paleolithic to the Early Bronze Age*, Cambridge: Cambridge University Press, 2012, p. 5.

[2] Chen, X., *Zhongguo Shiqian Kaoguxueshi Yanjiu* 1895 – 1949, Beijing: Sanlian Shudian, 1997, pp. 185 – 204, 264 – 272.

[3] Chen, X., *Zhongguo Shiqian Kaoguxueshi Yanjiu* 1895 – 1949, Beijing: Sanlian Shudian, 1997, pp. 227 – 250, 310 – 329.

[4] Xia, N., Zhongguo kaoguxue de xianzhuang, *Wenwu Cankao Ziliao* 1, 1954, pp. 61 – 62; Chen, X., *Zhongguo Shiqian Kaoguxueshi Yanjiu* 1895 – 1949, Beijing: Sanlian Shudian, 1997, pp. 200 – 274.

The Chinese School of Archaeology

The Marxist Paradigm

The remaining archaeologists of the New China faced several challenges, not least how to adapt themselves to the changed political environment. Breaking ties with the West and creating bonds with the Soviet Union, the nascent government modelled itself upon the latter to upgrade its science and education sectors. [1]Archaeologists, like other intellectuals mostly trained in Western universities and pro-West national universities, had little choice but to learn the "advanced experiences (*xianjin jingyan*)" from their Soviet colleagues through intense scholarly exchange and systematic translation of Soviet publications;[2] as a result they revolutionised Chinese archaeological institutions, fieldwork methodology and interpretive paradigms. [3]

A variety of publications, including textbooks, articles and course plans of Soviet archaeologists such as S. V. Kiselev (1905 – 1962), A. V. Artsikhovskiĭ (1902 – 1978) and A. L. Mongait (1915 – 1974) inspired Chinese archaeologists to imbue the discipline with Marxist theories,[4] and to provide the guidelines for the first Chinese archaeology textbooks in the 1950s. In addition, Marxist classical works by Friedrich Engels (1820 – 1895) and Joseph Stalin (1878 – 1953) were by now part of the regular history curriculum in China to

---

[1] Pepper, S., Education for the new order, in R. MacFarquhar, J. K. Fairbank ed., *The Cambridge History of China*, Cambridge: Cambridge University Press, Vol. 14, Part 1, 1987, pp. 185 – 217.

[2] Su, B., Ruhe shi kaogu gongzuo chengwei renmin de shiye, in B. Su ed., *Su Bingqi Kaoguxue Lunshu Xuanji*, Beijing: Wenwu, 1984, pp. 277 – 282; Su, B., Muqian kaogu gongzuo zhong cunzai de wenti, in B. Su ed., *Su Bingqi Kaoguxue Lunshu Xuanji*, Beijing: Wenwu, 1953, pp. 284 – 289; Xia, N., Tianye kaogu xulun, *Wenwu Cankao Ziliao* 4, 1952, p. 90; Zheng, Z., Kaogu shiye de chengjiu he jinhou nuli de fangxiang, *Kaogu Tongxun* 2, 1956, p. 15.

[3] Zhang, L., Soviet inspiration in Chinese archaeology, *Antiquity* 85, 2011, pp. 1049 – 1059.

[4] Kiselev, S. V., *Jixieliefu Jiangyanji*, translated by Quanxin Zhang, Bingyi Chen, Zerong Liu, Langshan Liao, Beijing: Zhongsu Youhao Xiehui; Anonymous, 1955, Sulian "Kaoguxue tonglun" jiaoxue dagang, *Kaogu Tongxun* 1, 1955, pp. 71 – 77; Artsikhovskiĭ, A. V., *Kaoguxue Jichu*, translated by Yudong Lou et al, Beijing: Kexue; Avdushin, D. A., "Tianye kaogu gongzuo fangfa" jiaoxue dagang, translated by Yudong Lou, *Kaogu Tongxun* 1, 1956, pp. 80 – 84; Mongait, A. L., *Sulian Kaoguxue*, translated by Zhongguo Kexueyuan Kaogu Yanjiusuo Tushuguan, Unofficial publication, 1963.

offer a paramount framework for historical sciences. Marxist theories were not unknown to Chinese historians of the early twentieth century; in fact, they had already been spontaneously integrated into Neolithic and Bronze Age histories of China by Guo Moruo (1892 – 1978), Lü Zhenyu (1900 – 1980) and Yin Da.① However, it was not until the 1950s that they were thoroughly assimilated into Chinese archaeology.②

The adoption of the Marxist paradigms, however, was not an easy path; it took several years of agitation, including the coercive Anti-rightist Campaign (1957 – 1958) and the Great Leap Forward (1958 – 1960), to lodge them firmly in the archaeological discipline, which one may sense from Xia Nai's essay "*Xin Zhongguo de kaoguxue* (Archaeology of New China)".③ It is no coincidence that in 1958 a number of young enthusiasts called for the building of a lineal history of social formations and denounced the culture-historical and typological analyses as legacies of the "bourgeois archaeology",④ an episode reminiscent of the radical ideas of the Ravdonikas School around 1930 in the Soviet Union.⑤

The subjects of settlement, technology, economy and social relations were timely contributions that the Marxist paradigm—through the lens of Soviet archaeologists—brought to Chinese archaeology, which was dominated by the culture-historical paradigm in the Nationalist Era. In these subjects, Chinese archaeology anticipated what happened in Europe and the United States in the 1960s, where the culture-historical paradigm likewise lost its appeal to the proponents of New Archaeology and Social Archaeology, and new research subjects, including ecology, settlement pattern, specialised production and

---

① Lü, Z., *Shiqianqi Zhongguo Shehui Yanjiu*, Beiping: Beiping Renwen Shudian, 1934; Guo, M., *Zhongguo Gudai Shehui Yanjiu*, Beijing: Renmin, 1954; Yin, D., Zhongguo yuanshi shehui, in D. Yin ed., *Yin Da Shixue Lunzhu Xuanji*, Beijing: Renmin, 1989, pp. 8 – 226.

② For a fuller discussion of the adoption of Marxist ideas and theories, see Zhang, L., Soviet inspiration in Chinese archaeology, *Antiquity* 85, 2011, pp. 1049 – 1059.

③ Xia, N., Xin Zhongguo de kaoguxue, *Kaogu* 9, 1962, pp. 453 – 458.

④ Zhang, Z., Zhongguo kaoguxueshi de jidian renshi, in Z. Zhang ed., *Zhongguo Kaoguxue: Shijian, Lilun, Fangfa*, Zhengzhou: Zhongzhou Guji, 1994, pp. 49 – 50.

⑤ Trigger, B. G., *A History of Archaeological Thought*, Cambridge: Cambridge University Press, 1989, pp. 216 – 227.

social evolution sprang up like mushrooms to cope with ancient societies. ①

In the New China, however, the Marxist paradigm was sanctified in such a manner that archaeologists were expected to quote the dicta of Lewis Henry Morgan (1818 – 1881) and Engels and fit their fresh materials into them, rather than devise middle-range theories and methodologies to turn the subjects into empirical research topics. ②Consequently, the outdated scheme of social evolution, formulated by Engels and schematised by Stalin, lost its opportunity to be updated by the new ethnographic and archaeological data rapidly accumulating in the New China. Thus, after its initial enlightenment, the Marxist theories degenerated into the routine practice of perfunctory categorising of archaeological materials and scrupulous covering of original research with ideological camouflage. It was not long before Marxist archaeology lost its vitality.

The Culture-historical Paradigm and Typology

From the very beginning, Marxists were committed to liberating the ethnic peoples from the tyranny of imperialism and inequality, both within and beyond their nations. In keeping with this cause, the Soviet Union demanded careful study not only of their technologies, economies, cultures and social relations—so as to lift their socio-economic status to the socialist level③—but also their histories, with particular attention to their origins and stages of social development. ④It is not surprising that the culture-historical paradigm and typology, once condemned as "bourgeois scholarship" in the early 1930s, were

---

① Trigger, B. G., *A History of Archaeological Thought*, Cambridge: Cambridge University Press, 1989, pp. 245 – 328.
② Chang, K. C., Archaeology and Chinese Historiography, *World Archaeology* 13, 1981, p. 167.
③ Yang, K., *Minzuxue Gailun*, Beijing: Zhongguo Shehui Kexue, 1984, p. 133.
④ Suliankaoguxue Shelun, Sidalin guanyu yuyanxue wenti ji jingji wenti de zhuzuo yu sulian kaoguxuejiamen de renwu, translated by Yidong Zhang, *Kaogu Xuebao* 6, 1953, pp. 7 – 8.

highly valued in Soviet archaeology.①

Under the drive of rising national consciousness in the twentieth century, Chinese archaeologists had already begun to search for the origins of Chinese civilisations in the Nationalist Era;② they were now motivated by the Soviet mandate to further their work. Fieldwork, following the construction trends at the time, was taking place mostly outside the ethnic areas.③Consequently, the calls of ethnologists such as Fei Xiaotong (1910 – 2005) for archaeologists' help with the histories of contemporary nationalities went largely unheeded. ④Archaeological manpower was instead showered on the histories of the ethnic groups that founded the early dynasties in the Central Plain. The culture-historical paradigm and typology, likewise denounced in the anti-bourgeois-scholarship movement in 1958 but soon revived, turned out to be safe outlets of intellectual creativity.

The Sino-Soviet friendship declined after 1957 and ultimately froze in the 1960s. By then, Chinese archaeologists had already learned a great deal from Soviet archaeology and put it to good use. ⑤The Sino-Soviet split, however, inflicted a heavy blow on them. Having shut its window to the West in 1949, China now lost any opportunity of communicating with leading archaeological communities elsewhere; only in the 1980s was such contact resumed. In the absence of outside inspiration, Chinese archaeologists were left to play out their own talents. However, following the takeover of mainland China in 1949, intense political campaigns, tight ideological control of the academic community and the Cultural Revolution, all of which were characterised by a severe anti-

---

① Gening, V. F., *Ocherki po Istorii Sovetskoĭ arkheologii*: *U Istokov Formirovaniia Marksistskikh Teoreteskikh Osnov Sovetskoĭ arkheologii*, 20-e-pervaia polovina 30-kh gg., Kiev: Nauka, 1982, pp. 168 – 175.

② Chen, X., *Zhongguo Shiqian Kaoguxueshi Yanjiu* 1895 – 1949, Beijing: Sanlian Shudian, 1997, pp. 205 – 227, 276 – 309.

③ Zheng, Z., Kaogu shiye de chengjiu he jinhou nuli de fangxiang, *Kaogu Tongxun* 2, 1956, p. 15.

④ Fei, X., Kaizhan shaoshu minzu diqu he yu shaoshu minzu lishi youguan de diqu de kaogu gongzuo: zai kaogu gongzuo huiyishang de fayan, *Kaogu Tongxun* 3, 1956, pp. 1 – 10; Ligong, Jiaqiang shaoshu minzu diqu de kaogu gongzuo, *Kaogu* 10, 1956, p. 66.

⑤ Beijing Daxue Lishixi Kaogu Zhuanye, *Zhongguo Kaoguxue*, Unofficial publication; Zhongguo Kexueyuan Kaogu Yanjiusuo, *Xinzhongguo de Kaogu Shouhuo*, Beijing: Kexue, 1960.

The Chinese School of Archaeology

intellectualism, virtually made any theoretical thinking—even under the Marxist and Maoist rubric—a precarious venture. In this context, it was a courageous figure, Su Bingqi (1909 – 1997), who arose to steer archaeological thinking in the subsequent decades.

After graduating from the History Department of Peking Normal University in 1934, Su Bingqi joined the Institute for Historical Studies, National Peking Academy, and participated in the excavations of the pre-dynastic and dynastic Zhou (1600BC – 256BC) site Doujitai in Baoji, Shaanxi province, which aimed to discover the origins of the Zhou and Qin cultures/peoples. In 1935, he was charged with the task of writing an excavation report of the 104 tombs found there. For a beginner in this field, with few reference works to hand, the chronology of these data alone was a daunting challenge. ①Inspired by the methodology of Oscar Montelius ("Die Methode" in Montelius 1903), he took the ceramic li-tripod—which occurred most pervasively in the tombs—as his diagnostic chronological indicator, and carried out a meticulous morphological and technical examination of 59 specimens, including those uncovered from the cemetery and stray finds from neighbouring sites. He then divided them into four types (*xing*), and for each drew up an evolutionary path. For the moulded-body type he discerned three phases of development, in which the height of the body decreases while the depth of the belly increases in proportion. On these grounds he divided the cemetery into three periods and eleven sub-periods spanning the early Western Zhou (ca. 1045BC – 950BC) through to the post-Han period (220AD –   ). ②

This experimental application of Montelian typology in China was groundbreaking in that Su Bingqi imbued Montelius's method with his own interpretation. The selection of chronologically diagnostic ceramic wares as well as tomb structure as subjects of typological analysis, the division of a class of ceramic vessels into types, and the tracing of each type's evolutionary path were the first efforts of adapting Montelian typology to Chinese materials. Confident

---

① Su, B., Gei qingnianren de hua, in B. Su ed., *Huaren, Long de Chuanren, Zhongguoren: Kaogu Xungenji*, Shenyang: Liaoning Daxue, 1994, pp. 210 – 219.

② Su, B., Doujitai goudongqu muzang (excerpt), in B. Su ed., *Su Bingqi Kaoguxue Lunshu Xuanji*, Beijing: Wenwu, 1984, pp. 3 – 58.

about his method, Su persistently applied it, with modifications, to his studies of an Eastern Zhou (771BC – 256BC) cemetery at Luoyang and of Yangshao (4900BC – 2900BC) ceramics from Xi'an. ①In the case of the Luoyang cemetery, he took assemblages of ceramic types as the basis for chronological arrangement, having seriated each type according to their morphological changes. ②In the case of the Yangshao ceramics from Xi'an, he upset the widely held opinion that the Miaodigou phase came after the Banpo phase. After a detailed analysis of the pointed amphorae (*xiaokoujiandiping* in Chinese) and flower *Rosa multiflora*, *Dendranthema morifolium*, bird and fish designs of the two phases, he contended that they were actually two co-evolving regional variants of Yangshao. ③Incidentally, this idea is no longer valid; Chinese archaeologists have once again come to the agreement that the Miaodigou phase (3900BC – 3600BC) postdates the Banpo phase (4900BC – 3800BC). ④

  The study of the Yangshao culture, which spans the valleys of the middle Yellow River and its major tributary, the Wei River, marked another milestone in the development of Montelian typology in China. The term *shi*, for a chronological subtype, came into formal use; by now the terms *xing* (type) and *shi* (subtype) had become standard in Chinese typology. This new typology was further developed and adapted to Chinese materials by Su Bingqi and his disciples. Blessed with a comprehensive cultural sequence, Chinese archaeologists occupied themselves mostly with the chronology of a culture or a site, the question at issue being the integration of stratigraphic with typological data. Zou Heng, working with ceramic materials from Zhengzhou and Anyang, both of which were Shang (1600BC – 1046BC) urban centres, made an innovative attempt in this direction by assigning individual architectural features

---

  ① Su, B., Guanyu Yangshao wenhua de ruogan wenti, *Kaogu Xuebao* 1, 1965, pp. 51 – 82; Su, B., Luoyang Zhongzhoulu (Xigongduan) Jieyu, in B. Su ed., *Su Bingqi Kaoguxue Lunshu Xuanji*, Beijing: Wenwu, 1984, pp. 65 – 87.

  ② Su, B., Luoyang Zhongzhoulu (Xigongduan) Jieyu, in B. Su ed., *Su Bingqi Kaoguxue Lunshu Xuanji*, Beijing: Wenwu, 1984, pp. 65 – 87.

  ③ Su, B., Guanyu Yangshao wenhua de ruogan wenti, *Kaogu Xuebao* 1, 1965, pp. 51 – 82.

  ④ Yan, W., Lun Banpo leixing he Miaodigou leixing, in W. Yan ed., *Yangshao Wenhua Yanjiu*, Beijing: Wenwu, 1989, pp. 115 – 120.

The Chinese School of Archaeology

to stratigraphic sequences validated by artefact typology. ①Later Su Bingqi, Yin Weizhang, Zhang Zhongpei, Yan Wenming and Yu Weichao evaluated the respective strengths of typological analysis and stratigraphic evidence. ②To them, stratigraphic evidence provided only the sequence, and typological analysis was necessary to establish a compatible chronology. Su and Yin and Zhang even mounted an art-historical perspective to the typology by stating that the various types of artefacts of one period must show some common stylistic characteristics and must change in parallel from one period to another. ③

Regional Cultural Genealogy

Yin Da had already noticed that various regional cultures flourished simultaneously,④ but it was Su Bingqi who systemised and linked them with early ethnic groups recorded in ancient Chinese texts. In his 1965 article, Su compared regional phases of the Yangshao culture in Shaanxi and Henan provinces with the Dawenkou culture (4200BC – 2600BC) in Shandong and Jiangsu provinces, and the Qujialing culture (3400BC – 2500BC) in Hubei province. Because of the appearance of floral designs resembling roses (*Rosa multiflora* and *Dendranthema morifolium*; hua in Chinese) on Miaodigou wares, Su believed that the Yangshao tribes were the origin of the *Hua* or *Huaxia* (Chinese) nation, whereas Dawenkou and Qujialing represent neighbouring ethnic groups. Though contemporary, the Dawenkou culture appeared to be

---

① Zou, H., Shilun Zhengzhou xin faxian de Yin Shang wenhua yizhi, *Kaogu Xuebao* 3, 1956, pp. 77 – 103; Zou, H., Shilun Yinxu wenhua fenqi, *Beijing Daxue Xuebao* (Renwen kexue ban) 4, 1964, pp. 77 – 103 & 5, 1964, pp. 63 – 90.

② Su, B., W. Yin, Dicengxue and Qiwu xingtaixue, *Wenwu* 4, 1982, pp. 1 – 7; Zhang, Z., Dicengxue yu leixingxue de ruogan wenti, *Wenwu* 5, 1983, pp. 60 – 69; Yan, W., Kaogu ziliao zhengli zhong de biaoxingxue yanjiu, in W. Yan ed., *Zouxiang Ershiyi Shiji de Kaoguxue*, Xi'an: Sanqin, 1997, pp. 53 – 77; Yu, W., Guanyu "kaogu leixingxue" wenti, in W. Yu ed., *Kaogu Leixingxue de Lilun yu Shijian*, Beijing: Wenwu, 1989, pp. 1 – 35.

③ Su, B., W. Yin, Dicengxue and Qiwu xingtaixue, *Wenwu* 4, 1982, pp. 1 – 7; Zhang, Z., Dicengxue yu leixingxue de ruogan wenti, *Wenwu* 5, 1983, pp. 60 – 69.

④ Yin, D., Lun woguo xinshiqishidai de yanjiu gongzuo, *Kaogu Tongxun* 2, 1955, pp. 1 – 4.

· 11 ·

socio-economically more advanced than Yangshao. ①

This vision harked back to the New Historiography of the Nationalist era, which held that early Chinese history, instead of having a single origin and following a unilineal development, had multiple origins and developed along multiple regional trajectories. The historian Fu Sinian (1896 – 1950), for instance, perceived a division of the Yi (barbarians), embodied by the Longshan culture (2600BC – 2000BC) in Shandong province in the east, and the Xia (Chinese), embodied by the Yangshao culture in the west. ②Longshan was even taken to be the origin of the Shang civilisation, whereas Yangshao was alleged to be the origin of the Zhou. Another historian, Xu Xusheng (1888 – 1976), Su's mentor during his early career, added as a third group the Miaoman (Miao barbarians) block in the middle Yangzi River valley. ③The emphasis on multi-linealism and on the contributions of the "barbarian" cultures to Chinese civilisations also found expression in the works of contemporary archaeologists such as Li Ji (1896 – 1979). ④Since the late 1950s, however, the traditional historiography in which the "Chinese" were always assumed to be the most culturally advanced, outshining the barbarian cultures around them, has returned to centre stage. ⑤Su's observation that other ethnic cultures—at certain stages of their development—could be more advanced than Chinese cultures was a counterstrike to this perception.

Prompted by ever-accelerating industrialisation, archaeological fieldwork increased dramatically after the 1950s, and spatial and chronological gaps were quickly filled. The discoveries of the Zhengzhou Shang city (1600BC – 1300BC) and Erlitou (1900BC – 1500BC) linked up the Longshan and Anyang

---

① Su, B., Guanyu Yangshao wenhua de ruogan wenti, *Kaogu Xuebao* 1, 1956, pp. 51 – 82.

② Fu, S., Yi-Xia dongxi shuo, in S. Fu ed., *Fu Sinian Xuanji*, Tianjin: Tianjin Renmin, 1996, pp. 247 – 292.

③ Xu, X., *Zhongguo Gushi de Chuanshuo Shidai*, Guilin: Guangxi Shifan Daxue, 2003, pp. 42 – 147.

④ Li, J., Zhongguo kaoguxue zhi guoqu yu jianglai, in J. Li ed., *Li Ji Kaoguxue Lunwen Xuanji*, Beijing: Wenwu, 1990, p. 48.

⑤ Feili, H., Yu Zhang Guangzhi jiaotan, in G. Zhang ed., *Kaogu Renleixue Suibi*, Beijing: Sanlian Shudian, 1990, p. 213.

Shang periods (1200BC – 1046BC); a lineage of Chinese civilisation from Yangshao through the Qin Empire was thus established. By the beginning of the 1980s, Su's interest in regional cultural genealogy came to fruition in the formation of the so-called theory of "regional cultural genealogy and variations (*quxi leixing*)."① In this formulation, the accumulated archaeological data in China were grouped into six culture-historical regions: Shaanxi, Henan, Shanxi (central China), Shandong and neighbouring provinces (eastern China), Hubei and neighbouring provinces (Middle Yangzi), Lower Yangzi, Lake Poyang-Pearl River Delta (southern China), and the northern zone straddling the Great Wall. Each region comprised a number of sub-regions, whose cultural genealogies, as far as available data allow, are traced back to the Palaeolithic and followed through to the Late Neolithic. In 1975, contrary to the entrenched paradigm that viewed central China as the cradle from which Chinese civilisation radiated cultural rays to surrounding regions, Su emphasised that cultural influx moved mostly the other way.②

The theory of "regional cultural genealogy and variations" constitutes the backbone of the "Chinese school of archaeology", the birth of which Su announced in 1981 at a meeting of the Beijing Society for Historical Studies.③ Su himself, already in his seventies, often travelled across China to offer input and encouragement to local archaeologists to apply the concept to their data. He even initiated a research project on the cultural genealogy of the "circum-Bohai region", which gave impetus to the discovery of the piled-stone altar at Dongshanzui and the "goddess temple" at Niuheliang, both of which belong to the Hongshan Culture (4700BC – 3300BC) in western Liaoning province, where female figurines and jadeite artefacts were unearthed as well.④

---

① Su, B., W. Yin, Guanyu kaoguxue wenhua de quxi leixing wenti, *Wenwu* 5, 1981, pp. 10 – 17.

② Su, B., W. Yin, Guanyu kaoguxue wenhua de quxi leixing wenti, *Wenwu* 5, 1981, pp. 10 – 17; Su, B., *Zhongguo Wenming Qiyuan Xintan*, Shenyang: Liaoning Daxue, 2009, pp. 92 – 93.

③ Su, B., Jianguo yilai Zhongguo kaoguxue de fazhan, in B. Su ed., *Su Bingqi Kaoguxue Lunshu Xuanji*, Beijing: Wenwu, 1984, p. 305.

④ Su, B., Huanbohai kaogu yu Qingzhou kaogu, *Kaogu* 1, 1989, pp. 47 – 50; Su, B., *Zhongguo Wenming Qiyuan Xintan*, Shenyang: Liaoning Daxue, 2009, pp. 92 – 93.

The Multiple Origins of Chinese Civilisations

These discoveries inspired Su to take another bold step in his thinking. The origin of Chinese civilisations, an issue discussed as far back as the 1930s, had long been the focal question of Chinese archaeology. The conventionally held belief that China has a history of 5000 years has proved difficult to substantiate through received textual evidence—to date the writing can be traced back only to the Anyang Shang period, and the state-level society only to the Erlitou period.① However, in the 1980s, large proto-urban centres associated with prestigious goods (egg-shell pottery, jade tubes and discs, etc.), sizeable "palace" buildings, large clay drums and wealthy tombs dating to 3500BC – 2000BC were discovered in various regions (Guangdong, Zhejiang, Shandong, Liaoning, Gansu, Henan, Shanxi, etc.). In Marxist terminology, all these traits reflect the disintegration of "primitive society" and the coming of class differentiation and state society. Su believed that this Late Neolithic cultural florescence marked the beginning of Chinese civilisations.② He dubbed this simultaneous outburst of civilisations in many regions as "stars shining all over the sky (*mantian xingdou*)."③

While Su perceived that the surrounding regions were culturally superior to the Central Plain during the Neolithic, his disciple Yan Wenming had a different vision for the Bronze Age and thereafter. Organising Neolithic cultures into five regions, he offered a model of a "centripetal structure of a multi-petalled flower", in which the Central Plain played the central and leading role, spearheading the surrounding regions in the formation of civilisation. Combining with the culture-historical approach, both Su and Yan arrived at a historiographic paradigm that the multiple nationalities in China, while possessing their own origins, have intimately interacted with the Han Chinese in

---

① Liu, L., X. Chen, *The Archaeology of China: From the Late Paleolithic to the Early Bronze Age*, Cambridge: Cambridge University Press, 2012, pp. 262 – 278.
② Su, B., *Zhongguo Wenming Qiyuan Xintan*, Shenyang: Liaoning Daxue, 2009, p. 93.
③ Su, B., *Zhongguo Wenming Qiyuan Xintan*, Shenyang: Liaoning Daxue, 2009, p. 99.

history to the point that they together formed one overarching unity, "the Chinese nationality (*zhonghua minzu*)."① Incidentally, this idea turned out to echo the model of "multi-component unity (*duoyuan yiti*)" that Fei Xiaotong developed to characterize the formation history of the many nationalities within China.②

An immediate question arising out of the realisation that Chinese civilisations had multiple origins was how they emerged. To answer this question, Su advanced three models. One was fission, for which a ready case in point was the breakup of the Yangshao culture into the Banpo and Miaodigou phases. The second was collision; the Hongshan culture in the north-east, featuring dragon designs, collided with the Yangshao culture in the Guanzhong plain, featuring flower designs, to create the late Hongshan civilisation, which boasted the ensembles of altars, temples and mausoleums mentioned above. ③The third was assimilation; the Chalcolithic Taosi cemetery (2600BC – 2000BC) in southern Shanxi, for instance, absorbed the painted dragon design and tripodal pottery types from the area of the Great Bend of the Yellow River in Inner Mongolia, and jade knives from Zhejiang in the southeast. Each of these models addresses the question of the formation of the Chinese nation, another issue of key importance to Chinese archaeologists. Thus, unlike the unilineal model that depicted the gradual growth of the Chinese nation in central China, they provide an alternative, more dynamic and complex process.

The Chinese School

The Chinese school of archaeology thus portrayed has achieved far more than the proponents of the "Marxist Chinese archaeological system" had expected. It has not only built up a temporal and spatial framework for Chinese

---

① Yan, W., Zhongguo shiqian wenhua de tongyixing yu duoyangxing, *Wenwu* 3, 1987, pp. 38 – 50; Yan, W., Guanyu chongjian Zhongguo shiqianshi de sikao, *Kaogu* 12, 1991, p. 1117.

② Fei, X., Zhonghua minzu de duoyuan yiti geju, in X. Fei ed., *Zhongguo Minzu Duoyuan Titi Geju*, Beijing: Zhongyang Minzu Xueyuan, 1989, pp. 1 – 36.

③ Su, B., *Zhongguo Wenming Qiyuan Xintan*, Shenyang: Liaoning Daxue, 2009, p. 103.

archaeology and thus answered the question of the origin of Chinese civilisation, but it has also formulated its own working methods and interpretive theories. Montelian typology was developed and enriched in such a way that it not only has the power to define chronologies, but also to build regional cultural lineages. Its culture-historical approach—itself as flexible as any of its modules—depicts a complex picture of regional cultural traditions and their interactions, which compares well with the Western concept of "interaction sphere", applied by K. C. Chang (1931 – 2001) to the Yangshao period and Longshan period cultures in China. Multi-linealism has provided a fresh understanding of the origins of Chinese civilisations. [1]

While one might regret the lack of interaction with theoretical development outside China and the monotony of theories and approaches after decades of development of archaeology in China, one must bear in mind that the Chinese school was a product of specific socio-political circumstances that determined the questions asked and the solutions provided. [2] In the manic quest for Soviet "advanced" science and technology during the 1950s, Chinese archaeologists gained a great deal of Marxist archaeology and the ethno-centric approach and thereafter innovatively adapted these elements to their soil. Although in the anti-Soviet era (1960 – 1989) this history was almost forgotten, its legacy is still visible today. During the following decades, Chinese archaeologists suffered greatly from intellectual isolation and incessant anti-intellectual campaigns. Even so, they were able to rediscover Montelian typology and develop it to generate new models for interpreting China's ancient past, including regional cultural genealogies and the multiple origins of Chinese civilisations. This is a contribution that cannot be ignored. Even though they are, to a certain extent, pervaded by idiosyncratic, freelance and intuitive thinking, these models contain a kernel of usefulness and can potentially be applied to non-Chinese contexts.

---

[1] Chang, K. C., *The Archaeology of Ancient China*, New Haven (CT) & London: Yale University Press, 1986, p. 234.

[2] Wang, T., Establishing the Chinese archaeological school: Su Bingqi and contemporary Chinese archaeology, *Antiquity* 71, 1997, pp. 31 – 39.

Acknowledgement

The author wishes to express his profound gratitude to Professor Lothar von Falkenhausen for his critical reading of the draft. All errors remain the author's own.

New Developments in Chinese Archaeology*

Introduction

In April 2009, the State Administration of Cultural Heritage (hereafter SACH, a unit of the Ministry of Culture) of China released a new *Archaeological Fieldwork Manual*. Borrowing concepts and technical guidelines from British and Japanese manuals, the manual thoroughly revamps the previous version which was first published in 1984. The updated version aims to change profoundly archaeological survey, excavation, storage and conservation methodologies across the nation. ①

The New Manual

In 2005, SACH commissioned Beijing University to undertake a major revision of the 1984 manual, drawing upon global developments in archaeological thinking, fieldwork techniques, and storage and conservation guidelines. ②The new manual makes wide-ranging recommendations: for example, it calls attention not only to stratigraphy, but also to spatial organisation and formation processes; it stipulates the use of sieving and flotation to recover small animal bones, seeds and artefacts; it recommends that

---

* The article was originally published in *Antiquity* 88, 2014, The Project Gallery. It is reprinted in this anthology with minor changes.

① Zhao, H., Tianye kaogu gongzuo guicheng de xiuding, tuiguang he peixun, *Zhongguo Wenwubao*, 22 June 2012, p. 7.

② Zhao, H., L. Qin, H. Zhang, B. Sun, Xinxingshi xinxuyao xinguicheng: Xinxiuding, *Tianye Kaogu Gongzuo Guicheng* de xiangguan shuoming, *Nanfang Wenwu* 3, 2009, p. 2.

pottery and stone artefacts are not cleaned so as to preserve starch residues for future research. As a result of these and many other guidelines, archaeological projects should no longer focus narrowly on chronology and culture definition and should become more open to specialists from various other disciplines. Unlike in the past, archaeology and other sciences are to be closely integrated. ①

The manual also prescribes new data recording and publishing procedures. The former comprises three complementary parts: detailed documentation, mapping and photography/filming of all aspects of the excavation process. ②These documents, together with artefacts and samples, are to be properly archived so as to be accessible to scholars of any discipline. ③As regards publishing, although the old manual mandated full publication, in reality excavation reports were little more than a presentation of limited examples of features and artefacts, serving largely to illustrate chronology and cultural affiliation. ④This narrow focus significantly slowed, and sometimes rendered hopeless, the publication of reports and significantly constrained Chinese archaeology. ⑤The new manual, with its priorities in multi-disciplinary and comprehensive research, presses for faster and comprehensive publication of detailed descriptions of site formation, plans, archaeological features and all artefacts without distraction by time-consuming research articles. ⑥

In order to make these principles and standards operable, the new manual

---

① State Administration of Cultural Heritage, *Tianye Kaogu Gongzuo Guicheng*, Bejing: Wenwu, 2009; Zhao, H., Tianye kaogu gongzuo guicheng de xiuding, tuiguang he peixun, *Zhongguo Wenwubao*, 22 June 2012, p. 7.

② State Administration of Cultural Heritage, *Tianye Kaogu Gongzuo Guicheng*, Bejing: Wenwu, 2009, pp. 6–7.

③ State Administration of Cultural Heritage, *Tianye Kaogu Gongzuo Guicheng*, Bejing: Wenwu, 2009, p. 7.

④ Ministry of Culture, *Tianye Kaogu Gongzuo Guicheng*, Bejing: Ministry of Culture, 1984, p. 7.

⑤ Zhao, H., L. Qin, H. Zhang, B. Sun, Xinxingshi xinxuyao xinguicheng: Xinxiuding, Tianye Kaogu Gongzuo Guicheng de xiangguan shuoming, *Nanfang Wenwu* 3, 2009, pp. 3–4.

⑥ State Administration of Cultural Heritage, *Tianye Kaogu Gongzuo Guicheng*, Bejing: Wenwu, 2009, pp. 8–9; Zhao, H., L. Qin, H. Zhang, B. Sun, Xinxingshi xinxuyao xinguicheng: Xinxiuding, *Nanfang Wenwu* 3, 2009, p. 6.

provides technical guideline, including those for survey, excavation, mapping and sampling.① It also requires that conservation be incorporated into project design. In the past, individual excavators determined how much (or little) effort was placed on conservation; there was no mandatory requirement in the old Manual. Realising that cultural artefacts are most vulnerable to damage at the moment they are excavated, the new manual requires excavators to make provision for trained personnel and equipment for on-site conservation.

Trial Application

As with other national policies and regulations, SACH adopted a "test-and-refine" approach to the new manual. It commissioned several trial applications to assess its effectiveness and to detect potential problems.② For example, in 2011 a group of archaeologists from province- and local-level institutions undertook a systematic survey of the Chalcolithic walled settlement of Shimao in Shenmu county, Shaanxi province.③ The Shimao site had already been subject to earlier survey and excavation but remained poorly understood.④

The 2011 work included intensive field-walking to collect surface artefacts and the mapping of structures with GPS.⑤ Field survey of this kind was

---

① State Administration of Cultural Heritage, *Tianye Kaogu Gongzuo Guicheng*, Bejing: Wenwu, 2009, pp. 11 – 43.

② Zhao, H., Tianye kaogu gongzuo guicheng de xiuding, tuiguang he peixun, *Zhongguo Wenwubao*, 22 June 2012, p. 7.

③ Yang, L., Shenmu Shimao xinshiqi shidai juluo diaocha, in Shaanxi Province Institute of Archaeology ed., *Annual Reports of the Shaanxi Province Institute of Archaeology*, Unofficial publication, 2011, pp. 14 – 16.

④ Dai, Y., Shaanxi Shenmuxian Shimao longshan wenhua yizhi diaocha, *Kaogu* 3, 1977, pp. 154 – 157, 172; Banpo Museum, Shaanxi Shenmu Shimao yizhi diaocha shijue jianbao, *Shiqian Yanjiu* 2, 1983, pp. 92 – 100; Wang, W. Z. Sun, Shimao yuqi de niandai ji xiangguan wenti, *Kaogu yu Wenwu* 4, 2011, pp. 40 – 49.

⑤ Yang, L., Shenmu Shimao xinshiqi shidai juluo diaocha, *Annual Reports of the Shaanxi Province Institute of Archaeology*, Unofficial publication, 2011, pp. 14 – 16.

introduced to China during the 1990s through a number of joint projects. ①The Manual significantly raises the standards for such regional survey work, requiring detailed topographical environmental and archaeological recording in addition to the narrower obligations of the previous guidelines. For example, it requires the

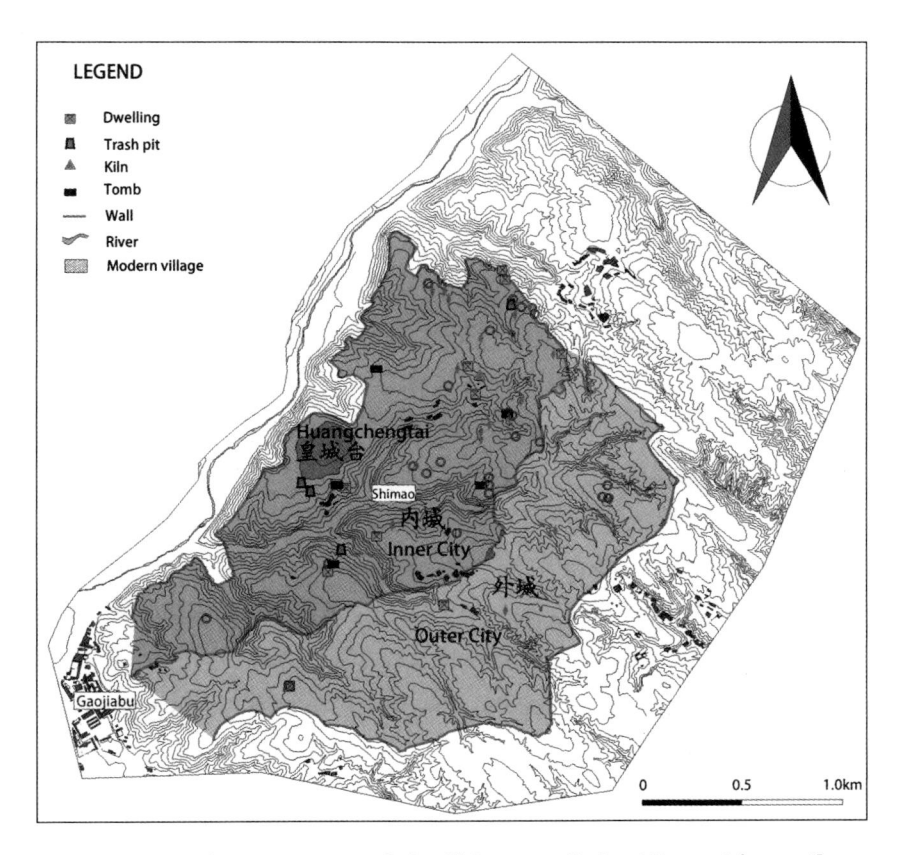

Fig. 1 - 2 - 1 A survey map of the Shimao walled settlement in northern Shaanxi province

(Extracted from Zhouyong Sun, Jin Shao, Nan Di, 2020, Shimao yizhi de kaogufax yu yanjiu zongshu, *Zhongyuan Wenwu 1*, 2020, Fig. 2)

---

① e. g. Sino-American Joint Huan Valley Fieldwork Team, Huanhe liuyu quyu kaogu yanjiu chubu baogao, *Kaogu* 10, 1998, pp. 13 - 22; Sino-American Joint Liangcheng Region Archaeological Team, Archaeological survey in the Rizhao region of Shandong Province, *Kaogu* 5, 2002, pp. 10 - 18; Chen, Xingcan, Li Liu, Hanwei Hua (Henry T. Wright), and Lin Ai, Social complexization in the heartland of Chinese civilizations: a study of settlement pattern in the Yi-Luo region, *Kaogu Xuebao* 2, 2003, pp. 161 - 218; Sino-American Joint Chifeng Archaeological Project, *Phase Report of the Regional Survey in Eastern Inner Mongolia (Chifeng)*, Beijing: Kexue, 2003.

preparation of large-scale maps and aerial photographic coverage in advance of fieldwork.①As a result, the Shimao survey accurately mapped the settlement's two wall circuits and established its size, 425ha. Pottery sherds indicate occupation during the late Longshan period (2600BC – 1900BC); this preliminary chronology will be refined by radiocarbon dates of samples collected during the survey.②The discovery of the hitherto neglected walled settlement, the accurate mapping of the site, and other abundant fresh data hence produced make the project a showcase of field survey for SACH (Fig. 1 – 2 – 1). Indeed, without the inspiration of the manual, it could have operated in the traditional manner and given much less data, albeit with contemporary technologies, as happened with the third nationwide survey of cultural heritage in China in 2007 – 2011.

Conclusion

In recent years regional survey, zooarchaeology and archaeobotany have been used by various projects in China, but by codifying and endorsing these practices on a national level, the new manual marks a milestone in the development of Chinese archaeology. Since 2009, the technical guidelines contained in the manual have been integrated into SACH's annual training programmes for fieldworkers as well as university curricula, and SACH monitors the implementation of the manual's guidelines through its inclusion in the review of excavation projects.③Although to date only a few trial applications have been undertaken, it will potentially have great influence on the practice of Chinese archaeology in years to come. As well as defining new standards for fieldwork, the new manual requires archaeological institutions to build storage facilities and

---

① State Administration of Cultural Heritage, *Tianye Kaogu Gongzuo Guicheng*, Bejing: Wenwu, 2009, pp. 1 – 3.

② Yang, L., Shenmu Shimao xinshiqi shidai juluo diaocha, in Shaanxi Province Institute of Archaeology ed., *Annual Reports of the Shaanxi Province Institute of Archaeology*, Unofficial publication, 2011, pp. 14 – 16.

③ Zhao, H., Tianye kaogu gongzuo guicheng de xiuding, tuiguang he peixun, *Zhongguo Wenwubao*, 22 June 2012, p. 7.

purchase new equipment, and encourages them to hire more conservators and to support more conservation centres. In addition, it advocates more rapid publication and higher-quality reporting, and consequently it will provide a solid foundation for future scholarship. As the guidelines in the new manual come into force, Chinese archaeology will be transformed.

Acknowledgement

Thank you to Professor Xingcan Chen for his valuable comments on the draft of this article. All errors remain my own.

Chinese Field Methods[*]

Introduction

Although the study of ancient artifacts has a long history in China, the modern science of archaeology was brought to China only in the late nineteenth century by foreign explorers and archaeologists. Since the 1920s, however, as the Nationalist government curbed foreigners' field activities in its land, native archaeologists, mostly Western-trained, from a few institutions (the Cenozoic Research Laboratory of the Geological Survey of China, the Institute of History and Philology of Academic Sinica and the Society for Historical Studies of National Beiping Academy) began to play the major role. [①]The political fragility and economic feebleness of the time, however, did not allow science to develop significantly. Although much progress was made in excavation techniques, including the division of strata and typological analysis of artifacts,[②] only a modest number of sites had been excavated and a small group of archaeologists had been trained by 1949, the year when the Communist Party took over the mainland China.

Dramatic changes came about after 1949. Having unified the country, the Chinese Communist Party set out to modernize its industry, science, and education. And having decided to dissect its relations with the West and side with the Soviet Union, it urged the academic community to learn the "advanced

---

[*] The article was originally published in Martin Carver ed., *Encyclopedia of Global Archaeology*, New York: Springer. It is reprinted in this anthology with minor changes, pp. 1443 – 1446.

[①] Chen, X., *Zhongguo Shiqian Kaoguxueshi Yanjiu* 1895 – 1949, Beijing: Sanlian Shudian, 1997, p. 87.

[②] Chen, X., *Zhongguo Shiqian Kaoguxueshi Yanjiu* 1895 – 1949, Beijing: Sanlian Shudian, 1997, pp. 145 – 162, 227 – 249, 310 – 329.

experience (Xianjin jingyan)" of the Soviet science. The archaeologists and their students, who were trained in the West or educated in the pro-West Nationalist Era, had little choice but to study Soviet theories and methods.① Archaeology, which now received lavish state support, continued to be cast as a subdiscipline of history as in the Nationalist Era, but it was now imposed upon a new paradigm: Marxist dialectical materialism and historical materialism. While dialectical materialism introduces the concept of social evolution, historical materialism brings the subjects of social relations, economy, and technology to archaeology.② The Soviet archaeology also demanded that archaeologists devote themselves to the life of the subject and down-trodden people, as a counterforce to their natural instinct, that is, to excavate tombs and monuments of the social elites. It does not follow, however, that Chinese archaeologists gave priority to settlements and tombs of the common people. In fact, apart from a few exemplary Neolithic settlements that were dug to fulfill the Marxist mandate, they continued to favor large urban centers, such as Erlitou, Anyang, Luoyang, and Chang'an, and monumental tombs for the purpose of uncovering treasures and wonders to illustrate the grandeur of Chinese history and civilizations.③

Key Issues/Current Debates/Future Directions/Examples

Chinese archaeologists translated many Soviet publications to avail themselves not only of ready-made models of integrating the Marxist theories into archaeological interpretation, but also of "advanced" fieldwork methodologies. As a result, they began their fieldwork with systematic survey, thereby acquiring the basic information of the location, chronology, and cultural definition of a single site as well as informing questions such as the geographic distribution and

---

① Zhang, L., Soviet inspiration in Chinese archaeology, *Antiquity* 85, 2011, p. 1052.
② Xia, N., Tianye kaogu xulun, *Wenwu Cankao Ziliao* 4, 1952, pp. 81–84.
③ Zhang, L., Soviet inspiration in Chinese archaeology, *Antiquity* 85, 2011, p. 1052.

the ecological environment of a culture.[①] In addition, Chinese archaeologists innovatively adopted the "Luoyang spade," a coring device which local treasure hunters had developed to search for tombs, as a prospecting tool. Skilled hands were trained to identify various types of features (tombs, architectural foundations, trash pits, riverbeds) from the soil samples taken from underground. Thanks to its efficiency and low cost, the tool is still popular today; one can often use it to get a good idea of the layout as well as stratigraphy of a site without excavation.

When Chinese archaeologists excavate a settlement, they usually lay out box pits of 2 ×2 m, which they replicate to expose large areas (Fig. 1 – 3 – 1). This method is very helpful because many settlements in China feature long habitation history and complex cultural deposit. Although it had also been used in the West, they were obliged by the ideology of the time to attribute the credit of inspiration to the Soviet archaeologist T. S. Passek (1903 – 1968). While earlier excavators were unable to discover houses at the Tripoly'e settlement because they had only opened narrow trenches and small areas, in the 1930s, Passek successfully discovered structures of 100 – 120m^2 in dimension with the box excavation. In a country blessed with long history and thick cultural deposit, this method appears to be very useful, as it provides a better stratigraphic control and a better understanding of a settlement: division of space and episodes of reconstruction.[②] Dubbed by Chinese archaeologists as "small excavation units but large-scale exposure," it was put to good use at the model Neolithic settlement of Banpo near Xi'an and Jiangzhai.[③] While the size of the unit is often adjusted to the specific circumstances and objectives of an excavation (it is now usually 5 ×5m or 10 × 10 m), the box-pit excavation

---

① Xia, N., Kaogu gongzuo de jinxi-liangtiao luxian de duibi. *Kaogu Tongxun* 2, 1958, pp. 1 – 4.

② Yan, W., Kaogu yizhi de fajue fangfa, in *Kaoguxue Yanjiu*, Beijing: Beijing Daxue, Vol. 2, 1994, p. 252.

③ Zhongguo Kexueyuan Kaogu Yanjiusuo, *Xi'an Banpo*, Beijing: Wenwu, 1963; Banpo Museum, Shaanxi Institute of Archaeology, Lintong County Museum, *Jiangzhai: A Report on the Excavation of a Neolithic Site*, Beijing: Wenwu, 1988.

remains the standard operational method today. ①

Ancient cities, especially those of the protohistoric and historical periods, demand a different approach. Following the Soviet guidelines, Chinese archaeologists first study historical documents to address questions about material production, social relations, and the spiritual life of the population. They can then turn to other questions such as spatial division, public amenities, and external economic connections. Since cities are much larger and more sophisticated than Neolithic settlements, it is unrealistic to implement the full-coverage excavation; small excavation units are instead deployed at particular sections to address particular questions, such as layout and chronology. Three phases of deposit are generally investigated to define their chronology: those formed during construction, those formed during occupation, and those after abandonment. This set of methods was effectively applied to the excavation of Chang'an, a capital of the Western Han Dynasty (206BCE – 9CE), near the present-day city of Xi'an. Together with the method of dividing cultural strata by soil content and color, it is still cherished as a working principle today. ②

Regional Genealogy and Variations

The intense learning of the Soviet archaeology came to a halt after the breakup of the Sino-Soviet brotherhood in the 1960s. Having turned away from the West in 1949, Chinese archaeologists were now secluded from the development of archaeological theories and methods over the world. Without external inspiration, they were left to move forward from what they had inherited from the Nationalist Era and learned from the Soviet. In the volatile political atmosphere that lingered from the 1950s through to the 1980s, however, theoretical thinking, even in the name of Marxist theories, was a life-threatening venture. Hence, no middle-range theories and methodologies were developed to

---

① Shi, X., Tianye kaogu fangfa-diaocha, fajue yu zhengli, in W. Yin ed., *Kaogu Gongzuo Shouce*, Beijing: Wenwu, 1982, pp. 18 – 19.

② Zhang, Z., Dicengxue yu leixingxue de ruogan wenti, *Wenwu* 5, 1983, p. 62.

第一部分　中国考古学史

Fig. 1 – 3 – 1　The "small unit/large exposure" (box system) in action on an excavation at Yangguanzhai, Shaanxi, in 2005 – 2006
(State Administration of Cultural Heritage, *Major Archaeological Discoveries in China in* 2006, Beijing: Wenwu, 2007, p. 16)

extrapolate the Marxist subjects of social relations, economy, and technology; discussion of these subjects was little more than filling fresh data into the old pigeonholes of Marxist theories. It was the typology and culture-historical paradigm inherited from the Nationalist Era, safeguarded by the sustained national consciousness, that had the chance of further development in the subsequent decades.

It was Su Bingqi (1909 – 1997), a courageous thinker for his time, who held the beacon for theoretical development in China. He began his theoretical venture in the 1930s when he attempted to work out a chronology for the cemetery at Doujitai in Baoji, Shaanxi province. Employing Montelius's typology but tempering it with his own interpretation, he selected the diagnostic ceramic ware li-tripod as the subjects of typological analysis, divided them into four types, and traced each type's evolutionary path. ①Since the 1950s, the division of *xing* (type), and *shi* (sub-type), which stands for the chronological subtype, became the standard method in Chinese typology. ②This method was further refined to fit the ever-growing excavation materials by Su Bingqi himself and his disciples. In his endeavor to set up chronologies for the Shang urban centers of Zhengzhou and Anyang, Zou Heng innovatively correlated stratigraphic and typological sequences of ceramic wares from these sites. ③

Su Bingqi's creativity did not end up at the typological analysis. He further developed a theory, namely, the "regional cultural genealogy and variations (*quxileixing*)," that offers a handy framework for organizing and explaining them. ④In this general and flexible formulation, the archaeological cultures that had been discovered by the 1970s were grouped into six macroscopic culture-historical regions; each region comprises of a few microregions, whose cultures are lined up from the Paleolithic Age through to the Bronze Age. Rejecting the conventional assumption that Central China was the cradle of Chinese

---

① Su, B., Doujitai goudongqu muzang (excerpt), in *Su Bingqi Kaoguxue Lunshu Xuanji*, Beijing: Wenwu, 1984, pp. 3 – 58.

② Su, B., Jieyu, in Zhongguo Kexueyuan Kaogu Yanjiusuo ed., *Luoyang Zhongzhoulu (xigongduan)*, Reprinted in *Su Bingqi Kaoguxue Lunshu Xuanji*, Beijing: Wenwu, 1984, pp. 65 – 87; Su, B., Guanyu Yangshao wenhua de ruogan wenti, *Kaogu Xuebao* 1, 1965, pp. 51 – 82.

③ Zou, H., Shilun Zhengzhou xin faxian de Yin Shang wenhua yizhi, *Kaogu Xuebao* 3, 1956, pp. 77 – 103; Zou, H., Shilun Yinxu wenhua fenqi, *Beijing Daxue Xuebao* (Renwen kexue ban) 4, 1964, pp. 77 – 103; 5, 1964, pp. 63 – 90.

④ Su, B., W., Yin, Guanyu kaoguxue wenhua de quxi leixing wenti, *Wenwu* 5, 1981, pp. 10 – 17; Su, B., W., Yin, Dicengxue yu qiwuxingtaixue, *Wenwu* 4, 1982, pp. 1 – 7.

civilizations lifting the outlying regions from backwardness, he emphasized instead that it was the outlying regions that outshined and enlightened Central China in the Prehistoric periods. Believing in the historicity of traditional texts, he further linked some of the regional cultures with early ethnic groups recorded in these texts. ①

New Development

The typological analysis and the "regional cultural genealogy and variations" theory were imbued into a national fieldwork manual issued in 1984.②Su Bingqi and his disciplines, all prominent figures in Chinese archaeology, frequently traveled across the nation to deliver them to his fellow colleagues, and urged them to patch up the gaps of the cultural lineages of their regions. Blessed by the growing excavations since the 1970s, each province was able to write its cultural history, more or less complete, from the Paleolithic Age well into the historical periods. ③They nevertheless brought much harm to Chinese archaeology in the meantime. Emphasizing on the importance of depositional strata and ceramic typology, they ignored many of other questions, such as the settlement pattern, and subsistence economy, as well as many types of data, such as soil, food residue, and botanical and faunal remains.

Since the late 1970s, however, China reopened itself to the World, and once again appreciated foreign archaeological theories and methods, mostly of the West and Japan. In 2005, the SACH commissioned the Archaeology Department of Beijing University, the leading institution in China, a major revision of the 1984 manual to catch up with the current development in archaeology over the globe. From manuals of Britain and Japan, the new

---

① Su, B., W., Yin, Guanyu kaoguxue wenhua de quxi leixing wenti, *Wenwu* 5, 1981, pp. 10 – 17; Su, B., W., Yin, Dicengxue yu qiwuxingtaixue, *Wenwu* 4, 1982, pp. 1 – 7.

② Ministry of Culture, *Manual of Archaeological Fieldwork*, Reprinted by the Experimental Teaching Center of Archaeology and Anthropology of Xiamen University, 2007.

③ Wenwu Editorial Committee ed., *Wenwu Kaogu Gongzuo Sanshinian*, Beijing: Wenwu, 1979; Wenwu Editorial Committee ed., *Wenwu Kaogu Gongzuo Shinian*, Beijing: Wenwu, 1991.

manual, which was issued in 2009, adopts the social archaeology of the West and the research subjects of settlement pattern, subsistence economy, craft production, and social organization. It asks excavators to pay attention not only to stratigraphy, but also to spatial organization and formation process of a site. It inserts sifting and flotation facilities into the excavation process so as to gather tiny animal bones, plant seeds, and artifacts for future analysis. In addition, it demands on-site conservation for the purpose of protecting fragile artifacts and features.[1] In line with the new standards, an excavation project is no longer targeted at narrow subjects such as chronology and culture definition, but becomes a platform for multidisciplinary cooperation; it is no longer a closed domain for the excavators alone, but an open territory for many specialists who examine various types of materials. In this way, Chinese archaeology will surely interact with the world communities more actively in the future.

---

[1] State Administration of Cultural Heritage, *Tianye Kaogu Gongzuo Guicheng*, Bejing: Wenwu, 2009.

Chinese Archaeology in the Twenty-First Century[*]

Chinese archaeology, after the devastating Cultural Revolution (1966 – 1976), finally embarked on a normal track of development. In the era of the "Reform and Open Door," the Marxist paradigm faded away from the academic sphere, whereas the regionalist paradigm arose to become the new beacon for Chinese archaeology. [①]This paradigm, juxtaposed with the rejuvenated historiographical and antiquarianist orientations, however, continued to hamper Chinese archaeology from playing out its full potential. [②]Since the late 1990s, while these forces remain omnipotent, a number of new developments have gradually mitigated their power. As a result of the rocket-like rise of economy, the entire country plunged into an unprecedented period of feverish modernization of infrastructure and urbanization. The grand construction projects and the rapidly growing state funding for research projects have injected vitality, perhaps too much and too fast, into the long-sluggish discipline. In the meantime, the influx of international expeditions and Western theories gradually transformed Chinese archaeology and triggered a thorough overhaul of the outdated fieldwork manual in 2009. The new manual, which was rigorously implemented by the State Administration of Cultural Heritage (hereafter SACH) to the entire country, has revolutionized the paradigm, methodology, and

---

* The article was originally published in C. Smith ed., *Encyclopedia of Global Archaeology*, https: //doi. org/10. 1007/978 – 3 – 319 – 51726 – 1_ 3365 – 1. It is reprinted in this anthology with minor changes.

① Von Falkenhausen, Lothar, The regionalist paradigm in Chinese archaeology, in Philip L. Kohl and Clare Fawcett ed., *Nationalism, Politics and the Practice of Archaeology*, Cambridge, UK: Cambridge University Press, 1996, pp. 198 – 217.

② Von Falkenhausen, Lothar, On the historiographical orientation of Chinese archaeology, *Antiquity* 67, 1993, pp. 839 – 849.

technological equipment of Chinese archaeology, which in turn has empowered it to reorient their research agenda, dispatch expeditions to foreign countries, and develop underwater archaeology.

Mega Infrastructure Modernization Projects

The Three Gorges Dam was designated to build up a dam in the middle of the Yangtze River; planned ever since the 1910s, it was put into execution in 1994. Within the affected area of 1074km^2, archaeological work had been sporadically done since the 1950s, and a number of important sites, including Longgupo in Wushan county, where an ape of 2 million years ago was found, had been uncovered; after the start of the project, an extensive archaeological survey was carried out which recorded 1074 sites, including 723 underground ones. These sites, however, had to be taken care of within mere 15 years, i.e., 1994 – 2009; thus, although over 30 universities and archaeological institutes from all over the country poured their manpower into this area, only a small fraction of them was subject to proper rescue excavation. The most extraordinary discovery was the salt production site at Zhongba in Zhong county, where 6 years of excavation exposed nearly 100 tombs, 300 house foundations, and 600 trash pits within an area of 6600m^2. [1]The cultural deposits, altogether 12.5m thick, comprised strata of the Neolithic Age through the Qing dynasty. [2]The discovery of a stratum of the Daxi culture at Liujiaba in Wushan county advanced the record of the earliest human activity in this area to as early as 5000BC. These sites, together with the historic site of Baidicheng in Fengjie county, whether or not completely excavated, were all submerged under water after 2009. [3]

---

[1] Liu, Yuchuan, Guangji Xu, and Hua Sun, Sanxia kaogu dahuizhan, *Civilization* 3, 2003, p. 65.

[2] Liu, Yuchuan, Guangji Xu, and Hua Sun, Sanxia kaogu dahuizhan, *Civilization* 3, 2003, p. 65.

[3] Liu, Yuchuan, Guangji Xu, and Hua Sun, Sanxia kaogu dahuizhan, *Civilization* 3, 2003, p. 64.

This ushered in a succession of grand projects. The South-North Canals Project, which was meant to deliver water from the Yangtze River to alleviate the draught that has long stricken northern China, consists of three lines, among which the Eastern and Middle Lines have been implemented. The Eastern Line, which links the Lower Yangtze River to the city of Tianjin, passes through Jiangsu, Shandong, and Hebei provinces. Utilizing the historical Grand Canal, rivers, and lakes along the way as well as building dozens of pumping stations, this line was started in 2002 and completed in 2014. Over 50 institutions from all over the country participated in the survey and excavation in the affected area within Jiangsu province alone, discovering a number of important sites, including the Han dynasty city of Liangwangcheng, the Han dynasty lineage cemetery of Shantou, and a cluster of tombs of the Yuan, Ming, and Qing dynasties pertaining to the active operation of the Grand Canal.[1] The Middle Line is used to draw water from the Danjiangkou Reservoir in Hubei province and transmit it through newly built canals in Henan and Hebei provinces and finally reach the cities of Tianjin and Beijing. Within the affected territory, over 600 sites had to be excavated within 9 years (2004 – 2013). About 24 institutions were involved in the excavation campaign, and by 2009 a half of them were excavated. Among them, the Yangshao culture settlement of Longshangang in Xichuan county, the late Shang settlement of Guandimiao in Xingyang city, the Eastern Zhou Chu cemetery of Xujialing in Xichuan county, and the royal cemetery of the Northern Dynasties in Yecheng are all important sites.[2]

Preservation of Important Sites

All of the above projects, plus the West-East Gas Pipelines, the high-speed railway and freeway networks, as well as the rapid urbanization all over the country, put ancient urban centers, settlements, and cemeteries, especially

---

[1] Lü, Chunhua, Nanshui beidiao gongcheng Jiangsu duan kaogu fajue gongzuo de chengguo ji tedian, *Zhongguo Wenwubao*, 19 July 2013, p. 7.

[2] Zhang, Zhiqing, and Fawei Liang, "Nanshuibeidiao zhongxian gongcheng kaogu faxian yu yanjiu xueshu yantaohui" jiyao, *Huaxia Kaogu* 3, 2010, pp. 44 – 48.

those located within or adjacent to modern cities, at risk of destruction. Although the Chinese Cultural Relic Protection Law was issued in 1982 and amended several times thereafter, it is up to the discretion of the all-powerful governments of the Central and Provincial levels whether to respect it or not. The state and provincial administrations of cultural heritage could not challenge but usually bend to the desire of, or sometimes collaborate with, the governments. Many of the affected sites had been designated as National Cultural Heritage, but they were either perceived as peripheral matters or as annoying obstacles to economic development, or over-exploited as tourist attractions.[①]

Alarmed by the escalating destruction to the archaeological sites, particularly those of national significance, such as the late Shang capital at Anyang, and the Sui and Tang dynasties capital at Xi'an, the State Administration of Cultural Heritage (hereafter SACH) figured out two strategies. One is to increase the number of applications for adding sites to the World Cultural Heritage List. China joined the *Convention Concerning the Protection of the World Cultural and Natural Heritage* in 1985, and by 2002, it had put 23 major sites, i.e. the Paleolithic site of Zhoukoudian, the Dunhuang Grottoes, the Terracotta Army, the Longmen Grottoes, and the Yungang Grottoes, on the list. This helped to implement protection programs, to change the attitude of the local governments and populations, and to bring tourist revenues. Since 2001, the SACH became more active in organizing these applications, even setting up a department specifically handling them, and overseeing the protection of the World Heritage sites.[②] To date, 17 more archaeological sites, including the late Shang capital at Anyang, the city and mausoleums of the Koguryo kingdom in Ji'an, the Silk Road, the Grand Canal, the Yuan dynasty city of Shangdu, and the Ming and Qing dynasties complexes of Tusi, have been named as World Heritage sites.

---

① Lu, Jiansong, Zhongguo dayizhi baohu de xianzhuang, wenti ji zhengce sikao, *Fudan Xuebao* (Social Sciences Edition) 6, 2005, pp. 120 – 126.

② Li, Rang, Zhongguo shijie wenhua yichan baohu shiye buru xinjieduan, *Zhongguo Wenhua Yichan* 2, 2004, pp. 64 – 67.

The other strategy is to focus on the "Great Sites," that is, large and significant sites. Since 2002, the SACH has integrated programs of investigation, protection, and display of these sites into the national Five-Year Plans of development, which the local governments have to execute faithfully. In the beginning, 50 sites were included in the Eleventh Five-Year Plan (2006 – 2010), then 100 in the Twelfth Five-Year Plan (2011 – 2015), and 150 in the Thirteenth Five-Year Plan (2016 – 2020). These programs entail the freezing of the territory of the site from any major developments, very much to the distress of the local governments, who lose valuable land for social and economic development. As a practical way of easing the tension between their interests and the programs, site parks were advanced as a solution for sites within or adjacent to modern cities. This solution turns a site into a recreation area or tourist attraction, and allows the local government to use the surrounding land for development. Such solution had been tried at the site of the Qujiang Pond (1996 – 2007), the imperial garden of the Tang dynasty capital of Chang'an. Once exalted as "the Qujiang model," the project has invited much critique, because it destroyed any cultural deposits in the surrounding area. Nevertheless, the same solution is now being implemented at other "Great Sites".[1]

Archaeologists have participated in the planning and execution of both the World Heritage application and the "Great Sites" protection projects; for both objectives, they have carried out a great deal of fieldwork for the sake of understanding the dimensions, cultural value, and preservation strategy of the target sites. Among them, Liangzhu figures very prominently. In the 1980s, the site was discovered to have one large walled settlement and three aristocratic cemeteries, whose tombs were furnished lavishly with jade objects. But as it is located near the economically vibrant city of Hangzhou, it became increasingly entangled with the expansion of the city. In 2001, the provincial government of Zhejiang set up a protection zone for the Liangzhu site, in which a park was planned and urban development was barred, whereas the surrounding zone was urbanized. Since 2006, Liangzhu has been exalted as a model site, included in

---

[1] Wang, Xuerong, "Zhongguo dayizhi baohu yantaohui" jiyao, *Kaogu* 1, 2008, pp. 38 – 45.

the protection program of the SACH and placed on the list of application for World Cultural Heritage. Thanks to both programs, large-scale excavation was resumed, leading to the discovery of the water-diverting canals outside the complex and rice paddies near the large walled settlement. ①

The Origin of Chinese Civilizations Project

In 1996, a grand research project, "the Xia-Shang-Zhou Chronology," was initiated by Song Jian (1931 -   ), then head of the National Science Committee (now Ministry of Science and Technology), to refine the chronologies of the Xia, Shang, and Zhou dynasties, the earliest dynasties recorded in Chinese historical accounts. The chronology of the three dynasties had in fact been tackled by generations of scholars, both Chinese and international, in various fields. The existence of the Xia dynasty has been and is still doubted by some scholars; however, as Song and other top leaders of China were upset by the fact that the "Chinese civilization" is not as old as those of the Near East and Egypt, a project should be undertaken. Specialists from various research institutions were mobilized to work out a finer chronology, a modest yet difficult objective. Nine teams were organized to deal with nine subjects: historians (headed by Li Xueqin 1933 - 2019) were to collect records of datable events in received texts; archaeologists (headed by Li Boqian 1937 -   ) were to excavate at key sites such as Erlitou, Yanshi Shang city, Anyang, and Fengxi, to find diagnostic cultural strata for dating Xia, Early Shang, and Late Shang; astronomers (headed by Zhang Peiyu 1935 -   ) were to search oracle bone and bronze inscriptions for astronomical events that anchor the date of King Wu's conquest of the Shang dynasty and the reign dates of all the kings of the Western Zhou; dating scientists (headed by Qiu Shihua 1932 -   ) were to provide a fine-grained chronological series of radiocarbon dates. Marred by internal disagreement, the project was concluded in 2000 without producing the

---

① Renfrew, Colin, and Bin Liu, The emergence of complex society in China: The case of Liangzhu, *Antiquity* 92/364, 2018, pp. 975 - 990.

wished-for results. ①

The project nevertheless provided an ideal precedent for other large multi-year projects to come. In 2001, the grand project, "The Origin of Chinese Civilizations," was launched to further fulfill the aspiration of Song Jian. It was tailored to prove the long-held claim of the existence of "Five Thousand Years of Chinese Civilizations," which would make the Chinese civilizations rival with Near Eastern and Egyptian Civilizations. Some scholars, international and Chinese, are doubtful of this claim, which would require the Chinese civilization to have risen before 3000BC, in archaeological terms, within the Neolithic Age. The Ministry of Science and Technology was nevertheless fully supportive of the project. Under the leadership of two archaeologists Wang Wei and Zhao Hui, a multi-institutional and multi-disciplinary team was organized in the same manner as for the Xia-Shang-Zhou Chronology Project.

After 2 years of preparatory work, the project was officially activated. During its first official stage (2004 – 2005), the project was set to focus on the region of the Central Plain and the period of 2500BC – 1500BC, or the Longshan, Erlitou, and Early Shang periods, addressing five subjects: (1) a fine-grained radiocarbon chronology of the archaeological cultures in the region; (2) the natural environment; (3) settlement pattern and social structure; (4) economy and technology; and (5) the formation of Chinese civilization. When it came to the second stage (2006 – 2008), the same set of questions was posted to address the period of 3500BC – 2500BC, or the late Yangshao and the early Longshan periods; it was also extended to include the important sites of Shimao in the Ordos Plateau, Taosi in the middle Yellow River, Shijiahe in the middle Yangtze River, Liangzhu in the Lower Yangtze River, and Niuheliang in the Liao River Valley. A third stage (2009 – 2015) was undertaken to wrap up the project,② although no official reports have been published to date.

Based on the data it had acquired, the project proposed a new set of

---

① Xia-Shang-Zhou Duandai Gongcheng Zhuanjiazu, *Xia Shang Zhou Duandai Gongcheng* 1996 – 2000 *nian Jieduan Chengguo*, Beijing: Shijie Tushu, 2000.

② Wang, Wei, and Hui Zhao, Guanyu Zhonghua wenming tanyuan gongcheng, *Zhongguo Wenwubao*, 23 July 2012, p. 5.

material indicators of civilization: the development of agriculture and craft production; the building of monumental settlements and public structures that demand a great deal of labor investment; the building of palaces and temples that display royal power; the use of ritual objects that manifest sophisticated craftsmanship and high status. The Neolithic sites of Niuheliang in Liaoning province and Lingjiatan in Anhui province, dated to 3500BC and featuring large tombs furnished lavishly with jade objects and grand ritual structures, thus arrive at the threshold of civilization; the sites of Liangzhu and Taosi, dated to 3000BC – 2000BC and featuring grand settlements, massive palaces, and large tombs, have passed the threshold toward state-level society and civilization. During the next period, the imposing palaces, ritual bronzes, and bronze and turquoise workshops lift the Erlitou culture to the stage of "royal state," a homegrown term that designates the Shang and Zhou dynasties. The project thus inferred that civilization emerged in the Neolithic Age in several of the outlying regions, but all these civilizations disappeared to give way to the single "royal state" in the Central Plain in the Bronze Age (1750BC – 500BC) . [1]

After the completion of the project, the SACH funded another project "Discovering China." With an ambiguous yet trendy title, the project follows the spirit of the previous one to investigate the formation of civilizations in the Central Plain and the outlying regions, including the Ordos Plateau, the middle and the lower Yangtze River, highlighting the star sites of Shimao, Shijiahe, Liangzhu, and significant, newly discovered sites. Unlike the previous two, the project is directed by the SACH and executed by provincial institutes of archaeology; without any temporal and spatial constraint, it is flexible enough to incorporate any new discoveries of any period which bear on the origin of Chinese civilization, the origin of human beings in China, and the formation of the multi-ethnic unity of China: that is, grand walled settlements, monumental structures, rich cemeteries, even the imperial mausoleum of the Liao dynasty. Designated as a priority project of the SACH during the Thirteenth Five-Year

---

[1] Wang, Wei, and Hui Zhao, Guanyu Zhonghua wenming tanyuan gongcheng, *Zhongguo Wenwubao*, 23 July 2012, p. 5.

Plan period, it is yet in progress; as such, only some discoveries have been reported.①

International Fieldwork Projects in China

After the rise to power of the Chinese Party, political circumstances forced Chinese archaeologists to cut connections with the West in the 1950s, then with the Soviet Union in the 1960s, and thus with all the major archaeological communities of the world. By the late 1970s, only a few top Chinese scholars were sporadically in touch with foreign archaeologists. There were neither foreign research projects in China, nor Chinese field projects in foreign countries, with one exception. In the early 1960s, upon the request of North Korea, a joint Sino-Korean expedition was organized to investigate sites of the Neolithic and Bronze Ages, Koguryo, and Bohai periods in northeastern China. But the subsequent territorial conflict between the two countries caused the Chinese government to shut the door to international collaborative projects. It was only in the 1990s that China was reopened.②

The first international collaborative project on Chinese soil was that of Harvard University, led by Kwang-chih Chang (1931 – 2001), who had strenuously sought for such a project since the late 1970s. In 1990, his project of searching for the proto-Shang capital in the Shangqiu city was finally landed on the ground.③ This project was followed by other ones from the United States, France, and Japan. These international expeditions brought not only funds that China was badly lacking, but also new research agendas and methods. Among them, the teams of the Andover Foundation for Archaeological Research and

---

① Li, Yun, "Kaogu Zhongguo" xiangmu qude zhongyao jinzhan, *Guangming Daily*, 24 December 2018, p. 9.
② Zhang, Liangren, Woguo guoji kaogu hezuo de xianzhuang he wenti, in Xiaoyong Xiao ed., *Jucai Lancui Zhuxinpian: Meng Fanren Xiansheng Bazhi Huadan Songshou Wenji*, Beijing: Kexue, 2019, pp. 495 – 406; reprinted in this anthology.
③ Zhang, Liangren, Woguo guoji kaogu hezuo de xianzhuang he wenti, in Xiaoyong Xiao ed., *Jucai Lancui Zhuxinpian: Meng Fanren Xiansheng Bazhi Huadan Songshou Wenji*, Beijing: Kexue, 2019, pp. 495 – 406; reprinted in this anthology.

Harvard University came to Jiangxi and Hunan provinces to study the origin of rice agriculture.① The teams of Yale University, Minnesota University, and University of Pittsburg introduced the approach of regional survey to the Liangchengzhen site in Shandong province, the Huan River valley in Henan province, and the Chifeng region in Inner Mongolia. ② The team of the University of California, Los Angeles (UCLA), investigated the salt production site of Zhongba in the Three Gorges area before it was drowned. Among the French and Japanese teams, those from the National Scientific Research Center of France and the Buddhist University of Japan investigated a few ancient Buddhist monasteries deep in the Tarim Desert. ③ Thanks to these field projects, the study of Chinese archaeology in the West and Japan has grown significantly.

New Archaeological Fieldwork Manual

The "Xia-Shang-Zhou Chronology" and the "Origin of Chinese Civilization" projects as well as the international field projects brought new theoretical paradigms and new research strategies to Chinese archaeology, which prompted a thorough overhaul of the outdated *Archaeological Fieldwork Manual*. First issued in 1984, the manual was modeled upon the regionalist paradigm. The typological method was introduced to China and adapted to Chinese data by Bingqi Su (1909 – 1997).④ In the frenzied development of the "Marxist Chinese archaeological system" in the 1950s, typology was attacked as "bourgeois." Su nevertheless kept pondering over the regional cultural

---

① Zhang, Liangren, Woguo guoji kaogu hezuo de xianzhuang he wenti, in Xiaoyong Xiao ed., *Jucai Lancui Zhuxinpian: Meng Fanren Xiansheng Bazhi Huadan Songshou Wenji*, Beijing: Kexue, 2019, pp. 495 – 406; reprinted in this anthology.

② Zhang, Liangren, Woguo guoji kaogu hezuo de xianzhuang he wenti, in Xiaoyong Xiao ed., *Jucai Lancui Zhuxinpian: Meng Fanren Xiansheng Bazhi Huadan Songshou Wenji*, Beijing: Kexue, 2019, pp. 495 – 406; reprinted in this anthology.

③ Zhang, Liangren, Woguo guoji kaogu hezuo de xianzhuang he wenti, in Xiaoyong Xiao ed., *Jucai Lancui Zhuxinpian: Meng Fanren Xiansheng Bazhi Huadan Songshou Wenji*, Beijing: Kexue, 2019, pp. 495 – 406; reprinted in this anthology.

④ Hein, Anke, The Problem of Typology in Chinese Archaeology, *Early China* 39, 2016, pp. 21 – 52.

distinction of the Yangshao (5000BC – 2800BC) and Longshan (2800BC – 1800BC) periods. After examining archaeological cultures in more regions in the 1970s, he began to develop the theory of "regional cultural genealogy and variations," which sought to establish the cultural sequences of individual regions. In a time when most archaeologists, Chinese and international, held on to the traditional outlook that the only civilized part of China was the Central Plain, the theory gave due respect to the multilineal development of regional cultures, and gave rise to the notion of "multiple origins of Chinese civilizations". [1]

This theory, which constituted the backbone of what some call the "Chinese School" of archaeology, was the mother of the 1984 manual, a collective work compiled by Yin Weizhang (1936 –   ). The establishment of regional cultural sequences was thus taken to be the primary objective of Chinese archaeology. Since the 1990s, however, new theories and fieldwork methods streamed in from other countries, and the constraints of the 1984 manual appeared acute. Thus in 2005, the SACH commissioned Beijing University to conduct a major revision of the manual. From manuals of Britain and Japan, a whole set of survey, excavation, recording, storage, and conservation guidelines are borrowed.[2] A broad spectrum of subjects of settlement pattern, subsistence economy, craft production, and social organization are adopted. A full-coverage survey is instituted to investigate the distribution of artifacts, the natural environment, and local resources of a site. During excavation, attention is given to the spatial organization and the formation process of the site. Sifting and flotation are implemented to collect animal bones and plant seeds for further archaeobotanical and zooarchaeological studies. An excavation project is no longer aimed at narrow subjects such as the definition, chronology, and ethnic association of a culture, but at wider range of subjects and multi-disciplinary research. Much attention is paid to issues of conservation. Understanding that

---

[1] Zhang, Liangren, Chinese archaeological school, *Antiquity* 87, 2013, pp. 896 – 904.

[2] Zhang, Liangren, New developments in Chinese archaeology, *Antiquity* 88/339, 2014, The Project Gallery.

cultural artifacts are most vulnerable to damage at the moment when they are exposed to air, it stipulates that conservation personnel and apparatus be ready on site so that fragile artifacts can be taken care of instantly. ①Delicate artifacts are given instant consolidating treatment instead of being left to turn into powder; particularly small artifacts are transported in their original block of earth to laboratories to be excavated there under minute documentation rather than being taken out quickly in the field. ②

Before implementing the manual on all field projects in the country, the SACH commissioned several trial applications so as to demonstrate its advantages to the field archaeologists as well as to collect feedback for improvement. For instance, in 2011, a group of archaeologists of Shaanxi province undertook a systematic survey of the walled settlement of Shimao. An old-fashioned survey and a test excavation had been conducted there in the past, but the site remained poorly understood. This time the team carried out a full-coverage survey of a 20m-wide transect, recorded GPS data and architectural features, and gathered all pottery shards within the sampling zones. As a result, the knowledge of the settlement was augmented dramatically. The two circles of walls of the settlement were discovered and its dimension was accurately worked out as 425ha. ③

Chinese Field Projects in Foreign Countries

The new manual, vigorously promulgated by the SACH through field training programs and inspection of on-going fieldwork, leads not only to the improvement of fieldwork and research standards, but also to the upgrade of research facilities, including fieldwork equipment, conservation and research

---

① Zhang, Liangren, New developments in Chinese archaeology, *Antiquity* 88/339, 2014, The Project Gallery.

② Zhang, Liangren, New developments in Chinese archaeology, *Antiquity* 88/339, 2014, The Project Gallery.

③ Zhao, Hui, Shaanxi Shenmu Shimao yizhi kaogu fajue yanjiu de jinzhan jiqi yiyi, *Zhongguo Wenwubao*, 23 August 2016, p. 3.

laboratories, as well as university curriculum to catch up with the progress in the field. The annual "Top Ten National Discoveries" Award, started by *Zhongguo Wenwubao* in 1990, and the "Six National Great Discoveries" Award, started by the Institute of Archaeology of Chinese Academy of Social Sciences in 2010, compel archaeologists to refine their fieldwork and research. Among all the archaeological discoveries of the year all over the country, ten or six are selected for the awards. As time goes on, the awards ascribe increasing value to the fieldwork and research methodology of archaeologists as well as the scholarly significance of the discoveries. Highly visible in national media such as CCTV and Xinhua News, the award ceremonies of the two awards have become occasions of pompous gala like the "Oscar Award." Archaeological institutions and local governments scramble to use state-of-the-art technologies and conduct multi-disciplinary research, and conjure up national consciousness and the Party ideology of multi-ethnic unity of Chinese civilization, to win them. As a result, they have charged archaeological institutions with plentiful energy to update their fieldwork and research capacities, which quickly reach the threshold of excess. It is now not only possible but also necessary for them to export these capacities to foreign countries.

Chinese institutions began to send expedition to foreign land in 1998, when the Ministry of Commerce, upon the request of UNESCO, funded the Chinese Institute of Cultural Heritage to conserve the ancient city of Angkor Wat in Cambodia, which included archaeological investigation. In 2005, it funded another project in Mongolia, organized by the Inner Mongolian Institute of Cultural Relics and Archaeology, to investigate Xiongnu, Uighur, and Turkic cemeteries. After President Xi Jinping announced the "One-Belt One-Road" Initiative in 2013, the number of teams dispatched to foreign countries has increased significantly.[①] Most institutions, however, have to secure their own sources of funding, which are much less bountiful and sustainable; the SACH,

---

① Zhang, Liangren, Woguo guoji kaogu hezuo de xianzhuang he wenti, in Xiaoyong Xiao ed., *Jucai Lancui Zhuxinpian: Meng Fanren Xiansheng Bazhi Huadan Songshou Wenji*, Beijing: Kexue, 2019, pp. 495–406; reprinted in this anthology.

quite surprisingly, cannot help much. The first teams sent by the Heilongjiang and Jilin Province Institutes of Cultural Relics and Archaeology, as well as Jilin University, to the Far East of Russia in the early 2000s turned out to be ephemeral. [1]The project of Northwest University in Uzbekistan and Tajikistan was in a better situation, because it received a sizeable fund from the provincial government of Shaanxi. [2]

In a time of economic recession in many countries throughout the world, the Chinese teams provide not only much-needed funding for archaeological research, but also bring refined expertise and technical equipment to the target countries. [3]After several decades of fieldwork, Chinese archaeologists have developed an extraordinary expertise in field survey and excavation; in most regions of China, houses, ash pits, and tombs are built of earth materials, without using stone or mud-brick, and in most cases, they are hardly distinct. But Chinese archaeologists have mastered the skills and tools needed to discern them. The expedition of the Institute of Archaeology of the Chinese Academy of Social Sciences, to Uzbekistan, which was started in 2012, brought both of them to the site of Ming Tepa. The site was known to have one round of wall (500 × 800m) only, but after systematic application of the so-called Luoyang drill, a handy and efficient tool for survey work originally developed by grave robbers, it was found to have an outer wall, which effectively expanded its size to 2100 × 1300m. It was also found, again with the tool, to possess two roads, and a cemetery outside the eastern wall. The Chinese drill was also brought by a team of Nanjing University to Iran to define the boundary of Tepe Naderi in Northern Khorasan province. The area around the tepe has been buried under multiple layers of silt and washout from the tepe; the use of the drill in 2016

---

[1] Zhang, Liangren, Woguo guoji kaogu hezuo de xianzhuang he wenti, in Xiaoyong Xiao ed., *Jucai Lancui Zhuxinpian: Meng Fanren Xiansheng Bazhi Huadan Songshou Wenji*, Beijing: Kexue, 2019, pp. 495 – 406; reprinted in this anthology.

[2] Zhang, Liangren, Woguo guoji kaogu hezuo de xianzhuang he wenti, in Xiaoyong Xiao ed., *Jucai Lancui Zhuxinpian: Meng Fanren Xiansheng Bazhi Huadan Songshou Wenji*, Beijing: Kexue, 2019, pp. 495 – 406; reprinted in this anthology.

[3] Wang, Wei, Zhongguo kaoguxue guojihua de licheng yu zhanwang, *Kaogu* 9, 2017, pp. 3 – 13.

enabled the Sino-Iranian Joint Expedition to define the original ground and boundary of the tepe. ①

By the end of 2017, Chinese institutions have sent 22 expeditions to 13 countries over the globe. Most of them work in countries along the "Belt and Road," including Kazakhstan, Bangladesh, as far as Kenya. The rapid development of international projects in the last 18 years, however, has not been well prepared for. Most of the Chinese directors do not master the language and archaeology of the target countries. What's worse, no archaeological program at Chinese universities offers any training in the archaeology of any foreign country. Because of the lack of trained personnel, the excavation materials are published only in Chinese and the language of the target countries, thus inaccessible to most scholars of the international archaeological communities. To make the field projects in the foreign countries sustainable, such archaeological programs are urgently needed. ②

Underwater Archaeology

Owing to the growing economy of China, underwater archaeology has been rapidly developed as well. Underwater cultural heritage, i. e. shipwrecks, vexed the nerve of Chinese archaeologists in 1987, when an Australian company excavated 239,000 items of Chinese porcelains from a wrecked ship in the South China Sea and sold them on the international antiquities market. The Center for Underwater Archaeology was thus founded at the National History Museum; in the 1990s, young personnel were sent to Japan, United States, and the Netherlands, to learn underwater excavation techniques. In the meantime, the center began to survey Chinese waters, and discovered a number of

---

① Zhang, Liangren, Woguo guoji kaogu hezuo de xianzhuang he wenti, in Xiaoyong Xiao ed., *Jucai Lancui Zhuxinpian*: *Meng Fanren Xiansheng Bazhi Huadan Songshou Wenji*, Beijing: Kexue, 2019, pp. 495 – 406; reprinted in this anthology.

② Zhang, Liangren, Woguo guoji kaogu hezuo de xianzhuang he wenti, in Xiaoyong Xiao ed., *Jucai Lancui Zhuxinpian*: *Meng Fanren Xiansheng Bazhi Huadan Songshou Wenji*, Beijing: Kexue, 2019, pp. 495 – 406; reprinted in this anthology.

Chinese Archaeology in the Twenty-First Century

shipwrecks in subsequent decades.[1] A prominent discovery was made of an ancient commercial boat, "Nanhai I." Loaded with celadon wares of the Southern Song dynasty, the boat was entirely salvaged and delivered to a museum specifically built for it in 2007.[2] Since 2014, the boat "China Archaeology 01," specifically designed for underwater archaeology, and three research bases have been put into use, which augment the capacities of the center.[3]

Along with the growing number of field projects in foreign countries, the center, renamed the National Center for the Protection of Underwater Cultural Heritage and placed under the SACH in 2009, sent a team to Kenya. The well-known Chinese fleet dispatched by the early Ming Court in 1405 – 1433 reportedly reached East Africa, which seems to be well attested by abundant Ming dynasty ceramics found there.[4] A report of local descendants of Chinese sailors, who survived the capsizing of a ship, by The New York Times, caught the attention of the Chinese government. Suspecting that Zheng He, the commander of the fleet, actually landed there, the SACH sent specialists to investigate the site in 2005, and after 5 years of pilot survey, dispatched underwater archaeologists to the seabed of the Lamu Archipelago and Marindi Bay.[5] Although it failed to find substantial evidence for the landing of Zheng He, the team made a number of important discoveries, including a shipwreck dating to the sixteenth/seventeenth centuries and coming from Portugal found in

---

[1] Wu, Chunming, Zhongguo shuixia kaogu 20 zai, *Ocean World* 8, 2007, pp. 26 – 30.

[2] Zhang, Liangren, Woguo guoji kaogu hezuo de xianzhuang he wenti, In Xiaoyong Xiao ed., *Jucai Lancui Zhuxinpian: Meng Fanren Xiansheng Bazhi Huadan Songshou Wenji*, Beijing: Kexue, 2019, pp. 495 – 406; reprinted in this anthology.

[3] Zhang, Liangren, Woguo guoji kaogu hezuo de xianzhuang he wenti, in Xiaoyong Xiao ed., *Jucai Lancui Zhuxinpian: Meng Fanren Xiansheng Bazhi Huadan Songshou Wenji*, Beijing: Kexue, 2019, pp. 495 – 406; reprinted in this anthology.

[4] Zhang, Liangren, Woguo guoji kaogu hezuo de xianzhuang he wenti, in Xiaoyong Xiao ed., *Jucai Lancui Zhuxinpian: Meng Fanren Xiansheng Bazhi Huadan Songshou Wenji*, Beijing: Kexue, 2019, pp. 495 – 406; reprinted in this anthology.

[5] Zhang, Liangren, Woguo guoji kaogu hezuo de xianzhuang he wenti, in Xiaoyong Xiao ed., *Jucai Lancui Zhuxinpian: Meng Fanren Xiansheng Bazhi Huadan Songshou Wenji*, Beijing: Kexue, 2019, pp. 495 – 406; reprinted in this anthology.

Ngomeni Ras, which is filled with elephant tusks, copper ingots, mercury, copper molds, and glazed pottery.①

Conclusion

The development of Chinese archaeology in the twenty-first century, as the above review suggests, is phenomenal. Due to the limitation of space, this brief glosses over a few concurrent events, i. e. the rampant occurrence of tomb-robbing and the mushrooming of new museums, but it presents the major ones. Following the economic boom of China, the large-scale infrastructure projects, such as the Three Gorges Dam, the South-North Canals, plus the West-East Gas Pipelines, the high-speed railway and freeway networks, and rampant urbanization have brought long-dormant archaeological institutions a flood of rescue excavation and funding. On top of that, the state-funded preservation projects of the "Great Sites" and the research projects such as "the Origin of Chinese Civilizations" and "Discovering China" have further enhanced their vitality. On the one hand, the amount of fieldwork and data may have been too much and too fast for archaeological institutions to absorb. On the other hand, the lavish amount of funding and influx of new theories and methods have significantly boosted their capabilities, the momentum of which the SACH quickly picked up and disseminated to the entire country through the revised Archaeological Fieldwork Manual. The improved capacities have even enabled Chinese institutions to send expeditions to foreign countries and develop underwater archaeology. As a result, Chinese archaeologists have been able not only to free themselves from the prolonged yokes of the regionalist paradigm, the historiographic and antiquarianist orientations, but also to interact more actively with the international archaeological communities, by engaging themselves in more intense exchange of scholarship and fieldwork in foreign countries.

---

① Zhang, Liangren, Woguo guoji kaogu hezuo de xianzhuang he wenti, in Xiaoyong Xiao ed., *Jucai Lancui Zhuxinpian: Meng Fanren Xiansheng Bazhi Huadan Songshou Wenji*, Beijing: Kexue, 2019, pp. 495-406; reprinted in this anthology.

中国国际考古合作的现状和问题*

一 前言

2017年3月2日，中国考古界发生了一件大事，就是中国社会科学院考古研究所成立了外国考古研究中心。近20年来，中国的一些大学和文物考古机构陆续走出国门，到世界各国开展考古工作，已成燎原之势。① 不过，中国学者走出国门不久，仍然缺乏经验和人才。外国考古研究中心的成立，可以"整合各方力量，发挥协同作用"，可谓恰逢其时。② 借此之机，本文梳理中国开展外国考古的历程，总结经验，发现问题，为以后外国考古的发展建言献策。

二 关注外国考古

从20世纪20年代考古学传入中国开始，中国学者就一直关心中国文化的起源问题，他们发掘渑池仰韶、安阳殷墟、日照城子崖和宝鸡斗鸡台遗址，同时关注中亚和黑海北岸的考古资料，都是为了回答这个问题。中国考古学家真正关心外国的考古工作是从20世纪50年代开始的。当时中国各条战线都在学习苏联，考古学界也不例外。③

---

* 本文首先发表于肖小勇主编《聚才揽粹著新篇：孟凡人先生八秩华诞颂寿文集》，科学出版社2019年版，第495—406页。

① 袁靖：《境外考古热中的冷思考》，《光明日报》2017年4月11日第12版。
② 杨阳：《中国社会科学院成立外国考古研究中心》，《中国社会科学报》2017年5月12日。
③ Zhang, Liangren, Soviet Inspiration in Chinese Archaeology, *Antiquity* 85, 2011, pp. 1049-1059.

第一部分　中国考古学史

在此过程中，中国学者不仅翻译了苏联的教科书和教学大纲，[①] 而且翻译了一些中亚、西伯利亚的发掘资料和研究成果。[②] 1960 年以后又因为与苏联决裂，中国学术界为了批判，又翻译了一些苏联考古学资料。[③] 从 1976 年到 1984 年，林沄在吉林大学还开过《西伯利亚考古》课程，为此收集了苏联考古资料。[④]

由于外交工作的需要，从 20 世纪 50 年代到 80 年代，中国考古工作者还翻译介绍了其他一些国家的考古文献。他们主要关注的是社会主义阵营和亚非拉第三世界国家，其中包括朝鲜、[⑤] 蒙古、[⑥] 越南、柬埔寨、[⑦] 巴基斯坦、[⑧] 印度、[⑨] 阿尔巴尼亚、[⑩] 捷克斯洛伐克、[⑪] 罗马尼亚、[⑫] 埃及、[⑬]

[①] 文献颇多，这里仅举三例。А. Л. 蒙盖特：《苏联考古学》，中国科学院考古研究所译，内部发行，1963 年；Т. С. 帕谢克：《特黎波里居址的田野考查方法》，《考古通讯》1956 年第 3 期，第 101—112 页；佚名：《苏联"考古学通论"教学大纲》，《考古通讯》1955 年第 1 期，第 71—77 页。

[②] 文献颇多，这里仅举三例。М. Е. 马松、В. М. 马松：《中亚金石并用时代及青铜时代的考古文化》，《考古通讯》1960 年第 3 期，第 55—64 页；М. Л. 格里亚兹诺夫、О. И. 达维母、К. М. 斯卡郎：《阿尔泰巴泽雷克的五座古冢》，《考古》1961 年第 7 期，第 63—69、16 页；苏联大使馆新闻处供稿：《渤海王国的遗迹》，《考古》1960 年第 1 期，第 44 页。

[③] 吉林大学曾经组织一批论文，此举两例。林沄、杨建华：《舒藩河上出土的金代上享宜春县镜——兼驳苏修考古学家的谬论》，《吉林大学学报》（社会科学版）1979 年第 1 期，第 96—100 页；杨建芳：《"仰韶文化西来说"旧调的重弹——评瓦西里耶夫的两篇反华文章》，《四川大学学报》（哲学社会科学版）1977 年第 1 期，第 129—134 页。

[④] 林沄：《我的学术道路》，《我的学术思想》，吉林大学出版社 1996 年版。

[⑤] 宿白：《朝鲜安岳所发现的冬寿墓》，《文物参考资料》1952 年第 1 期，第 101—104 页。

[⑥] H. 赛尔奥德扎布：《蒙古人民共和国的考古遗存简述》，《考古》1963 年第 3 期，第 169—171 页。

[⑦] 夏鼐：《柬埔寨著名的历史遗产——吴哥古迹》，《考古》1972 年第 3 期，第 58—63 页。

[⑧] 夏鼐：《中巴友谊的历史》，《考古》1965 年第 7 期，第 357—364 页。

[⑨] 印度大使馆新闻处供稿：《印度河流域古文化的新发现》，《考古》1959 年第 3 期，第 167—168、176 页。

[⑩] 安志敏：《阿尔巴尼亚考古新发现及其发现》，《考古》1963 年第 4 期，第 173—180、187 页。

[⑪] 卢米尔·伊斯耳博士：《捷克斯洛伐克考古学概况》，《考古通讯》1958 年第 2 期，第 68—70、11—13 页。

[⑫] 家皓译：《罗马尼亚人民共和国最近的考古工作》，《考古通讯》1958 年第 6 期，第 59 页。

[⑬] 穆斯塔法·埃尔·埃米尔：《近年来的埃及发掘》，《考古通讯》1957 年第 2 期，第 113—117 页。

秘鲁、①墨西哥。②有些学者如夏鼐、安志敏、王仲殊和余明谦还访问过苏联、③伊朗、④阿尔巴尼亚、⑤保加利亚⑥和越南。⑦中国考古工作者偶尔也关注希腊、⑧澳大利亚、⑨西欧、⑩美国⑪和日本⑫的考古工作。虽然处于冷战时期，但是中国考古学者没有与世界隔绝，仍然从事一些学术访问和文献翻译。

三 "迎进来"考古

1978年改革开放以后，中国学术环境逐步宽松。一直关心中国考古的日本和西方学者纷纷来中国考察，收集资料，讨论学术合作；而中国学者出国访问日本和西方国家的机会逐渐增加，交流中国考古发现和研究成果。受此影响，中国考古学在外国迅速发展，成果和人才培养稳步增长。与此同时，区系类型学逐渐成为中国考古学界的指导思想，中国考古学家集中精力研究各个区域的文化序列和中国文明的起源问题。可惜的是，在20世纪80年代和90年代，中国学者对于外国考古的关

---

① 中国科学院考古研究所资料室：《秘鲁古代文化》，《考古》1972年第4期，第58页。
② 王仲殊：《墨西哥古代文化简述》，《考古》1973年第4期，第258页。
③ 王伯洪、王仲殊：《苏联考古工作访问记》，《考古》1959年第2期，第101—104页；1959年第4期，第201—202、211页；1959年第5期，第264—267、236页；1959年第9期，第496—504页。
④ 夏鼐：《近年中国出土的萨珊朝文物》，《考古》1978年第2期，第111—116页。
⑤ 夏鼐、王仲殊：《阿尔巴尼亚访问记》，《考古》1973年第5期，第313页；石兴邦：《欧洲旧石器文化略说》，《考古通讯》1958年第3期，第55—72页。
⑥ D. P. 基米特洛夫：《保加利亚的旧石器、新石器、金石并用和青铜时代》，《考古》1959年第9期，第494页。
⑦ 余明谦：《越南古迹记游》，《文物》1959年第2期，第53页。
⑧ 考古研究所翻译组编译：《希腊弗吉纳发现马其顿大墓》，《考古》1978年第3期，第210—212页。
⑨ 安志敏：《南澳大利亚的石器》，《考古》1974年第6期，第399—405页。
⑩ 黄培熙节译：《英国圣奥尔班发现古罗马时代文物》，《考古通讯》1957年第5期，第84页。
⑪ 邹志学节译：《美国早期石器时代文化考古简讯》，《考古通讯》1957年第5期，第82—84页。
⑫ 文献较多，仅举一例。杉原庄介：《日本农业文化的生成》，《考古通讯》1957年第5期，第90—94页。

心大幅度下降。①

1978年中美建交以后，哈佛大学的张光直教授曾极力推动中美之间的学术合作，当时哈佛大学和四川大学已经谈妥一个合作项目，但是因为考古界领导层的反对而流产。② 只是进入20世纪90年代以后，由于中国政府进一步开放，同时中国文物考古界严重缺乏经费和技术，封闭了30多年的国门才得以打开，外国考古学家开始进入中国开展考古工作。

最先发展起来的是中美合作项目。1990年，张光直教授为了寻找商文明，发起了商丘考古项目。为此，哈佛大学皮保德博物馆与中国社会科学院考古研究所开始了长达十年之久的合作，在商丘寻找最早的商城。③ 1992年，美国埃德沃考古学研究基金会（Andover Foundation for Archaeological Research）与江西省文物考古研究所合作，考察和试掘了江西万年、乐平、分宜等地的洞穴遗址，1993年和1995年发掘了万年县的仙人洞遗址，推动了稻作农业和陶器起源的研究。④ 2004年和2005年，为了进一步揭开稻作农业起源的面纱，美国哈佛大学人类学系与湖南省文物考古研究所在道县发掘了玉蟾岩遗址。⑤ 1995年以后，芝加哥自然历史博物馆、耶鲁大学和山东大学合作在山东省日照市两城镇开展区域调查和发掘。⑥ 1997年，美国明尼苏达大学科技考古实验室与中国

---

① 1985年，发表了三篇介绍外国考古的文章。蔡凤书：《日本考古的历史与现状》，《文史哲》1985年第5期，第35—41页；张光直：《当前美国和英国考古概况》，《考古与文物》1985年第3期，第104—110页；B. A. 切尔金、C. 克伦、J. C. 列别杰夫：《苏联考古学的成就和问题》，《史前研究》1985年第4期，第95—104页。后来期刊上就少见这类文章了。

② 夏鼐：《夏鼐日记》，1981年12月22日，华东师范大学出版社2009年版，第九卷，第96页。

③ 侯卫东：《商丘区域考古研究书评》，《华夏考古》2016年第4期，第139—146页。

④ 吴小红、张弛、保罗·格德伯格、大卫·科恩、潘岩、蒂娜·阿平、欧弗·巴尔-约瑟夫：《江西仙人洞遗址两万年前陶器的年代研究》，《南方文物》2012年第3期，第1—6页。

⑤ 吴小红、伊丽莎贝塔·博阿雷托、袁家荣、欧弗·巴尔-约瑟夫、潘岩、曲彤丽、刘克新、丁杏芳、李水城、顾海滨、韦琪·居、大卫·科恩、天朗·娇、保罗·戈德伯格、史蒂夫·韦纳：《湖南道县玉蟾岩遗址早期陶器及其地层堆积的碳十四年代研究》，《南方文物》2012年第3期，第7—15页。

⑥ 中美两城地区联合考古队：《山东日照市两城镇遗址1998—2001年发掘简报》，《考古》2004年第9期，第7—18页。

社会科学院考古研究所合作,在安阳市境内的洹河流域开展区域调查,并因此发现了洹北商城。① 1999 年,内蒙古文物考古研究所、中国社会科学院考古研究所、吉林大学边疆考古研究中心和匹兹堡大学组成的中美赤峰联合考古队在赤峰地区的锡伯河、半支箭河、西路嘎河和阴河做了区域考古调查。② 同年,加州大学洛杉矶分校、北京大学考古系和成都市文物考古研究所组成联合考古队,开始在四川省和重庆市调查古代盐业遗址,并发掘了忠县的中坝遗址。③ 这些项目不仅为中国带来了紧缺的经费和新技术,而且推动了中国考古学在美国的发展,哈佛大学、匹兹堡大学、加州大学洛杉矶分校和耶鲁大学纷纷培养中国考古学方向的研究生。

与此同时,一些欧洲国家也来到中国做合作项目。1993—2005 年,法国国家科研中心中亚考古研究所与新疆文物考古研究所联合,在新疆克里雅河下游做了连续的考古调查与发掘,因此发现了丹丹乌里克、喀拉墩和圆沙古城以及一些佛寺壁画和毛织品。④ 2000—2002 年,巴黎高等研究实践学院与武汉大学历史学院合作,发掘了河南南阳龚营遗址。⑤ 借着这些项目的东风,法国、德国和英国的一些大学也开始培养中国考古学方向的研究生。

随后日本学者也逐渐进入中国开展合作项目。1995 年以后,日本佛教大学与新疆文物考古研究所发掘了新疆尼雅遗址,发现了一座佛

---

① 唐际根、荆志淳、徐广德、瑞普·拉普:《洹河流域区域考古研究初步报告》,《考古》1998 年第 10 期,第 13—22 页。

② 塔拉、郭治中、朱延平、滕铭予:《内蒙古赤峰地区区域性考古调查阶段性报告(1999—2001)》,《边疆考古研究》(第 1 辑),科学出版社 2002 年版,第 357—368 页。

③ 李水城:《近年来中国盐业考古领域的新进展》,《盐业史研究》2003 年第 1 期,第 9—15 页。

④ 张玉忠:《"新疆克里雅河流域考古考察学术讨论会暨文物展示会"在法国巴黎举行》,《考古》2001 年第 5 期,第 92 页;王瑟:《揭开圆沙古城的神秘面纱》,《光明日报》2007 年 3 月 29 日第 5 版。

⑤ 杨宝成、杜德兰:《南阳附近的龚营遗址的发掘:方法和结果》,《考古发掘与历史复原》,中华书局 2006 年版;Alain Thote and Karine Michel, Une coopération franco-chinoise: les fouilles du site de Gongying, *Archéopages*, Hors-série 2, 2010, pp. 79–84.

寺和一处墓地。① 2002 年双方又调查发掘了丹丹乌里克佛寺。② 1995—1996 年，日本的东京共立女子大学、滋贺县立大学、茨城大学与宁夏文物考古研究所、固原博物馆和北京大学组成的"中日原州古墓考古队"，合作发掘了固原的唐代史道洛墓、北魏田弘墓。③ 1998 年，日本奈良国立文化财研究所与中国社会科学院考古研究所合作发掘西汉长安城遗址。④ 2003—2005 年，日本秋田县埋藏文化财中心与甘肃省文物考古研究所合作发掘武威磨咀子墓地。⑤ 与此同时，一些学术机构如千叶大学、九州大学、京都大学开始培养中国考古学方向的研究生。

四 "走出去"考古

20 世纪到 21 世纪之交，随着中国经济的好转，中国文物考古机构的工作经费逐渐充盈。在中国境内的国际项目仍然存在，但是得到审批的项目不多，到了今天还有八项（中日良渚、中美洮河流域、中美两城镇、中美大凌河流域、中美归城、中美曲阜、中美石寨山）。这是一件让人遗憾的事情。虽然中国考古机构现在不缺经费，但是开放国门仍然是非常重要的。中国考古学不仅要面向国内，还要面向世界，而外国学者的参与是最好的宣传中国考古和中国文明的方式。遗憾的是，研究中国考古学的外国学者本来就不多，近几年人数虽然还在增长，但是非常缓慢。

与此相反，中国文物考古机构开始走出去，由周边国家开始，逐渐

---

① 于志勇：《1995 年尼雅考古的新发现》，《西域研究》1996 年第 1 期，第 115—118 页。
② 新疆文物考古研究所：《新疆丹丹乌里克遗址新发现的佛寺壁画》，《边疆考古研究》2008 年第 7 辑，第 408—429 页。
③ 刘泉龙、梁娟：《中日考古新发现》，《宁夏画报》1996 年第 5 期，第 30—31 页。
④ 本刊记者：《中国社会科学院考古研究所与日本奈良国立文化财研究所联合举行中日合作发掘西汉长安城遗址新闻发布会》，《考古》1998 年第 5 期，第 95—96 期。
⑤ 王辉、赵雪野、李永宁、王琦、王勇、宁生银、大野宪司、村上义直、新海和广、魏美丽：《2003 年甘肃武威磨咀子墓地发掘简报》，《考古与文物》2012 年第 5 期，第 28—38 页。

走到了遥远的伊朗和中美洲。2012年以后,随着中国政府提出"一带一路"倡议,走出去的机构和发掘项目越来越多,迄今已经在13个国家开展了22个项目(表1-5-1)。需要说明的是,中国学者参与的外国考古项目,如2000年中国社会科学院考古研究所到德国发掘美伦艾克遗址,① 2017年武汉大学到吴哥城洞里萨特(Prasat Tonle Snguot)遗址的发掘,② 2017年中山大学到伊朗锡斯坦萨迪格(Tepe Sadegh)遗址发掘,③ 都不在本文的讨论范围。下面分区域来叙述。

表1-5-1　　　　　中国参与的外国考古项目统计表

国家	合作单位	项目	时间(年)
蒙古国	内蒙古自治区文物考古研究所	青铜时代、匈奴、突厥、回鹘遗址	2005—今
蒙古国	河南省文物考古研究院	高勒毛都2号墓地(匈奴)	2017—今
俄罗斯	黑龙江省文物考古研究所	哈巴罗夫斯克市郊遗址(新石器时代)	2001
俄罗斯	吉林大学边疆考古研究中心	特罗伊茨基墓地(渤海国)	2004
俄罗斯	中国社会科学院考古研究所	库纳列依斯克城址(渤海国)	2005
俄罗斯	吉林省文物考古研究所	克拉斯基诺城址(渤海国)	2011
俄罗斯	南京大学历史学院	卡勒望湖-Ⅰ和苏联路遗址	2015—今
朝鲜	延边大学	高句丽和渤海国遗址	2008—今
越南	四川省文物考古研究院、陕西省考古研究院	永福省义立遗址	2006
柬埔寨	中国文化遗产研究院、中国社会科学院考古研究所	周萨神庙遗址的发掘与保护	1998—1999
柬埔寨	中国文化遗产研究院	茶胶寺遗址的保护和修复	2009—2013
柬埔寨	中国文化遗产研究院	吴哥王宫遗址修复	2017—今
老挝	云南省文物考古研究所、四川大学历史文化学院	沙湾拿吉省Sepon矿区	2014—今
孟加拉	湖南省文物考古研究所	毗诃罗普尔遗址群	2014—今

---

① 袁靖:《境外考古热中的冷思考》,《光明日报》2017年4月11日第12版。
② 侯芝:《2017年柬埔寨洞里萨特医院遗址考古发掘纪实》,《中国文物报》2017年12月1日第7版。
③ 中山大学社会学与人类学学院谭玉华网页:http://ssa.sysu.edu.cn/teacher/2508。

续表

国家	合作单位	项目	时间（年）
印度	故宫博物院	奎隆港口	2017—今
乌兹别克斯坦	中国社会科学院考古研究所	明铁佩城址	2012—今
乌兹别克斯坦	西北大学丝绸之路文化遗产与考古学研究中心	撒马尔罕盆地遗址群	2012—今
哈萨克斯坦	陕西省考古研究院	拉哈特古城遗址	2017—今
伊朗	南京大学	纳德利土丘	2016—今
肯尼亚	中国国家博物馆、北京大学考古文博学院	拉穆群岛及其周边	2010—2013
肯尼亚	河南省文物考古研究院、山东大学	东非大裂谷吉门基石遗址	2017—今
洪都拉斯	中国社会科学院考古研究所	科潘城址	2015—今

（一）东亚和北亚

在东亚和北亚，中国考古机构在俄罗斯、蒙古和朝鲜开始了合作考古项目。

1. 俄罗斯

中国在俄罗斯的合作考古项目开始较早。2001年，黑龙江省文物考古研究所与俄罗斯科学院远东分院远东民族历史考古民族研究所一道，在哈巴罗夫斯克市郊发掘了一处遗址，获得了新石器时代早期（13000—9000BP）的30余件人工石器和陶器。[①] 2002年，中国社会科学院考古研究所派人赴海森崴，参加了库纳列依斯克城址的发掘，并考察了靺鞨时期的墓地和渤海时期的城址。[②] 2004年，吉林大学边疆考古研究中心与俄罗斯科学院西伯利亚分院考古与民族研究所组成考古队，发掘了靺鞨文化的特罗伊茨基墓地。发掘出土的人骨资料在长春市和新

[①] 黑龙江省文物考古研究所：《中俄专家首次联合探寻黑龙江流域文明起源》，新华网，2002年6月4日。

[②] 中国社会科学院考古研究所赴俄罗斯考古考察发掘团：《俄罗斯滨海地区2002年考古考察纪要》，《考古》2005年第8期，第74—90页。

西伯利亚市的实验室做DNA分析。[1] 时隔七年，吉林省文物考古研究所与俄罗斯科学院远东分院远东历史考古民族研究所合作发掘了渤海时期的克拉斯基诺城址。[2]

上述项目虽然为四家单位发起，但是由于种种原因，均历时一年即行终止。这种情况在南京大学的俄罗斯项目得到了改观。2014年，南京大学与俄罗斯联邦阿尔泰国立大学签订考古研究合作协议，共同调查发掘俄罗斯阿尔泰（包括阿尔泰共和国和阿勒泰边疆区）的青铜时代和早期铁器时代遗址，目的在于研究额尔齐斯河沿线的人群迁徙、冶金技术、农业和家畜传播。从2015年到2017年，联合考古队先后发掘了耶鲁尼诺文化（青铜时代中期）的聚落卡勒望湖－Ⅰ[3]和萨加雷文化（青铜时代晚期）的聚落苏联路－Ⅰ，[4] 都得到了大量的陶片、兽骨、铜渣、铜器和铜锭。2017年7月，双方利用合作平台举办了阿尔泰国际化考古实习，把南京大学多个学科的本科生带到阿尔泰共和国，发掘了一座古代游牧民族的墓地，并让他们开展多学科研究。[5]

2. 蒙古

与蒙古国的合作项目大不相同，不仅延续时间长，迄今已经连续工作了13年，而且规模大，前后有多家单位参与。合作单位主要为内蒙古自治区文物考古研究所、蒙古国游牧文化研究国际学院、蒙古国科学院考古研究所和蒙古国国家博物馆。从2005年开始，联合考古队调查了蒙古国中东部地区的后杭爱省、前杭爱省、布尔干省、中央省、乌兰巴托市和肯特省等7个省市的30多个苏木，发现了青铜时代的多日博勒斤祭祀遗址、匈奴时期的高勒毛都墓地、突厥时期的温格图祭祀遗址

---

[1] 冯恩学、阿尔金：《俄罗斯特罗伊茨基墓地2004年发掘的收获》，《边疆考古研究》第5辑，2006年，第211—215页。

[2] 吉林省文物考古研究所、俄罗斯科学院远东分院远东历史考古民族研究所：《2011年俄罗斯滨海边疆区克拉斯基诺城址考古勘探报告》，《北方文物》2016年第2期，第29—34页。

[3] 南京大学历史学院、俄罗斯阿尔泰国立大学历史系联合考古队：《俄罗斯蛇山市卡勒望湖Ⅰ号遗址的发掘》，《考古》2017年第9期，第14—21页。

[4] 水涛：《行走在中亚细亚草原上》，《中国文物报》2016年10月21日第7版。

[5] 周倩嘉、李灿、张良仁：《阿尔泰考古实习助力南大本科生"顶峰体验"》，http://news.nju.edu.cn/show_article_1_46495。

和回鹘时期的哈剌巴拉嘎斯古城，重点发掘了回鹘时期的胡拉哈墓地和浩莱山谷墓地。其中浩莱山谷5号墓园中发现的回鹘壁画墓，是蒙古国境内发现的第一座壁画墓。此外，在和日木塔拉遗址还发现了柔然墓葬。中蒙联合考古队一边工作一边整理，已经出版了三部（四册）考古报告，发表了十多篇简报及研究论文，成果颇为丰硕。①

2017年增加了一个中蒙合作项目。河南省文物考古研究院与蒙古国乌兰巴托大学合作，发掘匈奴时期的高勒毛都2号墓地。其中1号墓葬群是该墓地规模最大的，也是目前蒙古国境内同时期墓葬中规模最大的。在此之前，乌兰巴托大学已经连续10年发掘了这座墓地，清理了1座大型主墓葬和20余座陪葬墓，出土了保存完好的汉代马车、玉璧、玻璃器、金银器、铁器、陶器等遗物。②

3. 朝鲜

2008年以来，延边大学的高句丽渤海研究所与朝鲜社会科学院考古学研究所合作，调查发掘了朝鲜境内的高句丽和渤海王朝的遗址。其中高句丽王朝的城址为平壤一带的青岩洞土城、高坊山城、青湖洞土城。渤海王朝的遗址为咸镜北道清津市富居里的富居里石城（平原城）、富居里土城（山城）、独洞山城、延台峰烽火台、独洞烽火台、达莱沟墓群、延次沟墓群、合田墓群、玉生洞墓群、土城墓群、独洞墓群以及会宁的仁溪里土城、云头山城、童巾山城、弓心墓地。③合作富于成效，据报道，到2016年中方已经出版了六本考古报告。④

（二）东南亚

迄今为止，中国考古机构已经在柬埔寨、越南、老挝开展了考古工作。

---

① 陈永志、宋国栋、萨仁毕力格、程鹏飞：《中蒙考古合作十周年回顾与展望》，《草原文物》2015年第2期，第1—7页。

② 苏瑜、秦华：《河南首支境外考古队赴蒙古国发掘匈奴贵族墓地》，《郑州日报》2017年7月21日第8版。

③ 郑永振：《最近朝鲜境内的高句丽、渤海遗迹调查发掘成果》，《通化师范学院学报》（人文社会科学）2017年第4期，第1—7页。

④ 郑永振：《朝鲜境内历史遗迹调查报告》，http://skc.ybu.edu.cn/info/1040/1228.htm，2018年1月11日登录。

1. 柬埔寨

在柬埔寨的合作项目是商务部支持的援外项目。1998年，中国文物研究所接受中国政府的指令，参与联合国教科文组织领导的"拯救吴哥计划"。吴哥是9—15世纪柬埔寨的首都，历代君主曾先后建筑起三座都城，遗留下大量的古迹建筑。该所具体承担周萨神庙（Chausay）的维修与保护工作。周萨神庙位于吴哥城胜利门外，暹粒河西侧。目前尚未发现有关周萨神庙的历史记载，神庙也没有遗留下铭刻文字。根据法国学者的研究，周萨神庙为1113—1150年在位的苏利耶跋摩二世时期开始建造的。从1998年开始，该所做了实地考察并完成了基础测绘工作。按照国际通行的工作程序，在维修工程实施之前，需要实施考古勘查与发掘工作。为此中国文物研究所和中国社会科学院考古研究所组成考古组，从事周萨神庙的考古调查、勘探、发掘工作。[1]

周萨神庙的维修工作于2007年完成，当年中国文化遗产研究院（前身为中国文物研究所）又接受了二期援柬项目茶胶寺（Ta Keo）的维修工程。茶胶寺位于吴哥城胜利门外，周萨神庙以东。建于10世纪末11世纪初，属于吴哥王朝黯耶跋摩五世和苏耶跋摩一世时期的印度教国家寺庙。中国文化遗产研究院的主要任务为寺庙结构加固、材料修复和考古研究。经过三年的前期勘察，2011—2012年，项目组在茶胶寺内外做了考古调查。20世纪20和30年代，法国考古工作者就曾经调查了茶胶寺内的五座建筑，在这次工作中，中国文化遗产研究院系统测绘记录了这些建筑，并发现该寺出土的一些瓷器来自中国宋元时期南方窑口或受到中国的影响。[2] 2017年，中国文化遗产研究院又接受了吴哥城王宫遗址的发掘与修复工程。[3]

2. 越南

1992年夏天，四川省文物考古研究所和四川大学的学者听说越南

---

[1] 中国文物研究所、中国社会科学院考古研究所：《吴哥遗迹周萨神庙考古报告》，《考古学报》2003年第3期，第427—458页。

[2] 中国文化遗产研究院：《柬埔寨吴哥古迹茶胶寺周边遗址考古调查简报》，《考古》2017年第9期，第59—72页。

[3] 毛鹏飞：《中国援柬吴哥王宫遗址修复项目将探索吴哥文保新模式》，新华网，2018年6月6日。

冯原文化遗址出土了玉牙璋，可能与广汉县的三星堆遗址有联系。2006年，四川省文物考古研究院和陕西省考古研究院自筹经费，组成越南考古队，考察了越南北部红河流域的青铜至铁器时代的冯元文化、桐豆文化、扪丘文化和东山文化。① 同时，他们发掘了永福省的义立遗址，前后工作近三个月，获得了与三星堆文化有一定联系的一批遗物。后来两家单位与越南博物馆保持互访，共同编写了发掘报告。2016年报告出版，越南考古项目也随之结束。②

3. 老挝

2014年，云南省文物考古研究所开始了在老挝的考古工作。在完成了三个重点区域的考古调查以后，2015年该所联合四川大学以及老挝历史研究所，在沙湾拿吉省的维拉波利（Vilabouly）地区开展了考古调查和勘探，为下一步合作考古发掘做好了准备工作。③

（三）南亚

近几年在孟加拉和印度开始了合作考古工作，遗憾的是在巴基斯坦目前还没有合作项目。

1. 孟加拉

2014年，孟加拉国的阿格拉索·维克拉姆帕（Agrasor Vikrampar）基金会向中国大使馆请求，让中国考古工作者帮助发掘毗诃罗普尔（Vikrampura）佛教遗址群。据研究，它是8—12世纪孟加拉国的一个都城，著名的藏传佛教鼻祖阿底峡就在这里出生、学习和传教。在中国大使馆的协调下，湖南省文物考古研究所与阿格拉索·维克拉姆帕基金会签订了长期工作协议，双方组成联合考古队，共同发掘毗诃罗普尔遗址群的一个遗址纳特斯瓦尔（Nateswar）。发掘工作从2014年一直延续

---

① 雷雨：《从考古发现看四川与越南古代文化交流》，《四川文物》2006年第6期，第17—23页。
② 高大伦：《走出国门第一铲——记十年前的越南考古》，《光明日报》2016年6月10日第5版。
③ 佚名：《2015年度老挝考古调查勘探工作取得初步成果》，《东南亚考古研究》2016年1月13日更新。

到2017年,没有中断。①

2. 印度

喀拉拉邦位于印度半岛西南角。2014年,喀拉拉邦历史研究委员会(KCHR)在奎隆港口(Kollam Port)扩建工程中,陆续发现了大量的古代遗物。除了印度本地的陶器和铜币、地中海地区的玻璃器、两河流域的陶器,还有来自中国的瓷器碎片与铜钱。同年,委员会在帕特南遗址(Pattanam Site)也发现了一些中国瓷器碎片。应委员会的邀请,故宫博物院调查了两处遗址,并分类、记录和检测了两批中国文物。经鉴定,奎隆港口遗址出土的铜钱,年代约在8—14世纪;瓷器残片包含了产自浙江、江西、广东、福建等省的产品,年代约在10—14世纪;帕特南遗址出土的瓷器残片,主要是15—19世纪产自江西、福建的产品。2016年,故宫博物院与喀拉拉邦历史研究委员会、喀拉拉邦大学组成联合考古队,计划勘察和发掘奎隆港口遗址。②

(四)中亚

近几年来,中国已经在乌兹别克斯坦、塔吉克斯坦和哈萨克斯坦开始了合作项目。

1. 乌兹别克斯坦

2011年,中国社会科学院考古研究所与乌兹别克斯坦科学院考古研究所签订合作研究项目,计划用五年时间,系统调查与发掘费尔干纳盆地东部的明铁佩城址(Ming Tepa)。从2012年以来,双方组成联合考古队,从事考古勘探与发掘工作。到2016年为止,完成勘探面积5万平方米,发掘1100平方米。现在已经清楚,明铁佩城址有内城、外城两重城墙,内城城墙外侧分布有"马面"设施。城内发现有1号台基、2号台基和两条道路。发掘者认为,明铁佩城址是公元前2世纪至公元3世纪费尔

---

① 莫林恒:《佛国寻踪——孟加拉国毗诃罗普尔佛教遗址发掘记》,《大众考古》2016年第3期,第69—79页。
② 宫古:《2017年印度奎隆港口遗址考古工作正式启动》,《中国文物报》2017年1月6日第2版。

干纳盆地的一座王城等级的城市。①

在勘探过程中,联合考古队采用了中国的洛阳铲和钻探技术,因而发现了外城,使得明铁佩城址的面积从 500×800 米扩大到约 2100×1300 米。在内城南城墙内,联合考古队发掘了一处手工业作坊区遗迹,清理出土坯房址 5 间,房内发现了火灶、大陶瓮、堆石等遗迹以及磨石、兽骨残骸等遗物。发掘者初步推测这是一处可能与皮革加工有关的、功能完备的作坊遗址。在外城东墙附近发现了一处墓地,并清理了其中一个完整的墓葬。该墓葬人骨保存完整,出土随葬品丰富,包括陶器 4 件、铜戒指 1 件、玻璃珠 7 件。②

西北大学在新疆哈密市巴里坤县天山北麓做了 10 年的考古工作,由此萌生了到中亚追寻月氏人遗迹的想法。2011 年,西北大学先后考察了塔吉克斯坦和乌兹别克斯坦境内阿姆河、泽拉夫善河流域的铜石并用时代、希腊化时代、前贵霜时代、后贵霜时代遗址。③ 从 2014 年开始,在陕西省人民政府中亚考古专项经费资助下,西北大学与乌兹别克斯坦共和国科学院考古研究所组成联合考古队,先重点调查了撒马尔罕州南部的西天山北麓山前地带的萨扎干(Sazagan)和兹纳克(Zinak)古代游牧聚落遗址,发现了大量圆形石堆墓和土堆墓,时代可能为公元前 4 世纪至公元 4 世纪。西天山西端先后有塞种、萨尔马提亚、大月氏、嚈哒等古代游牧民族驻牧,撒马尔罕盆地南缘的游牧民族遗存很可能属于这些民族。④ 次年,联合考古队发掘了萨扎干遗址的五座墓葬和居住遗迹,根据出土的遗物,认为这些文物都属于公元前 2 世纪至公元 1 世纪的早期游牧

---

① 中国社会科学院考古研究所、乌兹别克斯坦科学院考古研究所联合考古队:《乌兹别克斯坦安集延州明铁佩城址考古勘探与发掘》,《考古》2017 年第 9 期,第 22—38 页。

② 刘涛、朱岩石、艾力江、何岁利:《乌兹别克斯坦明铁佩古城遗址发掘取得突破性收获》,《中国文物报》2017 年 1 月 13 日第 8 版。

③ 西北大学丝绸之路文化遗产保护与考古学研究中心、中国国家博物馆和陕西省考古研究院:《塔吉克斯坦、乌兹别克斯坦考古调查——前贵霜时代至后贵霜时代》,《文物》2015 年第 6 期,第 17—33 页;《塔吉克斯坦、乌兹别克斯坦考古调查——铜石并用时代至希腊化时代》,《文物》2014 年第 7 期,第 54—67 页。

④ 西北大学丝绸之路文物保护与考古学研究中心、边疆考古与中国文化认同协同创新中心、乌兹别克斯坦共和国科学院考古研究所:《2014 年乌兹别克斯坦撒马尔罕盆地南缘考古调查简报》,《西部考古》2015 年第 8 辑,第 1—32 页。

民族。①

2. 哈萨克斯坦

2017年，陕西省考古研究院向哈萨克斯坦派出考古队，开始调查与试掘拉哈特城址。拉哈特遗址位于天山北麓，伊塞克金人墓葬附近，传说是塞人的居址。拉哈特城址呈长方形，面积约25万平方米。考古队在城址内发掘了三条探沟，初步确定以一号高台为核心，以壕沟为界，周围分布若干居住区的格局。②

（五）其他国家

除了上述的周边国家，中国考古机构在较为遥远的伊朗、肯尼亚和洪都拉斯开启了合作考古项目。

1. 伊朗

由中亚再往西，中国考古学家的脚步沿着陆上丝绸之路迈进了伊朗。2016年，南京大学与伊朗文化遗产和旅游研究所（RICHT）签订了合作协议。同年，南京大学和伊朗文化遗产、手工和旅游组织北呼罗珊省办公室（相当于中国的省文物局）组成的联合考古队发掘了纳德利土丘（Tepe Naderi）。这座大型土丘位于阿特拉克（Atrak）河上游，北呼罗珊省希尔凡市区内，曾经是古代丝绸之路的一个中转站。根据前人的地表调查，纳德利土丘为一圆形土丘，使用年限从铜石并用时代一直延续到伊斯兰时期，前后延续5000多年。联合考古队采用洛阳铲找到了土丘的原始边缘，并发现了土丘外围的文化层。经测绘，土丘基础的直径达185米，土丘现存高度为20米，底部在现存地面以下5米。最后，发掘了一条长30米的探沟，跨越土丘内外，由此发现了从铜石并用时代到伊斯兰时期的文化堆积。③

---

① 西北大学丝绸之路文化遗产与考古学研究中心、乌兹别克斯坦共和国科学院考古研究所：《2015年度撒马尔罕萨扎干遗址发掘报告》，《西部考古》2016年第12辑，第1—28页。
② 陕西省考古研究院：《哈萨克斯坦伊塞克考古调查工作取得阶段性成果》，《中国文物报》2017年11月3日第8版。
③ 张良仁、水涛：《中伊合作考古，续写丝路故事》，《光明日报》2017年2月28日第12版。

2. 肯尼亚

在非洲，肯尼亚是"郑和下西洋"船队曾经抵达的地方，也是中国古代贸易经过的港口。20世纪70年代，夏鼐就注意到了东非出土的中国陶瓷。1994年，美国作家李露晔在《当中国称霸海上》中说，有个黑人告诉她，自己是中国人的子孙，是数百年前在拉穆群岛沉没的一条中国商船幸存者的后裔。之后《纽约时报》记者纪思道采访了当地的"中国人"后裔，并推测这些自称有中国血统的人，很可能是郑和部下的后裔。这个猜想不仅在国际上引起了广泛关注，而且很快引起了中国的关注。为此《人民日报》驻南非记者前往拉穆群岛，调查了传说中郑和船队的水手们上岸的地方。此地为上加村，公元8世纪至14世纪中后期是这一带的商贸中心，后因战乱频繁和淡水缺乏逐渐荒废。①

由于中国社会的高度关注，2005年国家文物局派人前往肯尼亚，考察拉穆群岛的古代遗址。② 经过五年的调查和水下考古培训，2010年，中国国家博物馆、北京大学考古文博学院和肯尼亚国家博物馆签订协议，决定在肯尼亚开展考古工作，为期三年，商务部将其作为重要援外项目，出资2000万元经费予以支持。2010年11月至2011年1月，联合考古队调查了拉穆群岛、马林迪海域的水下遗存，共发现了六处水下文化遗存线索、三处滨海散落遗存。③ 2013年11月至2014年1月，他们发掘了马林迪奥美尼角（Ngomeni Ras）的沉船遗址，完成了遗址东北部A区船体以上堆积，发现了较为清晰的船体结构以及象牙、铜锭、铜范、水银、硫化汞、绿釉陶器、有孔石器等重要遗物。经考证，此沉船为16—17世纪的葡萄牙船。④

肯尼亚曾出土约250万年前的人类化石，是"现代人"的起源地之

---

① 李新烽：《这里原是"中国村"》，《人民日报》2005年6月17日。
② 王庆环：《北京大学肯尼亚陆上考古记》，《光明日报》2016年8月18日，第8版。
③ 钟天阳：《在肯尼亚追寻郑和遗迹》，《第一财经日报》2010年3月4日第C4版；中国国家博物馆水下考古研究中心、肯尼亚国立博物馆沿海考古部：《2010年度中肯合作肯尼亚沿海水下考古调查主要收获》，《中国国家博物馆馆刊》2012年第8期，第88—99页。
④ 中国国家博物馆水下考古研究中心、肯尼亚国家博物馆滨海考古部：《肯尼亚马林迪奥美尼角沉船遗址2013年度水下考古发掘简报》，《中国国家博物馆馆刊》2014年第9期，第6—23页。

一。2017年,河南省文物考古研究院、山东大学和肯尼亚国家博物馆组成了联合考古队,到裂谷省的吉门基石遗址(Kimengich Site)工作。经过三天的调查,考古队在这里发现了三层堆积。上层为细石器堆积,中层为旧石器时代中期文化,而底层则发现了距今约200万年的早期石制品,发掘者推测是肯尼亚境内最早的人类文化遗存。①

3. 洪都拉斯

中美洲的玛雅文明与中国早期文明之间的联系,已经为不少学者所认识。只是相隔太平洋,以前没有条件前往实地考察,更遑论田野发掘了。2014年,中国社会科学院考古研究所与洪都拉斯人类学与历史研究所签订了合作协议,启动科潘遗址发掘、研究和保护项目。科潘为玛雅文明的一个城邦和都城,其遗址包括神庙宫殿区和贵族居住区两大部分。1885年,美国学者就开始开展考古工作,已经发现了仪式广场、金字塔、球场、王宫和贵族居住区等重要遗迹,出土了大量的雕刻、艺术品和文字。2015年,科潘项目列入中国社会科学院创新工程重大课题,中国和洪都拉斯联合考古队选择贵族居住区作为工作对象,开始了科潘遗址的发掘。② 为此项目,哈佛燕京学社资助开办了中美洲考古培训班,为东亚培养中美洲考古人才。③

五 经验和问题

回顾中国的国际考古合作史,可以看到一个迅猛发展的过程。1998年只有柬埔寨,到了2005年增加到了三项(柬埔寨、蒙古国、越南),2015年增加到了19家考古机构(含研究所和大学),到13个国家开展合作考古工作。据我们所知,中国社会科学院考古研究所正在酝酿在埃

---

① 侯彦峰、赵清坡:《肯尼亚吉门基石遗址考古初战告捷》,《中国文物报》2017年10月10日第1版。
② 中国社会科学院考古研究所科潘工作队:《洪都拉斯科潘遗址8N-11号贵族居址北侧晚期建筑》,《考古》2017年第9期,第39—58页;李新伟:《走近玛雅:科潘的发现和思考》,《中国社会科学报》2017年3月17日第5版。
③ 张春海:《中洪科潘遗址考古发掘"首战告捷"》,《中国社会科学报》2015年10月9日第1版。

◇❖◇ 第一部分 中国考古学史

及的发掘项目,① 河北师范大学正在酝酿在巴基斯坦的发掘项目。② 除了柬埔寨和肯尼亚的发掘项目为商务部支持以外,其他的均为各机构自筹经费。这说明中国迅速增长的经济实力为中国考古机构提供了经费支撑。这些项目中,除了周边国家的一些项目,其他项目与中国的学术问题都没有直接联系,这说明中国的考古机构已经有意识参与国际学术问题,走进国际学术舞台。

在西方国家考古经费日渐拮据、国际考古项目日渐萎缩的背景下,中国文物考古机构的加入无疑为外国考古注入了新的活力。蒙古国、柬埔寨、印度、乌兹别克斯坦、伊朗、洪都拉斯是过去一百多年来西方国家和俄罗斯考古学家最活跃的地方,中国考古队为它们增添了新力量。中国考古队不仅带去了资金和人力,而且带去了新方法和新技术。尽管中国考古学起步晚,但是中国考古学家在复杂的土遗址中摸爬滚打,练就了高超的钻探和发掘技术;20世纪90年代以来,通过与西方合作,向西方学习了全新的田野调查、测绘和记录手段。在此基础上,2009年,国家文物局颁布了新版《田野考古规程》,系统吸取了世界考古强国美国、英国和日本的理念和技术,整合成了一套新的田野考古规程,并向全国推广,迅速提升了中国考古学家的工作水平。③ 现在走出去考古的各个机构都按照先调查测绘、后有计划发掘和多学科研究、并实施文物保护的步骤开展工作。一些考古队将中国特有的洛阳铲和钻探技术带到了乌兹别克斯坦和伊朗,解决了一些重要问题。中国社会科学院考古研究所用洛阳铲找到了明铁佩城址的外城,而南京大学也用洛阳铲探明了纳德利土丘的边缘和外围的文化层。

当然,在国际考古迅猛发展的今天,我们需要时刻反省。中国考古机构走出去不久,存在一些短板不足为奇,但是有几个是急需解决的。一个是人才。一些学者已经敏锐地意识到,中国目前还缺乏懂外语和学

---

① 屈婷、龙瑶:《中国考古队将从孟图神庙"走进埃及"》,新华社北京1月7日电。
② 河北师范大学国际合作处:《巴基斯坦拉哈尔女子大学教师代表团访问我校》,http://www.hebtu.edu.cn/a/2016/12/06/20161206085400.html。
③ Zhang, Liangren, New developments in Chinese archaeology, *Antiquity* 88, 2014, The Project Gallery.

习外国考古的人才。① 从现有的情况来看，中国考古机构目前大多满足于发表发掘资料，并且大多用中文发表在国内期刊或发掘报告上，很少用外文发表在国际出版物上；在国际视野中利用这些考古资料，用外文写成论文在国际出版物上发表的更少。其根本原因就是中国缺乏外国考古人才。而中国高校的现行培养模式已经严重落伍，无法满足培养外国考古人才的需要。原因有二：第一，中国高校还没有外国考古专业，缺乏系统的外国考古课程，学生无法了解外国考古。第二，搞外国考古需要研读外文考古文献，学习外语。除了英语和日语这两门常用外语，搞外国考古还需要学习德语、法语、俄语、波斯语、西班牙语、乌兹别克语等。但是目前中国高校对于考古专业学生，本科生一般只要求他们达到英语四级或六级；对研究生中国高校迄今还没有要求学习第二外语，无法阅读用其他语言发表的文献。要改变这种现状，中国高校恐怕需要建立外国考古专业，专门培养外国考古人才。

另一个问题是经费。在一个国家的合作考古工作需要几十年的持续耕耘，才能达到取得成果、培养人才、滋润友谊的目的。现阶段只有中国文化遗产研究院在柬埔寨的考古和保护项目和国家博物馆在肯尼亚的水下考古项目作为商务部的援外项目得到了持续而充裕的经费支持。但是商务部资助的只能是援外项目，项目由所在国提出援助申请，周期漫长而口径狭窄，无法满足中国迅猛发展的外国考古项目。国家文物局虽然经费充裕，但是只能用于国内项目。现在它想了一些办法，解决了一些机构的燃眉之急，但也不是长久之计。目前大部分从事外国考古的机构带着科研目的，意图长期工作，但主要依靠自筹经费，难以为继。早年一些机构在俄罗斯、越南的合作项目运行仅一年就流产，恐怕与经费问题不无关系。一些学者提出设立稳定的学术经费用于支持外国考古，有意向的机构可以申请立项，立项后要至少支持五年，可以对每年的工作进行考核，考核合格后可以继续资助。② 这样的建议是非常适合的。

---

① 袁靖：《境外考古热中的冷思考》，《光明日报》2017年4月11日第12版。
② 王巍：《建议从两方面着手统筹设计"中国考古走出去"》，中国社会科学网，2017年3月11日。

六　结语

　　考古学在 20 世纪 20 年代进入中国，很快就中国化，成了探讨中国文明起源的工具。1949 年以后，中国文明起源问题仍然是中国考古学的核心问题，但是中国考古学家一方面向苏联学习，一方面受到国际共产主义运动的驱使，关心亚非拉国家的考古工作。20 世纪 80 年代以后，中国与西方关系缓和，但是中国考古学家不怎么关心外国考古，而集中精力解决中国各个区域的文化序列和文明起源问题。20 世纪 90 年代以后，日本和西方国家考古学家来到中国，开展合作考古，带来了中国紧缺的经费以及新的理念和方法。这些新理念和方法在 2009 年经过整理和补充，形成了 2009 年《田野考古规程》；这个规程经过国家文物局的强力推行，大大提高了中国考古学家的水平。到了世纪之交，中国经济腾飞，中国考古机构开始走出国门，带着研究经费和工作能力到周边国家开展合作考古工作。2012 年中国政府推行"一带一路"战略以后，外国考古项目就像星星之火，迅速蔓延开来。

　　但是，这种迅速发展的外国考古项目一方面展现了中国考古界的实力，另一方面也暴露了中国考古界的一些问题。几十年来中国考古学家已经练就了高超的田野工作技术，而 2009 年《田野考古规程》的推行确实提高了中国考古学家的理念和资料采集能力；因此，中国考古学家在外国考古项目中注入了调查、发掘和保护并举的理念，同时带去了卓越的田野工作经验和钻探技术。但是，与日本和西方国家相比，中国考古学家刚刚走出去，存在一些突出的问题。一是缺乏外国考古人才，目前中国考古学家大多只能用中文发表发掘资料，还没有能力在国际视野下利用这些资料，用外文写成论文发表在国际期刊上。中国大学的考古学科仍然只有中国考古专业，因此急需建立外国考古专业。二是外国考古项目需要长期稳定的经费来源，可以让考古学家长期从事外国考古，但是中国还没有这样的经费来源。现在的项目经费，大部分来自各个单位，但是这种来源不稳定，无法保障外国考古项目长期运行。

第二部分
考古学理论

Wucheng and Shang: A New History of a Bronze Age Civilization in Southern China*

Introduction

In 1989, an astonishingly sumptuous tomb was discovered at Chengjia Village in Dayangzhou District in Xin'gan County, Jiangxi province (Fig. 2-1-1). [1]Customarily known as Dayangzhou Tomb, it yielded a total of 475 bronze artifacts, 754 pieces of jades, and 139 pottery wares. Scholars who had been wrestling with scattered bronze objects from southern China were now blessed with a large assemblage embedded in a tomb context. [2]They were further blessed by the pottery materials that unmistakably associate the tomb with the Wucheng site, a walled settlement that has been continually excavated since the 1970s, and lodge it in a broad cultural context. The convergence of the Dayangzhou tomb and the Wucheng settlement, still a rare phenomenon in the Yangzi River Valley, cannot be more significant; together they present to us a well-developed civilization and hence dramatically change our perception of

---

* The article was originally published in *Bulletin of Museum of Far Eastern Antiquities* 78, 2010, pp. 53 – 78. It is reprinted in this anthology with minor changes.

[1] Excavation materials are published in: Peng Shifan, Liu Lin, and Zhan Kaixun, Jiangxi Xin'gan Dayangzhou Shangmu fajue jianbao, *Wenwu* 10, 1991, pp. 1 – 24; Jiangxisheng Bowuguan, Jiangxisheng Wenwu Kaogu Yanjiusuo, and Xin'ganxian Bowuguan, *Xin'gan Shangdai Damu*, Beijing: Wenwu, 1997.

[2] E. g. Hayashi Minao, Chōsa shutsudo so hakusho no jūni kami no yurai, *Toho Gakuho* 42, 1971, pp. 40 – 52; Kane, Virginia C., The independent bronze industries in the south of China contemporary with the Shang and Western Chou dynasties, *Archives of Asian Art* 28, 1974/1975, pp. 77 – 107; Peng, Shifan, Jiangxi diqu chutu Shangzhou qingtongqi de fenxi yu fenqi, *Zhongguo Kaogu Xuehui Diyici Nianhui Lunwenji*, Beijing: Wenwu, 1979, pp. 181 – 194; Gao, Zhixi, An introduction to Shang and Chou bronze nao excavated in South China, in K. C. Chang ed., *Studies of Shang Archaeology*, New Haven and London: Yale University Press, 1986, pp. 275 – 299; Gao, Zhixi, Lun Zhongguo nanfang chutu de Shangdai qingtongqi, in Wenwu ed., *Zhongguo Kaogu Xuehui Diqici Nianhui Lunwenji*, Beijing: Wenwu, 1989, pp. 76 – 88; Yin, Weizhang, Changjiang liuyu zaoqi yongzhong de xingtaixue fenxi, in *Wenwu yu Kaogu Lunji*, Beijing: Wenwu, 1986, pp. 261 – 270.

Bronze Age cultures in southern China. Chinese Bronze Age archaeology has notoriously progressed unevenly. ①

The focus of scholarly attention has been riveted on the so-called Central Plain at the sacrifice of the outlying regions. Thus while the Shang civilization could boast a succession of epochal discoveries, the contemporaneous societies around it could claim merely sporadic and modest finds. By the 1980s, there had been only a handful of systematically excavated sites in Southern China. These were the abovementioned Wucheng and Panlongcheng in Hubei province, also a walled settlement. The material culture from Panlongcheng was markedly identical to that of Erligang-Period Shang and the site was immediately recognized as a military outpost of the Shang kingdom. That from Wucheng is likewise replete with Shang elements. The two sites, the only then-known settlements of some cultural distinction in southern China, suggested that cultural development in this region was inspired by the Shang civilization. Unfortunately, this awareness further fed the entrenched image of "a single civilized center surrounded by a

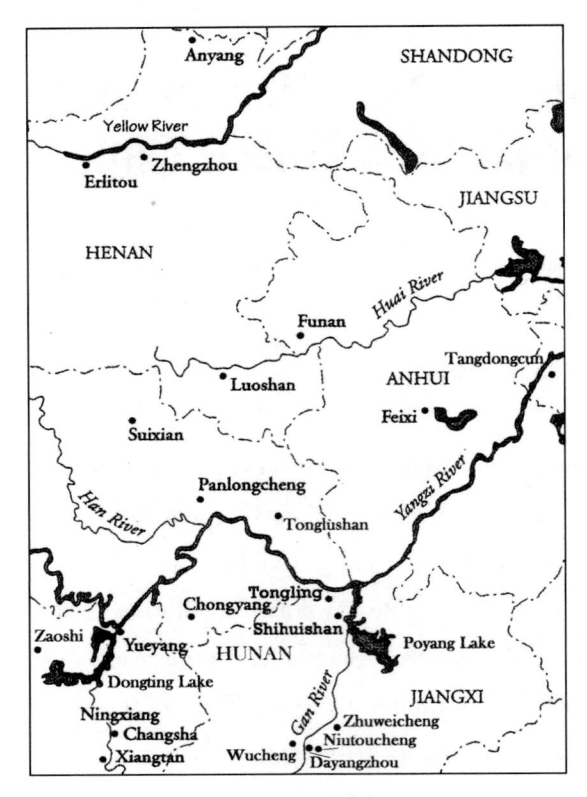

Fig. 2 - 1 - 1 **Map of Bronze Age sites in southern and northern China**

---

① This uneven development was believed to have been programmed largely by written history and the splendid Shang civilization found at Anyang, see Bagley, Robert W., An Early Bronze Age Tomb in Jiangxi Province, *Orientations* 24/7, 1993, pp. 20 - 36; Bagley, Robert W., Shang archaeology, in Michael Loewe and Edward L. Shaughnessy ed., *The Cambridge History of Ancient China*, Cambridge: Cambridge University Press, 1999, pp. 124 - 231. In my view, it was motivated by the aspiration to prove the indigenous origin of Chinese civilization and the concentration of construction projects, the major drive of archaeological excavation, in northern China.

Wucheng and Shang: A New History of a Bronze Age Civilization in Southern China

sea of barbarians."①

In the meantime, however, a few scholars began to challenge this Shang-centric outlook. ②They scrutinized artistically outstanding bronzes found in the Middle Yangzi River Valley, which had been construed to be imports from Shang foundries from this outlook. They came to discern many distinctive traits that are absent on their Shang counterparts. Dissatisfied with the import hypothesis, they postulated the existence of local bronze-producing civilizations in southern China. Yet qualified foundry sites had been found nowhere and this new proposition won over few scholars. The foundry remains found at Wucheng is characterized by stone molds, which are simply unsuitable for casting complex objects like bronze vessels and lend little aid to their proposition.

Since the 1980s, however, the pendulum tilted increasingly towards the local-civilization proposition. ③This was stimulated by a number of remarkable discoveries in southern China. Particularly important in this regard were the two sacrificial pits discovered at Sanxingdui, a walled settlement in Guanghan

---

① Chang, K. C., *The Archaeology of Ancient China*, Fourth edition, revised and enlarged, New Haven: Yale University Press, 1986, p. 361. Some scholars nevertheless recognized Wucheng as a local culture. See Li, Boqian, Shilun Wucheng wenhua, *Zhongguo Qingtong Wenhua Jiegou Tixi Yanjiu*, p. 228, Beijing: Kexue, originally published in *Wenwu Jikan* 3, 1981, pp. 133 – 143.

② Hayashi, Chōsa shutsudo so hakusho no jūni kami no yurai, *Toho Gakuho* 42, 1971, pp. 40 – 52; Kane, The independent bronze industries in the south of China, *Archives of Asian Art* 28, 1974/1975, pp. 77 – 107.

③ It has been postulated that this was driven by the loosening up of the grip of the then-dominant mononuclear paradigm that perceives all of Chinese civilization as originating from the Central Plain, see von Falkenhausen, Lothar, The Regionalist Paradigm in Chinese Archaeology, in Philip Kohl and Clare Fawcett ed., *Nationalism, Politics, and the Practice of Archaeology*, Cambridge: Cambridge University Press, 1995, p. 198. An alternative explanation is that archaeological data from regions outside the Central Plain had been very limited by the late 1980s for the reasons given in Footnote ① on Page 72. Chinese archaeologists were in fact fully motivated to recognize regional cultures and local innovations. For instance, by the 1980s a few scholars had already considered the Wucheng Culture to be an indigenous outgrowth, see Li, Boqian, Shilun Wucheng wenhua, in *Zhongguo Qingtong Wenhua Jiegou Tixi Yanjiu*, p. 228, Beijing: Kexue, originally published in *Wenwu Jikan* 3, 1981, pp. 133 – 143; Peng, Shifan, Jiangxi diqu chutu Shangzhou qingtongqi de fenxi yu fenqi, in *Zhongguo Kaogu Xuehui Diyici Nianhui Lunwenji*, Beijing: Wenwu, 1979, pp. 181 – 194.

county, Sichuan province.① Far beyond the imagination of any scholar, they yielded a massive ensemble of bronze artifacts. Except for a few vessels that are apparently outcomes of Shang influence, human masks and statues, and trees have never been seen at any Shang urban centers. There is little ground to claim the latter as imports from Shang foundries. Finally, the Dayangzhou tomb yielded an impressive collection of bronze vessels, most of which are stylistically different from Shang products. The accumulated evidence was so compelling that scholars found little basis to resist the "local-civilization" proposition.② Hence Robert W. Bagley, who had unswervingly espoused this proposition, announced that "what was once a minority view" has been turned into "a consensus."③

The "local-civilization" proposition, however, is not without contention. The key underwriting postulation, that the Dayangzhou bronzes were locally produced, cannot be ascertained at present. Clay molds suitable for producing them have not yet been found at Wucheng, the only known site in the vicinity that has yielded evidence of bronze production.④ In fact, Liu Li and Chen Xingcan, after a survey of metal working evidence during the Shang dynasty, declared that such clay molds have never been discovered outside Shang urban centers. And from this fact they inferred that the production of bronze vessels was monopolized by Shang rulers.⑤

Another point of contention centers on the relationship between Wucheng

---

① Excavation materials from the two pits are published in: Sichuansheng Wenwu Guanli Weiyuanhui, Sichuansheng Wenwu Kaogu Yanjiusuo, and Sichuansheng Guanghanxian Wenhuaju, Guanghan Sanxingdui yizhi yihao jisikeng fajue jianbao, *Wenwu* 10, 1987, pp. 1–15; Sichuansheng Wenwu Guanli Weiyuanhui, Sichuansheng Wenwu Kaogu Yanjiusuo, and Sichuansheng Guanghanxian Wenhuaju Wenguansuo, Guanghan Sanxingdui yizhi erhao jisikeng fajue jianbao, *Wenwu* 5, 1989, pp. 1–20; Sichuansheng Wenwu Kaogu Yanjiusuo, *Sanxingdui Jisikeng*, Beijing: Wenwu, 1999.

② Several Chinese scholars began to recognize a local civilization in southern China after the discovery of the Dayangzhou tomb. E. g. Gao, Zhixi, Tan Xin'gan Shangmu chutu tongqi de zhongda yiyi, *Zhongguo Wenwubao*, 6 December 1990, p. 3; Li, Xueqin, Faxian Xin'gan Shangmu de zhongda yiyi, *Zhongguo Wenwubao*, 29 November 1990, p. 3; Yin, Weizhang, Nanfang kaogu de zhongda tupo, *Zhongguo Wenwubao*, 22 November 1990, p. 3; Zou, Heng, Youguan Xin'gan chutu qingtongqi de jige wenti, *Zhongguo Wenwubao*, 6 December, 1990, p. 3.

③ Bagley, Robert W., An Early Bronze Age Tomb in Jiangxi Province, *Orientations* 24/7, 1993, p. 36.

④ The walled site Niutoucheng located near the Dayangzhou tomb likely co-existed with Wucheng, but systematic excavations have yet to be done to produce detailed information of the site.

⑤ Liu and Chen, *State Formation in Early China*, London: Duckworth, 2003, p. 133.

and Shang. The proponents of the "local-civilization" proposition are contented to entertain solely the stylistic and technical peculiarities of the Dayangzhou bronzes. [1] From such an art historical perspective, they deemed Wucheng as a self-contained local polity. From an anthropological perspective, however, Liu and Chen drew an opposite picture of the Wucheng society: it was a Shang colony by origin; its leaders, who were to be buried in tombs like the one at Dayangzhou, supplied local resources, copper ore and kaolin clay, to Shang rulers, and in return received manufactured bronze vessels from them. [2] This kind of relationship, in their view, parallels the core-periphery model as expounded by Immanuel Wallerstein. [3]

In reviewing the art historical and anthropological perspectives that previous studies have taken to interpret the Dayangzhou bronzes, I do not mean to pit one against another so as to favor either the "Shang-import" or "local-product" positions. Instead, I mean to synthesize the two perspectives. To me they are not antithetical but complementary, and when united they enable us to transcend the bipartisan controversy and to gain a more complex understanding of the Dayangzhou bronzes. In this article I will synthesize the insights that previous studies have to offer, but with the two perspectives in combination I will examine the entire database from Wucheng and Dayangzhou, which, regrettably, has not yet been done. The "local-product" theorists tend to overlook pottery materials, whereas the "Shang-import" theorists tend to under-appreciate the idiosyncratic traits of the Dayangzhou bronzes. The synthetic study I am pursuing turns out to be enlightening: it will unfold us a

---

[1] Gao, Zhixi, Tan Xin'gan Shangmu chutu tongqi de zhongda yiyi, *Zhongguo Wenwubao*, 6 December 1990, p. 3; Li, Xueqin, Faxian Xin'gan Shangmu de zhongda yiyi, *Zhongguo Wenwubao*, 29 November 1990, p. 3; Yin, Weizhang, Nanfang kaogu de zhongda tupo, *Zhongguo Wenwubao*, 22 November 1990, p. 3; Zou, Heng, Youguan Xin'gan chutu qingtongqi de jige wenti *Zhongguo Wenwubao*, 6 December 1990, p. 3; Sun, Hua, Guanyu Xin'gan Dayangzhou damu de jige wenti, *Wenwu* 7, 1993, pp. 19 – 26; Peng, Shifan, Jiangxisheng kaogu wushi nian, in Wenwu Chubanshe ed., *Xinzhongguo Kaogu Wushinian*, Beijing: Wenwu, 1999, pp. 216 – 230; Bagley, Robert W., An Early Bronze Age Tomb in Jiangxi Province, *Orientations* 24/7, 1993, pp. 20 – 36.

[2] Liu and Chen, *State Formation in Early China*, London: Duckworth, 2003, p. 135.

[3] Wallerstein, Immanuel, *The Modern World-System I: Capitalist Agriculture and the Origins of the European World-Economy in the Sixteenth Century*, San Diego et al: Academic Press, 1974.

brand-new history of the civilization embodied in the Wucheng walled settlement and the Dayangzhou tomb.

Wucheng as a Shang Colony[①]

Colonists from northern China found their way to southern China already during the Erlitou period (ca. 1880BC – 1521BC). [②]This is evidenced by the Shihuishan site located in De'an county in northern Jiangxi (Fig. 2 – 1 – 1). The site was excavated twice at small scales and two phases were discerned. [③]While the excavators dated them slightly earlier than Wucheng Phase I and Phase II respectively, which, as expounded below, are equivalent with Upper Erligang and the subsequent transitional period, I am inclined to link them with the Erlitou Period. Pottery wares of earlier periods are absent, attesting to that the site was uninhabited before. The ware types from this site closely resemble Erlitou types—*li*-tripod, *dou*-bowl, basin, *guan*-jar and *zun*-jar; in typology they correspond to Erlitou Phases III and IV respectively (Fig. 2 – 1 – 2). [④]This assemblage marks a rupture from that of the indigenous Neolithic Zhuweicheng Culture occupying the Gan River Valley and Poyang Lake

---

① This article adopts Gil Stein's definition of colony: "An implanted settlement established by one society in either uninhabited territory or the territory of another society. The implanted settlement is established for long-term residence by all or part of the population and is both spatially and socially distinguishable from the communities of a host society. The settlement onset is marked by a distinct formal corporate identity as a community with cultural/ritual, economic, military, or political ties to its homeland, but the homeland need not politically dominate the implanted settlement." Excerpt from Stein, Gil, Colonies without Colonialism: A Trade Diaspora Model of Fourth Millennium B. C. Mesopotamian Enclaves in Anatolia, in Claire L. Lyons and John K. Papadopoulos ed., *The Archaeology of Colonialism*, Los Angeles: The Getty Research Institute, 2002, p. 30.

② Xia-Shang-Zhou Duandai Gongcheng Zhuanjiazu, *Xia Shang Zhou Duandai Gongcheng 1996 – 2000 Nian Jieduan Chengguo Baogao*, Beijing: Shijie Tushu Publishing Company, 2000, pp. 76 – 77.

③ Excavation materials are published in: Jiangxisheng Wenwu Gongzuodui and De'anxian Bowuguan, Jiangxi De'an Shihuishan Shangdai yizhi shijue, *Dongnan Wenhua* 4 – 5, 1989, pp. 13 – 25; Jiangxisheng Wenwu Kaogu Yanjiusuo and Jiangxisheng De'anxian Bowuguan, Jiangxi De'an Shihuishan Shangdai yizhi fajue jianbao, *Nanfang Wenwu* 4, 1998, pp. 1 – 12.

④ The term "culture" used in this article only refers to a group of sites with common traits without implying a corresponding ethnic people.

Basin, in which both Shihuishan and Wucheng are located. ①Pottery assemblage of this culture, having little in common with those of Neolithic cultures in northern China, is characterized by the *ding*-tripod with three flat legs, the top-heavy *dou*-bowl, *hu*-jar, and the *he*-tripod (Fig. 2 – 1 – 3). These ware types are rare if not entirely absent at Shihuishan. Along with these ware types, Erlitou-type motifs such as cord designs and C-shaped design appeared at this site (Fig. 2 – 1 – 2). The absence of indigenous Neolithic ware types and the predominance of the Erlitou ware types and motifs attest to that a group of bearers of the Erlitou Culture arrived to settle in northern Jiangxi. This colonial culture, however, assimilated indigenous elements such as stone stepped axes and geometric designs.

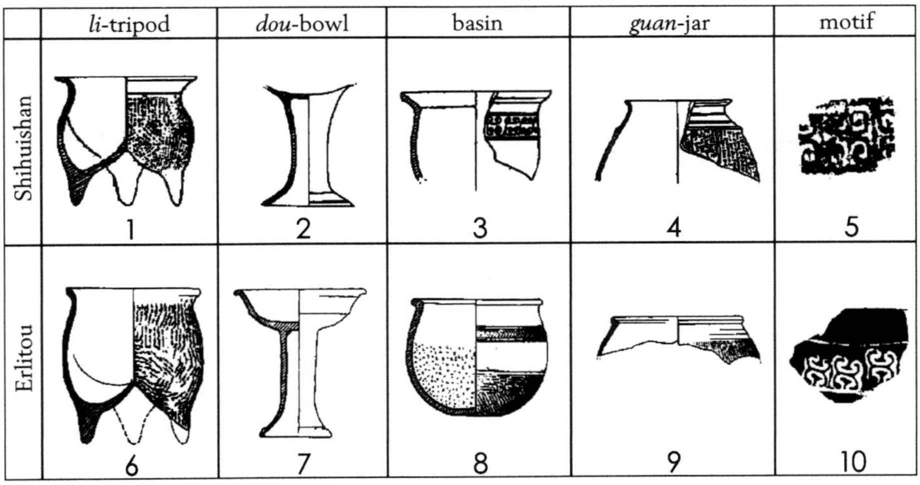

	li-tripod	*dou*-bowl	basin	*guan*-jar	motif
Shihuishan	1	2	3	4	5
Erlitou	6	7	8	9	10

Fig. 2 – 1 – 2 Ceramic ware types and motifs from Shihuishan and Erlitou

(1 – 5, Jiangxisheng Wenwugongzuodui and De'anxian Bowuguan, Jiangxi De'an Shihuishan Shangdai Yizhi Shijue, *Dongnan Wenhua* 4 – 5, 1989, Fig. 8: 1, 13, 14, 10, Fig. 10: 24. 6 – 10, Zhongguo Shehui Kexueyuan Kaogu Yanjiusuo, *Yanshi Erlitou: 1959 Nian*-1978 *Nian Kaogu Fajue Baogao*, Beijing: Zhongguo Dabaike, 1999, Fig. 206: 4, Fig. 242: 1, Fig. 210: 3, 10, Fig. 200: 14)

---

① General description of this culture can be found in Tang, Shulong, Shilun Zhuweicheng wenhua, *Nanfang Wenwu* 2, 1996, p. 56; Peng, Shifan, Jiangxisheng kaogu wushi nian, in Wenwu Chubanshe ed., *Xinzhongguo Kaogu Wushinian*, Beijing: Wenwu, 1999, p. 217.

◇❖◇ 第二部分 考古学理论

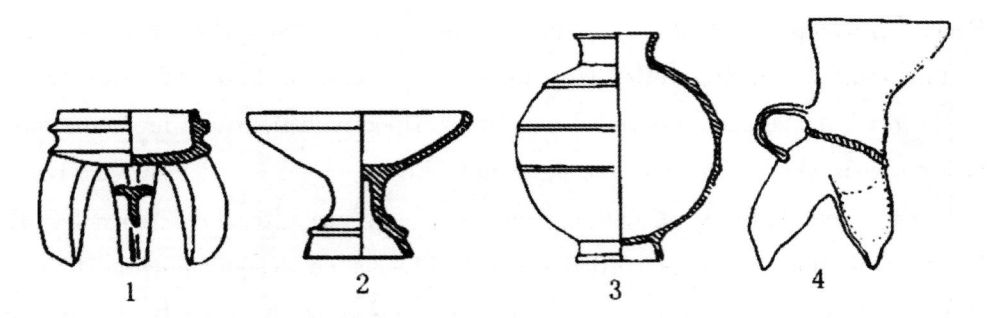

Fig. 2 – 1 – 3 **Major ceramic ware types of the Zhuweicheng Culture**
(1 – 4, Tang, Shulong, Shilun Zhuweicheng wenhua, *Nanfang Wenwu* 2, 1996, Fig. 2)

After a hiatus period equivalent to the Lower Erligang Phase, colonial activity was resumed during the Upper Erligang Phase (ca. 1476BC – 1415BC), as testified by the Wucheng walled settlement (Fig. 2 – 1 – 1).① Discovered in 1973, the site has been excavated for ten seasons.② After the first three seasons, archaeologists established a three-phase chronology (Fig. 2 – 1 – 4), which was tested by later seasons of excavation. The three phases have been correlated by excavators with the chronological range spanning the Upper Erligang and the Anyang period (1427BC – 1045BC).③ The five calibrated radiocarbon dates acquired in the 1970s, which correspond to 1810BC –

---

① Xia-Shang-Zhou Duandai Gongcheng Zhuanjiazu, *Xia Shang Zhou Duandai Gongcheng 1996 – 2000 Nian Jieduan Chengguo Baogao*, Beijing: Shijie Tushu Publishing Company, 2000, p. 65.

② Excavation materials from Wucheng have been partially published in several brief reports. See Jiangxisheng Bowuguan, Beijing Daxue Lishixi Kaoguzhuanye, and Qingjiangxian Bowuguan, Jiangxi Qingjiang Wucheng Shangdai yizhi fajue jianbao, *Wenwu* 7, 1975, pp. 51 – 71; Jiangxisheng Bowuguan and Qingjiangxian Bowuguan, Jiangxi Qingjiang Wucheng Shangdai yizhi disici fajue de zhuyao shouhuo, *Wenwu Ziliao Congkan* 2, 1978, pp. 1 – 13; Jiangxisheng Wenwu Gongzuodui, Xiamen Daxue Renleixuexi Basiji Kaoguzhuanye, and Qingjiangxian Bowuguan, Qingjiang Wucheng yizhi diliuci fajue de zhuyao shouhuo, *Jiangxi Lishi Wenwu* 2, 1987, pp. 24 – 35; Jiangxisheng Wenwu Kaogu Yanjiusuo, Xiamen Daxue Renleixuexi, and Zhangshushi Bowuguan, Zhangshu Wucheng yizhi diqici fajue jianbao, *Wenwu* 7, 1993, pp. 1 – 9; Jiangxisheng Wenwu Kaogu Yanjiusuo, Xiamen Daxue Renleixuexi, and Zhangshushi Bowuguan, Jiangxi Zhangshu Wucheng Shangdai yizhi dibaci fajue jiangbao, *Nanfang Wenwu* 1, 1995, pp. 5 – 23; Jiangxisheng Wenwu Kaogu Yanjiusuo and Zhangshushi Bowuguan, Jiangxi Zhangshu Wucheng Shangdai yizhi xichengqiang jiepo de zhuyao shouhuo, *Nanfang Wenwu* 3, 2003, pp. 5 – 18. They are comprehensively reported in Jiangxisheng Wenwu Kaogu Yanjiusuo and Zhangshushi Bowuguan, *Wucheng*, Beijing: Kexue, 2005.

③ Jiangxisheng Bowuguan, Beijing Daxue Lishixi Kaoguzhuanye, and Qingjiangxian Bowuguan, Jiangxi Qingjiang Wucheng Shangdai yizhi fajue jianbao, *Wenwu* 7, 1975, p. 61; Jiangxisheng Wenwu Kaogu Yanjiusuo and Zhangshushi Bowuguan, *Wucheng*, Beijing: Kexue, 2005, pp. 408 – 410.

965BC, generally corroborate the designated ceramic chronology. ①

The Wucheng site, which measures 61ha, is circumscribed by a moat and four walls. In terms of the given chronology of the Wucheng site, the walls were first constructed during Phase I and then widened during Phase II. ②Modest building foundations, kilns, and metalworking remains were more or less concentrated in certain areas within the fortress. ③Small tombs furnished with ceramic vessels were widely found inside the site; outside it a few relatively richer tombs furnished with isolated bronze artifacts have been found, but none is like the Dayangzhou Tomb. ④All these indicate that Wucheng is not comparable with Shang urban centers like Zhengzhou or Anyang. Stone molds, metal products likely cast out of them, copper ingots, crucibles, and slag found here attest to bronze casting at this site. ⑤In addition, the ten excavation seasons have brought to light a large number of inscriptions engraved on pottery wares and stone molds. ⑥

The excavators have already found that the staple pottery ware types—not to be confused with the stonewares uncovered at the same site⑦—of or likely of Phase I, including the *li*-tripod, *dou*-bowl, basin, *zun*-jar, high-necked jar, *guan*-jar, foot-ringed urn, and trumpet-mouthed jar resemble their Shang counterparts unearthed at Zhengzhou (Fig. 2-1-5). ⑧In fact all the ware types represented in the chronology chart are alien to the Zhuweicheng Culture.

---

① Jiangxisheng Wenwu Kaogu Yanjiusuo and Zhangshushi Bowuguan, *Wucheng*, Appendix II, Beijing: Kexue, 2005, p. 500.

② Jiangxisheng Wenwu Kaogu Yanjiusuo and Zhangshushi Bowuguan, *Wucheng*, Beijing: Kexue, 2005, p. 45.

③ Jiangxisheng Wenwu Kaogu Yanjiusuo and Zhangshushi Bowuguan, *Wucheng*, Beijing: Kexue, 2005, pp. 51-86.

④ Jiangxisheng Wenwu Kaogu Yanjiusuo and Zhangshushi Bowuguan, *Wucheng*, Beijing: Kexue, 2005, pp. 86-90.

⑤ Jiangxisheng Wenwu Kaogu Yanjiusuo and Zhangshushi Bowuguan, *Wucheng*, Beijing: Kexue, 2005, pp. 84-86.

⑥ Jiangxisheng Wenwu Kaogu Yanjiusuo and Zhangshushi Bowuguan, *Wucheng*, Beijing: Kexue, 2005, pp. 375-385.

⑦ This type of ceramic, frequently called hard-ware (yingtao) and proto-porcelain (yuanshici) in Chinese archaeological literature, is fired at a temperature above 1100°C and often imprinted with geometric designs and sometimes glazed. Li, Huibing, 1981, Yinwen tao yu yinwen yingtao, *Wenwu Jikan* 3, 1981, p. 90.

⑧ Jiangxisheng Wenwu Kaogu Yanjiusuo and Zhangshushi Bowuguan, *Wucheng*, Beijing: Kexue, 2005, pp. 411-413.

Other northern elements are legs of a *jue*-cup and a *jia*-cup, both of which are wine-drinking vessels, and a foot-ring of a *gui*-tureen, which is a food-serving vessel.① These ware types are without any doubt derived from Shang and indicative of the coming of Shang immigrants. Alternatively, one may argue that these Shang style wares appear in this region because local people adopted them. But the fact that local Neolithic ware types are almost entirely absent at Wucheng provides little foundation for this argument. In addition, it should be noted that Wucheng have not been inhabited prior to the Erligang period. It should also be noted that these Shang ware types fulfill the functions of cooking, serving, and storage, and possibly satisfy the daily life need of the residents.

In the meantime we should not lose sight of the fact that the Phase I ware types are not exact replica of Shang types. The appearance of ring bands, a motif originating on Shang bronze vessels, on the shoulders of *zun*-jars suggests that they are stylistically different from Shang pottery wares (Fig. 2 – 1 – 4).

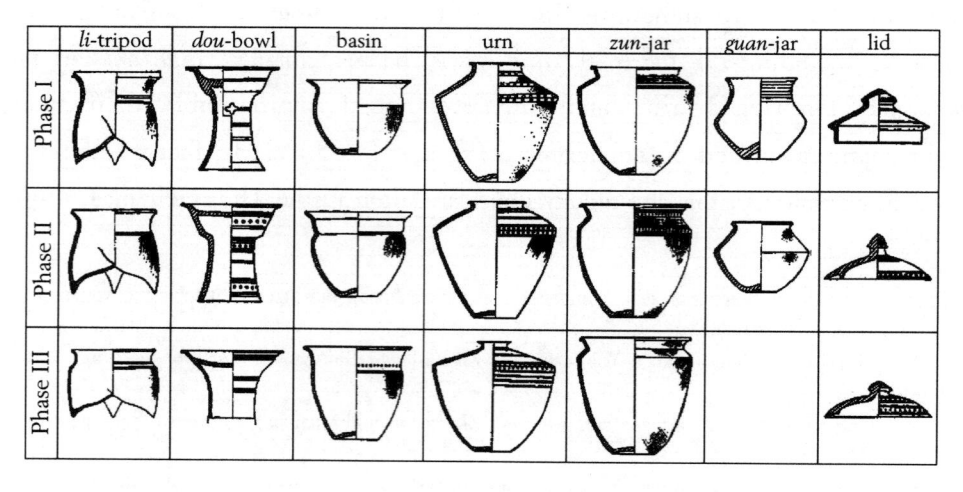

	li-tripod	*dou*-bowl	basin	urn	*zun*-jar	*guan*-jar	lid
Phase I							
Phase II							
Phase III							

Fig. 2 – 1 – 4 Wucheng ceramic chronology

(Adapted from Jiangxisheng Bowuguan, Beijing Daxue Lishixi Kaoguz huanye, and Qingjiangxian Bowuguan, Jiangxi Qingji ang Wucheng Shangdai yizhi fajue jianbao, *Wenwu* 7, 1975, Fig. 4)

---

① Jiangxisheng Wenwu Kaogu Yanjiusuo and Zhangshushi Bowuguan, *Wucheng*, Beijing: Kexue, 2005, pp. 301 – 303.

The Wucheng Culture is also noted for the high percentage of stoneware, which is made of local kaolin clay. According to one count, it occupies 4.07% during Phase I.① The ware types are *dou*-bowl, *zun*-jar, high-necked jar, whose forms are apparently modeled on Shang prototypes (Fig. 5: 2, 4, 9). The repertoire of decorative motifs comprises grids, basket designs, appliqué designs, S-like imprints, and ring bands, which are also derived from Shang.② It appears that the colonizers exploit the local resources to make ware types of their own choice.

The subsequent two phases come with several major changes (Fig. 2 – 1 – 4). Firstly, the six types of Shang wares undergo notable morphological alterations. The *li*-tripod vessels become stout, while the bowl parts of the *dou*-bowls turn shallower. The small *guan*-jars give rise to the large flat-bottomed ones. Secondly, the use of the dotted ring motif is spread onto pottery wares and stone tools such as knives.③ Third, the percentage of the stoneware grows. According to the abovementioned count, it arises to 5.08% during Phase II, and more dramatically to 29.2% during Phase III. During these two phases, the use of kaolin clay is extended to the *guan*-jar (Fig. 2 – 1 – 5: 10), trumpet-mouthed jar (Fig. 2 – 1 – 5: 12), urn, and bowl, the forms of which are derived ultimately from Shang pottery wares.④ As a result of these transformations, the ceramic style of Wucheng diverges further from the Shang Culture. It appears that large-scale migrations from the north come to a halt after Phase I, and that Wucheng residents no longer keep in pace with the Shang Culture, as they start to produce pottery wares to their own taste.

Another line of evidence underpinning the colony proposition is a large ensemble of inscriptions engraved on ceramic wares and stone molds

---

① Li, Keyou, and Shifan Peng, Lüelun Jiangxi Wucheng Shangdai yuanshi ciqi, *Wenwu* 7, 1975, p. 77.

② Li, Keyou, and Shifan Peng, Lüelun Jiangxi Wucheng Shangdai yuanshi ciqi, *Wenwu* 7, 1975, p. 78, Fig. 1.

③ Li, Keyou, and Shifan Peng, Lüelun Jiangxi Wucheng Shangdai yuanshi ciqi, *Wenwu* 7, 1975, Figs. 2 – 3.

④ Li, Keyou, and Shifan Peng, Lüelun Jiangxi Wucheng Shangdai yuanshi ciqi, *Wenwu* 7, 1975, p. 77.

◇❖◇ 第二部分 考古学理论

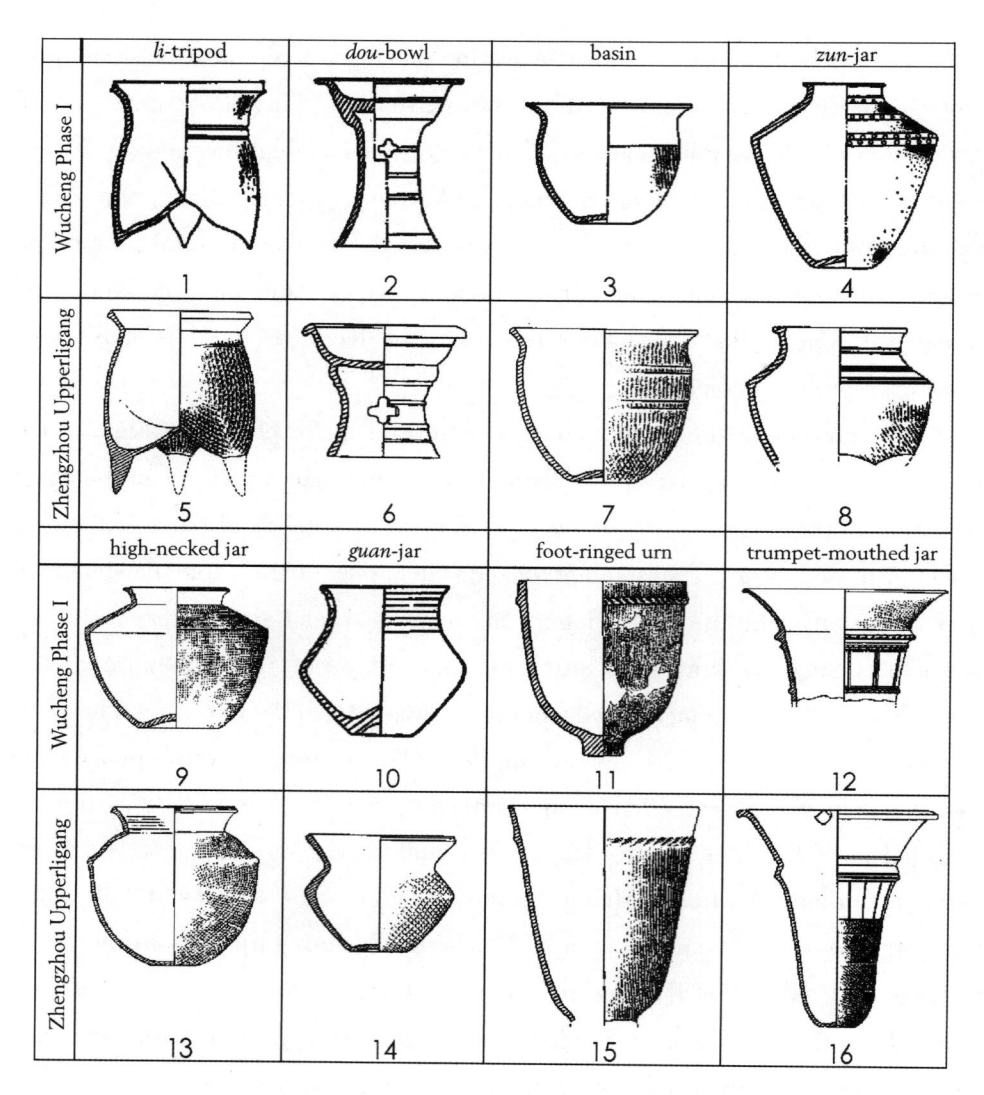

	li-tripod	dou-bowl	basin	zun-jar
Wucheng Phase I	1	2	3	4
Zhengzhou Upperligang	5	6	7	8
	high-necked jar	guan-jar	foot-ringed urn	trumpet-mouthed jar
Wucheng Phase I	9	10	11	12
Zhengzhou Upperligang	13	14	15	16

Fig. 2-1-5 Wucheng Phase I and Zhengzhou Upper Erligang ware types

(1 - 4, 10, Jiangxisheng Bowuguan, Beijing Daxue Lishixi Kaoguzhuanye, and Qingjiangxian Bowuguan, Jiangxi Qingjiang Wucheng Shangdai yizhi fajue jianbao, *Wenwu* 7, 1975, Fig. 4; 9, 11, 12, Jiangxisheng Wenwu Kaogu Yanjiusuo and Zhangshushi Bowuguan, *Wucheng*, Beijing: Kexue, 2005, Fig. 139: 6, Fig. 175: 1, Fig. 170: 4; 5 - 8, 13 - 16, Henansheng Wenwu Kaogu Yanjiusuo, *Zhengzhou Shangcheng: Yijiuwusan Nian—Yijiubawu Nian Kaogu Fajue Baogao*, Beijing: Wenwu, Vol. 2, 2001, Fig. 491: 1, Fig. 502: 3, Fig. 525: 6, Fig. 512: 7, Fig. 532: 1, Fig. 533: 4, Fig. 527: 1, Fig. 515: 6)

Wucheng and Shang: A New History of a Bronze Age Civilization in Southern China

(Fig. 2-1-6). ①The fourteen pieces of Phase I are long passages that comprise four to twelve characters. Many characters find analogies among Anyang oracle bone inscriptions, whereas others do not. One passage is read by Tang Lan as "? 止豆木口婦十中" (Fig. 2-1-6: 1). Such passages, which date to the Erligang period, may represent an earlier writing system that was used in the north and brought to Wucheng by Shang colonists. ②The inscriptions of Phases II and III comprise only one or two characters. Such characters as *qi* 七, *ge* 戈 (Fig. 2-1-6: 3), *shi* 矢, and *you* 有 (又) (Fig. 2-1-6: 2) are comparable with Anyang oracle bone as well as bronze inscriptions. It appears that some elements of the matured writing system of Shang continued to flow into southern China.

The foregoing description portrays to us a civilization in southern China. The Wucheng Culture features a walled settlement, bronze foundries, stoneware, and an embryonic writing system. These and the enormous number of bronze and jade artifacts recovered from the Dayangzhou tomb attest to that the local élite were able to mobilize a significant amount of material wealth. To date Wucheng remains the single archaeological culture

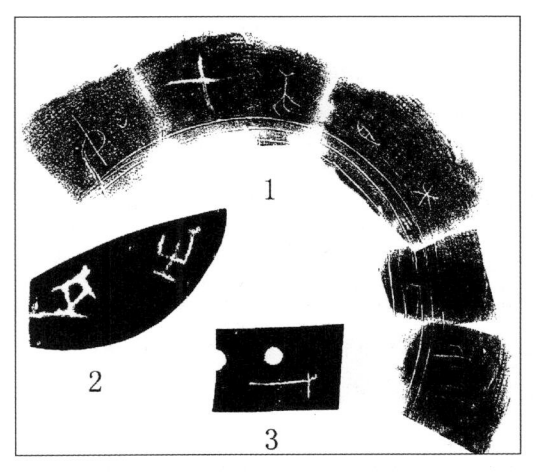

Fig. 2-1-6 Epigraphs from Wucheng

(Jiangxisheng Wenwu Kaogu Yanjiusuo and Zhangshushi Bowuguan, 2005, *Wucheng*, Beijing: Kexue, Fig. 225: 1, Fig. 227: 4, Fig. 229: 1)

---

① The inscriptions from the first three excavation seasons were thoroughly examined by the eminent paleographer Tang Lan. See Tang, Lan, Guanyu Jiangxi Wucheng wenhua yizhi yu wenzi de chubu tansuo, *Wenwu* 7, 1975, pp. 72-76; his readings were transcribed in Jiangxisheng Bowuguan, Beijing Daxue Lishixi Kaoguzhuanye, and Qingjiangxian Bowuguan, Jiangxi Qingjiang Wucheng Shangdai yizhi fajue jianbao, *Wenwu* 7, 1975, pp. 56-57, Table 1. The characteristics of these inscriptions were summarized in Beijing Daxue Lishixi Kaogu Jiaoyanshi Shangzhouzu, *Shangzhou Kaogu*, Beijing: Wenwu, 1979, p. 140.

② A rib found at the site of Erligang has ten characters that are very close to Anyang oracle bone inscriptions in style. See Henansheng Wenhuaju Wenwu Gongzuodui, *Zhengzhou Erligang*, Beijing: Kexue, 1959, p. 38.

furnished with such an array of civilizational elements in Bronze Age northern Jiangxi.

To further illustrate the archaeological manifestation of a Shang colony, it is enlightening to look at the Wannian Culture and the Panlongcheng site. The Wannian Culture designates a group of sites found in northeastern Jiangxi. It is considered to be an indigenous culture paralleling the Wucheng Culture in chronology. ①Despite the fact that materials of this culture came to light as early as in the 1960s, only a handful of sites have been subjected to test excavation. Settlements and cemeteries are little known, but ceramic sherds have been found in abundance. A careful comparison has enabled local archaeologists to find many distinctions between these sherds and those from Wucheng. The major ware types of the Wannian Culture are the *yan*-steamer with concave bottom, *ding*-tripod, *gui*-tripod with three pouch-shaped legs (not to be confused with the *gui*-tureen), and even stands, whereas those of the Wucheng Culture are the *li*-tripod, *guan*-jar, and *zeng*-steamer; the two assemblages are hence narrowly overlapped. The two cultures differ greatly in the ceramic production technique. Although the turning wheel is employed by both cultures, vessels of the Wannian Culture are formed in one piece, whereas those of Wucheng are assembled from separately prepared parts. ②Inter-cultural interaction is visible. The square spiral design and inscribed signs found upon Wannian wares are probably loaned from Wucheng. In the meantime, the distinctive Wannian *yan*-steamer with a concave bottom finds its way to Wucheng. ③

The Panlongcheng site, about 300km north of Wucheng, presents a contrasting picture. It consists of a small fortified town, a few "palace foundations" inside the walls, and several residential and burial areas outside

---

① A modest amount of excavation materials is published in: Jiangxisheng Wenwu Gongzuodui and Wannianxian Bowuguan, Jiangxi Wannian leixing Shang wenhua yizhi diaocha, *Dongnan Wenhua* 4-5, 1989, pp. 36-37; Li, Jiahe, Juyuan Yang, and Shizhong Liu, Jiangxi Wannian leixing Shang wenhua yanjiu, *Dongnan Wenhua* 3, 1990, pp. 142-160.

② Li, Jiahe, Juyuan Yang, and Shizhong Liu, Jiangxi Wannian leixing Shang wenhua yanjiu, *Dongnan Wenhua* 3, 1990, pp. 155-160.

③ Li, Jiahe, Juyuan Yang, and Shizhong Liu, Jiangxi Wannian leixing Shang wenhua yanjiu, *Dongnan Wenhua* 3, 1990, p. 156.

the walls. Human occupation at this site began in the Erlitou Period, but the walled town itself appeared in the early Upper Erligang Phase and fell out of use by the end of this phase. ①Nearly all the aspects of the material culture, including the rammed-earth technique employed in the construction of the walls, tomb structure and furnishings, and artifactual styles are identical to their Zhengzhou counterparts. ②A long-standing consensus is that Panlongcheng was a colony of the Shang kingdom and it collapsed when the Shang power withdrew from the Yangzi River Valley at the end of the Upper Erligang Phase. ③The Panlongcheng material culture, however, is not purely a replica of the Shang Culture. The presence of the concave-bottomed *yan*-steamer at Panlongcheng attests to trade with the Wannian populations in the east. ④

The Wucheng site, having much more peculiar traits than Panlongcheng, seems to defy the designation of a Shang colony. But if we look at the Wucheng material culture historically, we can well understand the origin of these traits. While the Phase I ceramic wares closely resemble Shang products, the Phase II and Phase III wares show a steady growth of idiosyncratic elements. Although we cannot precisely define the chronology of the three phases, it seems that the transition from Phase I to Phase II roughly occurs at the end of the Upper

---

① Brief excavation reports are seen in Hubeisheng Bowuguan, Yijiuliusan nian Hubei Huangpi Panlongcheng Shangdai yizhi de fajue, *Wenwu* 1, 1976, pp. 49 – 59; Hubeisheng Bowuguan, Panlongcheng Shangdai Erligangqi de Qingtongqi, *Wenwu* 2, 1976, pp. 26 – 41; Hubeisheng Bowuguan, and Beijing Daxue Lishixi Kaoguzhuanye, Panlongcheng yijiuqisi niandu tianye kaogu jiyao, *Wenwu* 2, 1976, pp. 5 – 15; Wuhanshi Bowuguan, Hubeisheng Wenwu Kaogu Yanjiusuo, and Huangpixian Wenwu Guanlisuo, 1997 – 1998 nian Panlongcheng fajue jianbao, *Jianghan Kaogu* 3, 1998, pp. 34 – 48. A comprehensive report is seen in: Hubeisheng Wenwu Kaogu Yanjiusuo, *Panlongcheng*, Beijing: Wenwu 2001, pp. 442 – 449.

② Hubeisheng Wenwu Kaogu Yanjiusuo, *Panlongcheng*, Beijing: Wenwu, 2001, pp. 493 – 498.

③ Hubeisheng Bowuguan and Beijing Daxue Lishixi Kaoguzhuanye, Panlongcheng yijiuqisi niandu tianye kaogu jiyao, *Wenwu* 2, 1976, pp. 5 – 15; Chang, K. C., *Shang Civilization*, New Haven: Yale University Press, 1980; Bagley, Robert W., P'an-lung-ch'eng: A Shang city in Hupei, *Artibus Asiae* 39. 3/4, 1977, p. 210; Bagley, Robert W., Changjiang bronzes and Shang archaeology, in National Palace Museum ed., *International Colloquium on Chinese Art History*, Taibei: National Palace Museum, 1992, p. 216; Bagley, Robert W., An early Bronze Age tomb in Jiangxi Province, *Orientations* 24. 7, 1993, pp. 20 – 36; Hubeisheng Wenwu Kaogu Yanjiusuo, *Panlongcheng*, Beijing: Wenwu, 2001, p. 498; Liu and Chen, *State Formation in Early China*, London: Duckworth, 2003, p. 118.

④ Hubeisheng Wenwu Kaogu Yanjiusuo, *Panlongcheng*, Beijing: Wenwu, 2001, p. 496, Fig. 348 [B]: 32.

Erligang phase. The withdrawal of the Shang power from the Yangzi River Valley that terminated the life of the Panlongcheng site probably also cut loose the connection between Wucheng and Shang, and left the Wucheng Culture to develop in its own way.

Wucheng in the Shang Trading Network

Liu and Chen were keen to find that the Wucheng élite supplied the two local resources—kaolin clay and copper ore—to Shang urban centers such as Zhengzhou and Anyang, citing compositional studies to back up their suppositions. ①Yet their discussion is rather hasty, and I will elaborate their argument here.

As discussed earlier, the stoneware production thrived during the time of the Wucheng Culture. The count cited above tells us that it starts with a ratio of 4.07% of ceramic sherds during Phase I; then it arises to 5.08% during Phase II, but during Phase III this culture it skyrockets to 29.2%. ②By contrast the Zaoshi site located in the neighboring province of Hunan does not bear any allusion to this industry. ③In the north, stonewares have been found at the Shang urban centers of Zhengzhou and Anyang in élite tombs; they are evidently prestige goods. In most likelihood, however, they are local products. A most compelling piece of evidence is that the Shang city at Zhengzhou has produced a number of deformed wares, which could not have been transported over long distance from Wucheng. ④In addition, the bluish green glaze on Zhengzhou stonewares is different from the bluish yellow one on Wucheng finds. ⑤

---

① Liu and Chen, *State Formation in Early China*, London: Duckworth, 2003, pp. 119 – 123.

② Li, Keyou, and Shifan Peng, Lüelun Jiangxi Wucheng Shangdai yuanshi ciqi, *Wenwu* 7, 1975, p. 77.

③ Hunansheng Wenwu Kaogu Yanjiusuo, Hunan Shimen Zaoshi Shangdai yicun, *Kaogu Xuebao* 2, 1992, pp. 185 – 219.

④ Chen, Tiemei, George Jr. Rapp, Zhichun Jing, and Nu He, Zhongzi huohua fenxi dui Shang shiqi yuanshici chandi de yanjiu, *Kaogu* 7, 1997, p. 39.

⑤ Li, Keyou, and Shifan Peng, Lüelun Jiangxi Wucheng Shangdai yuanshi ciqi, *Wenwu* 7, 1975, p. 80.

Wucheng and Shang: A New History of a Bronze Age Civilization in Southern China

The source of the raw material—kaolin clay—for producing the stonewares found in northern China has long concerned specialists. Li Keyou and Peng Shifan first noticed that the stonewares from Zhengzhou and Anyang are similar in elemental composition to those from Wucheng.[1] This is confirmed by two subsequent analyses. Chen Tiemei and his collaborators analyzed thirty-two stoneware fragments from Wucheng, Panlongcheng, Zhengzhou, and two other sites in northern China, and arrived at the conclusion that Wucheng was the actual source of kaolin clay for producing the stonewares found at the other four sites.[2] Zhu Jian and his collaborators analyzed four samples from Wucheng and two pieces from Zhengzhou, and obtained the same result. It appears that the Shang élite imported kaolin clay from Wucheng and produced stonewares locally.[3]

Another source that the Central Plain polities crave for is copper. The Middle and Lower Yangzi River Valley is well known for rich deposits of copper ores. Previous excavations at Tonglushan in the neighboring province of Hubei reveal that mining activities took place as early as Western Zhou (ca. 1046BC – 771BC).[4] The Tongling mines in northern Jiangxi were exploited even earlier.[5] The pottery wares, which were uncovered *in situ* in mining wells and ore processing workplaces, clearly suggest that the mines were opened back in the Erlitou period.[6] Radiocarbon dates (3330 ± 60BP, 3220 ± 70BP, 3120 ± 80BP) acquired by various laboratories in China and Australia confirm this dating.[7] Although there is no straightforward evidence to prove that the Wucheng

---

[1] Li, Keyou, and Shifan Peng, Lüelun Jiangxi Wucheng Shangdai yuanshi ciqi, *Wenwu* 7, 1975, p. 79.

[2] Chen, Tiemei, George Jr. Rapp, Zhichun Jing, and Nu He, Zhongzi huohua fenxi dui Shang shiqi yuanshici chandi de yanjiu, *Kaogu* 7, 1997, p. 45.

[3] Zhu, Jian, Changsui Wang, Yan Wang, Zhenwei Mao, Guangming Zhou, Changsheng Fan, Xiaoming Zeng, Yueming Shen, and Xicheng Gong, Shangzhou yuanshici chandi de zaifenxi, Appendix V in *Wucheng*, Beijing: Kexue, 2005, pp. 518 – 524.

[4] Huangshishi Bowuguan, *Tonglushan Gukuangye Yizhi*, Beijing: Wenwu, 1999, p. 183.

[5] Liu and Chen, *State Formation in Early China*, London: Duckworth, 2003, pp. 465 – 495.

[6] Liu, Shizhong and Benshan Lu, Jiangxi Tongling tongkuang yizhi de fajue yu yanjiu, *Kaogu Xuebao* 4, 1998, p. 468, Fig. 5: 3, 8.

[7] Liu, Shizhong and Benshan Lu, Jiangxi Tongling tongkuang yizhi de fajue yu yanjiu, *Kaogu Xuebao* 4, 1998, pp. 469 – 470.

◇❖◇ 第二部分 考古学理论

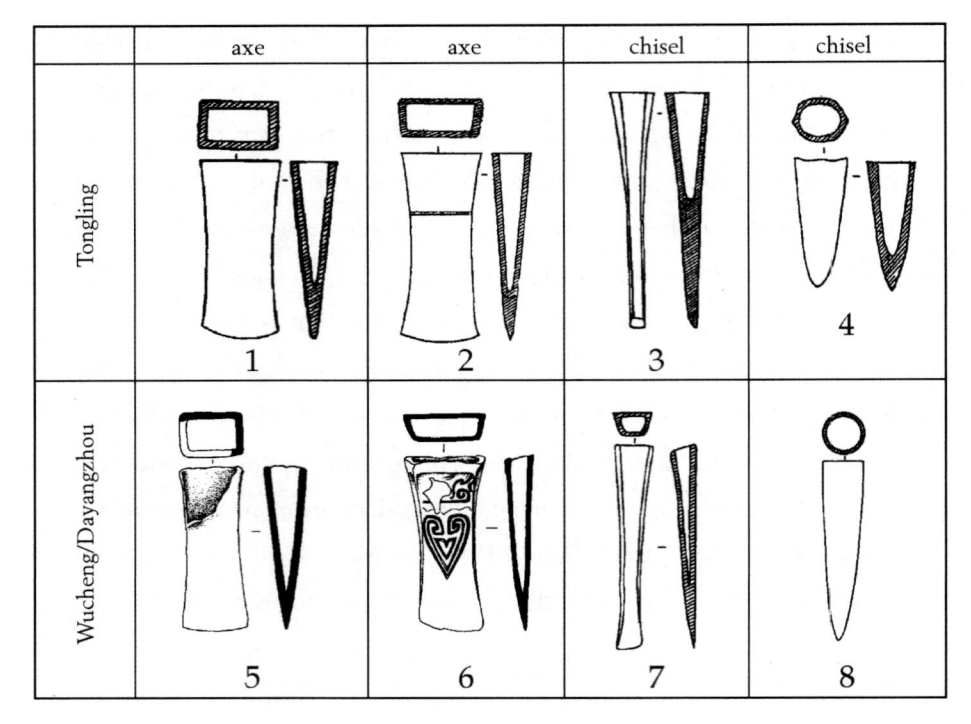

	axe	axe	chisel	chisel
Tongling	1	2	3	4
Wucheng/Dayangzhou	5	6	7	8

Fig. 2 – 1 – 7 Comparison of bronze tools from Tongling, Wucheng, and Dayangzhou

(1, 3, Liu Shizhong and Benshan Lu, Jiangxi Tongling tongkuang yizhi de fajue yu yanjiu, *Kaogu Xuebao* 4, 1998, Fig. 5: 2, 4; 2, 4, Jiangxisheng Wenwu Kaogu Yanjiusuo, Jiangxi Ruichang Tongling Shang Zhou kuangye yizhi diyiqi fajue jianbao, *Jiangxi Wenwu* 3, 1990, Fig. 10: 2, 3; 5 – 6, Jiangxisheng Wenwu Kaogu Yanjiusuo and Zhangshushi Bowuguan, *Wucheng*, Beijing: Kexue, 2005, Fig. 220: 1, 4; 7 – 8, Jiangxisheng Bowuguan, Jiangxisheng Wenwu Kaogu Yanjiusuo, and Xin'ganxian Bowuguan, *Xin'gan Shangdai Damu*, Beijing: Wenwu, 1997, Fig. 66: 1, Fig. 58: 6)

population was involved in mining, a few tools, such as two bronze chisels and two bronze axes, recall the bronze tools from the Dayangzhou tomb (Fig. 2 – 1 – 7).①They match the Dayangzhou and the Wucheng tools to such exactitude that one suspects that they were actually manufactured at Wucheng.

---

① Jiangxisheng Wenwu Kaogu Yanjiusuo, Jiangxi Ruichang Tongling Shang-Zhou kuangye yizhi diyiqi fajue jianbao, *Jiangxi Wenwu* 3, 1990, p. 7, Fig. 10: 2 – 3; Liu, Shizhong and Benshan Lu, Jiangxi Tongling tongkuang yizhi de fajue yu yanjiu, *Kaogu Xuebao* 4, 1998, p. 468, Fig. 5: 2, 4; Jiangxisheng Bowuguan, Jiangxisheng Wenwu Kaogu Yanjiusuo, and Xin'ganxian Bowuguan, *Xin'gan Shangdai Damu*, Beijing: Wenwu, 1997, p. 127, Fig. 66: 1; p. 114, Fig. 58: 6; Jiangxisheng Wenwu Kaogu Yanjiusuo and Zhangshushi Bowuguan, *Wucheng*, Beijing: Kexue, 2005, p. 368, Fig. 220: 1, 4.

Wucheng and Shang: A New History of a Bronze Age Civilization in Southern China

The chisels and axes were wood-cutting tools, but in the context of the Tongling site they were probably intended for working gallery and shaft propping timbers. One also suspects that the bronze industry at Wucheng was partly to make mining-related tools. Archaeological surveys carried out in the past ten years indicate that the Wucheng Culture actually occupied the Lower Gan River Valley and west of the Poyang Lake. ①One has good reason to speculate that the Wucheng polity controlled this region as well as the Tongling mines.

Archaeologists have long postulated that a group of Shang people established the Panlongcheng outpost to gain access to the Tonglushan mines. ②As a major polity in northern Jiangxi, Wucheng must have been erected with the same intention, although we are still short of analytical techniques to prove that it actually exported copper ores or ingots to Shang foundries in the north. Zicheng Peng and his collaborators, who examined the lead isotope ratio of Anyang bronzes, discovered that the copper ores for casting them all came from the Tonglushan mines. ③This result, grounded on a limited database, does not necessarily rule out the designated postulation. For now we simply leave the issue to future studies.

Remains indicative of bronze production have been recovered abundantly during the ten seasons of excavation at Wucheng. Formally demarcated foundry areas as we see at Zhengzhou and Anyang have not yet been found; only some "storage pits" yielded molds, carbon and copper residue, stone and ceramic tools, and daily life utensils. ④In a striking contrast to the situation at Shang urban centers, the majority of casting molds unearthed here were made of stone,

---

① Peng, Shifan, Jiangxisheng kaogu wushi nian, in Wenwu Chubanshe ed., *Xinzhongguo Kaogu Wushinian*, Beijing: Wenwu, 1999, p. 219.

② Chang, Kwang-chih, *Shang Civilization*, New Haven: Yale University Press, 1980, pp. 151 – 153; Liu and Chen, Cities and Towns: The Control of Natural Resources in Early States, China, *Bulletin of the Museum of Far Eastern Antiquities* 73, 2001, pp. 35 – 40.

③ Peng, Zicheng, Weidong Sun, Yunlan Huang, Xun Zhang, Shizhong Liu, and Benshan Lu, Gan E Wan zhudi gudai kuangliao quxiang de chubu yanjiu, *Kaogu* 7, 1997, pp. 53 – 61.

④ Jiangxisheng Bowuguan and Qingjiangxian Bowuguan, Jiangxi Qingjiang Wucheng Shangdai yizhi disici fajue de zhuyao shouhuo, *Wenwu Ziliao Congkan* 2, 1978, p. 4. The stone molds were taken to be a defining trait of the Wucheng Culture by some scholars, e. g. Peng, Shifan, Juemin Hua, and Zhongda Li, Jiangxi diqu zaoqi qingtongqi yezhujishu de jige wenti, *Zhongguo Kaogu Xuehui Disici Nianhui Lunwenji*, Beijing: Wenwu, 1983, p. 76. But this view is compromised by the fact that they have also been found at Erlitou, the first site witnessing bronze production in the Central Plain, e. g. Beijing Daxue Lishixi Kaogu Jiaoyanshi Shangzhouzu, *Shangzhou Kaogu*, Beijing: Wenwu, 1979, p. 138.

and they were not liable to high temperature and delicate carving. ①Therefore they could only be used to produce simple objects. In actuality, molds ever found at this site were intended for producing tools such as axes, adzes, and weapons such as arrowheads, knives, and daggers. ②Given the lack of clay molds at this site, which has been repeatedly testified by the ten excavation seasons, one cannot rule out the possibility that the bronze vessels from Dayangzhou were not produced at local foundries but at some unknown Shang foundries in the Central Plain, where clay mold casting technology had matured for centuries by the time of the Wucheng Culture.

The Dayangzhou Bronzes

The colony hypothesis sheds a new light on the bronzes found in the Dayangzhou tomb. The tomb was discovered when local villagers were quarrying the sand dune in which it was buried; neither the original burial structure nor skeletal remains existed at the moment of excavation—only what was presumably the bottom of the tomb where the accompanying goods were placed was preserved. Thus there is the opinion that the site was not a tomb but a hoard or a cultic spot. ③The excavators, however, found several features that favor a tomb designation. All the artifacts were placed within an ashy area (A) of 8.22m long and 3.6m wide, and without a central area (B) of 2.3m long and 0.85m wide. Area A contains organic remains, bronze fragments and lacquer pieces, whereas Area B contains more organic remains but less bronze fragments. Most of the bronze artifacts were found outside Area B, whereas jade ornaments, a

---

① Peng, Shifan, Juemin Hua, and Zhongda Li, Jiangxi diqu zaoqi qingtongqi yezhujishu de jige wenti, *Zhongguo Kaogu Xuehui Disici Nianhui Lunwenji*, Beijing: Wenwu, 1983, p. 77.

② The preliminary report identifies two stone molds [75T8(2)H3: 839, 75T8H1: 813] as for the legs of jia-cups and two others [75T8(2), p. 866, 75T8(2)H3: 847] as for parts of a vessel (Jiangxisheng Bowuguan and Qingjiangxian Bowuguan, Jiangxi Qingjiang Wucheng Shangdai yizhi disici fajue de zhuyao shouhuo, *Wenwu Ziliao Congkan* 2, 1978, p. 2. The former two pieces are missing in the final report; if the original interpretation is right, they can be explained as for mending broken legs of jia-cup. The latter two are re-identified as chariot fittings (Jiangxisheng Wenwu Kaogu Yanjiusuo and Zhangshushi Bowuguan, *Wucheng*, Beijing: Kexue, 2005, p. 146, Fig. 84: 11; p. 150, Fig. 86: 6).

③ See Sun, Hua, Guanyu Xin'gan damu de jige wenti, in Zhongguo Guojia Bowuguan and Jiangxisheng Wenhuating ed., *Shangdai Jiangnan: Jiangxi Xin'gan Dayangzhou Chutu Wenwu Jicui*, Beijing: Zhongguo Shehui Kexueyuan, 2006, pp. 337–340.

necklace, an exquisitely decorated bronze axe and a dagger, which were probably personal belongings, were found inside Area B. Thus Areas B and A probably represent the locations of an inner coffin and an outer chamber respectively.[①] In addition, 24 teeth that probably belong to one adult female, one child, and one infant were found also outside the chamber. They were probably sacrificial victims accompanying the primary occupant to the underworld.[②] Given these observations, the tomb is structurally and ritually reminiscent of Shang ones, which also lend support to the colony hypothesis.

Among the extraordinary ensemble of artifacts, the bronze and ceramic vessels are more diagnostic of the chronological position of the Dayangzhou tomb, as they are comparable with Shang bronzes and Wucheng ceramics respectively. The forty-eight bronze vessels seem to suggest a broad temporal scope, and many scholars date them to the temporal range spanning the Upper Erligang Phase and Anyang Phase II.[③] But Bagley, who has most thoroughly examined the Dayangzhou vessels, dates most of them to the thirteenth century, the transitional period between the end of the Upper Erligang Phase and Anyang Phase II, which I consider more convincing and will follow in this article.[④] The ceramic wares are identical to those of Wucheng Phase II.[⑤] Indeed, as Bagley comments, "in every aspect—shape, clays, glazes, decorative patterns and inscriptions of one or two characters"—the Dayangzhou materials match their

---

① Jiangxisheng Bowuguan, Jiangxisheng Wenwu Kaogu Yanjiusuo, and Xin'ganxian Bowuguan, *Xin'gan Shangdai Damu*, Beijing: Wenwu, 1997, pp. 5 – 6, 184 – 188.

② Han, Kangxin, Xin'gan Shangdai Damu renya jianding, in *Xin'gan Shangdai damu*, Beijing: Wenwu, 1997, p. 236.

③ Peng, Shifan, Lin Liu, and Kaixun Zhan, Guanyu Xin'gan Dayangzhou Shangmu niandai wenti de tantao, *Wenwu* 10, 1991, pp. 27 – 32; Sun, Hua, Guanyu Xin'gan Dayangzhou damu de jige wenti, *Wenwu* 7, 1993, p. 22; Sun, Hua, Guanyu Xin'gan damu de jige wenti, in Zhongguo Guojia Bowuguan and Jiangxisheng Wenhuating ed., *Shangdai Jiangnan: Jiangxi Xin'gan Dayangzhou Chutu Wenwu Jicui*, Beijing: Zhongguo Shehui Kexueyuan, 2006, p. 342; Jiangxisheng Bowuguan, Jiangxisheng Wenwu Kaogu Yanjiusuo, and Xin'ganxian Bowuguan, *Xin'gan Shangdai Damu*, Beijing: Wenwu, 1997, pp. 188 – 191.

④ Bagley, Robert W., An Early Bronze Age Tomb in Jiangxi Province, *Orientations* 24.7, 1993, p. 20.

⑤ Jiangxisheng Bowuguan, Jiangxisheng Wenwu Kaogu Yanjiusuo, and Xin'ganxian Bowuguan, *Xin'gan Shangdai Damu*, Beijing: Wenwu, 1997, pp. 191 – 192; Sun, Guanyu Xin'gan damu de jige wenti, in Zhongguo Guojia Bowuguan and Jiangxisheng Wenhuating ed., *Shangdai Jiangnan: Jiangxi Xin'gan Dayangzhou Chutu Wenwu Jicui*, Beijing: Zhongguo Shehui Kexueyuan, 2006, p. 342.

Wucheng counterparts. ①Two calibrated radiocarbon dates (3110 + 330 and 3360 + 160) corroborate this dating. ②It appears that the tomb is constructed no later than Anyang Phase II.

The forty-eight bronze vessels from the Dayangzhou tomb comprise thirty *ding*-tripods or -quadrupeds, five *li*-tripods, three *yan*-steamers, one pan, one *gui*-tureen, one *dou*-bowl, two *hu*-jars, three *you*-kettles, one *lei*-urn, one *pou*-jar, and one *zan*-beaker. Several stylistic analyses have come to discover "Shang" and "local" elements on them. In general, their forms are unequivocally derived from Shang. So are the *taotie* design, roundel, *kui*-dragon, turtle, coiled dragon, ring band, triangle, and flange that adorn these vessels. Yet they are stylistically heterogeneous. The excavators discern three styles among them: Shang, hybrid, and local. ③Those that replicate both form and decoration of Shang are ascribed to the Shang style category. Items of the hybrid style are those that integrate Shang prototypes and local innovations. The local style is not quite valid, for the bronze vessels it refers to, four in total, are actually radical variations of Shang prototypes. The *gui*-tureen (no. 43④) that has a false belly between the bowl and the ring foot is a playful combination of formal elements of the *dou*-bowl and *gui*-tureen. Items of this style therefore can be attributed to the hybrid style.

The local innovations have been examined by several scholars and most thoroughly by Bagley. ⑤The assemblage of the Dayangzhou bronzes lacks the wine wares of *jia*-cup and *jue*-cup, which are regular components of bronze assemblages of Shang tombs. Some decorative elements, including three-dimensional tigers, crested birds, a deer-like animal, and a two-dimensional swallow tail that are absent on the Shang bronzes are often present on the

---

① Bagley, Robert W., An Early Bronze Age Tomb in Jiangxi Province, *Orientations* 24.7, 1993, p. 20.

② Jiangxisheng Wenwu Kaogu Yanjiusuo and Zhangshushi Bowuguan, *Wucheng*, Beijing: Kexue, 2005, pp. 238 – 240.

③ Jiangxisheng Bowuguan, Jiangxisheng Wenwu Kaogu Yanjiusuo, and Xin'ganxian Bowuguan, *Xin'gan Shangdai Damu*, Beijing: Wenwu, 1997, p. 192.

④ This and the following serial numbers were assigned by the excavators to the Dayangzhou bronze vessels and bells, see Jiangxisheng Bowuguan, Jiangxisheng Wenwu Kaogu Yanjiusuo, and Xin'ganxian Bowuguan, *Xin'gan Shangdai Damu*, Beijing: Wenwu, 1997.

⑤ Bagley, Robert W., An Early Bronze Age Tomb in Jiangxi Province, *Orientations* 24.7, 1993, pp. 20 – 36.

Dayangzhou bronzes. Some motifs are borrowed from Shang but they are applied to vessel forms they do not belong to the Shang tradition. For instance, four *taotie* units on the aforementioned *gui*-tureen, and two intersecting tunnels in a square *you*-kettle (no. 47, Fig. 2 – 1 – 8: 3). It appears that the hybrid style items are artful manipulations of Shang forms and motifs, which reflect the idiosyncratic taste of the Wucheng élite. Such taste manifests more distinctly in the heavily molded rims of several vessels, the placement of standing animals on handles, and the rendering of the décor on each wall of five rectangular *ding*-quadrupeds [no. 9, no. 10, no. 11, no. 12 (Fig. 2 – 1 – 8: 1), no. 13], as well as an angular-shouldered *li*-tripod (no. 37). The appearance of local innovations upon these Shang-inspired bronzes fits in with the general trend of the localized colonial culture of Wucheng, which diverged from the Shang culture since Wucheng Phase II.

Where the Dayangzhou bronzes were produced, as commented above, is still uncertain. That the Shang style items were likely imports from Shang foundries is conceivable to all scholars; what remain in question are the hybrid style vessels. The distinctive traits have led many scholars to the conviction that they were locally produced, by implication, at Wucheng. [1]This proposition, however, has yet to account for the fact that the identifiable molds found at Wucheng were meant for casting tools, weapons, and a chariot fitting, but not for vessels. [2]The single mold (no. 29) found in the Dayangzhou tomb was intended for adze. [3]It is generally accepted that while the formally simple tools and weapons could have been produced at Wucheng, the formally sophisticated vessels are unlikely to have been produced there. A technical examination of the Dayangzhou bronzes even reveals that neither the vessels nor the tools and

---

[1] Bagley, Robert W., An Early Bronze Age Tomb in Jiangxi Province, *Orientations* 24.7, 1993, p. 29; Peng, Shifan, Jiangxisheng kaogu wushi nian, in Wenwu Chubanshe ed., *Xinzhongguo Kaogu Wushinian*, Beijing: Wenwu, 1999, p. 198.

[2] Jiangxisheng Wenwu Kaogu Yanjiusuo and Zhangshushi Bowuguan, *Wucheng*, Beijing: Kexue, 2005, pp. 143 – 148.

[3] Jiangxisheng Bowuguan, Jiangxisheng Wenwu Kaogu Yanjiusuo, and Xin'ganxian Bowuguan, *Xin'gan Shangdai Damu*, Beijing: Wenwu, 1997, p. 182, pl. II: 4.

weapons were produced out of stone molds; they were all cast out of clay molds.①While this finding renders inexplicable the stone molds found at Wucheng, it agrees well with the absence of clay molds there. All these facts defy the proposition that the bronze vessels from Dayangzhou were local products. As said above, clay molds suitable for casting vessels have not been found at any site in southern China.②It is equally hard to ascertain that they were produced at Shang foundries in the north, as Liu and Chen suggested.③No molds that have been found at Zhengzhou and Anyang were intended for casting the hybrid style vessels from Dayangzhou. The production issue has to be left unsolved at present.

Wherever the Dayangzhou bronzes were produced, one picture readily emerges from the foregoing stylistic examination. Rather than following the stylistic trend of the Shang bronzes, the Wucheng élite developed their own aesthetic taste by Wucheng Phase II, and they systematically imposed them on the products they commissioned. Such motifs as tigers and birds, swallow tails, ring bands, and flanges were applied to twenty-seven items (nos. 1, 2, 4, 14, 15, 16, 17, 18, 19, 20, 21, 22, 26, 27, 8, 9, 11, 12, 10, 33, 36, 34, 35, 37, 38, 43, 46) (Fig. 2 – 1 – 8: 1, 2). The group of motifs comprising tiger, ring band, and dragon-shaped leg were used to decorate nine *ding*-tripod

---

① Su, Rongyu, Juemin Hua, Shifan Peng, Kaixun Zhan, and Lin Liu, Xin'gan Shangdai damu qingtongqi zhuzao gongyi yanjiu, *Xin'gan Shangdai Damu*, Beijing: Wenwu, 1997, p. 293.

② The Panlongcheng site has yielded neither stone nor clay molds, but smelting residue has been found at the Yangjiazui and Louziwan loci (Hubeisheng Wenwu Kaogu Yanjiusuo, *Panlongcheng*, Beijing: Wenwu, 2001, pp. 357, 391), and smelting crucibles in the form of thick-walled jars pervasively inside and outside the walled town. It appears that copper smelting but not casting was operated at the site. The Zaoshi site, located in the neighboring province of Hunan, presents a similar situation. The site, rather modest in dimension, yielded a great number of Shang ware types, which suggest that the residents were also colonizers from Shang or their descendants. These vessels, by their forms, suggest that these colonizers settled at this site as early as the Upper Erligang Phase. Traces of bronze production have been found at the site. Apart from a furnace that might have been used to smelt copper ores, two stone molds for axes have been found in the residential area (Hunansheng Wenwu Kaogu Yanjiusuo, Hunan Shimen Zaoshi Shangdai yicun, *Kaogu Xuebao* 2, 1992, p. 191). Like the Wucheng foundry, this foundry produced only tools and weapons. One bronze awl, one hairpin, three arrowheads, and one fishing hook complete the evidence of bronze production. The Zaoshi foundry was apparently incapable to produce vessels either.

③ Liu and Chen, *State Formation in Early China*, London: Duckworth, 2003, p. 136.

Wucheng and Shang: A New History of a Bronze Age Civilization in Southern China

Fig. 2 - 1 - 8　Bronze vessels from Dayangzhou
(Extracted from: Jiangxisheng Bowuguan, Jiangxisheng Wenwu Kaogu Yan jiusuo, and Xin'ganxian Bowuguan, *Xin'gan Shangdai Damu*, Beijing: Wenwu, 1997, pl. IX: 2; pl. VI; pl. XVII: 5, pl. XXI: 1. 1. No. 12, h. 39. 5 cm; 2. No. 17, h. 44. 5cm; 3. No. 47, h. 28cm; 4. No. 64, h. 41. 5cm)

(nos. 14, 15, 16, 17, 18, 19, 20, 26, 27), and the design featuring one unit per side to four rectangular *ding*-quadrupeds (nos. 9, 10, 11, 12) (Fig. 2 – 1 – 8: 1), and the spiral design to the entire surface of three li-tripods (nos. 33a, ① 33b, 34).

The Dayangzhou bronzes are connected with not only finds in northern China, but also others in southern China. The four bells are most noteworthy, as several scholars have found them to be stylistically congruent with stray finds in the neighboring provinces of Zhejiang, Jiangsu, and Hunan.②Large bells like these are unknown in northern China but have been frequently found in southern China, and one may argue that they were produced in southern China. This point is again not verifiable at present because no bell molds have ever been found there.

The Dayangzhou bells consist of one *bo*-bell, which originally has a loop for suspension, and three *nao*-bells, which are positioned mouth-upward. The *bo*-bell (no. 63) bears a low-relief cow-head, a swallowtail motif and two bird miniatures, which are stylistically consistent with other Dayangzhou pieces. This is the earliest piece of its kind. ③The three *nao*-bells have their main decorations contained in two panels and highlighted by two raised eyes yet they differ otherwise. Two of them (nos. 65 and 66) have an elliptical section and a motif of sunken spiral lines. None of these pieces has found a close analogy in southern China. The other one (no. 64) features a hexagonal section and low-relief spiral lines in two sunken panels (Fig. 2 – 1 – 8: 4). It is nearly identical to a piece from Tangdong Village in Jiangning county, Jiangsu

---

① Two items were given one serial number, and they are differentiated here by affixing a and b.
② Gao, Zhixi, Tan Xin'gan Shangmu chutu tongqi de zhongda yiyi, *Zhongguo Wenwubao*, 6 December 1990, p. 3; Yin, Weizhang, Nanfang kaogu de zhongda tupo, *Zhongguo Wenwubao*, 22 November 1990, p. 3; von Falkenhausen, Lothar, Lun Jiangxi Xin'gan Dayangzhou chutu de qingtong yueqi, *Jiangxi Wenwu* 3, 1991, pp. 16 – 18; Bagley, Robert W., An early Bronze Age tomb in Jiangxi Province, *Orientations* 24.7, 1993, pp. 31 – 32.
③ von Falkenhausen, Lun Jiangxi Xin'gan Dayangzhou chutu de qingtong yueqi, *Jiangxi Wenwu* 3, 1991, p. 16; Bagley, Robert W., An early Bronze Age tomb in Jiangxi Province, *Orientations* 24.7, 1993, p. 31.

province. [1]No evidence is available to circumscribe the production site of these bells at present, but the match suggests that the Wucheng élite had contact with distant societies in southern China.

Conclusion

The foregoing discussion of the Wucheng fortress and the Dayangzhou tomb presents a fresh history of the rise of a Bronze Age civilization in southern China. Although how this civilization came to an end is still obscure, we know much about its origin and development. The Wucheng polity, initially a Shang colony, exploited the local resources kaolin clay, and very likely, copper ore, to be exported to Shang urban centers; but its culture diverged from that of Shang at the time when the Shang power retreated from the Yangzi River Valley and Wucheng was left an independent polity. Evidence of exchange of ceramic wares and bronze bells denotes that the Wucheng élite established broad connection with Wannian and other societies in southern China. The bronze vessels found at Dayangzhou attest to that the Wucheng élite had developed their own taste and systematically imposed it by Wucheng Phase II. The production site of the bronze vessels, however, is uncertain. The lack of clay molds at Wucheng undermines the local production proposition. The absence of such proper molds at Shang urban centers also hinders us from identifying them as Shang products. This question has yet to be enlightened by future discoveries.

This history demonstrates the value of combining the art historical and anthropological perspectives in the study of the Dayangzhou bronzes. Taken apart, either would tell us only a part of the history. The art historical perspective draws our attention to the stylistic eccentricities of the Dayangzhou bronzes at the price of the political and economic dynamics of the Wucheng polity. The anthropological perspective, on the contrary, leads us to discover the political and economic dynamics and the colonial origin of the Wucheng

---

[1] von Falkenhausen, Lun Jiangxi Xin'gan Dayangzhou chutu de qingtong yueqi, *Jiangxi Wenwu* 3, 1991, p. 16.

polity while ignoring the artistic development during its history. A complete history of the Dayangzhou bronzes can be told only when the two perspectives are combined.

This history also calls for a reflection on the Wucheng-Shang relationship, particularly the validity of the core/periphery model that has been applied to conceptualize it. ①The core/periphery model was formulated by Immanuel Wallerstein in 1974 to explain the polarization in the modern world. In his view, this was an outcome of the process of "peripheralization": core states in Western Europe converted by power those in Eastern Europe and the rest of the world into peripheral states, which were to supply raw materials to, and in the meantime, to consume the industrial products from the core states. Polarization occurred because the peripheral states were assigned to low-skill and low-value labor and thus surrendered a part of their surplus to the core states, which assumed the high-skill and high-value labor. ②

In the past three decades, however, this model has undergone rigorous critiques. There is no need here to give a comprehensive review of the vast literature; readers may get a good sense of it from the works of Philip Kohl and Gil Stein. ③I only intend to quote two essays that immediately illuminate the cases under consideration. One is that of Marshall Sahlins, who denied the passive role that the model assigns to the periphery. ④His comparative study of Chinese and Hawaiian reactions to European commercial penetration in the eighteenth-Century reveals that the core was not always determining the terms of contact. While the Chinese rejected England's primary exports as they

---

① Liu and Chen, *State Formation in Early China*, London: Duckworth, 2003, pp. 135 – 141.

② Wallerstein, Immanuel, *The Modern World-System*, San Diego et al: Academic Press, Vol. I, 1974, p. 350.

③ Kohl, Philip, The Use and Abuse of World Systems Theory: The Case of the Pristine West Asian State, in Michael B. Schiffer ed., *Advances in Archaeological Method and Theory*, San Diego et al: Academic Press, 1987, pp. 1 – 35; Stein, Gil, *Rethinking World-Systems*, Tuscon: The University of Arizona Press, 1999.

④ Sahlins, Marshall, Cosmologies of Capitalism: The Trans-Pacific Sector of "The World System," in Nicholas B. Dirks, Geoff Eley, and Sherry B. Ortner ed., *Culture/ Power/History*, Princeton: Princeton University Press, 1994, pp. 412 – 455.

considered themselves the only civilized land in the world, the Hawaiian were receptive to Euro-American goods as they perceived them as symbols of high status and divinity. The other is that of Domenico Sella, who contended that the core's gain does not necessarily mean the periphery's loss; the economic exchange between the core and periphery may be a win-win situation. ①These counter-theses practically eliminate all the underpinning premises of the Wallersteinian core/periphery model; without them, this model hardly offers any new insight for interpreting inter-societal relationship. ②

Yet the core/periphery model is so appealing to many archaeologists that they apply it to their own data—far beyond the geographical confine of Europe and the temporal confine of the modern era and much against the will of Wallerstein himself. ③In applying the model to the Wucheng-Shang relationship, Liu and Chen held the assumptions that Wucheng was under the dominance of Shang and that Shang gained wealth from the economic exchange with Wucheng. ④The two assumptions can be criticized not only from the perspective of the aforementioned counter-theses, but also from the perspective of this empirical study. First, it is true that Wucheng supplied raw materials to Shang, but it was not necessarily a passive periphery to Shang. As this study shows, the society became culturally and by implication politico-economically independent from Shang after Wucheng Phase I. The stylistically distinctive Dayangzhou bronzes undermine the image that they were gifts Shang rulers bestowed to the

---

① Sella, Domenico, The World System and Its Dangers, *Peasant Studies* 6, 1977, pp. 29 – 32.

② Stein, Gil, *Rethinking World-Systems*, Tuscon: The University of Arizona Press, 1999, p. 25.

③ Kohl, Philip, The Use and Abuse of World Systems Theory: The Case of the Pfigtine West Asian State, in Michael B. Schiffer ed., *Advances in Archaeological Method and Theory*, San Diego et al: Academic Press, 1987, pp. 1 – 35; Rowlands, Michael, Centre and Periphery: A Review of a Concept, in Michael Rowlands, Mogens Lawsen and Kristian Kristiansen ed., *Centre and Periphery in the Ancient World*, Cambridge et al: Cambridge University Press, 1987, pp. 1 – 11; Chase-Dunn, Christopher, and Thomas D. Hall, Conceptualizing Core/Periphery Hierarchies for Comparative Study, in Christopher Chase-Dunn and Thomas D. Hall ed., *Core/Periphery Relations in Precapitalist Worlds*, Boulder, San Francisco, and Oxford: Westview Press, 1991, pp. 5 – 44; Algaze, Guillermo, *The Uruk World System: The Dynamics of Expansion of Early Mesopotamian Civilization*, Chicago and London: The University of Chicago Press, 1993, revised and reprinted in 2005.

④ Liu and Chen, *State Formation in Early China*, London: Duckworth, 2003, pp. 135 – 141.

Wucheng élite in return for their raw materials. Wherever they were produced, the active role of the Wucheng élite in imposing their own taste on them cannot be ignored. Second, the remarkable amount of bronze vessels from the Dayangzhou tomb upsets the expectation that the Wucheng élite lost economic surplus to Shang. Given the small size of the Wucheng fortress, the appearance of so many bronze vessels is well beyond its economic capacity. Rather, it was more likely the other way round—the Wucheng élite profited substantially from the trade with Shang.

农业和文明起源*

文明起源在考古学上是一个复杂的问题，牵涉到人类社会的许多方面。其中一个重要方面就是农业。本文试图强调农业对文明起源所起的推动作用，并提出一些有关农业考古的看法，希望对目前正在进行的中华文明探源工程和类似课题有所帮助。

一

农业在人类社会发展中所起的作用很早就被考古学家认识到了。1928年，柴尔德（Gordon V. Childe）在《远古的东方》（*The Most Ancient East*）一书中首次指出了农作物的出现和动物的养殖是人类历史上的一次革命。在此书的1954年版中，柴尔德进一步阐述了这个"农业革命"说[①]：

> 食物的生产，即有意地培育植物食品——尤其是谷类植物，以及驯化、养殖和选择动物，是一场经济革命，是人类学会用火之后的最伟大的一次革命。它开辟了一个更为丰富而且更为可靠的食物来源，使人类依靠自身的能力可以控制并且能够几乎没有止境地扩大生产。由英格兰发生的工业革命的结果来看，这场革命可能带来了人口的激增。

现在看来，农业的起源并不是一场暴风骤雨式的革命，而是一个和风细雨式的渐变过程。实际上，采集渔猎经济在人类学会种植谷物以后

---

* 本文原刊于《考古》2011年第5期，第61—66页。收入本书时略有改动。
① Childe, Gordon V., *New Light on the Most Ancient East*, London: Routledge & Kegan Paul LTD., Revised in 1952 and reprinted with some corrections in 1954, p. 23.

的几千年时间里与农业共同存在。① 不过柴尔德所强调的是农业出现以后对于人口增长和社会发展的刺激作用。然而在西方，这个马克思主义唯物史观色彩很浓的思想在很长时间内没有得到考古学界的重视。近几十年来西方涌现的有关社会复杂化的理论往往考虑其他的因素，如战争、资源的再分配．专业化生产。其中一个重要的理论就是世界体系学说（world-system theory）。此学说的创始人华勒斯坦（Immanuel Wallerstein）的本意是想解释资本主义产生以后世界的财富如何从东方流向西方从而导致东西方之间的两极分化。他提出，工业革命以后的西欧通过各种方式（包括殖民），把其他地区纳入到一个以它为主导的世界经济体系。在这个体系中，西欧提供下游产品，扮演中心的角色，而其他地区提供原料和上游产品，扮演边缘的角色。这种中心—边缘的相互作用的结果就是西欧无形中从其他地区攫取了利润，因而导致了中心和边缘之间的贫富分化。②

世界体系学说发表之后，受到了很多学者的批评。萨林斯（Marshal Sahlins）指出，18世纪的中国和夏威夷并非处于被动地位，而西欧也并非处于主导地位。这与当地人的思维方式有关。中国人认为他们是世界上唯一的文明国家，所以拒绝了英国人提出的贸易请求。而夏威夷人则欢迎西欧的商品，因为他们认为它们来自外来的神明，是权力和地位的象征。③ 塞拉（Domenic Sella）强调中心的获利并不意味着边缘的损失，中心与边缘之间的贸易关系可能是双赢的关系。④ 这些反对意见动摇了华勒斯坦学说的一些支柱。在笔者看来，现代史上世界的两极分化，是因为工业革命使得西欧的商品生产能力以及价格竞争力迅速提高，导致其他地区的民族经济在开放市场（往往是被迫的）后迅速崩溃。

---

① 赵志军最近的有关稻作农业起源的研究提供了一个具体的例证。见赵志军：《栽培稻与稻作农业起源研究的新资料和新进展》，《南方文物》2009年第3期，第60—63页。

② Wallerstein, Immanuel, *The Modern World System I: Capitalist Agriculture and the Origins of the European World Economy in the Sixteenth Century*, New York: Academic Press, 1974.

③ Sahlins, Marshal, Cosmologies of Capitalism: The Trans-Pacific Sector of the World System, in Nicholas B. Dirks, Geoff Eley, and Shery B. Ortner ed., *Culture/ Power/ History*, Princeton: Princeton University Press, 1994, pp. 412 – 455.

④ Sella, Domenico, The World System and Its Dangers, *Peasant Studies* 6, 1977, pp. 29 – 32.

农业和文明起源

　　但是世界体系学说的中心—边缘理论受到了许多考古学家的推崇。尽管华勒斯坦本人在许多场合强调这个理论只适用于公元1500年以后的资本主义时代，但考古学家仍然满腔热忱地把它运用到考古材料上，并用它来解释古代的国家起源。一个著名的例子就是阿尔加泽（Guillermo Algaze）构造的乌鲁克时期美索不达米亚平原与北部的叙利亚山区和东部的伊朗高原之间的贸易关系。平原地区的城邦从北部山区和东部高原获得铜矿和石材，生产铜器、石器和纺织品，并把产品销往那些地区，从而获得利润并迅速积累财富。[①] 中心—边缘理论也出现在刘莉和陈星灿的著作中。他们的目的是利用该理论提供的时空框架重建起中原与周边地区之间的贸易网络。二里头时期和二里冈时期的中原王朝作为中心操控了这个贸易网，它们从边缘地区输入金属矿来生产青铜器同时向边缘地区输出青铜器。随着贸易网的形成，一个由四个级别组成的中央集权的行政系统也出现了。[②] 这里我们要感谢两位作者的努力，使得中原与周边地区之间的经济联系清晰地展现在我们的面前。

　　两位作者虽然有意回避上述的中心——边缘理论的两个困境，但是没有能够彻底摆脱它们的影响。其一，他们认为周边地区的城址，如盘龙城和吴城，都隶属于中原商王朝。这并不全对。说盘龙城是商王朝的一个据点大概是没有问题的，但是这样说吴城恐怕不行。吴城是二里冈上层时期商人建立的一个殖民地，但是这个时期以后它可能独立了。具体表现为它的铜器和陶器风格不再紧跟中原的变化路线了。尽管两位作者认识到了这一点，但是无意之中还是把吴城 II 期和同时期的新干大洋洲大墓纳入到商王朝的贸易网中。[③] 需要指出的是，尽管吴城在第二期

---

　　① Algaze, Guillermo, *The Uruk World System: The Dynamics of Expansion of Early Mesopotamian Civilization*, Chicago and London: The University of Chicago Press, 1993.
　　② Liu, Li, and Xingcan Chen, *State Formation in Early China*, London: Duckworth, 2003.
　　③ Liu, Li, and Xingcan Chen, *State Formation in Early China*, London: Duckworth, 2003. 尽管两位作者在第25页明确说明该书只讨论二里头和二里岗时期，但是此图反映出他们在无意之中涵盖了晚商时期。正如两位作者所说（第121页），相当于二里岗上层的吴城 I 期的遗存很少，只发现有一些陶片和铸造青铜工具的石范，因而不能印证他们提出的政治经济体系。能够表现这个体系的只有吴城 II 期和新干大洋洲大墓（出有475件青铜器，其中青铜容器48件），该书所指的也只有吴城 II 期和新干大洋洲大墓。而两位作者认为后面两种遗存的年代属于晚商时期（第121—122页）。

◇❖◇ 第二部分 考古学理论

可能继续向中原的商王朝提供铜矿和高岭土，但是它与后者可能是相对平等的贸易关系。其二，虽然他们没有否认农业的重要性，但是有关讨论一笔带过，通篇谈的则是资源掠夺在早期国家形成中的作用。给人的印象是，中原国家的形成是因为它们控制了铜矿的开采和青铜器的生产。不可否认，青铜器作为贵重器物（prestige goods）确实起到了推动和巩固中国早期王朝的作用。但是我们需要强调的是，商王朝之所以能够支撑庞大的铸铜作坊并且能够制造成千上万的青铜器，是因为它有坚实的经济基础，也就是农业。我们认为，青铜时代中原地区的社会发展速度之所以快于周边地区，是因为这里有大面积的肥沃平原，适于农业生产，因而中原地区很早就积累了雄厚的财富。而周边地区，尤其是资源产地，多为山地丘陵，可耕土地比较狭窄而贫瘠，经济基础相对薄弱。从这个角度来说，资源产地在与中原王朝的贸易活动中也获得了巨大的文化和物质利益。就吴城文化而言，同本地新石器时代文化相比，它在经济（大量青铜器和玉器）和技术水平（青铜铸造、原始瓷制造等）上可以说有了一个质的飞跃。

要正确地理解中原国家与周边地区的关系，我们恐怕需要正确地理解古代的政治经济学。这里我们有必要引入德阿特罗（Terence N. D. Altroy）和厄尔（Timothy K. Earle）的生存经济（staple finance 或 subsistence economy）和财富经济（wealth finance 或 political economy）学说。生存经济指的是下层必须交给统治者的税（谷物、动物、纺织品等）或者劳动力（为统治者耕作土地）。这种经济收入被用来维持官僚的生活需要。它的好处是简单直接，坏处是谷物和动物的运输费用高昂。所以它适合于小国，不适合大国或帝国。财富经济指的是生产和获得特殊产品（珍宝、原始货币）。它们或者直接来自下层，或者由王室支持的工匠制作。这种经济的好处是产品容易保存，便于长途运输。王室可以用它们来支付各级贵族官僚和附属人员的薪水，也可以用它们来交换所需要的贵重的原料和产品。[1] 总而言之，国家从下层人民获得生

---

[1] Altroy, Terence N. D., and Timothy K. Earle, Staple Finance, Wealth Finance, and Storage in the Inka Political Economy, *Current Anthropology* 26/2, 1985, pp. 187–206.

存经济，并用它来支持财富经济，以便维持国家机器的运转。青铜器的生产就属于财富经济，它是不能代替生存经济这个基础的。

因此，在探讨文明起源时，我们必须明确，土地和农业是古代社会主要的财富来源。在同等条件下，一个政体所统治的土地越多，农业越发达，那么它可以获得的财富就越多，它的物质文化就发展得越快。这也就是早期文明（如埃及、美索不达米亚、印度和中国）都出现在农业发达的平原地区而不是在铜矿丰富的山区的原因。

二

现在我们来进一步考察农业和社会发展的关系。首先来比较青铜时代的欧亚大陆和中国中原地区的文化发展程度。我们着重分析欧亚大陆的草原带和森林草原地带。在这里金属生产比中国中原地区起步要早，始于公元前 3500 年的青铜时代早期，即竖穴墓（Pit Grave）文化时期，生产的为纯铜。到了公元前 2500 年以后的青铜时代中期，即辛塔什塔（Sintashta）和阿巴舍沃（Abashevo）文化时期，开始砷青铜和锡青铜的生产，并且村落普遍从事金属的生产和贸易。按道理讲，这些村落应该积累了很多财富，并且出现了社会分化。但是根据我们的研究，在整个青铜时代，欧亚大陆的社会形态仍然是小型的村落，没有出现大型的类似于二里头和郑州商城的都市。社会分化出现于村落之间，但是没有形成很多等级。村落内部仍然是平等的。这种社会形态在传统的社会进化序列上还处于部落阶段。反观中国的中原地区，尽管青铜器已经出现于公元前 3 千纪的龙山时代，但那是零星的，迄今还没有见到这个时代的冶炼遗迹。大规模的青铜器生产肇始于二里头时代，而这时社会形态已经进入国家阶段。[1] 为什么欧亚大陆的草原和草原森林地带更早进入青铜时代，而在社会形态上反而落后于中国的中原地区呢？这是因为欧亚大陆的主要经济形态为畜牧经济，人们可能也从事农业，但是现有的证

---

[1] Zhang, Liangren, *Ancient Society and Metallurgy: A Comparative Study of Bronze Age Societies in Central Eurasia and North China*, PhD Dissertation, University of California, Los Angeles, 2007.

据非常薄弱。畜牧经济固然属于生产性经济，但是单位面积的产出远远低于农业，因而可以承载的人口密度很小。反观中国的中原地区，早在尚未出现金属的仰韶时代（公元前5000—前3000年），村落规模和人口密度就已经超过欧亚大陆的草原带和草原森林地带。如果说这个时代仍然处于比较平等的部落阶段，那么金属生产仍然处于萌芽状态的龙山时代（公元前3000—前2000年）就已经跨入酋邦阶段了。

我们再来看日本的情形。今村启尔（Imamura Keiji）为我们详细描绘了绳纹时代（公元前10000—前400年）向弥生时代（公元前400—公元300年）过渡的情况。[①] 在历时将近1万年的绳纹时代，人们的食物主要来自陆地上的野兽和植物果实、水中的鱼和贝壳。不过，由于日本群岛的野生食物资源丰富，所以人口较今天的许多采集渔猎社会密集。他们过着定居生活，村落规模较大，大者如千叶县的子和清水聚落有260座地穴式建筑和1000多个用于储存食物的袋状坑。同时人们可以生产大量的造型复杂而个体很大的陶器雕塑。不过，纵观绳纹时代，社会可以积累的财富不多，始终处于简单而平等的部落阶段。

在日本，公元前400年出现大规模的稻作农业，弥生时代也从此开始。现在一般认为，日本的稻作农业是从中国的长江中下游经朝鲜半岛传入的，与它同时传入的是青铜器和铁器。因此日本群岛跳过青铜器的使用时代，直接进入铁器的使用时代。稻作农业最早出现在九州岛北部，那里已经发现了许多水田遗址（如福冈县的野多目和板付），不过稻作农业在大约300年内传播到本州岛。这一时代社会开始分化。佐贺县的吉野里聚落规模很大，长1000米，宽400米，以环壕保护。聚落旁边发现有2000多座瓮棺葬和1座冢墓，其中冢墓下面的8座墓葬中，5座墓出土有青铜短剑和装饰品，地位明显高于其他墓葬。福冈县的吉武高木遗址群发现的一处墓地里，20座成人墓中的11座出土有随葬品。其中3号墓最为丰富，出土有4件青铜兵器和1件铜镜。由此看来，此时日本可能进入了酋邦阶段。到了公元5世纪，统一的国家开始

---

① Keiji, Imamura, *Prehistoric Japan: New Perspectives on Insular East Asia*, Honolulu: University of Hawaii Press, 1996.

出现。纵览日本的发展过程，稻作农业的传入是一个里程碑。

那么，日本的古代部落为什么会放弃渔猎采集经济转向稻作农业呢？今天我们恐怕无法给出一个准确的答案，因为这个转变过程可能不是若干年内完成的，应该是几十、几百年内完成的。20世纪60或70年代，许多学者认为，渔猎采集社会的生活比农业社会轻松，每天只需劳动若干小时就可以满足一天的需要，而且不破坏环境，所以他们把这些社会称为"富裕社会"。既然如此，这些社会就不必转向农业了。但是80年代以后，学者们发现他们的生活并没有如此美好。因为野生食物有季节性变化，同时它们在年份之间有所差异，渔猎采集社会不时地面临食物不足的窘境，因此他们需要储存食物来防止饥饿。① 相比之下，农作物更加稳定，产量很高而且易于贮存。根据贝尔伍德（Peter Bellwood）的计算，渔猎采集社会的一个家庭需要几个平方千米的土地才能维持，而农业社会的一个家庭只要几百平方米的土地就够了。② 因此随着渔猎采集社会的增长，他们逐渐地走向了农业生产的道路，或者被扩张的农业社会同化。

三

前面我们讨论了世界体系学说，重新树立了农业在古代社会发展中的地位。同时我们比较了欧亚大陆和中国中原地区青铜时代文化，回顾了日本古代社会的变化过程，再次突出了农业对于文明起源的推动作用。不过这些只是宏观的观察。如果我们要微观地分析农业和社会发展的关系，还有许多问题无法解释。就中国而言，第一，从仰韶时代到龙山时代再到青铜时代，中原地区稳步向复杂社会迈进。按照上述理论，农业应该在同步前进。因此我们需要知道同时期农业是怎么发展的。第二，长江流域的文化水平在仰韶和龙山时代与中原地区是并驾齐驱的，

---

① Lu, Tracey Lie Dan, *The Transition from Foraging to Farming and the Origin of Agriculture in China*, Oxford: John and Erica Hedges, 1999, pp. 136 – 137.

② Bellwood, Peter, *First Farmers: The Origins of Agricultural Societies*, Malden: Blackwell Pub, 2005, p. 14.

第二部分 考古学理论

为什么到了商代和西周社会发展就裹足不前甚至衰落了？我们知道长江中下游地区在古代是水稻的发源地，在今天是水稻的主要产地。我们需要知道是不是因为这里的稻作农业在商周时期衰落了？还是因为南方的稻作农业还不够发达，产量远远不如北方的旱作农业？

可喜的是，中国的农业考古在过去的几十年取得了长足的进展。尤其是在过去的20年里，由于新技术（浮选）的使用和新思维（关注经济方式）的指导，我们对中国农业的发展过程有了较为深入的认识。今天我们不仅清晰地了解了一系列农作物和家畜的培植和驯化过程，而且进一步触及古代社会的经济方式的变化。就农作物而言，粟和黍起源于中国的北方，并且从兴隆洼文化以后成为中国北方旱作农业的传统。[1] 进入龙山时代以后，人们开始种植稻谷和大豆。到了二里头时期，稻谷的种植快速增长；与此同时，起源于西亚的小麦传入中原。到了二里冈时期，小麦的种植规模增长，并开始取代粟和黍成为北方的主要粮食作物。随着农作物种类的多样化，土地的利用效率提高了，粮食的总体产量也因此增长了，同时气候变化对粮食生产的冲击也减小了。[2] 就家畜而言，我们同样可以看到这样一个多样化过程。公元前7000—前6000年，中国北方出现了家狗和家猪；到了公元前2500年，起源于西亚的黄牛和绵羊经由河西走廊传入中原地区；公元前1300年，可能起源于欧亚大陆的家马传入中原。[3] 它们的出现不仅丰富了人类的肉食资源，而且满足了中国社会复杂化以后日益增长的牺牲用动物。[4] 由此可见，农业的发展是中国中原地区文明发展的前提。

与此同时，我们对中国农业的多样化发展道路也有了一些初步的认

---

[1] 赵志军：《有关中国农业起源的新资料和新思考》，载《新世纪的中国考古学——王仲殊先生八十华诞纪念论文集》，科学出版社2005年版，第92—95页。

[2] 赵志军：《公元前2500年—公元前1500年中原地区农业经济研究》，载《科技考古》第二辑，科学出版社2007年版，第6—11页。

[3] 袁靖：《中国古代家马的研究》，载《中国史前考古学研究——祝贺石兴邦先生考古半世纪暨八秩华诞文集》，三秦出版社2003年版，第436—440页。

[4] 袁靖：《公元前2500年—公元前1500年中原地区动物考古学研究》，载《科技考古》第二辑，科学出版社2007年版，第32页；傅罗文、袁靖、李水城：《中国甘青地区新石器家养动物的来源及特征》，《考古》2009年第5期，第80—84页。

识。最新的研究表明，黄河中上游地区的家畜（猪和狗）养殖可以追溯到公元前6000年，到公元前4000年超越渔猎成为主流的经济方式。在长江中下游地区，猪狗饲养虽然也起步于公元前6000年，但是人们获取肉食的主要方式仍然是捕捞和狩猎。到公元前2000年家畜饲养才上升为主要经济方式。同样，尽管长江中下游地区是栽培稻的起源地，最早出现在公元前8000年，但是稻谷的种植发展相当缓慢，一直到公元前3200—前2100年才开始取代采集狩猎成为当地的主要经济。[①] 华南（岭南）地区以前被认为是栽培稻的发源地，最新的研究否定了这一点，而且公元前4500年以后出现的稻作农业可能是从长江流域传入的。不过，这里可能是块茎类粮食作物（芋）的发源地。[②]

这些新进展无疑是令人鼓舞的，也启发我们提出新的问题。上述的经济方式研究多局限于与目前正在开展的中华文明探源工程相关的黄河中游和长江下游以及公元前2500—前1500年。它们已经初步解释了中原地区文明得以稳步发展的原因，也解释了长江流域出现发达的良渚文化的原因。不过我们还需要对其他地区其他时间段展开研究，以便解决中国文明的后续发展和各地区发展的不平衡性问题，尤其是长江流域在青铜时代为什么落后于中原的问题。要研究这些问题，我们恐怕还要扩大研究范畴。除了农作物和家畜的驯化，我们还需要考虑种植（养殖）技术、农作工具和土地利用方式问题。当然，种植（养殖）技术和土地利用方式在考古遗存中很难观察到，将来要靠民族学材料来弥补，一方面要开展农作工具的微痕分析，以便讨论生产力的发展脉络，另一方面要分析古代植被来认识人类利用土地的能力。总之，农业考古是一个庞大的领域，非一时之力一人之功可以成就。我们希望将来有更多的学者、更多的经费能够投入到这个领域。

[①] 赵志军最近的有关稻作农业起源的研究提供了一个具体的例证。见赵志军：《栽培稻与稻作农业起源研究的新资料和新进展》，《南方文物》2009年第3期，第60—63页。

[②] 赵志军：《有关中国农业起源的新资料和新思考》，见《新世纪的中国考古学——王仲殊先生八十华诞纪念论文集》，科学出版社2005年版，第95—98页；赵志军：《对华南地区原始农业的再认识》，载《华南及东南亚地区史前考古——纪念甑皮岩遗址发掘30周年国际学术研讨会论文集》，文物出版社2006年版，第150、153页。

村落和社会进化[*]

一 序言

20世纪90年代以来,西方社会进化理论,尤其是美国人类学家塞维斯(Elman Service)的"游团—部落—酋邦—国家"四阶段论,逐渐进入我国,为我国文明与国家起源的探讨提供了新的研究思路。[①] 不过,我国学者只是引介或者使用理论,对于理论本身鲜有批判和修正。在西方,大多数社会进化论学者延续了20世纪初以来的奉行和谐论的思想传统,抛弃马克思主义的生产关系学说,因而看到了亲属关系和社会和谐,而没有看到早期社会存在的经济剥削和社会矛盾。同时,在讨论社会进化的行为主体时,过于看重个人(即部落首领、酋长和国王等)的作用,而忽略集体(即村落)的作用。因此他们的社会进化理论存在一些重要缺陷。在本文中,我们将结合马克思主义的生产关系学说,来重新诠释塞维斯的四阶段论。

二 西方社会进化理论

20世纪上半叶,进化论已在英美人类学界衰落了。以美国人类学家博厄斯(Franz Boas)为首的特殊论(Particulafigm)者完全否认了19世纪的单线进化论。相反,他们提倡研究单个文化;认为它们都是独特

---

[*] 本文原刊于《考古》2017年第2期,第85—96页。收入本书时略有改动。
[①] 陈淳:《文明与国家起源研究的理论问题》,《东南文化》2002年第3期;陈星灿等:《中国文明腹地的社会复杂化进程——伊洛河地区的聚落形态研究》,《考古学报》2003年第2期;乔玉:《伊洛地区裴李岗至二里头文化时期复杂社会的演变——地理信息系统基础上的人口和农业可耕地分析》,《考古学报》2010年第4期;郑建明:《史前社会复杂化进程的理论探索》,《华夏考古》2011年第2期。

的，拥有自己的历史。[1] 以英国人类学家马林诺夫斯基（Bronislaw Malinowski）、拉德克利夫－布朗（A. R. Radcliffe-Brown）和埃文思－普里查德（E. E. Evans-Pritchard）为首的功能主义（Functionalism）者同样回避了进化论，只关注单个社会。功能主义者也以不同的眼光来看待社会结构。19世纪的英国进化论者泰勒（Edward B. Tylor）认为社会是多种元素构成的集合体，而功能主义者认为社会是一个有机的整体；马克思主义者看到的是社会矛盾和冲突，而功能主义者看到的是社会团结与和谐。[2] 但是特殊论者和功能主义者花费了大量的精力做民族学调查，并且不断改进调查方法。正是由于他们的辛勤工作和方法创新，优质的民族学资料在20世纪迅速增长，为以后的社会进化理论的复活创造了条件。

与此同时，少数学者延续了进化论思想。英国考古学家柴尔德（Gordon V. Childe）在研究欧洲史前史时，就以农业生产技术的发展为主线，论述了聚落形态、贸易、专业化和社会分化的变化。但是他没有讨论社会进化模式。[3] 后来美国人类学家怀特（Leslie A. White）打破了特殊论的理论藩篱，重新拾起了进化论，并将特殊论和进化论视为一个硬币的两面："历史学关心的是单个事件，考虑其具体的时间和地点，而进化论关心的是事物和事件的类型，不考虑其具体的时间和地点。"[4] 对于20世纪60年代进化论的复活，美国人类学家斯图亚特（Julian Steward）也功劳不小。作为博厄斯的学生，他是一个特殊论者，但是他承认跨文化规律。在南美洲，斯图亚特发现了从狩猎—采集游团走向早期农业村落，最后走向国家级社会的进化过程。[5]

---

[1] Boas, Franz, The History of Anthropology, in *The Shaping of American Anthropology*, New York: Basic Books, Inc., 1974.

[2] Firth, Raymond, The Skeptical Anthropologist? Social Anthropology and Marxist Views on Society, in *Marxist Analyses and Social Anthropology*, London: Malaby Press, 1975.

[3] 戈登·柴尔德：《人类创造了自身》，上海三联书店2008年版，第40—134页；Childe, V. Cordon, *The Prehistory of European Society*, London: Penguin Books, 1958, pp. 150 - 161。

[4] White, Leslie, *The Evolution of Culture: The Development of Civilization to the Fall of Rome*, New York, Toronto, London: McGraw-Hill Book Company, Inc., 1959, p. 30.

[5] Steward, Julian H., *Theory of Culture Change*, Urbana: University of llinois Press, 1955, pp. 11 - 29.

◇❖◇　第二部分　考古学理论

　　上述人类学理论的发展和民族学资料的积累为20世纪50—60年代的理论创新铺好了道路。紧随而来的是美国人类学家萨林斯（Marshall D. Sahlins）和塞维斯（Elman R. Service），和怀特一样，他们区分了特殊进化（即特定自然和社会环境下的社会发展）和普遍进化（即人类社会共同经历的若干阶段）。正因为这个突破，塞维斯提出了"游团—部落—酋邦—国家"四阶段论。[①] 他借助于20世纪上半叶迅速增长的民族学资料，详细而准确地描绘了每个阶段的特征。不过他继承了功能主义者的和谐论。与强调社会矛盾和阶级斗争的马克思主义冲突论不同，和谐论强调团结和融合。塞维斯认为一个社会的构成成分越多，它就越需要维护这些成分的稳定，政治贵族因此出现以应对社会复杂化带来的挑战。这是人类学理论发展史上的一个里程碑，它既得到了学术界的广泛接受，也受到了不少批评。

　　其他学者提出了另外一些理论。美国人类学家弗莱德（Morton H. Fried）接受了马克思主义的生产关系学说，认为社会进化就是人们获得经济资源的差别。[②] 不过他的"平等—等级—阶级"阶段论不够准确。他的"平等社会"对应于塞维斯的"游团"，而"等级"和"阶级"压缩了"部落""酋邦"和"国家"。但是"游团""部落""酋邦"和"国家"这四个术语，更好地体现了人类社会进化中的复杂性。其后美国人类学家约翰逊（Allen W. Johnson）和厄尔（Timothy K. Earle）提出"家庭—地方群体—区域政治体"三阶段论。[③] 他们同样信奉和谐论，但抛弃了塞维斯的四阶段论，而采用社会政治组织的规模作标准。其"家庭"和"地方群体"阶段分别对应于塞维斯的"游团"和"部落"阶段，而"区域政治体"包含"酋邦"和"国家"两个阶段。但是这种将"酋邦"和"国家"叠加起来的做法不尽如人意，因

---

　　① Service, Elman R., *Primitive Social Organization: An Evolutionary Perspective*, Random House, 1962, pp. 59 – 177; Service, Elman R., *Origins of the State and Civilization: The Process of Cultural Evolution*, New York: W. W. Norton, 1975, pp. 3 – 103.

　　② Fried, Morton H., *The Evolution of Political Society: An Essay in Political Anthropology*, New York: Random House, 1967, pp. 52 – 191.

　　③ Johnson, Allen W., and Timothy Earle, *The Evolution of Human Societies: From Foraging Group to Agrarian State*, Stanford: Stanford University Press, 2000, pp. 32 – 35.

为这淡化了二者之间的差别。因此我们选取塞维斯的四阶段论，因为它更为准确地描绘了社会发展过程。同时我们接受弗莱德的生产关系学说，以便修正塞维斯四阶段论的缺陷。

三 社会进化的主角：个人或村落？

谁是早期社会发展的主角？这个问题常常为各种进化论理论所忽略。问题的核心是村落（community）或个人二者之间哪个是社会分化的主角。虽然19世纪的进化论者在古代社会里发现了以宗族为核心的村落，而且功能主义者调查了大量的民族学案例，普遍发现了这样的村落，但是村落的价值一直没有得到进化论者的重视。[1] 相反，他们把注意力都放在了个人即首领身上。

如上所述，塞维斯认为推动进化的主要动力是和谐而不是冲突。[2] 在他描述的四个阶段里，亲属关系扮演着维系整个社会的纽带角色。因此酋邦成为一个等级社会，而亲属关系根据出生顺序赋予个人不同的地位。在他看来，这条进化道路就是一个构成成分增多和复杂化增长的过程，而后者是人口增长和领土扩张的自然结果。因为看不到社会冲突，酋长如何得到权力，又如何统治其下属的村落自然就不清楚了。

弗莱德承认冲突的重要性，但其只看到个人之间的冲突。在他看来，等级分化的发生，是因为一个社会里存在的高级地位数量太少，而有能力担任这些职位的人数量太多；阶级分化的发生，是因为一个社会

---

[1] Malinowski, Bronislaw, *Angonauts of the Western Pacific*, New York: E. P. Dutton&Co, Inc., 1922; Malinowski, Bronislaw, *The Ethnography of Malinowski: The Trobriand Islands*, 1915-1918, London, Boston: Routledge & Kegan Paul, 1979; Radcliffe-Brown, A. R., *The Social Organization of Australian Tribes*, Melbourne: Macmillan &Co. Limited, 1931; 埃文斯-普理查德：《努尔人：对尼罗河畔一个人群的生活方式和政治制度的描述》，华夏出版社2002年版； Evans-Pritchard, E. E., *Kinship and Marriage among the Nuer*, Oxford: Oxford University Press, 1951; Fortes, Meyer, *Kinship and the Social Order*, Chicago: Aldine Publishing Company, 1963.

[2] Sahlins, Marshall D., Evolution: Specific and General, in *Evolution and Culture*, Ann Arbor: University of Michigan Press, 1960, pp. 23-44; Service, Elman R., *Primitive Social Organization: An Evolutionary Perspective*, Random House, 1962, pp. 21-23.

的成年人由于人口增长和资源有限而获得基本生产资料的机会不均等。① 但是这些看法解释不了等级如何分化，阶级如何产生。而且归根结底，村落内部的剥削是有悖于平等主义的。约翰逊和厄尔糅合了和谐论和冲突论，但是他们看到的只是酋邦阶段的"统治阶层"和"平民阶层"之间的分化。② 与塞维斯一样，他们认为酋邦的出现，是因为人口增长导致人们对经济资源的过度利用。酋长因而出现以承担管理责任，负责风险管理、灌溉系统建设、贸易和安全，以便减轻过度利用带来的问题。③ 所以酋长和统治阶层是因经济问题而产生的。亲属关系因此成为"统治阶层"和"平民阶层"结合成一个紧密的、和谐的集体的纽带。④ 不过这种看法无法解释一个阶层是如何取得统治地位的。

这些理论都强调首领的作用。有能力且有野心的首领在现有民族学资料中随处可见，但是将此当作社会进化的主角不无问题。人的野心和能力天然地制造了不平等，让一个村落内部出现个人威望和财富的不同。但是这种不平等，就像年龄和性别导致的不平等一样，是人类社会的普遍现象。而且由于这来源于个人的禀赋，会随着首领的死亡而转移，所以上述的"首领"论无法解释部落阶段的流动的小首领如何转变为酋邦阶段的稳定的、完全控制若干村落的大酋长。同时，这种观点完全忽略了村落的力量，将首领孤立于村落之外。如上所述，村落是重要的政治、经济和文化单位，强调内部团结和共同利益，拥有共同道德。因此首领必须在村落的框架内活动，利用集体力量，在实现村落共同利益的同时实现自己的价值。

村落是个历史产物，随着社会进化而变化。我们对于村落的认识主

---

① Fried, Morton H., *The Evolution of Political Society: An Essay in Political Anthropology*, New York: Random House, 1967, p. 52.

② Johnson, Allen W. and Timothy Earle, *The Evolution of Human Societies: From Foraging Group to Agrarian State*, Stanford: Stanford University Press, 2000, p. 250.

③ Johnson, Allen W., and Timothy Earle, *The Evolution of Human Societies: From Foraging Group to Agrarian State*, Stanford: Stanford University Press, 2000, p. 252.

④ Johnson, Allen W., and Timothy Earle, *The Evolution of Human Societies: From Foraging Group to Agrarian State*, Stanford: Stanford University Press, 2000, p. 249.

村落和社会进化

要来自于国家阶段以前的社会,尤其是部落阶段(其典型形态)的社会。① 一个村落首先是一个居住集体:它可以是若干家庭共同居住的定居村落;也可以是围绕一个中心分散居住的若干家庭。② 新几内亚高地的恩加人村落就属于分散类型,家庭没有集中居住,不过形成了村落,拥有共同的领土和自主权。③

村落也是一个亲属集体,其成员由血缘关系和婚姻维系在一起。一个亲属集体可以是宗族,或者是氏族。当成员通过血统追溯到共同的祖先时,这个集体就是宗族(lineage);当成员无法追溯到一个真实的祖先,只能追溯到一个传说的祖先时,这个集体就是氏族(clan)。实际上,凭借氏族制度,一个宗族可以灵活地吸纳另一个没有血缘关系的宗族,只要后者接受前者的祖先为共同祖先。因此一个村落属于一个宗族或氏族,④ 而一个宗族或氏族可拥有若干村落。⑤

村落的结构是可以变化的。在人口增长时,一个村落可分解为若干村落。由于宗族内在的机制,村落自然会按照血统分解。⑥ 举例来说,提科皮亚人(Tikopia)的宗族分解为好几个村落。⑦ 相反,一个村落可能容纳外来人口或战俘进入本宗族。⑧ 作为一个社会单元,一个村落可以和其他村落联合形成更大的社会组织。在澳大利亚,土著人的宗族村落组成部

---

① 现在一般将"community"翻译为"社区",但是这个译名并不理想。虽然村落也不是一个合适的译名,但能够准确地表达本文的意思,所以本文还是采用这个译名。
② Murdock, George P., *Social Structure*, London: Collier-Macmillan Limited, New York: The Free Press, 1949, pp. 79–90.
③ Johnson, Allen W., and Timothy Earle, *The Evolution of Human Societies: From Foraging Group to Agrarian State*, Stanford: Stanford University Press, 2000, p. 226.
④ Murdock, George P., *Social Srructure*, London: Collier-Macmillan Limited, New York: The Free Press, 1949, pp. 41–47.
⑤ Johnson, Allen W., and Timothy Earle, *The Evolution of Human Societies: From Foraging Group to Agrarian State*, Stanford: Stanford University Press, 2000, p. 210.
⑥ Evans-Pritchard, E. E., *Kinship and Marriage among the Nuer*, Oxford: Oxford University Press, 1951, pp. 279–287; Sahlins, Marshall D., The Segmentary Lineage: An Organization of Predatory Expansion, in *Comparative Political Systems*, Garden City, New York, 1967.
⑦ Firth, Raymond, *We, The Tikopia: A Sociological Study of Kinship in Primitive Polynesia*, second edition, London: George Allen & Unwin LTD, 1957, p. 354.
⑧ Evans-Pritchard, E. E., *Kinship and Marriage among the Nuer*, Oxford: Oxford University Press, 1951, pp. 254–260.

· 115 ·

落；在北美，村落组成胞族，胞族又组成部落，最后部落组成部落联盟。①

村落在政治、文化和经济领域都是一个独立的行事单元。② 村落首先是个经济单元。村落内的各个家庭都拥有土地的使用权，但是所有权掌握在村落首领的手上。③ 我们知道在提科皮亚人的马塔乌图（Matautu）村落，首领是大家公认的主人，是土地的拥有者和分配者。④ 虽然家庭是基本的经济生产单元，但是村落可以组织大规模生产活动，如狩猎、捕鱼和开垦等。同时，首领作为村落的领导人会参加区域性的聚餐（pooling）和分享（sharing）活动。

村落也是文化活动的主角。由于若干家庭共同生活在一个地方，它们通过合作和分享紧密地联系在一起。它们每天面对面交往，并参与集体工作和舞蹈（如提科皮亚人）。⑤ 这种亲密的交往产生了行为规范，村落也因此成为社会控制的主要场所。村民提倡遵守公共道德和规范，同时抵制出格举动。由于这些社会约束，一个村落的思想和行为固定下来；⑥ 由此也形成了共同的文化和观念。当然，这并不排除一个村落与其邻居的正常交往。⑦ 出于共同的文化传统、共同的生态和社会环境、共同的生活方式，一个村落还可能与其邻居享有共同的文化面貌。

村落也是基本的政治活动单元。虽然萨林斯认为家庭是基本的社会

---

① 摩尔根：《古代社会》，生活·读书·新知三联书店1957年版，第48—166页。
② Murdock, George P., *Social Structure*, London: Collier-Macmillan Limited, New York: The Free Press, 1949, pp. 81–84.
③ Johnson, Allen W., and Timothy Earle, *The Evolution of Human Societies: From Foraging Group to Agrarian State*, Stanford: Stanford University Press, 2000, p. 77.
④ Firth, Raymond, *We, The Tikopia: A Sociological Study of Kinship in Primitive Polynesia*, second edition, London: George Allen & Unwin LTD, 1957, p. 63.
⑤ Firth, Raymond, *We, The Tikopia: A Sociological Study of Kinship in Primitive Polynesia*, second edition, London: George Allen & Unwin LTD, 1957, p. 55.
⑥ 戈登·柴尔德：《人类创造了自身》，上海三联书店2008年版，第86页；Murdock, George P., *Social Structure*, London: Collier-Macmillan Limited, New York: The Free Press, 1949, p. 82.
⑦ Murdock, George P., *Social Structure*, London: Collier-Macmillan Limited, New York: The Free Press, 1949, p. 83.

单元，也隐约地表示它就是核心的政治活动单元，① 但是因为成员团结并忠诚于村落，所以村落可以在军事活动中统一行动，无论它是否拥有正式的首领（如酋长和议事会）。事实上，学者们都认为，村落是主要的政治活动单元，进可以攻击其他村落，退可以保护自己的成员。②

村落内部的气氛是平等的。在北美的易洛魁社会，村落成员拥有选举和罢黜首领的权力，承担援助、防卫和报复的义务，使用共同的墓地。首领和由成年人组成的议事会管理公共事务。③ 每个家庭都拥有一块土地的使用权，用自己的劳动获得生存资料。在这方面首领并没有特权；实际上他必须比其他成员更加辛勤地劳动，来生产更多的食物，以便在公共活动中分享。在推崇聚餐和分享的社会里，首领要比其他人贡献更多才能赢得威望。所以他不是个富裕的人，他也没有真正的权力推行他的命令。④ 如弗莱德所说，"首领可以领导，但是成员可以不听"⑤。实际上，他主要扮演村落的发言人，在部落活动中代表村落；同时扮演村落活动的主持人，为村落服务。⑥

即使在归属更高级别的社会组织以后，村落仍然保留了部分自治权。⑦ 在部落内，村落首领组成议事会，他们拥有同等的权力和地位，处理部落的公共事务，如发动战争、议和与结盟。部落首领并不固定，他由村落首领选举而来，而且面临罢黜的风险。此外，无论是酋长还是议事会都不能干预村落内部的事务；同等的村落首领组成的议事会才拥有绝对权力处理部落的共同事务。⑧

---

① Sahlins, Marshall D., *Tribesmen*, Englewood Cliffs, New Jersey: Prentice Hall, 1968, p. 21.
② Tylor, Edward B., *Anthropology: An Introduction to the Study of Man and Civilization*, New York: D. Appleton and Company, 1896, pp. 223 – 225; Evans-Pritchard, E. E., *Kinship and Marriage among the Nuer*, Oxford: Oxford University Press, 1951, pp. 166 – 172.
③ 摩尔根：《古代社会》，生活·读书·新知三联书店1957年版，第73、74页。
④ 摩尔根：《古代社会》，生活·读书·新知三联书店1957年版，第90页。
⑤ Fried, Morton H., *The Evolution of Political Society: An Essay in Political Anthropology*, New York: Random House, 1967, p. 133.
⑥ Sahlins, Marshall D., *Tribesmen*, Englewood Cliffs: Prentice-Hall, 1968, p. 21.
⑦ Sahlins, Marshall D., *Tribesmen*, Englewood Cliffs: Prentice-Hall, 1968, p. 22.
⑧ 摩尔根：《古代社会》，生活·读书·新知三联书店1957年版，第127—129页。

四　生产关系学说

如上所述，塞维斯、约翰逊和厄尔强调和谐，否认冲突，认为社会进化的动力来自于首领对专业化生产或军事或宗教的垄断。只有弗莱德强调冲突论，认为生产关系是产生社会不平等的根源。生产关系学说是马克思历史唯物主义解开人类社会发展之谜的一把钥匙，简单来说，它将社会分为两个阶级：有产阶级，即拥有生产资料（资本、土地和工具）的阶级；无产阶级，即不拥有生产资料而只拥有劳动力的阶级。因此，前者成为统治者和剥削者，后者成为被统治者和被剥削者。生产关系因此成为界定社会形态的标准，奴隶主—奴隶关系是奴隶制的标志，资本家—工人关系则是资本主义的标志。而社会进化就是社会形态的变化，根本的动力就是生产关系驱动的阶级斗争。

由于民族学资料有限，马克思历史唯物主义的生产关系学说和社会发展阶段学说在20世纪初未被西方人类学家接受。不过法国人类学家认为生产关系学说仍有价值。[1] 这是因为马克思和恩格斯对于资本主义社会的研究非常成功，而其生产关系学说就是从资本主义社会总结而来的。根据这个学说，法国学者研究了部落社会中"老者和少者，男人和女人，'大人'和普通人，主体宗族和附庸宗族"之间的不平等关系。[2] 在波利尼西亚酋邦社会里，他们区分出从事生产的普通人和"不从事生产的并且垄断政治、意识形态和宗教权力的贵族"。[3] 很可惜法国人类学

---

[1] Terray, Emmamuel, Cases and Class Consciousness in the Abron Kingdom of Gyaman, in *Marxist Analyses and Social Anthropology*, London: Malaby Press, 1975; Godelier, Maurice, *Perspectives in Marxist Anthropology*, Cambridge, New York: Cambridge University Press, 1977, p. 2; Bloch, Maurice, *Marxism and Anthropology*, Oxford: Clarendon Press, 1983, pp. 148–170.

[2] Godelier, Maurice, *Perspectives in Marxist Anthropology*, Cambridge, New York: Cambridge University Press, 1977, p. 32.

[3] Terray, Emmamuel, Cases and Class Consciousness in the Abron Kingdom of Gyaman, in *Marxist Analyses and Social Anthropology*, London: Malaby Press, 1975, p. 93; Godelier, Maurice, *Perspectives in Marxist Anthropology*, Cambridge, New York: Cambridge University Press, 1977, p. 87.

家就此止步，未效仿马克思和恩格斯进一步研究人类社会各个发展阶段的生产关系。

五　塞维斯四阶段论新解

下面我们来重新诠释塞维斯的四个阶段，即游团、部落、酋邦和国家。上面说到，我们接受他们的四阶段论，同时指出其缺陷，即否认冲突和强调个人的作用。为了弥补这些缺陷，我们融入了生产关系和村落学说，全面分析各个阶段的土地所有制、政治景观和村落形态，以便准确地认识各个阶段的特征；而且塞维斯引用的民族学材料严重不足，无法体现上述特征，为此我们又梳理了20世纪上半叶的西方民族学调查资料，做了补充。前面说到，功能主义人类学家关注单个社会，所以有关村落形态的调查资料相当丰富。但因为他们着重观察亲属关系和各级酋长，未关注生产关系和村落问题，所以停留在社会表象上，很少深入观察土地所有制和政治形态，有关的调查资料并不充足。基于现有民族学资料，我们将着重研究部落和酋邦阶段，因为它们体现了平等社会向阶级社会过渡的转变过程。同时，我们着重研究政治和经济方面，不涉及宗教信仰方面。需要强调的是，这个阶段论并不意味着一个社会一定从一个阶段走向另一个阶段；一个社会可能瓦解，或停滞，或跳过中间阶段而直接进入更高阶段。与萨林斯和塞维斯一样，我们尊重每个社会的特殊的发展道路。我们讲的阶段论只是一般的进化路线，人类社会的一般发展方向。

（一）游团阶段

属于游团阶段的只有狩猎—采集社会，而狩猎—采集社会并不都属于游团阶段。亲属关系是游团社会的核心纽带，其中大多为父系。不过斯图亚特提出一类父系和母系混杂的亲属关系。但是他引用的北阿尔贡卡（Algonkians，加拿大）、阿塔巴斯康人（Athabaskans，加拿大）、安达曼尼斯（Andamanese，澳大利亚）游团，虽然由若干没有血缘关系的家庭组成，但根本上还是父系，而不是混杂的游团。① 好在塞维斯不接受这些混杂的游团，但是他将所有狩猎—采集社会都看作"父系游团"就失之谬误了。② 达·玛思（David Damas）、李（Richard B. Lee）和德沃尔（Irven Devore）就列举了一些混合游团的例子，其中一对夫妇加入兄弟姐妹和父母的游团。所以亲属关系是双方的而不是父系或母系一方。③

摩尔根曾用"原始共产主义"来描述易洛魁部落，不过这个术语也可用来描述狩猎—采集社会的情况。这个术语并不是说每个人都能分享游团的财物，而是说所有家庭都能获得基本生产资料，因此既没有经济剥削，也没有政治压迫。土地的所有权属于游团。李（Richard B. Lee）这么描述非洲的空（！Kung）部落："土地没有私有权……生产是为了使用，而不是为了交换……当人们交换东西的时候，也是为了分享和互利。人们非常好客，反对财富积累。领导人是存在的，但是他们是财富的重新分配者，不是积累者。"④ 这些社会的首领既不是永久的，也不是很有权力。一个人因为能力成为首领，死了以后，他的影响就消失了；游团就重新选举首领。同时，首领需要说服而不是强迫人们服从他。⑤

狩猎—采集游团分布稀疏且居无定所。由于我们缺少民族学资料（资料丰富的美国西北海岸印第安人归入部落阶段），无法详细分析这个阶段的政治景观，所以我们只能谈几点想法。有些游团比其他的大些，经济和政治力量强些，因为它们的生态条件好些，但是它们都是自

---

① Steward, Julian H., *Theory of Culture Change*, Urbana: University of Illinois Press, 1955, pp. 143 – 150.

② Service, Elman R., *Primitive Social Organization: An Evolutionary Perspective*, Random House, 1962, pp. 65 – 66.

③ Damas, David, The Diversity of Eskimo Societies, in *Man the Hunter*, Chicago: Aldine Publishing Company, 1968; Lee, Richard B., and Irven Devore, Problems in the Study of Hunters and Gatherers, in *Man the Hunter*, Chicago: Aldine Publishing Company, 1968.

④ Lee, Richard B., Reflections on Primitive Communism, in *History, Evolution and Social Change*, Oxford, New York, Hamburg: BERG, 1988.

⑤ Service, Elman R., *Origins of the State and Civilization: The Process of Cultural Evolution*, New York: W. W. Norton, 1975, p. 56.

主的个体。在一个生态区域内所有的游团可能享有某些共同的文化特点，以应对共同的生态条件和生活方式，但是它们出于各自独特的政治、经济和文化活动，拥有一些独特的文化习惯。

（二）部落阶段

"部落"指的主要是农业和畜牧人群，但是也包括一些特别的狩猎、采集社会。其中就有美国西北海岸的印第安人，他们因为地处渔业资源丰富的区域，所以过着定居而富裕的生活。由于生产显著增长，部落比游团拥有更多的人口。它实际上是"游团的集合"，但是超越了游团社会，成为一个组织起来的社会。[1]

部落可以萎缩，也可以扩张，但是其依赖于牢固的亲属纽带把村落维系在一起。人类学家发现，部落是一个亲属集体，他们可追溯到一个传说的祖先或真实的祖先，因而形成了氏族或宗族。[2] 部落亲属制度的血统既不久远也不复杂。其中最为复杂的是尼格利亚的提夫（Tiv）人的宗族，其分支对应于领土的划分（图2-3-1）。[3] 不过我们不应该让亲属关系蒙蔽了眼睛：它是村落维系集体和扩大政治与经济利益的工具。

亲属制度如何影响部落社会的经济？亲属集体内土地如何分配？现有的研究文献没有很好地回答这些问题，大多数文献甚至没有触及这些问题。只有费司（Raymond Firth）在研究波利尼西亚的提科皮亚人时曾回答了这个问题。提科皮亚人生活在大洋洲，四个氏族分别由若干村落

---

[1] Sahlins, Marshall D., The Segmentary Lineage: An Organization of Predatory Expansion, in *Comparative Political Systems*, Garden City, New York, 1967, p. 93; Fried, Morton H., *The Evolution of Political Society: An Essay in Political Anthropology*, New York: Random House, 1967, p. 133.

[2] 摩尔根：《古代社会》，生活·读书·新知三联书店1957年版，第65页；Evans-Pritchard, E. E., *Kinship and Marriage among the Nuer*, Oxford: Oxford University Press, 1951, pp. 221-223; Firth, Raymond, *We, The Tikopia: A Sociological Study of Kinship in Primitive Polynesia*, second edition, London: George Allen & Unwin LTD, 1957, pp. 298-313; Service, Elman R., *Primitive Social Organization: An Evolutionary Perspective*, Random House, 1962, pp. 133-139; Sahlins, Marshall D., The Segmentary Lineage: An Organization of Predatory Expansion, in *Comparative Political Systems*, Garden City, New York, 1967, pp. 89-119; Fried, Morton H., *The Evolution of Political Society: An Essay in Political Anthropology*, New York: Random House, 1967, p. 133.

[3] Sahlins, Marshall D., *Tribesmen*, Englewood Cliffs, New Jersey: Prentice-Hall, 1968, pp. 50-51.

组成。每个氏族的酋长是"神的代表，代表他的人民祈求农作物的丰收"。他是土地的主人，有权分配氏族的土地，保护人民的共同利益。他甚至有权没收土地，但不能滥用权力。① 这种氏族首领土地所有制恐怕是部落社会的正常形态。

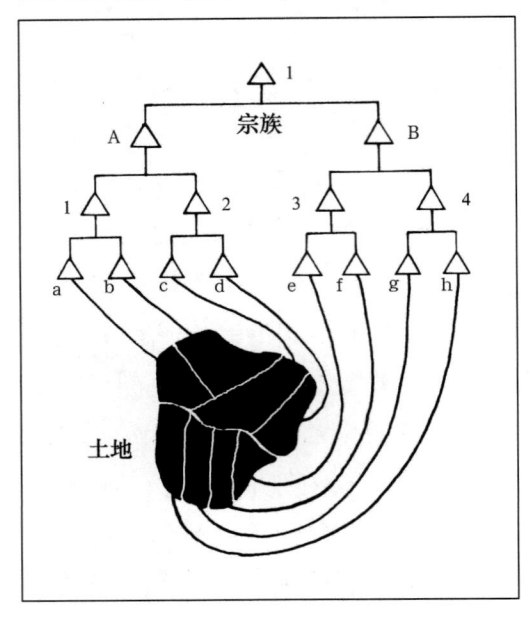

关于部落村落的经济形态，萨林斯提出了"家庭生产方式"说。② 他认为部落社会的经济生产是以单个家庭为单位进行的。每个家庭都会得到一块土地，自己耕种，因此其经济根本上是独立的。财富的积累也会因家庭而异，但是这种差异是随时变化而不是固定的。家庭生产方式本身会限制生产，因为家庭不生产超出自身需要的产品，它没有动机生产剩余产品。但是亲属关系会鼓励剩余产品的生产，首领会要求家庭提高产量以满足整个村落的需要。

图 2-3-1 尼格利亚提夫（Tiv）人的分解宗族制度示意图

(Sahlins, Marshall D., *Tribesmen*, Englewood Cliffs, New Jersey: Prentice Hall, 1968, p 3)

部落内部的村落之间是否存在贫富差异？过去的研究文献同样没有很好地回答这个问题。一些学者谈到了，但是没有深入。③ 因为每个村落都拥有自己的领土和资源，推测各个村落的经济因其规模和资源条件而有所差异。这个想法可得到约翰逊和厄尔的支持。在美国西北海岸的印第安人部落里，没有哪个村落

---

① Firth, Raymond, *We, The Tikopia: A Sociological Study of Kinship in Primitive Polynesia* second edition, London: George Allen & Unwin LTD, 1957, pp. 376-385.

② Sahlins, Marshall D., *Tribesmen*, Englewood Cliffs: Prentice-Hall, 1968, p. 75; Sahlins, Marshall D., *Stone Age Economies*, Chicago: Aldine Publishing Company, 1972, pp. 41-148.

③ Sahlins, Marshall D., *Tribesmen*, Englewood Cliffs: Prentice-Hall, 1968, p. 21; Turner, Jonathan H., *Human Institutions: A Theory of Societal Evolution*, Lanham et al: Rowman & Littlefield Publishers, Inc., 2003, p. 126.

酋长凌驾于其他村落。但是"有些村落会强于其他村落，因为他们的资源条件和政治、军事和管理技能有所差异"。[1] 这种村落之间差异的重要性需要引起我们的重视。如上所述，这是后来成长为酋邦和国家阶段阶级差别的种子。

实际上，部落内部村落之间的政治不平等在民族学资料中有很好的体现。委内瑞拉的亚诺麻莫部落和新几内亚的参巴加部落村落间的战争就是很好的例子。[2] 由于资源的缺乏，冲突和战争在亚诺麻莫部落非常普遍。虽然村落内部个人之间的矛盾可用血缘关系来平息，但是村落间争夺土地更容易引发暴力，即使这些村落属于同一个部落。举例来说，亚诺麻莫部落的诺莫特日（Nomoeteri）村分为四个村以后，其中一个子村落把母村落赶走，抢占了后者的土地。[3] 参巴加村是一个由分散的但是有亲属关系的家庭组成的村落，也用武力取代了另一个村落。[4] 这些例子充分显示，亲属关系本质上只是部落社会的意识形态：它既没有维系一个部落，也没有保障村落之间的和平。

因此，部落社会的成员就是政治和经济独立的但又存在差别的村落。不过政治景观是平等的，因为没有任何村落凌驾于其他村落之上。表现这种村落文化的现有民族学和考古学资料，很少有人讨论。不过可以推测，由于共同居住和共同生活，各个村落拥有独特的文化。由于共同的文化传统、共同的生态和社会环境、共同的生活方式，同一区域的村落之间会有一些共同的文化特征。

（三）酋邦阶段

酋邦的经典例子是波利尼西亚群岛上的酋邦，但是这类社会广泛发现

---

[1] Johnson, Allen W., and Timothy Earle, *The Evolution of Human Societies: From Foraging Group to Agrarian State*, Stanford: Stanford University Press, 2000, p. 216.

[2] Johnson, Allen W., and Timothy Earle, *The Evolution of Human Societies: From Foraging Group to Agrarian State*, Stanford: Stanford University Press, 2000, p. 77.

[3] Johnson, Allen W., and Timothy Earle, *The Evolution of Human Societies: From Foraging Group to Agrarian State*, Stanford: Stanford University Press, 2000, pp. 166–168.

[4] Johnson, Allen W., and Timothy Earle, *The Evolution of Human Societies: From Foraging Group to Agrarian State*, Stanford: Stanford University Press, 2000, p. 186.

第二部分 考古学理论

于北美洲、南美洲、欧洲和非洲。[1] 酋邦在许多方面超越了部落。首先，它拥有更多的人口，更大的领土，可称为"区域政治体";[2] 实际上，它是一个统一的政治体，管辖许多村落。[3] 其次，部落是个松散的村落集合体，而酋邦是高度统一的组织。[4] 而且部落首领是个靠能力争取到的、随时变化的位置，而酋邦的大酋长是个世袭的、永久的位置。[5] 最后，部落的村落享有完整的自主权，而酋邦的村落丧失了部分自主权，服从大酋长的统治;[6] 与此同时，村落首领与大酋长构成了藩属—宗主关系，前者向后者提供贡赋和劳役，并从后者获得保护和安全。[7]

学术界一般把酋邦描绘成等级社会。[8] 几乎所有的学者都认为，等级制度来自于部落阶段宗族的分解结构；这恐怕就是弗莱德把部落和酋邦都归入等级社会的原因。亲属关系是两个阶段的共同特征，不过二者存在显著的差异：部落的村落之间是平等的，而酋邦的村落之间是有等级差别的。[9] 酋邦的宗族结构复杂且呈金字塔形，包含了几代人、大宗

---

[1] Carneiro, Robert L., The Chiefdom: Precursor of the State, in *The Transition to Statehood in the New World*, Cambridge University Press, 1981.

[2] Johnson, Allen W., and Timothy Earle, *The Evolution of Human Societies: From Foraging Group to Agrarian State*, Stanford: Stanford University Press, 2000, p. 186.

[3] Carneiro, Robert L., The Chiefdom: Precursor of the State, in *The Transition to Statehood in the New World*, Cambridge University Press, 1981, p. 47.

[4] Oberg, Kalervo, Types of Social Structure among the Lowland Tribes of South and Central America, *American Anthropologist* 57, 1955, pp. 472–487.

[5] Service, Elman R., *Primitive Social Organization: An Evolutionary Perspective*, Random House, 1962, p. 163.

[6] Service, Elman R., *Primitive Social Organization: An Evolutionary Perspective*, Random House, 1962, p. 133; Carneiro, Robert L., The Chiefdom: Precursor of the State, in *The Transition to Slatehood in the New World*, Cambridge University Press, 1981.

[7] Johnson, Allen W., and Timothy Earle, *The Evolution of Human Societies: From Foraging Group to Agrarian State*, Stanford: Stanford University Press, 2000, p. 248.

[8] Service, Elman R., *Primitive Social Organization: An Evolutionary Perspective*, Random House, 1962, p. 163; Fried, Morton H., *The Evolution of Political Society: An Essay in Political Anthropology*, New York: Random House, 1967, p. 212; Sahlins, Marshall D., *Tribesmen*, Englewood Cliffs: Prentice Hall, 1968, p. 24.

[9] 由于民族学家往往只关注各级酋长之间的地位差别，而忽略了村落之间的地位差别，不过萨林斯的著作透露了一些萨摩亚和复活岛酋邦的村落的信息，见 Sahlins, Marshall D., *Social Stratification in Polynesia*, Seattle: University of Washington Press, 1958, pp. 30, 33–34, 54–55.

和若干小宗（图2-3-2），每个小宗离祖先距离越近，地位越高；离祖先越远，地位越低。我们或可设想，酋邦内存在远近不同而高低错落的小宗。但是在现实中，大宗和小宗都是同代的，他们是"兄弟"。在这个制度里，长子继承制发挥了重要作用。它规定长子的大宗地位最高，其他小宗随排行而依次降低。不过实际上，差别只见于大宗和小宗之间，并不见于小宗之间。① 不过这种制度是把双刃剑。首先，它为酋邦建立了一个等级秩序；其次，当小宗不满于自己低下的地位时，可以分解出去建立自己的酋邦。因此等级不全是血统决定的，政治力量也是一个决定因素。②

上面描绘的画面是一个纯粹的血缘社会，但这不是现实情况。在部落阶段，战争是为了"土地和其他资源，敌人要么杀掉，要么赶走"，而到了酋邦阶段，战争"是为了扩大政治经济，掠夺土地和劳动力"。③ 因此酋邦可以占领一个大区域，统治许多原本没有血缘关系的村落。④ 虽然现有的民族学资料没有告诉我们一个酋邦是如何起源的，但我们推测真实的情况是一个领头的村落及其联盟控制了一些被征服的村落，并且把它们纳入

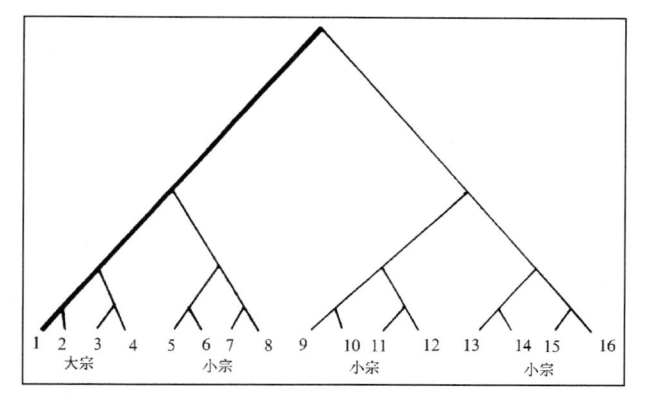

图2-3-2 酋邦锥形氏族结构示意图

(Johnson, Allen W., and Timothy Earle, *The Evolution of Human Societies From Foraging Group to Agrarian State*, Stanford: Stanford University Press, 2000, p. 283, Fig. 12)

---

① Johnson, Allen W., and Timothy Earle, *The Evolution of Human Societies: From Foraging Group to Agrarian State*, Stanford: Stanford University Press, 2000, p. 282.

② Johnson, Allen W., and Timothy Earle, *The Evolution of Human Societies: From Foraging Group to Agrarian State*, Stanford: Stanford University Press, 2000, pp. 32-35.

③ Johnson, Allen W., and Timothy Earle, *The Evolution of Human Societies: From Foraging Group to Agrarian State*, Stanford: Stanford University Press, 2000, p. 249.

④ Johnson, Allen W., and Timothy Earle, *The Evolution of Human Societies: From Foraging Group to Agrarian State*, Stanford: Stanford University Press, 2000, p. 250.

到自己的宗族系统，其首领也成为大酋长。与此同时，被征服村落的土地为领头村落占有，也为大酋长占有。血统因此成为一个有用的意识形态，可以将这个秩序合法化。

如此说来，不能简单地视酋邦为等级社会，它实际上是一个阶级社会。大酋长是酋邦的最高领导人，他是祖先的直系后代，因此是权力的合法继承人。[①] 他不仅仅是政治首领，而且是酋邦所有土地的所有者。但是跟部落首领不同，他是一个神圣的人物，不能从事体力劳动。相反，他依赖平民缴纳的剩余产品生活。此外，他的家庭和宗族成员成为村落首领或者武士和各种专职工作者，也依赖剩余产品生存。大酋长还从平民那里征劳役和兵役。在这个意义上，酋邦是一个阶级社会，因为它包含了一个剥削阶级和一个被剥削阶级。

与游团和部落相比，村落的形态发生了很大的变化。政治景观不再平等，因为出现了最高中心。最高中心是大酋长居住的地方，也是最大的村落，血缘关系最为混杂，因为该村落从下级村落中征召了一些工匠、侍从和武士。因此它成为一个大型村落。在夏威夷这样的复杂酋邦里，在高级中心下面还有一些二级中心，因为大酋长委派他的盟友或亲属去管理领土。这样的二级酋长可以完全控制他们的领土，但是在地位上低于大酋长，并且必须满足大酋长的各种需求。这些中心与最高中心结构相似，但规模要小些。在这个政治金字塔的底层是平民的村落。这些村落保留了部落阶段的许多特征，它们仍然是居住和亲属集体，但丧失了部分政治、经济和文化自主权，受到高级中心和二级中心的控制。这些村落的首领或者为植入（外来）或者为提拔（内部），但都承担一些义务，如向最高中心和二级中心提供劳役、士兵和贡赋。他们还需要接受酋邦的统一的文化习俗和行为规范。

（四）国家阶段

酋邦之后就是国家。这个阶段可以按照复杂程度分为若干类型，但是与本文相关的是古老型，也就是最简单的形态。这种国家延续了酋邦

---

① Sahlins, Marshall D., *Tribesmen*, Englewood Cliffs: Prentice-Hall, 1968, p. 25.

的政治、经济和意识形态。国王是土地的所有者，并且把部分所有权分给各个级别的贵族。亲属制度仍然决定着贵族的地位和政治经济特权。国王和贵族把土地的使用权交给原来的村落，作为交换后者向前者提供劳役和剩余产品。国王和贵族不再从事农业生产，负责维持秩序和安全，因此构成了统治阶级。他们利用宗教和礼仪将自己的特权和地位神圣化和合法化，与平民区分开来。

与此同时，国家超越了酋邦，不仅领土更大，人口更多，数以万计或数百万计。而且人口来源复杂，所面临的管理难度更大，因此国家建立了复杂的官僚制度来征收赋税和管理各级政府事务。统治阶级凌驾于村落之上，与其没有血缘关系。它利用军队来维持内部秩序，发动战争，获得新的土地和人口。它还利用宗教来神化国家和统治阶级。

在政治景观上，国家延续了酋邦阶段的趋势，并加以发展。由于领土和人口有所扩大，等级制度更为森严和复杂。在最高权力中心和平民村落之间，出现了多级管理中心。国家机器也开始打破村落组织。国家能够迁徙人口或者调动村落来建立新的居住集体，来满足经济（作坊）或军事（边塞）需要。此外，国家可以从传统的村落抽调士兵或技术工人，从而打破了它们的居住和亲属纽带。正如历史告诉我们的，村落的瓦解是个缓慢的过程，它一直延续到商品经济高度发达的现代社会，才得以彻底完成。

六　结语

前面我们归纳了已有的社会进化理论。我们不仅发现了它们的缺陷，而且发现了它们的优点。塞维斯、弗莱德、约翰逊和厄尔的阶段论，因为有迅速增长的民族学资料做支撑，所以较为扎实，而其中塞维斯的四阶段论最为准确。因此，我们接受这个阶段论和上述各位学者描绘的特征。

上述阶段论或者信奉和谐论或者信奉冲突论。和谐和冲突虽是对立的两面，但共存于一个社会。一方面，我们不能忽略血缘纽带的维系作用。另一方面，我们不能否认古代社会存在着经济剥削和政治压迫。通过梳理民族学资料，我们发现冲突的表现方式在不同阶段各不相同。游团和部落阶段，游团、村落之间存在横向的政治和经济差别，但不存在政治压迫和经济剥削；酋邦和国家阶段，出现领头村落和下属村落之间纵向的政治压迫和经济剥削。因此，马克思主义的生产关系学说继续启发着我们的社会进化理论。

不过，塞维斯、弗莱德、约翰逊和厄尔的阶段论都存在行为主体的问题。在他们看来，统治阶级是应对人口增长和资源缺乏而出现的，但是这种看法无法全面解释一批人如何取得统治地位而凌驾于另一批人之上。这种看法也无法解释流动的部落首领如何转变成世袭的酋邦大酋长。在我看来，其根本缺陷就在于忽略了村落。只有认识到村落的重要性，我们才能重新认识从平等的部落社会向分化的酋邦社会转变的过程。

因此，我们在重新定义塞维斯的阶段论时，把村落当成了关键的行为主体。狩猎—采集游团规模小，人口稀少，并且都是自主的群体。在部落阶段，一个村落自愿与其他村落结盟，组成部落，以实现他们的共同利益。村落之间存在政治和经济不平等，但是这不影响其自主权。村落内部也存在经济和社会不平等，但是它既不是固定的也不是剥削性的；村落的主导思想仍然是平等主义。当一个村落在联盟村落支持下，征服其他村落，建立一个稳定的统治秩序时，部落社会转变为酋邦社会。这个转变的核心是领头村落控制了领土和其他重要资源；这个村落和联盟村落构成了剥削阶级，而平民村落构成了被剥削阶级。一个野心勃勃而精明强干的首领当然是领头村落成功的重要因素。但是，他之所以能掌握最高权力，是因为他是领头村落的领导人，带领领头村落走向成功。国家统治了更大的领土和更多的人口，其统治需要复杂的官僚系统。

需要说明的是，压迫和剥削阶级的出现并非一定意味着被压迫和被剥削阶级受苦。在部落阶段战争随时随地发生于村落和部落之间，带来死亡和赔偿。[1] 虽然部落战争不一定意味着血腥和高死亡率，但是战争

---

[1] Hayden, Brian, Pathways to Power: Principles for Creating Socioeconomic Inequalities, in *Foundations of Social Inequality*, New York, London: Plenum Press, 1995.

和伤亡会直接影响双方的经济生活。在酋邦和国家阶段,虽然平民村落丧失了部分政治和经济自主权,但是他们得到了安全和秩序。这样村落可以把精力集中在生产上面,而由大酋长或国王来处理战争事务。从政治贵族的角度来说,他们的特权并非全是好处。虽然他们可以获得平民提供的剩余产品和劳动,享受更好的生活,但是他们都是武士或者祭司,负责保护平民的安全,保障他们的福祉。由于这种利益互补,由平等的部落社会向阶级分化的酋邦的转变悄无声息,以至于"社会成员都没有察觉到"这种转变。[①]

政治景观和村落组织在四个阶段中发生变化。在游团和部落阶段,村落是自主的,虽然它们之间可能存在政治和经济力量的差别。这种扁平的景观在酋邦阶段让位于金字塔形的景观。最高政治中心的规模更大,其人口的亲属构成更为复杂。在这个中心下面,可能会存在二级中心,其酋长就是大酋长的代理人。平民村落虽然仍保留其居住和血缘纽带,但丧失了部分自主权,服从最高和二级中心的统治。在国家阶段,传统村落的居住和血缘纽带开始遭到破坏,但是大体延续下来,只是在商品经济高度发达的现代社会才分崩离析。

[①] Fried, Morton H., *The Evolution of Political Society: An Essay in Political Anthropology*, New York: Random House, 1967, p. 183.

第三部分

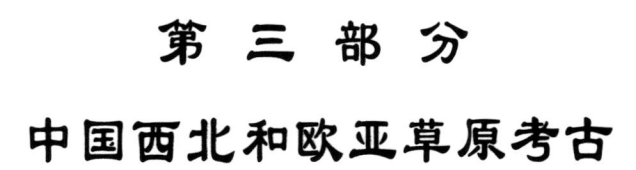

中国西北和欧亚草原考古

哈密地区史前考古*

一 前言

　　哈密地区位于新疆东部，包括现在的行政区域哈密市、伊吾县以及巴里坤哈萨克自治县。东天山横贯哈密地区全境，以南是哈密盆地，以北是巴里坤草原（图3-1-1）。哈密地区因为地处内陆，气候属于温带大陆性气候。巴里坤县和伊吾县境内的天山北麓地带由于天山的抬升作用，来自大西洋的水汽形成较为丰沛的降水，因而养育了大片的草场。而哈密盆地由于天山的阻隔，来自大西洋的水汽难以到达，所以降水稀少，蒸发量大，气候干燥，只是天山下来的雪水形成了哈密绿洲。不过东天山并没有阻隔哈密盆地和巴里坤平原，其间有峡谷相连，人们可以往来。而二者又通过伊吾县连接了河西走廊和吐鲁番盆地以西的区域，共同构成了古代丝绸之路上的一条重要通道。

　　19世纪末20世纪初，西方探险者先后来到新疆探险，揭开了新疆考古学研究的序幕。20年代末和30年代初，中瑞西北科学考察团的贝格曼、德日进、杨钟健分别调查了庙尔沟、三道岭和七角井，采集了一些陶片（含彩陶）和石器。[1] 1949年以后，西北文化局新疆维吾尔自治区文物调查工作组、新疆文管会和新疆少数民族社会历史调查组先后调查了全疆各个区域的古代遗址，哈密地区的考古工作也取

---

* 本文为国家社科基金项目《新疆史前金属器》（批准号11BKG007）的阶段性成果。原刊于《欧亚学刊》2016年第15辑，第1—18页，收入本书时略有改动。

[1] Bergman, F., *Archaeological Researches in Sinkiang*, Stockholm, Bokvörlags Aktiebolaget Thule, 1939, pp. 14-15; Teihard de Chardin, P., and C. C. Young, On some neolithic (and possibly palaeolithic) finds in Mongolia, Sinkiang and west China, *Bulletin of the Geological Society of China*, Vol. XII, No. 1-2, Peiping, 1933, pp. 83-104.

◇❖◇ 第三部分 中国西北和欧亚草原考古

得了一些进展。① 1957年，新疆维吾尔自治区文物管理所在三堡的焉布拉村、五堡的哈拉墩、巴里坤东面的石人子乡采集了一些陶器和石器。② 从此以后，考古工作者在哈密不仅做了更多的调查，而且发掘了一些墓地和聚落。③ 这一时期人们多将新疆的彩陶与中原比较，往往将出土彩陶的遗址视为新石器时代或者铜石并用时代。20世纪80年代以后，随着基本建设的推进，一大批遗址得到了发掘，其中重要的史前遗址有焉布拉克、五堡、天山北路、黑沟梁和东黑沟。与此同时，人们开始关注新疆本地的文化特征，将过去视为新石器时代或铜石并用时代的遗址修正为青铜时代和早期铁器时代。④

不过，虽然哈密地区的遗址发掘不少，研究也取得了不少进展，但是由于大多数重要遗址的发掘资料迟迟没有发表，因此研究严重滞后。其中一个重要的问题，即哈密地区的史前文化序列，仍然没有梳理清楚。韩建业、张凤和郭物先后整理了整个新疆的史前考古资料，韩建业和张凤还分出了三期。⑤ 不过，这些研究多注重埋葬习俗和陶器，而在金属器方面着墨不多；同时，哈密地区作为一个文化区域，其文化的发展过程仍然非常模糊。本文拟重新整理哈密地区的发掘资料，梳理该区域史前时期的文化序列，阐明各期文化的特征、传承和变迁。需要说明的是，本文并不涉及青铜时代以前的遗址。这是因为哈密地区和整个新疆一样，

---

① 陈戈、张玉忠：《世纪之交新疆考古学的回顾与展望》，《西域研究》1999年第1期，第3页。

② 李遇春：《新疆发现的彩陶》，《考古》1959年第3期，第153—154页。

③ 发掘资料见下列各遗址的注脚，这里只列举调查资料。史树青：《新疆文物调查随笔》，《文物》1960年第6期，第22—31页；吴震：《新疆东部的几处新石器时代遗址》，《考古》1964年第7期，第333—341页；新疆维吾尔自治区博物馆：《新疆出土文物》，文物出版社1975年版，图版七；新疆维吾尔自治区博物馆、新疆社会科学院考古研究所：《建国以来新疆考古的主要收获》，《文物考古工作三十年》，文物出版社1979年版，第170—171页；黄文弼：《新疆考古发掘报告》，文物出版社1983年版，第1—13页；王炳华：《新疆东部发现的几批铜器》，《考古》1986年第10期，第887—891页。

④ 陈戈：《关于新疆新石器时代文化的新认识》，《考古》1987年第4期，第343—351、322页；陈戈、张玉忠：《世纪之交新疆考古学的回顾与展望》，《西域研究》1999年第1期，第5页。

⑤ 韩建业：《新疆的青铜时代和早期铁器时代文化》，文物出版社2007年版；张凤：《新疆东部地区古文化探微》，《西域研究》2010年第2期，第44—52页；郭物：《新疆史前晚期社会的考古学研究》，上海古籍出版社2012年版，第42—57页。

虽然发现了一些打制石器和细石器，但是这类器物也出现在青铜时代和早期铁器时代遗址中。有关的遗址没有做过发掘，它们是否属于旧石器、细石器或新石器时代眼下还难以确定。①

二 三期文化

哈密地区先后经过发掘的遗址有焉布拉克、天山北路、南湾、黑沟梁、五堡、拉甫乔克、腐殖酸厂、艾斯克霞尔、寒气沟、上庙尔沟、拜契尔等墓地和东黑沟聚落（图3-1-1）。但是这些遗址中，只有焉布拉克墓地的发掘资料发表了一篇报告，大多数遗址只发表了简报，有的只发表了消息。与此同时，聚落发掘得很少，因此我们对于古代文化的认识有很大的局限。这里我们只整理和讨论发表了简报和报告的遗址。我们不仅考察埋葬习俗和陶器，而且考察金属器。根据这些遗址的总体情况，我们可以划分出三个前后相继而特征各异的文化：天山北路、焉布拉克和黑沟梁（表3-1-1）。

（一）天山北路文化

以天山北路墓地为代表的遗址曾一度没有正式的名称，后来才有人命名为"天山北路文化"。②过去一些人把腐殖酸厂、南湾和萨伊吐尔墓地归入该文化，但是下面我们看到，它们应属于焉布拉克文化。因此属于天山北路文化的遗址目前只有同名墓地一处。天山北路墓地位于今哈密市火车站以南，西坝河上游小河沟西侧，原为戈壁荒滩，后来随着哈密市的发展而成为市区（图3-1-1）。③根据发掘者常喜恩的回忆，该墓地的墓葬

---

① 陈戈：《新疆史前文化》，《西北民族研究》1995年第1期，第50页；陈戈、张玉忠：《世纪之交新疆考古学的回顾与展望》，《西域研究》1999年第1期，第7—8页。
② 韩建业：《新疆的青铜时代和早期铁器时代文化》，文物出版社2007年版，第41页；郭物：《新疆史前晚期社会的考古学研究》，上海古籍出版社2012年版，第42页。
③ 此部分根据作者与常喜恩的个人交流（2003年2月16—25日）以及常喜恩《哈密市雅满苏矿、林场办事处古代墓葬》，《中国考古学年鉴》，文物出版社1989年版，第274—275页；哈密墓地发掘组：《哈密林场办事处、雅满苏矿采购站墓地》，《中国考古学年鉴》，文物出版社1989年版，第330—331页；吕恩国、常喜恩、王炳华：《新疆青铜时代考古文化浅论》，《新疆石器时代与青铜时代》，文物出版社2008年版，第325—348页。

◇❖◇ 第三部分 中国西北和欧亚草原考古

实际上在1987年最早发现于今天山北路西侧的居民区内。1988年哈密地区雅满苏矿采购站和哈密林场办事处修建办公楼时发现了多座墓葬，引起了他的注意，于是紧急组织力量发掘。因此该墓地曾有"林雅墓地"的名称。[①] 1989年以后哈密市修建与其相连的天山北路，发现了大量的同类墓葬，于是实施大规模发掘，墓地名称因此改成天山北路。至1997年，新疆文物考古研究所和哈密地区文管所经过数次发掘，前后清理了705座墓葬。实际上，墓地范围不限于上述发掘区域，在天山北路两侧钻探发现还有墓葬，面积达1.5万平方米。

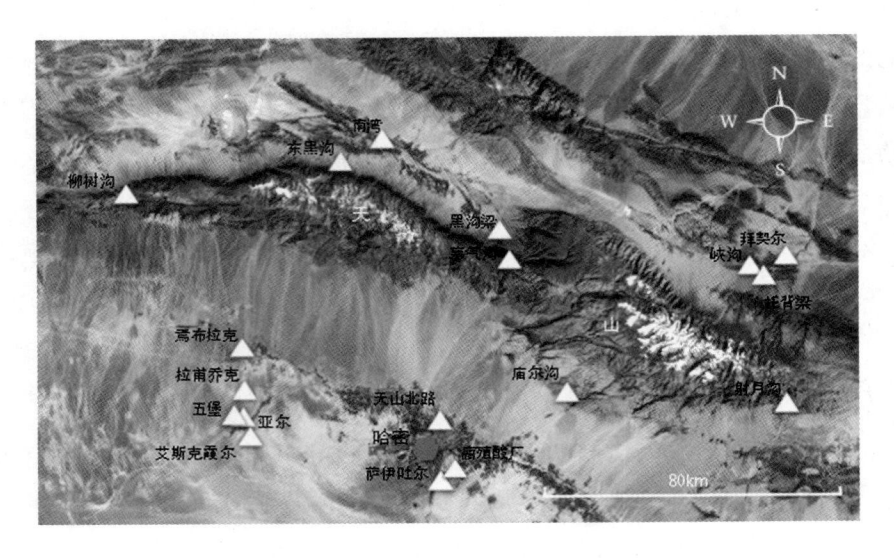

图3-1-1 哈密地区遗址分布图

在天山北路墓地，墓葬分布相当密集，打破、叠压关系很多。形制多为长方形的竖穴土坑，部分土坑坑壁用土坯加固，长1—2米，宽0.6—1米。葬式以侧身屈肢葬为主，头向多为东北和西南，死者多为单人葬（图3-1-2）。随葬品一般较少，种类有陶器、铜器、银器、骨器、珍珠和海贝，此外还有羊骨和牛骨。可惜时隔二十余年，发掘报告仍然没有出版，只有零星资料出现在两篇论文中。在其中的一篇论文中，吕恩国、

---

① 李水城：《从考古发现看公元前二千纪东西方文化的碰撞与交流》，《新疆文物》1999年第1期，第58页；李水城：《天山北路墓地一期遗存分析》，《吐鲁番学研究》2009年第1期，第1—3页。

· 136 ·

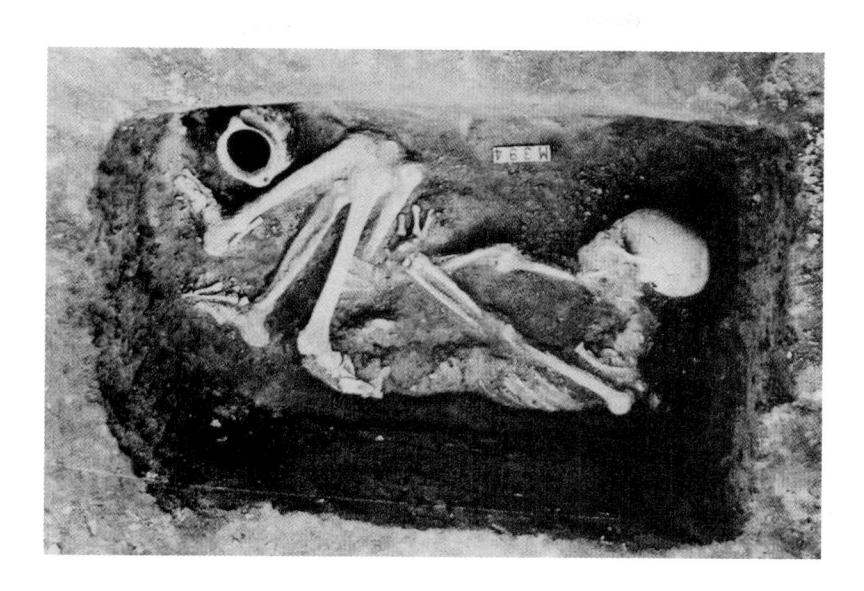

图 3-1-2　天山北路墓地 M358

（哈密博物馆：《哈密文物精粹》，科学出版社 2013 年版，第 23 页）

常喜恩和王炳华将天山北路的墓葬分为四期八段，绝对年代范围为公元前 19—前 13 世纪。此分期因为发掘资料没有出版，无法验证。不过从公布的分期图来看，其第一、二期的陶器，无论器类还是器形，都对应于张掖市西城驿遗址的第二、三期的同类器物，也就是四坝文化的第一和第二期。①

天山北路墓地出土的陶器中，大多数为夹砂褐陶，少数为灰陶。不少陶器表面施红色陶衣，上面绘黑彩，图案主要为直线、之字纹、三角纹、网格纹、菱格纹、手形纹和叶脉纹。这些陶器基本为平底器，束颈鼓腹，颈部和腹部常常带单环耳和双环耳。器类有双耳罐、单耳罐和单耳杯（图 3-1-3）。李水城曾经分析了天山北路墓地出土的陶器，指出它们至少可以分为两组，其中甲组陶器居多，与四坝文化存在很多相似的地方，"不少器形、花纹接近……如出一辙，如彩陶双耳罐、双耳素陶罐、四系罐、单把杯（或尊形器）、双耳盆等"。"多数与四坝文化中期近似，个别接近四坝文化晚期，估计绝

---

① 张良仁、王辉：《张掖市西城驿遗址的彩陶》，《北方民族考古》第 2 辑，2015 年，第 91—101 页。

◇❖◇ 第三部分 中国西北和欧亚草原考古

对年代应在公元前1800—前1600年之间。"① 乙组仅包含一种陶器，即双贯耳罐，来自南西伯利亚、蒙古西部和新疆北部的切木尔切克文化。实际上，上述的A组陶器无论在陶质、陶色、器类组合和器形方面都与四坝文化接近。天山北路文化的主体可能就是从四坝文化移植过来的。

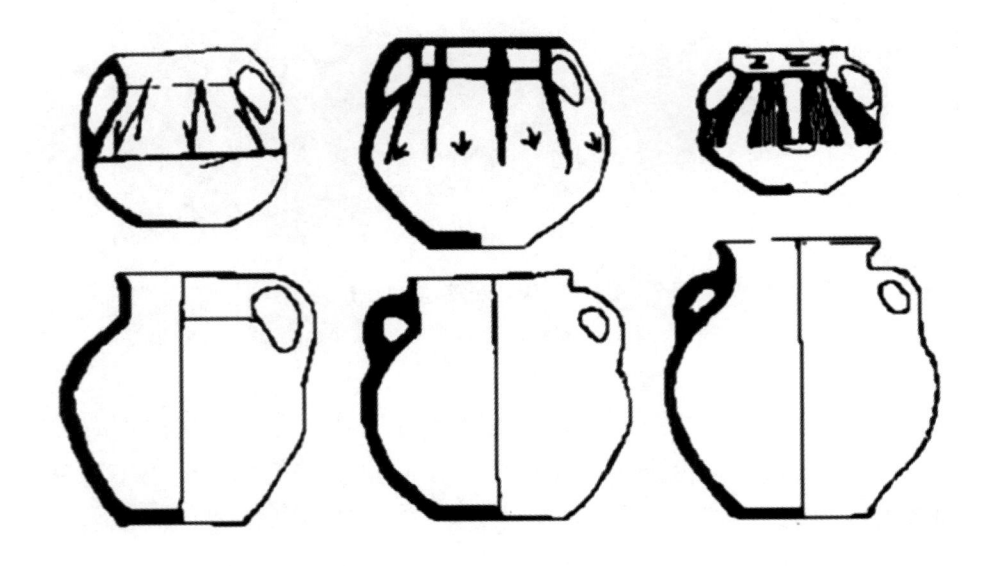

图 3-1-3 天山北路文化的陶器

（吕恩国、常喜恩、王炳华：《新疆青铜时代考古文化浅论》，载宿白主编《苏秉琦与中国当代考古学》，科学出版社2001年版，图一二：1、3、4、10；图一三：7、8）

天山北路墓地已经发掘的705座墓葬出土了大量的金属器，其中大部分收藏在哈密博物馆。据笔者的观察，其数量在3000件以上。这些金属器的线图见于报道的不多，可分为两批，一批32件，另一批36件。② 其中一类为短剑，只有一件（M626：2）有柄，有格和叉

---

① 李水城：《从考古发现看公元前二千纪东西方文化的碰撞与交流》，《新疆文物》1999年第1期，第59—60页。
② 北京科技大学冶金与材料史研究所、新疆文物考古研究所、哈密地区文物管理所：《新疆哈密天山北路墓地出土铜器的初步研究》，《文物》2001年第6期，第80页，图1；吕恩国、常喜恩、王炳华：《新疆青铜时代考古文化浅论》，载宿白主编《苏秉琦与中国当代考古学》，科学出版社2001年版，第182—183页，图一五至图一八。

形筋以及杏仁形刃（图3-1-4：10），①与哈萨克斯坦梅尔日科（Myrzhik）出土的安德罗诺沃短剑相似。②但是这里不见后者典型的器类柳叶形短剑、横銎斧、槽形手镯和螺旋形耳环。梅建军曾经想证明安德罗诺沃文化的影响出现在了哈密地区，但是他只找到了一些采集品，没有在天山北路墓地找到例证，③而潜伟干脆否认了安德罗诺沃文化的影响。④无论如何，天山北路墓地出土的金属器与安德罗诺沃文化关系不大。

20世纪90年代以来，梅建军和潜伟先后分析了108个样品的成分，发现其中79个为锡青铜（73%），12个为纯铜，9件为砷青铜。⑤这种成分组合显然与米奴辛斯克盆地的卡拉苏克文化相似，但是这里锡青铜如此之高的比例又与卡拉苏克文化不同。天山北路金属器的器类和器形也存在类似的情况。一类为刀，有10件，均为环首，弧背，工字形柄（如M679：4；图3-1-4：9）。⑥一类为直銎斧，形体细长，前面切出马蹄形口，与上口相同，而銎内底部也有台阶，挡住柄头向前挤压。⑦这些器物和杏仁孔刀（M307：4和M366：5）、铜泡（图3-1-4：14）、联珠泡（图3-1-4：4）、串珠、铜管（图3-1-4：3）、耳环（图3-1-4：6）、铜扣（图3-1-4：5、7）、铜镜、铜镯（图3-1-4：2）、铜手链、铜刀（图3-1-4：1）和铜凿与卡拉苏克文化的同类器接近。不

---

① 北京科技大学冶金与材料史研究所、新疆文物考古研究所、哈密地区文物管理所：《新疆哈密天山北路墓地出土铜器的初步研究》，《文物》2001年第6期，第80页，图1：7。

② Kadyrbaev, M. K., Zh. Kurmankulov, *Kul'tura Drevnikh Skotovodov i Metallurgov Sary-Arki*, Alma-Ata: Gylym, 1992, p. 59, Fig. 30.

③ Mei, J., *Copper and Bronze Metallurgy in Late Prehistoric Xinjiang*, BAR International Series 865, Oxford: Archaeopress, 2000, p. 38.

④ 潜伟：《新疆哈密地区史前时期铜器及其与邻近地区文化的关系》，知识产权出版社2006年版，第101页。

⑤ Mei, J., *Copper and Bronze Metallurgy in Late Prehistoric Xinjiang*, BAR International Series 865, Oxford: Archaeopress, 2000, p. 38；潜伟：《新疆哈密地区史前时期铜器及其与邻近地区文化的关系》，知识产权出版社2006年版，第38页；北京科技大学冶金与材料史研究所、新疆文物考古研究所、哈密地区文物管理所：《新疆哈密天山北路墓地出土铜器的初步研究》，《文物》2001年第6期，第81—87页。

⑥ 北京科技大学冶金与材料史研究所、新疆文物考古研究所、哈密地区文物管理所：《新疆哈密天山北路墓地出土铜器的初步研究》，《文物》2001年第6期，第80页，图1：6。

⑦ 吕恩国、常喜恩、王炳华：《新疆青铜时代考古文化浅论》，载宿白主编《新疆石器时代与青铜时代》，科学出版社2001年版，图一七：9。

过，天山北路墓地不见卡拉苏克文化的竖銎斧、镰刀、弓形器、铜斧、多角形铜泡和锯齿形缀饰。铜刀和铜镞的式样没有卡拉苏克文化的多，后者的臂钏、镂空镞和兽首铜刀不见于前者。① 而天山北路墓地的镂空铜牌（图3-1-4：11）、铜螺旋管（图3-1-4：15）、铜铃和亚腰形铜牌（图3-1-4：12）不见于卡拉苏克。装饰品中有一类为双齿别针（图3-1-4：13），往往由铅制作而成，也不见于卡拉苏克。从成分、器类和器物形态来看，天山北路墓地的金属器似乎不是从米奴辛斯克盆地的卡拉苏克文化直接输入的，而可能是本地生产的；其冶金技术似乎也不是直接来自卡拉苏克文化，而来自于别处。根据我们最新的研究，四坝文化的金属器的成分、器形和器类与卡拉苏克文化接近，其冶金技术可能来源于后者。结合天山北路墓地的彩陶生产技术来源于四坝文化，其金属器所需要的冶金技术可能也来自于四坝文化。

天山北路墓地出土的颅骨保存不好，王博等人收集了13具（男6，女7）做了分析。结果表明，墓主多数为东亚蒙古人种，亦有少量高加索人种，而且部分颅骨同时带有两个人种的特征，反映二者之间存在通婚与混血现象。

关于天山北路墓地的年代，中国社会科学院考古研究所考古科技实验研究中心采集了六个人骨样品，得到了六个碳十四数据。但是它们的校正年代中，一个（6118BC—5687BC）过早，其他五个（752BC—200BC，181BC—235BC，807BC—430BC，1111BC—845BC，919BC—803BC）过晚。② 学术界只能通过比较它与四坝文化的关系来推断，因

---

① 文中提到的参照器物见于 Griaznov, M. P., M. N. Komarova, I. P. Lazaretov, A. V. Poliakov, M. N. Pshenitsyna, *Mogil'nik Kiurgenner Èpokhi Pozdneĭ Bronzy Srednego Eniseia*, Sankt-Peterburg, 2010, Fig. 38：4, Fig. 32：21, Fig. 36：17, 15; Ziablin, L. P., *Karasukskiĭ mogil'nik Malye Kopëny* 3, Moscow, 1977, Fig. 30：27, Fig. 13：2, 1; Chernykh, E. N., *Ancient Metallurgy in the USSR: The Early Metal Age*, Cambridge University Press, 1992, Fig. 91：15; Jettmar, K., The Karasuk Culture and Its South-eastern Affinities, *Bulletin of the Museum of Far Eastern Antiquities* 22, 1950, pp. 83 - 140, pl. 2：31, pl. 3：1; Chlenova, N. L., *Chronologiia Pamiatnikov Karasukskoĭ Èpokhi*, Moscow: Science Press, 1972, Plate 7：3, Plate 10：53。

② 中国社会科学院考古研究所考古科技实验研究中心：《放射性碳素测定年代报告（二三）》，《考古》1996年第7期，第70页。

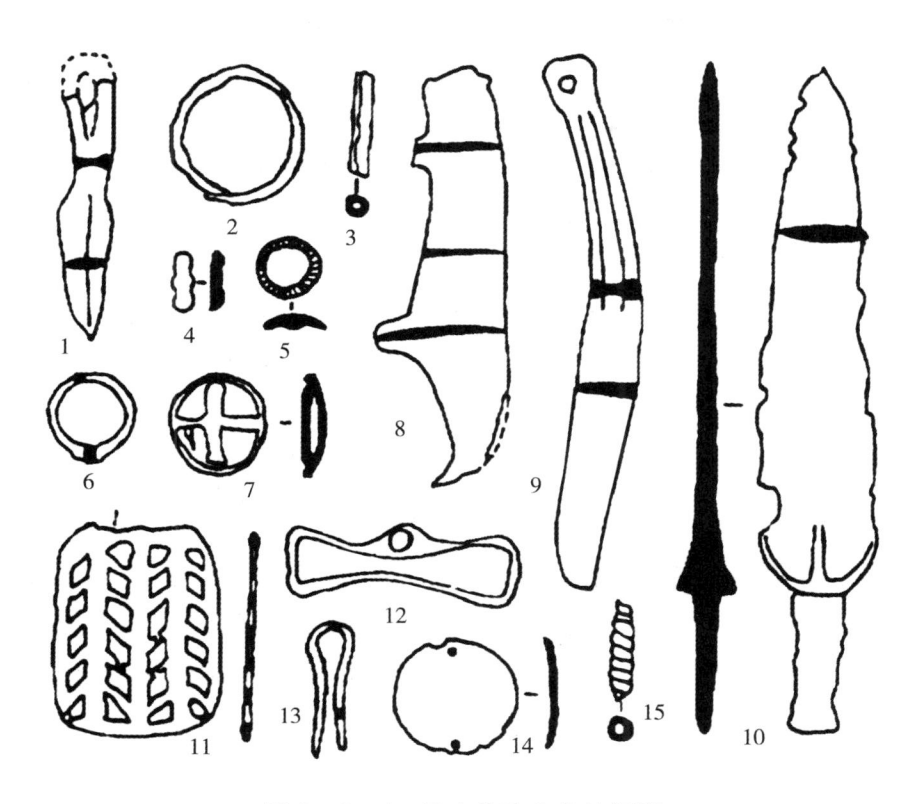

图 3-1-4　天山北路文化的铜器

1. M1∶4；2. M487∶5；3. M500∶6；4. M487∶5b；5. M500∶3；6. M456∶4；7. M608∶3；8. T1322；9. M679∶41；10. M626∶21；11. M604∶3；12. M511∶2；13. M513∶1；14. M698∶31；15. M683∶7（北京科技大学冶金与材料史研究所、新疆文物考古研究所、哈密地区文物管理所：《新疆哈密天山北路墓地出土铜器的初步研究》，《文物》2001年第6期，图1）

此曾经有公元前19—前13世纪，[①] 2000BC—1000BC，[②] 2000BC—1200BC的说法。[③] 有人根据一件马厂类型的彩陶，提出天山北路墓地可以早到马厂晚期。[④] 最近几年我们发掘了张掖西城驿遗址，得到了

---

① 吕恩国、常喜恩和王炳华：《新疆青铜时代考古文化浅论》，载宿白主编《苏秉琦与中国当代考古学》，科学出版社2001年版，第184页。

② 北京科技大学冶金与材料史研究所等：《新疆哈密天山北路墓地出土铜器的初步研究》，《文物》2001年第6期，第81页。

③ 潜伟：《新疆哈密地区史前时期铜器及其与邻近地区文化的关系》，知识产权出版社2006年版，第87页。

④ 韩建业：《新疆的青铜时代和早期铁器时代文化》，文物出版社2007年版，第99页。

三个连续的建筑层,因而将该遗址分为三期:马厂晚期、四坝一期、四坝二期。① 同时,我们从各个层位的遗迹采集了系列测年样品,将其年代分别定为2135BC—1900BC、1880BC—1680BC 和 1670BC—1530BC。从发表的陶器来看,他们所分的第一、二和三期对应于四坝一期和四坝二期,其年代为1880BC—1530BC。而其第四期的年代更晚一些,其双耳罐和简洁的三角纹与下述的焉布拉克文化接近,应该归入后者。

(二) 焉布拉克文化

可以归入焉布拉克文化的遗址已经发现不少,如上述的焉布拉克、天山北路、腐殖酸厂、② 南湾、③ 五堡、④ 拜契尔、⑤ 艾斯克霞尔、⑥ 拉甫乔克、⑦ 亚尔、⑧ 萨伊吐尔⑨和寒气沟⑩(图3-1-1)。它们分布于东天山南北两侧,但是集中在哈密盆地里,说明古代居民主要从

---

① 张良仁、王辉:《张掖市西城驿遗址的彩陶》,《北方民族考古》第2辑,2015年,第91—101页;张雪莲、张良仁、王辉、卢雪峰、陈国科、王鹏:《张掖市西城驿遗址的碳十四测年及初步分析》,《华夏考古》2015年第4期,第38—45页。

② 张成安、常喜恩:《哈密腐殖酸厂墓地调查》,《新疆文物》1998年第1期,第36—40页。

③ 常喜恩:《巴里坤南湾墓地66号墓清理简报》,《新疆文物》1985年第1期,第4、16页;新疆考古研究所:《巴里坤县南湾M95号墓试掘简报》,《考古与文物》1987年第5期,第7—8页。

④ 新疆文物考古研究所:《新疆哈密五堡墓地151、152号墓葬》,《新疆文物》1992年第3期,第1—10页。

⑤ 托乎提·吐拉洪:《新疆伊吾县拜契尔墓地进行抢救性考古发掘》,《中国文物报》2005年2月4日。

⑥ 此部分原始材料来自新疆文物考古研究所、哈密地区文物管理所《新疆哈密市艾斯克霞尔墓地的发掘》,《考古》2002年第6期,第30—41页。

⑦ 新疆文物考古研究所:《哈密拉甫乔克发现新石器时代晚期墓葬遗址》,《考古与文物》1984年第4期,第105—106页。

⑧ 胡望林:《哈密市亚尔墓地考古发掘》,《2013—2014文物考古年报》,第15—16页。

⑨ 新疆文物考古研究所:《哈密市花园乡萨伊吐尔墓地考古发掘报告》,《新疆文物》2014年第1期,第65—75页;胡望林:《哈密市萨伊吐尔墓地考古发掘》,《2013—2014文物考古年报》,第13—14页。

⑩ 此部分取自两篇内容大体相同但是编辑水准不同的简报,见新疆文物考古研究所、哈密地区文管所:《新疆哈密寒气沟墓地发掘简报》,《新疆文物》1996年第2期,第23—30页;新疆文物考古研究所、哈密地区文管所:《新疆哈密市寒气沟墓地发掘简报》,《考古》1997年第9期,第33—38页。

事农业，但是也经营畜牧业。由于篇幅有限，我们无法展开讨论各个墓地的材料，只能集中在代表遗址即焉布拉克墓地上。

焉布拉克（或写作焉不拉克）墓地位于哈密市西北约60千米的三堡乡西北方的小土岗上（图3-1-1）。土岗北高南低，长1250米，宽250米，一条由北而南的小泉将其分为东西两块，土岗西侧还有一条相同流向的小泉。土岗表面为小砾石，比较平坦，周围为水草地。在其南端，有一座小城，南北60米，东西50米，20世纪50年代南墙和西墙还保存较好，北墙和东墙已倒塌，现已破坏殆尽。[①] 早在20世纪50年代，这里就不断发现完整陶器，1957年考古工作者为此曾前往调查。[②] 1958年中国科学院考古研究所的黄文弼在这里做过小规模发掘，在小城开了三条探沟，墙基宽3米左右，用夯土和土坯砌筑。在南墙外有两间房屋，二房相连，中间有过道相通。城墙内外和房屋内出土有彩陶片、石磨盘和石球。他在土岗又发掘了14座墓葬。[③] 墓地地表为戈壁砾石，墓葬分布密集。因为表面没有痕迹，所以发掘者采取了开方发掘的办法。墓葬的结构非常简单，大体为长方形竖穴土坑，大多用土坯砌筑墓室，但是都比较窄小，无棺椁。人骨零散，随葬品很少。单人侧身屈肢葬和多人合葬都有，婴幼儿一般袝葬在成人墓旁，头向多为东南或西北（图3-1-5）。[④] 从小城和墓葬出土的陶器来看，二者的年代基本一致。[⑤] 1986年新疆维吾尔自治区文化厅委托新疆大学历史系举办的文博干部专修班在这里实习，共发掘墓葬76座。[⑥] 这批墓地的地层简单，墓葬都压在扰乱层（第2层）下，打破生土。同20世纪50年代发掘的14座墓葬一样，这批墓葬的人骨大多残碎杂乱或只有少量残骨，说明这些墓

[①] 新疆维吾尔自治区文化厅文物处、新疆大学历史系文博干部专修班：《新疆哈密焉布拉克古墓地》，《考古学报》1989年第3期，第326页。

[②] 李遇春：《新疆发现的彩陶》，《考古》1959年第3期，第153页。

[③] 黄文弼：《新疆考古发掘报告（1957—1958）》，文物出版社1983年版，第1—9页。

[④] 吕恩国、常喜恩、王炳华：《新疆青铜时代考古文化浅论》，载宿白主编《苏秉琦与中国当代考古学》，科学出版社2001年版，第187页。

[⑤] 黄文弼：《新疆考古发掘报告（1957—1958）》，文物出版社1983年版，第9页。

[⑥] 新疆维吾尔自治区文化厅文物处、新疆大学历史系文博干部专修班：《新疆哈密焉布拉克古墓地》，《考古学报》1989年第3期，第327页。

第三部分 中国西北和欧亚草原考古

葬为二次葬。随葬品主要是陶器，铜器有刀、镜、镞、锥、针、纺轮、扣和管等，石器有砺石和石珠，木器有人俑、盘、碗、桶等。其他还有少量铁、金、贝器和毛织物。①

发掘者按墓葬形制将焉布拉克墓地分为三期：一期为竖穴土坑墓，规模较大，有二层台；二期为竖穴土坑，无二层台；三期为地面上的土坯墓，三期墓葬大体由北而南分布，由多人合葬而单人葬。绝对年代为公元前1300—前565年。② 墓地上限年代相当于天山北路三、四期，下限年代已为早期铁器时代。③ 以该墓地为典型遗址，发掘者命名了焉布拉克文化，并将拉甫乔克④和五堡水库墓地也归入该文化，归属早期铁器时代。⑤ 后来发掘者又把哈拉墩、卡尔桑遗址（上层）、腐殖酸厂墓地归入该文化。⑥ 但是发掘报告提供的资料和分期后来引起了争议，而发掘和整理工作的主持人又两次撰文予以回应。⑦ 王博和覃大海重新整理了焉布拉克墓

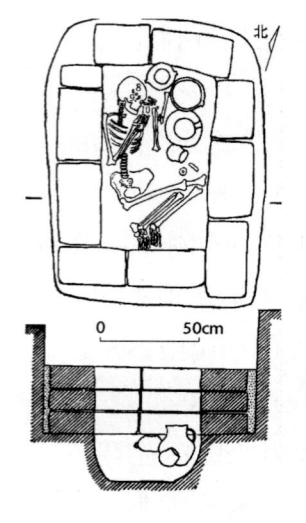

图3-1-5 焉布拉克墓地 M31

（新疆维吾尔自治区文化厅文物处、新疆大学历史系文博干部专修班：《新疆哈密焉布拉克古墓地》，《考古学报》1989年第3期，图一一）

---

① 新疆维吾尔自治区文化厅文物处、新疆大学历史系文博干部专修班：《新疆哈密焉布拉克古墓地》，《考古学报》1989年第3期，第337—352页。
② 新疆维吾尔自治区文化厅文物处、新疆大学历史系文博干部专修班：《新疆哈密焉布拉克古墓地》，《考古学报》1989年第3期，第354—355页；新疆文物事业管理局、新疆文物考古研究所：《新疆维吾尔自治区文物考古五十年》，《新中国考古五十年》，文物出版社1999年版，第483页；陈戈：《略论焉不拉克文化》，《西域研究》1991年第1期，第84页。
③ 陈戈：《略论焉不拉克文化》，《西域研究》1991年第1期，第84页。
④ 新疆考古研究所东疆队：《新疆哈密拉甫乔克发现新石器时代晚期墓葬》，《考古与文物》1984年第4期，第105—106页。
⑤ 新疆维吾尔自治区文化厅文物处、新疆大学历史系文博干部专修班：《新疆哈密焉布拉克古墓地》，《考古学报》1989年第3期，第356页。
⑥ 李遇春：《新疆发现的彩陶》，《考古》1959年第3期，第153页；吴震：《新疆东部的几处新石器时代遗址》，《考古》1964年第7期，第334—335页；哈密地区文管所：《哈密沁城白山遗址调查》，《新疆文物》1988年第1期，第12—16页；张承安、常喜恩：《哈密腐殖酸厂墓地调查》，《新疆文物》1998年第1期，第6—40页。
⑦ 陈戈：《来稿照登》，《新疆文物》1991年第1期，第97—99页；陈戈：《焉不拉克文化补说》，《新疆文物》1991年第1期，第48—52页。

· 144 ·

地的地层，提出所有墓葬都在一个层位上，根据墓葬叠压关系和陶器形式排比分了四期。① 吕恩国也对墓地的地层资料和墓葬之间的叠压打破关系提出了疑问。② 李文瑛再次整理墓地的单人葬和合葬的分布情况，然后根据墓葬类型和陶器类型，分了三期，但是得到的墓地使用顺序完全相反。先后为土坑竖穴墓、二层台墓和土坯墓，由南而北分布，由单人葬而变为多人合葬。在年代上，焉布拉克文化整体上晚于天山北路文化。③ 后来邵会秋再次整理了墓地的地层资料和类型分析，提出墓地可以分为两期。属于焉布拉克文化的其他墓地（如五堡、艾斯克霞尔、寒气沟）大体可以归入这两期，但是上庙儿沟墓地要晚于焉布拉克墓地，属于该文化的第三期。④ 作者注意到一座墓葬实际包含两座墓葬，但是这样一个地层关系略显不足，其他地层关系没有考虑进去，非常可惜。⑤

在哈密市以西的五堡墓地，新疆文物考古研究所先后发掘了114座墓葬，可惜的是，迄今为止只发表了M151和M152两座。⑥ 它们均为椭圆形竖穴土坑，坑内有土坯垒砌的墓壁，上面覆盖经过砍削的胡杨圆木，圆木之间的缝隙填塞小木棍，上面再铺芨芨草编扎的草帘。这种棚木和尸床与苏贝希文化相似，原先可能也见于焉布拉克文化的其他墓地，但是因为其他墓地潮湿，早已消失。⑦ 在东天山内的寒气沟墓地，

---

① 王博、覃大海：《哈密焉不拉克墓葬的分期问题》，《新疆文物》1990年第3期，第30—38页。

② 吕恩国：《论新疆考古学研究中存在的几个问题》，《新疆文物》1995年第2期，第71页。

③ 李文瑛：《哈密焉不拉克墓地单人葬、合葬关系及相关问题探讨》，《新疆文物》1997年第2期，第23—30页。

④ 邵会秋：《从M75看焉不拉克墓地的分期》，《新疆文物》2006年第2期，第84—90页。

⑤ 吕恩国、王博、覃大海、李文瑛已经注意到，焉布拉克墓地发掘报告所列的18例叠压打破关系（加上邵会秋发现的，共19例）中有一半属于婴幼儿埋在成人墓葬旁边的衬葬，但是还有一半是需要重新考虑的。

⑥ 一说113座。见新疆文物事业管理局、新疆文物考古研究所：《新疆维吾尔自治区文物考古五十年》，《新中国考古五十年》，文物出版社1999年版，第482页；吕恩国、常喜恩、王炳华：《新疆青铜时代考古文化浅论》，载宿白主编《苏秉琦与中国当代考古学》，科学出版社2001年版，第187页。

⑦ 张良仁、吕恩国、张勇：《吐鲁番地区早期铁器时代考古》，《早期中国研究》第2辑，文物出版社2016年版，第116—155页。

第三部分 中国西北和欧亚草原考古

1994年新疆文物考古研究所抢救发掘了四座墓葬，编号M1—4。它们的地表有鹅卵石封堆，受山体坡度的影响，多向偏低一侧倾斜。墓葬为竖穴土坑，部分墓室四周用片石砌筑石室，墓口覆盖片石或圆木。多个体男女合葬较多，屈肢葬较多，墓室内普遍随葬羊、马。石封堆、石室和牛羊牲不见于焉布拉克和上述其他墓地，但是出土的陶器和金属器都属于焉布拉克文化。器类有单耳圜底罐、单耳豆、单耳壶和双耳罐；彩陶纹样有十字纹、之字纹和平行线纹。这些器类、形态和纹样都与焉布拉克墓地出土的陶器群相同。铜器5件（管、双羊牌饰、刀、刻刀、锥），骨器4件，也与焉布拉克墓地相似。发掘者认为该墓地属于焉布拉克文化，但是又带有天山以北草原文化的一些因素，因此定名为寒气沟类型。墓主倾向于欧罗巴人种，但是带有部分蒙古人种的体质特征，如铲形门齿。[①]

焉布拉克文化的陶器器类有单耳杯、单耳罐、单耳钵、腹耳壶、豆、盆、双耳罐（图3-1-6）。与天山北路文化相比，该文化的陶器群既有连续性，也有显著的变化。焉布拉克墓地多单耳杯（图3-1-6：3）、单耳罐、单耳钵、腹耳壶、豆、盆。单耳罐（图3-1-6：1）和单耳钵（图3-1-6：2）有平底者，也有圜底者。腹耳壶侈口，高领，圆腹，圜底或平底（图3-1-6：7）。豆的盘类似于单耳钵，下接喇叭形圈足（图3-1-6：4）。其中单耳钵（图3-1-6：2）、腹耳壶和豆为天山北路文化所不见，而四耳罐和双耳罐（图3-1-6：6）虽然见于天山北路文化，但是形态大不相同。它们高领，敛口，圆腹，部分陶器绘彩，纹样流行横向之字纹、平行线纹、S纹和十字纹（图3-1-6：1、2、4、7）。它们都不见于天山北路文化，而天山北路文化的网格纹、菱格纹和手形纹也不见于焉布拉克文化。与前述的天山北路文化一样，本文暂不拟分期。

---

① 新疆文物考古研究所、哈密地区文管所：《新疆哈密寒气沟墓地发掘简报》，《新疆文物》1996年第2期，第23—30页；新疆文物考古研究所、哈密地区文管所：《新疆哈密市寒气沟墓地发掘简报》，《考古》1997年第9期，第33—38页。

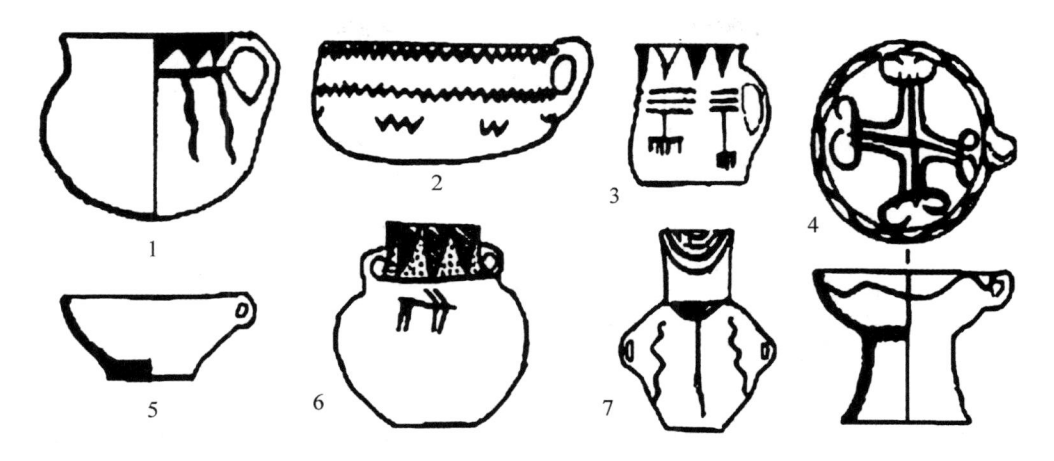

图 3-1-6 焉布拉克文化的陶器

1. M40：4；2. M64：8；3. T3：1；4. M60：1；5. M358：5；6. C：6；7. M75：18.（新疆维吾尔自治区文化厅文物处、新疆大学历史系文博干部专修班：《新疆哈密焉布拉克古墓地》，《考古学报》1989年第3期，图二〇：4、15、18，图二一：7、10，图二二：3、12）

在焉布拉克和拜契尔墓地都发现了一些金属器。它们继承了天山北路的大部分金属器，仍然以装饰品居多，工具和武器较少。但是器形有些变化，个体变小，制作趋于粗糙，已经走向明器化；铜镯和铜牌消失；新出现了耳坠和刻刀。铜扣边缘出现了锯齿纹，部分桥形钮加宽，较天山北路的完整，铸痕不明显（图3-1-7：7）；出现个体小而桥形钮大而窄的类型。铜泡圆鼓，中央有穿孔（图3-1-7：4）；也有扁平而中央有穿孔者；还有圆形个体较大者，两侧各有一个小孔。铜管（图3-1-7：9）仍然存在，有长有短，但是螺旋管消失了。铜耳环一端粗，一端细，类似鱼钩（图3-1-7：2、8）；也有粗细均匀者，也有两端锤扁者。新出现铜耳坠，为铜丝盘成螺旋状，再卷成铜耳环，下端增加喇叭形坠（图3-1-7：3）。铜镞多样化，有手掌形者，銎首；有管形者，也有铲形者，銎腔增大，但是体形较短而两翼较宽（图3-1-7：10、11）。铜刀的刀柄缩短而刀体加宽（图3-1-7：1）。在拜契尔墓地，除了铜器，还有铁器（刀、镯、耳环）。

第三部分 中国西北和欧亚草原考古

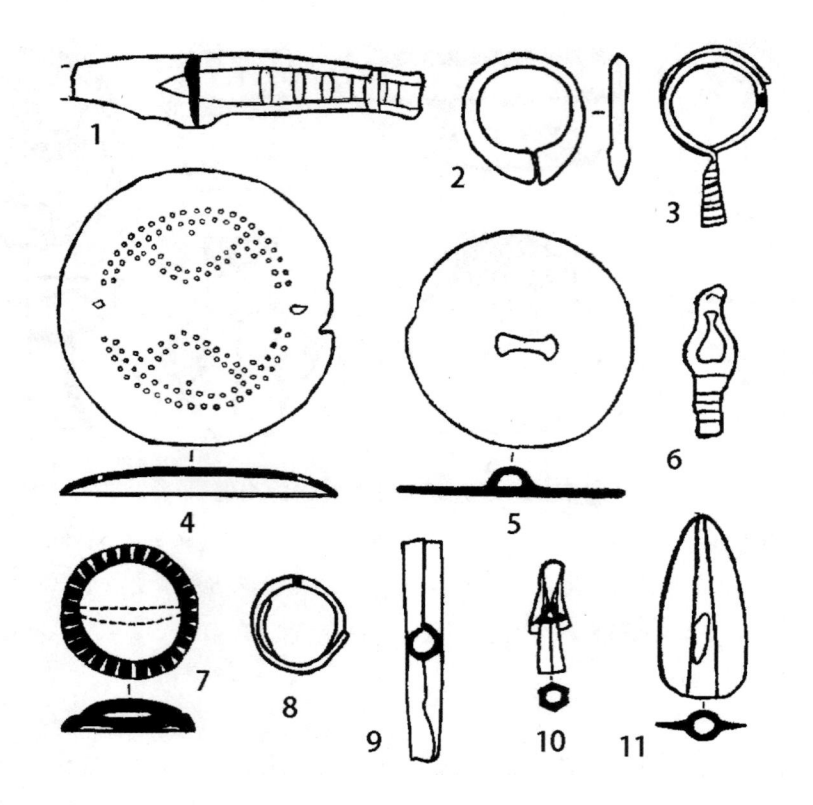

图 3-1-7 焉布拉克文化的铜器

1. M33:1；2. M48:2；3. M45:4；4. M46:1；5. M64:3；6. M75:23；7. M68:15；8. M6:9；9. M18:3；10. M68:2；11. M6:2（新疆维吾尔自治区文化厅文物处、新疆大学历史系文博干部专修班：《新疆哈密焉布拉克古墓地》，《考古学报》1989年第3期，图二三、二四）

关于焉布拉克墓地出土的金属器，梅建军和潜伟先后采集了12个样品，做了成分分析。[①] 其中锡青铜5个，纯铜4个，砷铜3个。这种多金属材料与天山北路接近，而锡青铜居多也与之相似。从拜契尔墓地出土的金属器中，潜伟和凌勇先后分析了18个铜器样品，发现其金属材质比较多样，有锡青铜（9）、纯铜（5）、铜锡砷（1）、铜砷锡（1）、砷铜（1）和铜砷铅（1）。因此，与天山北路和焉布拉克一样，

---

① Mei, J., *Copper and Bronze Metallurgy in Late Prehistoric Xinjiang*, Table 4.4, BAR International Series 865, Oxford: Archaeopress, 2000, p.40；潜伟：《新疆哈密地区史前时期铜器及其与邻近地区文化的关系》，知识产权出版社2006年版，第38页，表3.3。

锡青铜占据主流。① 五堡墓地出土的铜器很少，梅建军从中取了两个样品，成分均为砷铜。②

韩康信对焉布拉克墓地出土的29具头骨做了形态和测量分析，发现其中21具属于蒙古人种（72%），8具属于高加索人种（28%）。经过进一步分析，发现蒙古人种与西藏东部的卡姆类型和甘肃青铜时代的头骨接近，而与卡姆类型更为接近。而焉布拉克墓地出土的高加索人种头骨与孔雀河下游古墓沟的接近。表明焉布拉克墓地的人口为蒙古人种和高加索人种混合而成。③ 五堡墓地出土的人骨，经分析，既有蒙古人种的成分，又有欧洲人种的成分。④

关于焉布拉克文化的年代，人们从若干墓地采集了样品。发掘者从南湾墓地采集了木材样品1个，经国家文物局文物保护科学技术研究所碳十四实验室测得数据距今3000年左右。不过中国社会科学院考古研究所测了18个木头样品，得到了1685BC—838BC的年代范围。⑤ 发掘者从五堡墓地采集了4个圆木样品到国家文物局文物保护科学技术研究所碳十四实验室进行测定，得到的年代范围为1350BC—1050BC。后来又取了两个尸床样品到北京大学碳十四实验室进行测定，得到的数据为距今1620BC和950BC年，均未经树轮校正。⑥ 因此该墓地的年代范围应该是1350BC—950BC。发掘者曾将寒气沟M4的木质葬具取样送中国社会科学院考古研究所碳十四实验室做年代测定，年代为距今2205±93年，树轮校正后为

---

① 潜伟：《新疆哈密地区史前时期铜器及其与邻近地区文化的关系》，知识产权出版社2006年版，第144页，附表B-4。凌勇：《新疆公元前第一千纪的金属技术研究》，北京科技大学博士学位论文，2008年，第66—67页，续表3.3.1。

② Mei, J., *Copper and Bronze Metallurgy in Late Prehistoric Xinjiang*, BAR International Series 865, Oxford: Archaeopress, 2000, p.40, Table 4.4.

③ 韩康信：《新疆哈密焉不拉克古墓人骨种系成分研究》，《考古学报》1990年第3期，第388—389页。

④ 王博、崔静：《新疆哈密五堡古墓M151、M152出土颅骨种族人类学研究》，《新疆文物》1995年第1期，第28—43页。

⑤ 中国社会科学院考古研究所编：《中国考古学中碳十四年代数据集（1965—1991）》，文物出版社1991年版，第318—320页。

⑥ 新疆文物考古研究所：《新疆哈密五堡墓地151、152号墓葬》，《新疆文物》1992年第3期，第9页；中国社会科学院考古研究所编：《中国考古学中碳十四年代数据集（1965—1991）》，文物出版社1991年版，第318页。

◇❖◇　**第三部分　中国西北和欧亚草原考古**

公元前 359—前 40 年，[①] 年代偏晚。从焉布拉克墓地人们采集了 12 个木头样品，得到了 12 个碳十四数据。经过校正后，他们给出了两个年代范围：2111BC—1103BC 和 830BC—398BC。[②] 这两个年代范围都与焉布拉克墓地的相对年代不吻合，所以学术界给出了 1300BC—1000BC，[③] 1300BC—1100BC，[④] 1300BC—600BC 的范围。[⑤] 韩建业曾经将该墓地的陶器群和吐鲁番地区的苏贝希文化做了比较，器类和形态都接近，年代也接近。后者的碳十四年代数据有两组，一组为 920BC—710BC（经树轮校正），稍微偏晚；一组为 4 个羊毛样品的数据（来自 IM21 和 IM157）要早些，落在 1122BC—926BC 和 1261BC—1041BC 之间，可作为焉布拉克文化年代范围的参照。[⑥]

（三）黑沟梁文化

该文化得名于黑沟梁墓地，除此以外可以归入本文化的还有上庙尔沟、[⑦] 东黑沟、射月沟、[⑧] 柳树沟、[⑨] 峡沟[⑩]和托背梁[⑪]墓地。值得注意

[①] 新疆文物考古研究所、哈密地区文管所：《新疆哈密寒气沟墓地发掘简报》，《新疆文物》1996 年第 2 期，第 23—30 页；新疆文物考古研究所、哈密地区文管所：《新疆哈密市寒气沟墓地发掘简报》，《考古》1997 年第 9 期，第 33—38 页。

[②] 见潜伟：《新疆哈密地区史前时期铜器及其与邻近地区文化的关系》，知识产权出版社 2006 年版，第 125 页，附录 A。

[③] 新疆维吾尔自治区文化厅文物处、新疆大学历史系文博干部专修班：《新疆哈密焉布拉克古墓地》，《考古学报》1989 年第 3 期，第 355 页。

[④] 韩建业：《新疆的青铜时代和早期铁器时代文化》，文物出版社 2007 年版，第 40 页，表一〇。

[⑤] 潜伟：《新疆哈密地区史前时期铜器及其与邻近地区文化的关系》，知识产权出版社 2006 年版，第 71 页。

[⑥] 张良仁、吕恩国、张勇：《吐鲁番地区早期铁器时代考古》，《早期中国研究》第 2 辑，文物出版社 2016 年版，第 120 页。

[⑦] 新疆维吾尔自治区文物普查办公室、哈密地区文物普查队：《哈密地区文物普查资料》，《新疆文物》1991 年第 4 期，第 39 页；哈密地区文管所：《哈密黄田庙尔沟墓地调查》，《新疆文物》1998 年第 1 期，第 32—35、10 页。

[⑧] 新疆文物考古研究所、西北大学文化遗产保护与考古学研究中心、哈密地区文物局：《2008 年哈密市射月沟墓地考古发掘简报》，《新疆文物》2014 年第 2 期，第 4—8 页。

[⑨] 胡望林、张杰：《哈密市柳树沟遗址和墓地考古发掘》，《2013—2014 文物考古年报》，第 17—19 页。

[⑩] 新疆文物考古研究所、西北大学文化遗产保护与考古学研究中心、哈密地区文物局：《2008 年伊吾县峡沟墓地考古发掘简报》，《新疆文物》2014 年第 2 期，第 9—17 页。

[⑪] 西北大学文化遗产保护与考古学研究中心、新疆文物考古研究所、哈密地区文物局：《2008 年伊吾县托背梁墓地考古发掘简报》，《新疆文物》2014 年第 2 期，第 45—59 页。

的是，它们都分布在东天山的南北麓，而不见于哈密盆地；这说明本期的居民放弃了农业，专门从事畜牧业。限于篇幅，我们只能着重讨论黑沟梁和东黑沟遗址。

黑沟梁墓地原称伊吾军马场墓地，位于哈密市、伊吾县、巴里坤县交界处的伊吾军马场，地处天山北坡（图3-1-1）。1993年为了配合哈密—巴里坤公路改线工程，新疆文物考古研究所和哈密地区文管所对北山与天山主脉间的改线部分做了考古调查。黑沟梁大致呈南北走向，其东、西坡与梁顶公路改线部分遍布古代墓葬。发掘者由西而东分了四个墓地。其中一号位于西坡，墓葬百余座。墓葬多有石块封堆，中心多凹陷（图3-1-8：1）。封堆直径在2—7.5米之间，一般在4—5.5米之间。墓坑形制有两种：竖穴土坑和竖穴偏室。墓葬内为多人葬、仰身直肢、侧身屈肢和二次葬。随葬品有陶器、铁器、铜器、海贝、银器、漆器，此外还有殉牲骨骼。但是发掘墓葬的数量不明。发掘者认为这片墓地的年代上限为周，下限为汉代。二号墓地位于黑沟梁顶部及西坡上部，墓葬形制与一号相同，但是墓葬数量不清楚，似乎也没有发掘。三号墓地位于东坡，共有墓葬20座，可分两组，每组内有一座大墓和若干小墓，小墓呈弧形环绕大墓分布。四号墓地位于黑沟梁以东，墓葬总数在20座以上，也可分为两组。1993年和1994年在一号墓地清理了52座墓葬，在二号墓地清理了6座，在三号墓地清理了6座。出土随葬

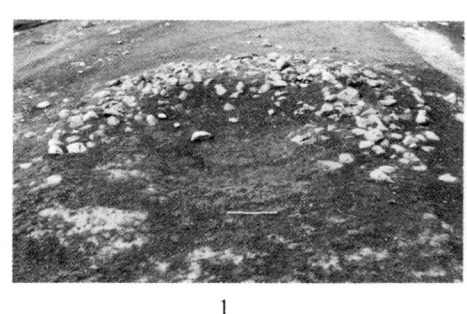

图3-1-8 黑沟梁文化的墓葬和房屋（黑沟梁、东黑沟）

1. 黑沟梁墓地封堆墓；2. 东黑沟房屋（哈密博物馆：《哈密文物精粹》，科学出版社2013年版，第185页上、第186页上）

◇❖◇ 第三部分 中国西北和欧亚草原考古

品有陶器、漆器、海贝、铜器和铁器等。

2006年新疆文物考古研究所和西北大学文化遗产与考古学研究中心在巴里坤县的东黑沟遗址清理了"石筑高台"1座、石围建筑4座和中小型墓葬12座。① 其中"石筑高台"为土石混合筑成的建筑，核心堆积以土为主，而边缘以石块居多（图3-1-8:2）。顶面长16.6米，宽10.4米，地面长30.3米，宽25.9米，北部高4米，南部高2米。该建筑有两个使用面，实际都是一座房屋的地面，总面积约166—180平方米。下层使用面的四周保存有石砌围墙，墙内有圆木。两层居住面的遗迹都有火塘和灰坑，下层有柱洞，上层还有灶坑。下层出土了铜刀、锥各1件。这种建筑实际上是厚墙围绕的木构建筑，不是真正的高台建筑。这类建筑过去在兰州湾子也发现过，只是发表的资料非常简短。② 大型石围建筑周围分布了若干方形石围建筑，均有石砌围墙，内有灰坑、灶和火塘。此外还有4座石围祭祀遗迹，石围均为圆形，其内发现残缺不全摆放凌乱的人骨。石围建筑大多为方形，一般由2个以上石围构成，最多的一个组合多达37个；石围墙体一般由1—5层石块构成，宽0.4—0.5米。石围面积大小不一，大者可达900平方米。这些建筑往往利用斜坡地形，一面围墙较高（F3的墙体现存高度0.8米），而其他三面围墙渐次降低，但是原始高度都不如大型石围建筑。从平面图来看，大型石围建筑叠压着石围建筑，年代晚于后者。

黑沟梁墓地的发掘报告没有出版，至今只发表了一篇语焉不详的简报，而且没有配发器物图片，我们无法做更精确的判断。③ 发掘所得器物现收藏在哈密博物馆，部分发表在该馆出版的图录上。④ 其中只有腹

---

① 新疆文物考古研究所、西北大学文化遗产与考古学研究中心：《2006年巴里坤东黑沟遗址发掘》，《新疆文物》2007年第2期，第32—60页；新疆文物考古研究所、西北大学文化遗产与考古学研究中心：《新疆巴里坤县东黑沟遗址2006—2007年发掘简报》，《考古》2009年第1期，第3—27页。

② 王炳华：《巴里坤县兰州湾子三千年前石构建筑遗址》，《中国考古学年鉴》，文物出版社1985年版，第255—256页。

③ 新疆文物考古研究所、哈密地区文管所：《哈密—巴里坤公路改线考古调查》，《新疆文物》1994年第1期，第9—10页。

④ 哈密博物馆：《哈密文物精粹》，科学出版社2013年版，第163—173页。

耳壶接近焉布拉克文化。单耳壶虽然见于焉布拉克文化，但是形态发生了很大的变化：环耳骑跨在腹部和颈部，易于倾倒液体。类似的器物还有带流罐；它和个体很大的双耳圜底釜都不见于焉布拉克文化（图3-1-9）。

图3-1-9 黑沟梁文化的陶器

（哈密博物馆：《哈密文物精粹》，科学出版社2013年版，第163—165、187—189页）

东黑沟墓地和聚落出土的器物不多。陶器大体可以分为两类，第一类为墓葬（M10、M12、M15）和部分石围建筑（X4）出土的单耳圜底罐、单耳平底罐、腹耳壶、双耳钵和圜底壶，它们与黑沟梁和上庙尔沟Ⅰ号墓地的接近，应该属于黑沟梁文化。第二类为石围建筑（F3）和大型石围建筑（GT1）出土的单耳高领罐、双耳敛口釜、盆、钵、杯、碗、双耳高领瓮、双耳罐和腹耳罐，个体较大；部分陶器上面绘三角网纹和平行之字纹。这类陶器显然不同于第一类，可惜哈密地区聚落发掘得少，我们了解得不多。其中双耳高领瓮和腹耳罐发现于南湾。同出的器物有铜刀、铜锥、大石磨盘、石磨棒、网坠和纺轮等，均为日常生产和生活器物，第二类陶器恐怕也是如此，而不同于墓葬随葬陶器。发掘者认为，墓葬、石围建筑和大型石围建筑属于同一时期；因为缺少比较材料，我们无法判断，暂且留待以后考虑。

金属器中，铜扣延续了下来，但是表面装饰鸟纹，与焉布拉克文化不同。铜泡也有很大变化，一种类似于铜镜，平整，一侧有柄，柄上有孔，可以系挂，但是形体很小；另一种大体圆形，中央穿孔。铜耳环沿用焉布拉克文化的复杂的组合耳环（坠子+环）。铜刀比焉布拉克文化的更为细长，类似于现代医生用的柳叶刀。铜锥更为细长，有的拧成麻花状。新出现了动物纹铜牌、带扣、带钩、马镳、铜铃、长柄短剑、铜钉（针形，但是有帽）和铜环（三角形）。铜镞仍为矛形双棱，但是銎腔更大，新出现了三棱镞。它们大多为游牧民族喜用的马具、工具、武器和装饰品（图3-1-10）。在上庙尔沟和托背梁墓地，我们看到了另一个变化。金属器中铁器居多，有短剑、刀、镞、带钩、带扣、泡、环、牌、珠、管、簪和锥。这些器类在焉布拉克时期用铜，现在改用铁制造。而且据发掘者的报道，在有随葬品的12座墓葬中，8座出土了铁器，可见铁器的使用相当普遍。

上述带有浓厚游牧文化特征的冶金技术来自何方？在哈密地区周围，与黑沟梁墓地同时的游牧文化发现于阿尔泰山区、米奴辛斯克盆地和图瓦。黑沟梁的环形柄铜镜、铆接柄的复合镜见于阿尔泰山区；[①] 三角形环首带钩、鸟形牌和圆形四孔节约见于米奴辛斯克盆地的塔加尔文化。[②] 鸟形带扣见于三个区域，但是其长方形双环者只见于图瓦；[③] 条形马镳和圆形+三角形环带扣也见于该区域。[④] 由此看来，虽然现有的资料不能说明黑沟梁的金属器来源于单个区域的启发，但是可以肯定黑沟梁接受了游牧民族的冶金技术和他们的生活方式。上述的石封堆和竖

---

① Rybakov, B. A. ed., *Stepnaia Polosa Aziatskoi chasti SSSR v Skifo-sarmatskoe Vremia*, Moscow: Science Press, 1992, Plate 63：45，Plate 64：25.

② Rybakov, B. A. ed., *Stepnaia Polosa Aziatskoi chasti SSSR v Skifo-sarmatskoe Vremia*, Moscow: Science Press, 1992, Plate 84：34，Plate 88：12，Plate 85：23.

③ Rybakov, B. A. ed., *Stepnaia Polosa Aziatskoi chasti SSSR v Skifo-sarmatskoe Vremia*, Moscow: Science Press, 1992, Plate 77：36.

④ Rybakov, B. A. ed., *Stepnaia Polosa Aziatskoi chasti SSSR v Skifo-sarmatskoe Vremia*, Moscow: Science Press, 1992, Plate 75：82，Plate 82：18.

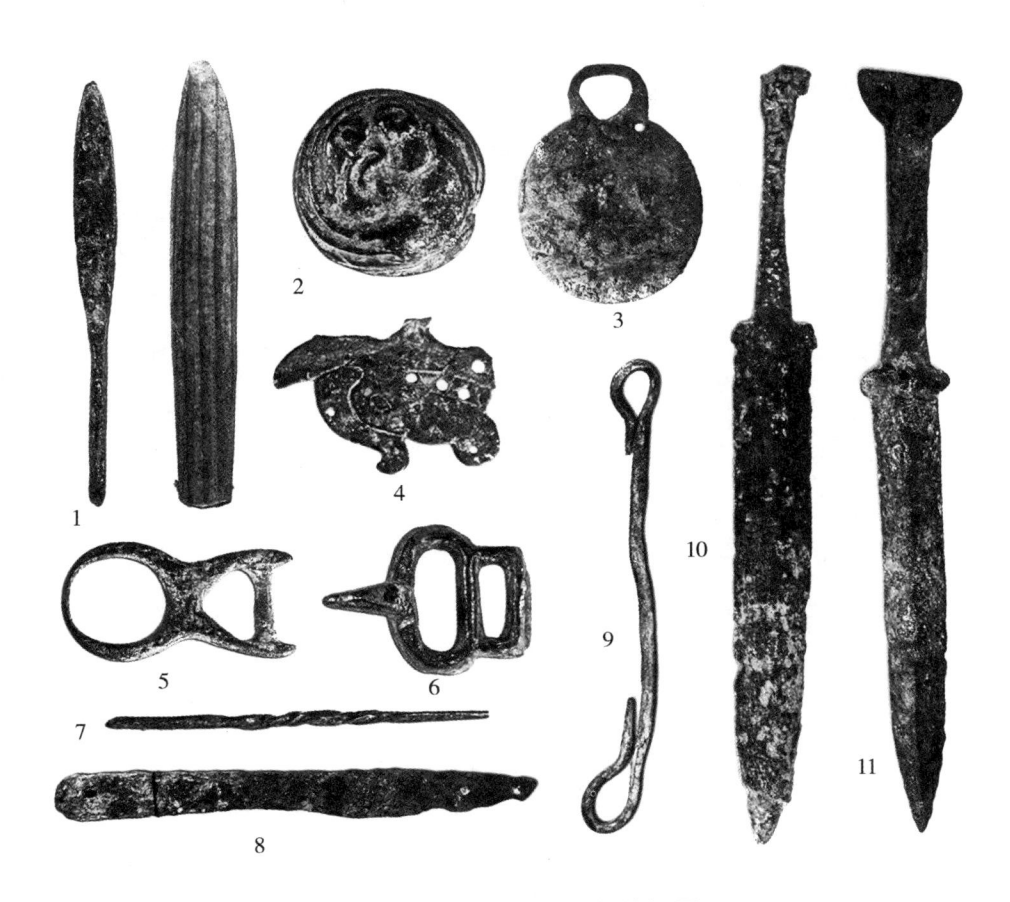

图 3-1-10 黑沟梁文化的铜器

(哈密博物馆：《哈密文物精粹》，科学出版社 2013 年版，第 166—172 页)

穴偏室也是游牧民族的埋葬习俗。魏东等人从Ⅰ号墓地采集了 45 例个体，发现了 1 例个体的大转子和股骨脊发达，结合其他考古学证据，推测该个体曾经骑马。[1] 不过，黑沟梁墓地不见上述三个区域的游牧文化的陶器，这说明黑沟梁居民只是部分接受了欧亚大陆草原带的游牧文化。

梅建军、潜伟和凌勇先后从黑沟梁墓地采集了 16 个铜器样品，发

---

[1] 魏东、曾雯、常喜恩、朱泓：《新疆哈密黑沟梁墓地出土人骨的创伤、病理及异常形态研究》，《人类学学报》2012 年第 31 卷第 2 期，第 183—184 页。

现其金属材质分别为锡青铜（8 个）、铜（6 个）和黄铜（铜锌合金，2个）。① 其中黄铜是新出现的材质，是否与游牧民族有关尚不得而知。

关于黑沟梁文化的年代范围，现有的碳十四测年数据不多。黑沟梁墓地只有两个木头样品的数据，结果相当一致，都在 768BC—402BC 之间。托背梁墓地有两个碳十四数据，M15 的人骨年代为 2160±30BP，M4 的人骨年代为 1945±35BP，分别相当于 210BC 和 5AD。这些年代数据与器物特征大体吻合，大体给出了 768BC—5AD 的年代范围。

上述墓地有人称为上庙尔沟类型。② 由上述分析来看，它们的陶器和金属器既继承了焉布拉克文化的一些器类和器形，又发生了很大的变化，而且埋葬习俗也发生了变化。其中体现游牧生活的马具、工具和装饰品类金属器把它们与焉布拉克文化区分开来。因此我们认为，命名一个新文化的条件已经成熟。其中黑沟梁墓地发现较早，而器物群也非常有代表性，因此我们建议命名为"黑沟梁文化"。

三　结论

前文提到的所有遗址（包括焉布拉克）都没有完全发表，绝大部分只发表了小部分资料，所以本文得到的结论只是阶段性的。不过，虽然上述三期的文化遗存之间缺乏地层证据，但是根据埋葬习俗、陶器和金属器的器类和形态，以及与周边文化的比较，这种划分是可以成立的（表3-1-1）。可惜碳十四数据仍然偏少，本文仍然无法准确地界定三期文化的年代范围。总的来说，本文一方面探讨了哈密地区的年代序列和文化变化问题，另一方面也揭开了问题，为以后的研究铺垫道路。

天山北路文化的遗址只有一处，也就是天山北路墓地。在该墓地大量墓葬已经发掘，出土了大量的陶器和金属器，资料极其丰富。可惜发掘报

---

① Mei, J., *Copper and Bronze Metallurgy in Late Prehistoric Xinjiang*, BAR International Series 865, Oxford: Archaeopress, 2000, p.40, Table 4.5；潜伟：《新疆哈密地区史前时期铜器及其与邻近地区文化的关系》，知识产权出版社 2006 年版，第 78 页，表 5.4；凌勇：《新疆公元前第一千纪的金属技术研究》，北京科技大学博士学位论文，2008 年，第 67 页，续表 3.3.1。

② 陈戈：《关于新疆远古文化的几个问题》，《新疆文物》1985 年第 1 期，第 33 页。

告至今没有出版，我们只能认识该文化的局部情况。该墓地流行竖穴土坑，部分土坑坑壁用土坯加固。人骨多单人侧身屈肢葬，多属于东亚蒙古人种，也有少量高加索人种和两个人种的混血。除了个别器类，该墓地的陶器在陶质、陶色、器类组合和纹样各个方面，都与河西走廊的四坝文化相似。同样，该墓地出土的许多金属器器类如直銎斧、铜泡、联珠泡、串珠、铜管、耳环、铜扣、铜镜、耳环、铜手链、铜刀和铜凿见于米奴辛斯克盆地的卡拉苏克文化；与此同时，其材质以锡青铜为主，还有纯铜和砷铜，这种组合也与卡拉苏克文化相近。这些器类和材质也与四坝文化相近。由陶器和金属器材料，我们可以推测，天山北路的冶金技术可能起源于卡拉苏克文化，但是直接来源于四坝文化。但是天山北路的居民并非完全照搬卡拉苏克或者四坝的冶金技术，他们发明或者改造了一些器类，如镂空铜牌、铜螺旋管、铜铃和亚腰形铜牌。天山北路墓地缺乏确切的碳十四年代，但是通过与四坝文化相比对，推定其年代范围为1880BC—1530BC。

表3-1-1　　　　　　　　哈密地区史前文化分期

分期/文化	遗址
天山北路	天山北路
焉布拉克	焉布拉克、五堡、寒气沟、拜契尔、拉甫乔克、艾斯克霞尔、亚尔、南湾、萨伊吐尔
黑沟梁	黑沟梁、庙尔沟、东黑沟、射月沟、柳树沟、峡沟、托背梁

焉布拉克文化的遗址已经发现不少，如腐殖酸厂、南湾、五堡、拜契尔、艾斯克霞尔、拉甫乔克、亚尔、萨伊吐尔和寒气沟，分布于东天山南北两侧，主要分布于哈密盆地，也见于东天山的河谷。相对而言，焉布拉克墓地的发表资料比较丰富，但是人骨大多残碎；与天山北路墓地的墓主一样，他们大多属于蒙古人种，少数属于高加索人种。与天山北路文化相比，焉布拉克墓地的陶器群既有连续性，也有显著的变化，新出现了单耳钵、腹耳壶和豆，彩陶纹样中流行横向之字纹、平行线纹、S纹和十字纹。关于这些新因素的来源，我们现在还不清楚。同

样，焉布拉克墓地出土的金属器既继承了天山北路文化的特征，又有所变化。它们延续了大部分器类，仍然以装饰品居多，而工具和武器有所减少，其制作趋于粗糙、小型化。其材质包括锡青铜、纯铜和砷铜，而以锡青铜为主。这种多金属材料与天山北路接近，而锡青铜居多也与之相似。除了铜质器物，本期还出现了铁器。关于焉布拉克墓地的年代，现有12个碳十四数据，不过经过校正后的年代范围都与焉布拉克墓地的相对年代不吻合。与之接近的苏贝希文化，碳十四测年数据在1122BC—926BC和1261BC—1041BC之间，可作为焉布拉克文化年代范围的参照。

已经发掘的黑沟梁文化遗址为数已经不少，有黑沟梁、庙尔沟、射月沟、柳树沟、东黑沟、峡沟和托背梁。其中除了墓地，还有聚落。这些遗址只分布于东天山南北麓，不见于哈密盆地。与天山北路和焉布拉克文化相比，该文化的面貌既有所继承，也发生了很大的变化。墓室除了竖穴土坑，还有竖穴偏室，上面覆盖圆形和环形封堆。陶器中只有腹耳壶接近焉布拉克文化。带流罐和双耳圜底釜则不见于焉布拉克文化，也不见于米奴辛斯克盆地的塔加尔、图瓦的乌尤克、阿尔泰山区的巴泽雷克文化以及蒙古和贝加尔湖周围的匈奴文化。这些新器类从何处来目前尚不得而知。金属器中，新出现了动物纹铜牌、带扣、带钩、马镳、铜铃、长柄短剑、铜钉（针形，但是有帽）、铜环（三角形）。它们都是游牧民族喜用的马具、武器和装饰品，而且流行动物纹样，说明该文化居民吸收了公元前一千纪欧亚草原带塔加尔、乌尤克与巴泽雷克等文化的养分。此外，铁器更为普遍，部分原先用铜制作的器物如刀、镞、带扣现在用铁制作。该文化的年代大体在768BC—AD5之间。

吐鲁番地区早期铁器时代考古[*]

一 前言

吐鲁番盆地位于新疆东部，三面环山，由北面和西面的天山和南面的觉罗塔格山包围，东面敞开。盆地海拔低，平均只有30米，其中心的艾丁湖更是低至-154.31米。这里阳光辐射强烈，热量难以散发，因此夏天温度高，7月份日均温度为32.2℃，最高达48.1℃；而冬天寒冷，1月份日均温度为-7.6℃，最低达-28.9℃；同时又地处内陆，来自太平洋和印度洋的水汽无法到达这里，而来自大西洋的水汽因为天山截留，无法进入盆地，所以盆地内雨水稀少，年降雨量只有15.7毫米。高温少雨的温带大陆性气候形成了大面积的沙漠以及横亘盆地中部的火焰山。不过天山下来的雪水养育了盆地内的绿洲，为农业的发展提供了保障；因此吐鲁番盆地成为古代丝绸之路的一个重要中转站，向东经哈密盆地、河西走廊连接中原的都城长安和洛阳，向西沿天山北麓通往欧亚草原或者沿天山南麓抵达中亚和南亚；所以欧亚草原、中亚、南亚和中原的人群曾经迁徙到这里，在这里交往和融合，因此盆地内积累了丰富多样的古代遗迹和遗物；而干燥的气候又使得这里的地上和地下有机物长年不腐，保存至今。

19世纪后期和20世纪以来，许多外国学者和探险家进入我国新疆，进行各种调查发掘活动，由此掀开了吐鲁番地区古代文化研究的序幕。1928年，我国学者参与了瑞典学者斯文赫定组织的"西北科学考察团"，开始了对吐鲁番等地的科学考察。其中黄文弼于1928年和1931年两次对吐鲁番高昌故城和交河故城及其附近的墓葬作了考察和发掘，还调查

---

[*] 本文原刊于《早期中国研究》第2辑，文物出版社2016年版，第116—155页。收入本书时略有改动。

◇❖◇ 第三部分 中国西北和欧亚草原考古

了古遗址和寺窟。20世纪50年代末以后，新疆的田野工作一度集中在阿斯塔那—哈拉和卓墓地和交河故城上。1976年这些发掘工作结束以后，人们的注意力才逐渐转移到史前遗址上。他们先后发掘了阿拉沟东口、苏贝希一号、艾丁湖、东风机器厂、博斯坦、洋海、三个桥、交河沟西、胜金店[①]和加依墓地[②]（图3-2-1）。学术界过去曾将这些遗址归入雅尔湖沟北类型，后来归入苏贝希文化。有人认为它与文献记载中的西汉以前的小国姑师对应，因此命名了姑师（车师）文化。因为苏贝希文化的年代与分布范围都与之重合，这种看法不无道理。[③]

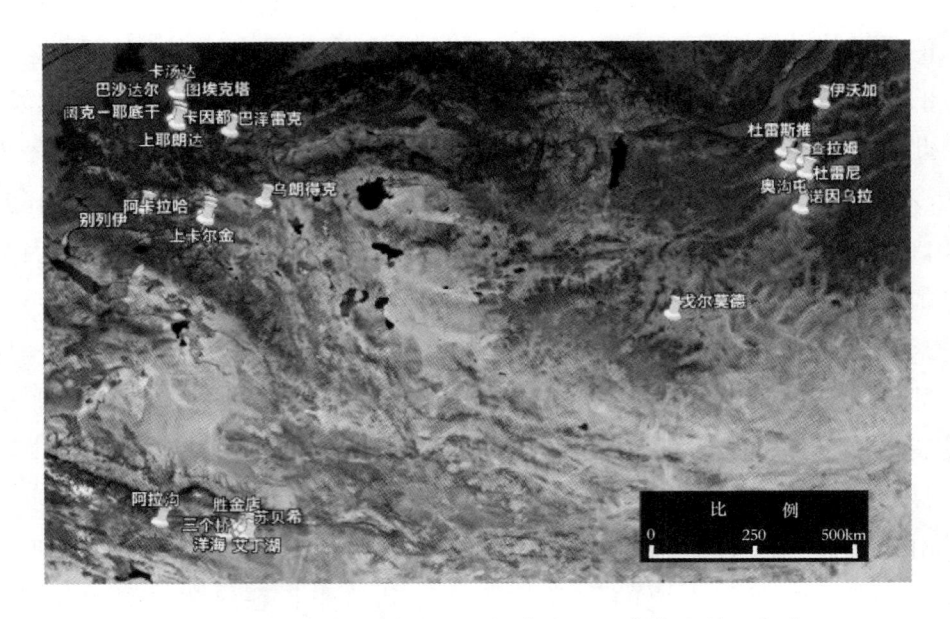

图3-2-1 吐鲁番地区、阿尔泰山区、蒙古和外贝加尔
早期铁器时代遗址分布图

由于高昌故城、交河故城、阿斯塔纳墓地、柏孜克里克、胜金口石窟等遗址的发现和发掘，我们了解了历史时期的各种宗教和文

---

① 新疆维吾尔自治区文物局编：《概述》，《新疆维吾尔自治区第三次全国文物普查成果集成——吐鲁番地区卷》，科学出版社2011年版，第3—4页。
② 承蒙吕恩国见告，此墓地发掘于2013年，简报即将发表。
③ 陈戈：《新疆史前时期又一种考古学文化——苏贝希文化试析》，载宿白主编《苏秉琦与当代中国考古学》，科学出版社2001年版，第167—170页。

化进入吐鲁番地区并生根发芽的情况。但是这里的史前文化是如何起源和发展的？本文将试图回答这个问题。当然，以前不少研究者回答了这个问题，取得了一些认识。① 不过本文将着重比较分析吐鲁番地区和欧亚草原的同时期文化，以便观察当时的文化互动和人群迁徙。在上述墓地中，洋海墓地经过大规模发掘，发表资料也比较丰富。本文将根据这个墓地的分期，统一吐鲁番地区史前墓地的分期，归纳各期文化的特征。在此基础上分析他们与欧亚草原的同时期文化即巴泽雷克和匈奴之间的联系，探讨吐鲁番史前居民的生活方式和来源。

二　吐鲁番地区墓地分期

（一）洋海墓地

洋海墓地位于火焰山南麓，鄯善县吐峪沟乡洋海阿斯喀勒村西北。墓葬主要分布在相对独立的三块台地上，其中Ⅰ号墓地（西）长300米、宽50米，面积1.5万平方米，有1000余座墓葬；Ⅱ号墓地（东）长300米、宽80米，面积2.5万平方米，有1500余座墓葬；Ⅲ号墓地（南）长150米、宽100米，面积1.5万平方米，墓葬约500座（图3-2-2）。除此之外，在西北和东南部的许多类似的小台地上，还零星分布着一些墓葬。墓地地表为沙砾戈壁，下面为第四纪黄土层。三片墓地是附近农民维修坎儿井时发现的，20世纪80年代以后不断遭受盗掘。其中1987年最为严重，80座墓葬遭到破坏。② 因此，1988年新疆文物考古研究所在Ⅰ、Ⅱ号墓地抢救发掘了82座墓葬（包括被盗、被扰的在内），但是这批墓葬的发掘资料迄今没有发表。③

---

①　如韩建业：《新疆的青铜时代和早期铁器时代文化》，文物出版社2007年版；郭物《新疆史前晚期社会的考古学研究》，上海古籍出版社2012年版。

②　新疆维吾尔自治区文物普查办公室、吐鲁番地区文物普查队：《吐鲁番地区文物普查资料》，《新疆文物》1988年第3期，第31—34页；新疆文物考古研究所：《"鄯善古墓被盗案"中部分文物之介绍》，《新疆文物》1989年第4期，第34—40页；吐鲁番地区文物局：《鄯善洋海墓地出土文物》，《新疆文物》1998年第3期，第44页。

③　邢开鼎：《鄯善县洋海古墓葬》，《中国考古学年鉴1989》，文物出版社1990年版，第274页。

第三部分 中国西北和欧亚草原考古

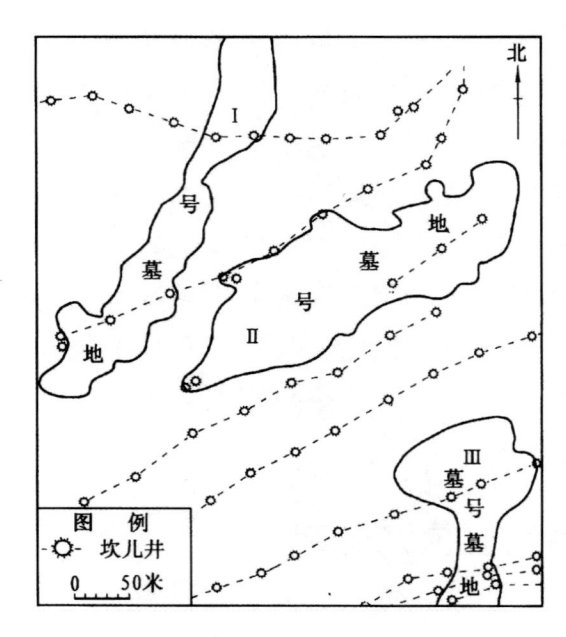

图 3-2-2 洋海墓地分布图

（新疆吐鲁番学研究院、新疆文物考古研究所：《新疆鄯善洋海墓地发掘报告》，《考古学报》2011年第1期，图二）

2003年春，又有40座墓葬被盗，同年3—5月，新疆文物考古研究所和吐鲁番地区文物局共同组建考古队，对洋海墓地实施了抢救性发掘。共清理、发掘墓葬521座，其中一号墓地218座，① 二号223座，② III号80座。此墓地的发掘资料已经部分发表，③ 完整的发掘报告已经整理完毕，目前正在编辑准备出版。④

发掘者将墓葬分为四类，并按照墓葬类型分了四期。⑤ A类为椭圆形竖穴墓，有的底部周围有生土二层台。此类墓有29座，发掘者选择报道了4座（IM21、IM67、IM145、IM150），可惜IM67和IM145出土的器物都没有发表（部分墓葬报道了器物，而没有报道形制和葬俗）。B类为竖穴二层台墓，但是形状为长方形，墓底或墓口的周围有二层台。此类墓65座，发掘者选择报道了5

---

① 一说209座，新疆文物考古研究所、吐鲁番地区文物局：《鄯善县洋海一号墓地发掘简报》，《新疆文物》2004年第1期，第3页。

② 一说213座，新疆文物考古研究所、吐鲁番地区文物局：《鄯善县洋海二号墓地发掘简报》，《新疆文物》2004年第1期，第29页。

③ 本节材料主要来自新疆吐鲁番学研究院、新疆文物考古研究所：《新疆鄯善洋海墓地发掘报告》，《考古学报》2011年第1期，第99—149页；新疆文物考古研究所、吐鲁番地区文物局：《鄯善县洋海一号墓地发掘简报》，《新疆文物》2004年第1期，第1—27页；《鄯善县洋海二号墓地发掘简报》，《新疆文物》2004年第1期，第28—49页；《鄯善县洋海三号墓地发掘简报》，《新疆文物》2004年第1期，第50—68页。新疆文物考古研究所、吐鲁番地区文物局：《新疆鄯善县洋海墓地的考古新收获》，《考古》2004年第5期，第3—7页。

④ 承蒙该墓地发掘工作的主持人吕恩国见告。

⑤ 关于洋海墓地的分类，发掘者的认识有个演化过程。他们曾经将墓葬分为七类（编号A—F），见新疆文物考古研究所、吐鲁番地区文物局：《鄯善县洋海一号墓地发掘简报》，《新疆文物》2004年第1期，第48页。后来合并为四类（编号A—D），见新疆吐鲁番学研究院、新疆文物考古研究所：《新疆鄯善洋海墓地发掘报告》，《考古学报》2011年第1期，第100页。

座（ⅠM5、ⅠM20、ⅠM90、ⅠM157、ⅡM284），另外7座（ⅠM80、ⅠM48、ⅠM99、ⅠM130、ⅠM113、ⅠM142、ⅢM366）只报道了部分资料，没有报道出土器物（部分墓葬报道了器物，而没有报道形制和葬俗）。C类为长方形竖穴土坑墓，墓室小而浅，无二层台。此类墓370座，发掘者选择报道了17座（ⅠM1、ⅠM169、ⅠM189、ⅠM195、ⅡM14、ⅡM60、ⅡM86、ⅡM154、ⅡM202、ⅡM260、ⅡM272、ⅡM273、ⅡM2054、ⅡM2063、ⅡM2211、ⅢM353、ⅢM364），另外8座（ⅠM75、ⅡM2005、ⅡM2038、ⅡM2042、ⅡM2052、ⅢM358、ⅢM360、ⅢM362）只报道了部分资料，没有报道出土器物。这三类的部分墓葬底部有木床，由四圆木足和方木床架（四足与床架由榫卯连接）构成框架，然后由细木铺成床面。同时它们的二层台或墓口安放木头，上面放置细木，再放枯树、树枝和干草，最后填土。D类为竖穴偏室墓，即在长方形竖穴的一侧下部掏挖出偏室，部分墓葬的墓口部用木棒或土坯封堵，外面覆盖苇席。有些墓葬（ⅡM249）的地面上还有围墙和环形封堆。[①] 此类墓有57座，发掘者选择报道了10座（ⅢM1、ⅡM18、ⅢM39、ⅡM243、ⅡM2206、ⅡM2211、ⅢM315、ⅢM329、ⅢM371、ⅢM376），其他

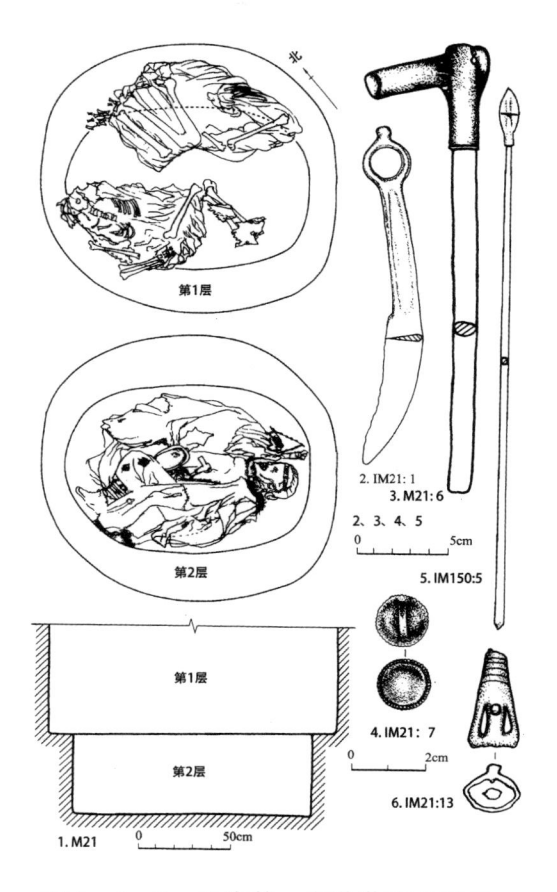

图3-2-3　洋海第一期墓葬和金属器

1. ⅠM21，2. ⅠM21∶1；3. ⅠM21∶6；4. ⅠM21∶7；5. ⅠM150∶5；6. ⅠM21∶13（新疆吐鲁番学研究院、新疆文物考古研究所：《新疆鄯善洋海墓地发掘报告》，《考古学报》2011年第1期，图六，图七∶1、4、5、19，图十∶11）

---

① 新疆文物考古研究所、吐鲁番地区文物局：《鄯善县洋海一号墓地发掘简报》，《新疆文物》2004年第1期，第35页。

4座（ⅡM249、ⅡM2005、ⅢM316、ⅢM318）只报道了部分资料，没有公布出土器物。与前三类不同的是，此类墓没有木床。各期的墓葬绝大多数为东西向，只有少数为南北向。

发掘者认为，A、B两类墓葬属于第一期，年代大约为公元前13—前9世纪。不过此前测得的两个（来自IM21和IM5）碳十四年代数据为920BC—710BC（经树轮校正，下同），稍微偏晚；后来测得的四个羊毛样品的数据（来自IM21和IM157）要早些，落在1122BC—926BC和1261BC—1041BC之间。① 这类墓葬很少出土陶器，而常常出土铜刀和铜斧，流行单人屈肢葬。该类IM21出土的铜铃、铜刀和铜泡和IM150出土的铜镞都与哈密地区焉布拉克墓地出土的同类器接近（图3-2-3）。② C类墓葬属于第二期，年代为公元前9—前3世纪。此前测得的两个（IM90、ⅡM63）数据分别为770BC—480BC和790BC—480BC。后来测得的大麻和葡萄藤样品（IM90、ⅡM213、ⅡM2069）的数据为630±95、805±13和305±65，也落在这个范围内。③ 本期墓葬大量出现单耳罐、单耳杯、壶和豆，并且绘竖条纹、涡纹、锯齿纹和网纹。本类墓葬IM189出土的角马镳和铜马衔与黑沟梁墓地出土的同类器接近，两者年代大体同时。IM20出土的陶单耳壶，细颈鼓腹，与哈萨克斯坦别列伊（Berel'）墓地8号冢出土的无耳陶壶接近，④ 只是前者施彩，而后者素面（图3-2-4）。D类墓葬属于第三期，年代为公元前2—公元2世纪，大体相当于匈奴时期或者两汉时期。已经测得的碳十四数据只有一个（ⅢM76），为490BC—160BC。本期墓葬流行仰身直肢葬，全为一次

---

① Beck, Ulrike, Mayke Wagner, Xiao Li, Desmond Durkin-Meisterernst, Pavel E. Tarasov, The Invention of Trousers and its Likely Affiliation with Horseback Riding and Mobility: A Case Study of Late 2nd Millennium BC Finds from Turfan in Eastern Central Asia, *Quaternary International* 348, 2014, pp. 224-235.

② 新疆文物考古研究所、新疆大学历史系文博干部专修班：《新疆哈密焉不拉克墓地》，《考古学报》1989年第3期，图二三：2、5。

③ 新疆文物考古研究所、吐鲁番地区文物局：《鄯善县洋海一号墓地发掘简报》，《新疆文物》2004年第1期，第2页。

④ Rubinson, Karen S., Burial Practices and Social Roles of Iron Age Mobile Pastoralists, in Soren Stark and Karen S. Rubinson with Zainolla S. Samashev and Jennifer Y. Chi eds., *Nomads and Networks: The Ancient Art and Culture of Kazakhstan*, Institute for the Study of Ancient World at New York University, Princeton University Press, 2012, pp. 77-90, Fig. 5-8.

葬。陶器已经不见彩陶，器类简单，只有单耳杯、单耳罐和钵，而环耳位于腹部；它们和弓箭、木冠和木盘一起构成了本类墓葬的常见组合。本期IIIM1出土的两枚铜牌，长方形，两端各钻两孔或一孔，常见于宁夏倒墩子墓地、①俄罗斯伊沃加（Ivolga）城址的房屋、②伊沃加墓地的墓葬、③杜雷斯推（Durestuǐ）墓地的墓葬（图3-2-5）。④

需要说明的是，这种按照墓葬类型分期的方法是值得商榷的。属于 B 类的 IM5 按照这种方法应归入第一期，但是该墓出土的长方形环首马衔、柳叶形铜刀和三孔角马镳，如果参照俄罗斯米奴

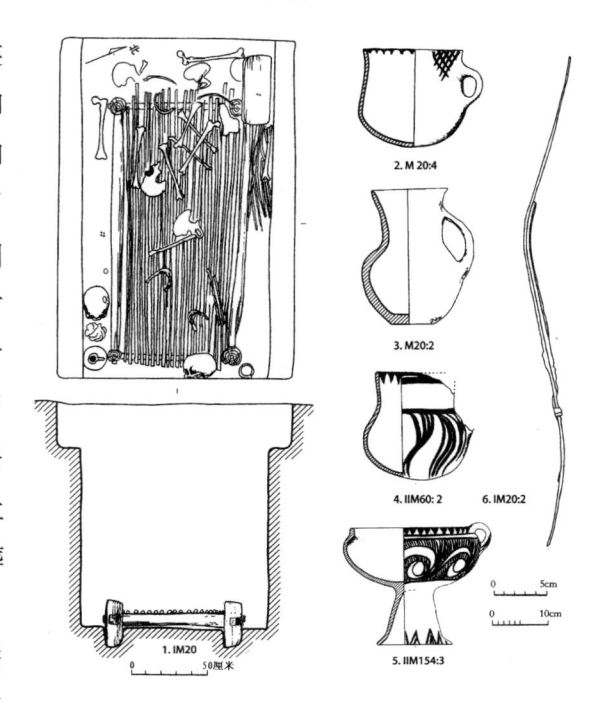

图 3-2-4 洋海第二期墓葬和随葬品

1. IM20；2. IM20：4；3. II154：4；4. IIM60：2；5. II154：3；6. IM20：2（新疆吐鲁番学研究院、新疆文物考古研究所：《新疆鄯善洋海墓地发掘报告》，《考古学报》2011年第1期，图十三，图十四：1、4，图三五：4、2，图三六：4）

辛斯克盆地的文化序列，与塔加尔文化接近。同样属于 B 类的 IM90 出土了一件陶杯，系泥质红陶，口沿内侧绘细密的锯齿纹，外壁绘粗大的三角纹，风格与 C 类的 IM169 出土的陶豆和 IIM60 出土的单耳罐的纹样

---

① Pan, Ling, Summary of Xiongnu Sites in Northern China, in Ursula Brossseder and Bryan K. Miller eds., *Xiongnu Archaeology: Multidisciplinary Perspectives of the First Steppe Empire in Inner Asia*, Vor- und Frühgeschichtliche Archäologie Rheinische Friedrich-Wilhelms-Universität Bonn, 2011, p. 465, Fig. 2：11, 12，分别为石质和骨质。

② Davydova, A. V., *Ivolginskiǐ Arkheologicheskiǐ Kompleks*, Tom 1：Ivolginskoe gorodishche, Sankt-Peterburg, 1995, Plate 16：1、2；Plate 53：7；Plate 69：25；Plate 71：5；Plate 96：16；Plate 107：5-7；Plate 157：1、15；Plate 167：9、16，大多为泥质，也有石质和铁质的。

③ Davydova, A. V., *Ivolginskiǐ arkheologicheskiǐ kompleks*, Tom 2：Ivolginskiǐ mogil'nik, Sankt-Peterburg, 1996, Plate 31：26；43：5-7；45：1-3；73：69、74，均为泥质。

④ Miniaev, S. S., *Dyrestuǐskiǐ mogil'nik*, Sankt-Peterburg: Evropeiskiǐ dom, 1998, Plate 36：1、2；88：3、4；98：2-8；104：15，部分为木质，部分为泥质。

◇❖◇ 第三部分 中国西北和欧亚草原考古

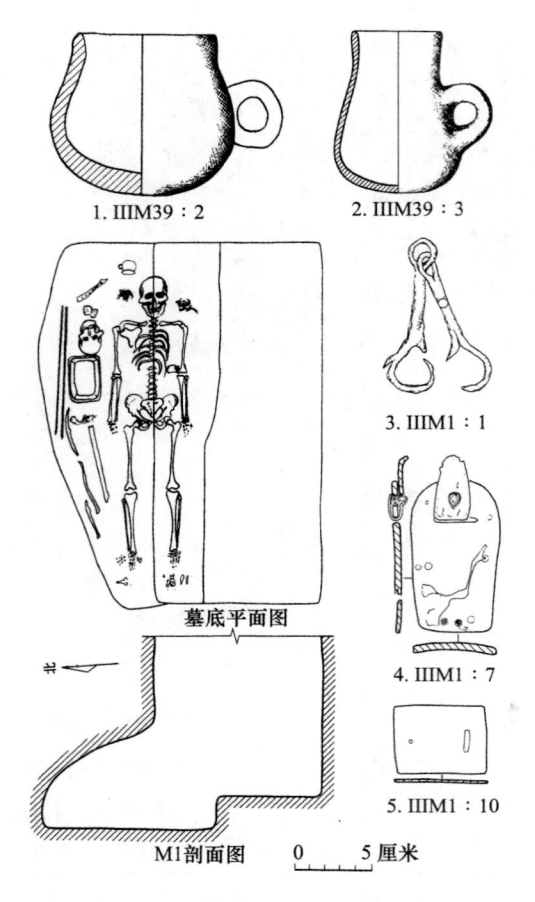

图 3-2-5 洋海墓地第三期墓葬和随葬品

1. ⅢM1：2，2. ⅢM39：2，3. ⅢM1：1，4. ⅢM1：7，5. ⅢM1：10，6. ⅢM39：3（新疆吐鲁番学研究院、新疆文物考古研究所：《新疆鄯善洋海墓地发掘报告》，《考古学报》2011年第1期，图三九，图四〇：1、14，2，图四六：1、3）

接近。它们与焉布拉克文化盛行的内填S纹的彩陶相距甚远，[①] 应晚于焉布拉克文化，应归入第二期。该墓出土的箜篌也与巴泽雷克二号冢出土的同类器（公元前5—前3世纪）相似，[②] 年代也接近，可为佐证。这样归总起来，上述墓葬重新分期如下（表3-2-1）：

[①] 新疆维吾尔自治区文化厅文物处等：《新疆哈密焉布拉克古墓地》，《考古学报》1989年第3期，第341页，图二一。

[②] Rudenko, Sergeĭ I., *Frozen Tombs of Siberia: The Pazyryk Burials of Iron-Age Horsemen*, translated by M. W. Tompson, Berkeley and Los Angeles: University of California Press, 1970, Fig. 146.

表 3-2-1　　　　　　　　　　洋海墓地分期

期别	A、B类	C类	D类
第一期 （焉布拉克）	IM21、IM67、 IM145、IM150、 IM157、IIM284		
第二期 （塔加尔）	IM1、IM5、 IM20、IM90	IM169、IM189、IM195、 IIM14、IIM60、IIM86、 IIM154、IIM202、IIM260、 IIM272、IIM273、IIM2054、 IIM2063、IIIM353、IIIM364	
第三期 （两汉）			IIIM1、IIIM18、IIIM39、IIM243、 IIM2206、IIM2211、IIIM315、 IIIM329、IIIM371、IIIM376

人们在洋海墓地收集了三批头骨材料，其形态特征和测量数据部分接近于欧罗巴人种，部分接近于蒙古人种，说明混血比较严重。[①]

因为地处戈壁，洋海墓地出土了大量的陶器、木器、骨器和皮毛质器物。其中有生火用的取火板，炊食用的陶罐、陶壶、木碗和木盘，纺织用的纺轮，奏乐用的竖琴，驭马用的皮辔、木鞭杆，狩猎用的木弓和木箭、皮射鞲、弓箭袋，装饰用的毛发罩、毛编织带，以及睡觉用的皮枕。此外还有不少服装。死者头戴羊皮帽，额头系彩色毛编织带，两耳戴金或铜耳环，身穿翻领毛大衣和毛织裤，脚穿长腰皮靴。有的死者随葬有栽绒毛毯（IM90、IM189），在红底上有蓝、绿和黄色水波纹，与部分彩陶的纹样相同。到了第三期，部分墓葬（IIIM329、IIIM376）出现了棉衣和棉裙。

洋海墓地出土的金属器很少，三期墓葬的变化明显。第一期墓葬除了铜斧、铜刀，还有铜铃和装饰射鞲和编织带的铜扣；第二期的金属器很少，只有铜马衔、铁马镳（发掘者称带扣）和铜刀，不见铜铃和铜扣；第三期也不多，只有铜牌、铁马衔、金箔和铁刀。因为目前

[①] 王博：《吐鲁番盆地青铜时代居民种族人类学研究》，载解耀华主编：《交河故城保护与研究》，新疆人民出版社 1999 年版，第 392 页。

见到的发掘资料不全,这种变化可能没有普遍性。不过该墓地显然缺乏金属器,这样看来吐鲁番地区的金属资源比较匮乏,可能主要依靠外来产品。

(二) 苏贝希墓地

苏贝希(曾称为苏巴什)村隶属于鄯善县吐峪沟乡,位于火焰山北侧,发源于博格达山的地下水在这里露出地面,形成吐峪沟。苏贝希为维语地名,意为水的源头,指苏贝希是吐峪沟的源头。吐峪沟切断火焰山,流向吐鲁番盆地。1980 年以来新疆考古工作者在该村周围发现了一处居址和三处墓地,其中 II 号墓地的大部分墓葬遭到盗掘;只有居址和 I、III 号墓地经过正式发掘。居址位于村南 3 千米的吐峪沟西侧的台地上。台地呈三角形,长宽约 90 米,面积 4000 余平方米,高出周围的沟床最多 10 米。[①] 由于早年农民挖土积肥和盗掘,遗址破坏严重,地表散落了许多石器、陶器和毛织品碎片。1992 年新疆文物考古研究所和吐鲁番地区博物馆在居址的北面、东南和西南面各开了一个探方,发现了三座房屋和进出台地的三条道路。其中 F1 保存较好,由三个单间构成,长 13.6 米,宽 8.5 米,里面发现了长方形池、圆池和火膛。发掘者认为其中一间用于居住,一间用于圈养牲畜,一间用于制陶,不过房子只发现了磨盘、石杵和一些陶片,证据似乎不足。[②] 所有的器物都出土于表土层,里面有马鞍形石磨盘、石磨棒和石纺轮。陶器可复原的很少,据称器形有釜、罐、钵和杯,常见彩陶多为壶和杯,纹样主要有涡纹和网纹。[③]

I 号墓地位于居址以北 600 米处,西邻山冈,东临吐峪沟,面积

[①] 吕恩国:《苏贝希发掘的主要收获》,载解耀华主编:《交河故城保护与研究》,新疆人民出版社 1999 年版,第 373 页。

[②] 新疆文物考古研究所、吐鲁番地区博物馆:《新疆鄯善县苏贝希遗址及墓地》,《考古》2002 年第 6 期,第 42—57 页。

[③] 吕恩国:《苏贝希发掘的主要收获》,载解耀华主编:《交河故城保护与研究》,新疆人民出版社 1999 年版,第 374—375 页。

3000余平方米。该墓地共发现52座墓葬。1980年新疆博物馆和吐鲁番地区文管所曾发掘8座，1985年该墓地遭到盗掘，50多座墓葬遭到破坏。① 1988年编号为一号，以便与二、三号相区分。1992年新疆文物考古研究所和吐鲁番地区博物馆发掘5座，其余39座全部被盗。墓葬的地表一般都有黑色砾石封堆，长3米，宽2米，高0.2米；墓室形制有竖穴土坑和竖穴偏室两种，竖穴偏室墓是在竖穴墓道的一侧掏挖墓室，埋人后墓室口部用圆木封闭，墓道口部用树枝、芦苇和杂草封闭，上面堆积封土。但是两类墓葬在其他方面差别不大。它们大多东西向，部分墓底放置木床，木床用木头或树枝做框架，上面铺树枝或毛毡做床面，停放1男2女或1男1女，有的时候还有幼儿，均仰身直肢，他们应该是夫妻或者家庭合葬墓。填土中有时再次埋人。此墓地的墓葬在形制和葬俗上与洋海墓地差别较大。②

Ⅲ号墓地位于苏贝希居址西南180米。墓地所在台地宽16米，长40米，地表覆盖了一层长年冲积而成的沙石层，不见遗物，也不见封堆，因此不为人所知，保存完好。1991年冬，吐峪沟乡修建由火焰山南麓的乡政府连接苏贝希村和312国道的道路，沿途开山填壑，因此推出了三座墓葬，吐鲁番地区博物馆随即清理了其中的两座，后来新疆文物考古研究所和吐鲁番地区博物馆联合布方发掘，清理了墓葬30座，将这个墓地发掘完毕。墓葬分布均匀，没有打破和叠压现象。墓葬方向多为东西向。三号墓地只有一座竖穴偏室墓M25，与一号墓地一样，墓室口部栽圆木，外敷芦苇和干草，与Ⅰ号墓口的覆盖物相似。其余29座均为竖穴土坑墓，一般为深达2米的长方形土坑，坑底铺垫细沙，上面放置芦苇捆扎的垫子。墓内往往埋有男女二人，有时还有幼儿，可能也是夫妻或家庭合葬墓。死者仰身屈肢，头前或身侧放置

---

① 吐鲁番地区文管所：《新疆鄯善县苏巴什古墓群的新发现》，《考古》1988年第6期，第502—506页。

② 此段材料来自吐鲁番地区文管所：《新疆鄯善苏巴什古墓葬》，《考古》1984年第1期，第41—50页；新疆文物考古研究所：《鄯善苏贝希墓群一号墓地发掘简报》，《新疆文物》1993年第4期，第1—13页；一号墓地的部分发掘资料再次发表于新疆文物考古研究所、吐鲁番地区博物馆：《新疆鄯善县苏贝希遗址及墓地》，《考古》2002年第6期，第42—57页。

◇❖◇ 第三部分　中国西北和欧亚草原考古

随葬品。墓室内没有填土，墓口搭棚木，上面压草绳捆扎的芦苇，再放一层草垫，顶部用黄泥或石块压实。①

两处墓地在地面设施和葬具上都非常接近，应该属于同一个文化，同一个时期。虽然 III 号墓地的死者头部下面往往有皮枕，但是他们在服装和服饰上与 I 号墓地差异不大。竖穴土坑墓 M11 下层墓主的服装保存较好。与洋海墓地不同的是，男性头戴盔形毡帽；女性梳双辫，分别套黑色的发套，盘绕在头上，用木笄固定或固定在圈形毡托上，头戴尖筒形皮帽。但是其他服装与洋海相似，男性上身穿圆领长袖毛织衣，外套开襟羊皮大衣，下身穿毛织裤，外套过膝长腰毡靴；女性上身同样穿黑色圆领长袖毛织衣，外套开襟长袖羊皮大衣，但是下身穿彩色毛织裙，脚穿短腰皮靴，左手戴一只皮手套，面部盖毛布和羊皮覆面各一块；婴儿裹毛布。所有死者的身上都裹着毛毡。②

发掘者认为两类墓葬代表两个前后延续的两期，竖穴土坑墓在前，竖穴偏室墓在后。这样做是不无道理的，因为两类墓葬的随葬品也存在显著的不同。竖穴土坑墓出土的陶器有单耳壶，有圆腹者，也有平底者，也有绘连续涡纹者。这些器物与甘青地区的卡约文化接近。双耳錾釜和双耳錾钵的耳錾为安装在器物上的横向把手，这种器物与阿尔泰山区巴泽雷克文化墓地的同类器相似。③ 其他器类还有豆、高足杯、钵，它们见于洋海墓地，但不同的是，彩陶较少。竖穴偏室墓器类较少，有双耳釜、单耳罐、单耳杯和钵，它们的环耳都在腹部，这些特征都与洋海墓地相同。此外，这类墓葬还有带流罐，器形与察吾呼文化相同，但

---

① 新疆文物考古研究所、吐鲁番地区博物馆：《鄯善县苏贝希墓群三号墓地》，《新疆文物》1994 年第 2 期，第 1—20、32 页。

② 新疆文物考古研究所、吐鲁番地区博物馆：《新疆鄯善县苏贝希遗址及墓地》，《考古》2002 年第 6 期，第 53—54 页；新疆文物考古研究所、吐鲁番地区博物馆：《鄯善县苏贝希墓群三号墓地》，《新疆文物》1994 年第 2 期，第 2、7、9 页。

③ Kiriushin, Iu. F., N. F. Stepanova, and A. A. Tishkin, *Skifskaia Èpokha Gornogo Altaia*, Chast' II, Pogrebal'no-pominal'nye kompleksy pazyrykskoĭ kul'tury, Barnaul: Press of Altai State University, 2003, Fig. 26:12; Fig. 196:1; Fig. 51:4.

是没有彩绘。①

如此看来，竖穴土坑墓和竖穴偏室墓确实代表了两期，分别相当于中原的东周和西汉时期。经与洋海墓地的陶器资料比较，可知二者分别对应后者的 C 类和 D 类，也就是第二、三期。发掘者采集了 4 座墓葬的木头做了年代测定，经树轮校正后，IM8、IM13、IIIM15（第二期）的年代分别为 3335±145BP、2420±90BP、2520±95BP 和 2285±90BP，前者明显偏老，后三者接近真实年代，本期年代应该是公元前 5—前 3 世纪。IM3（第三期）的年代为 2220±85BP，大体相当于西汉。发掘者认为两期都属于苏贝希文化，都是姑师人留下的遗存。② 从上述分析来看，两期的文化面貌有延续性，但是二者在服饰、发饰和随葬品方面存在很大的差别，这种差别是风格的变化还是人群的差异造成的，目前还难以判断，两期是否属于同一文化也不好确定。

除了上述的陶器和服装，苏贝希两处墓地的其他物质文化与洋海墓地接近。这里也出土了日常生活所用的取火板、木碗、化妆棒和角梳，狩猎用的弓箭和弓箭袋。不过苏贝希墓地的有机质遗物保存更好，出土了洋海墓地所没有的皮鞍以及女性面部所盖的羊皮和毛布。同时，两处墓地的人种构成也非常接近。苏贝希墓地出土的金属器也很少。这固然与墓地被盗有关，恐怕本来就少。除了第二期的两件铜耳环和铜镜；第三期除了铜兽首、铜觿和铜牌各一件，其他都是铁器。这反映了当时铁开始普及，已经取代铜来生产刀、扣、马衔和带钩等传统铜质产品。

---

① 此段材料来自吐鲁番地区文管所：《新疆鄯善苏巴什古墓葬》，《考古》1984 年第 1 期，第 43 页，图 4；新疆文物考古研究所、吐鲁番地区博物馆：《鄯善县苏贝希墓群三号墓地》，《新疆文物》1994 年第 2 期，第 1—20、32 页；III 号墓地的部分资料再次发表于新疆文物考古研究所、吐鲁番地区博物馆：《新疆鄯善县苏贝希遗址及墓地》，《考古》2002 年第 6 期，第 54 页，图一八。

② 吐鲁番地区文管所：《新疆鄯善苏巴什古墓葬》，《考古》1984 年第 1 期，第 49—50 页；新疆文物考古研究所：《鄯善苏贝希墓群一号墓地发掘简报》，《新疆文物》1993 年第 4 期，第 12 页；新疆文物考古研究所、吐鲁番地区博物馆：《鄯善县苏贝希墓群三号墓地》，《新疆文物》1994 年第 2 期，第 20 页；新疆文物考古研究所、吐鲁番地区博物馆：《新疆鄯善县苏贝希遗址及墓地》，《考古》2002 年第 6 期，第 57 页；吕恩国：《苏贝希发掘的主要收获》，载解耀华主编：《交河故城保护与研究》，新疆人民出版社 1999 年版，第 384 页。

苏贝希两处墓地出土的19具头骨通过人类学观察与测量，13具接近大欧洲人种（分属原始欧洲、地中海和中亚两河三个类型），3具接近蒙古人种（东北亚、南亚类型），3具属于混合人种。其中三号墓地M17出土了4具头骨，其中2具为欧洲人种，1具蒙古人种，1具混合人种。因此如果同墓出土的4人属于同一家庭，那么它们构成了一个混血家庭。①

（三）胜金店墓地

胜金店墓地位于火焰山北侧的山坡上，胜金乡胜金店村南，西距吐鲁番市40千米。由于墓葬表面覆盖了很厚的淤积层，地表没有任何迹象，因此没有遭受盗掘。在配合312国道复线工程建设的考古调查中，新疆的考古工作者发现了这个墓地。2006年5月新疆文物考古研究所在公路北侧做了一次发掘，2007年修路时，挖掘机在公路南侧的山坡上取土时，挖出了人骨和器物。同年10月，吐鲁番学研究院考古研究所在此发掘了26座墓葬。2008年4月又发掘了5座墓葬。两次共发掘墓葬31座。现存墓地呈椭圆形，南北长42米，东西宽23米。墓葬分布均匀，间隔3—8米，排列有序，没有打破、叠压现象。少量成人墓旁有儿童祔葬墓。

墓葬形制有三类，相当于洋海墓地的B、C、D类。B类为竖穴土坑二层台墓，墓室两侧有二层台，上面有圆木或厚木板搭成的棚顶，上面覆盖毛毡或芦苇编成的席子，其上再覆盖枸杞、芦苇、糜子、香蒲、麦的茎秆。最后用黏土压实，将墓口封严。C类为长方形竖穴土坑墓，没有二层台，但是墓口搭建有类似于B类的覆盖物。D类为竖穴偏室墓，墓室以成排的木梁封闭，上面再覆盖毛毡或草席，其上再覆盖植物茎秆。墓口以同样的方式再次封闭。三类墓葬均有木床，床上还有用柳枝和皮条捆扎而成的拱形床罩（图3-2-6）。②

---

① 陈靓：《苏贝希出土人骨的人种学考察及相关问题》，载解耀华主编：《交河故城保护与研究》，新疆人民出版社1999年版，第397—399、402—403页。
② 吐鲁番学研究院：《新疆吐鲁番市胜金店墓地发掘简报》，《考古》2013年第2期，第29—31页。

图 3-2-6 胜金店 B 类墓葬（M9）：木床、棚盖

（吐鲁番学研究院：《新疆吐鲁番市胜金店墓地发掘简报》，《考古》2013 年第 2 期，图六）

上述墓葬中，B 类报道了 M9 和 M13 两座；C 类报道了 M3 和 M29 两座；D 类报道了 M2 和 M20 两座。[①] 发掘者认为这些墓葬都属于苏贝希文化，而苏贝希文化延续时间很长，上达青铜时代，下至西汉。尽管它们的形制有些变化，但是发掘者认为整个墓地都属于西汉时期，碳十四测年数据 2200—2050 年可为佐证；同时发掘者推测墓主是姑师人。[②] 可以看到，这些墓葬的器物组合为单耳杯、双耳罐、钵和木盘，而且单耳杯和双耳罐的耳鋬都位于中腹，与洋海墓地的第三期墓葬相同。有些陶器虽然也施红色陶衣，但是都是素面，没有彩绘，也和洋海墓地的第三期相同。

由于气候干燥，尽管墓地曾经遭受洪水，但胜金店墓地仍然出土

[①] 吐鲁番学研究院：《新疆吐鲁番市胜金店墓地发掘简报》，《考古》2013 年第 2 期，第 29—55 页；吐鲁番学研究院：《新疆吐鲁番胜金店 2 号墓发掘简报》，《文物》2013 年第 3 期，第 20—24 页。

[②] 吐鲁番学研究院：《新疆吐鲁番市胜金店墓地发掘简报》，《考古》2013 年第 2 期，第 52 页。

了许多木器、骨器、皮革制品和毛织物。与洋海墓地一样，木器中的弓箭是男性墓主的标准装备。有些墓主还随葬石器、玛瑙珠和玻璃珠等装饰品，但是金属器很少。上述墓葬中，M2 和 M9 没有出土金属器。其余四座出土的金属器中，没有铜质工具和武器，只有镜和耳环是铜质的；铁刀较多，见于三座墓葬；原先为铜质器物的带扣现在也用铁来制作。金耳环与洋海一期的不同，上面镶嵌了红玛瑙和绿松石；同时串珠用红玛瑙、绿色和紫色玻璃等各种颜色的材料制作而成。看来本期的居民更加注重颜色的丰富。

（四）三个桥墓地

三个桥墓地位于鄯善县鲁克沁镇三个桥村南约 1.5 千米，鲁克沁绿洲以南的荒漠戈壁上，集中于两个台地上。20 世纪 80 年代后期，该墓地遭到较大规模的盗掘，挖开的墓葬随处可见，人骨、兽骨遍地分布。1990 年新疆文物考古研究所、吐鲁番地区博物馆和鄯善县文化局进行了抢救发掘，编号 36 座墓葬，实际清理 27 座。[①] 其中属于历史时期的墓葬 9 座；属于史前时期的墓葬 18 座，竖穴土坑墓 17 座，竖穴偏室墓 1 座。上述墓葬都是东西向。由于大部分墓葬被盗，死者的葬式、服饰和随葬品都不完整。但是从保存较好的墓葬来看，三个桥墓地的文化内涵与苏贝希墓地十分接近。常见多人葬，女性与儿童合葬者，也有一男三女合葬者；仰身直肢葬有之，侧身屈肢葬也有之。死者头下有皮枕，身穿皮衣、皮靴、皮套，因简报叙述简略，详情不明。从出土的陶器来看，两类墓葬没有差别，都有单耳壶、单耳罐、单耳杯，其中有圜底者，也有平底者；彩陶较少，图案均为变形三角纹和爪纹。单耳杯的耳都在口沿与上腹之间，杯都还有鸡冠鋬。因此两类墓葬都相当于洋海的第二期。其他随葬品与苏贝希文化的其

---

① 最早的简报说有 33 座，但是其中含 6 座殉马坑。见新疆文物考古研究所、新疆大学历史系 88 级考古专业、吐鲁番地区博物馆、鄯善县文化局：《新疆鄯善县三个桥古墓葬的抢救清理发掘》，《新疆文物》1997 年第 2 期，第 1—21 页。部分发掘资料再次发表于新疆文物考古研究所、新疆大学历史系、吐鲁番地区博物馆和鄯善县文化局：《新疆鄯善三个桥墓葬发掘简报》，《文物》2002 年第 6 期，第 46—62 页。

他墓地相似，有木盘、木拐杖、直角木器、骨梳、石化妆棒、砺石。服饰有皮大衣、彩色毛织裙，样式与苏贝希墓地的相同。不过一位墓主（M13）的发饰非常独特，头发向后梳至枕骨分为两股，然后插入两条假辫中，再套上两个辫罩；这种发饰不见于洋海、苏贝希和胜金店墓地。三个桥墓地还随葬羊肉和糜制食品。不过该墓地还有六个殉马和殉驼坑，发掘者认为与史前时期的墓葬相关，若此，那也是该墓地与苏贝希文化其他墓地不同的地方。

（五）艾丁湖墓地

艾丁湖墓地位于吐鲁番艾丁湖公社西北8千米的一片黄土地。1980年，艾丁湖乡团结三队的两名社员发现了这个墓地。由于风蚀严重，所有墓葬的上半部分已经消失，只剩下0.2—0.5米的墓室底部，不少墓葬的随葬品露出地表。新疆维吾尔自治区博物馆和吐鲁番地区文管所发掘了50座已经扰乱的墓葬，另外还采集了陶器60余件和一些铜器、铁器、石器。墓葬全部为竖穴土坑墓，均为单人葬，葬式均为仰身直肢，头均向西。人骨保存不好，而皮质和毛质服装都没有保存下来。陶器器类有壶、单耳罐、盆、钵和杯，有平底者，也有圜底者，彩陶纹样有锯齿纹、涡纹、网纹和变体三角纹。此外还有带有鸡冠鋬的盆和吐鲁番地区少见的三足鼎和盂。发掘者根据墓地出土的马纹铜牌和铜镜，认为该墓地的年代为西汉时期。[①] 但是从墓葬形制、陶器和其他遗物来看，该墓地的年代属于早期铁器时代，与洋海的第二期接近。

（六）喀格恰克墓地

喀格恰克墓地位于托克逊县喀格恰克村内戈壁滩上的一个高岗上。这里一共发现了18座墓葬，1983年4月，该墓地遭到不同程度的破坏，盗掘出土的彩陶、毛织物和皮制品散落在地面上。同年，吐鲁番地区文管所清理了这些墓葬。其中3座已经完全破坏，其余15座墓葬得

[①] 新疆维吾尔自治区博物馆、吐鲁番地区文管所：《新疆吐鲁番艾丁湖古墓葬》，《考古》1982年第4期，第365—372页。

到了清理。2座经过扰乱，13座基本完好。地表没有明显的封堆，墓葬全为竖穴土坑墓，大体东西向。墓室较小而浅，长1.5—2米，宽1—1.2米，深1.2—1.76米。由于墓底潮湿，人骨大多已经腐朽；但是墓室上部干燥，封闭墓口的木棍和苇席保存完好。其上原先有封土，后因木棍和苇席腐朽塌入墓室。其布局与苏贝希Ⅲ号墓地相同。因地面被破坏，墓上情况不明。陶器器类有单耳壶、单耳罐、杯、钵和盆，彩陶纹样有网纹、平行线、涡纹和三角纹。这些特征与苏贝希墓地一致，但彩陶更为丰富，约占陶器的一半左右。不过该墓地出土的陶质明器和木俑，是其他墓地所不见的。发掘者认为该墓地相当于苏贝希墓地的早期，即洋海墓地的第二期。发掘者采集了一个木棍样品，得到的碳十四年代为2715±120年（经树轮校正），可为佐证。同时，发掘者提出该墓地属于姑师王国。[①] 该墓地不见铁器，也不见青铜器。

（七）英亚依拉克墓地

英亚依拉克墓地位于托克逊县托台区喀格恰克村同名居民点，坐落在山前戈壁的一个高岗上。这里大约有30座墓葬，1983年有人盗掘墓葬，将彩陶片、毛织品和皮制品碎块抛撒遍地，吐鲁番地区文管所随即收集了墓葬周围的出土器物，加以编号。墓地地表有卵石封堆，高0.2—0.4米，直径约2米。墓葬均为竖穴土坑墓，南北向，墓口也用木棍和苇席封闭，然后堆置卵石。墓地采集的陶器有彩陶单耳壶和素陶单耳罐，从器形和彩陶纹样来看，与洋海第二期接近。发掘者认为该墓地属于春秋—战国时期的姑师文化。他们采集了一个木棍样品，得到的碳十四年代为2000±95（经树轮校正），稍微偏晚。[②]

（八）交河沟西墓地

交河沟西墓地位于交河故城西南，隔阿斯喀瓦孜河与之相望，西南以

[①] 吐鲁番地区文管所：《新疆托克逊县喀格恰克古墓群》，《考古》1987年第7期，第597—603页。

[②] 吐鲁番地区文管所：《新疆托克逊县英亚依拉克古墓群调查》，《考古》1985年第5期，第478—479页。

伊什果勒沟与盐山毗邻，东南为雅尔乃孜沟。台地本身为第四纪黄土，西北高而东南低，全长5300米，宽1000米。这里已经发现了细石器、史前时期、车师王国时期和高昌王国与唐代西州时期的家族茔院。1902—1921年日本大谷光瑞调查团曾经来到交河故城及其附近，但是没有发掘沟西台地的墓葬。1928年，黄文弼作为中瑞西北科学考察团成员在沟西台地做了发掘，但是他的工作集中在高昌至西州时期的家族茔院。1956年，新疆首届考古专业人员训练班在沟西台地实习，发掘了高昌王国和西州时期的家族茔园，但是也没有接触史前时期的墓葬。①

史前时期的墓葬位于沟西台地的东南端。1996年，新疆文物考古研究所与早稻田大学合作在这里发掘了23座墓葬，有竖穴土坑和竖穴偏室两种，前者15座，后者8座。这批墓葬的上半部分早年被人取土挖去1米左右厚的土层，原先是否存在封堆不得而知；残存的墓室较浅，大多深度不足1米。墓葬大多东西向。由于靠近水源，此墓地的有机质遗物都保存不好，仅部分墓葬保存有木床；值得注意的是，部分墓葬还有木棺和苇席。从M7出土的6根木棍来看，墓口原先封闭。竖穴偏室墓的墓室有用土坯封闭的。人骨保存不好，多单人葬，也有多人合葬，大多仰身直肢。部分墓葬随葬马头。②

部分墓葬空无一物，部分墓葬的随葬陶器残破，看不出形态特征。但是其他墓葬，无论是竖穴土坑墓还是竖穴偏室墓，出土的陶器均为红陶或灰陶，器胎厚，而且没有彩陶。其中单耳罐和盆很常见，也很有特征。单耳罐侈口，球形腹，单耳位于腹部；盆圜底或近平底。此外还有陶单耳杯，平底直腹。与洋海墓地的第三期和苏贝希的晚期接近。M16出土器物比较丰富，其中有装饰五星纹的单耳罐，三翼铁镞、牛头纹和马头纹金牌以及五铢钱，比较特殊。发掘者采集了三个木头样品，得到了三个碳十四年代数据，其中一个明显偏晚，其他两个分别为公元82—237年和公元85—241年，因此他们认为这批

---

① 新疆文物考古研究所：《交河沟西：1994—1996年度考古发掘报告》，新疆人民出版社2001年版，第2—3页。

② 新疆文物考古研究所：《交河沟西：1994—1996年度考古发掘报告》，新疆人民出版社2001年版，第1—41页。

墓葬的年代为两汉至魏晋时期。① 这批墓葬出土的五铢钱和星云纹铜镜为西汉时期的遗物，墓葬的年代应为两汉时期。

（九）阿拉沟墓地

阿拉沟是天山山脉里的一条山沟，介于托克逊县、乌鲁木齐市和静县之间，行政上属于乌鲁木齐市南山矿区。在南疆铁路阿拉沟工区的基建工程中，人们发现了大片古代墓葬。1976—1978年，新疆维吾尔自治区博物馆考古队在阿拉沟东口、鱼儿沟车站发掘了85座墓葬，其中竖穴石室墓71座，墓室用卵石砌成，墓口多数有盖木。其中有合葬，埋葬十几人到二三十人不等，随葬彩陶和木器较多；也有木棺葬，随葬彩陶较少。竖穴木椁墓7座，规模比较大，有封堆，周围有石围，墓室埋葬一二人，仰身直肢。② 发掘者发表了其中的4座竖穴木椁墓，由于铁路施工，墓葬封土已经遭到破坏。从残留痕迹来看，原来地表都有封堆。其中M30的封堆圆形直径5.5米，高0.5米，四周还有卵石砌成的矩形围墙，长14.5米，宽11米。墓室均为长方形竖穴，基本为东西向，长3.2米，宽1.6米，深6.1米。墓室底部铺黄土和薄木板，再用松木垒砌木椁四壁和顶部，上面再覆盖薄木板和草，然后依次填塞巨石、卵石、细沙和黄土。死者仰身直肢，头骨和肋骨还涂抹朱红色。这些墓葬出土了铜器、陶器、漆器、木盆和兽骨。其中陶杯敛口折沿，腹部有单耳；盆同样敛口折沿，圜底；单耳杯带流，腹部有单耳。二者的形态与洋海墓地的第三期相似。发掘者曾采集两个木头样品，得到了碳十四年代2345±75和2040±95，因此定为战国到西汉时期，并认为跟塞种有关。不过这些墓葬规格高，随葬品丰富，包含狮纹、虎纹金牌、银器、漆器和方座铜盘（图3-2-7），因此墓主应该是本地贵族。③

---

① 新疆文物考古研究所：《交河沟西：1994—1996年度考古发掘报告》，新疆人民出版社2001年版，第43页。

② 王博：《吐鲁番盆地青铜时代居民种族人类学研究》，载解耀华主编：《交河故城保护与研究》，新疆人民出版社1999年版，第388页。

③ 新疆社会科学院考古研究所：《新疆阿拉沟竖穴木椁墓发掘简报》，《文物》1981年第1期，第15—22页。

图 3-2-7 阿拉沟 M30 出土的金属器

（新疆社会科学院考古研究所：《新疆阿拉沟竖穴木椁墓发掘简报》，《文物》1981年第1期，图版捌：3、4、7）

1986年，在阿拉沟河谷西岸进行建筑施工时，人们破坏了三座墓葬。吐鲁番地区文管所做了清理，但是墓葬已经彻底遭到破坏，陶片和骨骼散落遍地。这些墓葬与上述四座相似，均为竖穴土坑木椁墓，基本为东西向。其中一座为儿童墓，其他两座为成人墓，一座长3.4米，宽1.4米，深1.95米。墓室内用直径15—20厘米的圆木砌筑木椁，上面用大石头覆盖，但是其他情况就不清楚了。由于墓室已经被扰，出土器物无法按墓编号，金属器也非常稀少。出土的陶器有单耳壶、单耳罐、单耳钵，有平底者，也有圜底者；环耳位于单耳壶的腹部，单耳罐的口沿。其中有些彩陶，绘三角纹和变体三角纹。发掘者认为这批墓葬的年代为战国—西汉时期，不过这些特征都与洋海墓地第三期接近，年代与之相差不大。这里出土的单耳尖底罐和单耳彩陶罐比较特别。[1]

---

[1] 吐鲁番地区文管所：《阿拉沟竖穴木棺墓清理简报》，《新疆文物》1991年第2期，第18—20页。

阿拉沟墓地出土的58个头骨，49个属于欧洲人种，7个属于蒙古人种，2个属于混合人种。① 其中M1出土的9个头骨中，欧洲人种6个（原始欧洲、中亚两河类型），蒙古人种2个，混合人种1个；M21出土的17个头骨中，欧洲人种15个（地中海、原始欧洲和中亚两河类型），蒙古人种2个；M3出土的8个头骨中，欧洲人种7个，蒙古人种1个。这些都说明阿拉沟的古代居民不仅混有不同人种，而且混有不同亚种。②

（十）交河沟北一号台地墓地

在交河故城的西北方和西南方有四个台地，现在编号为一号至四号，一号台地位于西北方，南北长350米，东西宽35—370米，台地本身为第四纪黄土，表面有一层砂砾和细砂；东西两侧为河床和农田，北侧与天山山前宽阔的戈壁滩相连。1994年，在中国、日本和联合国教科文组织联合组织的保护维修交河故城工程中，新疆文物考古所发掘了一号台地，在此发现了史前时期和历史时期的墓葬。其中经过发掘的史前时期遗迹有55座墓葬以及73座殉马坑。③

一号台地的墓葬习俗与上述墓地有些不同。墓地中央为一座大型墓葬，其地表有石块封堆，其周围有大量的附葬墓和殉马坑。发掘者清理了两座封堆墓M1和M16，以及一座封堆周围的墓葬（图3-2-8）。M1的封堆为环形，直径15—20米；封堆下面有一个土坯围墙，直径10.3米，原始高度应该在1.6米左右。围墙以内有一座偏室墓和一座殉马（驼）坑，以外有15座墓葬和23座殉马（驼）坑。M16的封堆也为环形，直径26米；封堆下面同样有土坯围墙，直径10.2—10.9米，宽约0.26米，最高0.8米。围墙里面有两座墓葬，外面有9座墓葬和25座殉马（驼）坑。少数墓葬（M16的中心墓葬）的墓口周围也用土坯砌了围

---

① 王博：《吐鲁番盆地青铜时代居民种族人类学研究》，载解耀华主编：《交河故城保护与研究》，新疆人民出版社1999年版，第388—390页。
② 王博：《吐鲁番盆地青铜时代居民种族人类学研究》，载解耀华主编：《交河故城保护与研究》，新疆人民出版社1999年版，第394—395页。
③ 本部分材料来自联合国教科文组织驻中国代表处、新疆文物事业管理局、新疆文物考古研究所：《交河故城——1993、1994年度考古发掘报告》，东方出版社1998年版，第15—74页。

墙；墓室里面或附近往往有一个殉马或殉驼坑，一个殉马坑埋葬一匹或两匹整马；M16 的围墙北侧有两排 18 座这样的殉马或殉驼坑，应该是对应中心墓葬的。同时，M1 和 M16 的中心墓葬远远大于周围的墓葬，其周围又有土坯围墙。而且 M16 也是出土金属器最多的墓葬。因此它们的地位显然高于后者。在另外一座封堆的周围发掘了 28 座墓葬和 23 座殉马（驼）坑。与吐鲁番地区同时期的其他墓地相比，交河沟北一号台地墓地的这些特征说明当时的社会已经出现了明显的社会分化。

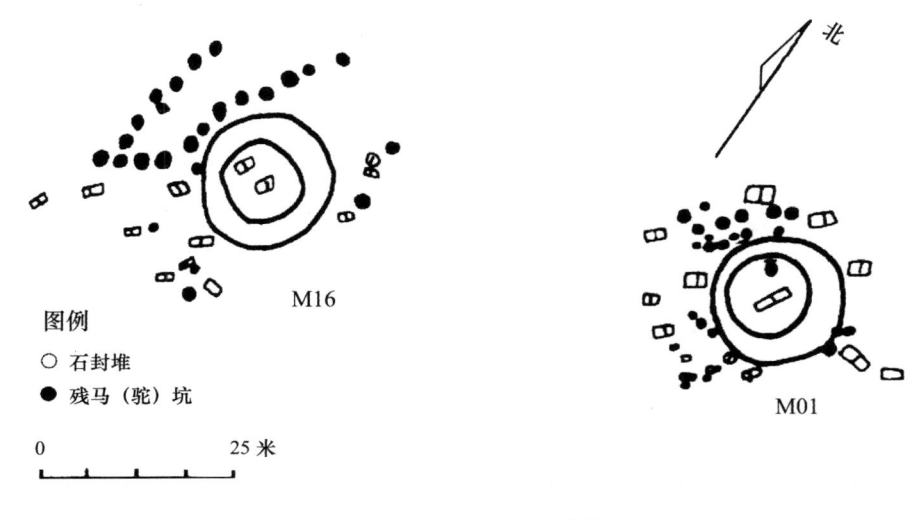

图 3-2-8 交河沟北一号台地墓地平面图

（联合国教科文组织驻中国代表处、新疆文物事业管理局、新疆文物考古研究所：《交河故城——1993、1994 年度考古发掘报告》，东方出版社 1998 年版，图一一）

不过，交河沟北一号台地墓地在其他方面又与上述墓地相同。它们大多东西向，为男女合葬或者加上儿童（可能为家庭合葬）。其中既有竖穴土坑墓，又有竖穴偏室墓。有的墓葬口部用棚木覆盖；偏室墓的口部也用了圆木封闭。墓室底部放置木床或者铺草垫或垫圆木。随葬陶器大多为素面夹砂红陶，主流器类有单耳罐、盆、单耳钵、单耳杯，此外还有双耳罐、单流罐和单耳壶等少数器类。少数陶器为彩陶，绘有三角纹和爪纹。整体而言，这些器类与上述墓地一致。

交河沟北一号台地墓地曾经遭到盗掘，随葬品遗失和破坏都很严重，但是也保存了一些具有时代和文化特色的器物。除了下面将要提到的陶器和骨器，比较突出的有骨、铜、金、银等材质加工成的鹿、牛首、驼、对鸟和鹰等形象，波浪、角、花瓣、锥等形状以及串珠、管、泡、扣等装饰品。其中鹿首圆雕，细致地刻画出了鹿的鼻子、眼睛和双角。其他金属器不多，有两面铜镜和1枚五铢钱，以及鹤嘴斧、马衔、马镳等铁器。木器不少，包括游牧民族常用的箭、盘、弓箭袋、取火板和木盒。木俑为此墓地所独有，系用圆木雕刻出人的头部和五官，然后上敷白色颜料，画出双眼，嘴唇涂红，头顶抹黑色以象征头发。纺织品中除了毛织品，还有绢、罗和棉布。

交河沟北一号台地墓地出土了不少球形腹单耳罐，其单耳位于腹部。同时，一件双耳罐的肩上出现了三圈凸弦纹和凸起的莲花纹。这些器物与交河沟西墓地的年代相近。上述的莲花纹见于伊沃加（Ivolga）城址出土的陶罐和铜镜，此外，这些墓葬还出土了各种桃形骨牌、长方形骨牌、角质弓弭与杜雷斯推墓地（Durestuǐ）、[1] 伊沃加城址[2]与伊沃加墓地、[3] 奥拉特（Orlat）墓地[4]出土的同类器接近，而该墓地出土的鹰搏虎金牌与乌尔本（Urbiun）III[5] 出土的一件铜牌接近，后者都是匈奴时期的遗物

---

[1] Miniaev, S. S., *Dyrestuǐskiǐ mogil'nik*, Sankt-Peterburg, 1998, Plate 5: 6, Plate 29: 11, Plate 98: 2 – 9, Plate 103: 1 – 2, Plate 112: 1 – 4.

[2] Davydova, A. V., *Ivolginskiǐ arkheologicheskiǐ kompleks*, Tom 1: Ivolginskoe gorodishche, Sankt-Petersburg, 1995, Plate 16: 1 – 2, Plate 125: 13.

[3] Davydova, A. V., *Ivolginskiǐ arkheologicheskiǐ kompleks*, Tom 2: Ivolginskiǐ mogil'nik, Sankt-Petersburg, 1996, Plate 15: 9 – 11, Plate 31: 26, 27, Plate 72: 24 – 25.

[4] Ilyasov, J. Y., D. V. Rusanov, A study on the bone plates from Orlat, *Silk Road Art and Archaeology* 5, 1997/1998, pp. 107 – 159, pl. 4 – 5, 转引自 Ursula Brosseder, Belt Plaques as an Indicator of East-West Relations, in Brosseder, Ursula, and Bryan K. Miller eds., *Xiongnu Archaeology: Multidisciplinary Perspectives of the First Steppe Empire in Inner Asia*, Vor- und Frühgeschichtliche Archäologie Rheinische Friedrich-Wilhelms-Universität Bonn, 2011, p. 397, Fig. 46: 35 – 39.

[5] Devlet, M. A., Sibirskie poiasnye azhurnye plastiny II v. do n. e. -I v. n. e. *Arkheologiia SSSR*, *Svod Arkheologicheskikh Istochnikov*, Moscow, 1980, D4 – 7, pl. 29, 117, 转引自 Brosseder, Ursula, Belt Plaques as an Indicator of East-West Relations, in Brosseder, Ursula, and Bryan K. Miller eds., *Xiongnu Archaeology: Multidisciplinary Perspectives of the First Steppe Empire in Inner Asia*, Vor- und Frühgeschichtliche Archäologie Rheinische Friedrich-Wilhelms-Universität Bonn, 2011, p. 380, Fig. 29: 2.

（图3-2-9）。发掘者从 M01 和 M16 分别取了一个木炭样品，其中 M01 的样品年代偏晚，M16 的样品年代为 2154±52，树轮校正年代为 178BC—36AD，因此他们认为一号台地墓地的年代为西汉时期。这个推断似乎可以成立，M01 的一座祔葬墓出土的一枚五铢钱为西汉初铸五铢时的产品，可为佐证。

根据上述分析，我们可以将吐鲁番地区的墓地分为三期（表3-2-2），分别相当于焉布拉克、巴泽雷克和匈奴时期。其中洋海墓地历时三期，苏贝希跨越两期，其他都集中在第二期或第三期。需要指出的是，这三期的文化延续性很强，墓葬均为竖穴土坑和竖穴偏室墓，墓室口部用木棍和苇草覆盖，上面再堆石，有时还要砌石围。墓室东西向，里面放置木床。死者头戴发冠，耳垂耳环，身穿皮毛衣服，足套皮靴，使用取火板生火，弓箭狩猎作战，壶、罐、杯、盘等木器和陶器做饭盛饭。这些现象表明，使用这些墓地的墓主都是游牧民族。但是短剑、矛和战斧很少发现，与米奴辛斯克盆地、图瓦和阿尔泰的同时期游牧民族的埋葬习俗有所不同，其原因可能在于本地缺乏获得金属原料的渠道。

与此同时，三期墓葬的文化面貌发生了很大变化。一期有较多的铜扣、铜铃、铜斧和铜刀；到了第二期，金属器工具和武器减少，只有少量的铜扣、铜刀、马衔和马镳。到了第三期，铁器大量出现，用于制造马衔和刀等实用器物，而金银铜等材质则用来制作装饰品。第二期彩陶较多，到了第三期彩陶减少，只见于若干墓地，而素陶和木器增加，取代了陶器。与此同时，第一、二期盛行毛皮衣服；到了第三期开始出现棉、罗和绢布衣服，它们的出现体现了与中亚和中原的文化联系。

表3-2-2　　　　吐鲁番地区早期铁器时代墓地分期

一期	二期	三期
洋海	洋海	洋海
	苏贝希	苏贝希
	三个桥	
	艾丁湖	

续表

一期	二期	三期
	喀格恰克	
	英亚依拉克	
		胜金店
		阿拉沟
		交河沟西
		交河沟北一号

三 文化联系

在吐鲁番盆地，早于洋海一期的青铜时代和新石器时代遗址还没有发现，因此洋海墓地的早期居民应该是外来的移民。可惜目前已经公布的洋海一期墓葬比较少，供比较研究的陶器没有发表，我们无从讨论。从出土的金属器来看，这些墓葬与哈密地区的焉布拉克文化接近。本期墓葬 IM21 和 IM150 出土的皮靴和马镳头反映了游牧生活，它们不见于焉布拉克文化，也不见于米奴辛斯克盆地，这可能是因为它们是有机物，在哈密和米奴辛斯克保存不下来。因此，洋海墓地的居民究竟来自何处，目前还不清楚。

前面已经提到了洋海二期墓葬与欧亚大陆同时期文化的联系。在米奴辛斯克盆地、图瓦和阿尔泰山区和东哈萨克斯坦，这个时期活跃着斯基泰时期的塔加尔、巴泽雷克、乌尤克文化。前面已经提到，吐鲁番地区的洋海二期墓葬与巴泽雷克文化关系较为密切。巴泽雷克文化分布于俄罗斯和哈萨克斯坦境内的阿尔泰山区，目前我们对于该文化的认识大部分来自于冢墓。最早的发掘可以追溯到 18 世纪的彼得大帝时代，1860 年以后科学的考古发掘大规模展开，其中人们熟悉的"国王/贵族"墓地有巴泽雷克（Pazyryk）、卡汤达（Katanda）、别列伊（Berel'）、希别（Shchibe）、图埃克塔（Tuèkta）、巴沙达尔（Bashadar）、阿卡拉哈（Ak-Alakha）和上卡尔金（Verkh-Kal'dzhin）—II；考古学家还发现了不少低等级墓地如卡因都（Kaĭndu）、特克斯肯（Tytkesken'）—Ⅵ、上耶朗达（Verkh Elanda）—Ⅱ、阔克—耶底干（Kok-Èdigan）、乌朗得克（Ulandryk）—Ⅰ（图3-2-1）。这样看来，其分布范围为俄罗斯和哈萨克斯坦境内的阿尔泰山区。[①] 其年代范围原来推算为公元前5—前3世纪，[②] 后来从阿卡拉哈和上卡尔金大冢的49个原木系列年轮样品和3个马骨样品得到的树轮校正数据的年代范围为415BC—287BC，[③] 支持了前面的推算结果。

前面在讨论各个墓地的年代时，我们引述了巴泽雷克文化的一些器物。为了讨论吐鲁番地区与上述文化之间的联系，下面再讨论几类有关的遗物和葬俗。

（一）葬俗

如上所述，吐鲁番地区洋海二期的史前墓葬普遍有石块或土石混合封堆，它与年代更早的哈密地区天山北路墓地的无封堆墓葬不同，而与阿尔泰山区和山前地带的切木尔切克和巴泽雷克文化的封堆墓接近。同时，仰身直肢和头西脚东的葬俗也再现了巴泽雷克文化的传统。这些显然都是草原地区民族的文化传统，不过，吐鲁番地区的史前墓葬还有石围，与切木尔切克和巴泽雷克文化不同。吐鲁番地区的偏室墓、木床和原木覆盖物也不见于后者。在巴泽雷克文化的墓葬一般随葬陶壶和羊骨，经常随葬铜质和骨质服装装饰品；在大型墓葬中随葬品更为丰富，还有金器和马匹。在吐鲁番地区，金器少见，马匹完全不见。与此同

[①] Kiriushin, Iu. F., N. F. Stepanova, and A. A. Tishkin, *Skifskaia Èpokha Gornogo Altaia*, Chast' Ⅱ, Pogrebal'no-pominal'nye kompleksy pazyrykskoĭ kul'tury, Barnaul: Press of Altai State University, 2003, pp. 8–37.

[②] Griaznov, M. P., Altaĭ i prialtaĭskaia step, in Rybakov, B. A. ed., *Stepnaia Polosa Aziatskoĭ Chasti SSSR v Skifo-sarmatskoe Vremia*, Moscow: Science Press, 1992, pp. 166–169.

[③] Zaifert, M., and I. Iu. Sliusarenko, Dendrokhronologicheskiĭ analiz pazyryskikh pamiatnikov, in Derevianko, A. P., and V. I. Molodin eds., *Fenomen Altaĭskikh Mumiĭ*, Novosibirsk: Press of Institute of Archaeology and Ethnography SORAN, 2000, p. 263; Von Görsdorf, È., and G. Parzinger, Radiouglerodnoe datirovanie loshchadinykh kosteĭ, in Derevianko, A. P., V. I. Molodin eds., *Fenomen Altaĭskikh Mumiĭ*, Novosibirsk: Press of Institute of Archaeology and Ethnography SORAN, 2000, p. 265.

时，巴泽雷克文化墓葬经常出现的鹿石不见于洋海二期的墓葬。[①]

（二）单耳壶

单耳壶是吐鲁番地区早期铁器时代墓地普遍出土的陶器。这种器物瘦长，长颈，微鼓腹，平底或者圜底（图3-2-10：1）。类似的器物大量发现于俄罗斯阿尔泰山区巴泽雷克文化的墓地，见于低等级墓地如卡因都（Kaĭndu）、特克斯肯（Tytkesken'）—VI（图3-2-10：2）、上耶朗达（Verkh Elanda）—II、阔克—耶底干（Kok-Èdigan）、乌朗得克（Ulandryk）—I 和高等级墓地如巴泽雷克和上卡尔金—II。[②] 这些器物有些绘了蝌蚪纹和蛇纹，有些绘了羊角錾和附加堆纹，有时还烧成黑陶。实际上，它们模仿的是同时期的皮质壶和角质壶，后者见于巴泽雷克、阿卡拉哈—III（图3-2-10：3）和上卡尔金—II墓地。[③] 模仿得比较逼真的陶器见于拉孜敦（Razdum'e）—VI号墓地（图3-2-10：4）。[④]

（三）皮枕和毡毯

苏贝希和三个桥墓地因为干燥，有机质遗物保存完好。不少死者

[①] Griaznov, M. P., Altaĭ i prialtaĭskaia step, in Rybakov, B. A. ed., *Stepnaia Polosa Aziatskoĭ Chasti SSSR v Skifo-Sarmatskoe Vremia*, Moscow: Science Press, 1992, pp. 164-165.

[②] Kiriushin, Iu. F., N. F. Stepanova, and A. A. Tishkin, *Skifskaia Èpokha Gornogo Altaia*, Chast' II, Pogrebal'no-pominal'nye kompleksy pazyrykskoĭ kul'tury, Barnaul: Press of Altai State University, 2003, Plate 8：1-6；Plate 9：2, 3, 6-8；Plate 10：1-8；Kiriushin, Iu. F., and N. F. Stepanova, *Skifskaia Èpokha Gornogo Altaia*, Chast' III, Pogrebal'nye kompleksy skifskogo vremeni sredneĭ Katuni, Barnaul: Press of Altai State University, 2004, Fig. 6：1-3, 6-8；Fig. 12：5-7, 8-10；Derevianko, A. P., V. I. Molodin eds., *Fenomen Altaĭskikh Mumiĭ*, Novosibirsk: Press of Institute of Archaeology and Ethnography SORAN, 2000, Fig. 141；Fig. 167；Fig. 169；Rudenko, Sergei I., *Frozen Tombs of Siberia: The Pazyryk Burials of Iron-Age Horsemen*, Berkeley and Los Angeles: University of California Press 1970, Plate 55：A, B, C.

[③] Derevianko, A. P., V. I. Molodin eds., *Fenomen Altaĭskikh Mumiĭ*, Novosibirsk: Press of Institute of Archaeology and Ethnography SORAN, 2000, Fig. 171, Fig. 172, Fig. 173, Fig. 174；Fig. 175；Fig. 185：1-3；Rudenko, Sergei I., *Frozen Tombs of Siberia: The Pazyryk Burials of Iron-Age Horsemen*, Berkeley and Los Angeles: University of California Press, 1970, Plate 152：B；Plate 59：A, B.

[④] Derevianko, A. P., V. I. Molodin eds., *Fenomen Altaĭskikh Mumiĭ*, Novosibirsk: Press of Institute of Archaeology and Ethnography SORAN, 2000, Fig. 187.

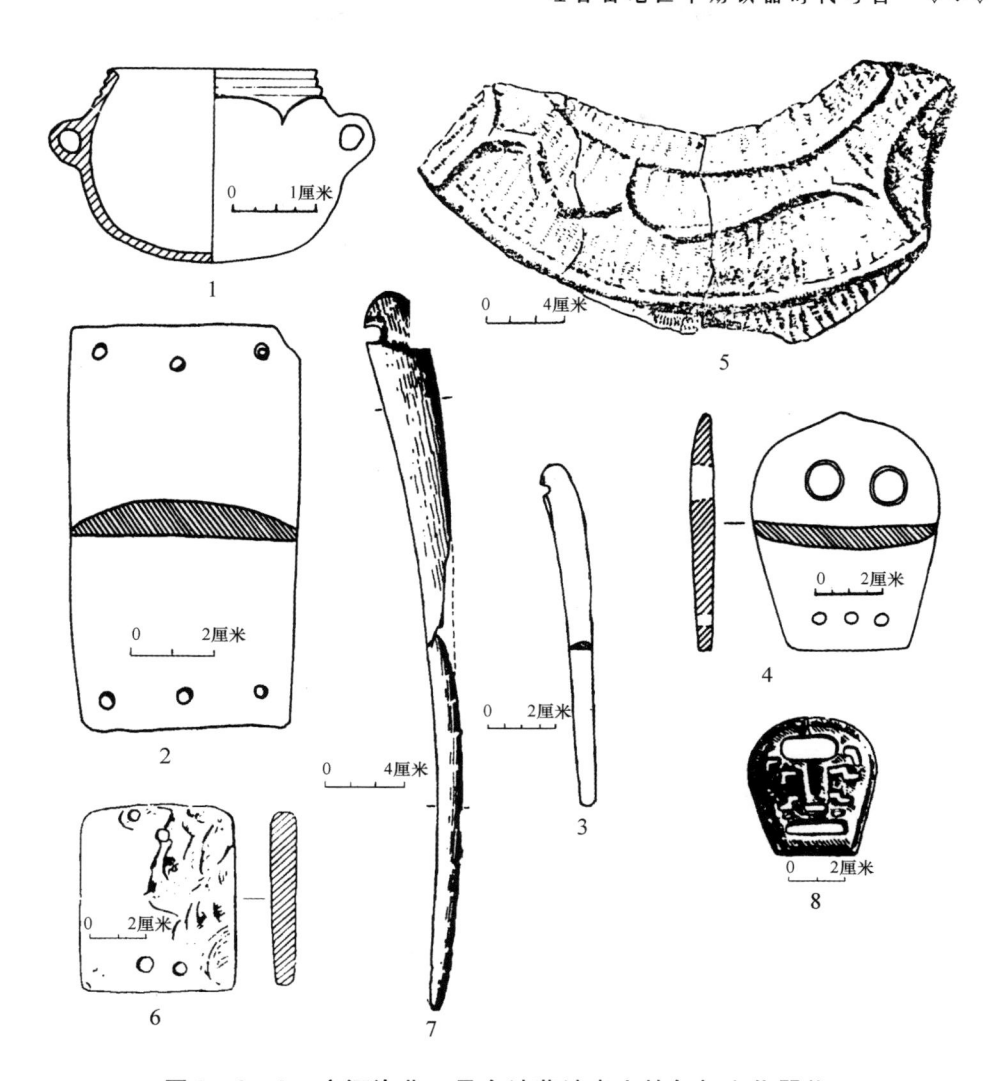

图 3-2-9 交河沟北一号台地墓地出土的匈奴文化器物

1—4，交河沟北一号台地（联合国教科文组织驻中国代表处、新疆文物事业管理局、新疆文物考古研究所：《交河故城——1993、1994 年度考古发掘报告》，东方出版社 1998 年版，图四一：1，图四三：5，图四六：9，图五○：3）

5—8，伊沃加城址（图片来源：Davydova, A. V., 1995, *Ivolginskiĭ Arkheologicheskiĭ Kompleks*, Tom 1: Ivolginskoe Gorodishche, pl. 142：9, pl. 16：2, pl. 125：9, pl. 125：13, Sankt-Peterburg）

第三部分 中国西北和欧亚草原考古

图3-2-10 洋海、特克斯肯—VI、阿卡拉哈—III 和拉孜敦—VI 出土器物比较

1. 洋海（新疆吐鲁番学研究院、新疆文物考古研究所：《新疆鄯善洋海墓地发掘报告》，《考古学报》2011年第1期，图一四：2）；2. 特克斯肯—VI（Kiriushin, Iu. F., N. F. Stepanova, and A. A. Tishkin, *Skifskaia Èpokha Gornogo Altaia*, Chast' II, Pogrebal'no-pominal'nye kompleksy pazyrykskoĭ kul'tury, Barnaul: Press of Altai State University, 2003, Plate 9: 2）；3. 阿卡拉哈—III（Derevianko, A. P., V. I. Molodin eds., *Fenomen Altaĭskikh Mumiĭ*, Novosibirsk: Press of Institute of Archaeology and Ethnography SORAN, 2000, Fig. 184: 6）；4. 拉孜敦—VI（Derevianko, A. P., V. I. Molodin eds., *Fenomen Altaĭskikh Mumiĭ*, Novosibirsk: Press of Institute of Archaeology and Ethnography SORAN, 2000, Fig. 187）

头靠着皮枕，身下铺着毡毯。皮枕用羊皮做成枕套，然后在里面塞碎皮条或干草，放在死者头下（图3-2-11：1）。这种死者头下放枕头的做法不见于同时期的中原和甘青地区，而见于俄罗斯境内的阿尔泰山区。在巴泽雷克墓地的1—5号冢墓出土了木质枕头，呈花生状（图3-2-11：2）。[①] 在阿卡拉哈—III和巴泽雷克墓地，死者头下放了毡枕，里面塞了羊毛，身下也铺了毡毯（图3-2-11：3）。[②] 看来，阿尔泰山区和吐鲁番盆地的早期铁器时代的居民共同拥有一些埋葬习俗。

[①] Rudenko, Sergei I., *Frozen Tombs of Siberia: The Pazyryk Burials of Iron-Age Horsemen*, Berkeley and Los Angeles: University of California Press, 1970, Plate 53: A, B, C.

[②] Derevianko, A. P., V. I. Molodin eds., *Fenomen Altaĭskikh Mumiĭ*, Novosibirsk: Press of Institute of Archaeology and Ethnography SORAN, 2000, p. 72; Rudenko, Sergei I., *Frozen Tombs of Siberia: The Pazyryk Burials of Iron-Age Horsemen*, Berkeley and Los Angeles: University of California Press, 1970, Plate 56.

吐鲁番地区早期铁器时代考古

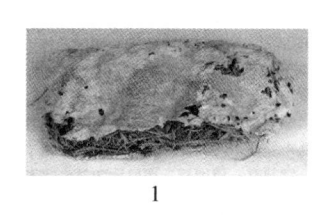

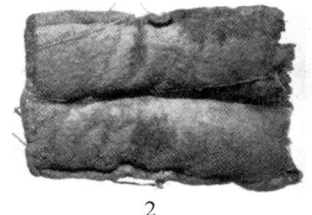

1　　　　　　　　　　　2　　　　　　　　　　　3

图 3-2-11　苏贝希、巴泽雷克和阿卡拉哈—Ⅲ 墓地出土的皮枕

1. 苏贝希墓地（吐鲁番学研究院：《新疆吐鲁番市胜金店墓地发掘简报》,《考古》2013 年第 2 期,图三七）；2. 巴泽雷克墓地（Rudenko, Sergei I., *Frozen Tombs of Siberia*: *The Pazryryk Burials of Iron-Age Horsemen*, Berkeley and Los Angeles: University of California Press, 1970, Plate 53：A, B, C）；3. 阿卡拉哈—Ⅲ 墓地（Derevianko, A. P., V. I. Molodin eds., *Fenomen Altaĭskikh Mumiĭ*, Novosibirsk: Press of Institute of Archaeology and Ethnography SORAN, 2000, p. 72）

（四）发饰

苏贝希墓地的墓主的发饰保存完好。男性头戴盔形毡帽；女性梳双辫，盘绕在头上，外套黑色的发网，头上再戴圆锥形毡筒，外面同样套黑色的发网（图 3-2-12：2）。① 这种女性的发辫外套发网和头顶尖筒形皮帽的做法也见于巴泽雷克墓地女性发饰上，只是后者的头发分两髻，但是同样把头发固定在一个圈形的毡托上，头上再竖立圆锥形毡筒（图 3-2-12：1）。②

（五）服装

洋海和苏贝希墓地都出土有毛质和皮质服装。其中苏贝希墓地出土的一件比较完整，黄色，圆领，对襟开，筒形袖，袖很宽很长，下摆外张（图 3-2-13：1）。同类的上衣发现于俄罗斯阿尔泰山区的阿卡拉哈—Ⅲ 墓地 1 号冢（女性）（图 3-2-13：2）和巴泽雷克墓地 2 号冢（男性），

---

① 新疆文物考古研究所、吐鲁番地区博物馆：《新疆鄯善县苏贝希遗址及墓地》,《考古》2002 年第 6 期,第 53—54 页；新疆文物考古研究所、吐鲁番地区博物馆：《鄯善县苏贝希墓群三号墓地》,《新疆文物》1994 年第 2 期,第 2、7、9 页。

② Derevianko, A. P., V. I. Molodin eds., *Fenomen Altaĭskikh Mumiĭ*, Novosibirsk: Press of Institute of Archaeology and Ethnography SORAN, 2000, Fig. 77, Fig. 80.

◇❖◇ 第三部分　中国西北和欧亚草原考古

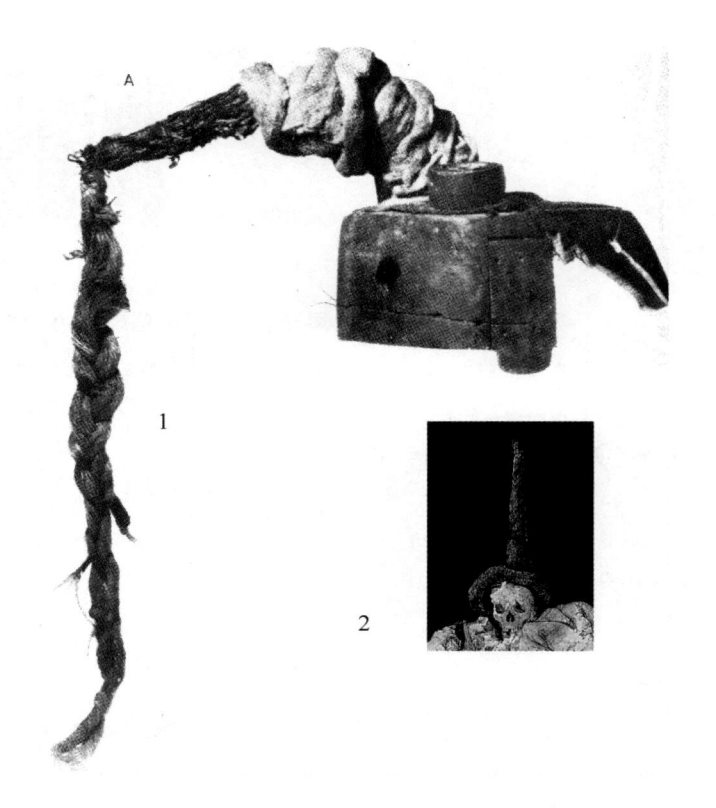

图 3-2-12　巴泽雷克和苏贝希墓地出土的发饰

1. 巴泽雷克墓地（Rudenko, Sergei I., *Frozen Tombs of Siberia*: *The Pazryryk Burials of Iron-Age Horsemen*, Berkeley and Los Angeles: University of California Press, 1970, Plate 66: A）；2. 苏贝希墓地（新疆文物考古研究所、吐鲁番地区博物馆：《新疆鄯善县苏贝希遗址及墓地》，《考古》2002 年第 6 期，图版伍: 1）

袖长及手指，只是后者为棉布制成，领口为圆领，下摆大开（图 3-2-13: 3）。[①] 这种上衣是古代和中世纪的许多民族都流行的款式。在阿尔泰山区的巴泽雷克文化墓葬中，毛织品虽然不如丝织品珍惜，但也是昂贵的材料。[②]

[①] Derevianko, A. P., V. I. Molodin eds., *Fenomen Altaĭskikh Mumiĭ*. Novosibirsk: Press of Institute of Archaeology and Ethnography SORAN, 2000, Fig. 67-68; Rudenko, Sergei I., *Frozen Tombs of Siberia*: *The Pazryryk Burials of Iron-Age Horsemen*, Berkeley and Los Angeles: University of California Press, 1970, Plate 63.

[②] Derevianko, A. P., V. I. Molodin eds., 2000, *Fenomen Altaĭskikh Mumiĭ*, p. 74. Novosibirsk: Press of Institute of Archaeology and Ethnography SORAN.

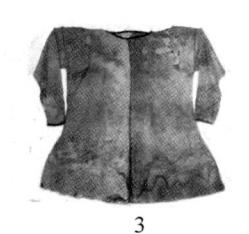

图 3-2-13 苏贝希、阿卡拉哈—III 和巴泽雷克墓地出土的服装

1. 苏贝希墓地（新疆维吾尔自治区文物事业管理局等主编：《新疆文物古迹大观》，新疆美术摄影出版社 1999 年版，图版 03042）；2. 阿卡拉哈—III 墓地 1 号冢（Derevianko, A. P., V. I. Molodin eds., *Fenomen Altaĭskikh Mumiĭ*, Novosibirsk: Press of Institute of Archaeology and Ethnography SORAN, 2000, Fig. 67—68）；3. 巴泽雷克墓地（Rudenko, Sergei I., *Frozen Tombs of Siberia: The Pazryryk Burials of Iron-Age Horsemen*, Berkeley and Los Angeles: University of California Press, 1970, Plate 63）

（六）毡袜

洋海和苏贝希墓地还出土了各种低腰和高腰靴。在洋海，两者都是用牛皮做底，用羊皮做帮。① 在苏贝希，低腰靴出土在女性死者的右脚；高腰靴出土在男性死者左脚上，靴帮高至腿根，用皮绳系在腰带上，以防止靴帮滑落。二者都是外面包皮，底部和腰部衬毡（图 3-2-14：1）。② 这种高腰靴也发现于阿卡拉哈—III 墓地 1 号冢（图 3-2-14：2）和巴泽雷克墓地 2 号冢，不过后者帮口贴了红色毡片云纹，靴底和靴帮也贴了红色毡片。而这种高腰靴常见于巴泽雷克文化的男女墓葬中，在男性死者身上，高腰靴套在裤子外面；在女性死者身上，高腰靴穿在裙子下面，也都用皮绳拴系在腰带上（图 3-2-14：3）。③

诚然，洋海二期遗存与巴泽雷克文化的共同特征远不止于此。类似的还有弓箭、马筇、马嚼和马镳。这些器物涵盖了饮食器皿、服装和兵

---

① 新疆吐鲁番学研究院、新疆文物考古研究所：《新疆鄯善洋海墓地发掘报告》，《考古学报》2011 年第 1 期，图八：3，4；图一〇：9，10；图二〇：12，13；图二四：6。
② 新疆文物考古研究所：《鄯善苏贝希墓群一号墓地发掘简报》，《新疆文物》1993 年第 4 期，第 7—8 页，图 4：1，3。
③ Derevianko, A. P., V. I. Molodin eds., *Fenomen Altaĭskikh Mumiĭ*, Novosibirsk: Press of Institute of Archaeology and Ethnography SORAN, 2000, Fig. 74.

◇❖◇ 第三部分 中国西北和欧亚草原考古

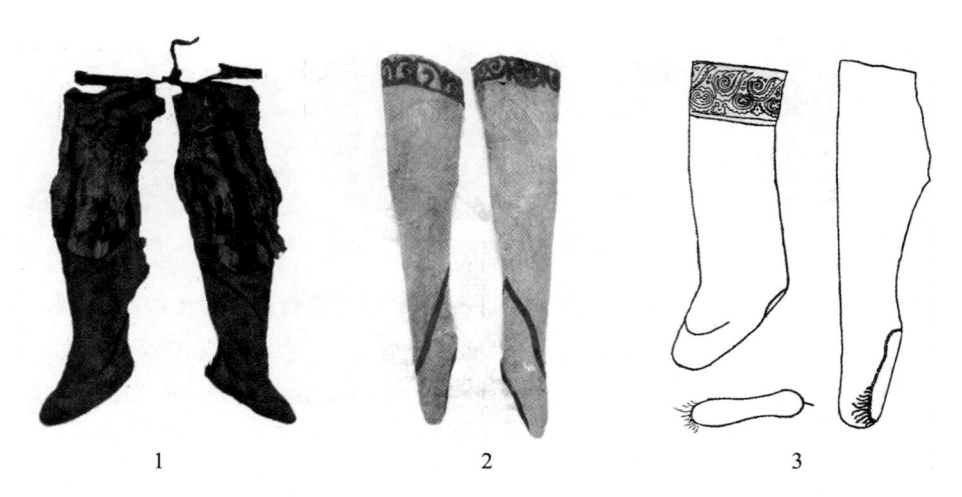

图 3-2-14 苏贝希、阿卡拉哈—Ⅲ、巴泽雷克墓地出土的毡靴

1. 苏贝希墓地（新疆文物考古研究所、吐鲁番地区博物馆：《新疆鄯善县苏贝希遗址及墓地》，《考古》2002 年第 6 期，图版肆：2）；2. 阿卡拉哈-Ⅲ墓地 1 号冢（Derevianko, A. P., V. I. Molodin eds., *Fenomen Altaĭskikh Mumiĭ*, Novosibirsk: Press of Institute of Archaeology and Ethnography SORAN, 2000, Fig. 74）；3. 巴泽雷克墓地 2 号冢（Rudenko, Sergei I., *Frozen Tombs of Siberia: The Pazryryk Burials of Iron-Age Horsemen*, Berkeley and Los Angeles: University of California Press, 1970, p. 88, Fig. 31）

器，充分说明本地的居民过着游牧生活。至于这些居民是否来自巴泽雷克和匈奴文化，它们还不足以说明问题。吐鲁番地区与巴泽雷克的陶器群不同，彩陶图案也迥然相异。但是因为游牧民族善于吸收其他文化，所以这并不能排除吐鲁番地区的古代居民来自阿尔泰山区、蒙古和外贝加尔的可能性。从洋海、苏贝希和阿拉沟的人骨材料来看，吐鲁番地区的古代居民由欧洲人种、蒙古人种和二者的混血人种构成，以欧洲人种为主流；而阿尔泰山区的巴泽雷克文化的居民同样包括欧罗巴人种和欧罗巴—蒙古人种的混血。二者的人种构成颇为接近，[1] 说明洋海二期的居民，或者部分，可能是从阿尔泰山区迁徙而来的。

---

[1] Rudenko, Sergei I., *Frozen Tombs of Siberia: The Pazryryk Burials of Iron-Age Horsemen*, Berkeley and Los Angeles: University of California Press, 1970, p. 52; Chikisheva, T. A., Antropologicheskaia kharakteristika mumii, in Derevianko, A. P., V. I. Molodin eds., *Fenomen Altaĭskikh Mumiĭ*, Novosibirsk: Press of Institute of Archaeology and Ethnography SORAN, 2000, p. 188.

前面提到了吐鲁番地区的洋海三期墓葬出土的匈奴文化器物，如洋海墓地出土的长方形牌、交河沟北一号台地墓地出土的莲花纹陶罐、桃形骨牌和角质弓弭。有关匈奴的考古工作开始于19世纪，20世纪以后俄罗斯、蒙古和其他国家的考古学家陆续在蒙古北部和外贝加尔先后发掘了外贝加尔的诺因乌拉（Noin-Uul）墓地、杜雷尼（Dureny）墓地、伊沃加城址和墓地、杜雷斯推（Durestuǐ）墓地、查拉姆（Tsaraam）墓地、图瓦的奥沟屯（Orgoiton）、蒙古境内的布尔罕—托尔沟（Burkhan Tolgoi）、戈尔莫德（Gol-Mod）、塔希汀—霍特沟（Takhiltyn Khotgor）、杜里—那斯（Duulig Nars）和宁夏的倒墩子墓地。迄今为止，匈奴文化的遗址已经发现于外贝加尔和蒙古全境。[1] 据不完全统计，目前已经发现了70多处墓地，4000多座墓葬。[2] 现已发现的墓葬大体可以分为大型墓和中小型墓，大型墓规模大，地表有长方形封堆，地下有墓道和方斗形墓室，墓室内有二椁一棺或一椁一棺；其周围有许多陪葬的中小型墓葬和殉牲。中小型墓的地表有方形和圆形封堆，地下有竖穴土坑，内有木棺；墓主仰身直肢，大多头北脚南，少数头东脚西。随葬品除了武器和工具、身体—服装—腰带装饰品和马具，还有灰陶高领罐、灰陶侈口罐和灰陶盆以及木质和漆木容器。[3] 匈奴墓葬大体可以分为两期，绝对年代大约为公元前3世纪—公元2世纪。[4]

根据我国的文献记载，匈奴曾经数次控制新疆的部分区域。公元前177—前161年间，匈奴两次大败月氏，占据了大月氏人的故地。有人认为此故地就是现在的东天山，也就是巴里坤平原，而且认为巴里坤平原就是匈奴右方王的王庭。最近十年来考古学家在巴里坤平原的天山北

---

[1] Brosseder, Ursula, and Bryan K. Miller, State of Research and future directions of Xiongnu studies, in Brossseder, Ursula, and Bryan K. Miller eds., *Xiongnu Archaeology: Multidisciplinary Perspectives of the First Steppe Empire in Inner Asia*, Vor- und Frühgeschichtliche Archäologie Rheinische Friedrich-Wilhelms-Universität Bonn, 2011, Fig. 1.

[2] 马健：《匈奴葬仪的考古学探索》，兰州大学出版社2011年版，第15页。

[3] Mogil'nikov, V. A., Khunnu Zabaikal'ia, in Moshkova, M. G. ed., *Stepnaia Polosa Aziatskoi Chasti SSSR v Skifo-Sarmatskoe Vremia*, Moscow: Science Press, 1992, pp. 259–266；马健：《匈奴葬仪的考古学探索》，兰州大学出版社2011年版，第166—168页。

[4] Mogil'nikov, V. A., Khunnu Zabaikal'ia, in Moshkova, M. G. ed., *Stepnaia Polosa Aziatskoi Chasti SSSR v Skifo-Sarmatskoe Vremia*, Moscow: Science Press, 1992, p. 257.

第三部分 中国西北和欧亚草原考古

麓发掘了岳公台—西黑沟和红山口—东黑沟两个遗址群,他们推测前者为大月氏的遗存,而以东黑沟遗址和黑沟梁墓地为匈奴的遗存。[①] 公元前120年,汉王朝势力进入新疆以后,与匈奴反复争夺对新疆的控制权。不过吐鲁番地区的姑师以及后续的车师作为独立政体保留下来,或者依附于匈奴,或者依附于汉王朝的西域都护府。[②] 从考古学材料来看,吐鲁番地区洋海三期的墓葬延续了二期的许多特征,如上面描述的"墓葬均为竖穴土坑和竖穴偏室墓,墓室口部用木棍和苇草覆盖,上面再堆石,有时还要砌石围。墓室东西向",而与匈奴墓葬的葬俗迥然不同。而这些葬俗体现的是人们的精神世界,不容易改变。前面提到的匈奴类型的器物则反映了本地文化与匈奴文化交流的结果;[③] 由于它们大多属于奢侈品,可能反映了本地上层与匈奴帝国上层之间的礼物往来。

最后,还有几件残铜镜值得一提。在胜金店墓地的M13和M29,出土了两块铜镜残片,一块形状不规则,一块三角形(图3-2-15:1),都镶嵌在带柄木框上。木框由原木削成,圆盘形,带圆柱形手柄。这种铜镜残片镶在木框上的做法,也见于阿卡拉哈—III墓地的1号冢。后者的铜镜残片大体正方形,镶嵌在圆盘上,带有长方形手柄(图3-2-15:2)。[④] 有意思的是,交河沟北一号台地墓地的M01的一座袝葬墓出土了同样的木托铜镜,木盘呈圆形,一侧有长方形柄,正面镶了一块半圆形铜镜。[⑤] M16的一座袝葬墓M16me出土了一件这样的木托,平面为椭圆形,一端有柄,正面刻出"蘑菇形"凹槽(图3-2-15:4)。[⑥] 另一件木托呈扇形,一端

[①] 王建新、席琳:《东天山地区早期游牧文化聚落考古研究》,《考古》2009年第1期,第33—36页;马健:《匈奴葬仪的考古学探索》,兰州大学出版社2011年版,第206—209页。

[②] 余太山主编:《西域通史》,中州古籍出版社2003年版,第49、52、56—57、63、68页。

[③] 王炳华:《交河沟西考古收获》,载王炳华《西域考古历史论集》,中国人民大学出版社2008年版,第605—606页。

[④] Derevianko, A. P., V. I. Molodin eds., *Fenomen Altaĭskikh Mumiĭ*, Novosibirsk: Press of Institute of Archaeology and Ethnography SORAN, 2000, Fig. 81, 82, 83.

[⑤] 材料来自联合国教科文组织驻中国代表处、新疆文物事业管理局、新疆文物考古研究所《交河故城——1993、1994年度考古发掘报告》,东方出版社1998年版,第60页,图四五:1。

[⑥] 联合国教科文组织驻中国代表处、新疆文物事业管理局、新疆文物考古研究所:《交河故城—1993、1994年度考古发掘报告》,东方出版社1998年版,第60页,图四五:2。

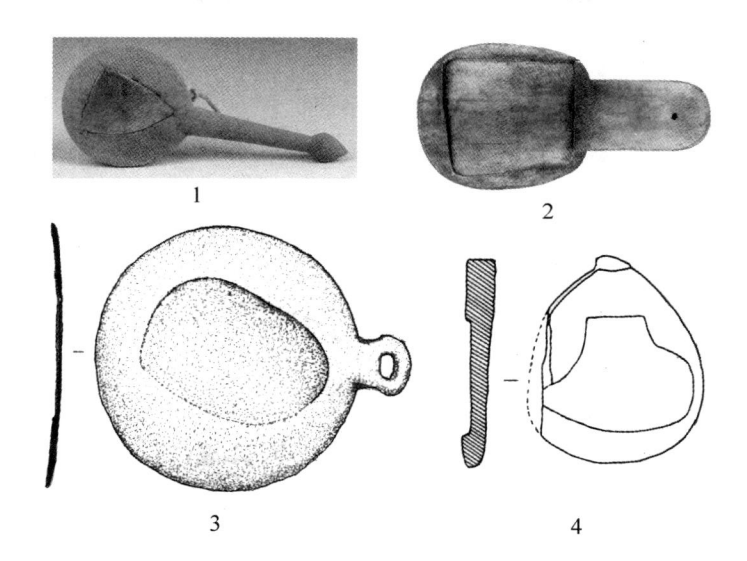

图 3-2-15 胜金店、阿卡拉哈—III、特克斯肯—VI 和交河沟北一号台地墓地出土的残铜镜比较

1. 胜金店墓地（吐鲁番学研究院：《新疆吐鲁番市胜金店墓地发掘简报》，《考古》2013 年第 2 期，图一八）；2. 阿卡拉哈—III（Derevianko, A. P., V. I. Molodin eds., *Fenomen Altaĭskikh Mumiĭ*, Novosibirsk: Press of Institute of Archaeology and Ethnography SORAN, 2000, Fig. 81, 82, 83）；3. 特克斯肯—VIII 4 号冢（Kiriushin, Iu. F., N. F. Stepanova, and A. A. Tishkin, *Skifskaia Èpokha Gornogo Altaia*, Chast' II, Pogrebal'no-pominal'nye kompleksy pazyrykskoĭ kul'tury, Barnaul: Press of Altai State University, 2003, Fig. 15：1）；4. 交河沟北一号台地墓地 M01（联合国教科文组织驻中国代表处、新疆文物事业管理局、新疆文物考古研究所：《交河故城——1993、1994 年度考古发掘报告》，东方出版社 1998 年版，第 60 页，图四五：1）

也有柄，正面挖出扇形凹槽。两者可能就是铜镜残片的木托，凹槽就是原先安放残片的地方，可惜铜镜已经遗失。类似的木托还见于苏贝希墓地（M15：2）[①] 和特克斯肯—VI14 号冢（图 3-2-15：3）。[②] 需要说

[①] 新疆文物考古研究所、吐鲁番地区博物馆：《新疆鄯善县苏贝希遗址及墓地》，《考古》2002 年第 6 期，图一二：12。此器发掘者原称为木勺，但是挖槽浅而且平，应为木托。

[②] Kiriushin, Iu. F., N. F. Stepanova, and A. A. Tishkin, *Skifskaia Èpokha Gornogo Altaia*, Chast' II, Pogrebal'no-pominal'nye kompleksy pazyrykskoĭ kul'tury, Barnaul: Press of Altai State University, 2003, Fig. 15：1.

明的是，胜金店、苏贝希和交河沟北出土的木托或木托铜镜都属于洋海三期，也就是两汉/匈奴时期，而可资对比的阿尔泰山区的同类器物均属于巴泽雷克文化。而外贝加尔和蒙古北部的匈奴时期墓葬出土了残铜镜，如额吉河（Ègiĭn gol）、伊里莫瓦（Il'movaia）和切列姆霍夫（Cheremuovaia）墓地，但是没有出土木托。① 不过，从吐鲁番地区和阿尔泰山区的材料来看，它们原先可能有木托，用于日常生活。

四　结语

根据洋海墓地的分期，笔者将吐鲁番地区已经发表的11处墓地分为三期。第一期相当于哈密地区的焉布拉克期，第二期相当于阿尔泰地区的巴泽雷克期，第三期相当于匈奴时期。这三期的文化内涵有延续性，从弓箭、服装和马具来看，这三期的居民均为游牧民。与此同时，文化内涵也有显著的变化。其中第一期具有较多的铜扣、铜铃、铜斧和铜刀。第二期金属工具和武器减少，但是出现了仿皮质壶和角质壶的陶单耳罐和陶单耳壶。到了第三期，彩陶减少，而铁器大量出现；同时棉、罗和绢布衣服出现。

吐鲁番地区早期铁器时代文化来自何处？目前还缺乏清楚的证据予以说明。从上述的铜器、单耳壶、残铜镜、皮枕和毡毯、发饰、服装和毡靴来看，吐鲁番地区先后受到了哈密地区的焉布拉克文化、阿尔泰山区的巴泽雷克文化与外贝加尔和蒙古的匈奴文化的影响。而在洋海、苏贝希和阿拉沟墓地的人骨材料中，欧罗巴人种占主流，也有部分蒙古人种，而且还有混合人种。在欧罗巴人种中，有地中海、原始欧罗巴和中亚人种，说明吐鲁番地区的人种构成非常复杂，其中可能有来自阿尔泰山区、蒙古和外贝加尔的游牧民。而洋海第三期的遗存则是洋海第二期的自然延续，不过出现了一些匈奴类型的器物，而且是奢侈品。学术界推测洋海第二期和洋海第三期遗存可能属于汉文文献里的姑师和车师，如是，这些奢侈品可能反映了本地上层与匈奴上层之间的礼物交换。

---

① 马健：《匈奴葬仪的考古学探索》，兰州大学出版社2011年版，图三—17，图三—56。

关于吉尔赞喀勒墓地用火遗物的一点看法[*]

吉尔赞喀勒墓地位于新疆塔什库尔干县提孜那甫乡曲曼村东北的塔什库尔干河西岸的吉尔赞喀勒台地上，海拔约 3070 米。这个区域为喀喇昆仑山脉、兴都库什山脉和阿赖山脉的连接处，与塔吉克斯坦、阿富汗和巴基斯坦接壤，是古代新疆通往印度河流域和中亚的交通要道。本地属于高寒干旱—半干旱气候，冬季漫长，干旱少雨。台地西侧是干燥荒凉的山脊，但是塔什库尔干河谷水源丰富，地势平坦，适合农业和畜牧。经过地面调查，墓地可以分为 A、B、C、D 四区：A 区 7 座，B 区 34 座，C 区 8 座，D 区 5—6 座墓葬（图 3-3-1）。2013 年，中国社会科学院考古研究所新疆工作队、喀什地区文物局、塔什库尔干县文物管理所在 A 区和 B 区发掘了 10 座墓葬，2014 年在 A、B、C、D 四区发掘了 29 座墓葬。[①] 其中 2013 年发掘的 10 座墓葬和 2014 年发掘的 9 座墓葬的资料已经发表。[②] 发掘者从 2013 年发掘的墓葬得到的人骨、木材、炭屑和织物提取了 15 个样品做了碳十四测年，得到了 2600BP—2400BP 的年代范围。[③]

---

[*] 本文原刊于《元史及民族与边疆研究集刊》第 38 辑，2020 年，第 198—208 页。收入本书时略有改动。

[①] Xueye Wang, Zihua Tang, Jing Wu, Xinhua Wu, Yiqun Wu, and Xinying Zhou, Strontium isotope evidence for a highly mobile population on the Pamir Plateau 2500 years ago, *Scientific Reports* 6, 2016, 35162; doi: 10.1038/srep35162.

[②] 中国社会科学院考古研究所新疆工作队：《新疆塔什库尔干吉尔赞喀勒墓地发掘报告》，《考古学报》2015 年第 2 期，第 229—230 页；中国社会科学院考古研究所新疆工作队、新疆喀什地区文物局、塔什库尔干县文管所：《塔什库尔干县吉尔赞喀勒墓地考古发掘简报》，《新疆文物》2014 年第 1 期，第 4—31 页；《新疆塔什库尔干吉尔赞喀勒墓地 2014 年发掘报告》，《考古学报》2017 年第 4 期，第 545—573 页。

[③] 中国社会科学院考古研究所新疆工作队：《新疆塔什库尔干吉尔赞喀勒墓地发掘报告》，《考古学报》2015 年第 2 期，第 247—257 页。

◇❖◇ 第三部分 中国西北和欧亚草原考古

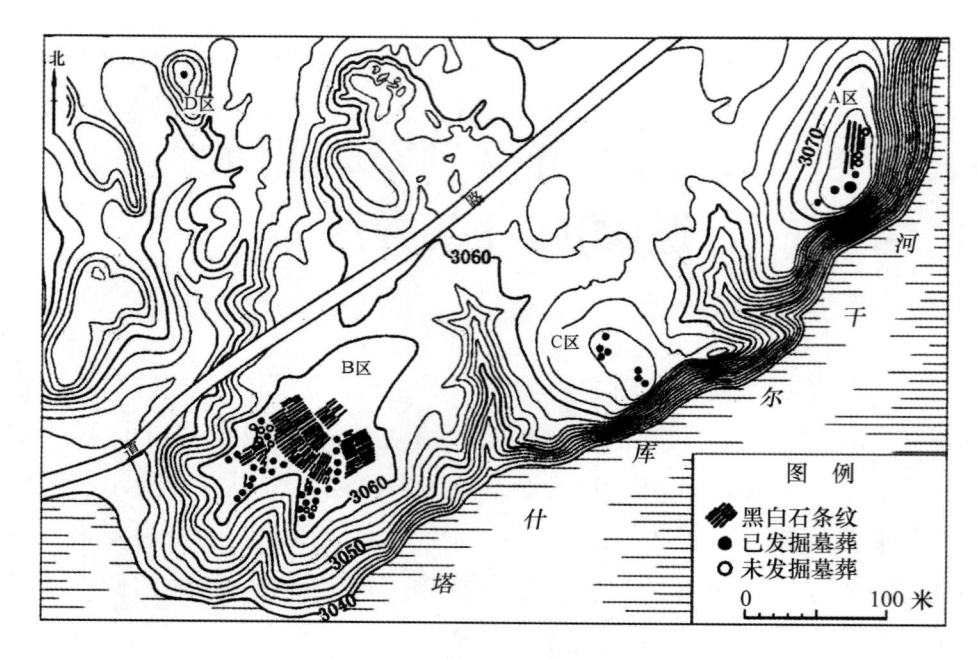

图 3-3-1 吉尔赞喀勒墓地平面图

（中国社会科学院考古研究所新疆工作队、新疆喀什地区文物局、塔什库尔干县文管所：《新疆塔什库尔干吉尔赞喀勒墓地2014年发掘报告》，《考古学报》2017年第4期，图一）

从现有的发表资料来看，吉尔赞喀勒墓地存在一些独特之处。一是在A区和B区的地表覆盖了许多黑色和白色鹅卵石铺成的条纹，两种条纹相间错落，黑白分明，蔚为壮观。这些条纹位于墓葬的东北或西南方向，呈放射状分布，长5—23米，宽0.8—2米。部分条纹压在墓葬上，与墓葬的封堆相连。它们在A区不多，而在B区的数量很大，成片分布。发掘者认为它们分为若干组，每组与一座墓葬对应。[①]但是他们发表的B区墓葬分布图显示，墓葬和条纹各自成组分布，并没有对应关系。二是9座墓葬出土了12件木质和1件陶质火盆，里面装满了黑色和白色鹅卵石，火盆内壁和鹅卵石都经过火烧。[②]

[①] 中国社会科学院考古研究所新疆工作队：《新疆塔什库尔干吉尔赞喀勒墓地发掘报告》，《考古学报》2015年第2期，第231页。
[②] 发掘者直接称之为火坛，有些不妥。如本文所述，这种器物并非拜火教所用的"火坛"，而可能是烧烤大麻籽的火盆。按照考古学命名原则，称之为火盆更为妥当。

关于吉尔赞喀勒墓地用火遗物的一点看法

上述黑白色条纹和木质、陶质火盆都是首次发现,在世界范围内没有先例,但是发掘者很快就联想到了琐罗亚斯德教(又称拜火教和袄教),并且在我国国家媒体新华社下属的新华网上发布了新闻,宣称吉尔赞喀勒墓地是最早的琐罗亚斯德教遗存,而且强调拜火教可能起源于帕米尔高原。[①] 琐罗亚斯德教曾经是古代波斯的重要宗教,也是国际学术界关心的问题,所以发掘者提出的是一个重要论点。[②] 按照学术规则,我们既需要"大胆假设",也需要"小心求证",所以我们需要仔细地审视发掘者的论据。

发掘者的论点包含两个要点:第一,吉尔赞喀勒墓地是琐罗亚斯德教遗址;第二,它是最早的琐罗亚斯德教遗址。我们先来看第二个要点。要证明吉尔赞喀勒墓地是最早的琐罗亚斯德教遗址,不是一件容易的事情。琐罗亚斯德教是世界各国尤其是伊朗学者长期关注的问题,他们已经取得了不少成果,研究者需要首先吸收消化这些成果。在这个方面,发掘者做了一些功课,但是他主要依赖的是我国学者的成果和译作,国外有关琐罗亚斯德教历史和考古学研究的权威著作和论文收集的不多,对国际研究现状不甚了解。据《阿维斯陀》经记载,琐罗亚斯德教是在公元前 2000 年的中亚形成的。其兴起在伊朗语支与印度—雅利安语支分离之后,在 1000BC 左右一些伊朗部落迁入伊朗高原之前。此后中亚的伊朗部落继续向西、北和东扩散,把琐罗亚斯德教带到了中亚和伊朗各地,因此粟特人、塞克人和和田人在阿契美尼德时期和后世为该教教徒。先知琐罗亚斯德抛弃了印度—伊朗语系的信仰,转而传播经过改革的宗教。19 世纪以来学者们皓首穷经,希望搞清楚这次改革的内容和教义的变化。但是历史遗留下来的

[①] 张鸿墀:《探秘离太阳最近的拜火教墓地遗址》,《新华每日电讯》2013 年 6 月 16 日第 3 版。王瑟:《帕米尔高原惊现拜火教遗址》,《光明日报》2014 年 8 月 14 日。Anonymous, Zoroastrian cemetery found in Xinjiang, Tashkurgan Tajik Autonomous county, Jirzankal, 2013, http://www.kaogu.cn/en/News/New_discoveries/2013/1026/43277.html, 2018 年 9 月 21 日登录。

[②] 2016 年 11 月 26 日,笔者在访问伊朗考古中心和伊朗文化遗产和旅游研究所时,伊朗官员说伊朗电视台发布了一则新闻,内容是我国新疆的一座墓地发现了最早的琐罗亚斯德教遗迹。

◇❖◇ 第三部分　中国西北和欧亚草原考古

文献资料非常有限，其经典《阿维斯陀》原为说唱诗歌，可能形成于公元前 2000 年和公元前 1000 年，然后口头流传下来，大概在 9 世纪以后形成文字，但是现存最早的版本是 13 和 14 世纪的。所以《阿维斯陀》既不能弃之不用，因为它包含了一些早期史料；但是也不能全盘接受，因为它经过了各个时期的修改增补。因此要使用《阿维斯陀》，就要用考古资料和出土文献来分析各个篇章的创作年代，就像我国的《尚书》，而不能拿来就用。同时期的文献资料只有波斯波利斯、苏萨和其他地方发现的波斯国王（居鲁士、大流士、薛西斯和阿塔西斯）铭文、希腊历史文献和埃兰文书，但是这些资料提供的有关阿契美尼德时期拜火教的教义和祭礼并不丰富。[1]

早期琐罗亚斯德教遗址一直是国际学术界关注的问题。伊朗人（以及印度—伊朗人）出身于游牧人群，其祭祀遗址主要为露天的，位于地势高处或高台之上，但是与拜火有关的遗迹在阿契美尼德时期以前已经有所发现。[2] 最早的一处可能是北大夏（Northern Bactria）的加尔库坦神庙（Jarkutan），年代为 1400BC—1000BC。神庙坐落在一座山峰上，里面有一处长方形建筑，规模为 60×44.5 米。在一个房间里人们发现了一个灰烬和烧骨的堆积。根据这些发现，发掘者认为这处建筑是"拜火庙"（图 3-3-2）。[3] 更为有名的是土库曼斯坦玛吉亚纳绿洲的托格洛克（Togolok）—I"神庙"、托格洛克（Togolok）—XXI"神庙"和贡鲁尔（Gonur）"火庙"，年代为公元前 1000 年左右。发掘者在这些建筑里发现了拜火遗迹和圣汁遗物（即《阿维斯陀》中的胡摩），因而认为是"印度—伊朗语系雅利安部落的原始琐罗亚斯德神庙"。[4] 但是这种看法遭到了其他学者的反对，他

---

[1] Skjærøv, Prods Oktor, Avesta and Zoroastrianism under the Achaemenids and early Sasanians, in Potts, D. T. ed., *The Oxford Handbook of Ancient Iran*, Oxford University Press, 2013, pp. 549 – 550.

[2] Shenkar, Michael, Temple Architecture in the Iranian World before the Macedonian Conquest, *Iran & the Caucasus* 11/2, 2007, pp. 169 – 194.

[3] Askarov, A., T. Shirinov, The Palace, Temple and Necropolis of Jarkutan, *Bulletin of Asia Institute* 8, 1994, p. 23.

[4] Sarianidi, V., *Margiana and Protozoroastrianism*, Athens, 1998, p. 102.

们认为拜火和圣汁是印度—伊朗语系的普遍习俗，不限于琐罗亚斯德教。"原始琐罗亚斯德"一词尤其受人诟病，因为我们不知道琐罗亚斯德生活于何时何地。①

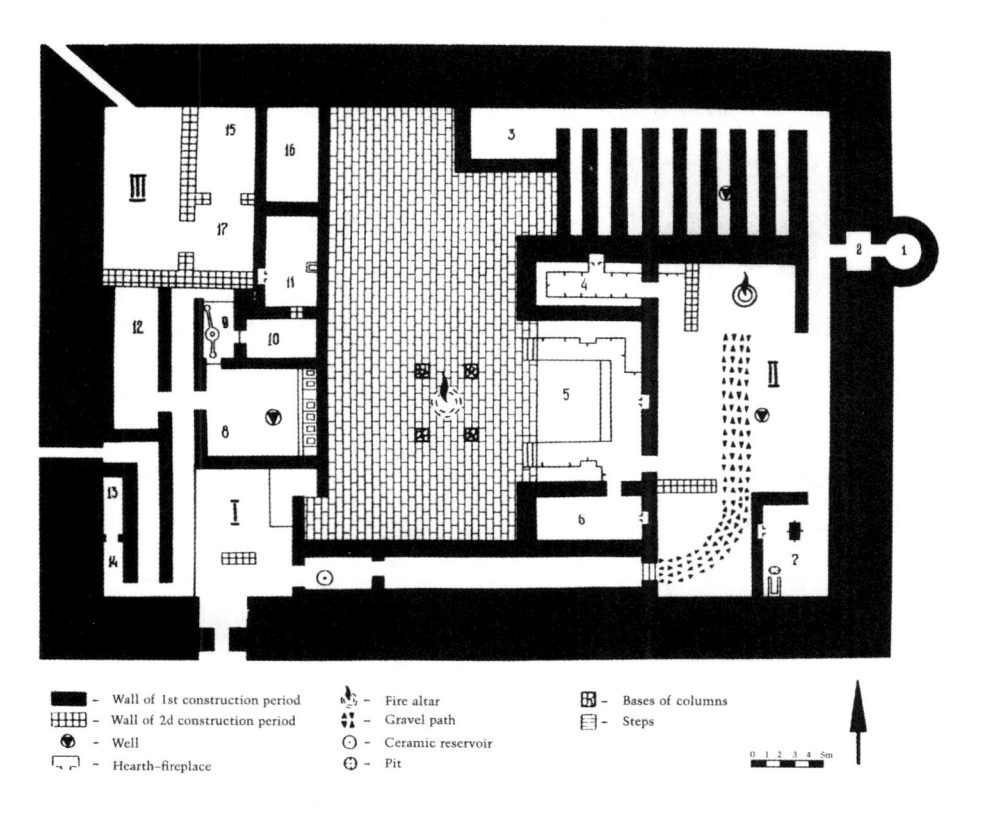

图 3-3-2 加尔库坦"火庙"

（Askarov, A., T. Shirinov, The Palace, Temple and Necropolis of Jarkutan, *Bulletin of Asia Institute* 8, 1994, Fig. 4）

琐罗亚斯德教是否为阿契美尼德帝国的国教，现在学术界还没有统一的看法。有些学者认为阿契美尼德人不信琐罗亚斯德教，有些学者认为它是国教。尽管皇家铭文和《阿维斯陀》有些对应之处，大流士一世以后的波斯诸王也的确尊阿胡拉马兹达为最高神（但不是唯一神），但是

---

① Shenkar, Michael, Temple Architecture in the Iranian World before the Macedonian Conquest, *Iran & the Caucasus* 11/2, 2007, p. 171; Tadikonda, Kalpana K., Significance of the Fire Altars Depicted on Gandharan Buddhist Sculptures, *East and West*, 57. 1/4, 2007, p. 30.

上述问题尚未解决。① 不过，现在已经发现了两座阿契美尼德时期的神庙。一座是位于锡斯坦（Sistan）的达罕依古拉曼（Dahān-i-Ghulāmān），公元前6世纪末和前5世纪初修建于一座聚落（可能是地方都城）内。神庙呈方形，内有庭院，四墙中间有门廊面朝庭院，布局类似波斯波利斯的宫廷建筑。在庭院中央修建了三座阶梯形土坯坛，周围分布了大量的灰烬，里面掺杂了动物油脂和骨骼。焚烧动物牺牲是当时的琐罗亚斯德教净礼绝对不能容忍的，所以有人认为它是本地宗教的遗迹。当然，我们现在无法知道阿契美尼德帝国的人是否都遵守净礼。② 另一座位于花拉子模的塔什齐尔曼（Tash-K'irman）土丘，年代为公元前4世纪初，发掘者以为肯定是琐罗亚斯德教早期的火庙。这座庙里面有一个高台、一个小庭院和密集复杂的房屋。一些房屋里面发现了厚厚的灰烬；一些房屋里面发现了火坛。这种布局仅此一见。显然这是一处古代祭祀遗迹，但是说它是琐罗亚斯德教拜火庙并不可取。③

除了神庙，在中亚的阿契美尼德时期的一些房屋里发现了疑似火坛的遗迹。在花拉子模的江巴斯—卡尔（Djanbas-Kale）发现的一座大型建筑中，有一间房屋（7.25×4米），中央放置了一个椭圆形座，绕墙一周长凳。地面覆盖着一层灰烬，上面叠压着一层锡。这个座可能就是一个火坛。在伊朗西部，帕萨加德（Pasargadae）东北部的祭祀区（Sacred Precinct）存在两根2米多高的石柱。南面的一根底部有阶梯形的基座，形状类似于大流士一世墓葬浮雕上面的火坛形象（图3-3-3）。事实上，在阿契美尼德时期墓葬的浮雕上可见国王站在阶梯形台基上，面对火坛，其中的柱子就跟这些石柱相似。④

---

① Shenkar, Michael, Temple Architecture in the Iranian World before the Macedonian Conquest, *Iran & the Caucasus* 11/2, 2007, p. 174; Stausberg, Michael, On the State and Prospects of the Study of Zoroastrianism, *Numen*, 55/5, 2008, p. 577.

② Shenkar, Michael, Temple Architecture in the Iranian World before the Macedonian Conquest, *Iran & the Caucasus* 11/2, 2007, p. 175.

③ Shenkar, Michael, Temple Architecture in the Iranian World before the Macedonian Conquest, *Iran & the Caucasus* 11/2, 2007, p. 176.

④ Shenkar, Michael, Temple Architecture in the Iranian World before the Macedonian Conquest, *Iran & the Caucasus* 11/2, 2007, pp. 176-177.

关于吉尔赞喀勒墓地用火遗物的一点看法 ◇❖◇

图 3-3-3　大流士一世墓葬浮雕（张良仁摄）

　　由此来看，在中亚和伊朗，人们已经发现了一些与拜火有关的遗迹，其中有早至公元前 1000 年前的，也有阿契美尼德时期的。但是这些遗迹是否为拜火教遗迹，学术界并不确定。要论证吉尔赞喀勒墓地是最早的琐罗亚斯德教遗址，发掘者就要推翻上述的遗址为琐罗亚斯德教遗址的看法。但是吉尔赞喀勒墓地并不存在年代优势，也没有建筑遗迹，所以说它是最早的琐罗亚斯德教遗址并没有什么过硬的证据。

　　吉尔赞喀勒墓地是否为琐罗亚斯德教遗址也是值得重新考虑的问题。在这方面，发掘者非常努力，从 2013 年开始发掘以来，一直在寻找新的证据，来支持自己的看法。在最近发表的一篇论文中，他汇总了吉尔赞喀勒墓地的"琐罗亚斯德教文化元素"。[①] 为了方便讨论，这里简要复述如下：

　　第一，C 区为一片荒漠高地，地表没有黑白色鹅卵石条纹，而且墓葬只有形式而没有内容，发掘者推测是琐罗亚斯德教《阿维斯陀》经文中的"达克玛（Dakhma）"。

[①] 巫新华：《新疆吉尔赞喀勒墓群蕴含的琐罗亚斯德教文化元素探析》，《西域研究》2018 年第 2 期，第 95—107 页。

第二，上述的 A 区和 B 区的黑色和白色鹅卵石条纹，在发掘者看来，是早期琐罗亚斯德教徒崇拜阿尼朗（Aneyran，意为"漫无边际的光源"）留下的遗迹。

第三，墓葬的圆形石圈、火盆内的圆形鹅卵石、天珠上的白色圆圈纹象征着琐罗亚斯德教主神阿胡拉·马兹达和诸善神。在《贝希斯敦铭文》上可以看到，阿胡拉·马兹达递给大流士一世一个圆环，这个圆环就象征着君权神授。

第四，A 区和 B 区的黑白色条纹基本都指向夏至日方向，而与之相对的墓葬位于冬至日方向。两者对应于琐罗亚斯德教历法的大夏季（1—7 月）和大冬季（8—12 月）崇拜习俗。

第五，A 区和 B 区的黑白色条纹寓意着琐罗亚斯德教的"善恶二元对立"的宇宙观。

第六，上述木质和陶质火盆是为了方便琐罗亚斯德教徒携带的"火坛"。根据希腊历史学家希罗多德的记载，阿契美尼德时期的教徒习惯到最高的山峰上，在那里向宙斯奉献牺牲。吉尔赞喀勒墓地出土的火盆小巧灵便，是教徒手持的礼器。火盆内检测到了大麻酚，发掘者认为它是胡摩（Haoma）汁的残留物。在祭祀仪式中，祭司和教徒把胡摩汁洒在圣火上，用来净化圣火。

第七，9 件木质火盆装了 1、8、10、14、15、23、27 枚鹅卵石。发掘者认为这些数字指的是每月的某一天，象征着每天的保护神阿胡拉·马兹达和其他神。

第八，11 座墓葬出土了大量的小木棍。这些小木棍手指粗细，长短不等，树皮均已削去。发掘者认为它们就是琐罗亚斯德教徒行祭礼时手持的巴尔萨姆枝。

第九，4 座墓葬出土了带孔的小木棍，它们往往和上述的小木棍一起出土。这些小木棍上钻了 1—16 个小孔。发掘者认为它们不是实用的钻木取火工具，而是祭祀用品，上面的小孔的数目同样是诸神的象征。

第十，几座墓葬出土了黑底白纹的 7 颗蚀花玛瑙珠，发掘者认为它们是琐罗亚斯德教徒崇拜的灵石。其黑白两色体现了"光明与黑暗二元对立"的宇宙观。

关于吉尔赞喀勒墓地用火遗物的一点看法

第十一，在 13 座墓葬中发现了二次葬。琐罗亚斯德教徒不允许人的尸体直接埋在土里，不能火葬，不能丢在水里，只能天葬：尸体只有在经过动物吃掉皮肉之后才能下葬。发掘者认为这种二次葬是天葬的遗物。

第十二，两座墓葬出土了鹰头骨和鹰爪骨。发掘者认为它们反映了琐罗亚斯德教徒的巴赫拉姆（鹰）崇拜。

第十三，12 座墓葬出土了铁刀，它们放在木盘内或套管内。发掘者认为它们不是实用器，而是祭祀用器。

第十四，两座墓葬出土了木质箜篌。发掘者认为它们是琐罗亚斯德教的重要乐器。

上面列出的证据看上去不少，可惜都经不起推敲。看一种遗迹、现象和遗物是否为琐罗亚斯德教的文化元素，我们要看它是否为该宗教的特定行为。为此我们要遵循两个原则，一是唯一性，就是这种遗迹、现象和遗物只见于琐罗亚斯德教的遗址；二是普遍性，就是遗迹、现象和遗物不能只见于一个遗址，应该见于琐罗亚斯德教的其他遗址。以唐卡为例，我们一见到它就会想到藏传佛教，就是因为它们不见于佛教其他宗派的寺院，另一方面又普遍见于藏传佛教的各个寺院。由此来检验上述论据，我们发现上述论据存在各种弱点。

第一条证据着眼于 C 区的地貌特征。但是 C 区不是空旷的荒漠，该区发现了 8 座墓葬；这些墓葬虽然人骨和遗物少，但是发表的 M44、M45、M48 三座墓葬都出土了木器或者毛织物，不能否认它们是墓葬。

第二、四、五条指向 A 区和 B 区的黑色和白色鹅卵石条纹。但是这种遗迹目前不见于其他遗址，也就是无法满足第二个原则。如果说它是拜火教的特征，那么它应该在同时期的其他遗址中反复出现。考古学家在中亚和伊朗发现了不少同时期和更晚的墓地，其中应该有琐罗亚斯德教徒的墓地，但是迄今没有发现这类遗迹。

第六条的火盆、第七条的鹅卵石数目和第十二条的鹰头骨、鹰爪骨同样违背了第二条原则。要证明它们是琐罗亚斯德教的文化元素，就要在其他琐罗亚斯德教遗址中找到同类的遗物和现象。可惜这三条目前只见于吉尔赞喀勒墓地一处。

其他七条违背了第一条原则。第三条着眼于圆形，但是圆形石围和

· 205 ·

◇❖◇ 第三部分　中国西北和欧亚草原考古

圆形图案是一种西伯利亚和新疆非常普遍的现象，并不限于吉尔赞喀勒墓地，圆形石围就见于和静县的察吾呼墓地。① 第十一条的二次葬、第十二条的铁刀和第十三条的箜篌也是如此。二次葬墓葬普遍见于新疆早期铁器时代的墓地，如吐鲁番的洋海，② 和静的察吾呼。③ 只不过吉尔赞喀勒墓地的人骨颅腔内发现了蝇蛆，但是这也只是暴尸后细菌滋生的结果，而不是琐罗亚斯德教的规制。铁刀（以及铜刀）是游牧人群吃饭时削肉用的，在新疆和西伯利亚的早期铁器时代墓葬里，铁刀既可以挂在死者的腰带上，也可以放在木盘内或者插在动物骨骼上。前者见于吐鲁番的苏贝希一号墓地M10、三号墓地M27，后者见于吐鲁番的洋海墓地IM5。④ 箜篌发源于两河流域，然后传播到南亚、中亚、新疆和阿尔泰山脉。迄今为止已经发现于阿尔泰山脉的巴泽雷克和巴沙达尔墓地（2件，巴泽雷克文化，公元前5—前3世纪），新疆且末县的扎滚鲁克墓地（3件）、吐鲁番的洋海墓地、哈密市艾斯克霞尔南墓地（11件，焉布拉克文化，公元前7—前6世纪）。⑤

第八条的小木棍和第九条的带孔小木棍实际上是成套的钻木取火工具；从已经发表的材料来看，后者的小孔直径为1厘米，而前者的直径也是1厘米，正好匹配。在2013年发掘的M14和2014年发掘的M28、M29中，二者一起出土，并且都有灼烧的痕迹，显然是使用过的

---

① 新疆吐鲁番学研究院、新疆文物考古研究所：《新疆鄯善洋海墓地发掘报告》，《考古学报》2011年第1期，第4—8、22—45、155—166、225—233、255—263页。
② 新疆吐鲁番学研究院、新疆文物考古研究所：《新疆鄯善洋海墓地发掘报告》，《考古学报》2011年第1期，第142页。
③ 新疆文物考古研究所：《新疆察吾呼大型氏族墓地发掘报告》，东方出版社1999年版，第46页。
④ 新疆文物考古研究所、吐鲁番地区博物馆：《新疆鄯善县苏贝希遗址及墓地》，《考古》2002年第6期，图一七、图八，发掘者将木盘称之为"木俎"；新疆吐鲁番学研究院、新疆文物考古研究所：《新疆鄯善洋海墓地发掘报告》，《考古学报》2011年第1期，图一一。
⑤ 杨洪冰、贾嫚：《从西亚到新疆——箜篌自西向东的流播路径》，《西域研究》2015年第3期，第119—124页；贺志凌、王永强：《哈密五堡艾斯克霞尔南箜篌的音乐考古学研究》，《中国音乐》2018年第4期，第117—122页；新疆吐鲁番学研究院、新疆文物考古研究所：《新疆鄯善洋海墓地发掘报告》，《考古学报》2011年第1期，第115页。

（图 3-3-4）。开始发掘者承认它们是钻木取火工具，①但是后来予以否认，并专门写了一篇文章来证明它们是琐罗亚斯德教的巴尔萨姆枝。② 这无疑是削足适履的做法。类似的成套工具已经发现于其他墓地，如吐鲁番洋海墓地、托克逊县阿拉沟和鱼儿沟墓地、鄯善县苏贝希墓地、和静县察吾呼墓地和伊吾县拜其尔墓地，年代为青铜时代或早期铁器时代，被人们称为取火板和钻杆。③

图 3-3-4 吉尔赞喀勒墓地出土钻木取火器

M29：1（中国社会科学院考古研究所新疆工作队、新疆喀什地区文物局、塔什库尔干县文管所：《新疆塔什库尔干吉尔赞喀勒墓地2014年发掘报告》，《考古学报》2017年第4期，图版拾：5）

不同之处在于，吉尔赞喀勒墓地部分墓葬出土的取火棒数量较大，2014年发掘的M25出土了20根，M32出土了10根，M44出土了44根。这只能说明生者有意给死者随葬了这种材料，以满足其某种需要。

第十条讲的是蚀花玛瑙珠（发掘者进一步称之为"天珠"）。发掘者专门写了一篇文章，论述它们的制作工艺；为此他征引了同时期的哈萨克斯坦维加罗克墓葬、新疆塔什库尔干县香宝宝墓地、河南省淅川县下寺墓地出土的同类器物。④ 这些案例说明，蚀花玛瑙珠不是琐罗亚斯

---

① 中国社会科学院考古研究所新疆工作队：《新疆塔什库尔干吉尔赞喀勒墓地发掘报告》，《考古学报》2015年第2期，第244页。

② 中国社会科学院考古研究所新疆工作队、新疆喀什地区文物局、塔什库尔干县文管所：《新疆塔什库尔干吉尔赞喀勒墓地2014年发掘报告》，《考古学报》2017年第4期，第572页；巫新华：《试论巴尔萨姆枝的拜火教文化意涵——从新疆吉尔赞喀勒墓群的出土文物谈起》，《世界宗教文化》2017年第4期，第119—127页。

③ 于志勇：《新疆考古发现的钻木取火器初步研究》，《西部考古》第三辑，2008年，第197—215页；蒋洪恩：《吐鲁番洋海墓地出土的钻木取火器研究》，《中国文物报》2018年5月4日第6版。

④ 巫新华：《浅析新疆吉尔赞喀勒墓群出土蚀花红玉髓珠、天珠的制作工艺与次生变化》，《四川文物》2016年第3期，第33—55页。

◇❖◇ 第三部分 中国西北和欧亚草原考古

德教特有的礼器。琐罗亚斯德教是否规定死者随葬蚀花玛瑙珠，教徒是否遵循这样的规定，还需要考古材料的检验。

在上述14条证据中，发掘者尤为倚重于第6条和第7条的火盆和里面的鹅卵石。木火盆是在圆木中间挖出一个窝，有的两侧各有一个錾，便于手持。陶火盆目前只发现了一件，也有两个錾。它们的大小不同，最大者为2014年发掘的一件（M9：2），长35厘米，宽20厘米，高14.2厘米，窝长16厘米，宽12厘米（图3-3-5）。这些火盆的内壁往往有厚达1厘米的炭化层；部分（M11、M15）火坛里面放置了烧过的鹅卵石。作者起初比较谨慎，认为这是明火埋葬的火坛，[①] 可能与琐罗亚斯德教有关。后来，在11座墓葬中发现了12个这样的木火盆。发掘者也迈出了新的一步，认为吉尔赞喀勒墓地出土的是"世界上迄今发现最早、最原始的拜火教火坛"。[②] 在他看来，火盆与太原北齐徐显秀墓（571年）和娄叡墓（570年）出土的瓷灯相似。但是这种联系非常牵强。后者经施安昌考证，与太原北周虞弘墓（592年）出土的火坛相同，并见于西安安伽墓木门、安阳北齐贵族墓内双阙、片治肯特Ⅵ.1区10号北墙、瓦拉赫萨（Varakhsha）东厅的拜火图；娄睿墓出土的瓷灯上还有琐罗亚斯德教的新月托日符号。徐、娄二墓除了这些瓷灯，还有古代伊朗神灵森莫夫（Senmurv）的图像。[③] 除了这些拜火图，火坛形象还见于米底国王Cyaxares（公元前625—前585在位）的陵墓大门、阿契美尼德国王陵墓大门、波斯波利斯出土的三枚印章、塔吉克斯坦片治肯特的壁画和纳骨瓮上。[④] 可以看到，它随着时间和地域而有所变化，但是火盆之下有个很高的底座。吉尔赞喀勒墓地出土的火盆既无底座，又缺乏佐证，恐怕不能比定为火坛。

不过，关于这些"火盆"，我们可以提出另外一种解释：它们可能是用来熏烤大麻的。大麻纤维可以纺织衣服，在旧大陆人类从新石器时代

[①] 中国社会科学院考古研究所新疆工作队：《新疆塔什库尔干吉尔赞喀勒墓地发掘报告》，《考古学报》2015年第2期，第249页。
[②] 王瑟：《拜火教只存在于当地人群中》，《光明日报》2016年12月21日第5版。
[③] 施安昌：《北齐徐显秀、娄叡墓中的火坛和礼器》，《故宫博物院院刊》2004年第6期，第41—48页。
[④] 陈文彬：《祆教美术中的火坛》，《丝绸之路研究集刊》第二辑，2018年，第189—204页。

就开始利用;其籽具有麻醉和致幻作用,熏烤大麻籽是游牧人群的普遍习俗。事实上,发掘者已经认识到,吉尔赞喀勒墓地的墓主是从事畜牧业的,也就是游牧人群。封土堆和石圈都是游牧人群的埋葬习俗,见于和静县的察吾呼墓地;①出土的毛毡、铜节约、铜泡、铜镜、石眉笔都是游牧人群的常见用品,见于吐鲁番的洋海墓地;②棚木、尸床见于吐鲁番的洋海墓地。③事实上,研究者分析了吉尔赞喀勒墓地出土木火坛内壁的烧灼残留物,发现了大麻酚(Cannabinol,CBN),即四氢大麻酚(Tetrahydrocannabinol,THC)的降解产物,可见木火坛内曾经燃烧过大麻。④发掘者提出这些烧灼残留物为琐罗亚斯德教徒往火坛内浇胡摩(haoma,发掘者译为豪麻)汁的产物,纯属想当然:大麻酚是大麻的成分。胡摩汁是《阿维斯陀》(《吠陀》经称苏摩,soma)的圣汁,那么胡摩到底是什么植物呢?这是一个困扰了国际学术界几个世纪迄今未能解决的问题。19世纪曾经有学者指认为肉珊瑚(Sarcostemma acidum),后来的学者倾向于麻黄(Ephedra)。⑤麻黄的成分是麻黄碱,是一种兴奋剂,而不是致幻剂。

图3-3-5 吉尔赞喀勒墓地出土火盆

M12:4(中国社会科学院考古研究所新疆工作队:《新疆塔什库尔干吉尔赞喀勒墓地发掘报告》,《考古学报》2015年第2期,图版拾伍:5)

---

① 新疆文物考古研究所:《新疆察吾呼大型氏族墓地发掘报告》,东方出版社1999年版,第4—8、22—45、155—166、225—233、255—263页。
② 新疆吐鲁番学研究院、新疆文物考古研究所:《新疆鄯善洋海墓地发掘报告》,《考古学报》2011年第1期,第143—144页。
③ 新疆吐鲁番学研究院、新疆文物考古研究所:《新疆鄯善洋海墓地发掘报告》,《考古学报》2011年第1期,第142—143页。
④ 任萌、杨益民、巫新华、王永强、蒋洪恩:《新疆出土2500年火坛内壁烧灼物分析》,载新疆维吾尔自治区文物考古研究所编:《2015—2016文物考古年报》,第127页。
⑤ Houben, Jan E. M., The Soma-Hauma problem: Introductory overview and observations on the discussion, *Electronic Journal of Vedic Studies* 9.1, http://www.ejvs.laurasianacademy.com/ejvs0901a.txt.

◇❖◇ 第三部分　中国西北和欧亚草原考古

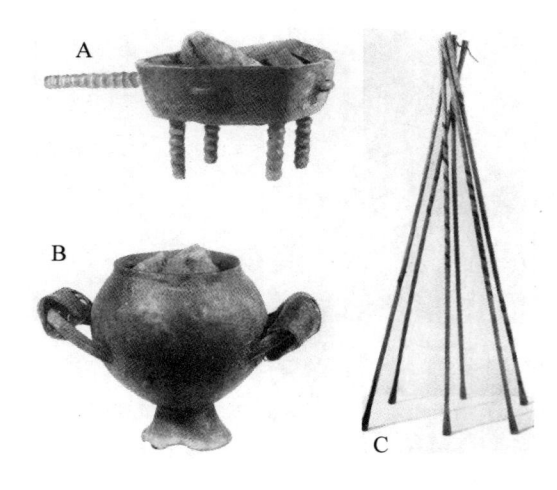

图3-3-6　巴泽雷克2号冢

（Rudenko, Sergei, *Frozen Tombs of Siberia*: *The Pazyryk Burials of Iron Age Horsemen*, Berkeley and Los Angeles: University of California Press, 1970, Plate 62）

希罗多德详细记载了黑海北岸大草原斯基泰人的丧葬习俗。他们种植大麻，在埋完死人后，他们在一个三根木棍搭成的架子上，小心地蒙上羊毛布，让其严丝合缝；在这个小帐篷内他们放入一个钵，上面放着一些烧红的石头。然后他们抓一些大麻籽，爬进小帐篷，把大麻籽扔到烧红的石头上。大麻籽马上起烟，烟雾腾腾，比起希腊的蒸汽浴有过之而无不及。斯基泰人坐在里面，呼吸大麻烟，会愉快地大喊。① 这条文献记载得到了今俄罗斯阿尔泰共和国的巴泽雷克墓地的验证。1947年，俄罗斯考古学家在此墓地发掘了四座"国王"级别的大冢，在2号冢里面发现了一个1.2米高的木支架帐篷；帐篷里面发现了一只铜锼（图3-3-6）。在此墓中发现了另一个木支架和一只铜锼。两只铜锼里面盛放着一些石头和少量大麻籽，部分大麻籽已经炭化。它们可能是燃烧着埋入墓葬的。此外，还发现了一个装了大麻籽的皮囊和分散的大麻籽和香菜。② 这些墓葬的年代为公元前5—前3世纪。据报道，在乌克兰也发现了早期铁器时代斯基泰人使用大麻的物证。③ 不过，在欧亚草原，吸食大麻烟在青铜时代即已见于罗马尼亚和北高加索。④

---

　　① Herodotus, *The Histories*, with an English translation by A. D. Godley, Books III and IV, London: William Heinemann, and New York: G. P. Putnam's Sons, 1920, pp. 273-274.

　　② Rudenko, Sergei, *Frozen Tombs of Siberia*: *The Pazyryk Burials of Iron Age Horsemen*, translated by M. W. Thompson, Berkeley and Los Angeles: University of California Press, 1970, pp. 284-285.

　　③ Pashkevich, G., New Evidence for Plant Exploitation by the Scythian Tribes during the Early Iron Age in the Ukraine, *Acta Palaeobot*, Suppl. 2, Krakow, 1999, pp. 597-601.

　　④ Ecsedy, I., *The People of the Pit-grave Kurgans in Eastern Hungary*, Akadémiai Kiadó, Budapest, 1979.

综上所述，在中亚和伊朗，迄今为止已经发现了若干公元前1000年前后的火庙和火坛。虽然它们在时间、空间和特征上都契合琐罗亚斯德教，但是由于阿契美尼德时期的宗教多样性以及文献的缺少，学术界仍然无法确定它们的性质。吉尔赞喀勒墓地没有发现上述遗迹，起源地之说难以成立。发掘者提供的14条证据比较薄弱，不能证明吉尔赞喀勒墓地是一处琐罗亚斯德教遗址。相反，现有发掘资料和研究成果表明，该墓地的居民为游牧人群，其关键物证火盆可能是游牧人群熏烤大麻籽和其他致幻植物的器物。

张掖市西城驿遗址的彩陶[*]

1948年，甘肃省山丹县培黎学校在县城以南的四坝滩挖水渠时，发现了一处遗址与一批陶器和石器。1953年，该校创办人新西兰籍路易·艾黎（Rewl Alley）函告夏鼐，建议派人前去发掘。[①] 1954年他将所有遗物移交给甘肃省文管会。1956年中国科学院考古研究所的安志敏在甘肃省文管会看到了这批器物，并且前往遗址调查，采集了一部分陶器和石器。[②] 他发现该遗址出土的器物可以分为三组，其中主体的乙组和甘肃省境内当时已知的甘肃仰韶文化（后来改名为马家窑文化）、齐家文化和沙井文化都不同，陶器质料粗糙，彩陶颜料浓厚而且凸起，因此它可能代表了一个新的文化类型，其年代晚于甘肃仰韶文化，早于沙井文化，而与齐家文化相当；根据当时掌握的资料，可知其分布范围为酒泉、山丹、民乐和永昌一带。从遗址出土的农业生产工具和墓葬出土的猪头骨，说明该文化的居民过着定居生活，从事农业和家畜养殖。[③] 虽然当时只有一些调查资料，安志敏暂时命名了四坝文化，[④] 但

---

[*] 本文原刊于《北方民族研究》第2辑，2015年，第91—101页。收入本书时略有改动。
[①] 有关路易·艾黎写信之事引自李水城《四坝文化研究》，《考古学文化论集》（三），文物出版社1993年版，第80页。重印于李水城《东风西渐——中国西北史前文化之进程》，文物出版社2000年版，第58—105页。
[②] 安志敏：《甘肃山丹四坝滩新石器时代遗址》，《考古学报》1959年第3期，第7—16页。
[③] 安志敏：《甘肃山丹四坝滩新石器时代遗址》，《考古学报》1959年第3期，第13—14页。
[④] 安志敏：《甘肃古文化及其有关的几个问题》，《考古通讯》1956年第6期，第17页。而他本人在1959年发表的文章里，没有提"四坝文化"这个命名。可能当时考古界对该文化的命名还有争议，安志敏出于谨慎起见搁置了1956年命名的"四坝文化"。

是很快宁笃学和严文明采用了这一名称。① 尽管当时资料缺乏，但是他对文化面貌的认识在今天看来大体都是正确的。当然，他将其定为新石器时代并把该遗址出土的金环和青铜刀残片归入沙井文化，现在来看是错误的。但这是囿于当时的资料限制，不能求全责备。

四坝滩遗址以后，考古工作者陆续发现了民乐县的东灰山、西灰山、② 天祝县的董家台、民勤县的沙井、山丹县的山羊堡滩、酒泉县（现为酒泉市）的下河清；③ 而且他们在酒泉下河清遗址还发现了四坝文化晚于马厂文化的地层。④ 1976年，在玉门市的火烧沟墓地发掘了312座墓葬，出土金属器200余件和镞范若干。⑤ 遗憾的是，这批发掘材料至今仍未发表，只有65件金属器的检测资料见诸报道。其中有红铜、砷铜和锡青铜，从而确定了四坝文化属于青铜时代。⑥ 1990年，该墓地做了第二次发掘，清理了17座墓葬。⑦ 1986年，北京大学考古学系与甘肃省文物考古研究所在河西走廊做了调查，并且在安西县（瓜州县）鹰窝树清理墓葬3座。⑧ 1987年两家单位又在

---

① 宁笃学：《民乐县发现的二处四坝文化遗址》，《文物》1960年第1期，第74—75页；严文明：《甘肃彩陶的源流》，《文物》1978年第10期，第62—76页。但是同年甘肃省博物馆发表的（《甘肃古文化遗存》，《考古学报》1960年第2期，第23—24页）采用的是"四坝式"遗址，1979年发表的《甘肃省文物考古三十年》又采用"火烧沟类型"。后来许永杰还曾用过"火烧沟·四坝文化"的名称，但是1991年甘肃省文物考古研究所发表《甘肃省文物考古工作十年》（《文物考古工作十年》，文物出版社1991年版，第317页），之后"四坝文化"一名就固定下来。

② 宁笃学：《民乐县发现的二处四坝文化遗址》，《文物》1960年第1期，第74—75页。

③ 甘肃省博物馆：《甘肃古文化遗存》，《考古学报》1960年第2期，第23—24页。

④ 甘肃省博物馆：《甘肃古文化遗存》，《考古学报》1960年第2期，第23—24页。山羊堡滩遗址见第29页，表一。

⑤ 甘肃省博物馆：《甘肃省文物考古工作三十年》，《文物考古工作三十年》，文物出版社1979年版，第139—159页。

⑥ 北京钢铁学院冶金史组：《中国早期铜器的初步研究》，《考古学报》1981年第3期，第287、289页；孙淑云、韩汝玢：《甘肃早期铜器的发现与冶炼、制造技术的研究》，《文物》1997年第7期，第77—78页；严文明：《甘肃彩陶的源流》，《文物》1978年第7期，第77—78页。

⑦ 北京科技大学冶金与材料史研究所、甘肃省文物考古研究所：《火烧沟四坝文化铜器成分及制作技术的研究》，《文物》2003年第8期，第86—96页。

⑧ 李水城、水涛：《甘肃西部地区考古调查》，《中国考古学年鉴》，文物出版社1987年版，第270页；李水城：《四坝文化研究》，《考古学文化论集》（三），文物出版社1993年版，第101—102页。

当时的酒泉县的干骨崖发掘了 107 座墓葬,① 同年甘肃省文物考古研究所与吉林大学北方考古研究室在民乐县东灰山发掘了 249 座墓葬。② 2003—2004 年,在当时的酒泉县的西河滩遗址发掘了一处聚落,发现了 50 多座房屋,400 多座烧烤坑,以及储藏坑、祭祀坑、陶窑和墓葬,不过发掘资料还没有发表。③ 因此,四坝文化的遗址主要分布于河西走廊中西部,南抵祁连山北麓,北近巴丹吉林沙漠的西南边缘,西北达瓜州县城的疏勒河南岸,东至山丹县一带(图 3-4-1)。④ 据最近报道,考古工作者在额济纳旗周围发现了一些四坝文化的陶片,说明四坝文化向北扩散到了这里。⑤

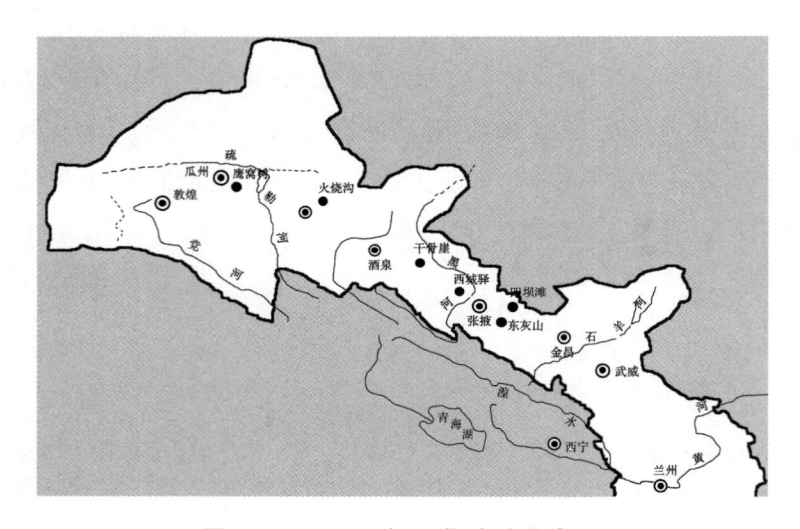

图 3-4-1 四坝文化遗址分布图

---

① 李水城、水涛:《酒泉县丰乐乡干骨崖遗址》,《中国考古学年鉴》,文物出版社 1987 年版,第 271 页;北京大学考古文博学院、甘肃省文物考古研究所:《甘肃酒泉干骨崖墓地的发掘与收获》,《考古学报》2012 年第 3 期,第 351—368 页。

② 许永杰:《民乐县东灰山火烧沟四坝文化遗址》,《中国考古学年鉴》,文物出版社 1988 年版,第 246 页;甘肃省文物考古研究所、吉林大学北方考古研究室:《民乐东灰山考古——四坝文化墓地的揭示与研究》,科学出版社 1998 年版。

③ 赵丛苍:《西河滩遗址发掘主要收获及其意义》,《西北大学学报》(哲学社会科学版)2005 年第 35(3)期,第 50—51 页。

④ 李水城:《四坝文化研究》,《考古学文化论集》(三),文物出版社 1993 年版,第 103—104 页。

⑤ 甘肃省文物考古研究所、北京大学考古文博学院:《河西走廊史前考古调查报告》,文物出版社 2011 年版,第 408—411 页。

有关四坝文化分期，李水城的《四坝文化研究》同甘肃省文物考古研究所与吉林大学北方考古研究室合编的《民乐东灰山考古——四坝文化墓地的揭示与研究》和张忠培的《东灰山墓地研究》做了讨论。其中《四坝文化研究》发表于1993年，作者主要根据干骨崖墓地及火烧沟墓地的部分墓葬资料，提出了五期说。干骨崖墓地属于三—五期，而火烧沟墓地属于一—三期，二者衔接，没有间断，它们的碳十四年代为公元前2000年至前1600年。① 四坝文化的来源，作者认为是河西的马厂文化。不过二者之间还存在一个过渡类型（乙类），其遗存既有别于马厂，也不同于四坝文化，同时又具有马厂和四坝文化的一些特征。② 四坝文化还存在一部分齐家风格的陶器，而前者的彩陶也出现在后者（即甲类）。③ 张忠培根据东灰山墓地的地层关系和器物演变，将其分为三期。他认为东灰山三期基本上与火烧沟吻合，而早于干骨崖墓地。④ 根据当时取得的九个碳十四数据（公元前1900—前1585年），张忠培认为四坝文化落在夏纪年之内或夏商之际。他同意马厂文化是四坝文化的源头，但是他提出马厂文化与四坝文化存在一段时间距离（大约相差一百年）；至于李水城提出的"过渡类型"是介于马厂与四坝之间的考古学文化，还是马厂或者四坝的一个阶段，他认为还要进一步研究。四坝文化与齐家文化也存在"广泛深入的文化交流"。⑤ 虽然四坝文化的

---

① 干骨崖墓地有四个碳十四测年数据，校正后年代范围很大，在1890BC—1250BC之间，李水城选取了1850BC—1600BC；火烧沟墓地也有四个数据，校正后年代范围为1940BC—1630BC，李水城选取了2000BC—1800BC。最后归总为2000BC—1600BC，三次处理都没有说明根据。见李水城《四坝文化研究》，《考古学文化论集》（三），文物出版社1993年版，第90、94、103页。

② 李水城：《四坝文化研究》，《考古学文化论集》（三），文物出版社1993年版，第109页。

③ 李水城：《四坝文化研究》，《考古学文化论集》（三），文物出版社1993年版，第108页。

④ 张忠培：《东灰山墓地研究》，《中国文化研究所学报》，香港中文大学，1997年第6期，第297页，重印于张忠培《中国考古学：走向与推进文明的历程》，紫禁城出版社2004年版，第253—286页。

⑤ 张忠培：《东灰山墓地研究》，《中国文化研究所学报》，香港中文大学，1997年第6期，第300、302—303、305页，重印于张忠培《中国考古学：走向与推进文明的历程》，紫禁城出版社2004年版。

第三部分　中国西北和欧亚草原考古

去向不明，但是它的一些因素传播到新疆哈密市的天山北路墓地。①

上述分期都推动了四坝文化的研究。本文尝试在此基础上利用西城驿遗址的发掘资料提出一个新的分期。西城驿遗址位于甘肃省张掖市西北171千米，距离黑河7—9千米。经过测绘，该遗址总面积达35万平方米；但是遗址区内分布有古河道和若干座大沙丘，将遗址区分为三个部分，所以我们分了A、B、C三区。A、B两区为隔古河道东西相望的两片台地，而C区则在一座大沙丘的东侧。A区的堆积最厚，厚度在150厘米以上。2010年以来，我们已经连续五年在这里做了发掘，不仅发现了很多房屋建筑和灰坑，而且发现了大量的彩陶和其他陶片。与此同时，我们发现了连续地层，可以对该遗址的建筑遗迹和遗物进行分期。目前发掘仍在继续，已经发表了一篇发掘简报，②另一篇发掘简报和前期的一些科技考古论文也即将问世。本文将利用2010年的发掘资料提出一个初步的分期。

前文说到，有关四坝文化的分期前人都做过研究，如何处理以往的分期成果是每个发掘者都要面临的问题。一种方法是无视原有的分期成果，另起炉灶；一种方法是把新材料套进原先的分期成果。两种方法在我国考古界都很常见，但是都有问题。文化分期与其他学术问题一样，存在各种局限，需要经过不断检验而得到修正和升华。这就要求后人接力棒似地对前人的工作进行剖析，看看旧分期存在哪些问题，新材料又能解决什么问题。如果旧分期没有问题，那就没有必要提出新的分期。如果有问题，那么就利用新材料解决这个问题。这样前人的工作不至于浪费，后人也不用再做前人做过的功课，其他研究者也无需面对几套大相径庭的分期无所适从而烦恼。后种方法往往是出于对前人的尊重乃至敬畏，不敢碰其分期成果，其结果是浪费了新材料带来的新认识，文化分期也只能裹足不前，停留在前人的成果上。文化分期是一项必要的基础工作，但是它不是考古学

---

① 李水城：《四坝文化研究》，《考古学文化论集》（三），文物出版社1993年版，第108—109页。
② 甘肃省文物考古研究所、北京科技大学冶金与材料史研究所、中国社会科学院考古研究所、西北大学文化遗产学院：《甘肃张掖市西城驿遗址》，《考古》2014年第7期，第3—17页。

研究的中级目标（解决具体学术问题，如经济形态、社会组织），更不是高级目标（认识人类社会的发展规律）。可惜的是，我国的考古学界不注重学术传承，不注重学术批评，各自为政，导致很多人消耗很多精力甚至停留在这种基础工作上。

　　李水城和张忠培二人的分期，都是当时能够达到的最高水平。但是两位学者也清醒地认识到，他们缺乏地层材料，所能做的就是尽量发挥类型学的作用。所以西城驿遗址的连续地层和丰富的陶片为我们创造了有利的条件，其优势是纯粹的类型学所不可比拟的。尽管地层出土陶片比较破碎，缺乏完整器形，但是通过观察各个地层单位（含灰坑、墓葬、房屋等遗迹单位）出土的陶片，利用类型学，我们可以归纳出更为明确细致的陶器演变规律。我们要做的是利用新材料来建立分期，然后来检验他们的分期，而不是把新材料套进他们的分期。在分期时，我们要观察各个层位的陶器的变化大小，合并小的，区分大的，形成分期。与此同时，由于我们的分期不仅是为自己服务的，也是为其他研究者服务的，所以要简单明了，各期特征也容易掌握，便于检验应用。由一个探方的发掘资料形成分期，还要对照其他探方予以验证，不对的修正，不足的补充。如果发掘了新的探方，也要予以验证。将来如果发掘了其他聚落，也要与之验证，使分期得到及时的更新，同时提高它的适用范围。这样就不用发掘一个遗址就提出一个新的分期，我们只要对原有分期进行补充修正就行了。其他研究者也不用从头再搞一次文化分期，而可以集中精力去研究其他问题。

　　上述的简报中发表了2011年的部分发掘资料，但是没有公布地层资料。西城驿遗址的发掘是从A区台地东北角遭到破坏的豁口开始的，刮开台地的壁面后，可以清晰地看到三大层堆积（图3-4-2）。以灰沟底部为界，以上为第一大层，表面为建筑F3；以下的F4、F8及其上面的一层为第二大层；F4、F8以下为第三大层，里面也包含若干层建筑。这样的分期后来在整理陶器时得到了验证；我们在第一、二大层之间以及第二、三大层之间都观察到了比较明显的变化，而各大层内则变化不明显。因此我们将西城驿遗址的堆积分为三期，同时我们重新整理了简报发表的陶器资料，做了一张分期图（图3-4-3）。

第三部分　中国西北和欧亚草原考古

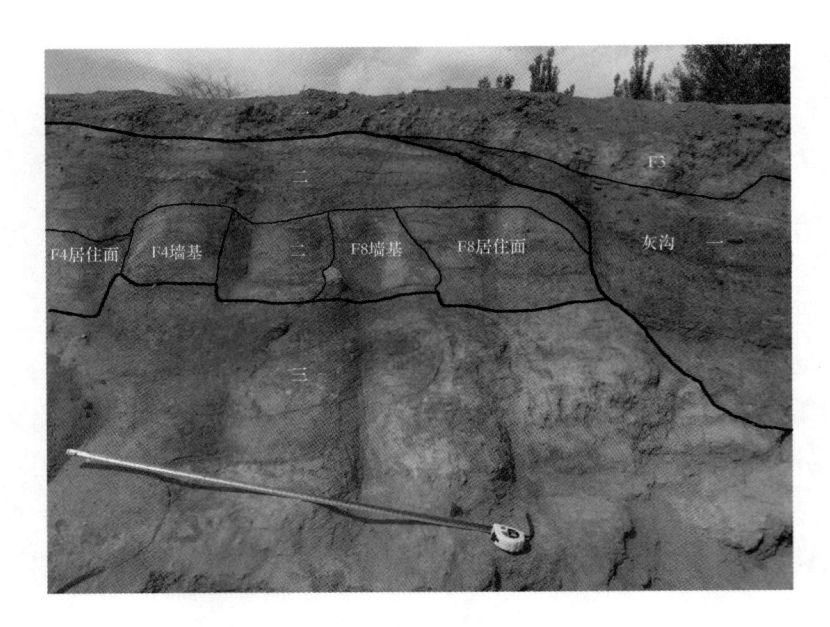

图3-4-2　西城驿遗址缺口剖面图（张良仁摄）

西城驿遗址的三期陶器的各方面特征延续性很强，均包含粗砂、细砂和泥质陶，前两类均有灰陶和砖红陶，后一类均为红陶。器类与已经发表的东灰山墓地的接近，均有双耳罐、无耳罐、腹耳壶、豆、双耳盆、盘、器盖和瓮，说明四坝文化的居民死后随葬日常使用的陶器。它们以素面为主，但也有彩陶、绳纹、篮纹、戳印纹和珍珠（有窝）。三期器类没有大的变化，只是第三期出现了钵和单耳杯。下述的三期陶器的变化发生在器形和花纹上，体现的是一个渐变的过程。

第一期：第三大层。陶质坚硬清脆，表面经过刮抹磨光，鲜艳亮泽。陶色大多为砖红色，但也有橙红色和深红色。绳纹深而清晰。绘彩陶者大多直接绘于器表，少数绘于白色或紫红衣之上。图案有竖线、横线、竖行连续菱格纹、网格纹、涡纹、对三角纹、三角形网格纹、菱格网纹、"M"形纹、"人"形纹和"X"形纹。线条纤细均匀。所用颜料有墨汁状，也有泥粉状，漆黑发亮。有些陶器镶嵌珍珠。罐高领，直口，尖圆唇或圆唇，有指压纹花边，双耳上端紧贴器口；壶类器高领，直口，尖唇，圆肩，深腹。其他器类有切口罐。此外还发现齐家文化的薄胎大耳罐、圆肩篮纹罐、鬲足、鼎足，其中薄胎大耳罐折腹，形体瘦高。

·218·

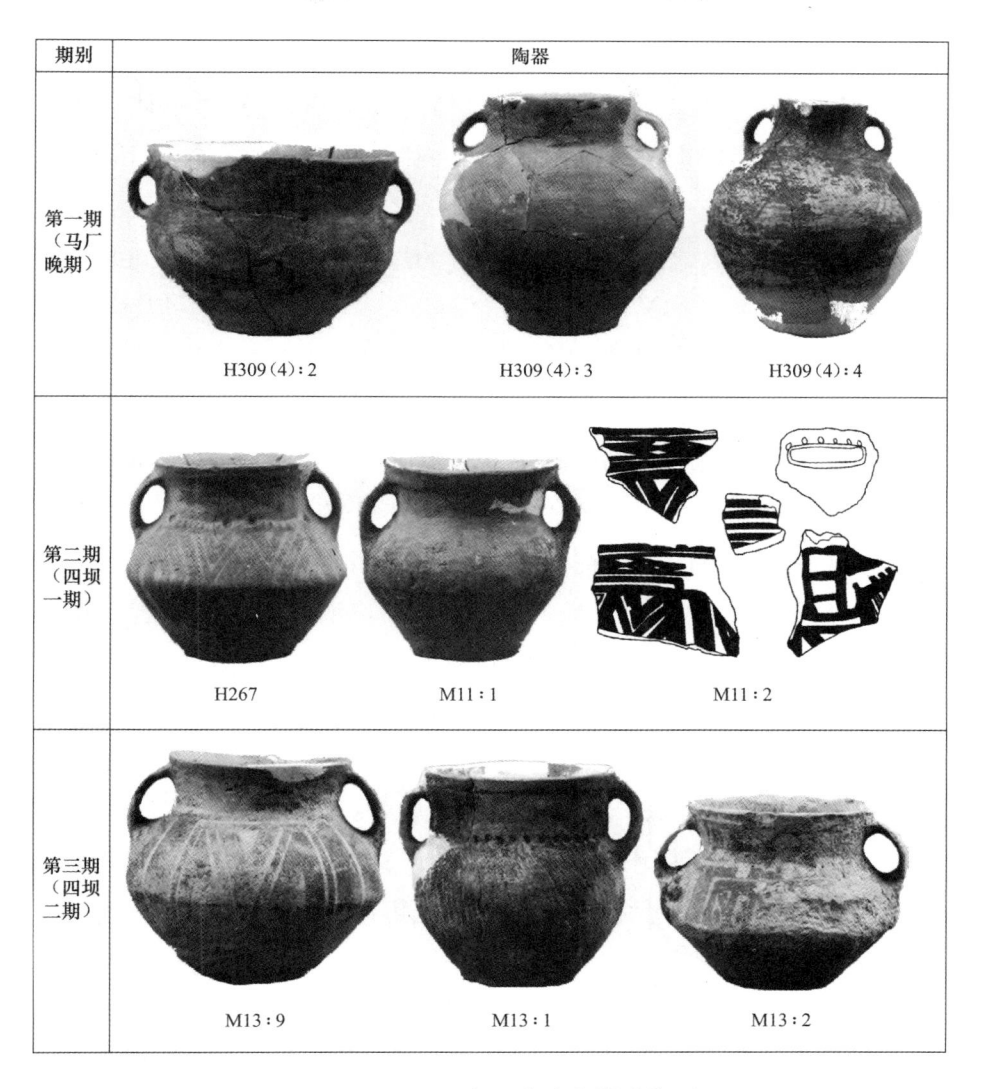

期别	陶器
第一期（马厂晚期）	H309(4):2　　H309(4):3　　H309(4):4
第二期（四坝一期）	H267　　M11:1　　M11:2
第三期（四坝二期）	M13:9　　M13:1　　M13:2

图 3-4-3　西城驿遗址陶器分期图

第二期：第二大层。陶色稳定，呈砖红色，表明制陶技术趋于成熟。表面虽然经过磨光，但是工艺退化，失去光泽。无论粗砂陶还是细砂陶都普遍在表面施白衣，使得色泽灰暗混浊。绳纹浅而模糊。彩陶直接绘于器表者减少，而多绘于紫红或白色陶衣上。所用颜料为泥粉状，易起皮脱落。图案为网格、棋盘格、折线、三角纹、菱形网格、横线和竖线，线条粗犷。有些器物镶嵌珍珠。罐和壶一般侈口或敞口，厚唇，有指压纹花边。双耳上端移至唇下。本期器物普遍变得厚重，但是继续

◇❖◇ 第三部分 中国西北和欧亚草原考古

出有齐家文化的鬲足。

第三期：第一大层。陶色稳定，呈砖红色，同时器物个体无论是厚胎器物还是薄胎器物都有所增大，表明制陶技术更为成熟。但是磨光技术退化，更加依赖施白衣或紫红衣来装饰表面，色泽更为暗浊。彩陶普遍绘于白衣或紫红衣之上，所用颜料更为厚重，色泽发白；同时图案更为丰满，线条更为粗犷，更加显得富丽堂皇。只是颜料更加容易脱落，而且线条不易识别，看上去黑乎乎一片。图案有三横线、折线、三角纹、回纹。不见镶嵌珍珠者。壶和罐的口沿加宽，更加外张，呈侈口或敞口，同时腹部外鼓。罐的双耳上端下移至颈的中部。本期出有齐家文化的薄胎大耳罐和鬲足，前者胎增厚，形体变矮。

上述分期显然不同于以往的分期，对于陶质、陶色、器形、彩陶陶衣和纹样方面的认识更为清晰。这一切要归功于西城驿遗址提供的连续地层和丰富的陶片。那么上述三期陶器与以往讨论的马厂文化和四坝文化有什么联系呢？下面将着重讨论这个问题。

首先我们来看西城驿遗址的一期陶器与马厂文化晚期的关系。关于马厂文化的分期，瑞典学者巴尔姆格伦（Nils Palmgren）最早利用采集或征购得来的陶器，使用艺术史方法提出了一套方案。[1] 尽管其材料比较零星，但是其观察角度和分析方法不无可取之处，可惜该分期出于种种原因没有得到中国考古学家的重视。1970 年以后，随着考古发掘的进展，人们利用新发现的墓葬材料整理出了若干分期。1976 年，考古工作者根据地层关系将当时在青海省乐都县柳湾墓地发掘的 227 座墓葬分为三期。[2] 至 1979 年发掘结束时，墓葬数量增至 872 座，但是发掘者维持了此前的三期说。[3] 1973 年和 1974 年，考古工作者在永昌县鸳鸯池墓地发掘墓葬 189 座，后来将其分为三期，提出早期属于半山类

---

[1] Palmgren, Nils, *Kansu Mortuary Urns of the Pan Shan and Ma Chang Groups*, Palaeontologia Sinica Series D, Volume Ⅲ, Beiping: The Geological Survey of China, 1934.

[2] 青海省文物管理处考古队、北京大学历史系考古专业：《青海乐都柳湾原始社会墓葬第一次发掘的初步收获》，《文物》1976 年第 1 期，第 69 页。该文有关各期特征的叙述文字漏印较多，完整者见严文明《甘肃彩陶的源流》，《文物》1997 年第 7 期，第 70—71 页。

[3] 青海省文物管理处考古队、中国社会科学院考古研究所：《青海柳湾——乐都柳湾原始社会墓地》，文物出版社 1984 年版，第 239—242 页。

型，中期和晚期都属于马厂类型，相当于后者的早期和晚期。[1] 这个分期与 1977—1978 年发掘的兰州市红古区土谷台墓地（发掘 84 座墓葬）类似。[2] 后来李伊萍将柳湾墓地分为四期，随之将马厂文化也分为四期。[3] 后来李水城更为系统地整理柳湾墓地出土的彩陶的器形和花纹，也将之分为四期。[4] 上述各位学者认识到的陶器演变规律都大体相似，都是器形由胖而瘦，彩绘由红黑复合彩而黑彩，纹样由写实而抽象。

根据李水城的描述，马厂文化从二期开始进入河西走廊西段（酒泉以东），三期进一步扩张至酒泉以西，四期马厂文化衰落，在河西走廊消失。[5] 西城驿遗址的一期陶器与马厂二期相比，器类上缺少长颈瓶和高低耳壶，彩陶上缺少红黑复合彩。就可比较的器形双耳罐而言，前者比马厂二期的要瘦高。[6] 因此，西城驿遗址的一期显然不属于马厂二期。马厂三、四期的器形属于同一组，彩陶花纹变化不大，只是构图更为简单，风格更为粗放，[7] 可以合并为一期，其中的差别或许是墓葬之间的差别，而不是时间的差别。长颈瓶和高低耳壶基本消失，剩下小口瓮、单耳罐、双耳罐、双耳盆、钵、豆等，西城驿遗址的一期陶器器类与之大体重合。不同的是，马厂三、四期瓮的比例偏高，不过这可能反映的是文化喜好。纹样有些变化，红黑复合彩消失，剩下黑色单彩，而且陶器表面流行施深红色陶衣，与西城驿遗址的一期陶器相近。器形方面，西城驿一期的彩陶和夹砂双耳罐都是直口，高领，双耳上端与口沿平齐。这些特征与马厂三、四期的典型墓葬 M558、M1284、M564 和 M1290 出土的陶器接近。[8] 西城驿一期流行竖线、横线纹、竖行连续菱格、网格、涡纹、对三

---

[1] 甘肃省博物馆文物工作队、武威地区文物普查队：《甘肃永昌鸳鸯池新石器时代墓地》，《考古学报》1982 年第 2 期，第 222 页。

[2] 甘肃省博物馆、兰州市文化馆：《兰州土谷台半山—马厂文化墓地》，《考古学报》1983 年第 2 期，第 191—210 页。

[3] 李伊萍：《半山、马厂文化研究》，《考古学文化论集》（三），文物出版社 1993 年版，第 32—67 页。

[4] 李水城：《半山与马厂彩陶研究》，北京大学出版社 1998 年版，第 178—182 页。

[5] 李水城：《半山与马厂彩陶研究》，北京大学出版社 1998 年版，第 184—187 页。

[6] 李水城：《半山与马厂彩陶研究》，北京大学出版社 1998 年版，第 179—180 页，图六五。

[7] 李水城：《半山与马厂彩陶研究》，北京大学出版社 1998 年版，第 180—181 页。

[8] 四座墓葬的陶器图分别见《青海柳湾》上册图三八 B、图四六和图四九。

◇❖◇ **第三部分 中国西北和欧亚草原考古**

角纹、三角形网格纹、菱格网纹、"M"形纹、"人"形纹、"X"形纹也与马厂三、四期的花纹接近。不过后者仍然残留有人蛙纹、大圆圈纹和锯齿纹，为西城驿一期所没有，但是这可能是聚落的日常用品与墓葬的随葬用品的不同。总体而言，西城驿一期在器类、器形、彩陶风格与纹样方面与马厂三、四期接近，因此属于后者，也就是马厂晚期。[①]

西城驿遗址第三期陶器的器类、器形、花纹和风格与已经发表的山丹县四坝滩、玉门县火烧沟和民乐县东灰山出土的陶器，都属于典型的四坝文化。这里无需多说，需要着重讨论的是本期与前人所做的分期。如前所述，张忠培认为东灰山墓地的年代与李水城所分的火烧沟墓地相当，而早于干骨崖墓地。总体来看，李水城所分的五期中，三—五期与西城驿遗址的第三期相当。各期的彩陶双耳罐口沿外侈呈喇叭状，双耳上端移至颈中部，腹部圆鼓，腹部装饰下端张开的三角纹；夹砂双耳罐与之类似，口沿侈口呈喇叭状，双耳上端位于颈中部，腹部圆鼓。这些器形和花纹特征与西城驿第三期的接近，应该同时。也许将来地层资料增加，可以允许我们分得更细，但是目前我们只能作为一期。

西城驿遗址第二期相当于简报的第一期。从现有材料可以看出，本期与一期之间差别明显，两期应该分开。彩陶双耳罐微侈口，双耳上端下移至口沿下，腹部微鼓，夹砂双耳罐和无耳罐同样微侈口。它们类似于李水城分出来的"过渡时期"的陶器，既继承了西城驿第一期即马厂晚期的特征，也出现了西城驿第三期即四坝文化的特征。此外，李水城分出的四坝文化一至二期陶器，从陶器特征来看，也属于本期。与四坝文化分期不同，在划分"过渡时期"时，李水城依靠的是从若干遗址拼凑起来的陶器，根据就是他们体现出了一些介于马厂与四坝之间的特征。[②] 现在西城驿遗址提供的新资料把马厂与四坝文化连接起来，一方面证实了他的方法和思路，另一方面提供了他当时拥有的材料所无法比拟的完整资料。同样，将来等资料增加，也许有可能分得更细。只是

---

① 李水城将马厂第三期视为马厂晚期。《半山与马厂彩陶研究》，北京大学出版社1998年版，第180页。
② 李水城：《四坝文化研究》，《考古学文化论集》（三），文物出版社1993年版，第109—113页，图一一，图一二，图一三。

"过渡时期"一词已经不再合适。过渡现象是两个前后相继的文化之间经常出现的现象。往往前一个文化和后一个文化的第一期都会出现过渡特征，但是人们一般不会单独划出一个过渡时期。李水城研究的半山与马厂类型之间就是一个典型的例子。[①] 它本来就是一个暂时使用的名词，以应付资料有限，马厂与四坝文化之间的承接关系不清楚的需要。现在需要做的是，讨论该期到底属于马厂还是四坝。从西城驿第二期陶器的器形和花纹来看，它们更接近于第三期。因此，我们把西城驿遗址的第二、三期称为四坝文化的第一、二期。

在 2010 年，我们从三大层的地层和遗迹单位筛选出来的木炭和植物种子中选了一部分标本，送到中国社会科学院考古研究所考古科技中心碳十四实验室，供测年之用。现在测年数据已经出来，有关的分析论文也准备刊发。测年数据经过拟合以后，三期的年代范围分别为：一期，三个数据，2135BC—1900BC；二期，九个数据，1880BC—1680BC；三期，九个数据，1670BC—1530BC。[②] 总体而言，西城驿遗址的四坝文化一、二期年代范围与以往所得年代范围基本重合。如此看来，西城驿遗址的四坝文化历时 350 多年，这么长的历史只分两期似乎有点少，但是按目前的资料分只允许这么多。

总之，本文根据张掖市西城驿遗址的系列地层和彩陶，将四坝文化的彩陶分成三期。三期彩陶的器类、器形和纹样都具有很强的延续性，说明它们是前后延续发展的；同时，三期彩陶又各有自己的特征，可以代表三个阶段。其中第一期属于马厂晚期，第三期属于四坝文化，而第二期相当于过去的"过渡类型"。但是从彩陶特征来看，本期更接近于第三期，可以归入四坝文化。过去发掘的火烧沟、干骨崖和东灰山等墓地出土的彩陶可以归入这两期。根据最新获得的碳十四数据，三期的年代分别为 2135BC—1900BC、1880BC—1680BC 和 1670BC—1530BC。

---

① 李水城：《半山与马厂彩陶研究》，北京大学出版社 1998 年版，第 178 页。
② 张雪莲、张良仁、王辉、卢雪峰、陈国科、王鹏：《张掖市西城驿遗址的碳十四测年及初步分析》，《华夏考古》第 4 期，第 38—45 页。

Ancient Mud-brick Architecture of Northwest China[*]

Introduction

The continuous excavation in 2010 – 2015 at the Bronze Age settlement of Xichengyi near the historic town of Zhangye, Gansu province, has uncovered a good deal of interesting materials that bears upon the prehistoric east-west cultural interaction. Located in the middle of the Hexi Corridor, Zhangye was one of the "Four Commanderies" founded during the Western Han dynasty (206BC – 9AD) that constituted a crucial segment of the Silk Road. The appreciable amount of painted potsherds, copper ores, slag, animal bones, crop seeds, and mud-brick buildings found at Xichengyi makes it clear that the sedentary community was engaged not only in agriculture and metal production, but also in interaction with the East and West long before the advent of the commonly known "Silk Road." This paper will focus on the mud-brick buildings found at this site and present a new type of mud-brick construction technique that ingeniously fuses the mud-brick construction technique from the west and the earth ramming technique from the east.

Early Mud-brick Architecture

The earliest mud-brick architecture appeared in the Pre-Pottery Neolithic Age (9600BC – 8500BC) in the Near East, especially the Levant and Anatolia, used

---

[*] The article was originally published in *Paléorient* 44/1, 2018, pp. 93 – 103. It is reprinted in this anthology with minor changes.

mainly for erecting walls and sometimes for paving floors. ①②Modeled out of a mixture of clay, silt, sand, and vegetal temper, and later sun-dried, the early mud-brick was usually plano-convex or hog-backed in shape, "imitating the naturally occurring building material field stones widely used in the preceding Epipaleolithic Age, and discretely embedded in mud mortar made of the same mixture in the same way as field stones are set."③ As a durable and economical building material, mud-brick spread outward quickly to the settlement of Ganj Dareh in Central Zagros Mountains, possibly in 8000BC – 7800BC,④ the Jeitun culture in Central Asia, and the site of Mehrgarh in Pakistan in 7000BC – 6000BC. ⑤The mud-brick was laid in

---

① Aurenche, O., L'origine de la brique dans le Proche Orient ancient, in M. Frangipane, H. Hauptmann, M. Liverani, P. Matthiae, and M. Mellink eds., *Between the Rivers and Over the Mountains*: *Archaeologica Anatolica et Mesopotamica Alba Palmieri Dedicata*, Rome: Dipartimento di Scienze Storiche Archeologiche e Antropologiche dell'Antichità, Università di Roma (La Sapienza), 1993, pp. 73 – 76; Cauvin, J., *The Birth of the Gods and the Origins of Agriculture*, translated by Trevor Watkins, Cambridge: Cambridge University Press, 2000, p. 36; Biçakci, E., Observations on the early pre-Pottery Neolithic architecture in the Near East: 1. New building materials and construction techniques, in M. Özdoğan, H. Hauptmann, and N. Basgelen eds., *From villages to towns*: *early villages in the Near East*, studies presented to Ufuk Esin, Istanbul: Arkeoloji ve Sanat Publications, 2003, p. 394; Love, S., Architecture as material culture: Building form and materiality in the Pre-Pottery Neolithic of Anatolia and Levant, *Journal of Anthropological Archaeology* 32/4, 2013, pp. 746 – 758.

② Some scholars regard the clay balls in the walls of the houses below the PPNA layer at Jericho as "the rudimentary form of bricks" (Kenyon, K. M., *Excavations at Jericho*, The Architecture and Stratigraphy of the Tell, London: British School of Archaeology in Jerusalem, Vol. III, 1981, pp. 224 – 225; Robert Homsher, personal comm., 1 October, 2013).

③ Wright, G. R. H., *Ancient Building Technology*, Leidon and Boston: Brill, 2005, Vol. 2, Part 1, p. 97.

④ Smith, P. E. L., Architectural Innovation and Experimentation at Ganj Dareh, Iran, *World Archaeology* 21/3, 1990, p. 328; Aurenche, O., L'origine de la brique dans le Proche Orient ancient, in M. Frangipane, H. Hauptmann, M. Liverani, P. Matthiae, and M. Mellink eds., *Between the Rivers and Over the Mountains*: *Archaeologica Anatolica et Mesopotamica Alba Palmieri Dedicata*, Rome: Dipartimento di Scienze Storiche Archeologiche e Antropologiche dell'Antichità, Università di Roma (La Sapienza), 1993, pp. 78 – 79; Weeks, L. R., The development and expansion of a Neolithic way of life, in D. T. Potts, ed., *Oxford Handbook of Ancient Iran*, New York: Oxford University Press, 2013, p. 50.

⑤ Khlopin, I. N., *Geoksiurskaya Gruppa Poselenii Epokhi Eneolita*: *Opyt istoricheskogo Analiza*, Moscow and Leningrad: Science Press, 1964, p. 69; Masson, V. M., *Poselenie Dzheitun*, Leningrad: Leningrad Branch of the Science Press, 1971, p. 51; Sarianidi, V., Food-producing and other Neolithic communities in Khorasan and Transoxania: eastern Iran, Soviet Central Asia and Afghanistan, in A. H. Dani and V. M. Masson eds., *History of Civilizations of Central Asia*, Paris: UNESCO Publishing, 1999, Vol. 1, p. 118; Sharif, M., and B. K. Thapar, Food-producing communities in Pakistan and northern India, in A. H. Dani and V. M. Masson eds., *History of Civilizations of Central Asia* Paris: UNESCO Publishing, 1999, Vol. 1, pp. 130 – 136; Jarrige, C., J. -F. Jarrige, R. H. Meadow, G. Quivron, *Mehrgarh*: *Field Reports 1974 – 1985 from Neolithic Times to the Indus Civilization*, published by the Department of Culture and Tourism, Government of Sindh, Pakistan, in collaboration with the French Ministry of Foreign Affairs, 1995, pp. 211, 244; Jarrige, J. -F., Mehrgarh Neolithic: New Excavations, in M. Taddei and G. de Marco eds., *South Asian Archaeology* 1997, Rome: Istituto Italiano per L'Africa e L'oriente, 2000, pp. 264, 282; Jarrige, J. -F., Mehrgarh Neolithic, *Prāgdhārā* 18, 2007, p. 140.

a single row, full-length ones alternated with half-length ones and quarter-length ones.①

In the process of transmission the mud-brick manufacturing technique evolved in various ways. At the multilayered Neolithic settlement of Çatalhöyük (7400BC – 6000BC) in Central Turkey, while earlier mud-brick was tempered with straw, later sandy mud-brick emerged in use. A black mortar, mixed with ash and broken bones, was used to bind them.② In the meantime, the hand-modeling technique was replaced by the form-molding technique in the Near East, Central Asia, and South Asia, which gave rise to rectangular or square shapes with straight lines and right angles, thereby increasing the production and building efficiency, another revolution in building technology.③ When it came to the Bronze Age (3400BC – 1300BC), when urban centers were in their time of rapid expansion, such mud-brick was widely used in the Near East, Central Asia, and South Asia.④ It has even been discovered at the pastoralist settlements of Zamaraevo-Alekseevka in North-Central Kazakhstan and Tasbas in

---

① Aurenche, O., L'origine de la brique dans le Proche Orient ancient, in M. Frangipane, H. Hauptmann, M. Liverani, P. Matthiae, and M. Mellink eds., *Between the Rivers and Over the Mountains: Archaeologica Anatolica et Mesopotamica Alba Palmieri Dedicata*, Rome: Dipartimento di Scienze Storiche Archeologiche e Antropologiche dell'Antichità, Università di Roma (La Sapienza), 1993, p. 80.

② Mellaart, J., *Çatal Hüyük: A Neolithic Town in Anatolia*, New York: McGraw-Hill Book Company, 1967, p. 55.

③ Wright, G. R. H., *Ancient Building Technology*, Leidon and Boston: Brill, 2000, Vol. 1, p. 42; Wright, G. R. H., *Ancient Building Technology*, Leidon and Boston: Brill, 2005, Vol. 2, Part 1, p. 99; Dunham, S., Ancient Near Eastern Architecture, in D. C. Snell ed., *A Companion to the Ancient Near East*, Malden, Oxford, and Carlton: Blackwell Publishing, 2005, p. 270; Masson, V. M., Eneolit Srednei Azii, in V. M. Masson, and N. Ya., Merpert eds., *Eneolit SSSR*, Moscow: Science Press, Part I, 1982, pp. 17, 26, 35; Jarrige, C., J. -F. Jarrige, R. H. Meadow, G. Quivron, *Mehrgarh: Field Reports 1974 – 1985 from Neolithic Times to the Indus Civilization*, published by the Department of Culture and Tourism, Government of Sindh, Pakistan, in collaboration with the French Ministry of Foreign Affairs, 1995, p. 423.

④ Thapar, B. K., New traits of the Indus civilization at Kalibangan: an appraisal, in N. Hammon ed., *South Asian Archaeology: Papers from the First International Conference of South Asian Archaeologists held in the University of Cambridge*, Park Ridge, New Jersey: Noyes Press, 1973, pp. 86 – 87; Bisht, R. S., Structural Remains and Town-planning of Banawali, in B. B. Lal and S. P. Gupta eds., *Frontiers of the Indus Civilization*, New Dehli: I. M. Sharma of Books & Books, 1984, pp. 90 – 91; Tosi, M., S. M. Shahmirzadi, and M. A. Joeynda, The Bronze Age in Iran and Afghanistan, in A. H. Dani, and V. M. Masson eds., *History of Civilizations of Central Asia*, Paris: UNESCO Publishing, 1999, Vol. 1, pp. 207, 213.

Eastern Kazakhstan. [1]

In China, the earliest known examples of mud-brick buildings have been discovered, unexpectedly, not in Xinjiang or Hexi Corridor, but in the middle Yangzi River, at the site of Menbanwan, which is assigned to the Late Neolithic culture of Qujialing (3400BC – 2500BC). [2]By the Longshan period (2500BC – 1800BC), mud-brick architecture was widely constructed in the Yangzi River Valley and Northern China (Fig. 3 – 5 – 1). Extraordinarily well preserved houses have been discovered at the Bronze Age settlement of Erdaojingzi in Chifeng city, Inner Mongolia, [3]of the Lower Xiajiadian culture (2200BC – 1500BC). Wherever reported, mud-brick was made with vegetal temper and laid by the stretcher technique and bound with mortar. In Xinjiang and Gansu, mud-brick structure has only been reported from the Bronze Age settlements of Xintala and Donghuishan, which date loosely to 1904BC – 1043BC. [4]The material, however, was widely used to line walls of tomb pits of the Early Iron Age in Xinjang, which roughly date to 1300BC – 200BC (Fig. 3 – 5 – 1). Wherever reported, mud-bricks from Xinjiang and Gansu differ in being sandy and without vegetal temper; and albeit bound with mortar, they were laid one right upon another, again different from those of the Yangzi River Valley and Northern China. The origins of the mud-bricks ever found in the disparate regions of China, however, remain to be a mystery.

Partly because of their commonality, few ancient mudbrick buildings ever found in Central Asia and China have been properly reported and studied. [5]It is

---

[1] Spengler, R. N., M. D. Frachetti, P. N. Doumani, Agriculture in the Piedmont of Eastern Central Asia: The Late Bronze Age at Tasbas, Kazakhstan, *Quaternary International* 348, 2014, p. 149; Doumani, P. N., M. D. Frachetti, R. Reardmore, T. Schmaus, R. N. Spengler, A. N. Mar'yashev, Burial Ritual, Agriculture, and Craft Production among Bronze Age Pastoralists at Tasbas (Kazakhstan), *Archaeological Research in Asia* 1 – 2, 2015, p. 22.

[2] Hubeisheng Wenwu Kaogu Yanjiusuo, Neolithic site at Menbanwan in Yingcheng, Hubei, in Guojia Wenwuju ed., *Zhongguo Zhongyao Kaogu Faxian*, Beijing: Wenwu, 1999, p. 10.

[3] Neimenggu Wenwu Kaogu Yanjiusuo, Neimenggu Chifengshi Erdaojingzi yizhi de fajue, *Kaogu* 8, 2010, pp. 16 – 19; Fig. 1.

[4] Xinjiang Kaogusuo, Xinjiang Heshuo Xintala yizhi fajue jianbao, *Kaogu* 5, 1988, pp. 399 – 407, 476; Gansu Wenwu Kaogu Yanjiusuo and Jilindaxue Beifang Kaogu Yanjiushi, *Minle Donghuishan Kaogu: Siba Wenhua Mudi de Jieshi yu Yanjiu*, Beijing: Kexue, 1998, p. 8.

[5] An exception is a comprehensive survey of ancient architecture, mostly built of mud-bricks, in Central Asia written by Nasiba S. Baimatowa (2008, *5000 Jahre Architektur in Mittelasien: Lehmziegelgewölbe vom 4. /3. Jt. V. Chr. Bis zum Ende des 8. Jhs. N. Chr.*, Mainz: Verlag Philipp von Zabern).

◇❖◇ 第三部分 中国西北和欧亚草原考古

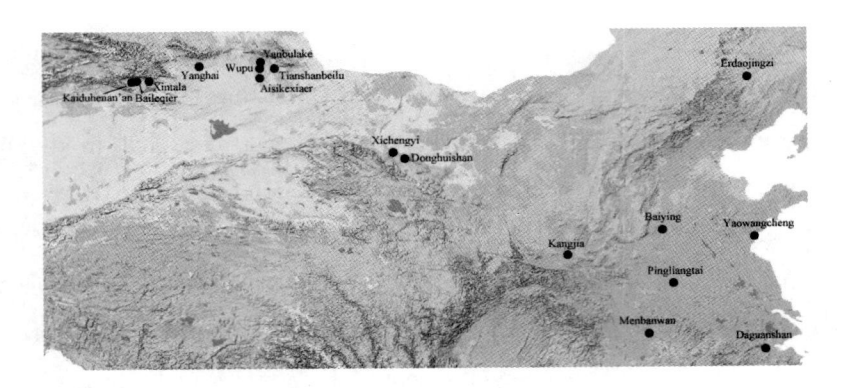

Fig. 3 – 5 – 1 **Distribution of mud-brick structures in China**

therefore striking to see that the mud-brick buildings found in the Near East (including Egypt, the Levant, and Anatolia) have been subject to extensive recording and measuring, to the point that one can tell the date of a building by the dimension of the mud-brick in it;[1] some of them have even been subject to various technical analyses to address the questions of material source and manufacturing style. [2]Such studies, as far as known to the authors, have not

---

[1] Wright, G. R. H., *Ancient Building Technology*, Leidon and Boston: Brill, 2005, Vol. 2, Part 1, pp. 102 – 103.

[2] Rosen, A. M., *Cities of Clay: The Geoarchaeology of Tells*, Chicago and London: The University of Chicago Press, 1986; Morgenstein, M. E., and C. A. Redmount, Mudbrick Typology, Sources, and Sedimentological Composition: A Case Study from Tell El-Muqdam, Egyptian Delta, *Journal of the American Research Center in Egypt* 35, 1998, pp. 129 – 46; Stevanović, M., Architecture, with contributions by Ina St. George, *Çatalhöyük Archive Report*, 2005, pp. 229 – 241, http: //www. catalhoyuk. com/archive_reports/; Love, S., Mudbrick and Mortar morphology, *Çatalhöyük 2005 Archive Report*, 2005, pp. 280 – 281, http: //www. catalhoyuk. com/archive_ reports/; Love, S., The Geoarchaeology of Mudbricks in Architecture: A Methodological Study from Çatalhöyük, Turkey, *Geoarchaeology: An International Journal* 27, 2012, pp. 140 – 156; Emery, V. L., and M. Morgenstein, Portable EDXRF Analysis of a Mud Brick Necropolis Enclosure: Evidence of Work Organization, El Hibeh, Middle Egypt, *Journal of Archaeological Science* 34, 2007, pp. 111 – 122; Tung, B., *Making Place, Doing Tradition: Exploring Intimate Knowledge at Neolithic Çatalhöyük*, PhD dissertation, University of California, Berkeley, 2008; Nodarou, E., C. Frederick, and A. Hein, Another (Mud) Brick in the Wall: Scientific Analysis of Bronze Age Earthen Construction Materials from East Crete, *Journal of Archaeological Science* 35, 2008, pp. 2997 – 3015; Barański, M. Z., Late Neolithic Architecture of Çatalhöyük, *Çatalhöyük 2011 Archive Report*, 2011, pp. 124 – 127, http: //www. catalhoyuk. com/archive_ reports/; Homsher, R. S., Mud Bricks and the Process of Construction in the Middle Bronze Age Southern Levant, *Bulletin of the American Schools of Oriental Research* 368, 2012, pp. 1 – 27.

been done to any mud-brick found in China. The recent discovery of mud-brick buildings at the Bronze Age settlement of Xichengyi provides a rare opportunity for us to investigate ancient mud-brick technique of Northwest China.

The Xichengyi Site

The settlement of Xichengyi (Fig. 3 – 5 – 1) is located 17 km to the northwest of the present-day Zhangye city, Gansu province. Located in the middle of the Hexi Corridor, which is a nearly 1000km-long passageway between Central China and Xinjiang, Zhangye was an important town along the Silk Road beginning in the Western Han dynasty (206BC – 9AD). The Xichengyi site itself was not part of the historic Silk Road story, but as we shall see later, it played a role analogous to Zhangye: the Silk Road was in function perhaps already in the Bronze Age. [1]Discovered in 1992, it barely escaped the forceful

Fig. 3 – 5 – 2 **Xichengyi site, the building of F3 (photo by L. Zhang)**

---

[1] Irene Good (2002, The archaeology of early silk, *Silk Roads, Other Roads: Proceedings of the 8th Biennial Symposium of the Textile Society of America*, September 26 – 28, 2002, Northampton, Massachusetts) gathered multiple discoveries of silk of the 2nd and 1st millennia in Central Asia and Eurasia, but except for those from Pazyryk tombs, the provenance of silk products is difficult to determine. Wei Wang (2013, Kaogu goule chu de hanqian sichou zhilu, *Guangming Daily* 14 December 2013, p. 12) cited the westward spread of millet from China, and the eastward spread of wheat, cow, and sheep, copper and iron metallurgy from West Asia in the Chalcolithic, Bronze Age, and Early Iron Age.

expansion of land reclamation effected by a local farm, and suffered heavily from the operations of bulldozers and excavators. It was the discovery of metalworking remains (ore, slag, metal artifacts) in 2007 – 2009 that triggered the excavation project. To date, this settlement is among only a few that have ever been excavated in the Hexi corridor and Xinjiang, but the resulting materials betray vibrant cross-regional interactions in prehistoric times. The mud-brick buildings present an outstanding episode of this broad and complex story.

Mud-Brick Buildings at Xichengyi

Based on the stratigraphy and ceramic typology of the site, the excavators have discerned three major periods of construction activities, the first belonging to the Chalcolithic Machang culture (2135BC – 1900BC) and later two to the Bronze Age Siba culture, 1880BC – 1680BC and 1670BC – 1530BC respectively.[①] Mud-brick buildings are profuse all over the Xichengyi site and from the first through the third period. But due to the constraint of the 4 × 4m excavation units, however, most of them are fragmentary; only a few are exposed in their entirety. One is what first appears to be an unusually large patch of sticky clay, but turns out to be a wall falling flat on the ground, with a large depression in the center, and a number of fragments scattered around. Albeit reddish in color, the wall bears no trace of burning; it is instead the natural appearance of the sticky clay, which was widely used in the ground preparation of the other mud-brick buildings at the site. The wall, a part of which was destroyed by the farm, was 3.5m long at the base, 1.4m at the top, and 2m high (Fig. 3 – 5 – 2). To the north of this wall there is a large post foundation, and on either side there is a patch of mud-brick paved floor. The post foundation consists of a post of 16cm

---

① Gansusheng Wenwu Kaogu Yanjiusuo, Beijing Keji Daxue Yejin yu Cailiaoshi Yanjiusuo, Zhongguo Shehui Kexueyuan Kaogu Yanjiusuo, and Xibei Daxue Wenhua Yichan Xueyuan, Gansu Zhangyeshi Xichengyi yizhi, *Kaogu* 7, 2014, pp. 3 – 17; Gansusheng Wenwu Kaogu Yanjiusuo, Beijing Keji Daxue Yejin yu Cailiaoshi Yanjiusuo, Zhongguo Shehui Kexueyuan Kaogu Yanjiusuo, and Xibei Daxue Wenhua Yichan Xueyuan, Gansu Zhangyeshi Xichengyi yizhi 2010 nian fajue jianbao, *Kaogu* 10, 2015, pp. 66 – 84; Zhang, Xuelian, Liangren Zhang, Hui Wang, Xuefeng Lu, Guoke Chen, and Peng Wang, Zhangyeshi Xichengyi yizhi de tanshisi cenian ji chubu fenxi, *Huaxia Kaogu* 4, 2015, pp. 110 – 120; Zhang, L, and H. Wang, Zhangyeshi Xichengyi yizhi de caitao, *Beifang Minzu Yanjiu* 2, 2015, pp. 95 – 98.

across placed at the center of a pit of 80 – 90 cm across and 38cm deep; the now-decayed wooden post was originally rested upon a 18cm thick layer of potsherds and the surrounding space was filled with earth, which was rammed hard to secure its position. This sturdy post, rather than the wall itself, was expected to uphold a heavy roof. No other wall of the building that it belongs to, labeled F3 (third period), is found. [1]It seems that the construction was called off after the failure of the wall; no trace of use is visible under the fallen wall.

Of all the other buildings, only the wall stumps and floors are preserved. Of the first period building F54, only two walls have been found in the excavation unit. One is fully exposed and 4.6m long, with four posts (0.20 – 0.48m apart) attached to one side of it; the other, perpendicular to the former, is partially exposed and only 0.45m long. A relatively intact one, labeled F4 (second period), is a multi-roomed building. Severely destroyed, it retains the floor and walls of three large rooms erected upon it, with a maximum length of 8m and a maximum width of 7.8m. The comparatively complete ones, labeled F1 and F2 (third period), might have been united as one building, in the top layer, also of the third period. Rectangular in shape, F1 is 5.34m by 2.36m and comprised of three rooms, and F2 is attached to the east of it, 6.32m long and 2.58m wide. Within the larger room in the north, F1 has two large post foundations of the F3 type, suggesting that it originally had a heavy roof; F2 has one in a small room (Fig. 3 – 5 – 3). The multi-room plans of F1, F2, and F4 are reminiscent of those of the Near East and Central Asia, and dramatically different from the model architectural plan of China proper, in which multiple rooms are arranged in one row. [2]A trademark of the PPN architecture in the Near East, [3] the compound layout spread out to Central Asia, as seen at the Neolithic and

---

[1] In Chinese archaeological terminology, letter F is conventionally used to designate buildings.

[2] The history of prehistoric architecture of China is an under-studied subject, but the lion-share, if not all, of documented multi-roomed buildings of the Neolithic and Early Bronze Age belongs unanimously to the linear arrangement. The Institute of Archaeology, Chinese Academy of Social Sciences, *Chinese Archaeology*, Volume of the Neolithic, Age Beijing: Chinese Social Sciences Press, 2010, Figs. 4 – 12, 4 – 30, 5 – 11, and 6 – 22, 6 – 34; The Institute of Archaeology, *Chinese Archaeology*, Volume of the Xia and Shang periods, Beijing: Chinese Social Sciences Press, 2003, Figs. 4 – 6.

[3] Cauvin, J., *The Birth of the Gods and the Origins of Agriculture*, translated by Trevor Watkins, Cambridge: Cambridge University Press, 2000, pp. 41, 98.

Chalcolithic (6000BC – 3000BC) settlements of Jeitun and Anau,[①] and persisted into the Bronze Age. All the walls of the aforementioned buildings are single-brick thick.

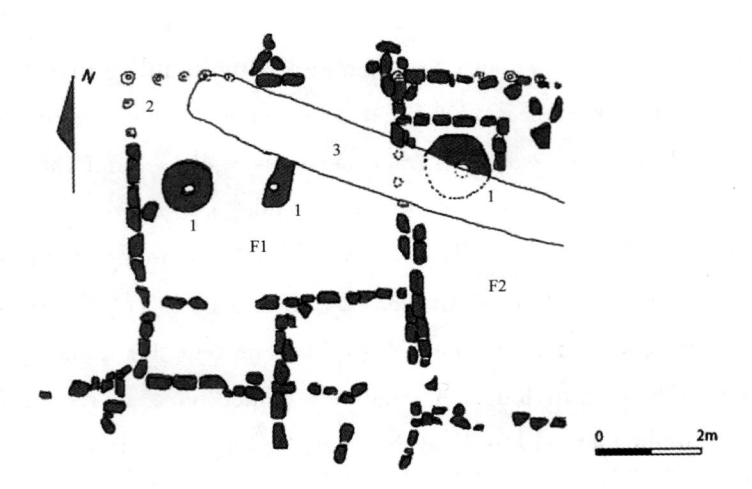

Fig. 3 – 5 – 3　Xichengyi site, Plan of F1 and F2
1. post foundation; 2. post hole; 3. modern ditch

External Properties of the Mud-brick

As a pilot study of the mud-brick buildings found at Xichengyi, this paper aims to characterize a few examples of them (Table 3 – 5 – 1). Based on field observation, the excavators have identified two types of mud-bricks. Both types are mold-made out of locally available silt, sand, and clay, but none is baked. No imprint of straw is visible. In this they are different from those of China proper and similar to those of Xinjiang and Gansu. It is worth mentioning that the local clay is sticky when wet and hard when dry, and traditionally used by local residents to make mud-brick. Type A mud-brick is compact and used throughout

---

① Sarianidi, V., Food-producing and other Neolithic communities in Khorasan and Transoxania: eastern Iran, Soviet Central Asia and Afghanistan, in A. H. Dani and V. M. Masson eds., *History of Civilizations of Central Asia*, Paris: UNESCO Publishing, 1999, Vol. 1, pp. 116 – 117, Fig. 1; Hiebert, F. T., and K. Kurbansakhatov, *A Central Asian Village at the Dawn of Civilization, Excavations at Anau, Turkmenistan*, Philadelphia: University of Pennsylvania Museum of Archaeology and Anthropology, 2003, pp. 114 – 115.

the three periods. Its size, however, varies widely from building to building, and even within one building. Examples of F4, for instance, are rectangular, 28 × 22 ×8cm at the top and 39 ×24 ×8cm at the bottom. Those of F3 are 24 × 16 × 9cm and 22 ×22 ×7cm. In general they are all quite thin. Type B mud-brick, by comparison, is rather bulky; it is used only for third-period buildings such as F1 and F2. Its size ranges remarkably from 42 ×20cm to 22 × 12cm in dimension and 18 – 23cm in thickness, even within one building.

Building Technique

The preservation condition of the mud-brick buildings does not allow us to fully reconstruct the construction process of the walls, but a careful observation of the mud-brick walls affords a few clues. The two types of mud-brick buildings, except for F3, are all erected upon foundations made of hardened red clay, but otherwise they differ enormously. In the case of Type A, mud-brick was laid along the designated line of the wall marked by small postholes in the ground (as seen in F1, Fig. 3 – 5 – 3). It was laid one directly upon another rather than interlocked (Fig. 3 – 5 – 4a). This masonry was structurally weak and readily succumbed to collapse. In fact, it is rarely seen in archaeological architecture; the single comparable case we have been able to find is that of a 3rd millennium BC building at Tappeh Hissar.[1] The solution of this problem was that mud-bricks were laid half wet, possibly two layers a time, and a wooden formwork was fixed upon the section; then the mud-brick was rammed hard so that it was bound to the ground and to another. The absence of mortar and the visible imprints of rammers of 5 – 8 cm in diameter upon the stem wall of F3 attest to this operation (Fig. 3 – 5 – 4b).

---

[1] Weisgerber, G., Schmucksteine im Alten Orient: Lapislazuli, Turkis, Achat, Karneol, in Thomas Stöller, Rainer Slotta, Abdolrasool Vatandoust eds., *Persiens Antike Pracht: Katalog der Ausstellung des Deutschen Bergbau-Museums Bochum* Bochum: Deutsches Bergbau-Museum Bochum, 2004, p. 70, Abb. 11.

第三部分 中国西北和欧亚草原考古

Table 3 – 5 – 1　　　Mud-brick samples from the Xichengyi site.

No.	Type	Building	Period	Chronology	Size (cm)	Color
1	A	F58	Late Machang	2135BC – 1900BC	17 × 14 × 7	5YR6/3
2	A	F54	Late Machang	2135BC – 1900BC	40 × 26 × 10	5YR6/3
3	A	F4	Siba I	1880BC – 1680BC	32 × 25 × 18	5YR5/3
4	A	Q1	Siba I	1880BC – 1680BC	31 × 23 × 14	5YR4/3
6	A	F3 – 1	Siba II	1670BC – 1530BC	Fragmentary	5YR5/3
5	A	F3 – 2	Siba II	1670BC – 1530BC	24 × 16 × 9	5YR5/3
7	A	F3 – 3	Siba II	1670BC – 1530BC	22 × 22 × 7	10YR 5/8
8	B	F1	Siba II	1670BC – 1530BC	22 × 12 × 18	10YR 7/6

Wooden posts of 10 – 15cm in diameter were pre-installed in the walls at the interval of ca 1.2m. Today both circular and semi-circular postholes are visible, and they possibly served to retain the walls rather than to secure the formwork. The placing of wooden posts in the wall recalls us of the buildings at Mureybet (8300BC – 7600BC) in the Near East,[1] which, however, has no later development there. This operation was repeated till the wall was completed. But unlike the painted building at Zaghe in Iran,[2] the buildings were without buttress. For Type B buildings, on the contrary, mud-brick was laid one course over another in the stretcher manner and a type of grey soil was used as mortar to fill the space between them, both horizontally and vertically. The walls of F1 and F2 nevertheless did not contain any timber post. In this Type B buildings resonate with those of both China proper and Central Asia.

Internal Properties

Apart from the aforementioned external properties and construction techniques, is there any internal difference between the two types of mud-bricks?

---

[1] Dunham, S., Ancient Near Eastern Architecture, in D. C. Snell ed., *A Companion to the Ancient Near East*, Malden, Oxford, and Carlton: Blackwell Publishing, 2005, p. 273.

[2] Negahban, Ezat, O., A brief report on the painted building of Zaghe (Late 7th-Early 6th Millennium B. C.), *Paléorient* 5, 1979, p. 243.

To answer this question, the authors submitted eight samples, which represent the three periods, to micro-structural and particle size analyses (Table 3 – 5 – 1). While the one from the building F1 is of Type B, the other are of Type A. The last two samples, from the buildings of F3 and F1, were analyzed at the State Key Laboratory of Tribology at Tsinghua University with FEI Quanta 200 FEG, and the laboratory of the School of Archaeology and Museology at Peking University with Mastersizer 2000 respectively. As they were submitted to the two laboratories right after the excavation in 2010, they retained moisture and their original colors. The first six samples, from the buildings of F58, F54, Q1 (a section of a wall), and F3 (-1, -2), were analyzed at the Lanzhou Institute of Chemical Physics, Chinese Academy of Sciences, with JSM 5600LV, and the MOE Key Laboratory of Western China's Environmental System, Lanzhou University, with Mastersizer 2000 respectively. These samples, which were submitted to the two laboratories in 2015, three or five years after the excavation, were already dehydrated and deprived of their original colors.

It turns out that the Type B mud-brick contains large pores and large agglomerates, which are loosely attached to each other (Fig. 3 – 5 – 5: h). The Type A items, in great contrast to them, do not have large pores; instead, their particles are fine and laminar, with only a few bubbles leftover (Fig. 3 – 5 – 5: a-g). Obviously they have received heavy compression, whereas the Type B

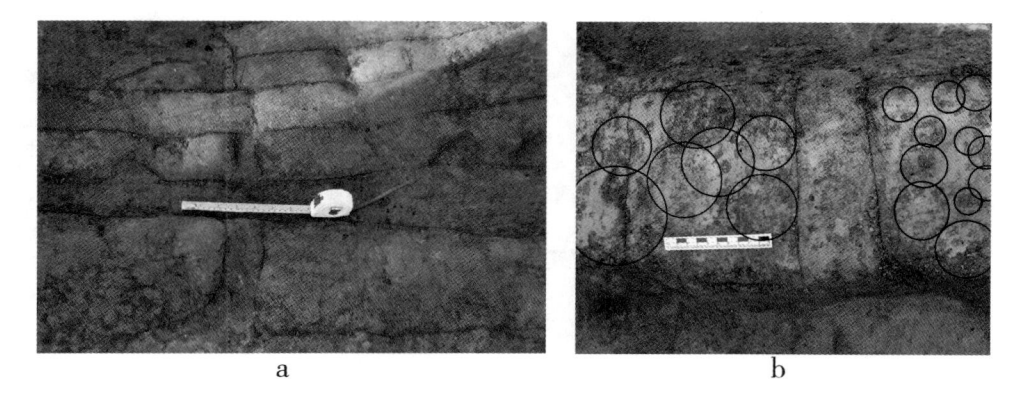

Fig. 3 – 5 – 4 **Xichengyi site, the stem wall of F3 (photo by L. Zhang)**
a. Layers of mud – bricks; b. imprints of rammers

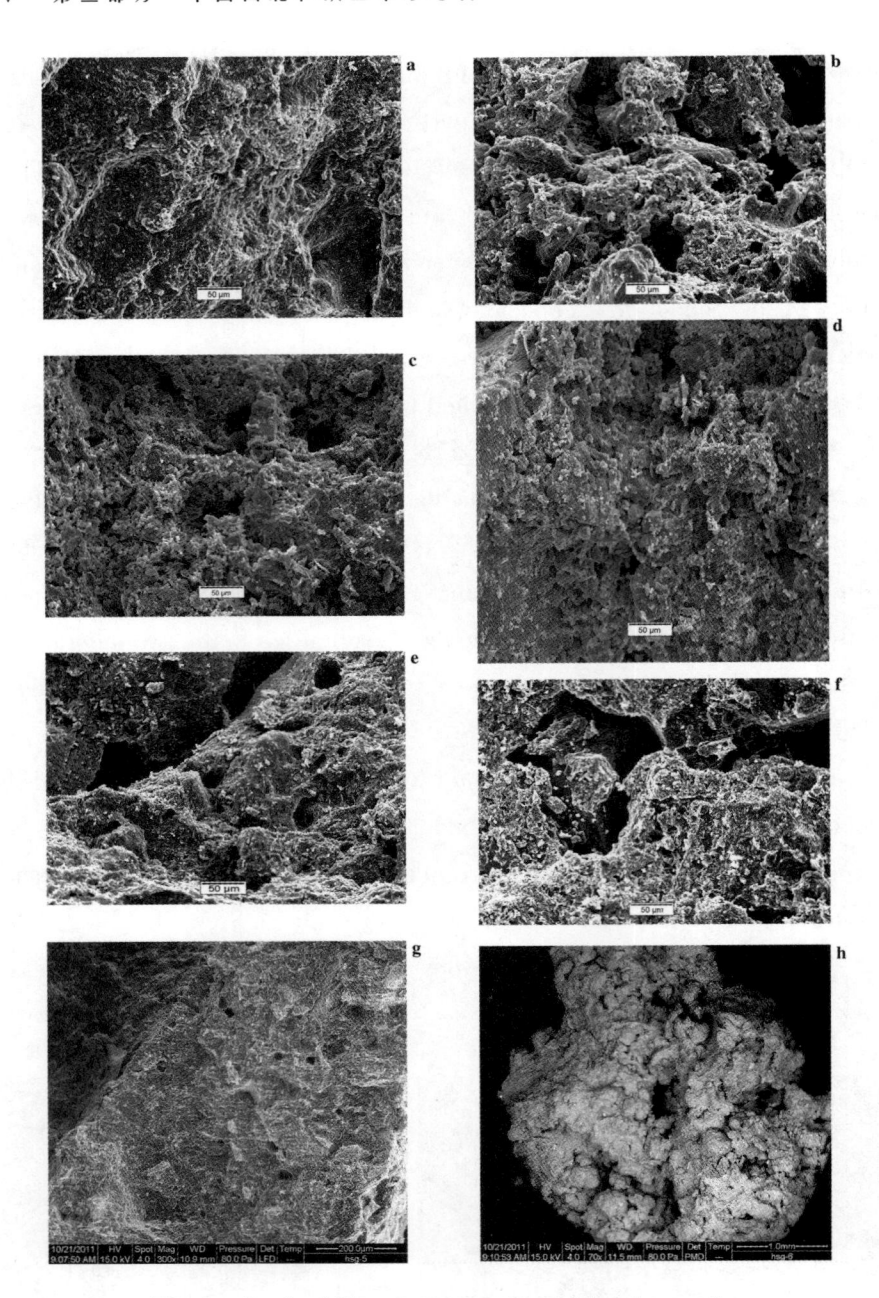

Fig. 3 – 5 – 5 Microstructure of mud-brick samples

a. F58; b. F54; c. F4; d. QI; e. F3 – 1; f. F3 – 2; g. F3 – 3; h. F1 (analyzed at the State Key Laboratory of Tribology at Tsinghua University, Beijing, and the Lanzhou Institute of Chemical Physics, Chinese Academy of Sciences, Lanzhou)

sample has not. Neither type shows any void of straw, which corroborates the above naked-eye observation. The particle size ranges of the eight samples are all confined to 0.317 – 1000μm, but the frequency distribution and accumulative weight curves of them diverge widely, without telling any structural difference between the two types of mud-bricks (Fig. 3 – 5 – 6: a-b). What is certain is that none of them is directly made out of natural deposit of river, but made of an intentional mixture of clay, silt, and sand.

A New Mud-brick Building Technique

The above research is merely a pilot work; a large-scale study of the mud-brick found at Xichengyi will be carried out after the completion of the excavation project. But the available data suffice to demonstrate that ancient residents manufactured two discrete types of mud-bricks. On the one hand, Type B mud-brick, which is bulky, was used together with mortar. On the other hand, Type A mud-brick came into use already during the first period of Xichengyi, and continued into the second and third periods. It was compact and thin; together with the sandy content and the multi-roomed compound layout of F1 and F4, it suggests that the mud-brick architecture as a whole was derived from Central Asia.

The fact that Type A mud-brick was bound by ramming rather than mortar merits some comment. As stated in the beginning of this paper, in China mud-brick architecture appeared first in the period of the Qujialing culture, and became widespread in North China during the Longshan period. Although mud-brick might have had local origins, it was not the mainstream building material in ancient and historical periods. In fact, the mainstream ones of the Neolithic Age were wattle-daub, as those found profusely at the Neolithic settlements of Banpo and Jiangzhai of the Yangshao Culture near the city of Xi'an, Shaanxi province, and earth ramming, which was invented in the late Yangshao period (3300BC – 2800BC) at the walled settlement of Xishan near the city of Zhengzhou, Henan province, and pervasively employed since the Longshan period for the construction of prestigious structures such as palaces, temples, and tombs, but sometimes also for vernacular buildings.① The mud-brick and earth ramming techniques, however, were never united in China proper.

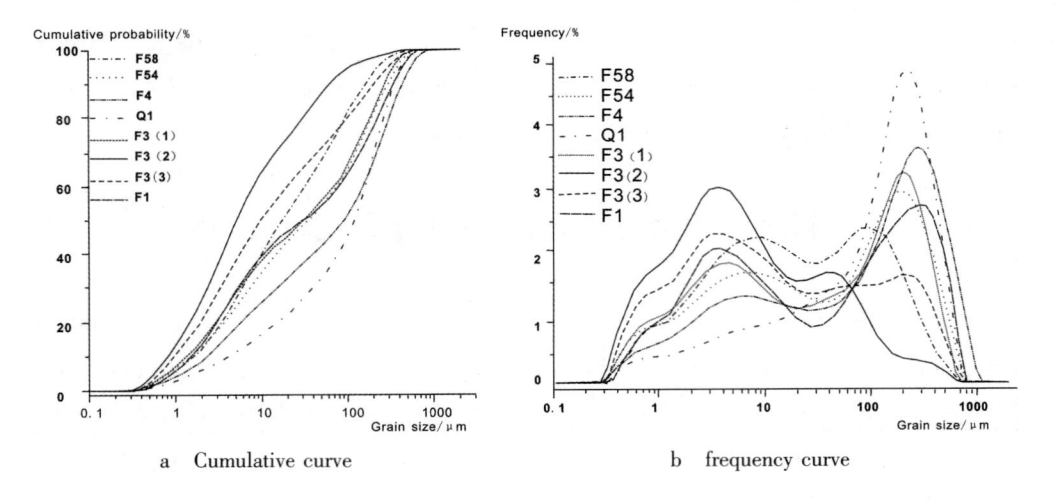

a Cumulative curve

b frequency curve

Fig. 3 – 5 – 6 Particle size distribution of mud-brick samples

(analyzed at the laboratory of the School of Archaeology and Museology at Peking University, Beijing, and the MOE Key Laboratory of Western China's Environmental System, Lanzhou University, Lanzhou)

In the Near East, there are references to earth ramming architecture during the Pre-Pottery Neolithic Age;② a mixture of soil, water, and a temper was

---

① Wang, Renxiang, Huanghe liuyu he beifang diqu xinshiqi shidai wanqi wenhua, in The Institute of Archaeology, Chinese Academy of Social Sciences ed., *Chinese Archaeology*, Volume of the Neolithic Age, Chapter IV, Beijing: Chinese Social Sciences Press, 2010, p. 232; Wu, Yaoli, Huanghe liuyu he beifang diqu xinshiqi shidai moqi wenhua, in The Institute of Archaeology, Chinese Academy of Social Sciences ed., *Chinese Archaeology*, Volume of the Neolithic Age, Beijing: Zhongguo Shehui Kexue, 2010, Chapter 6, p. 584.

② Aurenche, O., L'origine de la brique dans le Proche Orient ancient, in M. Frangipane, H. Hauptmann, M. Liverani, P. Matthiae, and M. Mellink eds., *Between the Rivers and Over the Mountains: Archaeologica Anatolica et Mesopotamica Alba Palmieri Dedicata*, Rome: Dipartimento di Scienze Storiche Archeologiche e Antropologiche dell'Antichità, Università di Roma (La Sapienza), 1993, p. 56; Cauvin, J., *The Birth of the Gods and the Origins of Agriculture*, translated by Trevor Watkins, Cambridge: Cambridge University Press, 2000, pp. 39, 41, 79.

pressed into a vertical formwork to erect a wall,[1] but it was replaced by mud-brick made of the same mixture after the latter came into being;[2] in the Mediterranean world, earth ramming technique was used since 814BC and boosted during the Roman period, presumably also in part of the Near East.[3] In Central Asia, evidence of prehistoric earth ramming architecture is sporadic; an earth ramming foundation was discovered at the Bronze Age settlement of Mundigak and Zaman-baba.[4] But throughout the history of the Near East, Central Asia, and South Asia, the conflation of the two techniques has never been heard of. The application of the earth ramming technique to mud-brick architecture was therefore an innovation of the Xichengyi residents.

Conclusion

Although many details remain obscure, it leaves no doubt that Type A mud-brick was a new construction material that ingeniously fused the time-honored mud-brick manufacturing technique, possibly from Central Asia, with the earth ramming technique from China proper, and the innovation was possibly

---

[1] Aurenche, O., L'origine de la brique dans le Proche Orient ancient, in M. Frangipane, H. Hauptmann, M. Liverani, P. Matthiae, and M. Mellink eds., *Between the Rivers and Over the Mountains: Archaeologica Anatolica et Mesopotamica Alba Palmieri Dedicata*, Rome: Dipartimento di Scienze Storiche Archeologiche e Antropologiche dell'Antichità, Università di Roma (La Sapienza), 1993, p. 58.

[2] Aurenche, O., L'origine de la brique dans le Proche Orient ancient, in M. Frangipane, H. Hauptmann, M. Liverani, P. Matthiae, and M. Mellink eds., *Between the Rivers and Over the Mountains: Archaeologica Anatolica et Mesopotamica Alba Palmieri Dedicata*, Rome: Dipartimento di Scienze Storiche Archeologiche e Antropologiche dell'Antichità, Università di Roma (La Sapienza), 1993, p. 60; Dunham, S., Ancient Near Eastern Architecture, in D. C. Snell ed., *A Companion to the Ancient Near East*, Malden, Oxford, and Carlton: Blackwell Publishing, 2005, p. 269.

[3] Jaquin, Paul A., Charles E. Augarde, and Christopher M. Gerrard, Chronological description of the spatial development of rammed earth techniques, *International Journal of Architectural Heritage* 2, 2008, pp. 384–385.

[4] Tosi, M., S. M. Shahmirzadi, and M. A. Joeynda, The Bronze Age in Iran and Afghanistan, in A. H. Dani, and V. M. Masson eds., *History of Civilizations of Central Asia*, Paris: UNESCO Publishing, 1999, Vol. 1, p. 215; Masson, V. M., The Bronze Age in Khorasan and Transoxania, in A. H. Dani and V. M. Masson eds., *History of Civilizations of Central Asia*, Paris: UNESCO Publishing, 1999, Vol. 1, p. 244.

made at the settlement of Xichengyi during the Late Machang period. It differs from Type B mud-brick in that it depends on ramming to bind the mud-brick to each other instead of mortar; and because of the ramming, it is more compact and stronger than Type B mud-brick. While its quality is superior to that of Type B mud-brick, the ignorance of proper footing preparation led to the ultimate failure of F3.

Acknowledgement

L. Zhang, the first and corresponding author of this article, wishes to express his gratitude to Serena Love, Burcu Tung, and Robert Homsher for providing references on mud-brick architecture of the Near East, and the Institute for the Study of Ancient World for providing a visiting fellowship, and the access to international research literature key to this article, without which the article would have been impossible to write up. He is also grateful for Karen S. Rubinson, who read an earlier draft and contributed valuable feedback. In addition, he owes gratitude to Prof. Chunmei Ma for generating the particle size graphs. All errors remain his own.

Metal Trade in Bronze Age Central Eurasia*

Introduction

In the study of ancient Eurasian metallurgy, the Seĭma-Turbino Phenomenon is a great conceptual breakthrough. [1]Formulated by Chernykh and Kuz'minykh,[2] this concept unites a total of 442 metal artefacts and 30 casting moulds that have been discovered in a vast territory in Eurasia, stretching from the Altai Mountains in the east to Finland in the west. [3]The lion's share of these objects comes from cemeteries at Seĭma, Turbino, Reshnoe, Rostovka, and Satyga. Much of the social and economic lives of the Seĭma-Turbino populations, however, remains enigmatic because the five cemeteries are mostly devoid of either human skeletons or ceramic vessels. No settlement has ever been discovered. Only the morphologically distinctive metal artefacts (socketed axes, forked-shank spearheads and double-edged knives) and the prevalence of tin bronze unify these finds into one cultural entity. [4]

Chernykh and Kuz'minykh have carried out thorough morphological and spectral analyses of the aforementioned 442 metal artefacts. [5]On the one hand,

---

* The article was originally published in Jianjun Mei and Thilo Rehren eds., *Metallurgy and Civilisation*: *Eurasia and Beyond*, London: Archetype, pp. 17 – 25, It is reprinted in this anthology with minor changes.

[1] The term "Seĭma-Turbino" was first coined by O. N. Bader, *Drevniaia Metallurgiia Zapadnogo Urala*, Moscow: Science Press, 1964. It was defined as a cultural community that subsumes both the cemeteries at Seĭma and Turbino, which represent two local cultures in the Kama and Oka river valleys.

[2] Chernykh, E. N. and S. V. Kuz'minykh, *Drevniaia Metallurgiia Severnoĭ Evrasiia*, Moscow: Science, 1989.

[3] Chernykh, E. N., *Ancient Metallurgy in the USSR*: *The Early Metal Age*, Cambridge: Cambridge University Press, 1992, p. 216.

[4] Chernykh, E. N. and S. V. Kuz'minykh, *Drevniaia Metallurgiia Severnoĭ Evrasiia*, Moscow: Science; Chernykh, E. N., 1992, *Ancient Metallurgy in the USSR*: *The Early Metal Age*, Cambridge: Cambridge University Press, 1989, pp. 218 – 219.

[5] Chernykh, E. N. and S. V. Kuz'minykh, *Drevniaia Metallurgiia Severnoĭ Evrasiia*, Moscow: Science, 1989.

they found certain artefact types such as socketed axes and some metal alloys such as tin bronze, common to the entire territory; on the other hand, they have discerned two separate regions: an eastern or Siberian region and a western or European region, which are divided by the Ural Mountains.① The Siberian region is characterized by the predominance of ornate socketed axes and tin bronze, whereas the European region is characterized by a greater variety of artefact types, including shaft-hole axes, spearheads, adzes and daggers, as well as a variety of metal alloys including pure copper, copper-arsenic and silver-copper alloys, and billon.

Chernykh and Kuz'minykh assume that the metal artefacts were produced locally by their users.② The discovery of 30 moulds testifies that some communities of the Seĭma-Turbino Phenomenon were engaged in metal production and were possibly responsible for a part of the 442 items. The ever-accumulating metallurgical data of metal artefacts of neighbouring cultures, however, point to another possibility. These data, in combination with the above-mentioned morphological and compositional analyses, have illuminated the idea that a significant portion of the Seĭma-Turbino metals were produced by external communities. In this paper I will substantiate this idea by delving into the ancient metal trade with a particular focus on the European region and the contemporaneous cultures of Abashevo and Sintashta. The term metal trade used here refers primarily to the cross-regional flow of ingots and actual artefacts; the bulky copper ores were less likely to be involved in long-distance trade. This task requires the use of data on the distribution of copper ores, chemical composition of metal artefacts and metalworking communities; fortunately these data, although far from sufficient, are now available.

---

① Chernykh, E. N., *Ancient Metallurgy in the USSR: The Early Metal Age*, Cambridge: Cambridge University Press, 1992, p. 220. In a recent statistic Chernykh et al. counted "slightly over five hundred" metal objects belonging to this phenomenon. Chernykh, E. N., S. V. Kuz'minykh, and L. B. Orlovskaia, Ancient Metallurgy of Northeast Asia: from the Urals to the Saiano-Altai, in K. M. Linduff ed., *Metallurgy in Ancient Eastern Eurasia from the Urals to the Yellow River*, Lewiston, Queenstone, Lampeter: The Edwin Mellen Press, 2004, pp. 15 – 36.

② Chernykh, E. N. and S. V. Kuz'minykh, *Drevniaia Metallurgiia Severnoĭ Evrasii*a, Moscow: Science, 1989.

Metal Trade in Bronze Age Central Eurasia

Database

Chernykh and Kuz'minykh, once again, have provided most of the data regarding the distribution of copper ores and the chemical composition of metal artefacts. In 1967 – 68, Chernykh located over 30 Bronze Age mines in the Eastern Urals (Trans-Urals in Russian) (Fig. 3 – 6 – 1). ①He was even able to define the compositional characteristics of the copper ores to be found in a number of them. The Elenovka and Ush-Katta mines yield ores that contain some tin (up to 1%) and nickel (up to 0.1%). This is a possible source for tin bronze. Other possible tin sources are located some considerable distance away in central Kazakhstan and further east in the Altai Mountains (including eastern Kazakhstan). The Tash-Kazgan and Nikol'skoe mines produce high arsenic and high silver ores, respectively. These are the sources for arsenic-copper and silver-copper alloys. ②Ores that are rich in gold and silver but with less arsenic have been found at Ishkino. ③Overall, the Eastern Urals is a rich source of polymetallic ores. ④Copper ores are also available in the Western Urals (Pre-Urals in Russian) in the valleys of the Kama River and its tributaries Belaia and Ufa, but they are all sandstones, which have very low contents of minor metals-arsenic, silver, nickel, lead and iron; antimony and gold are

---

① Chernykh, E. N., *Ancient Metallurgy in the Urals and the Volga River Valley*, Moscow: Science, 1970, pp. 35 – 49.

② The other arsenic-rich source is the Caucasian Mountains. Chernykh, *Ancient Metallurgy in the USSR: The Early Metal Age*, Cambridge: Cambridge University Press, 1992, p. 200, argues that active exploitation of this source took place in the time of Pit-Grave, Catacomb and Poltavka cultures, but had ceased in the time of the Seĭma-Turbino Phenomenon. This position is adopted by P. Kohl, *The Making of Bronze Age Eurasia*, Cambridge, New York: Cambridge University Press, 2007.

③ Zaykov, V. V., A. M. Yuminov, A. P. Bushmakin, E. V. Zaykova, A. D. Tairov, and G. B. Zdanovich, Ancient copper mines and products from base and noble metals in the Southern Urals, in K. Jones-Bley and D. G. Zdanovich eds., *Complex Societies of Central Eurasia from the 3rd to the 1st Millennium BC*, Washington DC: Institute for the Study of Man, 2002, pp. 417 – 442.

④ The mine at Dergamysh has been found to contain gold, but the mine at Vorovskaya Yama has not been defined compositionally. Zaykov, V. V., A. M. Yuminov, A. P. Bushmakin, E. V. Zaykova, A. D. Tairov, and G. B. Zdanovich, Ancient copper mines and products from base and noble metals in the Southern Urals, in K. Jones-Bley and D. G. Zdanovich eds., *Complex Societies of Central Eurasia from the 3rd to the 1st Millennium BC*, Washington DC: Institute for the Study of Man, 2002, pp. 417 – 442.

◇❖◇ 第三部分　中国西北和欧亚草原考古

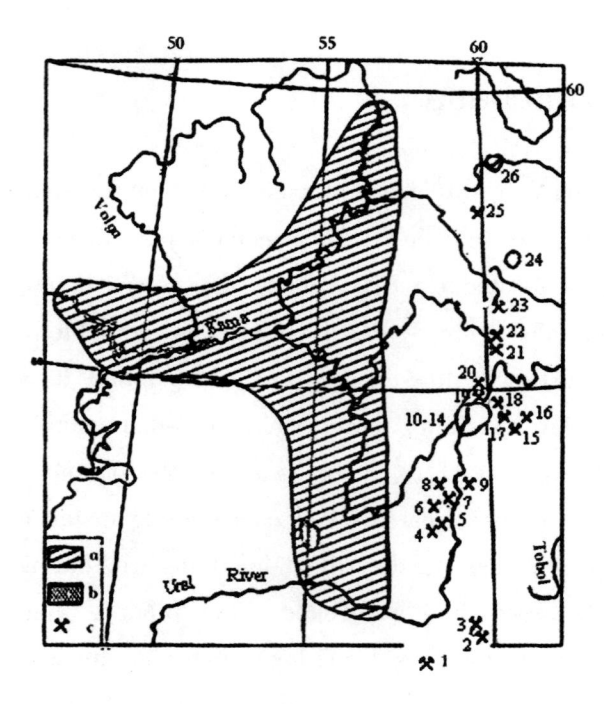

Fig. 3-6-1　Distribution of copper ores in the Eastern and Western Urals

a. area of copper sandstone ores; b. groups of copper ore mines; c. copper ore mines.　2. Ush-Katta; 3. Elenovka; 4. Ishkinino; 6. Dergamysh; 8. Bakr-Uziak; 9. Vorovskaia Yama; 17. Tash-Kazgan; 18. Nikol'skoe (adapted from Chernykh, E. N., *Drevniaia Metallurgiia Urala i Povol'zhia*, Moscow: Science, 1970, p. 37, Fig. 32)

completely absent here. ① This is the source for chemically pure copper. It follows that if a community in the Western Urals wished to produce arsenic and tin bronzes, it was bound to import ores from the Eastern Urals, or central Kazakhstan, or even farther away in the Altai Mountains. In the Donets River valley, particularly the Bakhmut basin, ancient copper ore mines and smelting sites have also been discovered. ② The sandstone ores available in this area are good for obtaining pure copper as well, however, they contain some silver and arsenic. As in the Western Urals, ancient communities in this region had to import tin-containing ingots if they wished to produce tin bronze. Certainly, communities in the regions that lack copper ores, such as the Lower Volga (from the Samara Bend to the end of the Volga River) and much of the territory of the Seĭma-Turbino Phenomenon, had to import either ingots or ready-made artefacts.

Information pertaining to Bronze Age metalworking communities comes mostly from settlements, but sometimes from cemeteries as well. Evidence of

---

① Chernykh, E. N., *Drevniaia Metallurgiia Urala i Povol'zhia*, Moscow: Science, 1970, p. 48.
② Tatarinov, S. I., O gorno-metallurgicheskom tsentre èpokhi bronzy v Donbasse, *Sovetskaia Arkheologiia* 4, 1977, pp. 192-206.

metal production has been discovered in a large number of settlements and cemeteries not only in the Eastern Urals, but also in the Western Urals, the Middle Volga (from Nizhniĭ Novgorod to the Samara Bend), and the Don and Donets River valleys. It is very likely that Seĭma-Turbino communities had intimate trade connections with contemporaneous metalworking communities of the Abashevo and Sintashta cultures as well as the Alakul' and Srubnaya cultures. [1]While the Srubnaya culture dates to the Late Bronze Age, roughly to 1690BC – 1390BC, [2] the Sintashta cultures date to the Middle Bronze Age, approximately 2040BC – 1730BC. [3]The Seĭma-Turbino Phenomenon thus spans the Middle and Late Bronze Age and dates roughly to 2040BC – 1390BC. Due to the limitation of space, this paper only deals with the trading activities among Seĭma-Turbino, Abashevo and Sintashta communities.

Metalworking communities have been widely discovered in the territory of the Abashevo culture, evidenced by settlements such as Shilovskiĭ in the Don River valley, Tochka in the Middle Volga valley, and Balanbash in the Western Urals. [4]Although they only had geographical access to sandstone ores in the Western Urals, the Middle Volga, and the Donets River valley, they were nevertheless able to acquire the desired metals by importing polymetallic ingots, or actual artefacts, from the Eastern Urals. By comparison, metalworking communities of the Sintashta culture, represented by a number of settlements and cemeteries, were located in the Eastern Urals, and geographically proximate to the polymetallic mines in this region (Fig. 3 – 6 – 2). It is reasonable to assume that Sintashta communities produced and supplied arsenic- and silver-

---

[1] Zhang, L., *Ancient Society and Metallurgy: A Comparative Study of Bronze Age Societies in Central Eurasia and North China*, PhD thesis, University of California, Los Angeles, 2007, pp. 223 – 37.

[2] Chernykh, E. N., Absoliutnaia khronologiia pozdnebronzovykh sloev Gornogo, in E. N. Chernykh ed., *Kargaly*, Tome II, Moscow: Languages of Slavonic Culture, 2002, p. 125; Görsdorf, J., C14 dates of specimens from Gornyĭ (in Russian), in E. N. Chernykh ed., *Kargaly*, Tome III, Moscow: Languages of Slavonic Culture, 2004, pp. 293 – 294.

[3] Epimakhov, A. V., B. Hanks, and S. Renfrew, Radiouglerodnaia khronologiia pamiatnikov bronzovogo veka zaural'ia, *Rossiĭskaia Arkheologiia* 4, 2005, pp. 92 – 102.

[4] Priakhin, A. D., *Poseleniia Abashevskoĭ Obshchnosti*, Voronezh: The Voronezh University Press, 1976; Sal'nikov, K. V., Abashevskaia kul'tura na Iuzhnom Ural'e, *Sovetskaia Arkheologiia* 21, 1954, Fig. 2.

containing metals for Abashevo communities. Sintashta communities such as Sintashta (the type site) and Arkaim were in fact specialised in metal production, as is evident from the ubiquitous metalworking remains in their settlements. ①

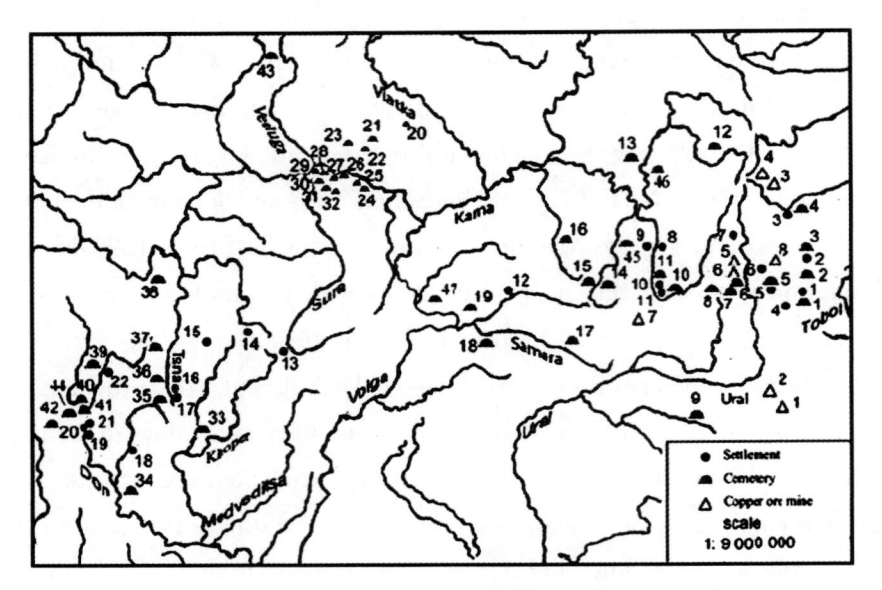

Fig. 3 – 6 – 2 Settlements and cemeteries of the Sintashta and Abashevo cultures and the Seĭma-Turbino Phenomenon

Settlements: 1. Sintashta; 5. Arkaim; 9. Balanbash; 10. Beregovskiĭ – I, – II; 12. Tochka; 21. Shilovskiĭ. *Cemeteries*: 1. Sintashta; 2 Kamennyĭ-Ambar-V; 4. Krivoe Ozero; 5. Bol'shekaraganka; 6. Al'mukhametovski-I; 8. Baishev-IV; 9. Tanabergen-II; 11 Beregovskiĭ – I; 12. Iukalekulevo; 13. Turbino-I, – II; 17. Nikiforovskiĭ; 33. Vlasov-I; 36. Selezni-II; 37. Staroĭur'evo; 38. Reshnoe; 40. Vvedenka; 43. Seĭma; 44. Khokhol'skiĭ; 45. Chukrakly; 46. Ust'-Gaiva; 47. Sokolovka; 48. Rostovka. *Copper ore mines*: 1. Ush-Katta; 2. Elenovka; 3. Tash-Kazgan; 4. Nikol'skoe.

(adapted from Priakhin, A. D. and A. Kh. Khalikov, 1987, Abashevskaia kul'tura, in O. N. Bader, D. A. Krainov, and M. F. Kosarev ed., *Èpokha Bronzy Lesnoĭ Polosy*, p. 126, Fig. 23, Archaeology of SSSR, Moscow: Science)

---

① Gening, V. F., G. B. Zdanovich, and V. V. Gening, *Sintashta—Arkheologicheskie Pamiatniki Ariĭskikh Plemen Uralo-Kazakhstanskikh Stepeĭ*, Cheliabinsk: South-Ural Book Publisher, 1992; Zdanovich, G. B., Arkaim: arii na Urale ili nesostoiavshaiasia tsivilizatsiia, in G. B. Zdanovich (ed.) *Arkaim: Po Stranitsam Drevneĭ Istrorii Iuzhnogo Urala*, Cheliabinsk: Kamennyĭ Poias, 1995, pp. 21 – 42.

Table 3 – 6 – 1   Chemical composition of metal-related samples from Sintashta and Abashevo communities

Community	Unit	Cu	Cu + As	Cu + Sn	Ag	Cu + Ni	Total
Sintashta	SS	7	60	2	2		71
		9. 9%	84. 5%	2. 8%	2. 8%		100%
	SC	27	118	11	11		167
		16. 2%	70. 6%	6. 6%	6. 6%		100%
Arkaim	AS	11	12				23
		47. 8%	52. 2%				100%
	BK		15		2	3	20
			75%		10%	15%	100%
Krivoe Ozero	KrO	3	13	4			20
		13%	65%	20%			100%
Abashevo *	ASH	22	62		3	1	88
		25%	70. 5%		3. 4%	1. 1%	100%

[Sources of data: Sintashta settlement (SS) (Zaĭkova, E. V., Sostav metallicheskikh izdeliĭ Sintashta, in G. B. Zdanovich et al eds., *Rossiia i Vostok: Problemy Vzaimodeĭstviia*, Cheliabsinsk: Cheliabinsk State University, Volume V, Book 2, 1995, pp. 152 – 157); Sintashta cemetery (SC) (Chernykh, E. N., and S. V. Kuz'minykh, Chemical compositions of 167 specimens from the Sintashta cemetery, Unpublished data, 2005); Arkaim settlement (AS) and cemetery (BK) (Bushmakin, A. F., Metallicheskie predmety iz Kurgana 25 Bol'shekaraganskogo mogil'nika, in D. G. Zdanovich ed., *Arkaim: Nekropol'*, Cheliabinsk: South-Ural Book Publisher, 2002, pp. 132 – 43); Krivoe Ozero cemetery (KrO) (Degtiareva, A. D., and S. V. Kuz'minykh, Rezul'taty analiticheskogo issledovaniia metalla mogil'nika Krivoe Ozero, in N. B. Vinogradov, *Mogil'nik Bronzovogo Veka Krivoe Ozero*, Cheliabinsk: South-Ural Book Publisher, 2003, pp. 285 – 309). * Abashevo (ASH) refers to sites in the Volga and Don River valleys (Chernykh, E. N., Metall donskogo varianta abashevkoĭ kul'tury, in A. D. Priakhin, *Abashevskaia Kul'tura v Podon'e*, Voronezh: The Voronezh University Press, 1971, p. 207)]

A significant number of settlements and cemeteries of the Abashevo and Sintashta communities have yielded copper ores, slag, moulds and metal artefacts, and thus indicate the presence of metalworking and/or metal-consuming communities. Altogether 88 specimens from Abashevo sites comprising artefacts, ores and slag, have been subjected to spectral analysis, while 301 specimens from Sintashta settlements and cemeteries have been similarly tested. [1] A total of 167 specimens were taken from the Sintashta cemetery (SC) and analysed by Chernykh and Kuz'minykh. [2]

Overall, the ever-progressing excavation and research endeavours have made it possible to consider the hypothesis of metal trade among Seĭma-Turbino, Abashevo and Sintashta communities. The following analysis will consider in particular two major aspects of this hypothetical trend: (1) the metal trade between Seĭma-Turbino and Abashevo and Sintashta communities and (2) the metal trade between Abashevo and Sintashta communities. The purpose of this focus is to highlight the extensity and intensity of ancient metal trade in Central Eurasia. Compositional and morphological data will be employed to elucidate the two themes.

Metal trade

The hypothesis of metal trade among Abashevo and Sintashta communities is first borne out by the chemical composition of their metal artefacts (Table 3 – 6 – 1). It must be noted that the factor of recycling has barely been probed in relation to the metal artefacts under discussion, but it cannot be ignored and therefore the points made here are not conclusive. The 301 tested specimens of the Sintashta culture include 167 pieces from the Sintashta

---

[1] Chernykh, E. N., Metall donskogo varianta abashevkoĭ kul'tury, in A. D. Priakhin, *Abashevskaia Kul'tura v Podon'e*, Voronezh: The Voronezh University Press, 1971, p. 207; Zaĭkova, E. V., Sostav metallicheskikh izdeliĭ Sintashta, in G. B. Zdanovich et al eds., *Rossiia i Vostok: Problemy Vzaimodeĭstviia*, Cheliabsinsk: Cheliabinsk State University, Volume V, Book 2, 1995, pp. 152 – 157; Bushmakin, A. F., Metallicheskie predmety iz Kurgana 25 Bol'shekaraganskogo mogil'nika, in D. G. Zdanovich ed., *Arkaim: Nekropol'*, Cheliabinsk: South-Ural Book Publisher, 2002, pp. 132 – 143; Degtiareva, A. D., and S. V. Kuz'minykh, Rezul'taty analiticheskogo issledovaniia metalla mogil'nika Krivoe Ozero, in N. B. Vinogradov, *Mogil'nik Bronzovogo Veka Krivoe Ozero*, Cheliabinsk: South-Ural Book Publisher, 2003, pp. 285 – 309.

[2] I would like to express my profound gratitude to E. N Chernykh and S. V. Kuz'minykh for their unmediated generosity in offering me unpublished data, some of which is quoted in this paper.

cemetery (SC), 71 pieces from the Sintashta settlement (SS), 23 from the Arkaim settlement (AS) and 20 from the Bol'shekaraganka cemetery (BK) associated with Arkaim, and 20 from the Krivoe Ozero cemetery (KrO). It appears that the percentage of objects made of pure copper (derived from sandstone ores), is lower than that of arsenic bronze artefacts, even among Abashevo specimens. This fact denotes a regular trade of arsenic-containing metal ingots and artefacts from Sintashta communities to their Abashevo partners, whether through direct trade of ingots or through indirect trade of recycled metals. Other metals are relatively modest in quantity. It appears that tin bronze and silver were regularly produced and used by Sintashta communities, as they have been found in both their settlements and cemeteries. They were also buried in tombs at Krivoe Ozero and Bol'shekaraganka. Thus, the three silver objects among the Abashevo specimens must have been imported from the Sintashta community. In addition, among the Abashevo specimens is one nickel and copper alloy, which finds three analogies among the specimens from Bol'shekaraganka. The provenance of this alloy might have been Arkaim.

The trade in metal artefacts is a subtle subject. Compositional data are insufficient, because one community may use recycled metals from a third party. It is necessary to introduce the morphological criterion, i.e. because of the complexity of provenancing metal objects, it is assumed that if two objects from two distant sites are both compositionally and morphologically close to each other, one is likely to be an import. One community may acquire metal by recycling metals from source communities, or its products may emulate the forms of metal artefacts of source communities. The likelihood that both situations occur at the same time is considered low. Although many artefacts from the Abashevo and Sintashta communities have been subjected to compositional analysis, many others have not been analysed. The most readily available data are in fact line drawings that show their formal characteristics. Thus, when compositional analysis is done and can be combined with stylistic analysis, it is possible to discern imported artefacts with greater certainty. When compositional data are not available, stylistic analysis is the only means of achieving this. In this case, it is assumed that local products are stylistically homogeneous and occur repetitively, whereas imported items are incongruent with the styles of local products and are relatively rare. Because moulds were handmade, artefacts from one community should not be expected to be identical. This line of analysis is merely suggestive, and is riddled with uncertainties given the above-mentioned caution that one community may emulate foreign forms.

I will now focus on the types of metal artefacts that are morphologically more sophisticated, and thus more expressive of the aesthetic and technical preferences of the producing communities. The first type to be considered is that of ornaments (Fig. 3 – 6 – 3). The double-ring pendant from Krivoe Ozero (KrO K10T14) is apparently an import from the Abashevo community because it rarely occurs in tombs of the Sintashta culture but is found frequently in those of the Abashevo culture.① On the contrary, the one-and-half twist earing has been found pervasively at the Sintashta, Arkaim, Krivoe Ozero and Kamennyĭ-Ambar-V cemeteries of the Sintashta culture, but it has only been discovered at the Nikiforovskiĭ and Khokhol'skiĭ cemeteries of the Abashevo culture.② The earrings from Sintashta and Abashevo cemeteries are uniform in shape (Fig. 3 – 6 – 3). The four tested pieces from the Sintashta cemetery,③ and one from the Arkaim settlement④ are all made of silver-based alloys (Table 3 – 6 – 2). This fact and the prevalence of this product at Sintashta cemeteries indicate that the Sintashta community produced and supplied these ornaments as they had better access to the silver-rich mines at Nikol'skoe.

As regards bracelets, most Abashevo specimens were made by bending

---

① This type of pendant was used widely in Bronze Age eastern Europe, but those from Abashevo communities find the closest match to those of Sintashta communities.

② Vasil'ev, I. B., and A. D. Priakhin, Beskurgannyĭ Abashevskiĭ mogil'nik u Nikiforovskogo lesnichestva v Orenburzh'e, *Sovetskaia Arkheologiia* 2, 1979, pp. 145 – 152; Chernykh, E. N., Metall donskogo varianta abashevkoĭ kul'tury, in A. D. Priakhin, *Abashevskaia Kul'tura v Podon'e*, Voronezh: The Voronezh University Press, 1971, pp. 208 – 209.

③ Chernykh, E. N., and S. V. Kuz'minykh, Chemical compositions of 167 specimens from the Sintashta cemetery, Unpublished data, 2005.

④ Bushmakin, A. F., Metallicheskie predmety iz Kurgana 25 Bol'shekaraganskogo mogil'nika, in D. G. Zdanovich ed., *Arkaim: Nekropol'*, Cheliabinsk: South-Ural Book Publisher, 2002, p. 138, Fig. 81: 7b.

Metal Trade in Bronze Age Central Eurasia

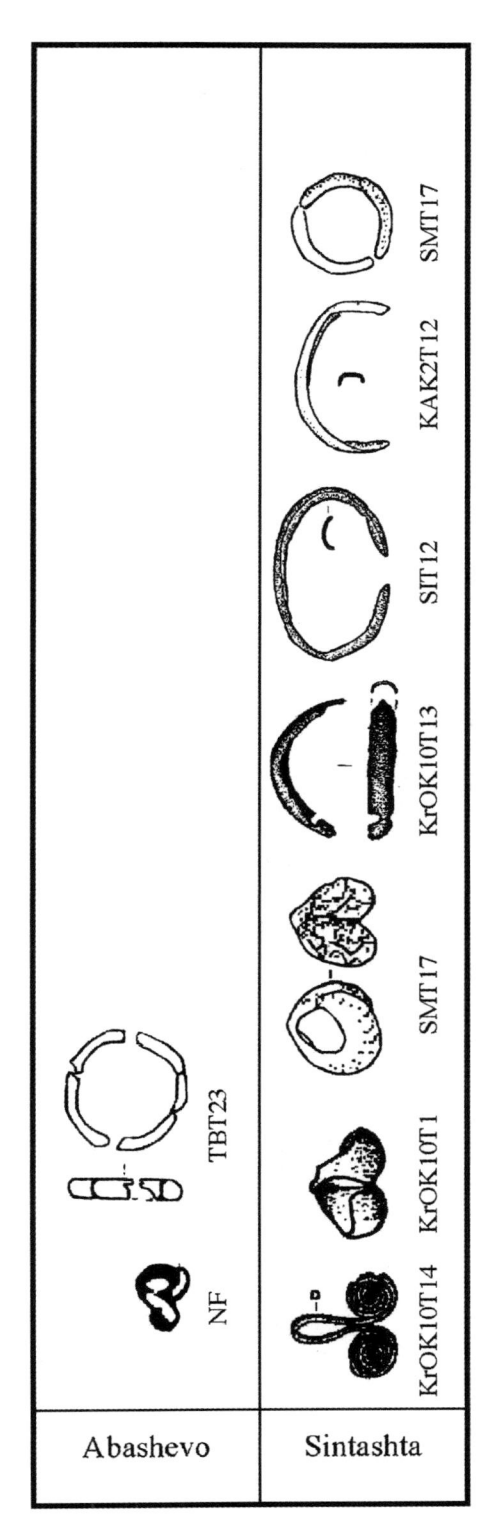

Fig. 3-6-3 Metal ornaments from Sintashta and Abashevo communities

NF – Nikiforovski., TB – Tanabergen-II [Sources of data: NF (Vasil'ev and Priakhin 1979: 147, Fig. 3: 20); KrO K10T14, KrO K10T1, KrO K10T13 (Vinogradov 2003: 14, Fig. 76: 1; 128, Fig. 55: 2; 172, Fig. 75: 12); SMT17, SMT17, SIT12 (Gening et al. 1992: 169, Fig. 82: 8, 10; 285, Fig. 159: 1); KA-2T12 (Kostiukov et al. 1995: 201, Fig. 25: 7); TBT23 (Tkachev 2004: 12, Fig. 4: 5)]

Table 3-6-2 Chemical composition of metal ornaments from Sintashta and Abashevo communities. Sources of data: Sintashta (SM, SI; Chernykh and Kuz'minykh 2005); Arkaim (BK-25; Bushmakhin 2002); Krivoe Ozero (KrO; Degtiareva and Kuz'minykh 2003); Khokhol'skii (KhKh; Chernykh 1971)

	Site	Cu	Sn	Pb	Zn	Bi	Ag	Sb	As	Fe	Ni	Co	Au	Mn
Bracelet	SMT2	core	12	0.2		0.005	0.06	0.1	0.03	0.004	0.003			
	SMT2	core	6	0.06		0.002	0.06	0.03	0.04	0.005	0.001			
	SMT2	core	6	0.1	0.02	0.004	0.2		0.03	0.07	0.001			
	SMT2	core	4	0.2	0.02	0.003	0.2	0.003	0.05	0.015	0.002			
	SMT13	core	7	0.3		0.003	0.0005	0.003	0.2	0.1	0.003		0.03	
	KrO	core	6.2	0.21	0.001	0.012	0.14	0.073	0.24	0.0037	0.0047	0.0014	0.0001	
	SIT11	core	0.006	0.0012	0.001	0.0003	0.032	0.027	2	0.063	0.047	0.0014	0.0015	
	SIT11	core	0.0017	0.001	0.0012	0.0003	0.027	0.027	2.7	0.086	0.064	0.0019	0.0019	
	SIT12	core	0.0022	0.001	0.001	0.0008	0.019	0.043	2.7	0.13	0.047	0.0015	0.0041	
	SIT12	core	0.002	0.0022	0.001	0.001	0.089	0.029	2.5	0.12	0.035	0.0014	0.0037	
	SIT12	core	0.0016	0.001	0.002	0.0016	0.0048	0.0076	1.8	0.0037	0.052	0.0012	0.001	
	KhKh	core		0.001			0.007		4.5	0.6	0.009	0.006	~0.001	0.005
	KhKh	core		0.001			0.04		3.5	0.3	0.005			0.001
Earring	SMT2	<40					core						<3	
	SMT2	<3					core						~30	
	SMT13	<1					~50						~50	
	SIT12	>30					core							
	BKK25	11.33			0.28	0.18	87.13		0.82					
	KhKh	10	little	yes	?	little	core	?	yes	little	little			yes

Metal Trade in Bronze Age Central Eurasia

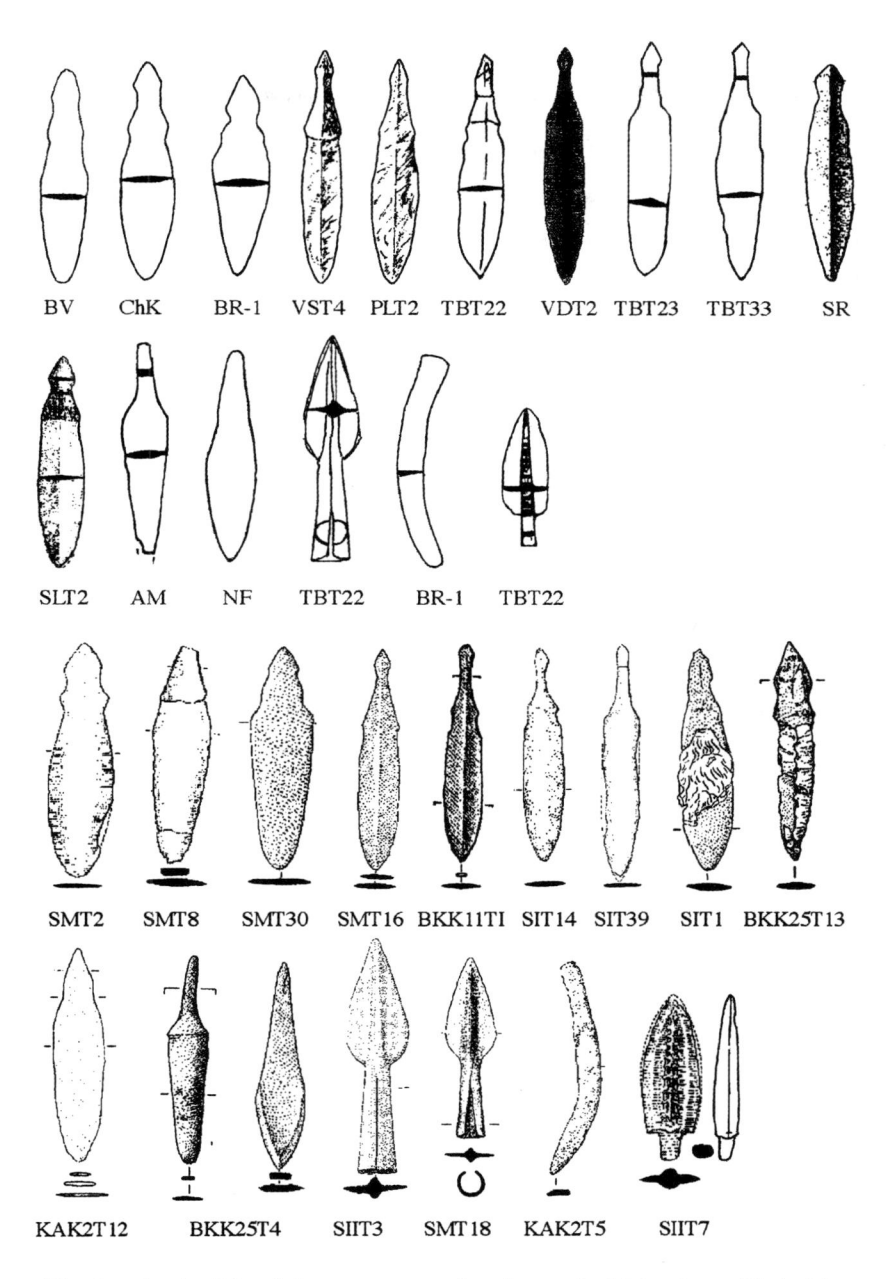

Fig. 3 – 6 – 4 Metal daggers, spearheads, and sickles from Sintashta and Abashevo communities

BV-Baishev-IV; ChK-Chukrakly, BR – I-Beregovskiĭ – I, VS-Vlasov-I, PL-Pavlovsk, TB-Tanabergen-II, VD-Vvedenka, SR-Staroiur'evo, SL-Selezni-II, NF-Nikiforovskiĭ, AM-Al'mukhametovskiĭ, Iuk-Iukalekulevo.

[Sources of data: BV (Obydënnov, M. F., and G. T. Obydënnova, *Pamiat'niki bronzovogo veka Iuzhnogo Urala*, Ufa: Press of Eastern University, 1996, Fig. 34: 1); ChK, BR – I, AM (Gorbunov, V. S., *Abashevskaia Kul'tura Iuzhnogo Priural'ia*, Ufa: Bashkir Pedinstitute, 1986, Fig. 14: 16; Fig. 18: 1, 15); VS, PL (Siniuk, A. T., and I. A. Kozirchuk, Nekotorye aspekty izucheniia Abashevskoĭ kultury v Basseĭne Dona, in I. B. Vasil'ev ed., *Drevnie Indoiranskie Kul'tury Volgo-Ural'ia*, 1995, Fig. 4: 2, Fig. 14: 10, Samara: The Samara State Pedagogical University); VDT2 (Siniuk, A. T. and Kileĭnikov, V. V., Kurgan u sela Vvedenka na Done, *Sovetskaia Arkheologiia* 1, 1976, Fig. 3: 5); SR (Priakhin, A. D., Kurgany pozdneĭ bronzy u s. Staroiur'evo, *Sovetskaia Arkheologiia* 3, 1972, Fig. 2: 1); SLT2 (Priakhin, A. D., N. B. Moiseev, and V. I. Besedin, *Selezni 2: Kurgan Dono-volzhskoĭ Abashevskoĭ Kul'tury*, Voronezh: The Voronezh University Press, 1998, Fig. 6: 1); NF (Vasil'ev, I. B., and A. D. Priakhin, Beskurgannyĭ Abashevskiĭ mogil'nik u Nikiforovskogo Lesnichestva v Orenburzh'e, *Sovetskaia Arkheologiia* 2, 1979, Fig. 4: 4); TBT22, T23, T22, T22 (Tkachëv, V. V., Pogrebal'nye kompleksy s shchitkovymi psaliiami v stepnom priural'e, in A. N. Usacuk ed., *Psalii*, Donetsk: Donetska Oblasti Folk Culture Museum, 2004, Fig. 2: 7; Fig. 4: 11; Fig. 2: 1, 8); SMT2, 8, 30, 16, 39, 18, SIT14, 1, 14, SIIT3 (Gening, V. F., G. B. Zdanovich, and V. V. Gening, *Sintashta— Arkheologicheskie Pamiatniki Ariĭskikh Plemen Uralo-Kazakhstanskikh Stepeĭ*, Cheliabinsk: South-Ural Book Publisher, 1992, Fig. 46: 6; Fig. 51: 13; Fig. 114: 1; Fig. 70: 2; Fig. 126: 21; Fig. 88: 3; Fig. 148: 18; Fig. 140: 4; Fig. 148: 20; Fig. 175: 10); BKK11T1 (Botalov, S. G., S. A. Grigor'ev, and G. B. Zdanovich, Pogrebal'nye kompleksy èpokhi bronzy Bol'shekaraganskogo mogil'nika, in G. B. Zdanovich ed., *Materialy po Arkheologii i Ètnografii Iuzhnogo Urala*, Cheliabinsk: Kamennyĭ Poias, 1996, Fig. 3: 4); BKK25T13, BKK25T4 (Zdanovich, D. G., Okhrannye raskopki v zone Bol'she-karaganskogo kar'era, in D. G. Zdanovich ed., *Arkaim: Nekropol'*, Cheliabinsk: South-Ural Book Publisher, 2002, Fig. 35: 2; Fig. 16: 1); KAK2T5, KAK2T12 (Kostiukov, V. P., Epimakhov, A. V. and Nelin, D., Novye pamiatnik sredneĭ bronzy v Iuzhnom Zaural'e, in I. V. Vasil'ev ed., *Drevnie Indoiranskie Kul'tury Volgo-Ural'ia*, Samara: Samara State Pedagogical University, 1995, Fig. 21: 1; Fig. 25: 1).]

solid wires. ①By contrast, the items from the Sintashta cemetery were predominantly bent from groove-shaped foils (Fig. 3 – 6 – 3). Two tested specimens from Khokhol'skiĭ were produced locally or by different communities of the same culture, although they were produced of arsenic bronzes, the raw materials of which came probably from the Eastern Urals (Table 3 – 6 – 2). Five tested samples from Sintashta and Krivoe Ozero contain high percentages of tin (4.2% – 8.3%) and a broad range of trace elements (Table 3 – 6 – 2). They were therefore more likely produced by the Sintashta community. Three analogous bracelets can be found at the Tanabergen-II cemetery of the Abashevo culture. ②Although the chemical composition of these items is as yet unknown, morphologically they all resemble the Sintashta items.

Daggers have been discovered in much greater quantity in tombs of both the Abashevo and Sintashta cultures. They are morphologically diverse and thus expressive of stylistic preferences of individual communities. Unfortunately, not many specimens have been compositionally tested. They fall into several types (Fig. 3 – 6 – 4). The distinctive type A specimen, which features a thin and broad leaf-like blade (SMT2), and type B specimen, which is thicker and narrower than type A, occur four times altogether at the Sintashta cemetery (SMT8), and once at the Baishev-IV (BV) and Chukrakly (ChK) cemeteries of the Abashevo culture. The frequency of occurrence attributes the source of these types of daggers to Sintashta communities.

Type C daggers have acute hilt and blade contours and include several variations. The piece from Sintashta (SMT16), the most precisely fashioned variation, finds analogies at the cemeteries of Bol'shekaraganka (BKK11T1) of the Sintashta culture, and Vlasov-I (VST4), Pavlovsk (PLT2) and Tanabergen-II (TBT22) of the Abashevo culture (Fig. 3 – 6 – 4). They were probably produced and supplied by the Sintashta community as this variation appears at the two neighbouring cemeteries of Sintashta and Bol'shekaraganka,

---

① Chernykh, E. N., O metalle abashevskoĭ kul'tury, in *Pamiatniki Kamennogo i Bronzovogo Veka Evrazii*, Moscow: Science, 1964, p. 107.

② Tkachëv, V. V., Pogrebal'nye kompleksy s shchitkovymi psaliiami v stepnom priural'e, in A. N. Usachuk ed., *Psalii*, Donetsk: Donetska Oblasti Folk Culture Museum, 2004, p. 12, Fig. 4: 5 – 7.

whereas analogous finds are widely dispersed at Abashevo sites. A second variation, which features a slender hilt and long blade, appears three times at Sintashta (only two, SIT14 and SMT39, are shown in Fig. 3-6-4) and once at Bol'shekaraganka (BKK11T1, not shown in Fig. 3-6-4) of the Sintashta culture, and twice at Tanabergen-II (TBT23, T33) and once at Vvedenka (VDT2) of the Abashevo culture (Fig. 3-6-4). This distributional pattern again suggests that they were produced by Sintashta communities.

The type D dagger, featuring a short hilt and a blunt contour, occurs three times at Sintashta (SIT1), once at Bol'shekaraganka (BKK25T13) and Kamennyĭ-Ambar-V (KAK2T12) of the Sintashta culture, and once at Staroiur'evo (SR) and Selezni-II (SLT2) of the Abashevo culture (Fig. 3-6-4). The item from Krivoe Ozero[①] of the Sintashta culture, which has a fragmented body, may also fall within this type. The concentrated finds of this type at Sintashta cemeteries identify the associated communities as the producers/suppliers of this type of daggers. The following two types, however, are not easy to judge in terms of provenance because specimens are isolated. The type E dagger, which has an elongated rectangular hilt, is seen at Bol'shekaraganka (BK25T4) and Al'mukhametovskiĭ-I (AM) of the Abashevo culture (Fig. 3-6-4). The type F dagger, equipped with a long shank and a triangular blade, occurs once both at Sintashta (SIT3), and Nikiforovskiĭ (NF) (Fig. 3-6-4).

Other categories of metal artefacts-spearhead, knife and sickle-are limited in quantity. Spearheads, which have robust sockets and wide blades, have been found at Sintashta (SMT18) and Kamennyĭ-Ambar-V (KAK2T5) of the Sintashta culture, and Tanabergen-II (TBT22) of the Abashevo culture (Fig. 3-6-4); bent sickles have been found at Sintashta (SI14) of the Sintashta culture, and Beregovskiĭ-I (BR-I) of the Abashevo culture (Fig. 3-6-4). In addition, the unique metal arrowheads found at Sintashta (SII7) recur at Tanabergen-II (TB22) (Fig. 3-6-4). The Tanabergen-II

---

① Vinogradov, N. B., *Mogil'nik bronzovogo veka Krivoe Ozero*, Cheliabinsk: South-Ural Book Publisher, 2003, Fig. 68: 10.

piece imitates the Sintashta items not only in general contour but also in the vertebrae-like stalk. Due to the lack of metallurgical analysis, the provenance of these types of artefacts cannot be determined at present. But their concentration at cemeteries of Sintashta communities suggests that they were produced and supplied by Sintashta communities.

  The metal trade between Sintashta and Abashevo communities and Seĭma-Turbino communities becomes apparent when the formal and compositional characteristics of Seĭma-Turbino artefacts are examined. The 442 artefacts comprise 115 socketed axes, 73 spearheads, 126 knives, 21 daggers, 9 shaft-hole axes, 12 adze-chisels, 22 bracelets, 19 rings and 45 other objects. ①The percentage of the total made from similar alloys was as follows: tin-copper and tin-arsenic-copper alloys (37.2%); arsenic-copper and arsenic-antimony-copper alloys (44%); pure-copper (10.8%); copper-silver (3.3%) and silver-copper alloys (4.7%). ②The major ore sources were the arsenic- and silver-containing ores from the Eastern Urals and the sandstone ores from the Western Urals and from the Abashevo and Sintashta communities that dominated these regions. Alternatively, they might have been acquired from recycled metal artefacts, which were originally made of metals from these sources. When chemical composition is considered together with formal characteristics, four varieties emerge. First, there are the items that are morphologically absent in cemeteries or settlements of Abashevo and Sintashta cultures, for instance the socketed axes, fork-like spearheads and double-edged knives. There is little likelihood that they were imports from Sintashta and Abashevo communities; rather, they were probably local products or imports from elsewhere. This variety falls further into two different groups. Some are tin bronzes, and the communities might have obtained metals for their production from Elenovka and Ush-Katta, central Kazakhstan and the Altai Mountains; the others are pure copper or non-tin alloys, and they were made of metal ingots imported from

---

 ① Chernykh, E. N., and S. V. Kuz'minykh, *Drevniaia Metallurgiia Severnoĭ Evrasiia*, Moscow: Science, 1989, p. 38.
 ② Chernykh, E. N., and S. V. Kuz'minykh, *Drevniaia Metallurgiia Severnoĭ Evrasiia*, Moscow: Science, 1989, p. 188.

Sintashta and Abashevo communities. Secondly, there are those that are morphologically close to specimens from Sintashta and Abashevo communities. This variety likewise falls into two different categories. Some are tin bronzes, and their production locations are ambiguous because Seĭma-Turbino communities could have obtained tin from the Altai Mountains themselves. What deserves our greatest attention are those artefacts that are analogous to finds at Sintashta and Abashevo communities, and are made of pure copper and non-tin alloys. They are the subject of the following discussion.

The spearhead that has rhombic sections from Ust'-Gaiva, and the two from the Sintashta cemetery are similar in shape (Fig. 3-6-5), and all were made of copper-arsenic alloys.[①]This is in sharp contrast to the spearheads with fork-like shanks of the Seĭma-Turbino Phenomenon.[②]While the fork-like spearheads were likely produced by the Seĭma-Turbino community or imported from elsewhere, the spearhead from Ust'-Gaiva was probably manufactured by the Sintashta community. One spearhead from Reshnoe[③]has a similar form but with an added side loop made of a copper-arsenic alloy; it might likewise have come from the Sintashta community (Fig. 3-6-5). Two daggers from Turbino-I and Seĭma, the hilts of which have triangular tips, resemble the specimen from the Sintashta cemetery (SIT1) (Fig. 3-6-5). The one from Turbino-I is a copper-arsenic alloy, and the other from Seĭma contains antimony in addition to this alloy.[④]The sources of these daggers must also have been the Sintashta community.

The two shaft-hole axes from Seĭma and Sokolovka morphologically match the two items from the Sintashta cemetery (SMT3, SMT39), except that the latter two have small butts protruding from the shaft barrel (Fig. 3-6-6).

---

① Chernykh, E. N., and S. V. Kuz'minykh, *Drevniaia Metallurgiia Severnoĭ Evrasiia*, Moscow: Science, 1989, Table 2.1: nos. 4, 6, 7.

② Chernykh, E. N., and S. V. Kuz'minykh, *Drevniaia Metallurgiia Severnoĭ Evrasiia*, Moscow: Science, 1989, table 2.1: nos. 9-49.

③ Chernykh, E. N., and S. V. Kuz'minykh, *Drevniaia Metallurgiia Severnoĭ Evrasiia*, Moscow: Science, 1989, Table 2.1: no. 57.

④ Chernykh, E. N., and S. V. Kuz'minykh, *Drevniaia Metallurgiia Severnoĭ Evrasiia*, Moscow: Science, 1989, Table 3.1: nos. 2, 5.

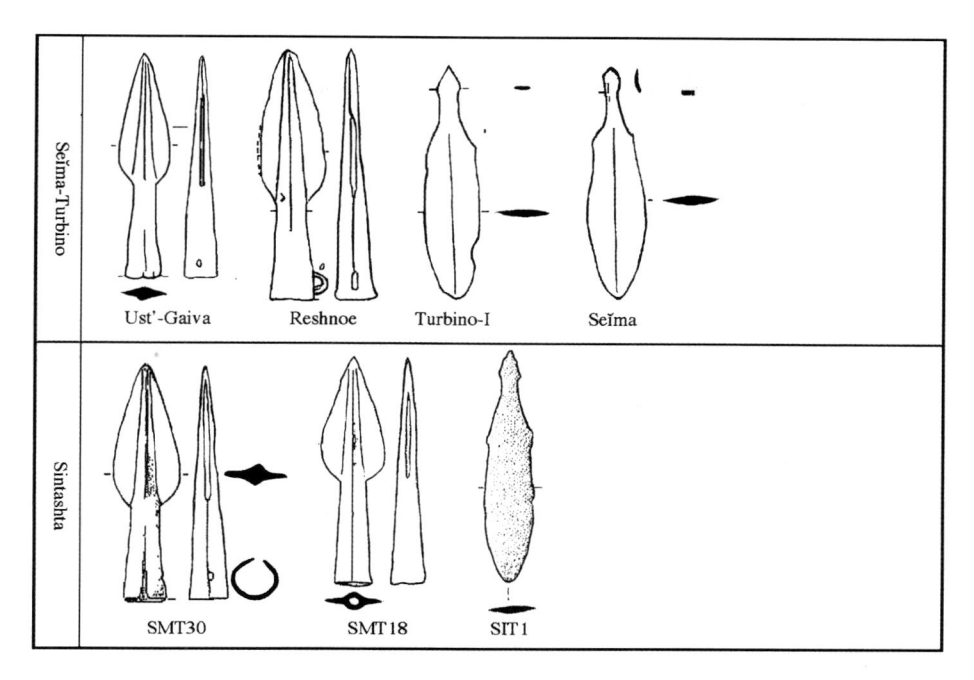

Fig. 3-6-5 **Spearheads and daggers from Sintashta, Potapovka and Seǐma-Turbino communities**

[Sources of data: Ust'-Gaiva, Reshnoe, SM30, SM18 (Chernykh, E. N., and S. V. Kuz'minykh, *Drevniaia Metallurgiia Severnoǐ Evrasiia*, Moscow: Science, 1989, Fig. 25: 2, Fig. 40: 1); Turbino-I, Seǐma (Chernykh, E. N., and S. V. Kuz'minykh, *Drevniaia Metallurgiia Severnoǐ Evrasiia*, Moscow: Science, 1989, Fig. 58: 2, 5); SI1 (Gening, V. F., G. B. Zdanovich, and V. V. Gening, *Sintashta—Arkheologicheskie Pamiatniki Ariǐskikh Plemen Uralo-Kazakhstanskikh Stepeǐ*, Cheliabinsk: South-Ural Book Publisher, 1992, Fig. 140: 1)]

The former were made of a copper-arsenic-antimony and a copper-arsenic alloy, respectively. [1]The two Sintashta pieces are copper-arsenic-nickel alloys. The chemical compositions of the Seǐma-Turbino pieces are not identical but are close to those of the two Sintashta axes. The three adzes from Turbino-I and Ust'-Gaiva repeat the forms of samples from Sintashta and they chemically belong

---

[1] Chernykh, E. N., and S. V. Kuz'minykh, *Drevniaia Metallurgiia Severnoǐ Evrasiia*, Moscow: Science, 1989, Table 6. 1: nos. 5.

to the copper-arsenic alloy type.①The formal and compositional resemblance identifies Sintashta as the producing/ supplying community of these shaft-hole axes and adzes.

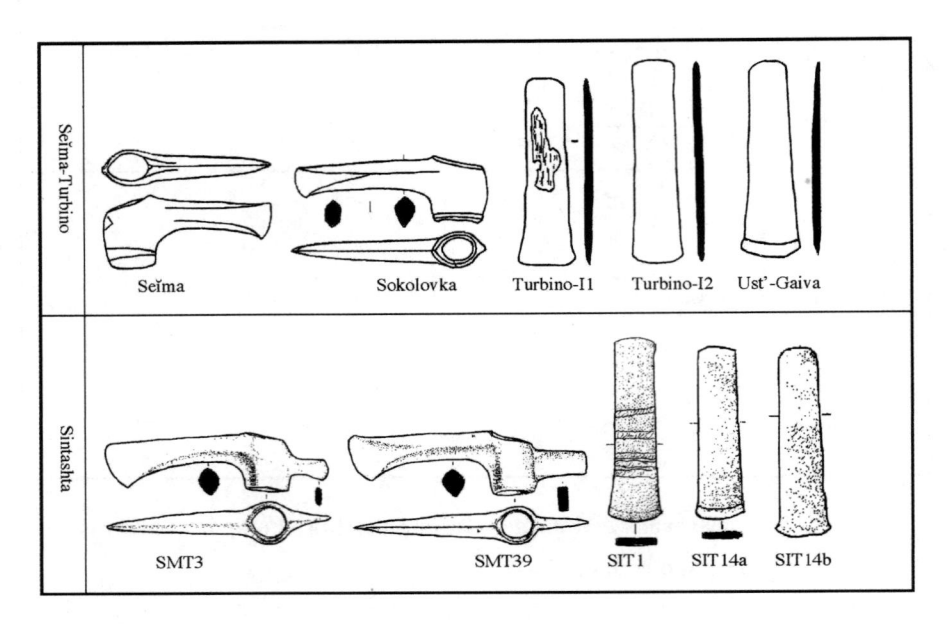

Fig. 3 – 6 – 6   Shaft-hole axes and adzes from cemeteries of the Sintashta culture and the Seĭma-Turbino Phenomenon

[Sources of data: Seĭma, Sokolovka (Chernykh, E. N. , and S. V. Kuz'minykh, *Drevniaia Metallurgiia Severnoĭ Evrasiia*, Moscow: Science, 1989, Fig. 70: 5, 6); SM3, SM39 (Gening, V. F. , G. B. Zdanovich, and V. V. Gening, *Sintashta—Arkheologicheskie Pamiatniki Ariĭskikh Plemen Uralo-Kazakhstanskikh Stepeĭ*, Cheliabinsk: South-Ural Book Publisher, 1992, Fig. 49: 6, Fig. 127: 1); Turbino-I1, Turbino-I2, Ust'-Gaiva (Chernykh, E. N. , and S. V. Kuz'minykh, *Drevniaia Metallurgiia Severnoĭ Evrasiia*, Moscow: Science, 1989, Fig. 71: 4, 5, 8); SI1, SI14a, SI14b (Gening, V. F. , G. B. Zdanovich, and V. V. Gening, *Sintashta—Arkheologicheskie Pamiatniki Ariĭskikh Plemen Uralo-Kazakhstanskikh Stepeĭ*, Cheliabinsk: South-Ural Book Publisher, 1992, Fig. 140: 7; Fig. 148: 15, 16)]

---

① Chernykh, E. N. , and S. V. Kuz'minykh, *Drevniaia Metallurgiia Severnoĭ Evrasiia*, Moscow: Science, 1989, Table 7. 1: nos. 5, 4, 8.

Metal Trade in Bronze Age Central Eurasia ◇❖◇

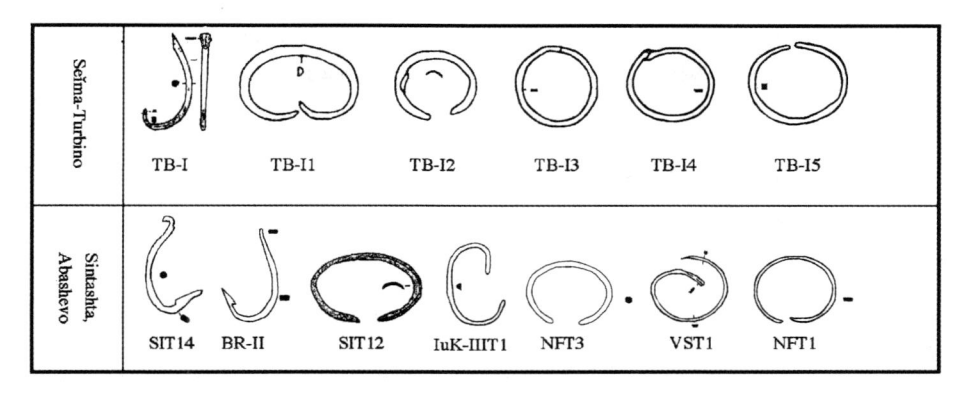

Seĭma-Turbino	TB-I	TB-I1	TB-I2	TB-I3	TB-I4	TB-I5
Sintashta, Abashevo	SIT14 · BR-II · SIT12 · IuK-IIIT1 · NFT3 · VST1 · NFT1

Fig. 3 – 6 – 7　Fishing hooks and bracelets from Sintashta, Abashevo and Seĭma-Turbino communities

[TB-Turbino, Sources of data: TB – I, TB – I1, 2, 3, 4, 5 (Chernykh, E. N. , and S. V. Kuz'minykh, *Drevniaia Metallurgiia Severnoĭ Evrasiia*, Moscow: Science, 1989, Fig. 72: 24; Fig. 73: 17, 21, 15, 10, 8); SIT14, SIT12 (Gening, V. F. , G. B. Zdanovich, and V. V. Gening, *Sintashta—Arkheologicheskie Pamiatniki Ariĭskikh Plemen Uralo-Kazakhstanskikh Stepeĭ*, Cheliabinsk: South-Ural Book Publisher, 1992, Fig. 148: 2; 274, Fig. 153: 1); BR – II, IuK – IIIT1 (Gorbunov, V. S. , *Abashevskaia Kul'tura Iuzhnogo Priural'ia*, Ufa: Bashkir Pedinstitute, 1986, Fig. 15: 7, 20); NFT3, NFT1 (Vasil'ev, I. B. , and A. D. Priakhin, Beskurgannyĭ Abashevskiĭ mogil'nik u Nikiforovskogo lesnichestva v Orenburzh'e, *Sovetskaia Arkheologiia* 2, 1979, Fig. 3: 3, 1); VST1 (Siniuk, A. T. , and I. A. Kozirchuk, Nekotorye aspekty izucheniia Abashevskoĭ kultury v Basseĭne Dona, in I. B. Vasil'ev ed. , *Drevnie Indoiranskie Kul'tury Volgo-Ural'ia*, Samara: The Samara State Pedagogical University, 1995, Fig. 4: 1)]

The fishing hooks from Turbino-I (TB – I) are morphologically common among the finds from Sintashta (e. g. SIT14) and Abashevo (e. g. BR – II) sites; their chemical compositions, unanimously copper-arsenic alloys,[①] indicate that they were imported from Sintashta and Abashevo communities (Fig. 3 – 6 – 7). In the meantime, among the 29 bracelets[②] of the Seĭma-Turbino Phenomenon, 25 are made of solid wires that are circular, rectangular and triangular in section. These forms recall specimens of the Abashevo culture.

[①] Chernykh, E. N. , and S. V. Kuz'minykh, *Drevniaia Metallurgiia Severnoĭ Evrasiia*, Moscow: Science, 1989, Table 9. 2.

[②] Chernykh, E. N. , and S. V. Kuz'minykh, *Drevniaia Metallurgiia Severnoĭ Evrasiia*, Moscow: Science, 1989, Fig. 73: nos. 1 – 8, 10 – 28, 30 – 34.

Three pieces from Turbino-I (TB – I3, 4, 5) in particular resemble the four pieces from the cemeteries at Iukalekulevo (IuK – 3T1), Nikiforovskiĭ (NFT3, NFT1) and Vlasov-I (VST1) (Fig. 3 – 6 – 7). One bracelet is made of a copper-silver alloy.①Two other pieces from Turbino-I (e. g. TB – I1, 2), however, have groove-shaped sections, and match specimens from the Sintashta cemetery (SIT12) (Fig. 3 – 6 – 7). The two bracelets are made exclusively of copper-arsenic alloys.②These bracelets again reflect the vibrant trade from Sintashta and Abashevo communities to their Seĭma-Turbino partners.

Conclusions

Due to the sparseness of compositional data, many of the foregoing hypotheses cannot be confirmed, but the combination of available compositional and morphological data are strongly indicative of dynamic and expansive trading networks that involved Sintashta, Abashevo and Seĭma-Turbino communities. In such networks, not only copper ingots, but also ready-made metal artefacts were circulated. As far as these data go, the major directions of the flow of metal goods were from Sintashta communities to their Abashevo counterparts, and from Sintashta and Abashevo communities to their Seĭma-Turbino counterparts. Sintashta communities were therefore the hubs of these trading networks. The ultimate reason for this pattern of metal trade lies in the concentration of the much-desired polymetallic ores in their territories, the Eastern Urals. The metal types of arsenic-copper and silver-copper alloys from this region were constantly in demand.

This paper therefore not only offers a new understanding of the Seĭma-Turbino metals, but also supplies a new perspective to the issue of social development in eastern Europe. Communities of the Sintashta culture as a whole were economically and, by implication, politically stronger than those of the

---

① Chernykh, E. N., and S. V. Kuz'minykh, *Drevniaia Metallurgiia Severnoĭ Evrasiia*, Moscow: Science, 1989, Table 10. 1: no. 15.
② Chernykh, E. N., and S. V. Kuz'minykh, *Drevniaia Metallurgiia Severnoĭ Evrasiia*, Moscow: Science, 1989, Table 10. 1: nos. 19, 22.

Abashevo culture. This superiority is manifested in the larger fortified settlements and greater deposits of metal artefacts and other prestige goods in tombs of the Sintashta culture. ①The probable underlying mechanism is that metals commanded great economic and social value in ancient societies, and the metal producing and supplying communities gained greater economic wealth and political power than the consuming communities. This is not the place to extrapolate this theme at length, but it is worth advancing the point that metal trade may throw new light onto early social evolution.

---

① Gening, V. F. , G. B. Zdanovich, and V. V. Gening , *Sintashta—Arkheologicheskie Pamiatniki Ariĭskikh Plemen Uralo-Kazakhstanskikh Stepeĭ*, Cheliabinsk: South-Ural Book Publisher, 1992; Botalov, S. G. , S. A. Grigor'ev, and G. B. Zdanovich, Pogrebal'nye kompleksy èpokhi bronzy Bol'shekaraganskogo mogil'nika, in G. B. Zdanovich (ed.), *Materialy po Arkheologii i Ètnografii Iuzhnogo Urala*, Cheliabinsk: Kamennyĭ Poias, 1996, pp. 64 – 88; Vinogradov, N. B. , *Mogil'nik Bronzovogo Veka Krivoe Ozero*, Cheliabinsk: South-Ural Book Publisher, 2003; Zdanovich, D. G. , Okhrannye raskopki v zone Bol'shekaraganskogo kar'era, in D. G. Zdanovich ed. , *Arkaim: Nekropol'*, Cheliabinsk: South-Ural Book Publisher, 2002, pp. 110 – 116; Epimakhov, A. V. , *Rannie Kompleksnye Obshchestva Severa Tsentral'noĭ Evrazii*, Book 1, Cheliabinsk: Cheliabinsk House of Printing, 2005; Zhang, L. , *Ancient Society and Metallurgy: A Comparative Study of Bronze Age Societies in Central Eurasia and North China*, Ch. IV, PhD thesis, University of California, Los Angeles, 2007.

西西伯利亚南部的青铜时代分期[*]

西西伯利亚西起于乌拉尔山脉,东止于叶尼塞河,南起于阿尔泰山脉,北止于北冰洋。在这片辽阔的土地上,纵向流淌着叶尼塞河、鄂毕河、额尔齐斯河、依辛河(Ishin')和托博尔(Tobol')河,同时横向排列着草原、森林草原、森林和苔藓带。根据历史文献记载,自早期铁器时代以来,草原和森林草原带的游牧民族同南方的波斯、中亚和中国的农业文明发生了密切的经济文化交往。而更早的历史情况,由于文献记载的匮乏,一直是考古工作者们关注的对象。考古工作在此始于19世纪,蓬勃发展于苏联时代,不断地更新着学术界的认识。迄今为止,人们已经发现数千座墓地和聚落,并且命名了不少考古学文化。

本文的宗旨是为西西伯利亚南部的草原带和草原森林带已经发现的青铜时代文化建立一个清晰的年代框架。众所周知,对于年代的认识往往与考古学的发展是同步的。苏联时代的俄罗斯考古学,因为意识形态的缘故,是在非常封闭的情况下发展起来的,随着时间的推移,已建立起一套独特而复杂的类型学。即在确定一个文化的相对年代时,一般使用所谓的"文化因素分析法",并赋予其强大的功能。他们仔细地划分一个文化的陶器、石器和金属器的器类和纹样,并将它们与其他文化的同类因素对比,以此来确定它的相对年代。至于绝对年代,碳十四数据长期以来增长缓慢,远远落后于田野发掘的进度。尽管在俄罗斯碳十四测年实验室早在20世纪60年代就已建成,但是考古学家经常持怀疑态度,积累的数据不足

---

[*] 本文原刊于《考古学集刊》2017年第20集,第232—271页。收入本书时略有改动。

以界定一个文化的年代范围。在过去的几十年中，苏联考古学家常常比照中国安阳商文化和希腊迈锡尼文化来确定年代，他们认为这些文化有文献记载，所以年代比较可靠。

20世纪90年代以来，随着冷战的结束，考古学思想的交流日益频繁。中国考古学在20世纪50年代学习了许多苏联考古学的先进经验，[1] 但在此后的几十年里同样走了一条封闭的发展道路。上述苏联的文化因素分析法是有缺陷的，只考虑了共享若干形态或纹饰因素的文化是同时期的，并没有考虑也可能是不同时期的。中国学者运用的器物形态学或许可以弥补这个缺陷，[2] 本文就介绍这种新的类型学，它继承和发展了蒙特琉斯（Oscar Montelius）的类型学，不强调个别器类，不强调个别纹饰，而强调器物群整体的风格，并指出一个时期的各类器物在风格上是统一的，随着时间的推移，各类器物的风格整体发生变化，因而与前期不同。由此看来，一个文化并不是不同因素拼凑起来的大杂烩，而是一个反映人类审美趣味的有机体。因此，这种方法不仅适用于一个文化，还适用于一个地区的若干文化。大家知道，在欧亚大陆，由于没有地理障碍，器物和思想的流通可以畅行无阻，因此器物风格的变化不仅发生于一个文化，而且会传播到其他许多文化。由此看来，我国和苏联考古学家使用的"时代（horizon）"一词贴切地反映了这种大范围的文化变迁，但考古学家们只用"同时期的文化"，很少用它来描述大范围的文化变迁。[3]

笔者将依据碳十四测年数据，来分析西西伯利亚南部的青铜时代文化的绝对年代问题。苏联考古学家常用的类比中国和希腊材料的方法并不科学，这种断代方法使西西伯利亚青铜时代文化的年代晚了许多。虽然近10年来碳十四数据增加了不少，但是利用现有的数据还不能够界定部分文化的年代。因此，笔者利用自己建立的东欧（俄罗

---

[1] Zhang, Liangren, 2011, Soviet Inspiration in Chinese Archaeology, *Antiquity* 85, 2011, pp. 1049–1059.

[2] 苏秉琦、殷玮璋：《地层学与器物形态学》，《文物》1982年第4期，第1—7页。

[3] 俄罗斯考古学家用得较多，已见有"Sredny Stog-Khvalynsk horizon（铜石并用时代）""Yamnaya horizon（青铜时代早期）""Novykumak horizon（青铜时代中期）"。这些名词只限于东欧（俄罗斯）境内；西西伯利亚青铜时代考古学没有使用"horizon"的情况。

斯境内顿河—乌拉尔河之间）的年代框架作为参考（表3-7-1），[①]再予以断代。主要是因为东欧不仅积累了很多年代数据，而且与西西伯利亚之间的文化联系也较为密切，其器物变化规律可为研究西西伯利亚南部青铜时代文化的年代提供重要的参照依据。

一 东欧的年代框架

笔者认为东欧的青铜时代可以分为三期（见表3-7-1）。早期包括竖穴墓文化（Yamnaya），其年代大体为公元前3300—前2100年。[②] 中期包括辛塔什塔（Sintashta）文化，其年代大体为公元前2040—前1730

表3-7-1 东欧与西西伯利亚青铜时代分期和绝对年代

分期	东欧	分布地域	碳十四年代	西西伯利亚	分布地域	碳十四年代
早期	竖穴墓（Yamnaya）	伏尔加河下游和乌拉尔河流域的草原带和半沙漠带	公元前3300—前2100年	阿凡纳谢沃（Afanas'evo）	米奴辛斯克盆地、图瓦、蒙古、阿尔泰山前和谢米巴拉琴思科（哈萨克斯坦）	公元前3650—前2240年
				切木尔切克（Chemurchek）	中国、蒙古和哈萨克斯坦的阿尔泰山前地带	公元前2840—前1680年
				奥库涅沃（Okunevo）	米奴辛斯克盆地、图瓦和阿尔泰山前地带	公元前2885—前1693年
中期	辛塔什塔（Sintashta）	乌拉尔山脉南部东侧的森林草原带	公元前2040—前1730年	安德罗诺沃（Andronovo）	西至乌拉尔河，东至叶尼塞河，北至森林带南缘，南至中亚的草原带	公元前1750—前1400年
				耶鲁尼诺（Elunino）	鄂毕河上游	公元前2500—前1700年
				克罗托沃（Krotovo）	鄂毕河和额尔齐斯河之间的草原带和森林草原带	公元前1400—前1100年

---

① Zhang, Liangren, *Ancient Society and Metallurgy: A Comparative Study of Bronze Age Societies in Central Eurasia and North China*, Archaeopress, 2012.

② Zhang, Liangren, *Ancient Society and Metallurgy: A Comparative Study of Bronze Age Societies in Central Eurasia and North China*, Archaeopress, 2012, p. 26.

续表

分期	东欧	分布地域	碳十四年代	西西伯利亚	分布地域	碳十四年代
晚期	木椁墓（Srubnaya）	顿河、伏尔加河和乌拉尔河流域的草原带	公元前1690—前1390年	卡拉苏克（Karasuk）	米奴辛斯克盆地	公元前1400—前800年
				伊尔敏（Irmen'）	西至额尔齐斯河，东至鄂毕河，南至南阿尔泰，北至鄂毕河和楚勒姆河的交汇处	公元前1890—前1130年
				萨穆西（Samus'）	新西伯利亚以北，权耶河以南，秋明以东，托木河下游以西的森林和森林草原带	公元前1500—前1200年

年。[1] 晚期包括木椁墓（Srubnaya）文化，其年代大体为公元前1690—前1390年。[2] 熟悉欧亚大陆青铜时代考古的读者会马上注意到，这个年代框架与目前俄罗斯的主流观点相左，但也有不少学者把阿巴舍沃和辛塔什塔文化归入青铜时代晚期。[3] 如果依据新的类型学，即依据金属器和陶器的变化规律分析，这个分期框架是可以成立的。

在金属器方面，早期的竖穴墓文化的铜器绝大多数为纯铜，[4] 但是南高加索地区的同时期文化已经掌握了砷铜铸造技术。它们与竖穴墓文化有着紧密的文化交流关系，因此笔者赞同E. N. 切尔内赫（Chernykh）的观点，把竖穴墓文化归入青铜时代。在中期的辛塔什塔文化阶段，人们开始掌握砷铜技术，而到了晚期的木椁墓文化阶段，人们掌握了锡青铜技术（这样的分期就能清楚地反映冶金技术发展的三个阶段）。[5]

---

[1] Zhang, Liangren, *Ancient Society and Metallurgy: A Comparative Study of Bronze Age Societies in Central Eurasia and North China*, Archaeopress, 2012, p. 50.

[2] Zhang, Liangren, *Ancient Society and Metallurgy: A Comparative Study of Bronze Age Societies in Central Eurasia and North China*, Archaeopress, 2012, p. 90.

[3] 如 Chernykh, E. N., *Ancient Metallurgy in the USSR: The Early Metal Age*, translated by Sarah Wright, Cambridge, New York, and Melbourne: Cambridge University Press, 1992.

[4] Kuz'minykh, S. V., and S. A. Agapov, Medistye peschaniki priural'ia i ikh ispol'zovanie v drevnosti, *Stanovlenie i razvitie proizvodiashchego khoziaĭstva na Urale*, Sverdlovsk, 1989, pp. 178–197; Chernykh, E. N., *Ancient Metallurgy in the USSR: The Early Metal Age*, translated by Sarah Wright, Cambridge, New York, Melbourne: Cambridge University Press, 1992, p. 133.

[5] Chernykh, E. N., *Ancient Metallurgy in the USSR: The Early Metal Age*, translated by Sarah Wright, Cambridge, New York, Melbourne: Cambridge University Press, 1992.

类似的变化规律也见于这些文化的其他方面（表3-7-2）。早期的竖穴墓文化的墓葬为屈肢葬，墓底往往撒赤铁粉。陶器纹饰都很简单，主要有窝纹、松针纹和垂弧纹。在辛塔什塔阶段，不再使用赤铁粉，陶器的器形增加，主要有侈口鼓腹平底罐以及敛口直腹平底罐。与早期器物不同的是，纹饰丰满华丽，主要有回纹、三角纹和折线纹，其他还有碗和盘。晚期的木椁墓文化继承了辛塔什塔文化的一些因素，器物个体缩小，纹饰变得简单粗糙。

表3-7-2　　　　　　　　东欧青铜时代器物分期

分期	文化	典型器物					
		陶罐		铜横銎斧	铜矛	铜短剑	铜耳环、手镯
早期	竖穴墓文化						
中期	辛塔什塔文化						
晚期	木椁墓文化						

二　西西伯利亚青铜时代早期

属于本期的文化有阿凡纳谢沃（Afanas'evo）、切木尔切克和奥库涅沃（Okunevo），代表本期的两个阶段（见表3-7-1），在文化面貌和年代上，都与东欧的竖穴墓文化相对应。

（一）阿凡纳谢沃文化

阿凡纳谢沃是叶尼塞河上的一座山岗的名称（Afanas'eva gora）。20世纪20年代，S. A. 捷普劳霍夫（S. A. Teploukhov）在此发掘了几座墓葬，并由此命名了阿凡纳谢沃文化。① 此后，尤其是20世纪90年代以来，该文化的发掘资料逐渐增多，遗址集中发现于叶尼塞河流域，也发现于图瓦、蒙古、阿尔泰和谢米巴拉琴思科（哈萨克斯坦共和国境内）（图3－7－1）。② 其中大部分遗址为墓地，也发现了几处聚落遗址（如Kara- Tenesh），但是保存较差，只见灶坑和陶片。③ 在图瓦境内的叶尼塞

---

① Griaznov, M. P., *Afanas'evskaia Kul'tura na Enisee*, Sankt-Peterburg, 1999.

② Kiselev, S. V., *Drevniia Istoriia Iuzhnoĭ Sibiri*, Moscow: Science, 1951; Griaznov, M. P., and E. B. Vadezkaia, Afanas'evskaia kul'tura, *Istoriia Sibiri* 1, Leningrad, 1969, pp. 159 – 165; Ivanova, K. A., Mogil'nik podsukhanikha i nekotorye osobennosti Afanas'evskikh nadmogil'nykh sooruzheniĭ, *Kratkie Soobshcheniia Instituta Arkheologii* 114, 1968, pp. 58 – 69; Khlobystina, M. D., Drevnie mogil'niki Gornogo Altaiia, *Sovetskaia Arkheologiia* 1, 1975, pp. 17 – 34; Tsyb, S. V., Ranniaia gruppa Afanas'evskikh pamiatnikov i vopros o proiskhozhdenii Afanas'evskoĭ kul'tury, *Drevniaia Istoriia Altaia*, Barnaul, 1980, pp. 38 – 51; Larin, O. V., K istorii izucheniia afanas'evskoĭ kul'tury Gornogo Altaia, *Arkheologiia Gornogo Altaia*, Gorno-Altaisk, 1988, pp. 82 – 91; Larin, O. V., Afanas'evskie pamiatniki srednego techeniia Katuni, *Problemy Izucheniia Drevneĭ i Srednevekovoĭ Istorii Gornogo Altaia*, Gorno-Altaisk, 1990, pp. 3 – 30; Larin, O. V., *Afanas'evskaia Kul'tura Gornogo Altaia: Mogil'nik Sal'diar-1*, Barnaul: Press of Altai State University, 2005; Semenov, V. A., Pamiatniki Afanas'evskoĭ kul'tury v Saianakh, *Sovetskaia Arkheologiia* 4, 1982, pp. 219 – 222; Derevianko, A. P., and V. I. Molodin, *Denisova Peshchera*, Novosibirsk: Science, 1994; Vadetskaia, È. B., *Arkheologicheskie Pamiatniki v Stepiakh Srednego Eniseia*, Leningrad: Science Press, 1986; Surazakov, A. S., Afanas'evskie pamiatniki Gornogo Altaia, *Problemy Istorii Gornogo Altaia*, 1987, pp. 3 – 22, Gorno-Altaĭsk; Mogil'nikov, V. A., Nekotorye pamiatniki èpokhi rannego metalla iz Tsentral'nogo Altaia, *Probelmy Istorii Gornogo Altaia*, Gorno-Altaĭsk, 1987, pp. 23 – 34; Kubarev, V. D., D. V. Chereminsin, and I. Iu. Sliusarenko, Bike I, II: Pogrebal'nye pamiatniki Afanas'evskoĭ kul'tury na sredneĭ Katuni, *Drevnosti Altaia* 6, 2001, pp. 32 – 53; Tsybiktarov, A. D., Mogil'niki Afanas'evskogo tipa Mongolii i Tuvy, in M. V. Konstantinov and A. D. Tsybiktarov eds., *Tsentral'naia Aziia i Pribaĭkal'ia v Drevnosti*, Elan-Udè-Chita: Press of the Buriat' State University, 2001, pp. 42 – 52; Kiriushin, Iu. F., *Neolit, Ranniaia i Razvitaia Bronza Iuga-Zapadnoĭ Sibiri*, 2002, pp. 10 – 45, Barnaul; A. A. 科瓦列夫、D. 额尔德尼巴特尔：《蒙古青铜时代文化的新发现》，《边疆考古研究》2009 年第 8 期；Kubarev, V. D., *Pamiatniki Karakol'skoĭ kul'tury Altaia*, Novosibirsk: Press of Institute of Archaeology and Ethnography SORAN, 2009.

③ Pogozheva, A. P., Afanas'evskaia kul'tura, in V. I. Molodin ed., *Èpokha Èneolita i Bronzy Gornogo Altaia*, Barnaul: AzBuka, part 1, 2006, pp. 18 – 26.

河上的图拉达圩（Toora-dash）遗址中，在新石器的地层上和奥库涅沃文化地层下发现了阿凡纳谢沃文化的地层，清楚地表明其相对年代。①

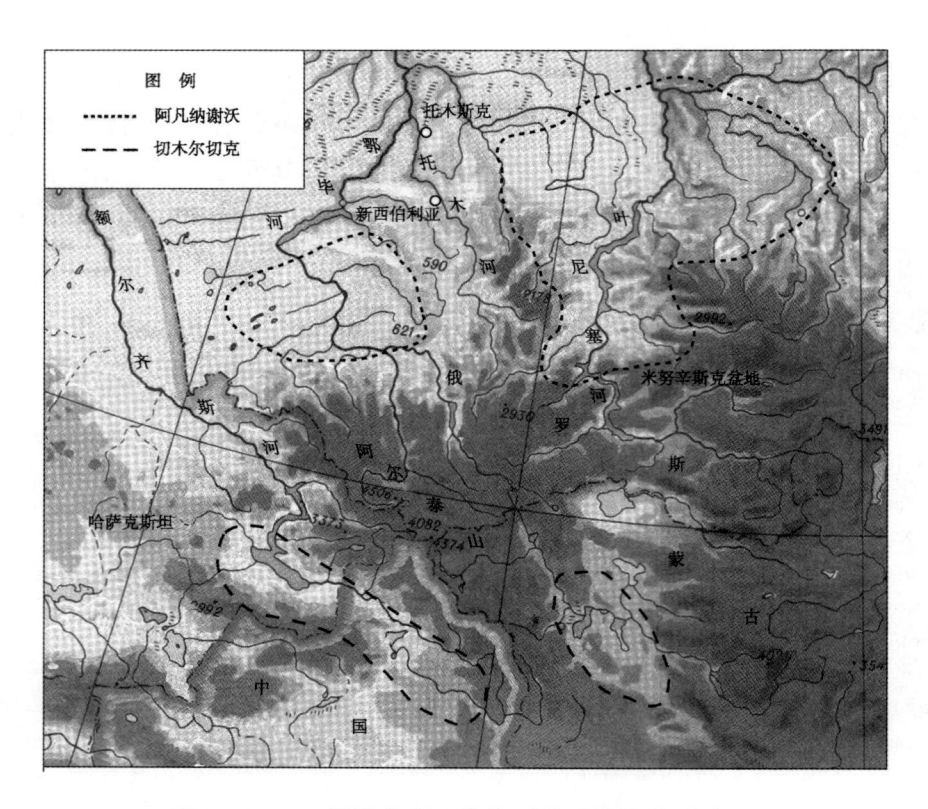

图 3-7-1　西西伯利亚青铜时代早期文化分布图

虽然有些学者认为阿凡纳谢沃是土生土长的文化，② 但它显然是东欧竖穴墓文化的后裔。墓葬都是竖穴坑，墓主头向一般为东北或西南。墓口盖木头或石板，坑上堆土或石块。有些墓葬周围有一圈石块砌成的围墙，有些墓葬没有封堆，只有石围。③ 一个土（石）堆下埋一座或更

---

① Semenov, V. A., Pamiatniki Afanas'evskoǐ kul'tury v Saianakh, *Sovetskaia Arkheologiia* 4, 1982, pp. 219 – 222.

② Semenov, V. A., Pamiatniki Afanas'evskoǐ kul'tury v Saianakh, *Sovetskaia Arkheologiia* 4, 1982, pp. 219 – 222; Bokovenko, N. A., and P. E. Mitjaev, Malinovyj Log, Ein Gräberfeld der Afanas'evo Kultur, *Eurasia Antiqua*, 2000, Band 6, pp. 13 – 33.

③ Ivanova, K. A., Mogil'nik podsukhanikha i nekotorye osobennosti Afanas'evskikh nadmogil'nykh sooruzheniǐ, *Kratkie Soobshcheniia Instituta Arkheologii* 114, 1968, p. 68.

多墓葬。大多数墓葬一人，也有葬两人或更多的。墓主多为仰身屈肢（例外的情况是向右侧身），下面铺草，然后撒赤铁粉。随葬品很少，一般只有一件陶器，有些还有金属器（图3-7-2：1）。陶器有橄榄形罐和球形罐两类。纹饰有戳印或压印的松针纹和弦纹（图3-7-2：2—4）。金属器中几乎不见武器，工具也很少，大多为装饰品（如耳环、管饰），也有一些加固木制容器的卡钉（图3-7-2：5—8）。除铜器外，还使用金器、银器和陨铁器。该文化的居民属于欧罗巴人种，与本地新石器时代居民及周围同时期的蒙古人种不同。[1] 另外，该文化也有一些与竖穴墓文化不同的地方。如陶器群包含一些黑海北岸洞室墓（Catacomb）文化的器物（见表3-7-1），尤其是形状独特的圈足豆（俄国文献称为香炉）；土（石）堆墓葬周围砌一圈石围；墓葬旁边普遍放置刻画精致的石人。这些差别并不能推翻上面所说的东欧起源说，这些可能只是竖穴墓居民为了适应本地环境进行的改变。

与竖穴墓文化相同，阿凡纳谢沃文化也被一些学者列入铜石并用时代。[2] 该文化的金属器数量不多，据2009年的一次统计为98件，[3] 其中装饰品（铜泡、指环、镯和串珠）居多，也有工具（锥、刀、铲）、武器（短剑）和加固木容器的部件（补丁、卡钉）（图3-7-2：5—8）。

---

[1] Griaznov, M. P., and E. B. Vadezkaia, Afanas'evskaia kul'tura, *Istoriia Sibiri* 1, 1968, p. 165, Leningrad; Griaznov, M. P., *Afanas'evskaia Kul'tura na Enisee*, Sankt-Peterburg, 1999, p. 52.

[2] M. P. Griaznov, M. P., and E. B. Vadezkaia, 1969, Afanas'evskaia kul'tura, *Istoriia Sibiri* 1, Leningrad, 1968, p. 161; Khlobystina, M. D., Drevnie mogil'niki Gornogo Altaiia, *Sovetskaia Arkheologiia* 1, 1975, p. 17; Vadetskaia, È. B., *Arkheologicheskie Pamiatniki v Stepiakh Srednego Eniseia*, Leningrad: Science Press, 1986; Surazakov, A. S., Afanas'evskie pamiatniki Gornogo Altaia, *Problemy Istorii Gornogo Altaia*, Gorno-Altaĭsk, 1987, pp. 3-22; Larin, O. V., K istorii izucheniia afanas'evskoĭ kul'tury Gornogo Altaia, *Arkheologiia Gornogo Altaia* 1, Gorno-Altaĭsk, 1988, pp. 82-89; Griaznov, M. P., *Afanas'evskaia Kul'tura na Enisee*, Sankt-Peterburg; Kiriushin, Iu. F., *Neolit, Ranniaia i Razvitaia Bronza Iuga-Zapadnoĭ Sibiri*, Barnaul, 1999, pp. 10-45; Grushin, S. P., E. A. Tiurina, S. V. Khavrin, Drevneĭshiĭ metall Iuzhnoĭ Sibiri, in S. P. Grushin ed., *Altaĭ v Sisteme Metallurgicheskikh Provintsiĭ Bronzovogo Veka*, Barnaul: Press of Altai State University, 2006; Pogozheva, A. P., Afanas'evskaia kul'tura, in V. I. Molodin ed., *Èpokha Èneolita i Bronzy Gornogo Altaia*, Barnaul: AzBuka, part 1, 2006, pp. 18-26.

[3] Tiurina, E. A., and S. P. Grushin, Èpokha èneolita (Afanas'evskiĭ metallokompleks), in *Altaĭ v Sisteme Metallurgicheskikh Provintsiĭ Èneolita i Bronzovogo Veka*, Barnaul: Press of Altai State University, 2009, p. 7.

◇❖◇　第三部分　中国西北和欧亚草原考古

还有四件采集的横銎斧，形态与阿凡纳谢沃的石斧接近，可能属于该文化。这些器物形制上与东欧环黑海冶金省（包括竖穴墓文化）的同类器接近。[1] 据发掘者观察，这些器物大多数为纯铜（50件），有些为自然铜，有些铜含砷、锑和银。青铜器（16件）、银器（6件）、金器（4件）和铁器（3件）的数量较少。[2] 米奴辛斯克盆地图贝（Tuby）河谷出土的铜器包括矛、凿和刀各一件，发掘者认为皆为青铜，而不是纯铜。铜矛不是阿凡纳谢沃文化普遍采用的锻造法制成，而是铸造而成的。[3] 同样被认定为青铜的还有叶尼塞河上的马里淖维劳格（Malinovyj Log）墓地、卡通河上的萨依加尔（Sal' diar）墓地和蒙古巴彦乌列盖省古尔干格维（Kurgak Govi）墓地出土的几件铜器（锥、耳环、刀各1件）。[4] 这些器物是否为青铜，需要经过检测才能够确定。

近10年来，研究者利用X射线荧光光谱仪对阿凡纳谢沃文化的金属器做了无损分析。结果表明，米奴辛斯克盆地（Afanas'eva gora、Karasuk-II、Barsuchikha-IV墓地）出土的9件铜器中，3件为自然铜，6件含有<1或1%—3%的砷。[5] 戈尔诺—阿尔泰（如Elo-I、Kuium、Sal'diar-I等墓地）出土的20件金属器中，1件为陨铁器，2件为金器，其余均为铜器。其中部分为纯铜，部分含有2%—6%的砷。[6] S. V. 哈夫林（Khavrin）推测铜矿本身含有很高的砷，所以这些铜器不一定是砷铜。20

---

[1] Grushin, S. P., E. A. Tiurina, S. V. Khavrin, Drevneĭshiĭ metall Iuzhnoĭ Sibiri, in S. P. Grushin ed., *Altaĭ v Sisteme Metallurgicheskikh Provintsiĭ Bronzovogo Veka*, Barnaul: Press of Altai State University, 2006, pp. 21 - 22.

[2] Grushin, S. P., E. A. Tiurina, S. V. Khavrin, Drevneĭshiĭ metall Iuzhnoĭ Sibiri, in S. P. Grushin ed., *Altaĭ v Sisteme metallurgicheskikh Provintsiĭ Bronzovogo Veka*, Barnaul: Press of Altai State University, 2006, pp. 30 - 32.

[3] Zimina, V. M., Afanas'evskoe pogrebenie iz Tuby, in A. P. Okladnikov ed., *Drevniaia Sibir'*, Novosibirsk: Science, Issue 2, 1966, p. 160.

[4] Bokovenko, N. A., and P. E. Mitjaev, Malinovyj Log, Ein Gräberfeld der Afanas'evo Kultur, *Eurasia Antiqua*, 2000, Band 6, p. 18; Larin, O. V., *Afanas'evskaia Kul'tura Gornogo Altaia: Mogil'nik Sal'diar-1*, Barnaul: Press of Altai State University, 2005, p. 17; А. А. 科瓦列夫、D. 额尔德尼巴特尔:《蒙古青铜时代文化的新发现》，《边疆考古研究》2009年第8期，第247页。

[5] Khavrin, S. V., Drevneĭshiĭ metall Saiano-Altaia, *Izvestiia Altaĭskogo Gosudarstvennogo Universiteta*, Seriia: Istoriia, Barnaul, 2008, Issue 4/2 (60), p. 212, Plate 4.

[6] Khavrin, S. V., Drevneĭshiĭ metall Saiano-Altaia, *Izvestiia Altaĭskogo Gosudarstvennogo Universiteta*, Seriia: Istoriia, Barnaul, 2008, Issue 4/2 (60), p. 212, Plate 5.

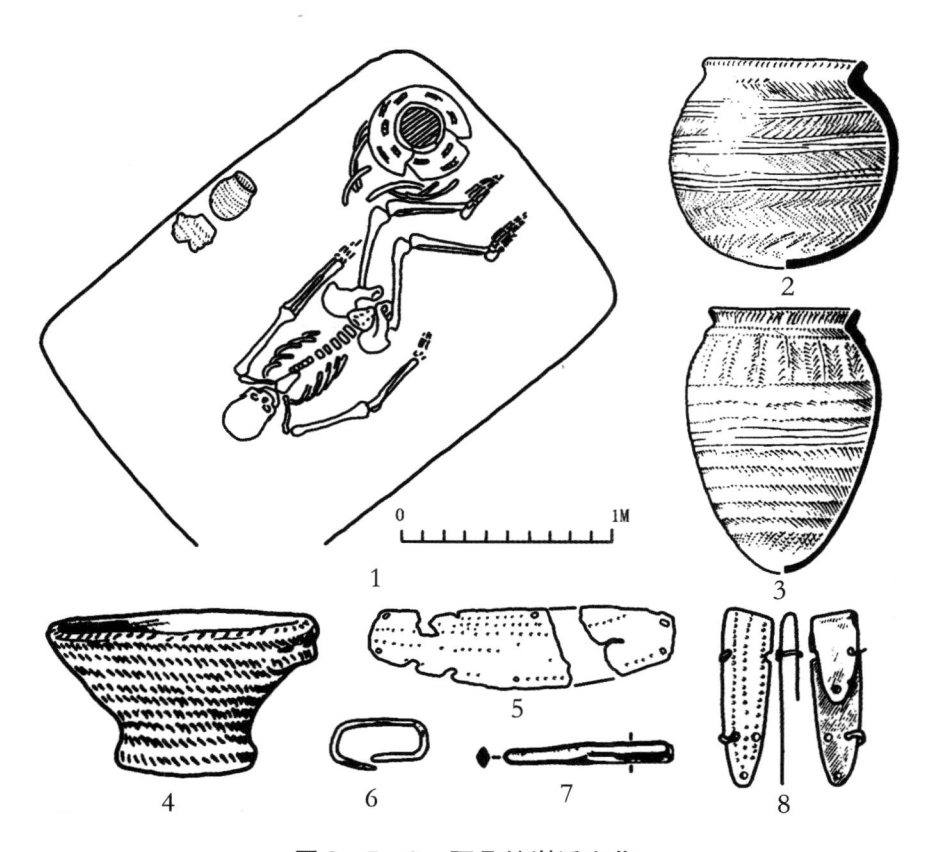

图 3-7-2 阿凡纳谢沃文化

1. M9；2、3. 陶罐；4. 陶豆；5、8. 铜泡；6. 铜卡钉；7. 铜锥

（1—8. Afanas'eva Gora；图片来源：znov, M. P., *Afanas'evskaia Kul'tura na Enise*, St. Peterburg, 1999, Fig. 4：6, Fig. 5：9, Fig. 6：12、13、21、25, Fig. 11：9、10）

世纪60年代初，曾对18件样品做过金相分析，其中塔斯哈札（Tas-Khazaa）墓地出土的一件耳环含有2%的砷和7%的锡，应为锡青铜。[①]

这里必须提到最近发表的弗拉季米洛夫卡（Vladimirovka）采矿遗址。[②] 该遗址位于阿尔泰共和国的卡拉格姆（Karagem）河上。1955年苏联地质学家在特列科特（Terekta）山北麓寻找钴矿时发现了古代的巷

[①] Khavrin, S. V., Drevneĭshiĭ metall Saiano-Altaia, *Izvestiia Altaĭskogo Gosudarstvennogo Universiteta*, Seriia：Istoriia, Barnaul, 2008, Issue 4/2（60）, p. 211, Plate 2.

[②] Bazhenov, A. I., V. B. Borodaev, and A. M. Maloletko, *Vladimirovka na Altae-Drevneĭshiĭ Mednyĭ Rudnik Sibiri*, Tomsk：Tomsk State University, 2002.

◇❖◇ 第三部分　中国西北和欧亚草原考古

道和石锤，后来又做过若干次的调查。因为地处高寒区，这里还发现了牛角（内塞木头）工具、木棒和鹿皮等有机质遗物。根据石锤的形制断定，巷道是阿凡纳谢沃时期的，碳十四测年数据也证实了这个年代。令人意外的是，考古学家一般认为早期使用的铜矿都是氧化矿，但这里只发现了硫化矿（$CuFeS_2$）。

随着发掘资料的积累，有学者将阿凡纳谢沃文化分为两期。早期墓葬只有小石块垒成的石围，墓室用木头覆盖，墓主人头向东北；晚期墓葬使用大石板竖砌成石围，墓室也用大石板覆盖，墓室上有石堆，墓主人头向西南。[1] 后来有学者指出上述特征在早、晚期都存在，因此这种分期不准确。[2] 关于阿凡纳谢沃文化的绝对年代，迄今为止已经测得40个数据。其中6个来自德尼索娃山洞（Denisova Peshchera），年代范围为公元前3340±40—前2240±30。5个来自中阿尔泰，年代为公元前3900—前3170年，但都没有经过校正。[3] 4个来自马里淖维劳格墓地的数据年代集中在公元前3650—前3400年。[4] 7个来自苏昌尼察（Suchanicha）墓地的数据年代集中在公元前3000±90—前2520±30年。[5] 4个来自耶罗—I（Elo-I）墓地的数据为公元前2770±25年、公元前2800±50年、公元前2460±50年和公元前3150±50年。[6] 7个来自古尔干格维墓地的数据年代范围为公元前2870—前2490年。[7] 近几年，从阿凡纳谢沃山和卡拉苏

---

[1] Tsyb, S. V., Ranniaia gruppa Afanas'evskikh pamiatnikov i vopros o proiskhozhdenii Afanas'evskoĭ kul'tury, *Drevniaia Istoriia Altaia*, Barnaul, 1980, pp. 38–51.

[2] Stepanova, N. F., K voprosu ob otnositel'noĭ khronologii pamiatnikov Afanas'evskoĭ kul'tury Gornogo Altaia, in *Problemy Khronologii i Periodizatsii Arkheologicheskikh Pamiatnikov Iuzhnoĭ Sibiri*, Barnaul, 1991, pp. 50–53.

[3] 参考 Larin, O. V., K istorii izucheniia afanas'evskoĭ kul'tury Gornogo Altaia, *Arkheologiia Gornogo Altaia*, Gorno-Altaĭsk, 1988, p. 85.

[4] Bokovenko, N. A., and P. E. Mitjaev, Malinovyj Log, Ein Gräberfeld der Afanas'evo Kultur, *Eurasia Antiqua*, 2000, Band 6, pp. 13–33.

[5] Gorsdorf, J., H. Pazinger, and A. Nagler, ^{14}C Dating of the Siberian Steppe Zone from Bronze Age to Scythian Time, in Scott, E. Marian, Andrey Yu. Alekseev, and Ganna Zaitseva eds., *Impact of the Environment on Human Migration in Eurasia*, Dordrecht, Boston, and London: Kluwer Academic Publishers, 2003, p. 88.

[6] Kiriushin, Iu. F., *Neolit, Ranniaia i Razvitaia Bronza Iuga-Zapadnoĭ Sibiri*, Barnaul, p. 81.

[7] A. A. 科瓦列夫、D. 额尔德尼巴特尔：《蒙古青铜时代文化的新发现》，《边疆考古研究》2009年第8期，第258页，表一。

克—III 墓地采集了 7 个人骨样品，所得的年代范围为公元前 2874—前 2469 年。[①] 如果以前的数据因为木炭样品可能偏早，那么这次就比较准确了。总体而言，这些碳十四数据的年代范围应在公元前 3650—前 2240 年，与上述竖穴墓文化的年代大体接近（表 3-7-1）。将来还需要做工作，以便更为准确地界定阿凡纳谢沃文化的年代范围。

（二）切木尔切克文化

切木尔切克（原名克尔木齐）文化是我国考古学家王博和常喜恩根据位于阿勒泰市的同名乡命名的。[②] 1961 年新疆维吾尔自治区博物馆在当时的阿尔泰专区开展文物普查时，在下属的阿尔泰、哈巴河、布尔津、福海、富蕴和青河县发现了这类墓葬，1963 年新疆维吾尔自治区民族研究所在当时的克尔木齐公社发掘了 32 座墓葬。[③] 其中部分（至少 10 座）墓葬根据出土的铁器和铜镜可定为后期墓葬，部分属于青铜时代墓葬。后来的工作表明，该文化墓葬和可能属于该文化的岩画主要分布于阿勒泰地区的额尔齐斯河和乌伦古河流域。[④] 1998 年以后，A. A. 科瓦列夫组织的国际中亚考古队在哈萨克斯坦共和国东部和蒙古阿尔泰地区发现了更多的同类墓葬。[⑤] A. A. 科瓦列夫把俄罗斯阿尔泰边疆区和阿尔泰共和国出土的石容器和石人也归入了这个文化，[⑥] 因此现在所知的该文化的分布范围为中国、哈萨克斯坦共和国、蒙古、俄罗斯四国（图 3-7-1）。

目前经过发掘的切木尔切克文化遗址只有若干墓地。除了上面提到

[①] Sviatko, S. V., J. P. Mallory, E. M. Murphy, A. V. Poliakov, P. J. Reimer, R. J. Schulting, New radiocarbon dates and a review of the chronology of prehistoric populations from the Minusinsk Basin, Southern Siberia, Russia, *Radiocarbon* 51/1, 2009, pp. 246 – 247.

[②] 王博、常喜恩：《温宿县包孜东墓葬群的调查和发掘》，《新疆文物》1986 年第 2 期。

[③] 新疆社会科学院考古研究所：《新疆克尔木齐古墓发掘简报》，《文物》1981 年第 1 期。

[④] 王博：《切木尔切克文化初探》，《考古文物研究——西北大学考古专业成立四十周年文集 1956—1996》，三秦出版社 1996 年版，第 274 页。

[⑤] A. A. 科瓦列夫、D. 额尔德尼巴特尔：《蒙古青铜时代文化的新发现》，《边疆考古研究》2009 年第 8 期，第 249、258 页。

[⑥] A. A. 科瓦列夫、D. 额尔德尼巴特尔：《蒙古青铜时代文化的新发现》，《边疆考古研究》2009 年第 8 期，第 258 页。

◇❖◇ 第三部分 中国西北和欧亚草原考古

的切木尔切克墓地外，A. A. 科瓦列夫组织的国际中亚考古队在哈萨克斯坦共和国东部的阿尔卡贝克（Alkabek）河流域发掘了12座墓葬，在蒙古科布多省和巴彦乌列盖省发掘了10座墓葬；A. A. 提什金（Tishkin）率领的俄蒙联合考古队在科布多市附近发掘了3座墓葬。这些墓葬一般分为两种。一种为茔院式，用石板或石块砌成长方形围墙，其内包含1—6座墓葬（图3-7-3：1）；另一种为单墓式。无论是茔院式还是单墓式，墓葬中都有石棺，也有土坑，有些还有封堆。石棺没有被封堆覆盖，而是露天的。葬式有侧身屈肢和仰身屈肢，还有乱骨葬。墓葬方向一般呈东西向，也有北南向的。[①]

墓葬旁边常常埋置石人或石柱是切木尔切克文化的一个重要特点。石人面部以凸棱表现面部轮廓、眼圈、眉骨和鼻梁。[②] 其中科布多省的亚格辛霍多（Iagshin Khodoo）3号冢东侧发现的石人是一个男人形象，圆脸，头戴头盔，胸膛敞开，双手分别持"弯钩"和弓（图3-7-3：2）。[③] 因为切木尔切克墓地的部分墓葬出土有铜镜和铁器，所以不少学者长期将这类墓葬的年代定为突厥时期。[④] 但也有学者注意到这类墓葬的陶器和一些葬俗与阿凡纳谢沃文化接近，因此将其年代推到青铜时代和早期铁器时代或青铜时代，也有学者直接将其归入阿凡纳谢沃文化，[⑤] 还有一些学者认为，切木尔切克墓地的材料与阿凡纳谢沃文化很不相同，应当属于

[①] 新疆社会科学院考古研究所：《新疆克尔木齐古墓发掘简报》，《文物》1981年第1期；A. 科瓦列夫、D. 额尔德尼巴特尔：《蒙古青铜时代文化的新发现》，《边疆考古研究》2009年第8期。

[②] 王博：《切木尔切克文化初探》，《考古文物研究——西北大学考古专业成立四十周年文集1956—1996》，三秦出版社1996年版，第276页，图2。

[③] A. A. 科瓦列夫、D. 额尔德尼巴特尔：《蒙古青铜时代文化的新发现》，《边疆考古研究》2009年第8期，第250页，图二：3。

[④] 新疆社会科学院考古研究所：《新疆克尔木齐古墓发掘简报》，《文物》1981年第1期；王博：《切木尔切克文化初探》，《考古文物研究——西北大学考古专业成立四十周年文集1956—1996》，三秦出版社1996年版，第274页。

[⑤] 陈戈：《新疆远古文化初论》，《中亚学刊》1995年第4期，第38页；王炳华：《新疆地区青铜时代考古文化试析》，《新疆社会科学》1985年第2期；王博：《切木尔切克文化初探》，《考古文物研究——西北大学考古专业成立四十周年文集1956—1996》，三秦出版社1996年版；Kuz'mina, E. E., *The Prehistory of the Silk Road*, edited by Vitor H. Mair, Philadelphia: University of Pennsylvania Press, 2008, p. 85.

另一个文化。①

切木尔切克文化墓葬的随葬器物包括陶器、石器（含容器和工具）、骨器和金属器几类，数量不多。其中切木尔切克墓地出土的压印鱼鳞纹的橄榄形圜底罐和圈足豆（俄国文献称香炉）与阿凡纳谢沃的同类器接近（图3-7-3：3—5），②这是切木尔切克文化与阿凡纳谢沃文化有过交往的证据。切木尔切克墓地出土的橄榄形石罐、卵形石罐、半球形素面石罐、兽柄石勺、半球形素面陶罐（图3-7-3：9）是该文化的典型器物。③ 同样属于该文化的特色器物还有巴彦乌列盖省的古拉拉乌拉、古尔干格和古米季格维墓地出土的骨刀和亚格辛霍多墓地出土的铅耳环和铜耳环（图3-7-3：6—8）。④其中亚格辛霍多Ⅰ号墓出土的铜耳环经过检测，为锡青铜。⑤ 根据已有的碳十四测年数据可知，这是欧亚大陆出现的较早的锡青铜。由此来看，切木尔切克文化大体与阿凡纳谢沃文化同时且邻近，文化上有些接触。有学者进一步指出，该文化与阿凡纳谢沃文化不同，起源于法国大西洋沿岸的新石器时代文化。⑥ 蒙古境内出土的头骨经鉴定都属于欧罗巴人种。⑦ 类似于切木尔切克文化的石人只见于法国。⑧ 同时，墓室上没有封堆，有长方形围

---

① 王博：《切木尔切克文化初探》，《考古文物研究——西北大学考古专业成立四十周年文集 1956—1996》，三秦出版社 1996 年版；А. А. 科瓦列夫、D. 额尔德尼巴特尔：《蒙古青铜时代文化的新发现》，《边疆考古研究》2009 年第 8 期。
② 王博：《切木尔切克文化初探》，《考古文物研究——西北大学考古专业成立四十周年文集 1956—1996》，图 4：3、6，三秦出版社 1996 年版；祁小山、王博：《丝绸之路—新疆古代文化》，第 222 页，图 1、4，新疆人民出版社 2008 年版。
③ 王博：《切木尔切克文化初探》，《考古文物研究——西北大学考古专业成立四十周年文集 1956—1996》，图五：3，图六：4、6、8，三秦出版社 1996 年版；А. А. 科瓦列夫、D. 额尔德尼巴特尔：《蒙古青铜时代文化的新发现》，《边疆考古研究》2009 年第 8 期，图 3：9。
④ А. А. 科瓦列夫、D. 额尔德尼巴特尔：《蒙古青铜时代文化的新发现》，《边疆考古研究》2009 年第 8 期，图 2：8，图 3：4—7。
⑤ А. А. 科瓦列夫私人通信，2011 年 2 月 18 日。
⑥ А. А. 科瓦列夫、D. 额尔德尼巴特尔：《蒙古青铜时代文化的新发现》，《边疆考古研究》2009 年第 8 期，第 258—259 页。
⑦ А. А. 科瓦列夫、D. 额尔德尼巴特尔：《蒙古青铜时代文化的新发现》，《边疆考古研究》2009 年第 8 期。
⑧ А. А. 科瓦列夫、D. 额尔德尼巴特尔：《蒙古青铜时代文化的新发现》，《边疆考古研究》2009 年第 8 期。

第三部分 中国西北和欧亚草原考古

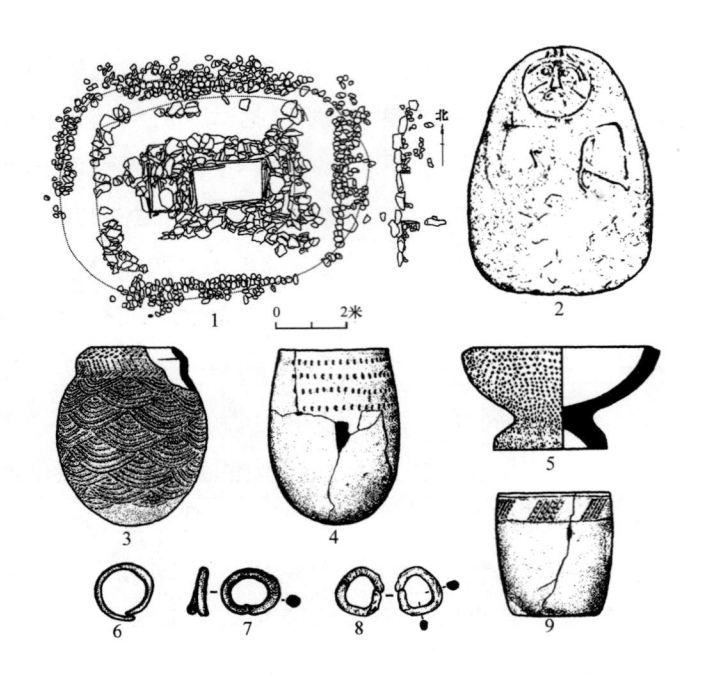

图 3-7-3 切木尔切克文化

1. 墓葬；2. 石人；3、4. 陶罐；5. 陶豆；6—8. 铜耳环；9. 石罐。
1. 哈维音山谷 M1；2、6、8. 亚格辛霍多 III；3—5、7、9. 切木尔切克乡
（图片来源：1、2、6、8，A. A. 科瓦列夫、D. 额尔德尼巴特尔：《蒙古青铜时代文化的新发现》，《边疆考古研究》2009 年第 8 期，图三：1、3、5—7；3—5、7、9，新疆社会科学院考古研究所：《新疆克尔木齐古墓发掘简报》，《文物》1981 年第 1 期，图三：1—3、图五）

墙，石块层和土层交错覆盖的做法也与西欧新石器时代墓葬相似。[1] 哈萨克斯坦共和国东部墓葬的围墙东侧还有大石板构成的通道，也与法国西部的接近。[2] 证据虽然不少，但是切木尔切克文化西来说恐怕还需要更为坚实的证据。从墓葬形制和器物特征来看，将其视为阿凡纳谢沃的姐妹文化更为合适。

切木尔切克与阿凡纳谢沃文化的许多共同特征说明了二者是共存

---

[1] A. A. 科瓦列夫、D. 额尔德尼巴特尔：《蒙古青铜时代文化的新发现》，《边疆考古研究》2009 年第 8 期。

[2] A. A. 科瓦列夫、D. 额尔德尼巴特尔：《蒙古青铜时代文化的新发现》，《边疆考古研究》2009 年第 8 期。

的，现有的碳十四测年数据也证明了这一点。迄今为止，已经从蒙古的切木尔切克墓葬采集了 29 个测年样品（其中人骨 19 个），根据所得碳十四年代数据，A. A. 科瓦列夫将该文化的年代范围定为公元前 2300—前 1700 年，[1] 不过数据本身集中在公元前 2840—前 1680 年（概率为 95.4%）（见表 3-7-1），与阿凡纳谢沃重合较多。

（三）奥库涅沃文化

1947 年，M. N. 科马诺娃（Komarova）根据奥库涅沃（Okuneva Ulusa）发现的一座冢墓命名了奥库涅沃文化，认为其属于安德罗诺沃文化的早期。[2] 但切尔诺瓦娅（Chernovaia）—M 墓地发现之后，G. A. 马克西缅科夫（Maksimenkov）将其视为一个独立的文化，[3] 原先归入阿凡纳谢沃文化的一些遗址如塔斯哈札（Tas-Khazaa）和别伊特勒（Bel'tyry）就被划入该文化中，[4] 以及 1992—1995 年发掘的维巴特（Uĭbat）—II 和维巴特—V 墓地。[5] 此外，在一些墓地发现了包含阿凡纳谢沃冢墓的奥库涅沃墓葬。[6] 在图拉达坪（Toora-Dash）墓地，奥库涅

---

[1] A. A. 科瓦列夫、D. 额尔德尼巴特尔：《蒙古青铜时代文化的新发现》，《边疆考古研究》2009 年第 8 期，第 252—258 页。

[2] Komarova, M. N., Pogrebeniia Okuneva Ulusa, *Sovetskaia Arkheologiia* 9, 1947, pp. 47-60.

[3] Maksimenkov, G A., Okunevskaia kul'tura i ee sosed na Obi, *Istorii Sibiri*, Leningrad, T. 1, 1968, pp. 165-172.

[4] Lipskiĭ, A. N., and È. B. Vadetskaia, Mogil'nik Tas-Khazaa, in D. G. Savinov, M. L. Podol'skiĭ, A. Nagler, and K. V. Chugunov eds., *Okunevskiĭ Sbornik* 2：*Kul'tura i ee Okruzhenie*, Sankt-Peterburg, 2006, pp. 9-52; Lipskiĭ, A. N., and È. B. Vadetskaia, Afanas'evskie i okunevskie pogrebeniia v Mogil'nike Bel'tyry, in D. G. Savinov, M. L. Podol'skiĭ, A. Nagler, and K. V. Chugunov eds., *Okunevskiĭ Sbornik* 2：*Kul'tura i ee Okruzhenie*, Sankt-Peterburg, 2006, pp. 73-81.

[5] Lazaretov, I. P., Okunevskie Mogil'niki v doline reki Uĭbat, in D. G. Savinov and M. L. Podol'skiĭ eds., *Okunevskiĭ Sbornik*：*Kul'tura, Iskusstvo, Antropologiia*, Sankt-Peterburg, 1997, pp. 19-79.

[6] Maksimenkov, G. A., Vpusknye mogily okunevskogo ètappa v Afanas'evskikh kurganakh, *Sovetskaia Arkheologiia* 4, 1965, pp. 206-207; Maksimenkov, G. A., Okunevskaia kul'tura v Iuzhnoĭ Sibiri, *Materialy i Issledovaniia po Arkheologii SSSR*, Issue 130, Moscow, Leningrad, 1965; Leont'ev, S. N., Pamiatnik Okunevskoĭ kul'tury kurgan Chernovaia XI, *Arkheologiia Ètnografiia i Antropologiia Evrazii* 4/8, 2001, pp. 116-123.

◇❖◇ 第三部分　中国西北和欧亚草原考古

沃的地层压在阿凡纳谢沃地层之上，年代上要晚于阿凡纳谢沃文化。[1] 至今该文化遗址已经发现于米奴辛斯克盆地、图瓦和阿尔泰（见图 3 - 7 - 1）。[2] 在米奴辛斯克盆地发现的遗址大多数为墓地，也发现若干聚落遗址，其中包括山头上的堡垒，但没有发现房屋，只发现有陶片。[3]

奥库涅沃文化的埋葬习俗也很特殊，其冢墓容纳多座墓葬，不同于阿凡纳谢沃文化。墓主属于不同性别和年龄，可能为同一家庭。墓室由石板竖砌而成，有时石棺砌在更大的墓坑内，二者之间的空隙用石块填满，成人与儿童一起埋葬。在两座墓内发现一具人骨架和两个头骨，其他墓内则只有人骨架。塔斯哈札和色达（Syda）—V 墓地颇为独特，石围为正方形，部分墓坑中葬有多具人骨，其中有男有女，有老有小，似为家庭墓。[4] 墓主一般头枕石块，墓内放置许多祭奠用品。随葬品很少，

---

[1] Semenov, V. A., Pamiatniki Afanas'evskoĭ kul'tury v Saianakh, *Sovetskaia Arkheologiia* 4, 1982, p. 220.

[2] Levasheva, V. P., Raskopki Mogil'nika Okunevskoĭ kul'tury v Abakane v 1945 g., in A. P. Okladnikov and A. P. Derevianko eds., *Arkheologiia Severnoĭ i Tsentral'noĭ Azii*, Novosibirsk, 1975, pp. 99 - 104; Savinov, D. G., Problemy izucheniia Okunevskoĭ kul'tury (v istoriograficheskoĭ aspekte), in *Okunevskiĭ Sbornik: Kul'tura, Iskusstvo, Antropologiia*, Sankt-Peterburg, 1997, pp. 7 - 18; Lazaretov, I. P., Okunevskie Mogil'niki v doline reki Uĭbat, in D. G. Savinov and M. L. Podol'skiĭ eds., *Okunevskiĭ Sbornik: Kul'tura, Iskusstvo, Antropologiia*, Sankt-Peterburg, 1997, pp. 19 - 79; Kovalev, A. A., Mogil'nik Verniĭ Askiz I, kurgan 2, in *Okunevskiĭ Sbornik: Kul'tura, Iskusstvo, Antropologiia*, Sankt-Peterburg, 1997, pp. 80 - 112; Pshenitsna, M. N., and B. N. Piatkin, Kurgan Razliv X-pamiatnik Okunevskoĭ kul'tury, in *Okunevskiĭ Sbornik 2: Kul'tura i ee Okruzhenie*, Sankt-Peterburg, 2006, pp. 82 - 94; Sher, Ia. A., and S. P. Grushin, Mogil'nik rannego bronzovogo veka Cheremushnyĭ Log I, in *Okunevskiĭ Sbornik 2: Kul'tura i ee Okruzhenie*, Sankt-Peterburg, 2006, pp. 95 - 103; Nagler, A., and G. Partsinger, Novye pamiatniki okunevskoĭ kul'tury v tsentral'noĭ chasti Minusinskoĭ kotloviny, in *Okunevskiĭ Sbornik 2: Kul'tura i ee Okruzhenie*, Sankt-Peterburg, 2006, pp. 104 - 119; Gul'tov, S. B., M. L. Podol'skiĭ, and I. N. Tsygankov, Okunevskiĭ kurgan "94 - ĭ kilometr," in *Okunevskiĭ Sbornik 2: Kul'tura i ee Okruzhenie*, Sankt-Peterburg, 2006, pp. 120 - 124.

[3] Semenov, V. A., Pamiatniki Afanas'evskoĭ kul'tury v Saianakh, *Sovetskaia Arkheologiia* 4, 1982, pp. 219 - 222; Gotlib, A. I., Gornye arkhitekturno-fortifikatsionnye sooruzheniia Okunevskoĭ èpokhi v Kharasii, in *Okunevskiĭ Sbornik: Kul'tura, Iskusstvo, Antropologiia*, Sankt-Peterburg, 1997, pp. 134 - 151.

[4] Lipskiĭ, A. N., and È. B. Vadetskaia, Mogil'nik Tas-Khazaa, in D. G. Savinov, M. L. Podol'skiĭ, A. Nagler, and K. V. Chugunov eds., *Okunevskiĭ Sbornik 2: Kul'tura i ee Okruzhenie*, Sankt-Peterburg, 2006, pp. 9 - 52; Griaznov, M. P., and M. N. Komarova, Syda V-Mogil'nik okunevskoĭ kul'tury, in *Okunevskiĭ Sbornik 2: Kul'tura i ee Okruzhenie*, Sankt-Peterburg, 2006, pp. 53 - 72.

有些墓仅有几件陶罐和金属器，有些墓则空无一物。切尔诺瓦娅—VII墓地的一些头骨上撒有赤铁粉，少数墓随葬野熊、牛、马的头骨，鹿、狼的骨骼以及狍、绵羊的矩骨。① 在米奴辛斯克盆地和阿尔泰，冢墓用石块砌成，石堆外还有一圈石围；而在图瓦，冢墓是用土堆成的。

奥库涅沃文化还有一个引人关注的特点是，墓内常放置刻有人物和动物形象的石雕和岩画（图3-7-4：1），② 无论写实或者抽象，人物雕刻一般描绘头部以及头上的华丽装饰，且均为女性。根据西伯利亚的民族学资料，她们属于女性萨满，反映的是女性萨满崇拜。③ 这些石雕本身出现在墓室的墙内，因此奥库涅沃居民认为是用来砌筑墓室的石块，没有特别的含义。④ 另外，在拉孜里夫（Razliv）墓地发现了一个人物雕像；⑤ 在阿尔泰的奥泽尔诺耶（Ozernoe）和喀拉克尔（Karakol'）发现的岩画在构成墓室的围墙的同时，也形成了横向的壁画。⑥ 这样看来，这些岩画应该是在修筑墓葬前特意雕刻的。

如上所述，有些学者将奥库涅沃文化归入安德罗诺沃文化早期，⑦ 有些

---

① Vadetskaia, È. B., Mogil'nik Chernovaia VIII – ètalonnyĭ pamiatnik Okunevskoĭ kul'tury, in È. B. Vadetskaia, N. V. Leont'ev, and G. A. Maksimenkov eds., *Pamiatniki Okunevskoĭ Kul'tury*, Leningrad, 1980.

② Leont'ev, S. N., V. F. Kapel'ko, and Iu. N. Esin, *Izvaianiia i Stely Okunevskoĭ Kul'tury*, Abakan: Khakass Book Publisher, 2006.

③ Vadetskaia, È. B., Mogil'nik Chernovaia VIII – ètalonnyĭ pamiatnik Okunevskoĭ kul'tury, in È. B. Vadetskaia, N. V. Leont'ev, and G. A. Maksimenkov eds., *Pamiatniki Okunevskoĭ Kul'tury*, Leningrad, 1980, p. 76.

④ Vadetskaia, È. B., Mogil'nik Chernovaia VIII – ètalonnyĭ pamiatnik Okunevskoĭ kul'tury, in È. B. Vadetskaia, N. V. Leont'ev, and G. A. Maksimenkov eds., *Pamiatniki Okunevskoĭ Kul'tury*, Leningrad, 1980, p. 54.

⑤ Pshenitsna, M. N., and B. N. Piatkin, Kurgan Razliv X-pamiatnik Okunevskoĭ kul'tury, in *Okunevskiĭ Sbornik* 2: *Kul'tura i ee Okruzhenie*, Sankt-Peterburg, 2006, pp. 82 – 94.

⑥ Kubarev, V. D., *Pamiatniki Karakol'skoĭ Kul'tury Altaia*, Novosibirsk: Press of Institute of Archaeology and Ethnography SO RAN SO RAN, 2009.

⑦ Komarova, M. N., Pogrebeniia Okuneva Ulusa, *Sovetskaia Arkheologiia* 9, 1947, pp. 47 – 60; Savinov, D. G., Problemy izucheniia okunevskoĭ kul'tury (v istoriograficheskom aspekte), in *Okunevskiĭ Sbornik*: *Kul'tura, Iskusstvo, Antropologiia*, Sankt-Peterburg, 1997, pp. 7 – 18; Semenov, V. A., Okunevskie pamiatniki Tuvy i Minusinskoĭ kotloviny (Sravnitel'naia kharakteristika i khronologiia), in *Okunevskiĭ Sbornik*: *Kul'tura, Iskusstvo, Antropologiia*, Sankt-Peterburg, 1997, pp. 152 – 160.

第三部分 中国西北和欧亚草原考古

学者则归入阿凡纳谢沃文化晚期,[1] 也有学者认为与萨穆西文化同时,[2] 甚至还有学者认为与阿凡那谢沃文化同时,[3] 笔者认为是阿凡纳谢沃与安德罗诺沃的过渡阶段。在该文化的墓葬中,葬式为仰身屈肢,有时撒有赤铁粉。陶罐表面饰有锯齿纹、印纹或几何纹。主要器类有圆锥形平底罐和橄榄形平底罐(图3-7-4:2—4),与阿凡纳谢沃文化的同类器物接近,还有豆。与阿凡纳谢沃不同的是,除纯铜外,该文化还发现了较多的锡青铜(比例达50%)和少量砷铜和铅青铜。[4] 需要指出的是,本地发现的铜渣与铜锭不含锡,米奴辛斯克盆地和克拉斯诺亚尔边疆区南部的锡矿也很少,因此推测上述铜器中的锡可能是外来的。已知出产锡矿的地区为哈萨克斯坦共和国东部的卡尔巴—纳雷姆。[5] 金属器类仍限于短剑、刀、指环、锥和针(图3-7-4:5—8)。铜刀个体小,表面宽平,呈片状。指环由铜丝拧弯而成,有尖头。整体来看,奥库涅沃文化更接近阿凡纳谢沃文化而不是安德罗诺沃文化。

与阿凡纳谢沃文化相同,奥库涅沃的居民也属于欧罗巴人种,但具有森林带蒙古人种的一些特征。[6] 维巴特冢墓的女人骨架兼有欧罗巴人种和

---

[1] Kyzlasov, L. R., Afanas'evskie kurgany na rekakh Uïbat i Biur', *Sovetskaia Arkheologiia* 2, 1962, pp. 112 – 123.

[2] Matiushchenko, V. I., Andronovskaia kul'tura na Verkhniĭ Obi, *Iz Istorii Sibiri*, Issue 11, Tomsk: Press of Tomsk University, 1973; Chlenova, N. A., Est' li skhodstvo mezhdu okunevskoĭ i Karasukskoĭ kul'turami, *Problemy Arkheologii Evrazii i Severnoĭ Ameriki*, Moscow, 1977, pp. 96 – 112.

[3] Tiurina, E. A., and S. P. Grushin, Èpokha èneolita (Afanas'evskiĭ metallokompleks), *Altaĭ v Sisteme Metallurgicheskikh Provintsiĭ Èneolita i Bronzovogo Veka*, Barnaul: Press of Altai State University, 2009, p. 18.

[4] Piatkin, B. N., Nekotorye voprosy metallurgii èpokhi bronzy iuzhnoĭ sibiri, *Arkheologiia Iuzhnoĭ Sibiri*, Issue 9, Kemerovo, 1977, pp. 22 – 33; Khavrin, S. V., Spektral'nyĭ analiz okunevskogo metalla, in *Okunevskiĭ Sbornik: Kul'tura, Iskusstvo, Antropologiia*, Sankt-Peterburg, 1997, pp. 157 – 167; Khavrin, S. V., Metallicheskie izdeliia Okunevskoĭ kul'tury, in *Okunevskiĭ Sbornik 2: Kul'tura i ee Okruzhenie*, Sankt-Peterburg, 2006, pp. 242 – 244; Khavrin, S. V., Drevneĭshiĭ metall Saiano-Altaia, *Izvestiia Altaĭskogo Gosudarstvennogo Universiteta*, Seriia: Istoriia, Barnaul, 2008, Issue 4/2 (60): Plate 4.

[5] Piatkin, B. N., Nekotorye voprosy metallurgii èpokhi bronzy iuzhnoĭ sibiri, *Arkheologiia Iuzhnoĭ Sibiri*, Kemerovo, Issue 9, 1977, pp. 24 – 25, 28.

[6] Alekseev, V. P., O brakhikrannom komponente v sostave naseleniia Afanas'evskoĭ èpokhi, *Sovetskaia Ètnografiia* 1, 1961, pp. 116 – 129; Maksimenkov, G. A., Vpusknye mogily Okunevskogo ètappa v Afanas'evskikh kurganakh, *Sovetskaia Arkheologiia* 4, 1965, pp. 206 – 207; Maksimenkov, G. A., *Andronovskaia Kul'tura na Enisee*, Leningrad, 1978, p. 85.

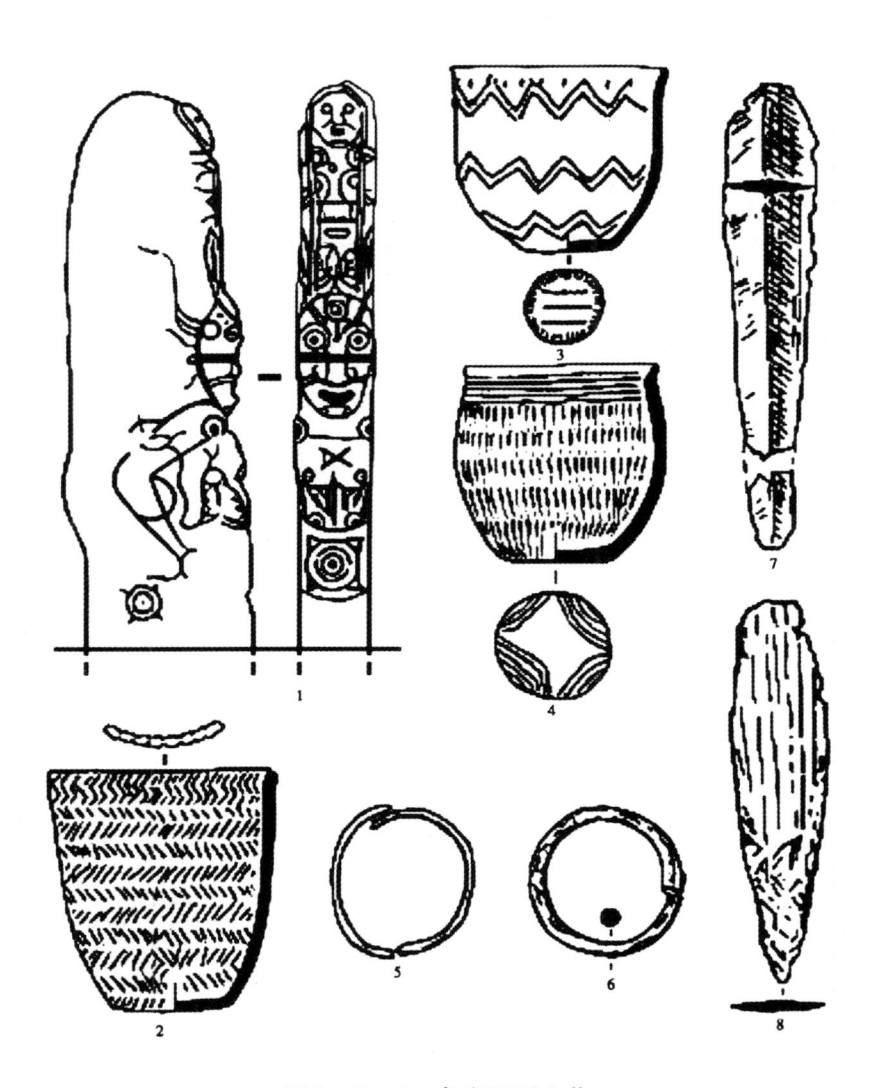

图 3-7-4 奥库涅沃文化

1. 石人；2—4. 陶罐；5、6. 铜指环；7、8. 铜短剑（1—8. Chernovaia-VII；图片来源：Vadetskaia, È. B., Mogil'nik Chernovaia VIII-ètalonnyĭ pamiatnik Okunevskoĭ kul'tury, in È. B. Vadetskaia, N. V. Leont'ev, and G. A. Maksimenkov eds., *Pamiatniki Okunevskoĭ Kul'tury*, Plate XIX：2, 6, 13, Plate XXI：5, Plate XXVII：10, Plate XXIX：4, 6, Plate XLIX：103, Leningrad, 1980）

蒙古人种的特征。因此该文化的居民是欧罗巴人种和蒙古人种混合的产物，而不是纯粹的阿凡纳谢沃居民的后裔。①

关于奥库涅沃文化的消失年代还没有确切的结论。少数学者认为在图瓦和米奴辛斯克盆地南部一直延续到了青铜时代晚期，后被卡拉苏克文化替代；而在米奴辛斯克盆地北部，该文化为安德罗诺沃文化所延续。② 该文化的年代范围，长期以来只有一个碳十四数据为公元前 2335—前 2190年，根据比较研究推定该文化年代为公元前 2000—前 1300 年。最近 10 年里，又获得了两批碳十四测年数据。第一批数据样品来自米奴辛斯克盆地的七个遗址，包括人骨和木炭，年代范围为公元前 2467—前 1693 年。第二批数据有 19 个，样品来自米奴辛斯克盆地的五个遗址（见表 3 -7 -1），均为人骨，年代集中在公元前 2885—前 2565 年，③ 由此得到的年代范围为公元前 2885—前 1693 年（见表 3 -7 -1）。

三 西西伯利亚青铜时代中期

本期最著名的是安德罗诺沃文化，笔者认为其对应于东欧的辛塔什塔文化。另外，耶鲁尼诺和克罗托沃文化也可以归入本期，因为其金属器与辛塔什塔、安德罗诺沃文化同类器物接近（表 3 -7 -1）。

（一）安德罗诺沃文化

安德罗诺沃文化是 20 世纪 20 年代由 S. A. 捷普劳霍夫（Teploukhov）命名的。从那时起该文化一直是苏联考古学界的热门话题，其遗址也广泛发现于西至乌拉尔河，东至叶尼塞河，北至森林带南缘，南至中亚的辽阔

---

① Maksimenkov, G A., Okunevskaia kul'tura i ee sosed na Obi, *Istorii Sibiri*, Leningrad, 1968, T. 1, p. 166; Lazaretov, I. P., Okunevskie Mogil'niki v doline reki Uĭbat, in D. G. Savinov and M. L. Podol'skiĭ eds., *Okunevskiĭ Sbornik: Kul'tura, Iskusstvo, Antropologiia*, Sankt-Peterburg, 1997, p. 40.

② Sviatko, S. V., J. P. Mallory, E. M. Murphy, A. V. Poliakov, P. J. Reimer, and R. J. Schulting: New radiocarbon dates and a review of the chronology of prehistoric populations from the Minusinsk Basin, Southern Siberia, Russia, *Radiocarbon* 51/1, 2009, p. 248.

③ Sviatko, S. V., J. P. Mallory, E. M. Murphy, A. V. Poliakov, P. J. Reimer, R. and J. Schulting, New radiocarbon dates and a review of the chronology of prehistoric populations from the Minusinsk Basin, Southern Siberia, Russia, *Radiocarbon* 51/1, 2009, p. 248.

土地上（图3-7-5）。① 另外，该文化遗址在新疆也有发现。② 该文化聚落遗址发现不多，经过大规模发掘的更少；相反墓地有大量发现，区域特征和共同特征都非常显著。墓葬中冢墓和地面（意为无封土，下同）墓都有，且以后者居多。一般两种墓葬都有石围，墓室内有木棺或石棺。大多数墓葬为土葬，但在一些墓地火葬也比较多。③ 土葬墓中人骨左侧身，屈肢，与辛塔什塔的埋葬习俗相同。安德罗诺沃的墓主头向大多为西南（图3-7-6：1），而辛塔什塔的头向大多为东北，与后者相同的是墓室大小和葬具依墓主的年龄而定，儿童墓总体上少于成人墓。④ 大多数墓葬只埋一人，但合葬墓也不少，一般是成人和儿童的合葬。然而，在巴拉巴平原儿童（0—15岁）墓数量超过成人墓，说明当时儿童的死亡率相当高。⑤ 有些儿童埋在单独的墓地内，⑥ 与辛塔什塔文化相同。大多数墓葬随葬陶器，只有少数墓还随葬金属器。此外，许多墓地还发现无人骨但有随葬品的墓葬（衣冠冢）。⑦

---

① Kiselev, S. V., *Drevniia Istoriia Iuzhnoĭ Sibiri*, Moscow: Science, 1951; Sal'nikov, K. V., *Ocherki Drevneĭ Istorii Iuzhnogo Urala*, Moscow, 1967; Maksimenkov, G. A., *Andronovskaia Kul'tura na Enisee*, Leningrad, 1978; Potëmkina, T. M., Alakul'skaia kul'tura, *Sovetskaia Arkheologiia* 2, 1983, pp. 13 – 33; Potëmkina, T. M., *Bronzovyĭ Vek Lesostepnogo Pritobol'ia*, Moscow: Science, 1985; Molodin, V. I., *Baraba v Èpokhu Bronzy*, Novosibirsk: Science, 1985; Matiushchenko, V. I., Andronovskaia kul'tura na Verkhniĭ Obi, *Iz Istorii Sibiri*, Issue 11, Tomsk: Press of Tomsk University, 1973; Kiriushin, Iu. F., *Neolit, Bronzovyĭ Vek Iuzhno-Taëzhnoĭ Zony Zapadnoĭ Sibiri*, Barnaul, 2004; Kuz'mina, E. E., *The Prehistory of the Silk Road*, Philadelphia: University Pennsylvania Press, 2008.

② Peng, K., The Andronovo bronze artifacts discovered in Gongliu county in Yili, Xinjiang, in V. H. Mair ed., *The Bronze Age of Early Iron Age Peoples of Eastern Central Asia*, Washington, DC: Institute for the Study of Man, Vol. 2, 1998, pp. 573 – 580; Mei, J., *Copper and Bronze Metallurgy in Late Prehistoric Xinjiang*, Oxford: Archaeopress, 2000; Kuz'mina, E. E., Historical Perspectives on the Andronovo and Early Metal Use in Eastern Asia, in Katheryn Linduff ed., *Metallurgy in Ancient Eastern Eurasia from the Urals to the Yellow River*, Lewiston, Queenston, and Lampeter: The Edwin Mellen Press, 2004, pp. 37 – 84；韩建业：《新疆的青铜时代和早期铁器时代文化》，文物出版社2007年版；郭物：《新疆史前晚期社会的考古学研究》，上海古籍出版社2012年版。

③ Matiushchenko, V. I., Andronovskaia kul'tura na Verkhniĭ Obi, *Iz Istorii Sibiri*, Tomsk: Press of Tomsk University, Issue 11, 1973, pp. 29 – 30.

④ Matiushchenko, V. I., Andronovskaia kul'tura na Verkhniĭ Obi, *Iz Istorii Sibiri*, Tomsk: Press of Tomsk University, Issue 11, 1973, p. 31.

⑤ Molodin, V. I., *Baraba v Èpokhu Bronzy*, Novosibirsk: Science, 1985, pp. 109 – 111.

⑥ Matiushchenko, V. I., Andronovskaia kul'tura na Verkhniĭ Obi, *Iz Istorii Sibiri*, Tomsk: Press of Tomsk UniversityIssue 11, 1973, p. 32.

⑦ Molodin, V. I., *Baraba v Èpokhu Bronzy*, Novosibirsk: Science, 1985, pp. 111 – 112.

◇❖◇ 第三部分 中国西北和欧亚草原考古

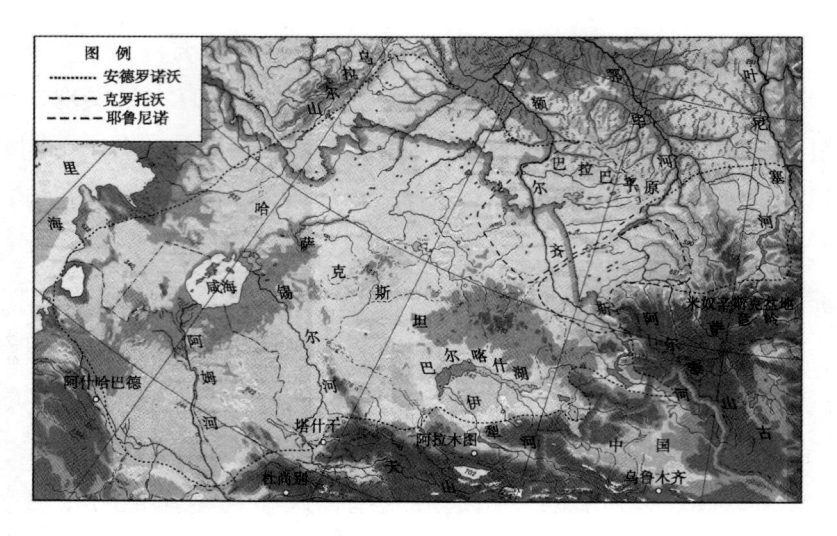

图 3-7-5 西西伯利亚青铜时代中期文化分布图

K. V. 萨尔尼科夫（Sal'nikov）根据东乌拉尔（俄文一般称外乌拉尔）的材料，认为安德罗诺沃文化可以分为三期，即费德罗沃（Fedorovo）、阿拉库伊（Alakul'）和萨马拉叶甫（Samaraev）。① M. F. 科马诺娃（Komarova）支持这个分期，② 但也有学者持不同观点。E. A. 费德诺娃—达维多娃（Fedorova-Davydova）提出，费德罗沃和阿拉库伊不是一个文化的两个阶段，而是两个并行的文化，③ 大多数考古学家接受此观点，不过在二者的相对年代问题上仍存在分歧。④ 基于二者存在共同特征，E. A. 费德诺娃—达维多娃命名了一个更高级别的涵盖二者的安德罗诺沃文化历史共同体（Andronovo cultural-historical community）。⑤ M. F. 科马诺娃认为，费德罗沃与阿拉库伊的差别在于陶器器形和纹饰上，⑥ 阿拉库伊文化的鼓腹平

---

① Sal'nikov K. V., *Drevneĭshee Naselenie Cheliabinskoĭ Oblasti*, Cheliabinsk, 1948; Sal'nikov, K. V., Bronzovyĭ vek Iuzhnogo Zaural'ia, *Materialy i Issledovaniia po Arkheologii SSSR* 21, 1951, pp. 94–151.

② Komarova, M. N., *Otnositel'naia khronologiia pamiatnikov Andronovskoĭ kul'tury*, *Arkheologicheskiĭ Sbornik* 5, 1962, pp. 50–75.

③ Fedorova-Davydova, E. A., Andronovskoe pogrebenie XV–XIII vv. do n. è., *Trudy Gosudarstvennyĭ Istoricheskiĭ Muzeĭ* 37, Moscow, 1960, pp. 56–59.

④ Stokols, V. S., 1972, *Kul'tura Naseleniia Bronzovogo Veka Iuzhnogo Zaural'ia*, Moscow.

⑤ Fedorova-Davydova, E. A., Andronovskoe pogrebenie XV–XIII vv. do n. è., *Trudy Gosudarstvennyĭ Istoricheskiĭ Muzeĭ* 37, Moscow, 1960, pp. 56–59.

⑥ Komarova, M. N., *Otnositel'naia khronologiia pamiatnikov Andronovskoĭ kul'tury*, *Arkheologicheskiĭ Sbornik* 5, 1962, pp. 50–75.

底罐为折肩，而费德罗沃文化的同类器为圆肩，这样的差别只是一个文化的地方差别而已，二者在埋葬习俗和器物风格上都是一致的。

安德罗诺沃文化的陶器类似于辛塔什塔的陶器，陶胎含砂，也有含滑石的，大多数为灰色。器类有鼓腹平底罐、直腹平底罐和碗。鼓腹平底罐是主要器类，制作精美，外表磨光，并装饰三角纹、折线纹、回纹和松针纹（图3-7-6：2、4）。直腹平底形罐（图3-7-6：3）和碗制作粗糙，装饰草率。[1] 所有器类和纹饰都与阿巴舍沃和辛塔什塔的接近，这表明在东欧和西西伯利亚存在着共同的器物风格。

俄罗斯（包括苏联时代）考古学家经常将阿拉库伊、辛塔什塔和木椁墓文化作比较，视为共时，[2] 只因为精美陶器与辛塔什塔的接近，而粗糙陶器与木椁墓文化接近。但这种分析方法忽略了一个文化是一个整体，它们位于乌拉尔山脉两侧，虽然在地域上相邻，但是三者在年代上是有差异的，分别属于青铜时代中期和晚期。阿拉库伊以及整个安德罗诺沃文化在文化面貌上与辛塔什塔接近，但安德罗诺沃文化的陶器特征多样化，不仅表现在拥有精美和粗糙的陶器，而且器类还丰富，显然是欧亚大陆青铜时代制陶技术的巅峰时代。相反，木椁墓文化的陶器在形态和纹饰上都显得单调呆板，表明其制陶技术已经走向衰落。

在金属器方面，安德罗诺沃文化也与辛塔什塔文化相似，反映出二者共同的生活方式。安德罗诺沃的金属器种类较多，包括武器（直銎斧、横銎斧、矛、短剑）、工具（刀、凿、锥）和装饰品（耳环、指环、串珠、垂饰、手镯、泡）。这些器类的风格与辛塔什塔大多不同，但也存在相同之处，限于篇幅，仅举几例。柳叶形短剑（图3-7-6：5）、矛（图3-7-6：9）、有格起脊短剑（图3-7-6：6）和两端带螺旋头的手镯是安德罗诺沃文化特有的器物，而横銎斧（图3-7-6：8）和三角形短剑

---

[1] Matiushchenko, V. I., Andronovskaia kul'tura na Verkhnii Obi, *Iz Istorii Sibiri*, Tomsk: Press of Tomsk University, Issue 11, 1973, Figs. 11–17.

[2] 如 Zdanovich, G. B., *Bronzovyi Vek Uralo-Kazakhstanskikh Stepei*, Sverdlovsk: Ural State University Press, 1988; Vinogradov, N. B., Pamiatniki petrovskogo tipa v iuzhnom zaural'e i severnom kazakhstane: kul'turnaia atributsiia i vnutrenniaia periodizatsiia, *Arkheologiia Urala i Zapadnoi Sibiri: K 80-letiiu so dnia rozhdeniia Vladimira Fedorovicha Geninga*, Ekaterinburg: Ural State University Press, 1995, pp. 129–133.

（图3-7-6：7），大多数指环、耳环和螺旋管都可以在辛塔什塔文化中找到同类器（图3-7-6：10—15），正因为如此，E. N. 切尔内赫把三个文化都归入欧亚大陆冶金省。[1] 另外，装饰品中不少是外包金箔的青铜和金质器物，装饰有珍珠纹或松针纹。[2]

人们已经从南乌拉尔、[3] 北哈萨克斯坦共和国、东哈萨克斯坦共和国、中哈萨克斯坦共和国、中亚、西西伯利亚和南西伯利亚提取了400个检测样品（包括铜器、矿石、炉壁、铜块），考察安德罗诺沃的冶金技术特征，[4] 发现其与辛塔什塔文化不同的是，即使是靠近外乌拉尔的托博尔河中游，金属器中锡青铜和纯铜占据主流，锡含量平均为5—6%，高者为10—15%。[5] 砷铜和锑青铜要少得多，占10%。砷、锑和铅与铜共生，不过古代工匠可能有意识地选择多金属铜矿来冶炼，因此这些金属含量较高的铜器也应该是青铜。[6] 不过，上述区域的青铜器在成分上带有浓重的本地特征，表明各个区域拥有自己的矿源。举例来说，托博尔河中游的安德罗诺沃部落利用哈萨克斯坦共和国北部的乌什—卡塔（Ush-Katta）以及乌拉尔河流域的铜矿，[7] 与此同时，它们在冶炼和铸造技术上相当一致，表明安德罗诺沃人在大规模迁徙时把技术带到了各个区域。在中哈萨克斯坦共和国的一

---

[1] Chernykh, E. N., *Ancient Metallurgy in the USSR: The Early Metal Age*, translated by Sarah Wright, Cambridge, New York, Melbourne: Cambridge University Press, 1992, pp. 191–215.

[2] Pozdniakova, O. A., and S. V. Khavrin, Srednĭĭ period bronzovogo veka (Andronovksĭĭ metallokompleks), in S. P. Grushin ed., *Altaĭ v Sisteme Metallurgicheskikh Provintsĭĭ Èneolita i Bronzovogo Veka*, Barnaul: Press of Altai State University, 2009, pp. 57–74.

[3] 含辛塔什塔文化金属器。——作者注

[4] Avanesova, N. A., *Kul'tura Pastusheskikh Plemen Èpokhi Bronzy Aziatskoĭ Chasti SSSR*, Tashkent: Press of "FAN" UzSSR, 1991, pp. 76–83.

[5] Kuz'minykh, S. V., and E. N. Chernykh, Spektroanaliticheskoe issledovanie metalla bronzovogo veka lesostepnogo pritobol'ia (predvaritel'nye resul'taty), in T. M. Potëmkina, *Bronzovyĭ Vek Lesostepnogo Pritobol'ia*, Moscow: Science, 1985, pp. 346–367; Piatkin, B. N., Nekotorye voprosy metallurgii èpokhi bronzy iuzhnoĭ sibiri, *Arkheologiia Iuzhnoĭ Sibiri*, Kemerovo, Issue 9, 1977, p. 29; Chernykh, E. N., *Ancient Metallurgy in the USSR: The Early Metal Age*, translated by Sarah Wright, Cambridge, New York, Melbourne: Cambridge University Press, 1992, p. 213.

[6] Avanesova, N. A., *Kul'tura Pastusheskikh Plemen Èpokhi Bronzy Aziatskoĭ Chasti SSSR*, Tashkent: Press of "FAN" UzSSR, 1991, pp. 73–74.

[7] Kuz'minykh, S. V., and E. N. Chernykh, Spektroanaliticheskoe issledovanie metalla bronzovogo veka lesostepnogo pritobol'ia (predvaritel'nye resul'taty), in T. M. Potëmkina, *Bronzovyĭ Vek Lesostepnogo Pritobol'ia*, Moscow: Science, 1985, pp. 365–366.

些遗址（如 Atasu）发现了熔炉、矿石和炉渣，说明安德罗诺沃的金属冶炼包含三个步骤，即焙烧矿石、炼粗铜和炼精铜。一些接近矿源的村落显然是从事冶金生产和金属贸易的。①

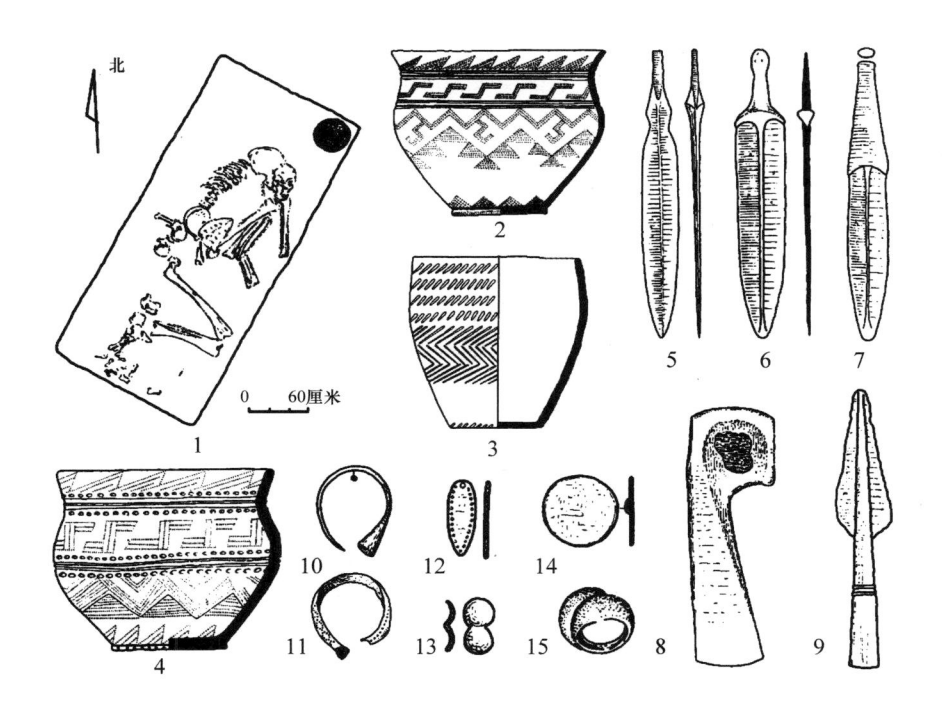

图 3-7-6 安德罗诺沃文化

1. 墓葬；2—4. 陶罐；5—7. 铜短剑；8. 铜横銎斧；9. 铜矛；10、15. 铜耳环；11. 铜镯；12、13. 铜泡；14. 铜镜

（1、4、15. Preobrazhenka II，图片来源：Molodin, V. I., *Baraba v Èpokhu Bronzy*, Novosibirsk：Science, 1985, Fig. 56, Fig. 44, Fig. 54；2. Abramovo-IV，图片来源：Molodin, V. I., *Baraba v Èpokhu Bronzy*, Novosibirsk: Science, 1985, Fig. 44: 7；3、8、10 - 14. Elovka II，图片来源：Matiushchenko, V. I., Andronovskaia kul'tura na Verkhniĭ Obi, *Iz Istorii Sibiri*, Tomsk: Press of Tomsk University, Issue 11, 1973, Fig. 45: 5, Fig. 43: 20、9、10、17、14、11；5. Lake Kungur，图片来源：Potëmkina, T. M., *Bronzovyĭ Vek Lesostepnogo Pritobol'ia*, Moscow: Science, 1985, Fig. 51: 3；6. River Varvarka，图片来源：Potëmkina, T. M., *Bronzovyĭ Vek Lesostepnogo Pritobol'ia*, Moscow: Science, 1985, Fig. 51: 4；7. Lake Shartash，图片来源：Potëmkina, T. M., *Bronzovyĭ Vek Lesostepnogo Pritobol'ia*, Moscow: Science, 1985, Fig. 51: 5；9. Tiumenskaia Oblast'，图片来源：Potëmkina, T. M., *Bronzovyĭ Vek Lesostepnogo Pritobol'ia*, Moscow: Science, 1985, Fig. 51: 6）

---

① Avanesova, N. A., *Kul'tura Pastusheskikh Plemen Èpokhi Bronzy Aziatskoĭ Chasti SSSR*, Tashkent: Press of "FAN" UzSSR, 1991, pp. 80 - 82.

◇❖◇ 第三部分　中国西北和欧亚草原考古

有关安德罗诺沃文化的起源，俄罗斯考古学家已经提出了不少假说，有学者说是阿凡纳谢沃，① 也有学者说是本地的铜石并用文化。② 在此笔者不讨论其源头，但要指出该文化精美的陶器和发达的冶金业在乌拉尔山两侧的欧亚大陆草原带和森林草原带传播得非常迅速。有关米奴辛斯克盆地和鄂毕河上游的人骨材料的研究表明，它们属于欧罗巴人种，不过具有蒙古人种的特征，③ 安德罗诺沃文化的居民，根据 C. F. 捷别茨（Debets）的研究，并非是来自本地的阿凡纳谢沃居民的后裔，而是来自西方的，④ 当然，这个证据并没有指认安德罗诺沃居民的家乡。众所周知，欧罗巴人种仍占据着西西伯利亚，并且与叶尼塞河以东的蒙古人种居民有着密切的交往。

迄今为止，获得的安德罗诺沃文化的碳十四测年数据不多。从叶尼塞河流域的遗址得到的九个数据中，四个偏早或偏晚，其余五个年代范围为公元前2100—前1300年。⑤ 在米奴辛斯克盆地遗址获得的五个数据的年代范围为公元前 1715±65—前 1420±40 年，⑥ 在阿尔泰北部遗址获得的四个数据中，来自捷列乌兹季乌兹沃兹（Teleutski Vzvoz）的为公元前 1500±50 年，两个来自图里那山（Turina Gora）的为公元前 1750±25 年和公元前 1620±20 年，一个来自图赫锡加特—IV（Tukh-Sigat-IV）的为公元前 1350±90 年。⑦ 最新获得的九个人骨测年数据校正后均在公元前

---

① Kiselev, S. V., *Drevniia Istoriia Iuzhnoĭ Sibiri*, Moscow: Science, 1951.

② Komarova, M. N., Otnositel'naia khronologiia pamiatnikov Andronovskoĭ kul'tury, *Arkheologicheskiĭ Sbornik* 5, 1962, pp. 50 – 75.

③ Matiushchenko, V. I., Elovsko-irmenskaia kul'tura, *Iz Istorii Sibiri*, Tomsk: Press of Tomsk University, Issue 12, 1974, p. 48.

④ 转引自 Formozov, A. A., K voprosu o proiskhozhdenii Andronovskoĭ kul'tury, *Kratkie Soobshcheniia Instituta Istorii Material'noĭ Kul'tury*, Issue 39, 1951, p. 5。

⑤ Maksimenkov, G. A., *Andronovskaia Kul'tura na Enisee*, Leningrad, 1978, p. 108.

⑥ Gorsdorf, J., H. Pazinger, and A. Nagler, 14C Dating of the Siberian Steppe Zone from Bronze Age to Scythian Time, in Scott, E. Marian, Andrey Yu. Alekseev, and Ganna Zaitseva eds., *Impact of the Environment on Human Migration in Eurasia*, Dordrecht, Boston, and London: Kluwer Academic Publishers, 2003, p. 88.

⑦ Kiriushin, Iu. F., *Neolit, Bronzovyĭ Vek Iuzhno-Taëzhnoĭ Zony Zapadnoĭ Sibiri*, Barnaul, 2004, p. 82.

1744—前1500年之间。① 这样，安德罗诺沃文化的年代范围大致为公元前1750—前1400年（表3-7-1），相对于辛塔什塔文化偏晚，当然，今后还需要更多的数据来给出一个更为精确的年代范围。

（二）耶鲁尼诺文化

耶鲁尼诺文化是Iu. F. 基留申（Kiriushin）根据位于鄂毕河上游的同名墓地命名的。② 该文化的遗址分布于从阿雷（Alei）河上游到楚梅什（Chumysh）河中游的阿尔泰山麓（见图3-7-5），已经发掘了若干墓地和聚落。值得一提的是，在桦树湾（Berezovkaia Luka）聚落发现了生产青铜的遗存，包括纯铜、青铜器、铅饰、矿石、炉渣和铜粒。埋葬习俗也别具特色，墓室为土坑，上面堆土，有的周围有壕沟，内填祭祀活动留下的兽骨。无论是单人葬还是合葬，墓主均左侧身屈肢，头一般向东，也有向北的，向南的很少。大多数人骨撒有赤铁粉。随葬品是陶器和大小家畜（包括马），其他种类的器物较少。

耶鲁尼诺文化的陶器与辛塔什塔文化的陶器相近，器类包括直腹平底罐、鼓腹平底罐以及碗，均为平底。但与辛塔什塔陶器不同的是，表面以及底部都布满纹饰，大部分为横向戳印的直线或曲线、附加堆纹、窝纹和乳丁纹。几何形图案如三角纹和菱格纹较少（图3-7-7：2—4）。金属器较少，包括1件双刃刀、2件单刃刀和1件带有雕塑的刀（图3-7-7：5—7）。③ 其中双刃刀弯曲，柄部装饰斜线三角纹。这种刀类似于塞依玛—图尔宾诺现象的青铜器，发现于图尔宾诺—1、塞依玛和罗斯托夫卡墓地。④ 其中38件经过检测，23件为锡青铜，其余为纯铜、纯铅和锡铅合金。其中部分样品为矿石，除了铜以外，还含有锡和铅等金属，说明这里的铜

---

① Sviatko, S. V., J. P. Mallory, E. M. Murphy, A. V. Poliakov, P. J. Reimer, R. and J. Schulting, New radiocarbon dates and a review of the chronology of prehistoric populations from the Minusinsk Basin, Southern Siberia, Russia, *Radiocarbon* 51/1, 2009, p. 251.

② Kiriushin, Iu. F., Itogi i perspektivy izucheniia pamiatnikov èneolita i bronzy Altaia, *Problemy Drevnikh Kul'tur Sibiri*, Novosibirsk, 1985, pp. 48–53.

③ 归入该文化的其他器物有矛、镞、锥、直銎斧和范。它们都是征集品，不一定属于该文化。

④ Kiriushin, Iu. F., *Neolit, Bronzovyĭ Vek Iuzhno-Taëzhnoĭ Zony Zapadnoĭ Sibiri*, Barnaul, 2004.

器是用阿尔泰本地生产的多金属共生矿制造的，不过锡还是从哈萨克斯坦共和国东部的卡尔巴和纳雷姆山脉进口的。① 此外，该文化遗址还出土石质雕塑（图3-7-7：1）。

耶鲁尼诺文化的居民构成很有趣，男人属于欧罗巴人种的地中海类型，而女人则有蒙古人种的特征。② 当然，当时的人种构成是否确实如此还需要更多的检测资料支持。Iu. F. 基留申认为，本地新石器和铜石并用时代的居民都属于蒙古人种，因此推测耶鲁尼诺时期中亚和地中海的东部居民曾经向东迁徙到阿尔泰。③ 他还认为耶鲁尼诺居民曾与克罗托沃和萨穆西居民有过交往，④ 并推测一支欧罗巴人种（主要是男性）来到鄂毕河—额尔齐斯河上游（即阿尔泰地区）与本地居民融合，形成了耶鲁尼诺文化。⑤

Iu. F. 基留申认为耶鲁尼诺文化早于安德罗诺沃文化，⑥ 但没有任何地层依据。在讨论该文化的相对年代时，他引用了一些自相矛盾的证据。一方面，他认为戳印纹和篦纹属于铜石并用时代，而附加堆纹属于安德罗诺沃时期；另一方面，他又把金属器与塞依玛—图尔宾诺现象联系起来。现有的碳十四数据（经过校正）支持耶鲁尼诺与安德罗诺沃文化同时的观点。至今从桦树湾聚落、捷列乌兹季乌兹沃兹—I（Teleutskii Vzvoz-I）和其他遗址已经获得了41个碳十四年代数据（经校正），年代范围为公

---

① Grushin, S. P., Ranniĭ period bronzovogo veka (Eluninskiĭ metallokompleks), in S. P. Grushin ed., *Altaĭ v Sisteme Metallurgicheskikh Provintsiĭ Èneolita i Bronzovogo Veka*, Barnaul: Press of Altai State University, 2009, pp. 46-48.

② Kiriushin, Iu. F., *Neolit, Bronzovyĭ Vek Iuzhno-Taëzhnoĭ Zony Zapadnoĭ Sibiri*, Barnaul, 2004, p. 73.

③ Kiriushin, Iu. F., *Neolit, Bronzovyĭ Vek Iuzhno-Taëzhnoĭ Zony Zapadnoĭ Sibiri*, Barnaul, 2004, p. 84.

④ Kiriushin, Iu. F., *Neolit, Bronzovyĭ Vek Iuzhno-Taëzhnoĭ Zony Zapadnoĭ Sibiri*, Barnaul, 2004, p. 85; Kiriushin, Iu. F., and S. P. Grushin, K voprosu o sootnoshenii Eluninskoĭ i Krotovskoĭ arkheologicheskikh kul'tur, *Istoriko-kul'turnoe Nasledie Severnoĭ Azii*, Barnaul: Press of Altai State University, 2001, p. 34.

⑤ Grushin, S. P., Kul'tura zhizneobespecheniia i proizvodstva naseleniia stepnogo i lesostepnogo Ob'-Irtysh'ia vo vtoroĭ polovine III-pervoĭ chetverti II tys. do n. è., Summary of doctoral dissertation of historical Science, Barnaul: Altai State University, 2013, p. 23.

⑥ Kiriushin, Iu. F., *Neolit, Bronzovyĭ Vek Iuzhno-Taëzhnoĭ Zony Zapadnoĭ Sibiri*, Barnaul, 2004, pp. 76-82.

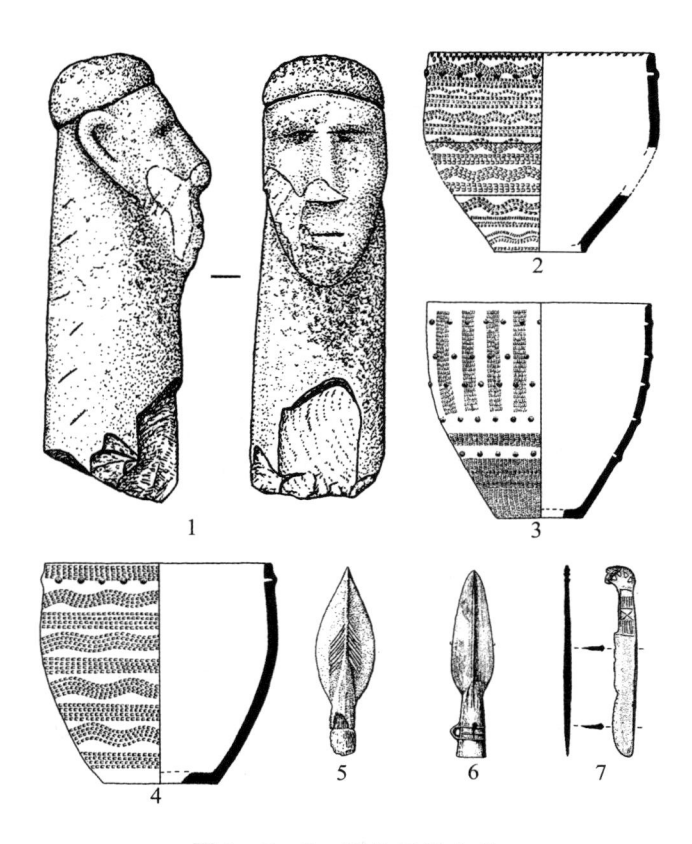

图 3-7-7 耶鲁尼诺文化

1. 石人；2—4. 陶罐；5、6. 铜矛；7. 铜刀

[1. Sakkushka；2、3、4. Kostenkova-Izbushka；5. Teleutskiǐ-Vzvoz-I；6. Charysh（征集）；7. Elunino；图片来源：Kiriushin, Iu. F., *Neolit, Bronzovyǐ Vek Iuzhno-Taëzhnoǐ Zony Zapadnoǐ Sibiri*, Barnaul, 2004, Fig. 72：2, 4, Fig. 76：3, Fig. 121：12, Fig. 131：1, Fig. 148, Fig. 151：1]

元前25—前18世纪或高于前2500—前1700年（见表3-7-1），[①] 与辛塔什塔文化的年代大体重合。

（三）克罗托沃文化

克罗托沃文化是V. I. 莫罗金（Moldin）命名的，遗址分布于鄂毕河

---

① Grushin, S. P., Kul'tura zhizneobespecheniia i proizvodstva naseleniia stepnogo i lesostepnogo Ob'-Irtysh'ia vo vtoroǐ polovine III-pervoǐ chetverti II tys. do n. è., Summary of doctoral dissertation of historical Science, Barnaul：Altai State University, 2013, p. 20.

和额尔齐斯河之间，尤其在巴拉巴平原。他认为克罗托沃文化早于安德罗诺沃文化，但与奥库涅沃没有多少共同点，并与安德罗诺沃文化也没有延续性。[①] 他率领的考古队在普列奥布拉任卡（Preoblazhenka）—II 和文格罗沃（Vengerovo）—II 发现了五座半地穴式单间和两间房屋，[②] 在巴拉巴平原的索普卡（Sopka）—II 和阿布拉莫沃（Abramovo）—XI 墓地以及鄂毕河上的奥丁斯科耶（Ordynskoe）—I 墓地发现了大量的墓葬（见图3-7-5）。前者发掘面积大，共清理 200 座墓，[③] 但发掘报告尚未出版，只有一些笼统的介绍见于其文章。大多数墓葬的头向为东北，多为单人葬，少数为二人或三人葬，葬式大多为仰身直肢，人骨架上撒有赤铁粉。[④]

克罗托沃文化的陶器独具特色，一是多孔易碎，内外壁都用木片或草或木棒磨光。这种技法阿凡纳谢沃和奥库涅沃文化的居民也使用过。器物大多数为大型直腹平底罐，小型直腹平底罐和鼓腹平底罐很少。器物通体装饰，纹饰大多为戳印点构成的平行线、折线和波纹。另一种技法为贴泥条，形成直线或曲线（图3-7-8：1、2、6）。特色器物还包括形体修长的石质和骨质镞、石质月牙形刀，以及有穿孔垂饰、鸟头骨雕和蛇形针。

冶金生产遗存已经发现于索普卡—II、普列奥布拉任卡—II 和文格罗沃—I1，包括范芯、坩埚、勺和铸造棒、直銎斧和矛的泥范。[⑤] 此外，索普卡—II 墓地出土了一大批铜器（图3-7-8：3—5，7—10），包括23件短剑；有长方形柄、三角形头和橄榄形刃（图3-7-8：9）。一件短剑还有带球形头的金属柄（图3-7-8：10）。另一类是弯曲的单刃刀（图3-7-8：4）。第三类是直銎斧，没有耳朵（图3-7-8：8）。第四类为手镯，由金属条弯曲而成，内侧有半圆形槽。大多数镯有两个螺旋头，跟安德罗诺沃的接近（图3-7-8：5）。指环有的铸造而成，有的表面包金叶，有的由金属条弯曲而成。还有金属条制成的细长的镯（图3-7-

---

① Molodin, V. I., *Èpokha Neolita i Bronzy Lesostepnogo Ob-Irtysh'ia*, Novosibirsk, 1977.
② Molodin, V. I., *Èpokha Neolita i Bronzy Lesostepnogo Ob-Irtysh'ia*, Novosibirsk, 1977, p. 49; b. Molodin, V. I., *Baraba v Èpokhu Bronzy*, Novosibirsk: Science, 1985, pp. 35-36.
③ Molodin, V. I., *Baraba v Èpokhu Bronzy*, Novosibirsk: Science, 1985, pp. 75-82.
④ Molodin, V. I., *Baraba v Èpokhu Bronzy*, Novosibirsk: Science, 1985, pp. 80-81.
⑤ Molodin, V. I., *Baraba v Èpokhu Bronzy*, Novosibirsk: Science, 1985, pp. 58-60.

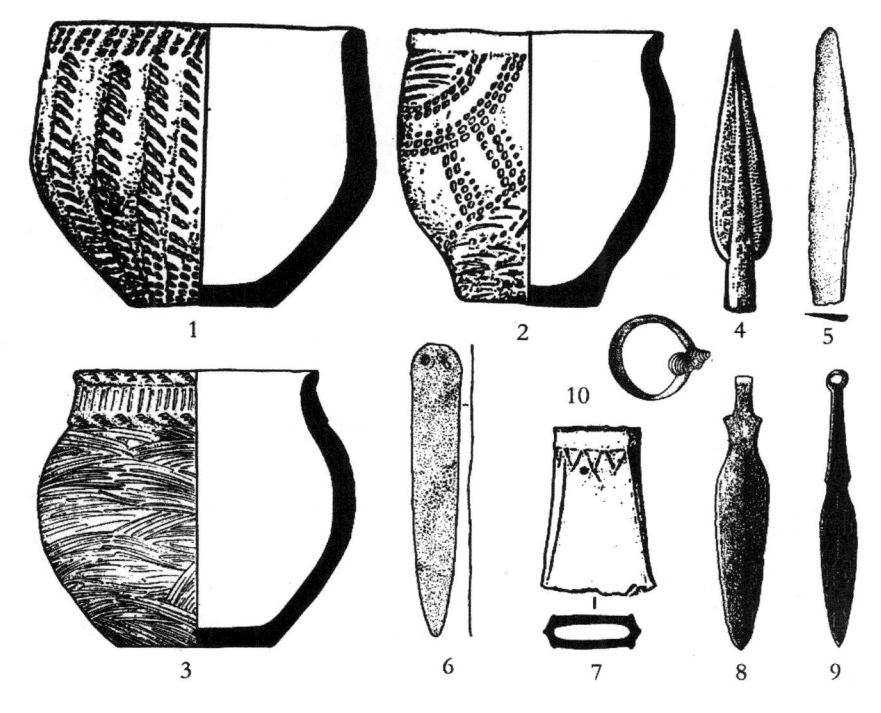

图 3-7-8　克罗托沃文化

1—3. 陶罐；4. 铜矛；5、6. 铜刀；7. 铜竖銎斧；8、9. 铜短剑；10. 铜镯

（1—10. Sopka-II；图片来源：Molodin, V. I., *Baraba v Èpokhu Bronzy*, Novosibirsk：Science, 1985, Fig. 15：1, 5, 6, Fig. 28, Fig. 29：1, 2, Fig. 30：10, 12, Fig. 31：3, Fig. 34：3）

8：5）。还发现一些铸造的带钮的铜扣和锤打的铜扣。大多数器物可以在安德罗诺沃文化找到类似器。

　　关于克罗托沃文化的相对年代，已经发现一些地层依据。一座墓葬被一座安德罗诺沃墓和一座伊尔敏（晚期）墓打破。在普列奥布拉任卡—II，克罗托沃地层被一座安德罗诺沃墓打破。因此发掘者认为其早于安德罗诺沃，[①] 而与奥库涅沃和萨穆西同时。[②] 这些文化的埋葬习俗（竖穴墓、仰身、二人葬、赤铁粉）以及随葬品（金属器类、陶器上的泥条和连环

[①] Molodin, V. I., *Baraba v Èpokhu Bronzy*, Novosibirsk：Science, 1985, pp. 82, 86.

[②] Molodin, V. I., O sootnoshenii Krotovskoĭ i Okunevskoĭ kul'tur, *Nekotorye Problemy Sibirskoĭ Arkheologii*, Moscow：Science, 1988, pp. 6–15; Molodin, V. I., *Èpokha Neolita i Bronzy Lesostepnogo Ob-Irtysh'ia*, Novosibirsk, 1977, p. 76.

纹）确实存在相似之处，但说它们是同时期的还欠妥，要解决这个问题，应当考虑陶器和金属器的风格。上面的比较研究说明克罗托沃与安德罗诺沃同时。此前 E. E. 库兹米娜（Kuz'mina）也指出，安德罗诺沃与克罗托沃的陶器共同出土于索普卡—II 墓地。① 到目前为止尚无有关该文化的碳十四数据。V. I. 莫洛金参照安德罗诺沃和塞依玛—图尔宾诺的年代，把克罗托沃的年代定为公元前 14—前 12 世纪或公元前 1400—前 1100 年（见表 3 - 7 - 1）。② 笔者认为这个年代太晚，还需要依靠碳十四测年来确定。

四　西西伯利亚青铜时代晚期

这是西西伯利亚青铜时代的最后一期，不过一些学者认为后面还有一个向铁器时代过渡的时期。一般将卡拉苏克（Karasuk）和伊尔敏（Irmen'）文化归入本期（见表 3 - 7 - 1）。根据陶器和金属器特征，本文将萨穆西（Samus'）文化也归入本期。

（一）卡拉苏克文化

卡拉苏克文化是 S. A. 捷普劳霍夫根据他首次发现该文化墓葬的同名河流命名的。许多遗址发现于米努辛斯克盆地，③ 零星的铜器和陶器发现于西西伯利亚、东西伯利亚、图瓦、蒙古甚至我国的鄂尔多斯（图 3 - 7 - 9）。因此一些学者如 M. P. 格廖兹诺夫（Griaznov）和 A. I. 马特诺夫（Martynov）将这些地域都归入该文化的范围，④ 但是也有学者如

---

① Kuz'mina, E. E., Historical Perspectives on the Andronovo and Early Metal Use in Eastern Asia, in Katheryn Linduff ed., *Metallurgy in Ancient Eastern Eurasia from the Urals to the Yellow River*, Lewiston, Queenston, and Lampeter: The Edwin Mellen Press, 2004, p. 57.

② Molodin, V. I., *Èpokha Neolita i Bronzy Lesostepnogo Ob-Irtysh'ia*, Novosibirsk, 1977, pp. 87 – 88.

③ Kiselev, S. V., *Drevniia Istoriia Iuzhnoĭ Sibiri*, Moscow: Science, 1951, p. 151.

④ Griaznov, M. P., Istoriia drevnikh plemen Verkhneĭ Obi, *Materialy i Issledovaniia po Arkheologii SSSR*, Issue 48, Moscow, Leningrad: Science, 1956; Martynov, A. I., Karasukskaia èpokha v Ob-Chulymskom mezhdurech'e, *Drevniaia Sibir'*, Novosibirsk, Issue 2, 1966, pp. 164 – 182; Griaznov, M. P., B. N. Piatkin, and G. A. Maksimenkov, Karasukskaia kul'tura, *Istoriia Sibiri*, Leningrad, T. 1, 1968, pp. 180 – 187.

N. A. 齐连诺娃（Chlenova）反对这种做法。①

至 1996 年，卡拉苏克文化已经发现 10 个聚落。②在卡缅卡（Kamenka）—V、特普塞（Tepsei）—XII 和卢加夫斯卡娅（Lugavskaia）—II，发现了一些小型半地穴式建筑。在乌斯琴基诺（Ustinkino）—II、卡缅勒劳格（Kamennyi Log）—I、通楚赫（Tunchukh）和斯多林罗佐克（Sidorin Lozhok），发现了 3—6 座大型半地穴式房屋。其中卡缅勒劳格—I 有 6 座冬季房屋，为地穴式，面积 100—200 平方米，其内出土的陶范表明每座房屋的居民都从事金属器生产。这些聚落只有零星的发掘资料见于报道，③只有托尔加扎克（Torgazhak）聚落经过了大面积的发掘，资料大部分已经发表。1988—1991 年，在托尔加扎克发掘 1300 平方米，揭露 7 座大型房屋，1—5 号为 II 形，开口向东。如 1 号面积为 262 平方米，四边形，房顶由若干柱子支撑，出土了 1 个石人、1 件陶勺，房屋用途不明。卡拉苏克房屋只有 4 个或 6 个等距的柱洞，其陶器大多为球形或炮弹形，部分发现于墓地，但实用器大多不见于墓地。这个聚落另一类独具特色的器物是很多刻有人物、动物形象和几何纹的石子，其中的一些图案见于奥库涅沃陶器，这些石子很独特。④

尽管绝大多数资料来源于墓地，但是墓地中经过大面积发掘且资料大批发表的没有几座，⑤而且大多数墓地在古代就已经被盗。与阿凡纳谢沃和安德罗诺沃文化不同的是，卡拉苏克的墓地埋有大量的墓葬，其数量常常超过 100。经过发掘的墓葬，在干湖（Sukhoe Ozero）—II 有 550 座，在小

---

① Chlenova, N. A., *Pamiatniki Kontsa Èpokhi Bronzy v Zapadnoĭ Sibiri*, Moscow, 1994.
② Savinov, D. G., *Drevnie Poseleniia Khakasii Torgazhak*, Sankt-Peterburg, 1996.
③ Vadetskaia, È. B., *Arkheologicheskie Pamiatniki v Stepiakh Srednego Eniseia*, Leningrad: Science Press, 1986, p. 59.
④ Vadetskaia, È. B., *Arkheologicheskie Pamiatniki v Stepiakh Srednego Eniseia*, Leningrad: Science Press, 1986, pp. 22, 16, 28, 44.
⑤ Ziablin, L. P., *Karasukskoĭ Mogil'nik Malye Kopëny 3*, Moscow, 1977; Vadetskaia, È. B., *Arkheologicheskie Pamiatniki v Stepiakh Srednego Eniseia*, Leningrad: Science Press, 1986, p. 53; Griaznov, M. P., M. N. Komarova, I. P. Lazaretov, A. V. Poliakov, and M. N. Pshenitsyna, *Mogil'nik Kiurgenner Èpokhi Pozdneĭ Bronzy Srednego Eniseia*, Sankt-Peterburg, 2010.

◇❖◇ 第三部分　中国西北和欧亚草原考古

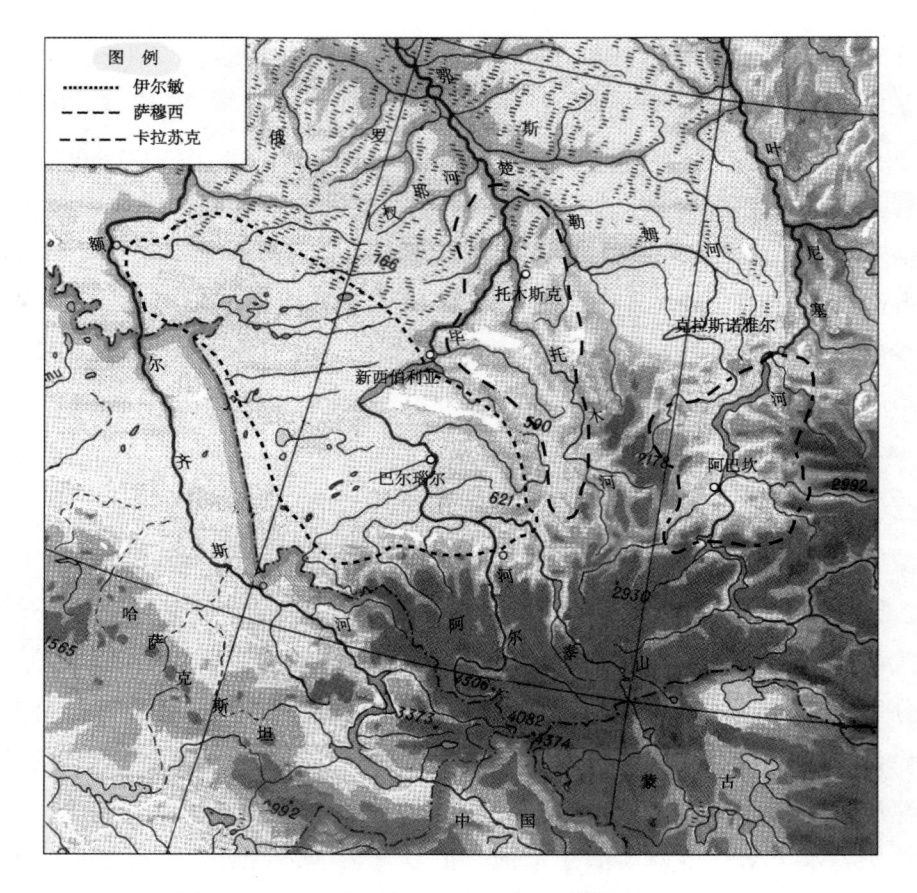

图 3-7-9　西西伯利亚青铜时代晚期文化分布图

卡票那（Malye Kopëny）—II 有 287 座，在丘尔格那（Kiurgenner）—I 有 184 座。① 如果加上未发掘和已经遭到破坏的墓葬，这些墓地的规模相当大。墓葬的周围往往有长方形或圆形的石板砌成的围栏，高约 0.5—0.9 米，圈数有时为 2 个或 3 个。一座茔院内一般有一座墓葬，同时一座中心茔院周围又附着 1 座或 2 座茔院。墓葬上面覆盖的封土不厚，其上再覆盖石块。② 在丘尔格那—I 墓地的部分石围的西南侧，也就是墓主的足端，发

---

① Pshenitsna, M. N., and B. N. Piatkin, Predislovie, in M. P. Griaznov, M. N. Komarova, I. P. Lazaretov, A. V. Poliakov, and M. N. Pshenitsyna eds., *Mogil'nik Kiurgenner Èpokhi Pozdneĭ Bronzy Srednego Eniseia*, Sankt-Peterburg, 2010, p. 7.
② Poliakov, A. V., Obshchaia kharakteristika materialov Mogil'nikov Kiurgenner I i II, in M. P. Griaznov, M. N. Komarova, I. P. Lazaretov, A. V. Poliakov, and M. N. Pshenitsyna eds., *Mogil'nik Kiurgenner Èpokhi Pozdneĭ Bronzy Srednego Eniseia*, Sankt-Peterburg, 2010, pp. 43–59.

现有竖立的石板，似乎为墓葬的标识。① 墓室用石板砌成，用石板覆盖。该文化的墓葬大多数为单人葬，可能为夫妻的男女合葬墓少见，但有幼儿、儿童和成年人（包括男女）的墓葬。② 墓主大多侧身向左，头向大多向东或东北。值得注意的是，卡拉苏克文化墓葬常随葬可能用于盛放酸奶的陶器和原先盛放于木盘（现已消失）里的几块肉。③

与早些的文化相比，卡拉苏克呈现出许多共同和独特的地方。陶器方面不同于安德罗诺沃的同类器，多为球形罐，高领、圜底，平底陶罐也存在，其中有些有束颈和双耳。也有些橄榄形罐，与青铜时代早期的阿凡纳谢沃陶器接近，似乎为复古现象。陶器表面压平磨光，大多拍印或戳印纹饰，使用较广的是斜线三角纹、松针纹、菱格纹、回纹和弦纹，与安德罗诺沃文化的陶器纹饰相似，但是一般只出现在器物的颈部和肩部，而且经过简化（图 3 - 7 - 10：1—4），因此在形态和纹饰上继承了阿凡纳谢沃和安德罗诺沃的一些因素，但与安德罗诺沃的陶器大不相同。奥库涅沃文化的人物和动物雕刻也见于卡拉苏克的陶器和石头。总体来说，卡拉苏克的情形很像木椁墓文化，展现了一个简化和衰落的趋势。在铜器中，大多数工具和武器（直刃刀、弯刃刀、短剑、矛、直銎斧、锥）以及装饰品（手镯、指环、耳环、垂饰、串珠、管、泡）与安德罗诺沃的器类接近（图 3 - 7 - 10：5—13），但刃接在柄上的折柄刀是卡拉苏克的发明（图 3 - 7 - 10：7）。④ 根据金相分析，卡拉苏克文化的铜刀均为铸造，其中大多经过冷煅，少数经过热锻。⑤ 在卡拉苏克的金属器中，锡青铜、砷锡青铜和砷铜都存

---

① Griaznov, M. P., M. N. Komarova, and M. N. Pshenitsyna, Materialy Mogil'nik Kiurgenner I i II, in *Mogil'nik Kiurgenner Èpokhi Pozdneĭ Bronzy Srednego Eniseia*, Sankt-Peterburg, 2010, pp. 9 – 42.

② Poliakov, A. V., Obshchaia kharakteristika materialov Mogil'nikov Kiurgenner I i II, in M. P. Griaznov, M. N. Komarova, I. P. Lazaretov, A. V. Poliakov, and M. N. Pshenitsyna eds., *Mogil'nik Kiurgenner Èpokhi Pozdneĭ Bronzy Srednego Eniseia*, Sankt-Peterburg, 2010, pp. 48 – 49.

③ Poliakov, A. V., Obshchaia kharakteristika materialov Mogil'nikov Kiurgenner I i II, in M. P. Griaznov, M. N. Komarova, I. P. Lazaretov, A. V. Poliakov, and M. N. Pshenitsyna eds., *Mogil'nik Kiurgenner Èpokhi Pozdneĭ Bronzy Srednego Eniseia*, Sankt-Peterburg, 2010, p. 52.

④ Chlenova, N. A., *Pamiatniki Kontsa Èpokhi Bronzy v Zapadnoĭ Sibiri*, Moscow, 1994, p. 271; Novgorodova, È. A., *Tsentral'naia Aziia i Karasukskaia Problema*, Moscow, 1970.

⑤ Naumov, D. V., Proizvodstvo i obrabotka Karasukskikh nozheĭ, in N. L. Chlenova, *Khronologiia Pamiatnikov Karasukskoĭ Èpokhi*, Moscow: Science Press, 1972, p. 140.

在，而且大多数墓地出土的金属器中砷铜占主流。① 然而，最近报道的丘尔格那—Ⅰ、Ⅱ墓地出土的金属器（墓地被盗，残留的金属器绝大多数为耳环、串珠等装饰品）半数为砷铜和纯铜，半数为锡青铜，有的含锡量高达25%。② 除了铜器以外，卡拉苏克文化的居民还使用金质装饰品，包括半月形垂饰、指环和耳环。③ 卡拉苏克金属器的铸范除了石范或陶范，还常使用金属范，较石范和泥范而言，金属范铸造的器物更加致密而且强度更高。④ 在图瓦还保留有不少古代采矿和冶炼遗址，遗憾至今尚未发掘。这里发现的一块可以同时铸造四件器物（两把刀、一把短剑和一把斧）的石范表明，卡拉苏克人曾经从事金属生产。⑤

关于卡拉苏克文化的起源，俄罗斯考古学家付出了不少努力。C. F. 捷别茨通过研究所有头骨和人骨架，发现一支可能属于蒙古人种的新人群进入米奴辛斯克盆地，并与当地的阿凡纳谢沃人的后裔结婚。⑥ 如果说安德罗诺沃人种是长脸型，那么卡拉苏克人是圆脸型，他认为这种新因素来自帕

---

① Naumov, D. V., Proizvodstvo i obrabotka Karasukskikh nozheĭ, in N. L. Chlenova, *Khronologiia Pamiatnikov Karasukskoĭ Èpokhi*, Moscow: Science Press, 1972, p. 141; Piatkin, B. N., Nekotorye voprosy metallurgii èpokhi bronzy iuzhnoĭ sibiri, *Arkheologiia Iuzhnoĭ Sibiri*, Kemerovo, Issue 9, 1977, pp. 29 – 30; Sunchugashev, Ia. I. , *Drevneĭshie Rudniki i Pamiatniki Ranneĭ Metallurgii v Khakassko-Minusinskoĭ Kotlovine*, Moscow, 1975; Sergeeva, N. F., *Drevneĭshaia Metallurgiia Medi Iuga-Vostochnoĭ Sibiri*, Novosibirsk: Science, 1981; Avanesova, N. A. 1, *Kul'tura Pastusheskikh Plemen Èpokhi Bronzy Aziatskoĭ Chasti SSSR*, Tashkent: Press of "FAN" UzSSR, 199; Bobrov, V. V., S. V. Kuz'minykh, and T. O. Teneishvili, *Drevniaia Metallurgiia Srednego Eniseia*, Kemerovo, 1997; Khavrin, S. V., Metall èpokhi pozdneĭ bronzy nizhneteĭskoĭ gruppy pamiatnikov (Torgazhak-Arban-Fedorov ulus), in S. N. Astakhov ed. , *Evraziia Skvoz Veka*, Sankt-Peterburg, 2001, pp. 117 – 125.

② Khavrin, S. V., Metall Mogil'nika Kiurgenner, in M. P. Griaznov, M. N. Komarova, I. P. Lazaretov, A. V. Poliakov, and M. N. Pshenitsyna eds. , *Mogil'nik Kiurgenner Èpokhi Pozdneĭ Bronzy Srednego Eniseia*, Sankt-Peterburg, pp. 102 – 106.

③ Chlenova, N. A., Zoloto v karasukskuiu èpokhu, *Sovetskaia Arkheologiia* 4, 1972, pp. 247 – 259.

④ Naumov, D. V., Proizvodstvo i obrabotka Karasukskikh nozheĭ, in N. L. Chlenova, *Khronologiia Pamiatnikov Karasukskoĭ Èpokhi*, Moscow: Science Press, 1972, p. 140.

⑤ Kyzlasov, L. R., 1993, K istorii karasukskoĭ metallurgii, *Rossiĭskaia Arkheologiia* 3, 1993, pp. 43 – 49.

⑥ Debets, G. F., Rasovye tipy Minusinskogo kraia v èpokhu rodovogo stroia, *Antropologicheskiĭ Zhurnal* 2, 1932, pp. 26 – 48; Debets, G. F., *Paleoantropologiia SSSR*, Trudy institute ètnografi, novyi serial, T. Ⅳ, Moscow and Leningrad, 1948, p. 82.

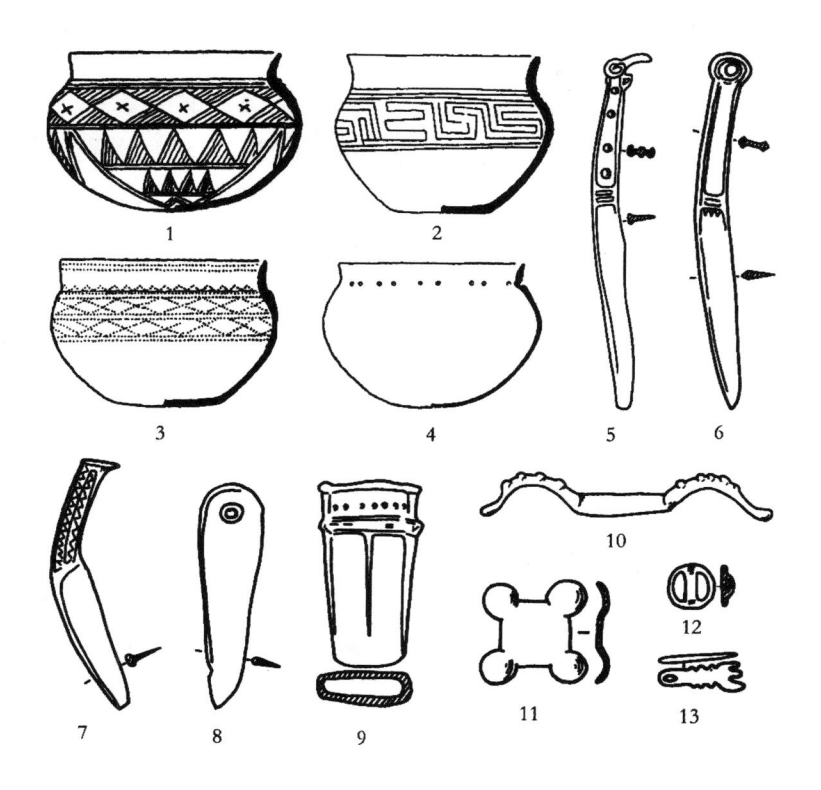

图 3-7-10　卡拉苏克文化

1—4. 陶罐；5—7. 铜刀；8. 铜镰刀；9. 铜竖銎斧；10. 铜弓形器；11. 铜泡；12. 铜扣；13. 铜坠饰

（1、2、3、4, Malye Kopëny 3, 图片来源：Ziablin, L. P., *Karasukskoĭ Mogil'nik Malye Kopëny 3*, Moscow, 1977, Fig 4：18, Fig 8：5, 7, 13；5、6、8. Abakan；7. Kugunck；9. Ladeynoe Pole；10. Askyz；11. Verkhny Askyz；12、13. Sartak. 图片来源：Chernykh, E. N., *Ancient Metallurgy in the USSR*: *The Early Metal Age*, translated by Sarah Wright, Cambridge, New York, Melbourne: Cambridge University Press, 1992, Fig 91：1, 4, 5, 6, 7, 9, 11, 15, 25, 26)

米尔—费尔干纳，后来的研究证实了这种欧罗巴和蒙古人种特征共存的观点。[①] 关于文化起源学者们已经提出了不少假说，S. V. 吉谢列夫认为是中国北部，[②] N. L. 齐连诺娃则将卡拉苏克铜器追溯到伊朗的鲁里斯坦

[①] Rykushina, G. V., Naselenie Srednego Eniseia v Karasukskuiu èpokhu, *Paleoantropologiia Sibiri*, Novosibirsk, 1980, pp. 47–63.

[②] Kiselev, S. V., *Drevniia Istoriia Iuzhnoĭ Sibiri*, Moscow: Science, 1951, p. 182.

(Lufigtan),① 但是 È. A. 诺夫格罗多娃（Novgorodova）表示怀疑，指出鲁里斯坦的铜器并不比卡拉苏克早多少。② È. A. 瓦捷茨卡娅（Vadetskaia）提出本地起源说，她引用的是卡拉苏克与安德罗诺沃和奥库涅沃之间的联系。在她看来，卡拉苏克人主要是安德罗诺沃和奥库涅沃的后裔，不过也见证了哈萨克斯坦共和国人的渗透。③ 卡拉苏克文化的埋葬习俗和陶器上的几何形图案显然来源于安德罗诺沃文化。④ 这些假说再次让我们想起了把文化因素等同于民族的文化历史方法。不过，在解释新因素时，除了人群迁徙，还应该考虑文化传播。

卡拉苏克文化的另一个重要问题是年代。其中的一个方面是该文化本身的分期，这在俄罗斯考古学家中间还没有形成共识。È. A. 诺夫格罗多娃认出了两类陶器，即卢加夫（Lugav）和卡拉苏克；⑤ M. D. 赫洛别思齐娜（Khlobystina）看到了青铜刀由折柄型演变为直柄型的过程，⑥ 同 N. L. 齐连诺娃（Chlenova）一并提出卢加夫类型要早于卡拉苏克。后来 M. P. 格廖兹诺夫用卡门诺娄格（Kamennolog）取代了卢加夫，并认为是卡拉苏克的晚期阶段，因为在墓葬形制和陶器上与塔加尔（Tagar）接近。⑦ 他的分期为大多数学者所接受，但是也有问题，因为折柄刀和直柄刀都见于奥库涅沃文化。另外，卡门诺娄格的典型特征（新葬俗、陶器和其他器物）很少一起出现而是单个出现在一个墓地中。⑧ 因此，È. A. 诺夫格罗多娃和 N. L. 齐连诺娃抛弃了两个阶段的分期法，提出了卡拉苏克有两个

---

① Chlenova, N. A., *Pamiatniki Kontsa Èpokhi Bronzy v Zapadnoĭ Sibiri*, Moscow, 1994, p. 275.
② Novgorodova, È. A., *Tsentral'naia Aziia i Karasukskaia Problema*, Moscow, 1970, pp. 24 – 25.
③ Vadetskaia, È. B., *Arkheologicheskie Pamiatniki v Stepiakh Srednego Eniseia*, Leningrad: Science Press, 1986, pp. 61 – 62.
④ Griaznov, M. P., M. N. Komarova, and M. N. Pshenitsyna, Materialy Mogil'nik Kiurgenner I i II, in M. P. Griaznov, M. N. Komarova, I. P. Lazaretov, A. V. Poliakov, and M. N. Pshenitsyna eds., *Mogil'nik Kiurgenner Èpokhi Pozdneĭ Bronzy Srednego Eniseia*, Sankt-Peterburg, 2010, p. 14.
⑤ Novgorodova, È. A., *Tsentral'naia Aziia i Karasukskaia Problema*, Moscow, 1970.
⑥ Khlobystina, M. D., *Bronzovye Nozhi Minusinskogo Kraia i Nekotorye Voprosy Razvitiia Karasukskoĭ Kul'tury*, Leningrad, 1962.
⑦ 转引自 Vadetskaia, È. B., *Arkheologicheskie Pamiatniki v Stepiakh Srednego Eniseia*, Leningrad: Science Press, 1986, p. 52.
⑧ Vadetskaia, È. B., *Arkheologicheskie Pamiatniki v Stepiakh Srednego Eniseia*, Leningrad: Science Press, 1986, p. 53.

并行的地方类型,分别在米奴辛斯克盆地和萨彦—阿尔泰地区独立发展起来。① 不过,M. P. 格廖兹诺夫的两期说在近几年重新得到推崇和发展,但是这些新研究仰仗的是中央与边缘墓葬之间的差异,仍然缺乏可靠的地层依据。② 从器物形态上看,卢加夫类型的陶器大多为球形或橄榄形圜底罐,腹部素面,仅口沿有简单的纹饰,体现了一个新的时代风格,似乎与塔加尔文化接近,但还是卡拉苏克陶器的发展形态,年代应该晚于卡拉苏克文化。金属器继承了卡拉苏克文化的许多器类,但是卡拉苏克的折柄刀、弓形刀和兽纹刀在卢加夫类型中很少见,只有环形柄仍流行。③

关于卡拉苏克文化的相对年代,注意到墓地中没有发现打破安德罗诺沃文化的墓葬,因此有学者认为它们是同时的。④ 不过 E. A. 瓦捷茨卡娅(Vadetskaia)注意到了两个现象,认为卡拉苏克要晚于安德罗诺沃。一是许多安德罗诺沃因素出现在卡拉苏克文化中,而安德罗诺沃文化不见卡拉苏克文化因素;二是卡拉苏克冢墓离安德罗诺沃冢墓很近,看起来好像是重新利用了安德罗诺沃墓地。⑤ 在特普塞山曾做了一个小区域调查,发现阿凡纳谢沃、安德罗诺沃和卡拉苏克文化的墓地紧挨着,但互相并不打破。⑥ 至于卡拉苏克与早期铁器时代的塔加尔文化的关系,N. L. 齐列诺娃列举了六个卡拉苏克早于塔加尔的地层关系,但也注意到卡拉苏克器物

---

① Novgorodova, È. A., *Tsentral'naia Aziia i Karasukskaia Problema*, Moscow, 1970, p. 176; Chlenova, N. A., Zoloto v karasukskuiu èpokhu, *Sovetskaia Arkheologiia* 4, 1972, pp. 247 – 259.

② Griaznov, M. P., Raboty Krasnoiarskoĭ èkspeditsii, *Kratkie Soobshchenii Instituta Arkheologii*, Moscow, Issue 100, 1965, pp. 62 – 71; Poliakov, A. V., Otnositel'naia khronologiia pogrebeniĭ Mogil'nika, in M. P. Griaznov, M. N. Komarova, I. P. Lazaretov, A. V. Poliakov, and M. N. Pshenitsyna eds., *Mogil'nik Kiurgenner Èpokhi Pozdneĭ Bronzy Srednego Eniseia*, Sankt-Peterburg, 2010, pp. 60 – 69.

③ Chlenova, N. A., *Khronologiia Pamiatnikov Karasukskoĭ Èpokhi*, Moscow: Science Press, 1972, pp. 194 – 207.

④ Vadetskaia, È. B., *Arkheologicheskie Pamiatniki v Stepiakh Srednego Eniseia*, Leningrad: Science Press, 1986, p. 61.

⑤ Vadetskaia, È. B., *Arkheologicheskie Pamiatniki v Stepiakh Srednego Eniseia*, Leningrad: Science Press, 1986, pp. 61 – 62.

⑥ Griaznov, M. P., and M. N. Komarova, Afanas'evskaia kul'tura, in *Kompleks Arkheologicheskikh Pamiatnikov u g. Tepseĭ na Enisee*, Novosibirsk, 1979, p. 160.

和墓葬与塔加尔文化的同类遗存共存的情况，① 因此她认为卡拉苏克与塔加尔部分同时。然而 A. 阿思卡诺夫（Askarov）、V. 沃尔科夫（Volkov）和 N. 塞尔—奥加夫（Ser-Odjav）认为卡拉苏克的卡门诺娄格阶段属于早期铁器时代。②

因为缺少碳十四测年数据，确定卡拉苏克文化的绝对年代是一个十分棘手的难题，以前只有两个数据 2930±60（公元前 980 年）和 2710±75（公元前 760 年），③ 后来从托尔加扎克遗址得到了两个数据公元前 820—前 782 年和公元前 834—前 758 年。④ 在这些年代出现以前，主要参照欧洲、西亚和中国等地的历史和考古资料，其中参照最多的是中国的器物。⑤ S. A. 捷普劳霍夫根据卡拉苏克折柄刀与东周刀币相似的现象，最早把卡拉苏克定为公元前 10—前 8 世纪。后来安阳商文化发现了折柄刀，因此学者们把目光又投向了安阳，但因为在这种刀的来源问题上存在分歧，给出的结果就大相径庭。C. B. 吉谢列夫认为商文化是这种刀的发源地，给出公元前 14—前 12 世纪的年代范围（当时他以为安阳商文化的年代是公元前 15—前 14 世纪），⑥ 后来他改变了观点，认为这种刀的发源地是米奴辛斯克盆地，因此把卡拉苏克文化的年代改为公元前 15—前 13 世纪。⑦ M. 罗越（Loehr）认为卡拉苏克早于安阳商文化，年代为公元前 1400—前 1300 年。⑧ E. A. 瓦捷茨卡娅参照了西西伯利亚的耶罗夫卡

---

① Chlenova, N. A., *Khronologiia Pamiatnikov Karasukskoĭ Èpokhi*, Moscow: Science Press, 1972, pp. 37 – 39.

② Askarov, A., V. Volkov, and N. Ser-Odjav, Pastoral and nomadic tribes at the beginning of the first millennium B. C., in A. H. Dani and V. M. Masson eds., *History of Civilizations of Central Asia*, Vol. 1, The dawn of civilization: earliest times to 700 B. C., Delhi: Motilal Banarsidass Publishers Private Limited, 1999, p. 460.

③ Chlenova, N. A., *Khronologiia Pamiatnikov Karasukskoĭ Èpokhi*, Moscow: Science Press, 1972, p. 39.

④ Savinov, D. G., *Drevnie Poseleniia Khakasii-Torgazhak*, Sankt-Peterburg, 1996, p. 46.

⑤ Chlenova, N. A., *Khronologiia Pamiatnikov Karasukskoĭ Èpokhi*, Moscow: Science Press, 1972, pp. 10 – 12.

⑥ Kiselev, S. V., *Drevniia Istoriia Iuzhnoĭ Sibiri*, Moscow: Science, 1951, pp. 178 – 179.

⑦ C. B. 吉谢列夫：《苏联境内青铜文化与中国商文化的关系》，《考古》1960 年第 2 期，第 52 页。

⑧ Loehr, M., Weapons and Tools from Anyang and Siberian Analogies, *American Journal of Archaeology* LIII, 1949, pp. 126 – 144.

（Elovka）文化，把卡拉苏克的年代定为公元前 11—前 8 世纪。[1] N. L. 齐连诺娃研究了中国和西西伯利亚的同类器物，确定了公元前 13—前 6 世纪的年代范围。[2] 近 10 年来，公布了 17 个数据，这样得到的范围是公元前 1420—前 830 年。[3] 最近又公布了 19 个人骨测年数据，校正后的年代范围为公元前 1400—前 800 年（见表 3-7-1）。[4] 不过 A. V. 波廖科夫（Poliakov）和 S. V. 司瓦科（Sviatko）结合卡拉苏克和石峡文化的相对年代，提出了一个更小的年代范围，即公元前 14—前 11 世纪或者公元前 1400—前 1000 年。[5]

（二）伊尔敏文化

伊尔敏文化是 N. L. 齐列诺娃在 1955 命名的。[6] 迄今为止该文化遗址发现于西至额尔齐斯河，东至鄂毕河，南至南阿尔泰，北至鄂毕河和楚勒姆河（Chulym）交汇处的广大地域内（见图 3-7-9）。[7] 最初该文化的遗址被归入卡拉苏克文化，随着资料的增加，与卡拉苏克之间的差别开始

---

[1] Vadetskaia, È. B., *Arkheologicheskie Pamiatniki v Stepiakh Srednego Eniseia*, Leningrad: Science Press, 1986, p. 65.

[2] Chlenova, N. A., *Khronologiia Pamiatnikov Karasukskoĭ Èpokhi*, Moscow: Science Press, 1972, pp. 61–63.

[3] Gorsdorf, J., H. Pazinger, and A. Nagler, 14C Dating of the Siberian Steppe Zone from Bronze Age to Scythian Time, in Scott, E. Marian, Andrey Yu. Alekseev, and Ganna Zaitseva eds., *Impact of the Environment on Human Migration in Eurasia*, Dordrecht, Boston, and London: Kluwer Academic Publishers, 2003, p. 88.

[4] Poliakov, A. V., and S. V. Sviatko, Radiouglerodnoe datirovanie arkheologicheskikh pamiatnikov neolita—nachala zheleznogo veka Srednego Eniseia: obzop resul'tatov i novye dannye, *Teoriia i Praktika Arkheologicheskikh Issledovanii*, Barnaul, Issue 5, 2009, pp. 20–56; S. V. Sviatko, J. P. Mallory, E. M. Murphy, A. V. Poliakov, P. J. Reimer, and R. J. Schulting, New radiocarbon dates and a review of the chronology of prehistoric populations from the Minusinsk Basin, Southern Siberia, Russia, *Radiocarbon* 51/1, 2009, p. 253.

[5] Poliakov, A. V., and S. V. Sviatko, Radiouglerodnoe datirovanie Arkheologicheskikh Pamiatnikov neolita—nachala zheleznogo veka Srednego Eniseia: obzop resul'tatov i novye dannye, *Teoriia i Praktika Arkheologicheskikh Issledovanii*, Barnaul, Issue 5, 2009, p. 35.

[6] Matveev, A. V., *Irmenskaia Kul'tura v Lesostepnom Priob'e*, Novosibirsk: Novosibirsk university, 1993, p. 8.

[7] Molodin, V. I., *Baraba v Èpokhu Bronzy*, Novosibirsk: Science, 1985, p. 139.

◇❖◇ 第三部分　中国西北和欧亚草原考古

引起 C. B. 吉谢列夫的注意，后来许多学者也认同，[①] 但 M. P. 格廖兹诺夫却认为托姆河（Tom'）、新西伯利亚州和鄂毕河上游的遗址只是卡拉苏克文化的地方类型。[②]

伊尔敏文化与西西伯利亚的大多数青铜时代文化不同，发现的聚落远远多于墓地。在鄂毕河流域的森林草原带，该文化的遗址极其密集。1993 年之前，在比亚（Biǐ）河与托姆河之间的河段发现将近 100 座聚落，在巴拉巴平原发现 14 座聚落，[③] 有些属于地穴式房屋。其中的伊尔敏—I 聚落的 No. 3 房屋保存最好，长 14 米，宽 12 米，深 1 米，内发现陶片和兽骨，以及铜锥、铜片、铜矿石、坩埚、范和小刀，周围还发现零星的范和人物雕塑，[④] 表明该聚落曾经是从事金属生产的。在贝斯特洛甫卡（Bystrovka）—IV 聚落发现 5 座房屋，其中的 No. 2 房屋保存较好，长 18 米，宽 15 米，深 0.5 米，中央有 1 个烧火坑。在所有的房屋内，沿着四壁和两条分割线分布有许多柱洞。在克拉斯诺亚尔（Krasnoǐ lar）的房屋外面的垃圾坑内发现三块陶范（用于铸造泡、直銎斧和一件不知名器物）。[⑤]

相对而言，已经发掘的墓地不多，但是埋葬习俗在该文化广阔的分布范围内却相当一致。其中最有代表性的是朱拉夫列沃（Zhuravlevo）—IV 墓地，发掘的面积最大，在 20000 平方米的范围内，有 22 座冢墓排成行列，有些冢墓周围有壕沟或石围。其中 No. 10 最有趣，在一块石头下面发现 9 个马头。这些冢墓都是集体葬，有些包含 10—17 座墓葬。中央的墓葬大多为男性长者，而周围为一列或一圈女性和儿童墓葬。墓葬大多直

[①] Chlenova, N. A., O kul'turakh bronzovoǐ Èpokhi lesostepnoǐ zony Zapadnoǐ Sibiri, *Sovetskaia Arkheologiia* 23, 1955, pp. 38 – 57; Matveev, A. V., *Irmenskaia Kul'tura v Lesostepnom Priob'e*, Novosibirsk: Novosibirsk university, 1993; Bobrov, V. V., Chikisheva, T. A., Mikhaǐlov, Iu. I., *Mogil'nik Èpokhi Pozdneǐ Bronzy Zhuravlevo* 4, Novosibirsk, 1993.

[②] Griaznov, M. P., *Istoriia drevnikh plemen Verkhneǐ Obi*, *Materialy i Issledovaniia po Arkheologii SSSR*, Issue 48, Moscow, Leningrad: Science, 1956.

[③] Matveev, A. V., *Irmenskaia Kul'tura v Lesostepnom Priob'e*, Novosibirsk: Novosibirsk university, 1993, p. 17; Molodin, V. I., *Baraba v Èpokhu Bronzy*, Novosibirsk: Science, 1985, p. 117.

[④] Matveev, A. V., *Irmenskaia Kul'tura v Lesostepnom Priob'e*, Novosibirsk: Novosibirsk university, 1993, pp. 33, 37.

[⑤] Matveev, A. V., *Irmenskaia Kul'tura v Lesostepnom Priob'e*, Novosibirsk: Novosibirsk university, 1993, p. 74.

接建在古代的地面上，而不是埋在土坑内。墓室大多为木材搭成，有时也用石板，体积都不大，只够容纳墓主屈肢的尸体，儿童墓要小于成人墓。无论性别和年龄，墓主都向右侧身，头向西南。有些骨架缺少手或腿或头骨，可能是二次葬。随葬品依年龄和性别而有所区别，一般都有铜泡，可能是头冠的装饰品。除此之外，男性墓再没有东西，而女性墓则还有许多装饰品，包括垂饰、耳环、指环、手镯、管和泡，还一般有 1 到 2 件陶器。[1]

伊尔敏文化的陶器器形矮而圆，同卡拉苏克的陶器相似，而与安德罗诺沃的截然不同。虽然陶器有些是圜底的，与卡拉苏克陶器相同，但大多数是平底的，束颈、圆肩，曲线优美，与卡拉苏克不同。碗的数量很多，其他器类数量不多，伊尔敏特有的器类是轮廓为菱形的罐。纹饰简单，只出现在颈部和肩部，很少出现在肩以下。常见的纹饰有乳丁纹（由内向外压出）、折线纹、网格纹。几何纹中多见斜线三角纹和并行三角纹（图 3-7-11：1—4）。

伊尔敏聚落和墓地出土的金属器数量不多，种类也较少。刀单刃，直柄，并有环首。这种刀与卡拉苏克文化的同类器接近。折背宽刃刀和柄头带环的弓背刀也见于卡拉苏克文化。镯是用铜片卷成的，有眼睛形或槽形截面。耳环有圆形泡和钉形柄。指环有时用铜片卷成，有时用铜丝卷成。其他还有带柄的三孔马镳、矛、直銎斧、圆铜镜和凿（图 3-7-11：5—15）。

伊尔敏文化显然出现在安德罗诺沃之后。在伊尔敏—I 聚落遗址，伊尔敏的地层压在安德罗诺沃之上。在克拉斯诺亚尔居址，一座伊尔敏的地穴式房屋坐落在安德罗诺沃文化的聚落上。[2] 在扎列曲诺耶（Zarechnoe）—I 墓地，伊尔敏的一座冢墓出土于安德罗诺沃的一座儿童墓之上。[3] 在普列奥

---

[1] Bobrov, V. V., Chikisheva, T. A., Mikhaǐlov, Iu. I., *Mogil'nik Èpokhi Pozdneǐ Bronzy Zhuravlevo 4*, Novosibirsk, 1993, pp. 77 – 83.

[2] Griaznov, M. P., Istoriia drevnikh plemen Verkhneǐ Obi, *Materialy i Issledovaniia po Arkheologii SSSR*, Issue 48, Moscow, Leningrad: Science, 1956; Chlenova, N. A., *Pamiatniki Kontsa Èpokhi Bronzy v Zapadnoǐ Sibiri*, Moscow, 1994, p. 11.

[3] Bobrov, V. V., Chikisheva, T. A., Mikhaǐlov, Iu. I., *Mogil'nik Èpokhi Pozdneǐ Bronzy Zhuravlevo 4*, Novosibirsk, 1993, p. 5.

布拉任卡—Ⅱ墓地，一座伊尔敏墓出现在一座安德罗诺沃墓之上，[①] 还有一条填满伊尔敏陶片的壕沟打破安德罗诺沃文化儿童墓地的一座墓。[②] 伊尔敏文化的绝对年代，有些学者定为公元前10—前7世纪，也有学者定为公元前12—前8世纪。[③] 目前得到的碳十四数据只有几个，来自贝斯特洛甫卡聚落的公元前1890±40，来自雅萨旭雷卢格（Iasashnyǐ Lug）聚落的公元前1870±60、公元前1570±30、公元前1951—前1848年、公元前1130±100、公元前1280±100、公元前1270±40、公元前1270±40和公元前1230±40。[④] 这些数据的大致范围为公元前1890—前1130年（表3-7-1）。N. L. 齐连诺娃并不接受这些年代，认为这些年代都偏早。但从卡拉苏克文化的年代范围来看，这些年代接近真实年代。还有一个来自普列奥布拉任卡—Ⅱ的是公元前880±25，显然偏晚。当然，要得到更为准确的年代还需要更多的碳十四测年数据支持。

（三）萨穆西文化

萨穆西文化是M. F. 科萨廖夫在1963年根据同名聚落命名的，分布于鄂毕河中游（新西伯利亚以北，权耶河以南，秋明以东，托木河下游以西）的森林和森林草原带（表3-7-1）。[⑤] 该文化与伊尔敏文化类似，以聚落遗址居多。典型的遗址是1954年由V. I. 马秋申科发现的萨穆西—

---

① Molodin, V. I., *Baraba v Èpokhu Bronzy*, Novosibirsk: Science, 1985, p. 142.

② N. L. Chlenova 收集了一些安德罗诺沃陶器与伊尔敏陶器共存的墓葬以及安德罗诺沃与伊尔敏陶器共存的墓地。但是这些例子并不能否定安德罗诺沃和伊尔敏的年代关系（Chlenova, N. A., *Pamiatniki Kontsa Èpokhi Bronzy v Zapadnoǐ Sibiri*, Moscow, 1994, pp. 11-12）。

③ Griaznov, M. P., Istoriia drevnikh plemen Verkhneǐ Obi, *Materialy i Issledovaniia po Arkheologii SSSR*, Issue 48, Moscow, Leningrad: Science, 1956; Kosarev, M. F., *Bronzovyǐ vek Zapadnoǐ Sibiri*, Moscow: Science, 1981; Savinov, D. G., and V. V. Bobrov, Titovskiǐ Mogil'nik Èpokhi Pozdneǐ Bronzy na reke Ine, in *Problemy Zapadnosibirskoǐ Arkheologii: Èpokha Kamnia i Bronzy*, Novosibirsk, 1981, pp. 122-135; Molodin, V. I., *Baraba v Èpokhu Bronzy*, Novosibirsk: Science, 1985, p. 143; Matveev, A. V., *Irmenskaia Kul'tura v Lesostepnom Priob'e*, Novosibirsk: Novosibirsk university, 1993, p. 132.

④ Chlenova, N. A., *Pamiatniki Kontsa Èpokhi Bronzy v Zapadnoǐ Sibiri*, Moscow, 1994, p. 22.

⑤ Matiushchenko, V. I., Drevniaia istoriia poseleniia lesnogo i lesostepnogo Priob'ia, Ch. 2: Samus'skaia kul'tura, *Iz Istorii Sibiri*, Issue 10, Tomsk: Press of Tomsk University, 1973; Kosarev, M. F., *Bronzovyǐ Vek Zapadnoǐ Sibiri*, Moscow: Science, 1981, p. 86; Molodin, V. I., and I. G. Glushkov, *Samus'skaia Kul'tura v Verkhnem Priob'e*, Novosibirsk: Science, 1989; Kiriushin, Iu. F., *Neolit, Bronzovyǐ Vek Iuzhno-Taëzhnoǐ Zony Zapadnoǐ Sibiri*, Barnaul, 2004, p. 41.

IV，1954—1972年曾连续发掘，发掘面积达5000平方米，发现5座地穴式房屋。这些房屋以过道相连，形成了一个单元。1号房屋5.1平方米见方，1.25米深，内有两个灶坑，也发现可能属于地面建筑的火坑。[①] 克拉哈廖夫卡（Krokhalevka）—I是另一个经过大面积发掘的聚落，这里发现了3座半地穴式房屋（64平方米）。1号房屋大致呈方形，南侧有突出的门道，门道内有一个火坑，房内北侧有一具狗骨架。火坑周围分布有木炭、烧骨、陶片和石器。房屋中央有4个大柱洞，用以支撑房顶，四壁的小柱洞则用以支撑墙壁。[②] 黑湖（Chernoozer'e）—VI聚落的周围有壕沟保护，发掘9座半地穴式房屋，面积平均为48平方米，深约0.4—0.6米，内有火坑和柱洞。[③]

萨穆西—IV继承了奥库涅沃文化的一些特征，出土的人物和动物雕刻很多（图3-7-12：1）。值得一提的是，这些人物雕刻的面貌特征，据体质人类学家V. A. 德涅莫夫（Dremov）观察，属于欧罗巴人种。而V. A. 德涅莫夫指出，萨穆西文化存在多个人种和民族，这些人物雕刻形象只反映了其中的一部分。[④] 其中一些雕刻呈靴形，上面有瓦楞装饰。类似的人物雕刻在土耳其查塔尔胡尤克（Chatal Hüyük）和土库曼斯坦南部古科苏（Giuksur）—I也有发现，表明萨穆西文化与近东和中亚存在文化联系。[⑤] 遗址中出土了一些熊和人骨骼，以及装饰兽头的陶器，还有青铜、石质和陶质的鸟、熊、熊头、人头雕塑。该文化中如此丰富的人物和动物形象雕塑在属于该文化的其他遗址不见。[⑥]

[①] Matiushchenko, V. I., Drevniaia istoriia poseleniia lesnogo i lesostepnogo Priob'ia, Ch. 2: Samus'skaia kul'tura, *Iz Istorii Sibiri*, Tomsk: Press of Tomsk University, Issue 10, 1973, pp. 61-64.

[②] Molodin, V. I., and I. G. Glushkov, *Samus'skaia Kul'tura v Verkhnem Priob'e*, Novosibirsk: Science, 1989, pp. 113-116.

[③] Kosarev, M. F., Pervyĭ period razvitogo bronzovogo veka Zapadnoĭ Sibiri (Samus'sko-seĭminskaia èpokha), in O. N. Bader, D. A. Krainov, and M. F. Kosarev eds., *Èpokha Bronzy Lesnoĭ Polosy SSSR*, Moscow: Science, 1987, p. 273.

[④] 转引自 Kiriushin, Iu. F., *Neolit, Bronzovyĭ Vek Iuzhno-Taëzhnoĭ Zony Zapadnoĭ Sibiri*, Barnaul, 2004, p. 35.

[⑤] 转引自 Kiriushin, Iu. F., *Neolit, Bronzovyĭ Vek Iuzhno-Taëzhnoĭ Zony Zapadnoĭ Sibiri*, Barnaul, 2004, pp. 35-36.

[⑥] Matiushchenko, V. I., Drevniaia istoriia poseleniia lesnogo i lesostepnogo Priob'ia, Ch. 2: Samus'skaia kul'tura, *Iz Istorii Sibiri*, Issue 10, Tomsk: Press of Tomsk University, 1973, p. 60.

◇❖◇ 第三部分 中国西北和欧亚草原考古

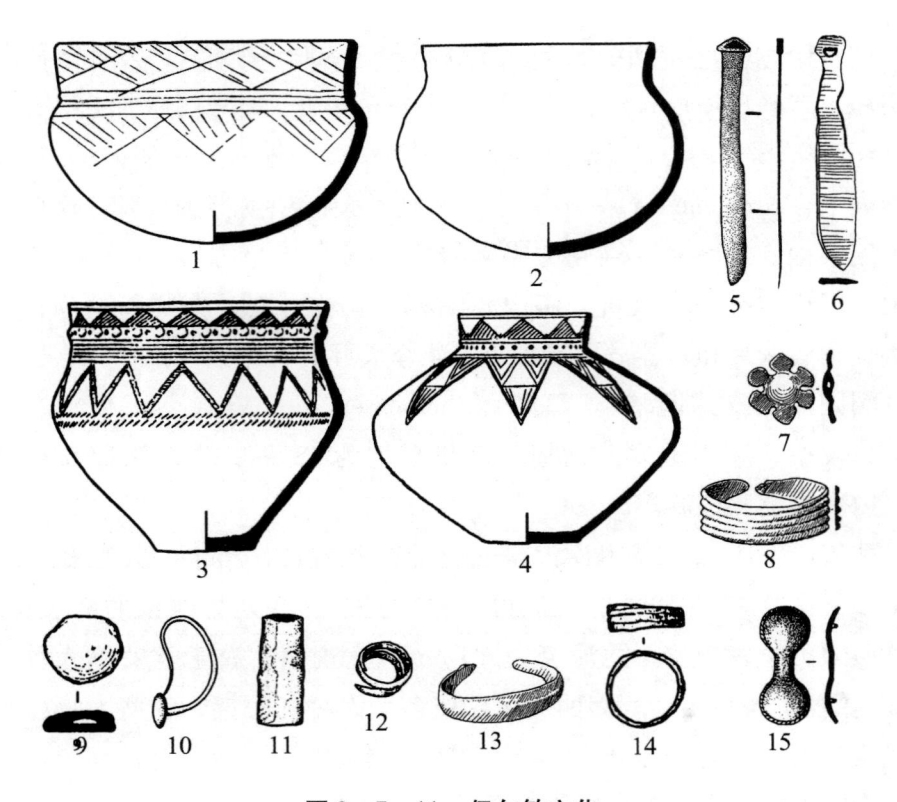

图 3-7-11 伊尔敏文化

1—4. 陶罐；5、6. 铜刀；7、15. 铜泡；8、13、14. 铜镯；9. 铜扣；10、12. 铜耳环；11. 铜管

（1、2、5、10、11、12. Preobrazhenka II；3. Irmen' I；4、15. Bystrovka IV；6、9、13、14. Ordynskoe I；7、8. Zhulavlev，图片来源：Matveev, A. V., *Irmenskaia Kul'tura v Lesostepnom Priob'e*, Novosibirsk：Novosibirsk university, 1993, Plate 18：3, 5；Plate 23：15, Fig. 14：2, 22, Plate 25：6, 9, 14, Fig. 39：9；Molodin, V. I., *Baraba v Èpokhu Bronzy*, Novosibirsk：Science, 1985, Fig. 61：9, Fig. 62：15, Fig. 63：1, 13, 19, 25）

萨穆西文化的陶器有三大类。一类是鼓腹平底罐，其中个体较高的与青铜时代中期辛塔什塔文化的同类器接近，而器物矮胖且为平底或圜底的则更接近于伊尔敏文化的同类器。第二类是直腹平底罐，大小不一。第三类是敛口器物。这类陶器一个显著的特征是通体饰戳印点和篦纹构成的松针纹、直线、波纹和之字纹或人物和动物形象，另外有人物和动物形象的陶器底部一般呈四边形或六边形（图 3-7-12：2—6）。根据这些陶器特点，V. I. 马秋申科（Matiushchenko）划分出了萨穆西

· 310 ·

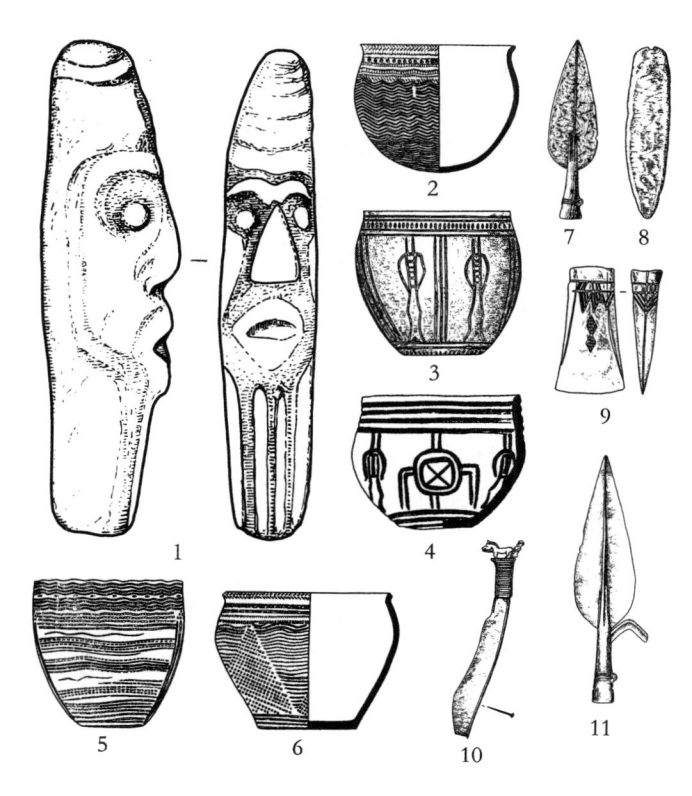

图 3-7-12　萨穆西文化

1. 石人；2—6. 陶罐；7、11. 铜矛；8、10. 铜刀；9. 铜直銎斧

[1—11. Samus'-IV，图片来源：Kosarev, M. F., Pervyĭ period razvitogo bronzovogo veka Zapadnoĭ Sibiri (Samus'sko-seĭminskaia èpokha), in O. N. Bader, D. A. Krainov, and M. F. Kosarev eds., *Èpokha Bronzy Lesnoĭ Polosy SSSR*, Moscow: Science, 1987, Fig. 100: 2, 7, 9, Fig. 101: 2, 3, 5, Fig. 102: 1, 3, 6, 9, Fig. 103: 18; Molodin, V. I., and I. G. Glushkov, *Samus'skaia Kul'tura v Verkhnem Priob'e*, Novosibirsk: Science, 1989, Fig. 37: 2]

和耶罗夫卡—伊尔敏两期，[1] 但因无地层依据，难以成立。[2]

萨穆西—IV 遗址出土了大量的金属器，包括青铜斧、锛、权杖头，也出土了范芯、勺和坩埚，以及 400 件石质和陶质范，可以铸造的器物有

---

[1] Matiushchenko, V. I., Drevniaia istoriia poseleniia lesnogo i lesostepnogo Priob'ia, Ch. 2: Samus'skaia kul'tura, *Iz Istorii Sibiri*, Issue 10, Tomsk: Press of Tomsk University, 1973, pp. 75-76.

[2] Kiriushin, Iu. F., *Neolit, Bronzovyĭ Vek Iuzhno-Taëzhnoĭ Zony Zapadnoĭ Sibiri*, Barnaul, 2004, pp. 29-30.

直銎斧、横銎斧、矛、刀和短剑（图3-7-12：7—11）。① 这些青铜器和范所铸造的器类 E. H. 切尔内赫和 C. B. 库兹明内赫作为塞依玛—图尔宾诺现象的一部分做过仔细的分析。塞依玛—图尔宾诺现象指的是一批青铜器和铸范，发现于一些墓地、窖藏和聚落，分布于欧亚大陆的一大片地域。其中萨穆西—IV 出土的直銎斧为长方体，六角形截面，与塞依玛墓地出土的同类器接近（图3-7-12：10）。② 不过塞依玛—图尔宾诺现象的青铜器，根据笔者的研究，可以分为两期，分别属于青铜时代中期和晚期。③ 萨穆西—IV 出土的铜器与青铜时代晚期的木椁墓文化接近，主要表现为宽刃的横銎斧、形体细长的矛和双耳直銎斧。毫无疑问，该聚落曾经是一个专门从事金属生产的村落，所用的金属原料可能来自阿尔泰和东哈萨克斯坦。通过分析5件器物和2件坩埚可知，萨穆西—IV 的金属器含有很高的锡铅或锡。④ 出有铜块、铜锥、矛范和坩埚的冶金作坊也见于鄂木斯克以北100千米的黑湖（Chernoozer'e）—IV 遗址。⑤ 同样，克拉哈廖夫卡—I 聚落出土的坩埚、范（矛、直銎斧、刀）和范芯表明，这里也曾从事金属生产。⑥

位于鄂木斯克附近的罗斯托夫卡（Rostovka）墓地因为出土许多铜器和陶器，与萨穆西—IV 文化出土的同类器接近，可以归入萨穆西文化。⑦ 1966—1969 年，V. I. 马秋申科发掘了该墓地，共清理38 座墓葬，分五排东西向和南北向排列。墓葬未经过盗掘或破坏，均为土坑墓，部分用木头加固。31 座为土葬，其中10 具人骨保存较好，8 具为仰身直肢，头向东，2

---

① Matiushchenko, V. I., *Drevniaia istoriia poseleniia lesnogo i lesostepnogo Priob'ia*, Ch. 2: Samus'skaia kul'tura, *Iz Istorii Sibiri*, Tomsk: Press of Tomsk University, Issue 10, 1973, pp. 71-74.

② E. H. 切尔内赫、C. B. 库兹明内赫：《欧亚大陆北部的古代冶金》，王博、李明华翻译，张良仁校对，中华书局2010年版，比较图78：5—6 和图17：1、3。

③ Zhang, Liangren, *Ancient Society and Metallurgy: A Comparative Study of Bronze Age Societies in Central Eurasia and North China*, Archaeopress, 2012, pp. 67-68, 108-109.

④ Matiushchenko, V. I., *Drevniaia istoriia poseleniia lesnogo i lesostepnogo Priob'ia*, Ch. 2: Samus'skaia kul'tura, *Iz Istorii Sibiri*, Prilozhenie 1, Tomsk: Press of Tomsk University, Issue 10, 1973, pp. 75-76.

⑤ Kosarev, M. F., *Bronzovyĭ Vek Zapadnoĭ Sibiri*, Moscow: Science, 1981, p. 91.

⑥ Molodin, V. I., and I. G. Glushkov, *Samus'skaia Kul'tura v Verkhnem Priob'e*, Novosibirsk: Science, 1989, pp. 51-52.

⑦ Kosarev, M. F., *Bronzovyĭ Vek Zapadnoĭ Sibiri*, Moscow: Science, 1981, pp. 95-96.

具为侧身屈肢。部分墓葬的人骨或被扰乱，或缺少头骨，或只有头骨。7 座墓为火葬，只发现木炭、烧土和烧骨。墓地北部还发现一个所谓的"火葬场"。这是一个南北向的土坑，周围有 15 个小柱洞，上面原来可能有覆盖的顶棚。随葬品分布不均匀，部分墓葬特别丰富，部分墓葬完全无遗物。随葬品种类多样，包含铜矛、铜斧、铜刀、铜短剑、金指环、石范、石刀、石器、骨器和陶器（含陶范）等，耐人寻味的细节是一些铜矛和铜刀是扎入墓底地面的。其中叉形柄矛与萨穆西—IV 出土的范对应，而陶碗、陶罐以及布满陶器的波纹和松针纹也与萨穆西—IV 相同。① 此外，墓地地面上还发现一些陶片和兽骨，经过鉴定有绵羊和马，而以后者居多。

  罗斯托夫卡墓地出土的金属器中有 47 件已经取样做了成分分析，39 件工具和武器类器物中，只有 1 件为砷铜，其余均为锡青铜，但部分还含有砷、铅和锑。8 件装饰品中 1 件为锡青铜，其余均为金。②

  萨穆西遗址的发掘者 V. I. 马秋申科认为萨穆西文化属于青铜时代早期，早于安德罗诺沃文化，其年代为公元前 16—前 13 世纪。③ M. F. 科萨列夫（Kosarev）、V. I. 莫罗金、I. C. 格鲁旭科夫（Glushkov）和 Iu. F. 基留申认为萨穆西遗址早于安德罗诺沃文化，但其绝对年代为公元前 1500—前 1200 年。④ 从比较研究的角度来看，萨穆西文化对应于东欧的青铜时代晚期。该文化的陶器包括直腹平底罐和小碗，形态与木椁墓文化非常接近，如束颈圜底罐（图 3-7-12：4）在形态上就与卡拉苏克和伊尔敏文化接近。⑤ M. F. 科萨列夫指出，罗斯托夫卡墓地和萨穆西—IV 居

---

  ① Matiushchenko, V. I., and G. V. Sinitsyna, *Mogil'nik u Derevni Rostovka vblizi Omska*, Tomsk：Press of Tomsk University, 1988, pp. 63 - 81, 89 - 98, 132.
  ② E. H. 切尔内赫、C. B. 库兹明内赫：《欧亚大陆北部的古代冶金》，王博、李明华翻译，张良仁校对，中华书局 2010 年版，第 210—238 页。
  ③ Matiushchenko, V. I., Drevniaia istoriia poseleniia lesnogo i lesostepnogo Priob'ia, Ch. 2：Samus'skaia kul'tura, *Iz Istorii Sibiri*, Tomsk：Press of Tomsk University, Issue 10, 1973, p. 59.
  ④ Kosarev, M. F., *Bronzovyĭ Vek Zapadnoĭ Sibiri*, Moscow：Science, 1981, p. 105; Molodin, V. I., and I. G. Glushkov, *Samus'skaia Kul'tura v Verkhnem Priob'e*, Novosibirsk：Science, 1989, p. 103; Kiriushin, Iu. F., *Neolit, Bronzovyĭ Vek Iuzhno-Taëzhnoĭ Zony Zapadnoĭ Sibiri*, Barnaul, 2004, p. 40.
  ⑤ Kosarev, M. F., Pervyĭ period razvitogo bronzovogo veka Zapadnoĭ Sibiri (Samus'sko-seĭminskaia èpokha), in O. N. Bader, D. A. Krainov, and M. F. Kosarev eds., *Èpokha Bronzy Lesnoĭ Polosy SSSR*, Moscow：Science, 1987, Fig. 102：3.

址出土的一些铜器（如弓形刀、带钩的矛）与卡拉苏克文化的同类器相近。[①] 虽然戳印纹和篦纹占主流，但安德罗诺沃文化的三角纹、菱格纹和折线纹也在使用，这种纹饰构成让我们想起了木椁墓文化。此外，上述一些铜矛、铜刀、铜短剑、金指环和铜竖銎斧的同类器物也见于木椁墓文化。[②]

五 结语

笔者依据苏秉琦和殷玮璋的器物形态学和东欧的青铜时代分期将西西伯利亚青铜时代文化分成了三期，基本理清了西西伯利亚青铜时代文化的发展脉络。

青铜时代早期，阿凡纳谢沃文化显然是东欧的竖穴墓文化派生出来的。墓主仰身屈肢，并撒有赤铁粉。陶器为橄榄形或球形，纹饰简单粗糙。金属器大多为装饰品，几乎不见武器，工具也极少。居民属于欧罗巴人种。奥库涅沃文化不同于阿凡纳谢沃文化，但同时继承了后者的很多因素。奥库涅沃的冢墓一般包含若干不同年龄和不同性别墓主的墓葬，且墓葬由石板竖砌而成。墓主仰身屈肢，有时撒有赤铁粉。出土陶器为橄榄形或锥形，接近阿凡纳谢沃的橄榄形罐，多为平底，装饰有简单的锯齿纹和几何纹。与阿凡纳谢沃文化不同的是，奥库涅沃文化除使用纯铜外，还使用了较多的青铜器，包括锡青铜、砷铜和铅铜。同时还生产武器和工具，如短剑、刀、指环、锥和针，但形态比较简单。如刀形扁平，个体小，为片状。奥库涅沃文化的居民与阿凡纳谢沃文化的居民相同，皆为欧罗巴人种。整体而言，奥库涅沃的物质文化更接近于阿凡纳谢沃文化。

青铜时代中期，一个庞大的安德罗诺沃文化出现。安德罗诺沃的冢墓和地面墓葬都出现石围，墓内出现木质或石质墓室。火葬在少数墓地占主流，但在土葬流行的墓地，墓主左侧身屈肢，与辛塔什塔文化的情

[①] Kosarev, M. F., *Bronzovyĭ Vek Zapadnoĭ Sibiri*, Moscow: Science, 1981, p. 96.

[②] Matiushchenko, V. I., and G. V. Sinitsyna, *Mogil'nik u Derevni Rostovka vblizi Omska*, Tomsk: Press of Tomsk University, 1988, pp. 68–81.

形接近。此外，墓葬的大小和葬具依墓主的年龄和性别而定，也与后者的情形接近。该文化的陶器同样与后者相似，器类多样，纹饰丰富。器类包括鼓腹平底罐、直腹平底罐和碗。其中鼓腹平底罐精致磨光，并装饰富丽的纹饰如三角纹、折线、回纹和松针纹。该文化的金属器器类多，包括多种武器、工具和装饰品，但也与阿巴舍沃和辛塔什塔文化接近。在风格上，安德罗诺沃陶器尽管不同于辛塔什塔文化，但也有与后者相同的地方。在安德罗诺沃的金属器中，锡青铜占主流。耶鲁尼诺文化在许多方面都具有特色，它与安德罗诺沃和辛塔什塔文化是同时的，主要表现在陶器器类同样包括直腹平底、鼓腹平底罐和碗。某些金属器如双刃刀和带有人物和动物形象的刀见于塞依玛—图尔宾诺现象，而后者与辛塔什塔文化有着密切的交往关系。克罗托沃文化在墓葬习俗、陶器和一些金属器形态方面的特色更为突出，但是克罗托沃的大部分青铜器带有安德罗诺沃特征的纹饰和形态。安德罗诺沃和耶鲁尼诺文化的居民属于欧罗巴人种，但也有蒙古人种的一些特征。看起来欧罗巴人种仍然占据西西伯利亚，但他们与叶尼塞河以东的蒙古人种有交往。

青铜时代晚期，卡拉苏克和伊尔敏文化比较接近。与阿凡纳谢沃和安德罗诺沃文化不同的是，墓地埋有大量的墓葬，数量常常超过100座。与安德罗诺沃墓葬相左的是，卡拉苏克墓葬的墓主仰身直肢，头向东或东北，而伊尔敏的墓主几乎都是右侧身，头向西南。卡拉苏克和伊尔敏的陶器均为球形或炮弹形，圜底。在平底器中，一些带有束颈和双耳。广为使用的纹饰为斜线三角纹、松针纹、菱格纹、回纹和弦纹，与安德罗诺沃文化的纹饰相近。但只出现在陶器的颈部或肩部，并且经过简化。因此在器形和装饰上继承了阿凡纳谢沃和安德罗诺沃的文化特征，但同时也进行了一些改变。奥库涅沃的人物和动物雕刻同样出现在卡拉苏克的陶器和石头上。在青铜器中，主要的工具、武器和装饰品都与安德罗诺沃文化接近，但卡拉苏克和伊尔敏自身的创新也不鲜见。折柄刀是其典型器。总的来说，卡拉苏克和伊尔敏的陶器很像木椁墓文化，显示出一个简化和衰退的倾向。人口是新来的，可能是蒙古人种进入米奴辛斯克盆地同本地的安德罗诺沃后裔通婚形成的。在萨穆西文化的陶器中，鼓腹平底罐在形态上与辛塔什塔文化的同类器相似，而那些矮胖的平底罐或圜底罐在形态上与伊尔敏文化的同类器接近。该文化的青铜器和金属生产的遗物极为丰富，其中400件石质和陶质铸范与木椁墓文化和塞依玛—图尔宾诺现象的金属器接近，这在宽刃横銎斧、形体修长的矛和双耳直銎斧表现得尤为明显。由于碳十四年代测定的数据不足，使我们无法精确地界定上述文化的年代范围，但可以依据现有的数据推断出一个粗略的年代范围，这个年代范围可以部分地支持本文开始提出的分期及其与东欧青铜时代文化的对应关系。关于阿凡纳谢沃文化，现有的20个数据在公元前3650—前2240年的范围，与竖穴墓文化大体相对应。奥库涅沃的年代范围为公元前2885—前1693年，与阿凡纳谢沃文化的年代部分重合。少数数据将安德罗诺沃文化的年代确定在公元前1750—前1400年，尽管这个年代范围与辛塔什塔文化的年代重合不多，但与该文化在青铜时代的位置是相符的。相比而言，耶鲁尼诺文化的年代可以定为公元前2250—前1550年，与辛塔什塔文化的年代非常接近。卡拉苏克和伊尔敏文化的年代分别为公元前1420—前830年和公元前1890—前1130年，与木椁墓文化的年代（公元前1690—前1390年）部分重合。

The Transmission of the Karasuk Metallurgy to the Northern Zone of China*

Introduction

The Northern Zone, which is situated between the Central Plain, the cradle of early Chinese civilizations, and the Eurasian steppe, the heartland of pastoralist cultures, has been in the limelight of research for nearly a hundred years. The early metal artifacts from this region, in particular, have been the central subject of the discourse pertaining to the origin of metallurgy of either the Karasuk culture in the Minusinsk Basin or the Shang civilization in the Central Plain. While some scholars held that they came from the Anyang Shang,[①] others advocated that they were originated in the Minusinsk Basin.[②] This debate

---

* 本文为国家社科基金课题"新疆东部史前冶金"(No. 11BKG007) 成果, 原刊于《史地》2017 年第 1 辑, 第 100—124 页。收入本书时有所改动。

[①] Karlgren, B., Some Weapons and tools form the Yin Dynasty, *Bulletin of the Museum of Far Eastern Antiquities* 17, 1945, p. 113; Jettmar, K., The Karasuk Culture and Its South-eastern Affinities, *Bulletin of the Museum of Far Eastern Antiquities* 22, 1950, p. 116, 121; Kiselev, S. V., *Drevniia Istoriia Iuzhnoĭ Sibiri*, Moscow: Science, 1951, pp. 178 – 179.

[②] Anderson, J. G., Selected Ordos Bronzes, *Bulletin of the Museum of Far Eastern Antiquities* 5, 1933, pp. 142 – 154; Loehr, M., Weapons and tools from Anyang and Siberian analogies, *American Journal of Archaeology* LIII, 1949, p. 129; Loehr, M., Ordos daggers and knives: new material classification and chronology, *Artibus Asiae* 14, 1951, pp. 136 – 137; Vadetskaia, È. B., *Arkheologicheskie Pamiatniki v Stepiakh Srednego Eniseia*, Leningrad: Science Press, 1986, pp. 61 – 62; Chlenova, N. L., *Pamiatniki Kontsa Èpokhi Bronzy v Zapadnoĭ Sibiri*, Moscow: Science, 1994; Bunker, E., The Bronze Age in Northwestern China: 13th-9th centuries BC, in E. C. Bunker, T. S. Kawami, K. M. Linduff, and E. Wu, eds., *Ancient Bronzes of the Eastern Eurasian Steppes from the Arthur M. Sackler Collections*, Arthur M. Sackler Foundation & the Arthur M. Sackler Museum, 1997, pp. 117, 127; Di Cosmo, N., The Northern Frontier in Pre-Imperial China, in M. Loewe & E. L. Shaughnessy, eds., *The Cambridge History of Ancient China*, New York: Cambridge University Press, 1999, pp. 893 – 896.

was later settled in favor of the "origin in the Minusinsk Basin." But the accumulating early metal arifacts from scientific excavations since the 1980s have prompted scholars to look at the Northern Zone itself, and the debate has evolved into another. Some scholars take up the idea of the autochthonous origin of metallurgy in the Northerm Zone,[1] whereas others look for its origin among the other cultures in the Eurasian steppe, mainly Andronovo and Seĭma-Turbino.[2] The readers may wonder: is there any profit to gain from visiting the old debate?

---

[1] Lin, Y., Bronzes of the Shang and of the Northern Zone, in K. C. Chang, ed., *Studies of Shang Archaeology*, New Haven and London: Yale University Press, 1986, pp. 237 – 273; Yuesitu, W., Yin zhi Zhouchu de beifang qingtongqi, *Kaogu Xuebao* 2, 1985, pp. 135 – 156; Yuesitu, W., Lun qingtongshidai changcheng didai yu ouya caoyuan xianglin diqu de wenhua lianxi, in The Institute of Archaeology, Chinese Academy of Social Sciences ed., *Ershiyi Shiji de Zhongguo Kaoguxue—Qingzhu Tong Zhuchen Xiansheng Bashiwu Huadan Xueshu Wenji*, Beijing: Wenwu, 2006, pp. 558 – 586; Tian, G., and S. Guo eds., *Eerduosishi Qingtongqi*, Beijing: Wenwu, 1986; Bai, Y., Zhongguo de zaoqi tongqi yu qingtongqi de qiyuan, *Dongnan Wenhua* 7, 2002, p. 36.

[2] Fiztgerald-Huber, L. G., Qijia and Erlitou: The Question of early Contacts with Distant Cultures, *Early China* 20, 1995, pp. 40 – 52; Mei, J., *Copper and Bronze Metallurgy in Late Prehistoric Xinjiang*, Oxford: Archaeopress, 2000, p. 74; Mei, J., Qijia and Seĭma-Turbino: The question of early contacts between Northwest China and the Eurasian steppe, *Bulletin of the Museum of Far Eastern Antiquities* 75, 2003, p. 19; Mei, J., Cultural Interaction between China and Central Asia during the Bronze Age, *Proceedings of the British Academy* 121, 2003, p. 38; Mei, J., G. Liu, and X. Chang, Xinjiang dongbu diqu chutu zaoqi tongqi de chubu fenxi he yanjiu, *Xiyu Yanjiu* 2, 2003, p. 8; Kuz'mina, E. E., Historical perspectives on the Andronovo and metal use in Eastern Asia, in K. M. Linduff ed., *Metallurgy in Ancient Eastern Eurasia from the Urals to the Yellow River*, Lewiston, Queenstone, and Lampeter: The Edwin Mellen Press, 2004, pp. 62 – 76; Li, S., Xibei yu Zhongyuan zaoqi yetongye de quyu tezheng ji jiaohu zuoyong, *Kaogu Xuebao* 3, 2005, p. 265; Linduff, K. M., The emergence and demise of bronze-producing cultures outside the Central Plain of China, in V. H. Mair, ed., *The Bronze Age and Early Iron Age Peoples of Eastern Central Asia*, Washington: Institute for the Study of Man, Vol. 2, 1998, p. 627; Linduff, K. M., Why have Siberian artefacts been excavated within ancient Chinese dynastic borders? in Adam Smith, David Peterson, and L. M. Popova eds., *Beyond the Steppe and The Sown: Integrating Local and Global Visions*, Leiden, Boston, Köln: Brill, 2002, p. 360; Linduff, K., and J. Mei, Metallurgy in Ancient Eastern Asia: Retrospect and Prospects, *Journal of World Prehistory* 22/3, 2009, pp. 274 – 275; Jaang, L., Long-Distance Interactions as Reflected in the Earliest Chinese Bronze Mirrors, in Lothar von Falkenhausen ed., *The Lloyd Cotsen Study Collection of Chinese Bronze Mirrors*, Los Angeles: Cotsen Occasional Press and UCLA Cotsen Institute of Archaeology Press, Volume II, 2011, p. 36; Mei, J., P. Wang, K. Chen, L. Wang, Y. Wang, and Y. Liu, Archaeometallurgical studies in China: some recent developments and challenging issues, *Journal of Archaeological Science* 56, 2015, pp. 221 – 232; Shelach-Lavi, G., Steppe Land Interaction and Their Effects on Chinese cultures during the Second and Early First Millennia BCE, in R. Amitai and M. Biran, eds., *Nomads as Agents of Cultural Change*, University of Hawaii Press, 2015, p. 21.

The Transmission of the Karasuk Metallurgy to the Northern Zone of China

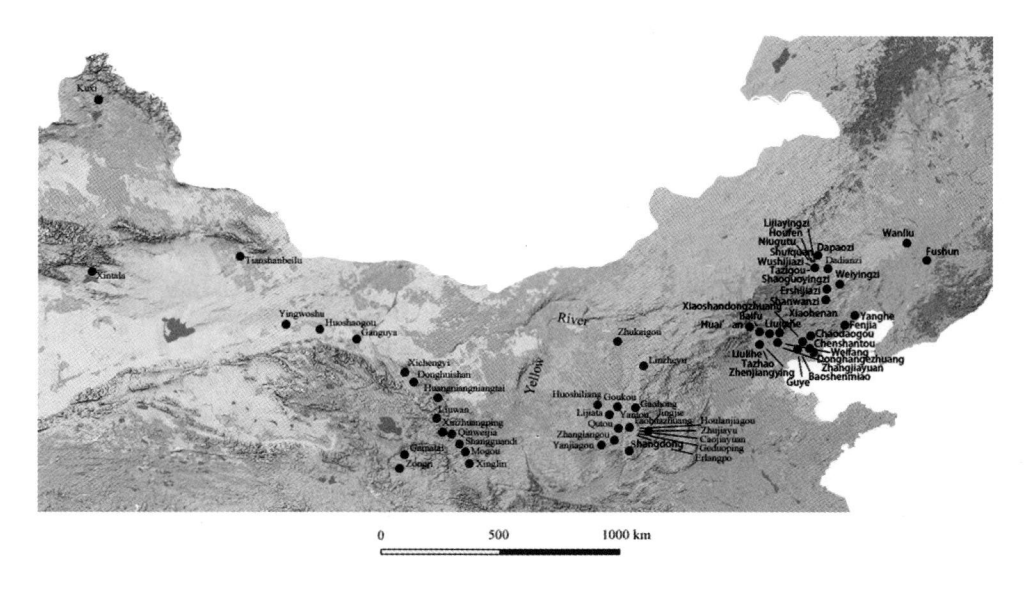

Fig. 3 – 8 – 1 Sites yielding Karasuk-type metal artifacts in northern China

The answer is yes. In fact, the two groups of scholars are mostly dealing with two discrete regions of the Northern Zone. The autochthonous-origin theorists are talking about the region from the Ordos Plateau to the Yanshan Mountain, without paying much attention to the region of Xinjiang, Gansu, and Qinghai provinces. On the contrary, the steppe-origin theorists are talking about the latter region, without giving much heed to the former one (Fig. 3 – 8 – 1). Both groups have categorically downplayed the contribution of the other cultures of the Eurasian steppe. This paper, by uniting the two regions, comes to draw a strikingly different picture: the Karasuk culture played a crucial role in the formation of the early metallurgy of the Northern Zone. Furthermore, by thoroughly re-examining the two regions, this paper identifies regional characteristics of them, and two possible transmission routes of the Karasuk metallurgy to the Northern Zone.

◇❖◇ 第三部分 中国西北和欧亚草原考古

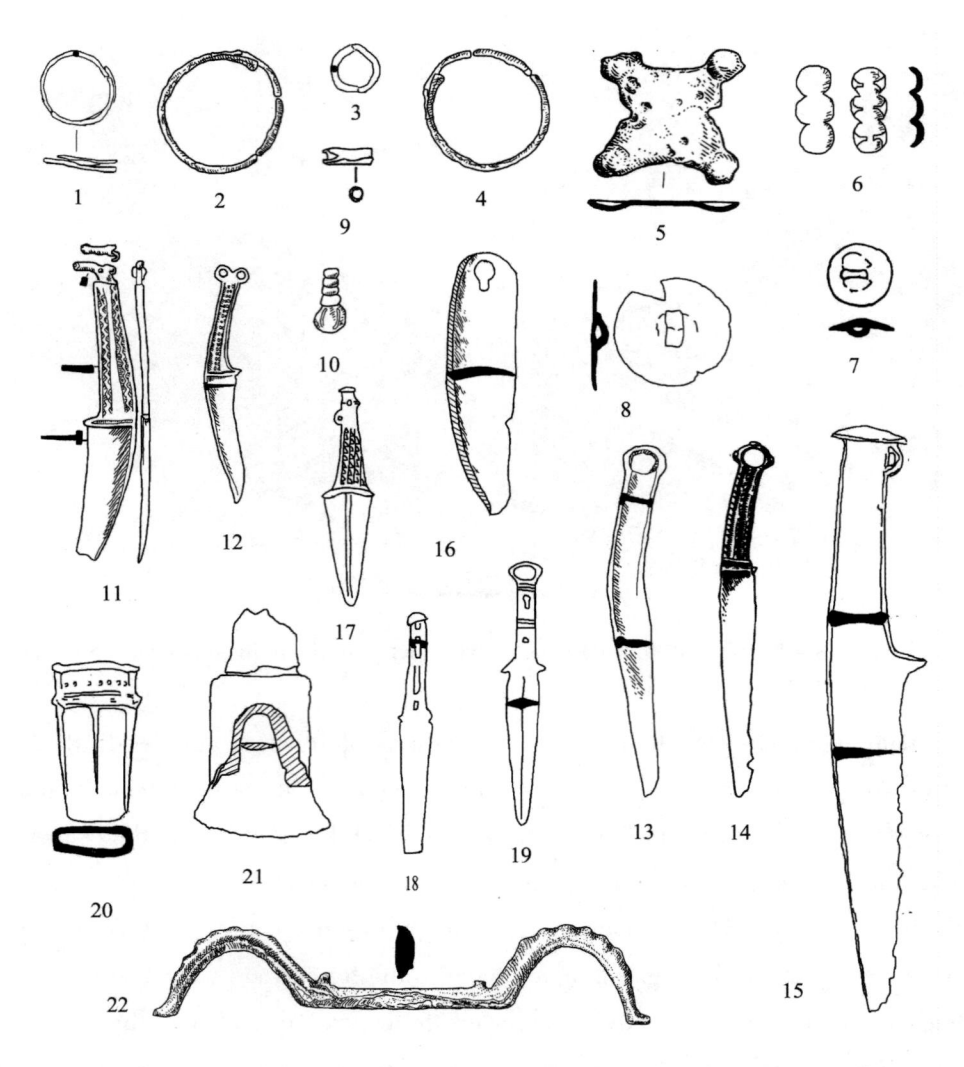

Fig. 3 – 8 – 2 Types of metal artifacts of Karasuk culture (No scale)

1, 3, 7, 8, 9, 15. Kiurgenner (extracted from Griaznov, M. P., M. N. Komakova, I. P. Lazaretov, A. V. Poliakov, and M. N. Pshenitsyna, *Mogil'nik Kiurgenner èpokhi pozdneĭ bronzy srednego Eniseia*, Sankt-Peterburg, 2010, Fig. 38:4; Fig. 32:21; Fig. 36:17, 15; Fig. 34:1); 2, 10. Malye Kopëny 3; 5, 22. Medvedka (extracted from Ziablin, L. P., *Karasuksiĭ Mogil'nik Malye Kopëny* 3, Moscow, 1977, Fig. 30:27, 22; Fig. 13:2, 1); 4. Sartak Hoard; 17. Karterevo; 18, 19. Krivaia; 20. Ladeĭĭskiĭ pol (Extracted from Chernykh, E. N., *Ancient Metallurgy in the USSR: The Early Metal Age*, translated by Sarah Wright, Cambridge, New York, Melbourne: Cambridge University Press, 1992, Fig. 91:15; Fig. 92:71; Fig. 92:3, 51; Fig. 91:9); 6. Karasuk; 21. Belaia River (extracted from Jettmar, K., The Karasuk Culture and Its South-eastern Affinities, *Bulletin of the Museum of Far Eastern Antiquities* 22, 1950, pl. 2:311, pl. 3:1); 11. Belaia River; 12. Uĭbat River; 13. Staroe kladbishche; 14. Uĭbat; 15. Karabilck (extracted from Chlenova, N. L. *Khronologiia Pamiatnikov Karasukskoĭ Èpokhi*, Moscow: Science Press, 1972, Table 9:3; Table 10:36; Table 7:3; Table 5:14; Table 10:53)

· 320 ·

The Transmission of the Karasuk Metallurgy to the Northern Zone of China

As a number of scholars have provided comprehensive overview of the Karasuk culture,[1] it suffices to make a few comments for the purpose of this paper. First, Karasuk inherits many features of the preceding cultures of Afanas'evo, Okunevo, and Andronovo but as usual makes many innovations.[2] The metal artifacts are typologically derived from Andronovo, including tools such as daggers, spearheads, and ornaments such as bracelets, finger-rings, earrings, beads, tubes, and plaques (Fig. 3-8-2: 1-3, 7-8, 18-20). But the curved back knives and beveled-socketed celts are the inventions of Karasuk.[3] Second, in the past ten years, two corpuses of radiocarbon dates, one 17 and the other 19, have converged upon the chronological range of 1400BC - 800BC.[4] This chronology, as Sophie Legrand suggests, represents the developed phase of Karasuk; that is to say, the rise of Karasuk could have been earlier.[5]

The Xinjiang-Gansu-Qinghai region

In Eastern Xinjiang, Gansu, and Qinghaiprovinces, Karasuk-type metal artifacts have been widely found (Fig. 3-8-1, Table 3-8-1). As they are

---

[1] Jettmar, K., The Karasuk Culture and Its South-eastern Affinities, *Bulletin of the Museum of Far Eastern Antiquities* 22, 1950, pp. 83-140; Novogorodova, È. A., *Tsentral'naia Aziia i Karasukskaia Problema*, Moscow, 1970; Legrand, S., The emergence of the Karasuk culture, *Antiquity* 80, 2006, pp. 843-879; Lazaretov, I. P., and A. V. Poliakov, Khronologiia i periodizatsiia kompleksov èpokhi pozdneĭ bronzy Iuzhnoĭ Sibiri, in A. B. Shamshin ed., *Ètnokul'turnye Protsessy v Verkhnem Priob'e i Sopredel'nykh Regionakh v Kontse Èpokhi Bronzy*, Barnaul: Kontsept, 2008, pp. 33-55.

[2] Jettmar, K., The Karasuk Culture and Its South-eastern Affinities, *Bulletin of the Museum of Far Eastern Antiquities* 22, 1950, p. 112; Grishin, Iu. S., *Metallicheskie Izdeliia Sibiri Èpokhi Èneolita i Bronzy*, Moscow: Science Press, 1971; Chernykh, E. N., *Ancient Metallurgy in the USSR: The Early Metal Age*, Translated by Sarah Wright. Cambridge, New York, Melbourne: Cambridge University Press, 1992; Legrand, S., The emergence of the Karasuk culture, *Antiquity* 80, 2006, pp. 843-879.

[3] Chlenova, N. L., *Pamiatniki Kontsa Èpokhi Bronzy v Zapadnoĭ Sibiri*, Moscow: Science, 1994, Fig. 2: 11-14.

[4] Gorsdorf, J., H. Pazinger, and A. Nagler, ^{14}C Dating of the Siberian Steppe Zone from Bronze Age to Scythian Time, in Scott, E. Marian, Andrey Yu. Alekseev, and Ganna Zaitseva eds., *Impact of the Environment on Human Migration in Eurasia*, Dordrecht, Boston, and London: Kluwer Academic Publishers, 2003, p. 88; Sviatko, S. V., J. P. Mallory, E. M. Murphy, A. V. Poliakov, P. J. Reimer, R. J. Schulting, New radiocarbon dates and a review of the chronology of prehistoric populations from the Minusinsk Basin, Southern Siberia, Russia, *Radiocarbon* 51/1, 2009, p. 253.

[5] Legrand, S., Karasuk metallurgy: Technological development and regional influence, in K. M. Linduff, ed., *Metallurgy in Ancient Eastern Eurasia from the Urals to the Yellow River*, Lewiston, Queenstone, and Lampeter: The Edwin Mellen Press, 2004, pp. 139-156.

chronologically, typologically, and compositionally close, they constitute one metallurgical region. At the cemetery of Tianshanbeilu in the Hami Oasis, about three thousand metal artifacts were found in the 1980s and 1990s. To date, however, the much-expected excavation report has not been published; consequently, a thorough typological study of the metal artifacts is not possible; only a number of examples have appeared in two publications.① Only six radiocarbon dates have been acquired, but after calibration they are either too early or too late for the cemetery.② Based on the ensemble of painted pottery, some scholars have considered the cemetery of Tianshanbeilu to be contemporaneous with the Siba culture, or even an offshoot of the latter.③

To the east, Karasuk-type metal artifacts have been found at the cemeteries of Ganguya, Donghuishan, Yingwoshu, and Huoshaogou of the Siba culture in the western Hexi Corridor,④ and the cemeteries of Dahezhuang, Xinzhuangping, Qinweijia, Zongri, Gamatai, Xinglin, and Mogou of the Qijia culture in the eastern Hexi Corridor and eastern Gansu and eastern Qinghai,⑤ (Fig. 3 – 8 – 1, Table 3 – 8 – 1) with the dividing line located approximately at the city of Wuwei. The chronology of Qijia has been loosely assigned to

---

① Lü, E., X. Chang, and B. Wang, Xinjiang Qingtong shidai kaogu wenhua qianlun, in B. Su, ed., *Su Bingqi yu Dangdai Zhongguo Kaoguxue* 3, Beijing: Kexue, 2001, pp. 172 – 19; Beijing Kejidaxue Yejin yu Cailiaoshi Yanjiusuo, Xinjiang Wenwu Kaogu Yanjiusuo, and Hamidiqu Wenwu Guanlisuo, Xinjiang Hami Tianshanbeilu mudi chutu tongqi de chubu yanjiu, *Wenwu* 6, 2001, pp. 79 – 89.

② Zhongguo Shehui Kexueyuan Kaogu Yanjiusuo Kaogu Keji Shiyan Yanjiu Zhongxin, Fangshexing tansu ceding niandai baogao (er, san), *Kaogu* 7, 1996, p. 70.

③ Li, S., Xibei yu Zhongyuan zaoqi yetongye de quyu tezheng ji jiaohu zuoyong, *Kaogu Xuebao* 3, 2005, p. 250; Jaang, L., Long-Distance Interactions as Reflected in the Earliest Chinese Bronze Mirrors, in Lothar von Falkenhausen ed., *The Lloyd Cotsen Study Collection of Chinese Bronze Mirrors*, Los Angeles: Cotsen Occasional Press and UCLA Cotsen Institute of Archaeology Press, Volume II, 2011, p. 40; Mei, J., Cultural Interaction between China and Central Asia during the Bronze Age, *Proceedings of the British Academy* 121, 2003, p. 19, p. 21; Liu, X., and W. Li, Shiqian qingtong zhilu yu zhongyuan wenming, *Xinjiang Shifan Daxue Xuebao* 35/2, 2014, pp. 81 – 82.

④ Beijingdaxue Kaogu Wenbo Xueyuan, and Gansusheng Wenwu Kaogu Yanjiusuo, Gansu Jiuquan Ganguya mudi de fajue yu shouhuo, *Kaogu Xuebao* 3, 2012, p. 366.

⑤ Xie, D., Qijia Wenhua, in The Institute of Archaeology, Chinese Academy of Social Sciences, ed., *Chinese Archaeology*, Volume of Xia and Shang, Beijing: China Social Sciences, 2003, p. 538.

The Transmission of the Karasuk Metallurgy to the Northern Zone of China

2190BC – 1630BC but that of Siba,① thanks to the multi-layered stratigraphy of the recently excavated settlement of Xichengyi, and a series of radiocarbon dates of the site, has been finely dated to 1880BC – 1530BC.②

This is by no means to suggest that the Karasuk-type metal artifacts were produced in the Minusinsk Basin and imported to the Xinjiang-Gansu-Qinghai region. For one reason, the metal artifacts in question display too many distinct morphological traits to warrant this idea. For another, many copper mines and metalworking settlements of the time have been discovered in the area of the Siba culture. ③The abovementioned settlement of Xichengyi, the only one that has been excavated, supplies ample evidence of metalworking. It was in fact the discovery of this evidence that has triggered the excavation project from 2010 through today. Apart from mud-brick buildings, a full gamut of materials, including ore, slag, furnace fragments, metal artifacts, has been found. ④Settlements like Xichengyi could have provided raw materials or ready products to those of the Siba and Qijia cultures, the latter of which are located in an area of little mineral resource.

Except for Donghuishan, the excavation materials of no site have been fully

---

① Xie, D., Qijia Wenhua, in The Institute of Archaeology, Chinese Academy of Social Sciences, ed., *Chinese Archaeology*, Volume of Xia and Shang, Beijing: China Social Sciences, 2003, p. 539; Jia, X., G. Dong, H. Li, K. Brunson, F. Chen, M. Ma, H. Wang, C. An, and K. Zhang, The development of agriculture and its impact on cultural expansion during the late Neolithic in the Western Loess Plateau, China, *The Holocene* 23/1, 2013, Table I; Dong, G., X. Jia, R. Elston, F. Chen, S. Li, L. Wang, L. Cai, and C. An, Spatial and temporal variety of prehistoric human settlement and its influencing factors in the upper Yellow River valley, Qinghai province, China, *Journal of Archaeological Science* 40, 2013, Table I.

② Zhang, X., L. Zhang, H. Wang, X. Lu, G. Chen, and P. Wang, Zhangyeshi Xichengyi yizhi de tanshisi cenian ji chubu fenxi, *Huaxia Kaogu* 4, 2015, pp. 38 – 45.

③ Li, Y., G. Chen, W. Qian, and H. Wang, Zhangye Xichengyi yizhi yezhu yiwu yanjiu, *Kaogu yu Wenwu* 2, 2015, p. 127.

④ Gansusheng Wenwu Kaogu Yanjiusuo, Beijing Kejidaxue Yejin yu Cailiaoshi Yanjiusuo, Zhongguo Shehui Kexueyuan Kaogu Yanjiusuo, and Xibei Daxue Wenhuayichan Xueyuan, Gansu Zhangyeshi Xichengyi yizhi, *Kaogu* 7, 2014, pp. 3 – 17; Gansusheng Wenwu Kaogu Yanjiusuo, Beijing Kejidaxue Yejin yu Cailiaoshi Yanjiusuo, Zhongguo Shehui Kexueyuan Kaogu Yanjiusuo, and Xibei Daxue Wenhuayichan Xueyuan, Gansu Zhangyeshi Xichengyi yizhi 2010nian fajue jianbao, *Kaogu* 10, 2015, pp. 66 – 84.

published, for that reason an accurate statistics of the metal artifacts from them is unavailable. From Table 1 one can tell that they are typologically rather diverse, especially at Tianshanbeilu, and the dominant types are body ornaments, including earrings/finger-rings, bracelets, plaques, and tubes, followed by knives and mirrors. The limit of space does not allow the author to discuss each type of artifact listed in Table 1; instead, he will only discuss the most pervasive types of knives, celts, earrings, bracelets, plaques, tubes, and mirrors, which serve most effectively the thesis of this paper.

Knives

Knives constitute a major category of metal artifacts of the Karasuk culture, and out of the diverse forms N. L. Chlenova classified fifteen types (Fig. 3 – 8 – 2: 11 – 15). [1]However, of the highly varied animal-pommeled knives of Karasuk, only one ram-pommeled knife was accidentally found in the Hami Oasis, [2] and it might have been an imported item from the Minusinsk Basin or a replica of a Karasuk prototype. [3]Of the other knives found in the Hami Oasis and Gansu and Qinghai provinces, some are fragments of the blades, whereas the intact ones and fragments of the hilts (32 in total) are all ring-pommeled and equipped with grooved handles. Four intact items have inward-curving blades (Fig. 3 – 8 – 3: 22), two outward-curving long blades (Fig. 3 – 8 – 3: 25), two long and straight blades (Fig. 3 – 8 – 3: 23), and the other three short and triangular blades, whose tips turn outward (Fig. 3 – 8 – 3: 15, 25). These knives, whose blades feature T-zoned section, correspond to Groups 11 and 12 of Chlenova. [4]

---

[1] Chlenova, N. L., *Khronologiia Pamiatnikov Karasukskoĭ Èpokhi*, Moscow: Science Press, 1972.

[2] Debaine-Francfort, C., Xinjiang and Northwestern China around 1000B. C., in R. Eichmann, and H. Parzinger, eds., *Migration und Kullturtransfer: Der Wandel vorder- und Zentralasiatischer Kulturen im Umbruch vom 2 – zum 1 Vorchristlichen Jahrtausend*, Bonn: Dr. Rudolf Habelt GmbH, 2001, p. 60.

[3] Chlenova, N. L., *Khronologiia Pamiatnikov Karasukskoĭ Èpokhi*, Moscow: Science Press, 1972, Table 9: 3.

[4] Chlenova, N. L., *Khronologiia Pamiatnikov Karasukskoĭ Èpokhi*, Moscow: Science Press, 1972, Table 6.

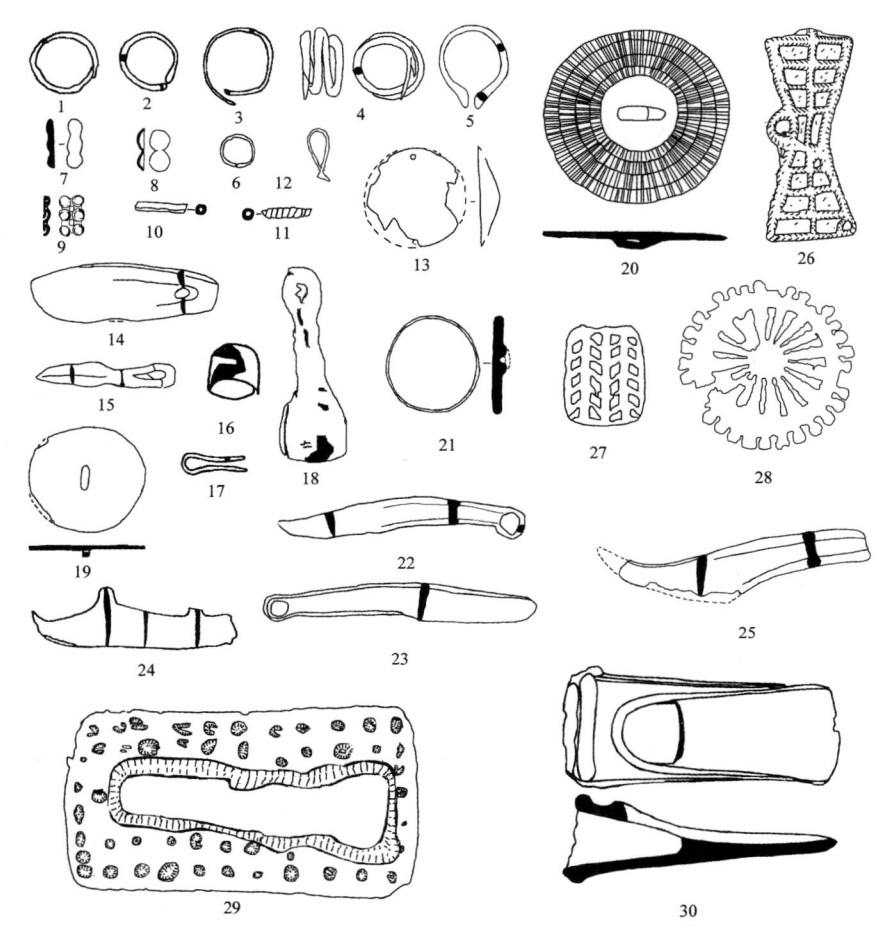

Fig. 3 – 8 – 3 Karasuk-type metal artifacts from the Xinjiang-Gansu-Qinghai zone (No scale)

1, 2, 3, 10, 11, 15, 17, 24, 26, 27, 31, Tianshanbeilu (extracted from Beijing Kejidaxue Yejin yu Cailiaoshi Yanjiusuo, Xinjiang Wenwu Kaogu Yanjiusuo, and Hamidiqu Wenwu Guanlisuo, Xinjiang Hami Tianshanbeilu mudi chutu tongqi de chubu yanjiu, *Wenwu* 6, 2001, Fig. 1: 15, 14, 13, 11, 10, 3, 8, 5, 21, 23, 7); 7, 8, 13, 14, 19, 20, 23, 29, Tianshanbeilu (extracted from Lü, E., X. Chang, and B. Wang, Xinjiang Qingtong shidai kaogu wenhua qianlun, in B. Su, ed., *Su Bingqi yu Dangdai Zhongguo Kaoguxue*, Beijing: Kexue, 2001, Fig. 15: 4, Fig. 16: 4, Fig. 15: 3, Fig. 18: 5, Fig. 17: 1, Fig. 18: 1, Fig. 17: 7, Fig. 15: 1); 18, 26, 28, Tianshanbeilu (redrawn from Hami Bowuguan, *Hami Wenwu Jingcui*, Beijing: Kexue, 2013, pp. 41, 96, 106); 4, 5, 9, 21, 22, 25, 30, Ganguya (extracted from Beijingdaxue Kaogu Wenbo Xueyuan, and Gansusheng Wenwu Kaogu Yanjiusuo, Gansu Jiuquan Ganguya mudi de fajue yu shouhuo, *Kaogu Xuebao* 3, 2012, Fig. 15: 9, 6, 11, 5, 2, 3, 1); 6, 12, 16, Mogou (redrawn from Xu, J., Gan-Qing diqu xinhuo zaoqi tongqi ji yetong yiwu de fenxi yanjiu, MA degree thesis, University of Science and Technology Beijing, 2009, Fig. 3 – 6: 10, 12, 1).

Celts

Celt is not a regular component of the paraphernalia that accompanies the deceased of the Karasuk culture to the afterworld; it only occasionally occurs in tombs. ①They are rectangular or elliptical at the mouth, and sometimes equipped with double loops and ribs at the rims. ②Celts figure prominently among the Seĭma-Turbino Phenomenon, counting 115 pieces out of the total 442 metal artifacts, but they markedly differ from the Karasuk ones, featuring elongated forms and sometimes the motif of rhombi. ③Only four items have been published from the Xinjiang-Gansu-Qinghai region. Two items from Xinglin in Minxian and Mogou in Lintan county are similar to Karasuk ones in possessing complete sockets and single loops for suspension. The other two from Tianshanbeilu and Ganguya have their rims reinforced with ribs, sockets beveled, and their internal walls of the sockets carved for securing the hafts (Fig. 3 – 8 – 3: 30). Their Karasuk counterparts are known only from stray finds. ④Differences in both types of celts are not immediately perceptible.

Earrings/finger-rings/bracelets

Earrings, finger-rings, and bracelets (26 in total) have often been uncovered in intact tombs of Karasuk (Fig. 3 – 8 – 2: 1 – 3). They are also common components of the assemblages of Andronovo tombs, but they differ from Karasuk artifacts in various ways. The Andronovo ornaments are mostly

---

① Novgorodova, È. A., *Tsentral'naia Aziia i Karasukskaia Problema*, Moscow, 1970, p. 100; Chlenova, N. L., *Khronologiia Pamiatnikov Karasukskoĭ Èpokhi*, Moscow: Science Press, 1972, Table 19: 1, 13.

② Chlenova, N. L., *Khronologiia Pamiatnikov Karasukskoĭ Èpokhi*, Moscow: Science Press, 1972, Table 19: 1, 13, 38, 43; Fig. 2: 20, 21.

③ Chernykh, E. N. and Kuz'minykh, S. N., *Drevniaia Metallurgiia Severnoĭ Evrasiia* (in Russian), Moscow: Science, 1989, Figs. 3 – 23.

④ Jettmar, K., The Karasuk Culture and Its South-eastern Affinities, *Bulletin of the Museum of Far Eastern Antiquities* 22, 1950, pl. 3: 1; Fig. 2: 21.

coiled out of thin foil and topped with spiral cones, which are absent among Karasuk artifacts, with a few items made of solid wires. ①The Karasuk ones are almost unanimously made of simple solid wires, which are often coiled for several rounds. ②The counterparts of the Karasuk ornaments have been widely found at Tianshanbeilu, Donghuishan, Ganguya, Yingwoshu, Xinzhuangping, Mogou, Gamatai,③ and Zongri (Fig. 3 - 8 - 3: 1 - 6, 12). Only two from Ganguya and Zongri are rendered in the same manner (Fig. 3 - 8 - 3: 4); the others vary from the Karasuk prototypes in forming single circles (Fig. 3 - 8 - 3: 1 - 3, 6). Their ends are often tapering or flattened into the shape of fan (Fig. 3 - 8 - 3: 5). Two earrings from Ganguya and Mougou, each of which has one tapering and one trumpet-like end (Fig. 3 - 8 - 3: 12), resemble the Andronovo prototypes, but they differ in having overly long pins.

Plaques

Plaques have been abundantly found in intact tombs of Karasuk and occur in several forms (Fig. 3 - 8 - 2: 5 - 8). Taking a convex boss as one unit, we encounter the varieties of single-, double-, triple-, four- (square), and six-unit (round) plaques. ④Their counterparts (43 in total) at Tianshanbeilu and several cemeteries of Siba and Qijia cultures are likewise rather diverse, comprised of single-, double-, triple-, and six-unit ones (Fig. 3 - 8 - 3: 7 - 9). While most of them closely resemble the Karasuk prototypes, the

---

① Kuz'mina, E. E., *Metallicheskie Izdeliia Èneolita i Bronzovogo Veka v Sredneĭ Azii*, Moscow: Nauka, Plate XIV, 1966; Avanesova, N. A., *Kul'tura Pastusheskikh Plemen Èpokhi Bronzy Aziatskoĭ Chasti SSSR*, Tashkent: Press of "FAN" UzSSR, 1991, Figs. 44 - 47; Chernykh, E. N., *Ancient Metallurgy in the USSR: The Early Metal Age*, translated by Sarah Wright, Cambridge, New York, Melbourne: Cambridge University Press, 1992, Fig. 71.

② i. e. Ziablin, L. P., *Karasuksiĭ Mogil'nik Malye Kopëny* 3, Moscow, 1977, Fig. 9: 12 - 14, Fig. 22: 5 - 17.

③ Xu, J., Gan-Qing diqu xinhuo zaoqi tongqi ji yetong yiwu de fenxi yanjiu, MA degree thesis, University of Science and Technology Beijing, 2009, Fig. 3 - 4: 2.

④ i. e. Chlenova, N. L., *Khronologiia Pamiatnikov Karasukskoĭ Èpokhi*, Moscow: Science Press, 1972, Table 17: 15, 33, 12, 2, 7.

six-unit piece is distinct in being rectangular. In addition, there are thin round pieces with a pair of holes symmetrically placed at either end (Fig. 3 - 8 - 3: 13). Unlike buttons, they depend on the two pairs of holes rather than loops for securing.

Tubes/Spiral tubes

Tubes, which are rolled out of sheets, and less so spiral tubes, which are rolled out of narrow tapes, have been found in Karasuk tombs (Fig. 3 - 8 - 2: 9).[1] According to Jettmar, they are components of necklaces.[2] The tubes appear already in Andronovo tombs, but not the spiral-tubes. In the Xinjiang-Gansu-Qinghai region, they (5 in total) have only been reported from Tianshanbeilu (Fig. 3 - 8 - 3: 10 - 11). The rough drawings, however, do not allow us to distinguish them from their Karasuk counterparts.

Mirrors

Mirror occurs rarely in Andronovo tombs, but often in Karasuk tombs. Several Karasuk mirrors are displayed in the Minusinsk City Museum, and sometimes known from excavation materials.[3] Presumably derived from round plaques, they generally take the form of plain disc with a loop on the back. Four mirrors have been reported from Tianshanbeilu, Gamatai, and Ganguya. Two are plain, and the other two are decorated with concentric rings of sunrays or hatched triangles (Fig. 3 - 8 - 3: 19 - 21). Without antecedent among Karasuk metals, the latter variant is probably a local innovation.

---

[1] i.e. Griaznov, M. P., M. N. Komarova, and M. N. Pshenitsyna, Materialy Mogil'nik Kiurgenner I i II, in M. P. Griaznov, M. N. Komarova, I. P. Lazaretov, A. V. Poliakov, and M. N. Pshenitsyna eds., *Mogil'nik Kiurgenner Èpokhi Pozdneĭ Bronzy Srednego Eniseia*, Sankt-Peterburg, 2010, Fig. 37: 25, 7.

[2] Jettmar, K., The Karasuk Culture and Its South-eastern Affinities, *Bulletin of the Museum of Far Eastern Antiquities* 22, 1950, p. 94.

[3] i.e. Griaznov, M. P., M. N. Komarova, and M. N. Pshenitsyna, Materialy Mogil'nik Kiurgenner I i II, in M. P. Griaznov, M. N. Komarova, I. P. Lazaretov, A. V. Poliakov, and M. N. Pshenitsyna eds., *Mogil'nik Kiurgenner Èpokhi Pozdneĭ Bronzy Srednego Eniseia*, Sankt-Peterburg, 2010, Fig. 66: 15; Fig. 2: 8.

The Transmission of the Karasuk Metallurgy to the Northern Zone of China

Among the other types of artifacts, jingle-bells (Fig. 3 - 8 - 3: 18), armlets (Fig. 3 - 8 - 3: 16), and sickles (Fig. 3 - 8 - 3: 14), also extrapolate the theme of adoption and re-invention. There are, however, a number of types that are exclusive to either the Minusinsk Basin or the Xinjiang-Gansu-Qinghai region. To the former are one bracelet of Karasuk, which is curved out of a substantial band and decorated with knobs and incised lines, and pediform pendants (Fig. 3 - 8 - 2: 4), the most diagnostic artifact of Karasuk.① To the Xinjiang-Gansu-Qinghai region are a torque from the cemetery of Mogou, which is a crescent-shaped band with a hole at each end,② and a knife, which has two humps from the cemetery of Tianshanbeilu.③ Rectangular plaques, which are characterized by bulging midribs, two holes, and rows of punched dots, and butterfly plaques, which are distinguished by butterfly-like wings and a loop for suspension, are prevalent at Tianshanbeilu; so are openwork plaques. ④

At this point, the keen readers may have found that my connection of the above-mentioned metal artifacts to Karasuk is at variance with the mainstream scholarship. In fact, only Gideon Shelach-Lavi has noticed the Karasuk-type artifacts in the Xinjiang-Gansu-Qinghai region, but he did not take the task of thoroughly exploring the subject.⑤ Other scholars have customarily talked about

---

① Novgorodova, È. A., *Tsentral'naia Aziia i Karasukskaia Problema*, Moscow, 1970, p. 144; Griaznov, M. P., M. N. Komarova, and M. N. Pshenitsyna, Materialy Mogil'nik Kiurgenner I i II, in M. P. Griaznov, M. N. Komarova, I. P. Lazaretov, A. V. Poliakov, and M. N. Pshenitsyna eds., *Mogil'nik Kiurgenner Èpokhi Pozdneĭ Bronzy Srednego Eniseia*, Sankt-Peterburg, 2010, Fig. 65: 13.

② Xu, J., Gan-Qing diqu xinhuo zaoqi tongqi ji yetong yiwu de fenxi yanjiu, MA degree thesis, University of Science and Technology Beijing, 2009, Fig. 3 - 6: 8.

③ Beijing Kejidaxue Yejin yu Cailiaoshi Yanjiusuo, Xinjiang Wenwu Kaogu Yanjiusuo, and Hamidiqu Wenwu Guanlisuo, Xinjiang Hami Tianshanbeilu mudi chutu tongqi de chubu yanjiu, *Wenwu* 6, 2001, Fig. 1: 5, Fig. 3: 24.

④ Beijing Kejidaxue Yejin yu Cailiaoshi Yanjiusuo, Xinjiang Wenwu Kaogu Yanjiusuo, and Hamidiqu Wenwu Guanlisuo, Xinjiang Hami Tianshanbeilu mudi chutu tongqi de chubu yanjiu, *Wenwu* 6, 2001, Fig. 1: 24, 23, 21, Fig. 3: 26, 27, 29.

⑤ Shelach-Lavi, G., Steppe land interaction and their effects on Chinese cultures during the second and early first millennia BCE, in R. Amitai and M. Biran, eds., *Nomads as Agents of Cultural Change*, University of Hawaii Press, 2015, p. 17.

◇❖◇ **第三部分 中国西北和欧亚草原考古**

the influence of Andronovo and the Seǐma-Turbino Phenomenon from Eastern Kazakhstan. ①This thesis is partly justified because several sites of the Andronovo culture have been discovered in Northwestern and Southwestern Xinjiang. But beyond these areas no site of the Andronovo type has been found. The authors took the tin bronze and arsenic copper among the Tianshanbeilu, Siba and Qijia metals as important evidence, but such metal types are not exclusive to Andronovo; they are actually present, quite commonly, in artifacts of the Karasuk culture. ②

---

① Fiztgerald-Huber, L. G., Qijia and Erlitou: The Question of Early Contacts with Distant Cultures, *Early China* 20, 1995, pp. 40 – 52; Mei, J., *Copper and Bronze Metallurgy in Late Prehistoric Xinjiang*, Oxford: Archaeopress, 2000, p. 74; Mei, J., Cultural Interaction between China and Central Asia during the Bronze Age, *Proceedings of the British Academy* 121, 2003, p. 38; Mei, J., Qijia and Seǐma-Turbino: The question of early contacts between Northwest China and the Eurasian steppe, *Bulletin of the Museum of Far Eastern Antiquities* 75, 2003, p. 19; Kuz'mina, E. E., Historical perspectives on the Andronovo and metal use in Eastern Asia, in K. M. Linduff ed., *Metallurgy in Ancient Eastern Eurasia from the Urals to the Yellow River*, Lewiston, Queenstone, and Lampeter: The Edwin Mellen Press, 2004, pp. 62 – 76; Li, S., Xibei yu Zhongyuan zaoqi yetongye de quyu tezheng ji jiaohu zuoyong, *Kaogu Xuebao* 3, 2005, p. 265; Linduff, K. M., An archaeological overview, in E. C. Bunker, ed., *Ancient Bronzes of the Eastern Eurasian Steppes from the Arthur M. Sackler Collections*, New York: The Arthur M. Sackler Foundation, 1997, p. 20; Linduff, K. M., The emergence and demise of bronze-producing cultures outside the Central Plain of China, in V. H. Mair, ed., *The Bronze Age and Early Iron Age Peoples of Eastern Central Asia*, Washington: Institute for the Study of Man, Vol. 2, p. 627; Linduff, K. M., Why have Siberian artefacts been excavated within ancient Chinese dynastic borders? in Adam Smith, David Peterson, and L. M. Popova eds., *Beyond the Steppe and the Sown: Integrating Local and Global Visions*, Leiden, Boston, Köln: Brill, 2002, p. 360; Linduff, K. M., What's mine is yours: the transmission of metallurgical technology in Eastern Eurasia and East Asia, in S. Srinivasan, S. Ranganathan, and A. Giumlia-Mair, eds., *Metals and Civilizations*, Banglaore: National Institute of Advanced Studies, 2015, p. 16; Linduff, K., and J. Mei, Metallurgy in Ancient Eastern Asia: Retrospect and Prospects, *Journal of World Prehistory* 22/3, 2009, p. 275; Liu, X., and W. Li, Shiqian qingtong zhilu yu zhongyuan wenming, *Xinjiang Shifan Daxue Xuebao* 35/2, 2014, pp. 81 – 82.

② Naumov, D. V., Proizvodstvo i obrabotka Karasukskikh nozheǐ, in N. L. Chlenova, *Khronologiia Pamiatnikov Karasukskoǐ Èpokhi*, Moscow: Science Press, 1972, pp. 140 – 157; Piatkin, B. N., Nekotorye voprosy metallurgii èpokhi bronzy iuzhnoǐ sibiri, *Arkheologiia Iuzhnoǐ Sibiri*, Kemerovo, Issue 9, 1977, pp. 22 – 33; Khavrin, S. V., Metall èpokhi pozdneǐ bronzy nizhnetěǐskoǐ gruppy pamiatnikov (Torgazhak-Arban-Fedorov ulus), in S. N. Astakhov ed., *Evraziia Skvoz Veka*, Sankt-Peterburg, 2001, pp. 117 – 125.

The Transmission of the Karasuk Metallurgy to the Northern Zone of China

The influence of the Andronovo metallurgy is nevertheless manifest in a few artifacts of Tianshanbeilu, Siba, and Qijia cultures. One dagger from Tianshanbeilu (Fig. 3 - 8 - 3: 31), which is analogous to an item found at Myrzhik in Central Kazakhstan,[1] and the trumpet-shaped earrings from Xiaohe,[2] Ganguya,[3] and Mogou (Fig. 3 - 8 - 3: 12) can be cited as testimonies. But beyond them few analogues can be found; the majority of types of metal artifacts belong to the Karasuk-type. As commented above, in metallurgy Karasuk inherits many elements from Andronovo but makes many innovations of its own. One may say that the Andronovo legacies have come to Eastern Xinjang, Gansu, and Qinghai through the Karasuk metallurgy. The Seĭma-Turbino phenomenon is a complicated conceptual entity in Eurasian archaeology; it suffices to remark that its diagnostic artifacts are spearheads and celts, not plaques, tubes, and ring-pommeled knives that characterize the Tianshanbeilu, Siba, and Qijia ensembles. And finally, we shall not forget that spearheads and celts are not exclusive to Seĭma-Turbino, they are also a part of the Karasuk repertoire. While some items of the two are similar, the other are quite different: the celts of Karasuk, for instance, often have their rims strengthened with raised ribs or their sockets beveled and internal walls carved.

The Ordos-Yanshan region

The Karasuk-type metal artifacts found in Ordos-Yanshan region, quite considerable in quantity, have been grouped under the "Ordos Style,"[4] or the

---

[1] Kadyrbaev, M. K., and Zh. Kurmankulov, *Kul'tura Drevnikh Skotovodov i Metallurgov Sary-Arki*, Alma-Ata: Gylym, 1992, Fig. 30.

[2] Mei, J., Y. Ling, K. Chen, A. Yidlisi, W. Li, and X. Hu, Xiaohe mudi chutu bufen jinshuqi de chubu fenxi, *Xiyu Yanjiu* 2, 2013, Fig. 4.

[3] Li, S., and T. Shui, Siba wenhua tongqi yanjiu, *Wenwu* 3, 2000, Fig. 2: 13.

[4] Tian, G., and S. Guo eds., *Eerduosishi Qingtongqi*, Beijing: Wenwu, 1986, p. 195; Tian, G., and S. Guo eds., Eerduosishi qingtongqi de yuanyuan, *Kaogu Xuebao* 3, 1988, pp. 257 - 275.

◇❖◇ 第三部分 中国西北和欧亚草原考古

"Northern Style."① A few scholars have linked the ancient metallurgy of this region with, some even attributed its origin to, the Xinjiang-Gansur-Qinghai region,② although others argued for a separate route of transmission.③ In the Ordos Plateau, the earliest datable items have been discovered at Zhukaigou in Yijinhuoluo Banner, the type site of the synonymous culture. These are a few finger-rings, armlets, bracelets, and one spiral tube of Period I, as well as a dagger and a knife of Period II. According to the chronology established by the excavators, they roughly date to 1900BC – 1700BC and 1500BC – 1200BC respectively.④ A good number of Karasuk-type metal artifacts have also been discovered in tombs along the 300km-long valley of the Yellow River (Fig. 3 – 8 – 1, Table 3 – 8 – 2). Based on the Central Plain style bronze vessels accompanying them, they have been dated to the Anyang Shang period

---

① Lin, Y., Bronzes of the Shang and of the Northern Zone, in K. C. Chang, ed., *Studies of Shang Archaeology*, New Haven and London: Yale University Press, 1986, pp. 237 – 273; Yuesitu, W., Yin zhi Zhouchu de beifang qingtongqi, *Kaogu Xuebao* 2, 1985, pp. 135 – 156; Yuesitu, W., Lun qingtongshidai changcheng didai yu ouya caoyuan xianglin diqu de wenhua lianxi, in The Institute of Archaeology, Chinese Academy of Social Sciences ed., *Ershiyi Shiji de Zhongguo Kaoguxue—Qingzhu Tong Zhuchen Xiansheng Bashiwu Huadan Xueshu Wenji*, Beijing: Wenwu, 2006, pp. 558 – 586; Li, B., Cong Lingshi Jinjie Shangmu de faxian kan Jin-Shaan gaoyuan qingtong wenhua de guishu, *Beijing Daxue Xuebao* 2, 1988, p. 23; Di Cosmo, N., The Northern Frontier in Pre-Imperial China, in M. Loewe & E. L. Shaughnessy, eds., *The Cambridge History of Ancient China*, New York: Cambridge University Press, 1999, pp. 896, 906; Yang, J., Yanshan nanbei Shang-Zhou zhiji qingtongqi yicun de fenqun yanjiu, in J. Yang, and G. Jiang, eds., *Gongyuanqian Erqianji de Jin-Shaan Gaoyuan yu Yanshan Nanbei*, Beijing: Kexue, 2008, p. 191.

② Bai, Y., Zhongguo de zaoqi tongqi yu qingtongqi de qiyuan, *Dongnan Wenhua* 7, 2002, p. 33; Mei, J., Zhongguo zaoqi yejinshu yanjiu de xinjinzhan, *Keji Kaogu* 3, 2011, p. 149; Mei, J., P. Wang, K. Chen, L. Wang, Y. Wang, and Y. Liu, Archaeometallurgical studies in China: some recent developments and challenging issues, *Journal of Archaeological Science* 56, 2015, p. 222.

③ Shelach-Lavi, G., Steppe Land Interaction and Their Effects on Chinese cultures during the Second and Early First Millennia BCE, in R. Amitai and M. Biran, eds., *Nomads as Agents of Cultural Change*, University of Hawaii Press, 2015, p. 252; Shelach-Lavi, G., Steppe Land Interaction and Their Effects on Chinese cultures during the Second and Early First Millennia BCE, in R. Amitai and M. Biran, eds., *Nomads as Agents of Cultural Change*, University of Hawaii Press, 2015, p. 21; Linduff, K., What's mine is yours: the transmission of metallurgical technology in Eastern Eurasia and East Asia, in S. Srinivasan, S. Ranganathan, and A. Giumlia-Mair, eds., *Metals and Civilizations*, Banglaore: National Institute of Advanced Studies, 2015, p. 20.

④ Tian, G., and J. Han, Zhukaigou wenhua yanjiu, *Kaoguxue Yanjiu*, Beijing: Kexue, 2003, p. 236.

(1300BC – 1046BC), [1] which postdate the Zhukaigou culture.

To the north and south of the Yanshan Mountain, Karasuk-type metals have been discovered in tombs, caches, and even settlements of the Lower Xiajiadian, Weiyingzi, Datuotou, and Upper Zhangjiayuan cultures. [2]The chronology of the Lower Xiajiadian is established to be 2000BC – 1200BC on the basis of forty radiocarbon dates. [3]Those of Datuotou, Weiyingzi, and Upper Zhangjiayuan, judged by Shang- and Zhou-style ritual bronzes found together with them, generally fall within the range of Shang and Western Zhou, or 1530BC – 1300BC, 1300BC – 1045BC, 1046BC – 771BC. [4]Unlike the Ordos Plateau, where isolated tombs and caches are located, several metal-yielding cemeteries and settlements have been excavated extensively in this region.

Unlike Xinjiang-Gansu-Qinghai, the Ordos-Yanshan region is a contact area between the Central Plain to the south and the Eurasian steppe to the north; Karasuk-type metal artifacts have often been found together with Shang and Western Zhou style ritual vessels, which provide more accurate chronological indicators. [5]Also unlike Xinjiang-Gansu-Qinghai, the Ordos-Yanshan region witnesses the vigorous diversification of weapons and tools at the expense of body

---

[1] Li, B., Cong Lingshi Jinjie Shangmu de faxian kan Jin-Shaan gaoyuan qingtong wenhua de guishu, *Beijing Daxue Xuebao* 2, 1988, p. 20; Wo, H., Jin-Shaan gaoyuan Shang-Zhou shiqi qingtongqi fenqun yanjiu, in J. Yang, and G. Jiang eds., *Gongyuanqian Erqianji de Jin-Shaan Gaoyuan yu Yanshan Nanbei*, Beijing: Kexue, 2008, pp. 56 – 67; Jiang, G., Nanliu Huanghe liang'an chutu qingtongqi de niandai yu zuhe yanjiu, in J. Yang and G. Jiang eds., *Gongyuanqian Erqianji de Jin-Shaan Gaoyuan yu Yanshan Nanbei*, Beijing: Kexue, 2008, p. 75; Cao, W., *Shanbei Chutu Qingtongqi*, Chengdu: Bashu Shushe, 2009, p. 38.

[2] Wang, W., Yanshan nanbei diqu, in The Institute of Archaeology, Chinese Academy of Social Sciences ed., *Chinese Archaeology*, Volume of Xia and Shang, Beijing: China Social Sciences Press, 2003, Fig. 1, Table 2.

[3] Shelach, G., R. D. Drennan, and C. E. Peterson, Absolute Dating, in Chifeng International Collaborative Archaeological Research Project ed., *Settlement Patterns in the Chifeng Region*, Pittsburg: University of Pittsburgh Center for Comparative Archaeology, 2011, pp. 19 – 22.

[4] Dong, X., Weiyingzi wenhua chubu yanjiu, *Kaogu Xuebao* 1, 2000, p. 12; Wang, W., Yanshan nanbei diqu, in The Institute of Archaeology, Chinese Academy of Social Sciences ed., *Chinese Archaeology*, Volume of Xia and Shang, Beijing: China Social Sciences Press, 2003, pp. 606, 611, 617; Dou, H., and D. Feng, Cong Zhenjiangying leixing kan xizhou wenhua zai Taihangshan donglu beiduan de fazhan, *Caoyuan Wenwu* 1, 2013, p. 53.

[5] Li, B., Cong Lingshi Jinjie Shangmu de faxian kan Jin-Shaan gaoyuan qingtong wenhua de guishu, *Beijing Daxue Xuebao* 2, 1988, p. 20; Wo, H., Jin-Shaan gaoyuan Shang-Zhou shiqi qingtongqi fenqun yanjiu, in J. Yang, and G. Jiang eds., *Gongyuanqian Erqianji de Jin-Shaan Gaoyuan yu Yanshan Nanbei*, Beijing: Kexue, 2008, pp. 56 – 67.

ornaments (Table 2). In addition, the bow-shaped objects that are pervasive here are absent in the Xinjiang-Gansu-Qinghai region. For the sake of space, we may confine our analysis to knives, daggers, spearheads, shaft-hole axes, bow-shaped objects, earrings/finger-rings/ bracelets, tubes, and plaques.

But like Xinjiang-Gansu-Qinghai, the metal artifacts could have been produced in the Ordos-Yanshan region. A few stone molds, which the excavators date to 1900BC – 1800BC, have been recently uncovered at the magnificent walled settlement of Shimao in the Ordos Plateau. It is noticeable, however, that the intended knife of one mold, also ring-pommeled, is of the Karasuk-type.[1] Ancient mines of copper and tin as well as smelting settlements of the Lower Xiajiadian culture have been profusely discovered.[2] Although no metalworking settlements have been discovered to date, the culture is not short of mineral resource for metal production.

Knives

Knives (51 in total) found in this region, most of which date to 1300BC – 771BC, are typologically diverse. The predominant type is the ring-pommeled knives, which count up to 41. They all have a long blade, but otherwise they differ significantly: some have real ring-pommels, whereas others have false ones in the form of perforation. An early item from Zhukaigou has a grooved handle and a sideway tang in place of guard (Fig. 3 – 8 – 4: 11). This type, as commented above, occurs in the Minusinsk Basin (Fig. 3 – 8 – 2: 13) and the Xinjiang-Gansur-Qinghai region. The ones from Houlanjiagou and Erlangpo have triangular rings and three butts (Fig. 3 – 8 – 4: 15), and formally resemble two items from the Minusinsk Basin.[3] The two items from Gaohong are

---

[1] Shao, J., and Z. Sun, Cong "xunnumu" kan Qijia yu Shimao, presentation at the International Forum on the Qijia Culture and the Huaxia Civilization, Guanghe County, Gansu Province, 14 – 15 October, 2016.

[2] Li, Y., Zhongyuan yu beifang diqu zaoqi qingtong chanye geju de chubu tansuo. *Zhongguo Wenwubao*, 28 February 2014, Page 5.

[3] Griaznov, M. P., M. N. Komarova, I. P. Lazaretov, A. V. Poliakov, and M. N. Pshenitsyna eds., *Mogil'nik Kiurgenner Èpokhi Pozdneĭ Bronzy Srednego Eniseia*, Sankt-Peterburg, 2010, Fig. 64: 8, 12; Fig. 65: 9; Fig. 2: 14.

both equipped with double rings and thickened backs (Fig. 3 – 8 – 4: 14). Their analogues are also found among Karasuk metals. ①

Among the Karasuk knives, there are many other varieties of pommels: ram head, sheep, elk, ibex, and mushroom. ②Only the ram, eagle, and mushroom-pommels are present among the Ordos-Yanshan metals. Of the mushroom-pommeled type, only one item has been found at Fengjia; it is an elaborate item, and the hilt is decorated with two parallel feather bands. ③Of the ram-pommeled knives there are seven items. The one from Chaodaogou is exquisitely crafted, with an exaggerated and loop-shaped ring and two horns; the eye-sockets and muzzle-sockets are all realistically rendered, and are now void but possibly filled with turquoise beads in the time of use (Fig. 3 – 8 – 4: 18). The hilt is decorated with two zones of raised butts and two rows of carved zigzag motifs at the borders; the blade and guard are likewise equipped with raised T-shaped backs. ④It is comparable with the Karasuk metals. ⑤A unique item from Xiaohenan has two naturalistically rendered horns and a broad and flat blade. ⑥It is analogous to the item from Wushijiazi, which differs only in that the horns are coiled and relatively abstract. ⑦The latter two, which find no parallel among the Karasuk metals, seem to be local innovations.

---

① Chlenova, N. L., *Khronologiia Pamiatnikov Karasukskoĭ Èpokhi*, Moscow: Science Press, 1972, Plate 10: 35 – 40; Fig. 2: 12.

② Chlenova, N. L., *Khronologiia Pamiatnikov Karasukskoĭ Èpokhi*, Moscow: Science Press, 1972, Plate 9: 1 – 10; Plate 19; Fig. 2: 11, 13, 15.

③ Wang, Y., G. Wang, and F. Li, Suizhong Fenjia faxian shangdai jiaocang tongqi, *Liaohai Wenwu Xuekan* 1, 1996, Fig. 3: 1; Fig. 4: 12.

④ Hebeisheng Wenhuaju Wenwu Gongzuodui, Hebei Qinglongxian Chaodaogou faxian yipi qingtongqi, *Kaogu* 12, 1962, Pl. 5: 3.

⑤ Chlenova, N. L., *Khronologiia Pamiatnikov Karasukskoĭ Èpokhi*, Moscow: Science Press, 1972, Fig. 2: 11.

⑥ Wang, F., Hebei Xinglongxian faxian Shang-Zhou qingtongqi jiaocang, *Wenwu* 11, 1990, pp. 57 – 58.

⑦ Shao, G., Neimenggu Aohanqi faxian de qingtongqi ji youguan yiwu, *Beifang Wenwu* 1, 1993, Fig. 49: 4.

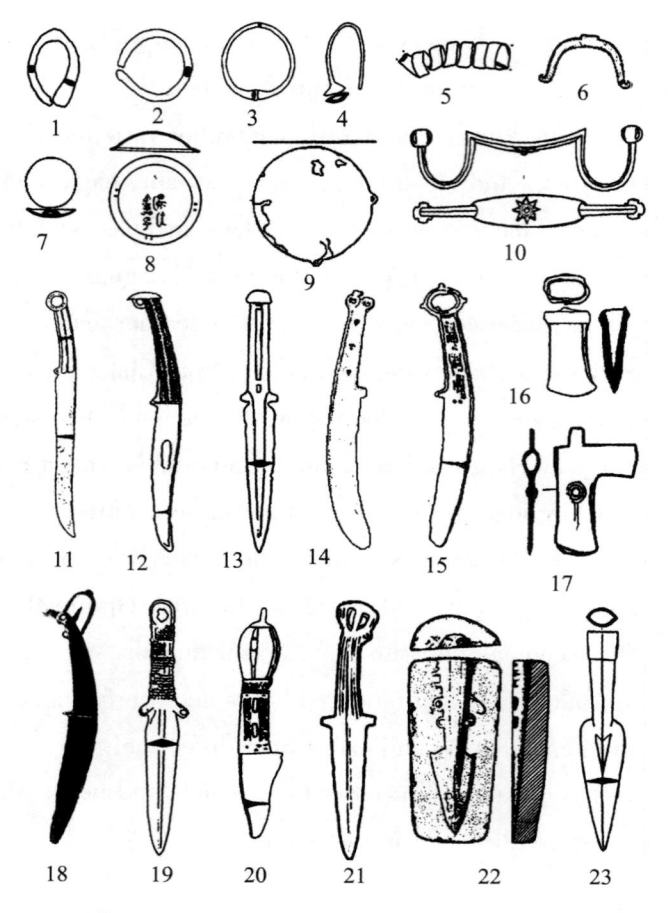

Fig. 3 – 8 – 4　Karasuk-type metal artifacts from the Ordos-Yanshan zone

1, 3, Dadianzi (Extracted from Zhongguo Shehui Kexueyuan Kaogu Yanjiusuo, *Dadianzi-Xiajiadian Xiaceng Wenhua Yizhi yu Mudi Fajue Bagao*, Beijing: Kexue, 1996, Fig. 86: 6); 2, 5, 11, 19, Zhukaigou (extracted from Neimenggu Wenwu Kaogu Yanjiusuo, and Eerduosi Bowuguan, *Zhukaigou-Qingtong shidai zaoqi yizhi fajue baogao*, Beijing: Wenwu, 2000, Fig. 213: 13, 10; Fig. 189: 6, 5); 4. Weifang (extracted from Tianjinshi Wenwu Guanlichu Kaogudui, Tianjin Jixian Weifang Yizhi Fajue Baogao, *Kaogu* 10, 1983, Fig. 8: 14); 6. Houlanjiagou (extracted from Guo, Y. , Shilou Houlanjiagou faxian Shangdai qingtongqi jianbao, *Wenwu* 4/5, 1962, Fig. 2); 7, Shuiquan (extracted from Shao, G. , Neimenggu Aohanqi faxian de qingtongqi ji youguan yiwu, *Beifang Wenwu* 1, 1993, Fig. 8: 7); 8, 9, Liulihe (extracted from Zhongguo Shehui Kexueyuan Kaogu Yanjiusuo, Beijingshi Wenwu Yanjiusuo, and Liulihe Kaogudui, Beijing Liulihe 1193 hao damu fajue jianbao, *Kaogu* 1, 1990, Fig. 5: 7; Fig. 8: 2); 10, 23, Jingjie (extracted from Shanxisheng Kaogu Yanjiusuo, *Lingshi Jingjie Shangmu*, Beijing: Kexue, 2006, Fig. 91, Fig. 136); 13, Baifu (extracted from Beijingshi Wenwu Guanlichu, Beijing diqu de youyi zhongyao kaogu shouhuo—Changping Baifu Xizhou muguomu de xinqishi, *Kaogu* 4, 1976, Fig. 9: 3); 14, 21, Gaohong (extracted from Yang, S. Shanxi Liulinxian Gaohong faxian Shangdai tongqi, *Kaogu* 3, 1981, Pl. 2, pl. 1); 12, 15, 16, 17, Fenjia (extracted from Wang, Y. , G. Wang, and F. Li, Suizhong Fenjia faxian shangdai jiaocang tongqi, *Liaohai Wenwu Xuekan* 1, 1996, Fig. 3: 1, 2; Fig. 2: 7; Fig. 5: 2); 18, Chaodaogou (extracted from Hebeisheng Wenhuaju Wenwu Gongzuodui, Hebei Qinglongxian Chaodaogou faxian yipi qingtongqi, *Kaogu* 12, 1962, pl. 5: 2); 20, Xiaohenan (extracted from Wang, F. , Hebei Xinglongxian faxian Shang-Zhou qingtongqi jiaocang, *Wenwu* 11, 1990, Fig. 2: 1); 22, Baoshenmiao (extracted from An, Z. , Tangshan shiguanmu jiqi xiangguan de yiwu, *Kaogu Xuebao* 7, 1954, Fig 6)

Jingle-bell-pommeled daggers common among Karasuk metals, but jingle-bell-pommeled knife is unknown among the Karasuk metals. Only one Jingle-bell-pommeled knife has been found in the Ordos-Yanshan region, that is, at Chaodaogou (Fig. 3 − 8 − 4: 20). The pommel is a depressed round jingle-bell with a slit cage; the hilt and the blade are grooved throughout, but they are separated by a petty butt. ①Another singular piece from Baifu, an eagle pommeled knife, is characterized by an extraordinarily slender but thick blade and a hilt evenly punctuated with seven perforations. ②This piece is again without parallel among the Karasuk metals and possibly a local innovation.

Daggers

Like the knives discussed above, daggers (15 in total) from the Ordos-Yanshan region are exceedingly diverse: their pommels occur in the forms of ring, jingle-bell, disc, ram, horse, mushroom, and eagle. As those of zoomorphic pommeled knives (i. e. Fig. 3 − 8 − 4: 18), they all date to the Anyang Shang and Western Zhou periods. The ring-pommeled dagger is a piece from Zhukaigou, which has an outstanding midrib and two hand guards (Fig. 3 − 8 − 4: 19). A ram-pommeled dagger from Chaodaogou, stylistically identical to the knife from the same site, features protruding brows and hollowed eye-sockets possibly filled with turquoise beads in the time of use; a long protruding midrib passes from the hilt all the way through the blade. ③Equally unique is a horse-pommeled dagger from Baifu. ④ Stylistically speaking, it has naturalistically rendered almond eyes and forward-pointing ears. The hilt has a set of rectangular sockets, one long and two short, meant for inlaying beads made of turquoise or other materials. An eagle-pommeled dagger from the same

---

① Hebeisheng Wenhuaju Wenwu Gongzuodui, Hebei Qinglongxian Chaodaogou faxian yipi qingtongqi, *Kaogu* 12, 1962, Pl. V: 1.

② Beijingshi Wenwu Guanlichu, Beijing diqu de youyi zhongyao kaogu shouhuo—Changping Baifu Xizhou muguomu de xinqishi, *Kaogu* 4, 1976, Fig. 8: 5.

③ Hebeisheng Wenhuaju Wenwu Gongzuodui, Hebei Qinglongxian Chaodaogou faxian yipi qingtongqi, *Kaogu* 12, 1962, Pl. 5: 5, 7.

④ Beijingshi Wenwu Guanlichu, Beijing diqu de youyi zhongyao kaogu shouhuo—Changping Baifu Xizhou muguomu de xinqishi, *Kaogu* 4, 1976, Fig. 9: 5.

cemetery is almost a copy of the horse-pommeled dagger and the abovementioned eagle-pommeled knife. ①

Of the jingle-bell-pommeled daggers, an item from Baifu consists of an elongated jingle-bell and a triangular blade.②The other items from Gaohong, Linzheyu, Yanjiagou, Caojiayuan, Shuiquan,③ and Baifu, are all stylistically homogeneous and akin to the Chaodaogou knife in the form of jingle-bell. Slight difference exists in the decor of the hilt. The two items from Yanjiagou and Shuiquan are characterized by one oval zone and three columns of punched dots, whereas the three from Gaohong, Linzheyu, and Caojiayuan by a flat zone and multiple grooves (Fig. 3 - 8 - 4: 21). All of them feature horizontal guards, vertical midribs, and elongated blades. This type of daggers is rare, if not unknown, in the Minusinsk Basin and seems to be a local innovation.

The mushroom-pommeled daggers are equipped with a different type of blades, which possess prominent midribs. Five of them are known from the Ordos-Yanshan region alone, and they are stylistically homogeneous with some minor differences. They are all characterized by a tube hilt, which carries rectangular perforations. The pommel of the Shaoguoyingzi item (M1 : 1) is comprised of four knobs;④ those from Baifu (M3 : 22 - 1, M3 : 22 - 2)⑤ and Xiaohenan⑥feature semi-spherical pommels. The latter resembles a piece from the Minusinsk Basin, but the Shaoguoyingzi item has no parallel there and seems to be a local innovation.

---

① Beijingshi Wenwu Guanlichu, Beijing diqu de youyi zhongyao kaogu shouhuo—Changping Baifu Xizhou muguomu de xinqishi, *Kaogu* 4, 1976, Fig. 9: 4.

② Beijingshi Wenwu Guanlichu, Beijing diqu de youyi zhongyao kaogu shouhuo—Changping Baifu Xizhou muguomu de xinqishi, *Kaogu* 4, 1976, Fig. 8: 4.

③ Shao, G., Neimenggu Aohanqi faxian de qingtongqi ji youguan yiwu, *Beifang Wenwu* 1, 1993, Fig. 8: 5.

④ Jianpingxian Wenhuaguan, and Chaoyangdiqu Bowuguan, Liaoning Jianpingxian de qingtongshidai muzang ji xiangguan yiwu, *Kaogu* 8, 1983, Fig. 2: 1.

⑤ Beijingshi Wenwu Guanlichu, Beijing diqu de youyi zhongyao kaogu shouhuo—Changping Baifu Xizhou muguomu de xinqishi, *Kaogu* 4, 1976, Fig. 9: 2, 3; Fig. 4: 13.

⑥ Wang, F., Hebei Xinglongxian faxian Shang-Zhou qingtongqi jiaocang, *Wenwu* 11, 1990, Fig. 2: 8.

Spearheads

No spearheads have been found in Karasuk tombs; only a few are known from stray finds. They are willow-shaped and equipped with tapering sockets. In the Ordos-Yanshan region, spearheads (15 in total) are quite popular and stylistically diverse, but quite removed from the Karasuk prototypes. The one from Gaohong is similar to them but extremely slender. A spearhead from Jingjie bears an indented triangle and a taotie motif on the socket (Fig. 3 – 8 – 4: 23). Of two examples found at Liulihe, one has its shaft-socket tapering into the blades, whereas the other has its shaft-socket terminating at the beginning of the blade, whose section is rendered into the form of an angular rhomb. ①Echoing the former are two molds found at Baoshenmiao. ②The item from Xiaohenan, however, has no loop but hexagonal shaft barrel and wide blades. The diverse types, especially the Jingjie item, appear to be local derivative of the Karasuk prototype.

Shaft-hole axes

Shaft-hole axes are likewise pervasive and stylistically diverse in the Ordos-Yanshan region. The eighteen known items are all comprised of a socket, a counter-weight butt, and a blade. Two types can be differentiated out of them: one with slender rectangular blade and the other bloated square blade. Of the former type, an item from the Chaodaogou appears to be a typical one. The butt is cylindrical and the blade is slender. ③The item from Yanghe and Fengjia are formally similar, but they differ in that they bear a feather motif or a

---

① Zhongguo Shehui Kexueyuan Kaogu Yanjiusuo, Beijingshi Wenwu Yanjiusuo, and Liulihe Kaogudui, 1981 – 1983 nian Liulihe Xizhou Yanguo mudi fajue jianbao, *Kaogu* 5, 1984, Fig. 9: 3; Zhongguo Shehui Kexueyuan Kaogu Yanjiusuo, Beijing Liulihe 1193 hao damu fajue jianbao, *Kaogu* 1, 1990, Fig. 5: 8.

② An, Z., Tangshan shiguanmu jiqi xiangguan de yiwu, *Kaogu Xuebao* 7, 1954, Fig. 5: 6; Fig. 4: 22.

③ Hebeisheng Wenhuaju Wenwu Gongzuodui, Hebei Qinglongxian Chaodaogou faxian yipi qingtongqi, *Kaogu* 12, 1962, pl. 5: 2.

bulging cap. ①The Chenshantou item is different from all the aforementioned pieces: it has a triangular blade and double butts. ②Of the latter type, two items from Fengjia③and Xiaohenan④bear a large circular hole at the center of the blade, but the hole of the Xiaohenan piece has raised rims at both sides. Both types, which have no analogue among Karasuk artifacts, are local innovations.

Bow-shaped objects

Bow-shaped objects are not proliferous among the Karasuk metals. ⑤They are absent in the Xinjang-Gansu-Qinghai region but popular (8 in total) in the Ordos-Yanshan region. Different from the Minusinsk item, which consists of a straight bar and two arced arms with four knobs, the Ordos-Yanshan items occur in two types, one large and one small. The large ones from Jingjie, which occur in pair in two tombs, bear the motif of an octagonal star on the curve, apart from the regular element of jingle-bell pommels at the tips of the two arms (Fig. 3-8-4: 10). An item from Liulihe features the motifs of double cicada wings and a concentric cap on the bar. ⑥The small ones from Taohuazhuang, Zhujiayu, and Houlanjiagou are without precedent in the Minusinsk Basin, possessing out-flaring ends and rectangular butts on the arcs. ⑦The Ordos-Yanshan items, stylistically distant from the Minusinsk counterpart, must have

---

① Jinzhoushi Bowuguan, Liaoning Xingchengxian Yanghe faxian qingtongqi, *Kaogu* 6, 1978, pl. 9: 2; Wang, Y., G. Wang, and F. Li, Suizhong Fenjia faxian shangdai jiaocang tongqi, *Liaohai Wenwu Xuekan* 1, 1996, Fig. 5: 2; Fig. 4: 17.

② Meng, Z., and L. Zhao, Hebei Luanxian Wanshang qingtongqi, *Kaogu* 4, 1994, Fig. 3.

③ Wang, Y., G. Wang, and F. Li, Suizhong Fenjia faxian shangdai jiaocang tongqi, *Liaohai Wenwu Xuekan* 1, 1996, Fig. 5: 1.

④ Wang, F., Hebei Xinglongxian faxian Shang-Zhou qingtongqi jiaocang, *Wenwu* 11, 1990, Fig. 2: 7.

⑤ Chlenova, N. L., *Khronologiia Pamiatnikov Karasukskoĭ Èpokhi*, Moscow: Science Press, 1972, Table 39: 6; Fig. 2: 22.

⑥ Zhongguo Shehui Kexueyuan Kaogu Yanjiusuo, Beijingshi Wenwu Yanjiusuo, and Liulihe Kaogudui, 1981-1983 nian Liulihe Xizhou Yanguo mudi fajue jianbao, *Kaogu* 5, 1984, Fig. 9: 4.

⑦ Xie, Q., and S. Yang, Shanxi Lüliangxian Shilouzhen you faxian tongqi, *Wenwu* 7, 1960, p. 52; Yang, S., Shanxi Shilou Chuajiayu, Caojiayuan faxian Shangdai tongqi, *Wenwu* 8, 1981, pp. 49-53; Yang, S., Shanxi Liulinxian Gaohong faxian Shangdai tongqi, *Kaogu* 3, 1981, pp. 211-212; Guo, Y., Shilou Houlanjiagou faxian Shangdai qingtong qi jianbao, *Wenwu* 4/5, 1962, Fig. 4: 6.

been local developments.

Earrings/finger-rings/bracelets

The earliest items are from Zhukaigou and Dadianzi, the earliest ones among the sites in question. As those of the Xinjiang-Gansu-Qinghai region, they are mostly made of copper and occasionally gold wires. Among them (79 in total) there are many varieties, some are penannular, with tapering or fan-like ends (Fig. 3 – 8 – 4: 1, 3); some has one end rendered into a trumpet and the other into a tapering tip entering the trumpet. The two from Dadianzi and Nanshangen are bent out of flattened gold wires with two fan-like ends (Fig. 3 – 8 – 4: 2), which are bound to each other. ①Andronovo type earrings, which have trumpet-like and tapering ends, also occur in this region. The earliest ones from Zhangjiayuan and Weifang in Tianjin belong to the Lower Xiajiadian culture,② the later one from Liujiahe, also made of gold, dates to 1400BC – 1300BC based on accompanying Transitional-Shang style bronze vessels. They differ from the Andronovo prototypes in that the trumpets are exaggerated and the pins are thin. ③As in the case of the Ganguya and Mougou items, it is a later, possibly passed from Karasuk, development. Two bracelets from Zhukaigou are cast into full circles, and the other two from the same cemetery are penannular ones with two tapering ends. The other two are formally similar to the aforementioned earrings from the same tomb in having two fan-like ends, but they are much larger with diameters of 12.5cm. ④

---

① Liaoningsheng Zhaowudameng Wenwu Gongzuozhan, and Zhongguo Kexueyuan Kaogu Yanjiusuo Dongbei Gongzuodui, Ningchengxian Nanshangen de shiguomu, *Kaogu Xuebao* 2, 1973, Pl. 5: 5.
② Tianjinshi Wenwu Guanlichu, Tianjin Jixian Zhangjiayuan yizhi shijue jianbao, *Wenwu Ziliao Congkan* 1, 1977, Fig. 17: 3; Tianjinshi Wenwu Guanlichu Kaogudui, Tianjin Jixian Weifang Yizhi Fajue Baogao, *Kaogu* 10, 1983, Fig. 8: 14.
③ Beijingshi Wenwu Guanlichu, Beijingshi Pingguxian faxian Shangdai muzang, *Wenwu* 11, 1977, p. 4.
④ Beijingshi Wenwu Guanlichu, Beijingshi Pingguxian faxian Shangdai muzang, *Wenwu* 11, 1977, Fig. 13.

Tube

Tube is rather rare in the Ordos-Yanshan region; only one spiral tube (M1070∶2) is known from Zhukaigou and it is analogous to those of Tianshanbeilu (Fig. 3 – 8 – 4∶5).

Plaques

As in the Xinjiang-Gansu-Qinghai region, plaques (304 in total) have been abundantly found in the Ordos-Yanshan region. But they date not before, but after 1500BC. Two types can be differentiated. One type is more akin to the Karasuk prototype, with the small loop placed on the concave side, present at Shuiquan, Dapaozi, Baifu, and Nanshangen (Fig. 3 – 8 – 4∶7). They are rather small, varying from 0.85 to 7.5cm in diameter. Plaques of the second type, which have been found at Liujiahe, are much larger, 11cm in diameter and 2.5cm high, and without loop, but they have two pairs of double holes. Of the same type are the items from Liulihe and Zhukaigou, which occur in different forms: round, rectangular, horse-hoof-shaped, and cruciform, and vary from 12.4cm to 18cm in diameter. Some of the Liulihe plaques are inscribed with the characters "医侯舞 (Marquis Wu of Yan)" or "医侯舞易 (bestowed by Marquis Wu of Yan)" (Fig. 3 – 8 – 4∶8). Equipped with pairs of holes, these plaques have reportedly been stitched to a shield and an armor.[①] The four human masks and five animal masks found in the same tomb, bearing pairs of holes at the rim, may have served the same purpose. These plaques likewise appear to have been local developments.

In sum, many types of artifacts of the Ordos-Yanshan region are analogous to the Xinjiang-Gansu-Qinghai counterparts. As in the Xinjiang-Gansu-Qinghai region, the earrings, finger-rings, and bracelets, which date loosely to 2000 BC – 1200BC, are made of solid wires (Fig. 3 – 8 – 4∶1 – 4); ring pommeled knives are prominent (Fig. 3 – 8 – 4∶11); a spiral-tube (Fig. 3 – 8 – 4∶5),

---

① Zhongguo Shehui Kexueyuan Kaogu Yanjiusuo, Beijingshi Wenwu Yanjiusuo, and Liulihe Kaogudui, 1981 – 1983 nian Liulihe Xizhou Yanguo mudi fajue jianbao, *Kaogu* 5, 1984, pp. 29 – 30.

armlet, small plaques (Fig. 3 - 8 - 4: 7 - 8), small mirrors (Fig. 3 - 8 - 4: 9), and celts (Fig. 3 - 8 - 4: 16), which date after 1500BC, are likewise present. Among the spearheads, an item from Jingjie (Fig. 3 - 8 - 4: 23), which bears an indented triangle on the socket, and a mold from Baoshenmiao (Fig. 3 - 8 - 4: 22), the intended product of which has multiple loops, are distinguished from the Karasuk prototypes. This ensemble of artifacts provides ample evidence to indicate that both the Xinjang-Gansu-Qinghai and Ordos-Yanshan regions are subject to the influence of the Karasuk metallurgy. This paper, therefore, does not accept the thesis of Novogorodova that traces many types of artifacts to the Mongolian and Ordos Plateaus.[①] As in the Xinjiang-Gansu-Qinghai region, evidence of earlier metallurgy is meager in this region; the Karasuk-type metals found there must have been inspired by the Karasuk metallurgy from the Minsusinsk Basin.

Another group of artifacts, however, is unique to the Ordos-Yanshan region. Zoomorphic pommel knives, zoomorphic pommel daggers, shaft-hole axes, bow-shaped objects, and large plaques, are absent in the Xinjiang-Gansu-Qinghai region. It must be noted that they date, based on contextual materials, to 1500BC - 771BC, and as a whole later than the ensemble of the Xinjiang-Gansur-Qinghai region. It appears that the Ordos-Yanshan region, apart from the first group, selectively absorbs a separate set of metal artifacts of Karasuk. The zoomorphic pommel knives, zoomorphic pommel daggers, and shaft-hole axes, although they find close analogues among Karasuk metals, sometime even take on Shang style motifs. The bow-shaped objects and large plaques are morphologically even far removed from the Karasuk prototypes, assuming diverse forms and Shang style motifs and inscriptions; they are apparently the results of local development.

Transmission Routes

In both the Xinjiang-Gansur-Qinghai and Ordos-Yanshan regions, Karasuk-type metals are neither imports nor copies of Karasuk prototypes; instead, they

---

① Novogorodova, È. A., *Tsentral'naia Aziia i Karasukskaia Problema*, Moscow, 1970.

are already adapted to local tastes, the fact of which is eloquently attested by their morphological features and decorative motifs. Large-scale migration of population and trade of products are hence insufficient for explaining them; it is likely that metallurgy alone was disseminated. The two regions, however, constitute two discrete regions of development of Karasuk metallurgy. In the Xinjiang-Gansu-Qinghai region, Karasuk-type metals are mostly ornaments, followed by tools and weapons, which resonate with the ensemble of metal artifacts of the Minusinsk Basin. In the Ordos Plateau, however, Karasuk-type tools and weapons are picked up and cultivated in the Anyang Shang and Western Zhou periods. This choice is probably effected by the cultural preference of the Shang-Zhou tradition, which suppresses personal ornaments in favor of tools and weapons. The Karasuk metallurgy therefore is transmitted to the two regions through separate routes and different filters.

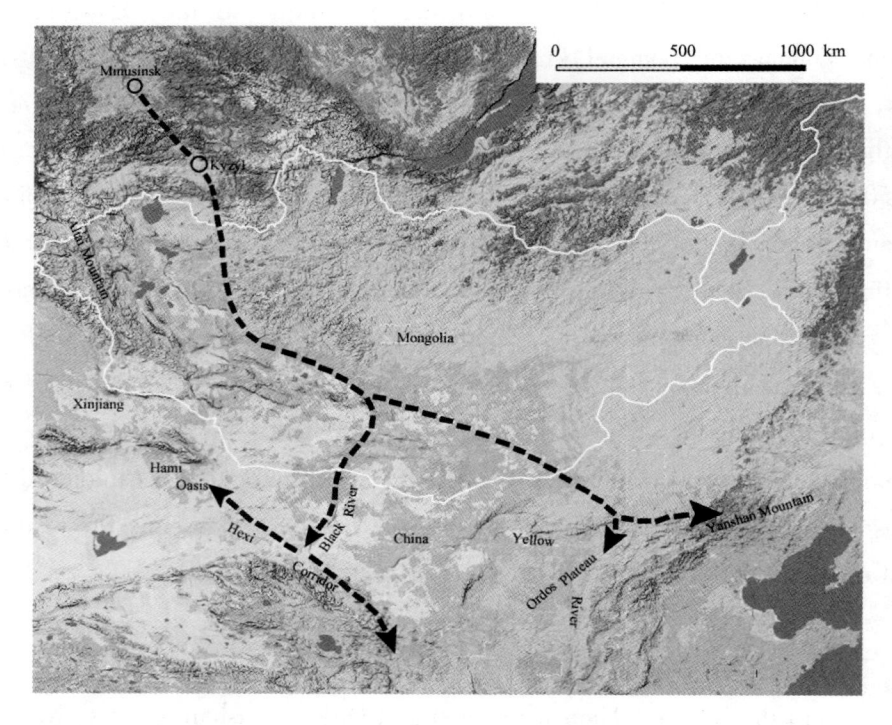

Fig. 3-8-5 Transmission routes of Karasuk metallurgy to the Northern Zone of China

The Transmission of the Karasuk Metallurgy to the Northern Zone of China

As the anthropology of technological transmission tells us, metal production is a "complex technological system" or chaine operatoire that involves multiple steps of labor, including smelting of ores, manufacture of refractory ceramics, and the production of metal artifacts. The transmission of metallurgy to a society without prior knowledge could not occur without direct instruction by skilled craftsmen. [1]Then what routes did the craftsmen take to deliver the Karasuk metallurgy to the two regions? E. N. Chernykh once describes two routes of transmission of the Karasuk metallurgy into China: 1, from the Saian-Altai through Xinjiang, and finally into Gansu; 2, from the Minusinsk Basin through Mongolia to the Ordos Plateau and the Yanshan Mountain. [2]In a general sense Katheryn Linduff and I agree with the second route. [3]Gideon Shelach-Lavi, however, proposes an alternative route that passes between the steppe and forest belts of northern Mongolia; [4] after arriving in the Yanshan Mountain, the Karasuk metallurgy spreads further to the Ordos Plateau. This route presupposes that the Karasuk-type metals of the Ordos Plateau postdate those of the Yanshan Mountain, but this is not true-the majority of the latter ensemble, excluding the ornaments from the Dadianzi cemetery, are later than the Ordos ensemble. The steppe route, which would spread metallurgy to both regions, seems more

---

[1] Schiffer, M. B., Transmission processes: A behavioral perspective, in M. J. O'Brien ed., *Cultural Transmission and Archaeology: Issues and Case Studies*, Washington, DC: Society for American Archaeology, 2008, p. 107; Van Pool, C. S., Agents and cultural transmission, in M. J. O'Brien ed, *Cultural Transmission and Archaeology: Issues and Case Studies*, Washington, DC: Society for American Archaeology, 2008, pp. 190–200; White, J. C., and C. Hamilton, The transmission of early Bronze Age technology to Thailand: new perspectives, *Journal of World Prehistory* 22, 2009, p. 360.

[2] Chernykh, E. N., Formation of the Eurasian steppe belt cultures: Viewed through the lens of archaemetallurgy and radiocarbon dating, in B. K. Hanks, and K. M. Linduff, eds., *Social Complexity in Prehistoric Eurasia: Monuments, Metals, and Mobility*, New York: Cambridge University Press, 2009, p. 141.

[3] Linduff, K. M., What's mine is yours: the transmission of metallurgical technology in Eastern Eurasia and East Asia, in S. Srinivasan, S. Ranganathan, and A. Giumlia-Mair eds., *Metals and Civilizations*, Banglaore: National Institute of Advanced Studies, 2015, p. 20.

[4] Shelach-Lavi, G., Violence on the Frontiers? Sources of Power and Socio-political Change at the Easternmost Parts of the Eurasian Steppe during the Late Second and Early First Millennia BCE, in B. K. Hanks and K. M. Linduff eds., *Social Complexity in Prehistoric Eurasia: Monuments, Metals, and Mobility*, Cambridge University Press, 2009, p. 252; Shelach-Lavi, G., Steppe land interaction and their effects on Chinese cultures during the second and early first millennia BCE, in R. Amitai and M. Biran eds., *Nomads as Agents of Cultural Change*, University of Hawaii Press, 2015, p. 21.

◇❖◇　**第三部分　中国西北和欧亚草原考古**

likely. The first route, which many authors have endorsed, requires some reconsideration. It may account for the Andronovo and Seĭma-Turbino artifacts discovered in the Xinjiang-Gansu-Qinghai region, but it does not explain the origin of the Karasuk-type metals found here, because they are totally absent in Eastern Kazakhstan and Xinjiang to the west of the Hami Oasis. Instead, it has been postulated that the Black River, which links up with the eastern foothill of the Altai Mountain, conveys Central Asian mirrors to the Qijia and Siba cultures.① It is also possible that the same route, which extends further to Tuva and the Minusinsk Basin, channels the Karasuk metallurgy into the Hexi Corridor and the Hami Oasis (Fig. 3 - 8 - 5).

The Chronological Dilemma

The propositions advanced above, however, are a hypothesis; it is currently compromised by a chronological dilemma of the cultures in question. As said earlier, the recent radiocarbon dates have placed Karasuk within the range of 1400BC - 800BC. The Siba and Tianshanbeilu cultures have been dated to 1880BC - 1530BC, and the Qijia culture roughly to 2190BC - 1630BC. In the Ordos-Yanshan region, the earliest Karasuk-type metals come from tombs of the Zhukaigou and Lower Xiajiadian cultures, and they date to 1900BC - 1200BC and 2000BC - 1200BC respectively. Provided this situation, one has good reason to suppose that the metallurgy was transmitted from the Xinjiang-Gansu-Qinghai and Ordos-Yanshan regions to the Minusinsk Basin instead.

This position, however, is difficult to reconcile with the overall picture of metallurgical development in the Eurasian steppe and the Northern Zone. First of all, the Xinjang-Gansu-Qinghai and Ordos-Yanshan regions constitute two discrete traditions of metallurgy; it is less conceivable for the metallurgy to

---

① Fiztgerald-Huber, L. G., Qijia and Erlitou: The Question of Early Contacts with Distant Cultures, *Early China* 20, 1995, p. 51; Jaang, L., Long-Distance Interactions as Reflected in the Earliest Chinese Bronze Mirrors, in Lothar von Falkenhausen ed., *The Lloyd Cotsen Study Collection of Chinese Bronze Mirrors*, Los Angeles: Cotsen Occasional Press and UCLA Cotsen Institute of Archaeology Press, Volume II, 2011, pp. 37, 39.

transmit from two regions to one area than the other way round. More importantly, little foundation has been paved for the Northern Zone to produce the Karasuk-type metal artifacts. After all, no prior metallurgy exists in Eastern Xinjiang; in Gansu province one tin bronze knife and one piece of slag have been discovered at the Majiayao culture (3000BC – 2500BC) site of Linjia, and one tin bronze knife at the Machang culture (2200BC – 1900BC) site of Jiangjiaping,[1] but the evidence is too scanty and distant to warrant the autochthonous origin of the complex ensemble of metal artifacts of Siba and Qijia. The same can be said of the Ordos Plateau, where no evidence of prior metallurgy has been found. On the contrary, metallurgy has a long undisrupted history of development in the Minusinsk Basin since the Afanas'evo period (3650BC – 2240BC). The metallurgy hence must have been transmitted from the Minusinsk Basin to the Xinjiang-Gansu-Qinghai region. The absence of a few Karasuk metal types denotes that the ancient populations of the Xinjiang-Gansu-Qinghai region do not accept all the types of Karasuk, whereas the appearance of new metal types indicates that they are quite innovative; they quickly adapt the acquired technology to produce the types of artifacts of their desire.

Albeit improvable at present, the hypothesis raised here is not without value. The chronological dilemma compels us either to look at the metal artifacts more carefully so as to come up with a better interpretation, or to ask for more and systematic radiocarbon dates for the Karasuk, Tianshanbeilu, Qijia, Zhukaigou, and Lower Xiajiadian so as to set up more accurate chronologies for them. One lesson can be learned from the progress in the archaeology of the Eurasian steppe and the Northern Zone in the last two decades is that the rapid increase of radiocarbon dates has greatly reshaped our knowledge of ancient cultures: it has not only advanced chronologies of Bronze Age cultures (i. e. Andronovo, Karasuk) of the Eurasian steppes for several hundred years, but also extended those of the Northern Zone (i. e. Lower Xiajiadian, Qijia) back

---

[1] Sun, S., and R. Han, Gansu zaoqi tongqi de faxian yu yelian, zhizao jishu de yanjiu, *Wenwu* 7, 1997, pp. 75 – 77.

for several hundred years. In this milieu, one may not exclude the possibility that in the future their chronologies change again to make the hypothesis more acceptable.

Conclusion

This paper, by extensively examining early metal artifacts found in the Xinjiang-Gansu-Qinghai and Ordos-Yanshan regions, comes to a new understanding of the development of early metallurgy in the Northern Zone. The majority of the Bronze Age metal artifacts are typologically analogous to those of the Karasuk culture in the Minusinsk Basin. The two regions nevertheless differ in the overall ensemble of Karasuk-type artifacts: while ornaments are prominent in the Xinjiang-Gansu-Qinghai region, tools and weapons are prominent in the Ordos-Yanshan region. This paper therefore proposes that metallurgy was transmitted from the Karasuk culture to the Northern Zone through two separate routes. The hypothesis is currently compromised by the chronological positions of the cultures in question, but the available evidence does not warrant the autochthonous origin of metallurgy in the two regions. It is more likely that the metallurgy was delivered from the Minusinsk Basin rather than the other way round. The Karasuk metallurgy, however, was selectively and innovatively adopted by the local populations, who dropped a number of types of metal artifacts and invented a number of local forms.

Acknowledgment

The author wishes to express his profound gratitude to the anonymous referees who have helped to improve the manuscript enormously by providing critical comments on the various versions of this paper. All the errors remain his own.

第四部分
东亚艺术史

Artistic Activities of Korean Envoys in China*

Introduction

Korea in the Chosǒn Dynasty (1392 – 1910) has often been described as a model tributary state of China. This was manifested in the persistent and frequent diplomatic missions it sent to China during the Ming (1368 – 1644) and Qing (1644 – 1911) Dynasties. From the very beginning of her life, the Chosǒn court sent to China three congratulatory envoys every year, one celebrating the Lunar Year, and the other two the birthdays of the emperor and heir apparent. At times there were many special missions, such as offering thanks (chinba), condolences (chinwi), obituary notices (kobu). The years between 1392 and 1450 were the prime, with an average of about seven per year.[①] This is congruent with the catalogue *Sahaeng-nok* 使行录, which is appended to the *Tongmun Hwigo* 同文汇考, a collection of Qing-Korea diplomatic activities published in 1881, which documents a total of 1250 missions during the 245 years between 1637 and 1881. Considering that a single envoy might assume several missions, the actual envoys to Beijing were 680, or almost 3 per year.[②] Thus if this rate is applied to the entire 518 years between

---

* 本文原刊于《史地》2018 年第 3 辑, 第 30—57 页, 收入本书时略有改动。

① Clark, Donald N., Sino-Korean tributary relations under the Ming, in Denis Twitchett and Frederick W. Mote eds., *The Cambridge History of China*, The Ming Dynasty 1368 – 1644, Cambridge University Press, 1998, part II, p. 280.

② Ledyard, Gari, Korean Travelers in China over Four Hundred Years, 1488 – 1887, in James B. Palais ed., *Occasional Papers on Korea*, Number two, The Joint Committee on Korean Studies, 1974, p. 5.

1392 – 1910, there would have been 1554 envoys altogether. This number, excluding the increased envoys, should be a modest estimation.

The diplomatic envoys not only served the political benefits of both nations, but also provided expedient opportunities of trading and cultural transmission. Under the name of tribute they submitted to Chinese imperial storage Korean products, such as ginseng, cloth, paper, and horses. In return they received a variety of Chinese products, including dragon robes, musical instruments, costumes, ornaments, silks, and books. Envoy members also engaged in private transaction on route as well as in Beijing. The business seemed rather profitable, for the Chosŏn government counted upon this side business, and paid envoy members relatively little from state funds. ①These gifts and commodities the Koreans brought back were bound to conduct the Chinese culture to Korea. It was owed to this mechanism that Chinese philosophy, laws, rituals, costumes, and other cultural institutions gained root in the Korean soil. It follows that the Koreans considered themselves as inheritors of the Chinese culture when the "barbarian" Manchu took over the power from the Ming Dynasty.

This paper aims to explore artistic activities of Korean envoys in China and their impact on the Korean art. The primary source presently available is the thirty-one travel diaries resulting from these envoys. One is the famous monograph *Yŏrha Ilgi* 热河日记, written by Pak Chi-wŏn 朴趾源（1737 – 1805）after his 1780 trip. The other thirty are compiled in the two-volume *Yŏnhaengnok Sŏnjip* 燕行录全集（the two volumes, originally marked with 上 and 下, will be referred to YS1 and YS2 in citation）, published by the Taedong Mun-hwa Yŏn'guwŏn of Sŏnggyun-gwan University in Seoul in 1960 – 1962. It is necessary to bear in mind that these diaries represent merely a tip of a gigantic iceberg. Ledyard relates that many envoys had over 40 ranking officials, and that Koreans used to keep diary in their travels. Thus a total of more than three

---

① Clark, Donald N., Sino-Korean tributary relations under the Ming, in Denis Twitchett and Frederick W. Mote eds., *The Cambridge History of China*, The Ming Dynasty 1368 – 1644, Cambridge University Press, part II, 1998, p. 281.

thousand diaries might have been produced for the Qing Dynasty alone. If added the Ming Dynasty, during which envoys were considerably more persistent and frequent, the number would surely multiply to a daunting figure. ①These documents certainly suffered enormous loss from the ravage of time, but we also believe that there must be many latent ones to be discovered.

Our concern with the number of diaries arises precisely from the fact that the currently available diaries turn out to be a relatively rich source for our inquiry of artistic activities of Korean envoys in China. The activities that this paper deals with refer specifically to viewing, exchanging and trading of paintings. Relevant information, however, is quite fragmentary and scattered. We should bear in mind one general image that Korean intellectuals were subject to more rigorous constraint of Confucianism, which regarded painting as marginal art, and they paid much less vigor to artistic matters, i. e. collecting, connoisseuring, and creating. The authors of these diaries overall shied away from a comprehensive description of their artistic activities, which certainly underrepresented the reality. Nevertheless the piecemeal information, when gleaned together, warrants us to envision that such activities were intensive and dynamic.

The impact of the artistic activities of Korean envoys on the Korean art has barely been appreciated. In accounting for the frequent dissemination of Chinese painting traditions, such as the Zhe School in the early and middle Chosŏn periods (1392 – 1700), and the Southern School in the late Chosŏn period (1700 – 1850), following the chronological framework of Ahn Hwijoon,② scholars tend to consider that a few imported painting manuals, such as the *Gushi Huapu* 顾氏画谱, *Jieziyuan huazhuan* 芥子园画传, played the overriding role. They also noticed that a few actual paintings were present in Korea, but the way they presented them creates an image that such works were

---

① Ledyard, Gari, Korean Travelers in China over Four Hundred Years, 1488 – 1887, in James B. Palais ed., *Occasional Papers on Korea*, Number two, The Joint Committee on Korean Studies, 1974, p. 5.
② Ahn Hwijoon, The Origin and Development of Landscape Painting in Korea, *Arts of Korea*, The Metropolitan Museum, 1998, pp. 310, 315, 322.

rare and peripheral to the training procedure of Korean artists.[1] A systematic survey of artistic activities of Korean envoys and their impact on the Korean art is well in order, and it will certainly advance our understanding of the mechanics of the dissemination of Chinese artistic traditions in Korea.

The significance of diplomatic communication in transmitting artistic tradition has well been recognized in recent studies in the case of Korean envoys to Japan. The rise of Japanese Southern School Nanga 南画, also inspired by Chinese sources, was a prominent episode in Japanese art history. Although located relatively secluded from the continent by sea, Japan maintained more active maritime trade with China than Korea. The trade necessarily brought in a great number of Chinese painting manuals and works, and even merchant artists such as Yi Fukiu.[2] Nevertheless new scholarship begins to acknowledge the role of Korean envoys in disseminating Chinese Southern School theories and techniques already transformed by Korean artists. Since the early seventeenth through the early nineteenth century, the Chosŏn court sent twelve diplomatic envoys to Japan. Intellectual officials and accompanying painters were engaged in constant artistic exchange with Japanese people, especially artists. These activities are amply manifest in the numerous diaries of Korean envoys, letters between artists of the two nations, memoirs left by Japanese artists, and even paintings done by Korean artists during their Japanese travels. Scholars believe that these direct contacts and actual paintings left a profound bearing on the growth of the Japanese Nanga School. An illuminating case is that Ooka Shunboku 大冈春卜, a distinguished Japanese artist, put a number of Korean paintings he obtained from his encounters with Korean painters in the painting manuals he commissioned, which were quite popular in Japan.[3]

---

[1] Kim-Paik, Kumja, The Introduction of the Southern School Painting Tradition to Korea, *Oriental Art* 36/4, 1990/1991, pp. 186 – 197; Jungmann, Burglind, Ike Taiga's Letter to Kim Yusŏng and his Approach to Korean Landscape Painting, *Review of Korean Studies* I, 1998, pp. 180 – 195.

[2] Jungmann, Burglind, Ike Taiga's Letter to Kim Yusŏng and his Approach to Korean Landscape Painting, *Review of Korean Studies* I, 1998, pp. 180 – 195.

[3] Yamannouchi, Chōzō, Ooka Shunboku no zufu lui, *Nihon Nangashi*, Tokyo: Ruri Shobó, 1981, pp. 91 – 94.

Artistic Activities of Korean Envoys in China

If we can take the significance of the Korean-Japanese encounters in the formation of the Japanese Nanga School, we should accord far more significance to the Korean-Chinese encounters in the Ming and Qing periods in the Korean art, whose intensity and intimacy make the former a petty case. The diaries under our investigation eloquently describe the rather intense artistic activities of Korean envoy members in China. The *Hangguk Misulsa Charyo Chipsong* 韩国美术史资料集成 compiled by Chin Hong-sop 秦弘燮, especially the fourth and sixth volumes (subsequently referred to as IV and VI in citation) collects a rich wealth of documents, memoirs, poems and essays that testify the astonishing number of Chinese paintings existing in Korea. These documents also cry out the impact of Chinese paintings on Korean artistic discourse and creation. The textual evidence compellingly convinces us that we should accord full credit to the significance of artistic activities of Korean envoys.

It is necessary to note that artistic exchange was not unidirectional. On the one hand, envoys, although much less frequently, were also dispatched from the Ming and Qing courts to Korea. Between 1392 and 1450, for example, ninety-five Ming envoys were sent to Korea, and between 1460 and 1506 twenty-six envoys.[1] The prominent cases are the ones led by Zhu Zhifan 朱之蕃 in 1607, and by Nian Gengyao 年羹尧 in 1769. Zhu was a literati artist, and he left many works in Korea,[2] whereas Nian, a meritorious general, brought a prominent artist, who held conferences with Korean court painters.[3] These Chinese envoys might well have brought some Korean paintings back to China. On the other hand, Korean envoy members also took Korean works to China. Pak Chi-wŏn saw a Korean painting album in a Chinese art shop. The album purportedly contains thirty pieces/sets of works of privileged Korean artists such as Kim Sik 金植 (1524 – 1593), Yi Kyŏng-yun 李庆胤 (1545 – 1611), Yi Ching 李澄 (1581-after 1645), Chŏng Sŏn 鄭歚 (1676 – 1759) and Kang Se-

---

[1] Clark, Donald N., Sino-Korean tributary relations under the Ming, in Denis Twitchett and Frederick W. Mote eds., *The Cambridge History of China*, The Ming Dynasty 1368 – 1644, part II, Cambridge University Press, 1998, p. 283.

[2] *Hangguk Misulsa Charyo Chipsong*, IV, pp. 107, 216; IV, p. 44.

[3] *Hangguk Misulsa Charyo Chipsong*, IV, p. 870.

hwang 姜世晃 (1713 – 1791). A Korean envoy member, who probably tried to test the Chinese art market, sold it to the owner of the shop.[①] Pak himself composed impromptu works at Shenyang (Mukden).[②] This direction of flow of art works, however, falls out of the scope of this paper, and will be not dealt with hereafter.

The Korean Envoys

We shall provide a brief overview of Korean diplomatic envoys, which will help us to understand their artistic activities. During the Ming and Qing dynasties, the diplomatic missions were the primary way for a Korean to get to China, although there were occasions of fishermen, and commuting officials blown to the Chinese coast by storms. Maritime travel seemed to be time-efficient, but still extremely precarious. Thus except for a few emergent occasions, Korean envoys went to China by land. Starting from Seoul, they usually took two weeks before crossing the Yalu River, and then they formally entered China at the customs station east of Fenghuang 凤凰关, which was a regular trading post for Koreans. The subsequent route, which did not vary much, would go through a long list of stations, including Shenyang, a political center in both Ming and Qing, and the formidable pass Shanhaiguan 山海关. On this route there were plenty of historical and cultural monuments open to Koreans, and they certainly did not waste the chances whenever their agendas allowed. The entire trip from Seoul to Beijing took about thirty[③] to sixty days.[④]

---

① Pak, Chi-wŏn, *Yŏrha Ilgi*, Sŏul Tŭkpyŏl-si: Taeyang Sŏjŏk, 1973, pp. 587 – 589.
② Pak, Chi-wŏn, *Yŏrha Ilgi*, Sŏul Tŭkpyŏl-si: Taeyang Sŏjŏk, 1973, pp. 547 – 550.
③ Clark, Donald N., Sino-Korean tributary relations under the Ming, in Denis Twitchett and Frederick W. Mote eds., *The Cambridge History of China*, The Ming Dynasty 1368 – 1644, part II, Cambridge University Press, 1998, p. 282.
④ Ledyard, Gari, Korean Travelers in China over Four Hundred Years, 1488 – 1887, in James B. Palais ed., *Occasional Papers on Korea*, Number two, The Joint Committee on Korean Studies, 1974, p. 10.

Artistic Activities of Korean Envoys in China

An envoy consists of around forty personnel in the Ming Dynasty,[①] but when it came to the Qing Dynasty, as a few diaries explicitly put it, the size locates anywhere between two hundred and four hundred. In either case, the envoy had one chief ambassador (chǒngsa 正使), one deputy ambassador (pusa 副使), and one Secretary (sǒjanggwan 书状官). They were selected from the most distinguished officials at court or even royal family members at times. Lower-ranking officials took a broad variety of functional positions, such as protocol officers, interpreters, translators, physicians, veterinarians, astrologers, clerks, and copyists. In general these officials were well educated, and conversant in Confucian classics, poetry, and history, but a few members even had discerning eyes for paintings, and some of them were renowned painters. The most prominent figure was the literati artist Kang Se-hwang (1713–1791), who was vice-ambassador of a 1784 envoy.[②] Five of his travel paintings are extant, depicting Chinese true scenery landscape.[③] The majority of the envoy members were servants, cooks, guides, soldiers, guards, and hostlers, and bearers, who constituted the retinue of the three top officials.[④]

To our interest, a court painter, and a calligrapher normally staffed the entourage, but they were lower-order officials.[⑤] In fact it was an institution that court painter accompanied envoys, and the *Sonjo Sillok* 宣祖实录 explicitly states that they bore the task of drawing detailed maps of the fortresses and passes of China, especially those close to the border of Korea.[⑥] Other regular duties of court painter were taking portraits of emperors every ten years, drawing

---

① Clark, Donald N., Sino-Korean tributary relations under the Ming, in Denis Twitchett and Frederick W. Mote eds., *The Cambridge History of China*, The Ming Dynasty 1368–1644, part II, Cambridge University Press, 1998, p. 280.

② Kang, Se-hwang, *P'yoam Yugo*, Songnam: Han'guk chongshin munhwa yon'guwon, 1979, p. 159.

③ Byun, Yong-sup, *P'yoam Kang Sehwang Hoehwa Yǒn'gu*, Seoul: Ilchisa, 1988, pp. 269–271.

④ Ledyard, Gari, Korean Travelers in China over Four Hundred Years, 1488–1887, in James B. Palais ed., *Occasional Papers on Korea*, Number two, The Joint Committee on Korean Studies, 1974, pp. 3–4.

⑤ YS1, p. 1158.

⑥ *Hangguk Misulsa Charyo Chipsong*, IV, pp. 817–818.

topography of royal mausoleums and palaces, and handling pictorial works in a variety of governmental documents. ①They also joined the reception crew for Chinese envoys, and demonstrated painting skill for them. ②To fulfill such varied duties these court painters had to acquire corresponding skills of drawing, designing, and creative painting. Because of this profession, they could have been active in artistic activities in China, and they indeed produced many travel paintings, as evidenced in the Painting of Arriving at Yan in the Jiachen Year 甲辰赴燕契会图 recorded by Yi Wôn-jông 李元祯（1622—1680）depicting the hardship of the sixty-two-day trip of his envoy to Beijing in 1670. ③But beyond this we can barely find other events in the documents at our disposal. The reason might be that they were lower in Korean official hierarchy, and were considered as peripheral staff. ④

  Once they arrived in Beijing, Korean envoys stayed in a permanent hostel established during the Ming Dynasty. It was located in the southeastern part of the city, and close to the Jade River Bridge; for that reason it was usually called Jade River Lodge 玉河馆. ⑤Koreans stayed in Beijing normally for a period from one month to several months. They would spend a few days fulfilling their official duties: submitting state letters and annual tributes, and most importantly, attending the imperial audiences. And in the end of their stay, they would also have finished all the trading business, and received the return letter from the imperial court. Beyond these duties, they had plenty of spare time to dispose of. However, in the entire period and early Qing, there were strict constraints regarding foreigners' movement within the capital, and a special Inspecting Official 提督 monitored the gate of the hostel to frustrate unauthorized excursions and visits. They nevertheless could receive streams of art merchants

---

  ① *Hangguk Misulsa Charyo Chipsong*, VI, p. 794.
  ② *Hangguk Misulsa Charyo Chipsong*, IV, p. 850.
  ③ *Hangguk Misulsa Charyo Chipsong*, IV, p. 352.
  ④ *Hangguk Misulsa Charyo Chipsong*, IV, p. 848.
  ⑤ Ledyard, Gari, Korean Travelers in China over Four Hundred Years, 1488–1887, in James B. Palais ed., *Occasional Papers on Korea*, Number two, The Joint Committee on Korean Studies, 1974, p. 4.

and artists in the hostel. And when the rules were relaxed around 1720,[1] the Koreans had chance to let their artistic interest go in this art world. They could engage in a broad range of activities, roaming in the spectacular capital, seeing historical and cultural monuments, meeting Chinese scholars, and visiting markets and churches.

Artistic Activities on Route

Artistic activities, defined here as viewing, exchanging and trading of paintings, occurred with both maritime and land envoys. As a rule they could take place in any prosperous city and town where historical and cultural monuments were present, or literati, artists, and art dealers converged. It should be noted that the thirty-one diaries, especially those supplying relatively desirable information, are primarily of the Qing Dynasty. Yet documents of artistic activities are too rich to allow a full description. We shall instead focus on the prominent ones.

Shenyang 沈阳 marks our opening point. It was the original capital of the Manchu regime, but it became the secondary one when the regime established the primary in Beijing. It was therefore a prosperous city in the northeast where Chinese officials, scholars, artists and art dealers converged. In 1636, Crown Prince Sohyŏn 昭显世子 and his brother Prince Pongnim 凤林大君 and five officials were held here as hostages, and during the period they often had conference with Meng Rongguang 孟荣光, a renowned Chinese painter disposed here. One member Kim Sang-hŏn 金尚宪（1570 – 1652）recorded that Meng painted for him the subject of Picking Chrysanthemum 採菊图,[2] which reflected their unyielding defiant sentiment of Koreans against the Manchu rule. A few of Meng's works survive, and one piece "Immortal Guest 仙客图"

---

[1] Ledyard, Gari, Korean Travelers in China over Four Hundred Years, 1488 – 1887, in James B. Palais ed., *Occasional Papers on Korea*, Number two, The Joint Committee on Korean Studies, 1974, pp. 11, 13.

[2] *Hangguk Misulsa Charyo Chipsong*, IV, pp. 173 – 174.

bearing the mark of the year Bingzi.①

Pak Nae-gyŏm 朴来谦（1780-after 1829）joined in 1829 a special envoy dispatched to Shenyang to attend the imperial audience, and stayed for thirty-three days. Pak was the secretary of the envoy, and he received service of Miao Mouxie 缪楳澥 and his two sons, who were in charge of serving the Korean envoys. Three days after the elder son came to Pak presenting an orchid painting. Another scholar, Chen Genglou 陈庚楼, granted him a work of "One Hundred Shou" with hundreds of stamps of the character of shou（寿）. Pak was invited to Chen's residence where he saw six paintings as well as antique tiles purportedly of the Qin and Han dynasties. When the envoy was about to leave, Chen brought another orchid painting, along with calligraphy and poem. Another associate Master Liu came with two volumes of the Cherished Words of Emperor Guan 关帝宝训, and a scroll depicting celestial officials.②Such encounters also took place at the pass Shanhaiguan where Yi An-nul 李安讷 （1571 – 1637）came across two Chinese artists Wang Yinglin 汪应遴 and Fu Qide 傅其德 in 1633, and obtained several landscapes from them.③

The subsequent stations supplied plenty of historical monuments. One locus that appealed to the Koreans was the Guzhucheng 孤竹城, the residence of the two Shang virtuous men Bo Yi and Shu Qi 叔齐, who allegedly refused to submit to the Zhou rule. Such virtuous heroes necessarily drew emperors and high officials here, and their commemorative works alone provided enough reason for the Koreans to make a side excursion.④Yi Ŭi-hyŏn 李宜显（1669 – 1745）, in his 1720 envoy, saw in a side temple a painting of vegetables, which he deemed as a lofty work. Earlier Korean visitors had made attempt to purchase it, but withheld at the prohibitive price. This time at a lower price he eventually obtained it.⑤Kang Se-hwang depicted the site in one of the five pieces

---

① National Museum of Korea, *Korean Paintings and Calligraphy of National Museum of Korea: A Comprehensive Catalogue*, National Museum of Korea, 1997, vol. VII, p. 20.
② YS1, pp. 890 – 899.
③ *Hangguk Misulsa Charyo Chipsong*, IV, pp. 165 – 166.
④ YS1, pp. 1003 – 1005.
⑤ YS2, p. 499.

mentioned above. Kim Kyŏng-sŏn 金景善（1788-after 1851）, in his returning way in 1833, he met one art dealer at the Yutian 玉田 station. What caught Kim's eyes was one magnificent calligraphy work of Su Shi 苏轼, which the dealer claimed as family heritage, and he had to sell it for starvation relief. ① At the final station Tongzhou, Yi Ŭi-hyŏn visited the Temple of Eastern Mount 东岳庙, a cultic temple dedicated to the Eastern Mount, or Taishan, and found calligraphy works of Manchu emperors, and of Zhao Mengfu 赵孟頫 and Dong Qichang 董其昌, who were both distinguished artists in Chinese art history. ②

When lodging at a town with official or gentry families, the Koreans often visited them to see their painting collections. The town of Funing 抚宁 riveted the attention of the Koreans primarily because of the prominent Xu family. The father Xu Henian 徐鹤年 earned a Jinshi title in the Qing court, and his two sons served as copyist in the imperial project of Siku Quanshu 四库全书. His family often hosted Qing officials, imperial families, and it was hospitable to Korean envoys. The contact began with Yun Sun 尹淳, a famed Korean calligrapher, who accidentally entered the Xu family. Xu showed all his collection of calligraphy and paintings, and in return Yun left a calligraphy work. Xu's hospitality became famed in Korea, and subsequent envoys chose to lodge in his residence so as to see his collection. When it came to the envoy of Pak Chi-wŏn in 1780, the father had died for many years, and his descendants disliked Korean guests because the large entourages of Korean envoys were rather disturbing. They only displayed some modest works. ③

The prosperous towns close to Beijing were very often the hubs of art trade as well. Many diarists documented their encounters with art dealers at a number of towns. At Funing, Yi Kap 李坤（1737-after 1778）, a member of a 1777 envoy, recorded that he saw Mi Fu's work "Western Travelers Submitting Tibetan Mastiff 西旅贡獒图," and a calligraphy album of Su Xian 苏贤, a

---

① YS1, p. 1122.
② YS2, p. 496.
③ Pak, Chi-wŏn, Yŏrha Ilgi, Sŏul Tŭkpyŏl-si: Taeyang Sŏjŏk, 1973, p. 587.

prominent artist of early Qing. ①Kim Kyŏng-sŏn, on his returning way in 1833, reported a dealer bringing a large scroll of calligraphy of Zhuzi (Zhu Xi 朱熹). ②Pak Sa-ho 朴思浩 (19th century) witnessed an art shop in this town in 1828. The shop was filled with books, calligraphy and paintings, and the Koreans spent some time there viewing and purchasing, although they could not tell genuine from fakery. ③

Fengrun 丰润 was more known for art dealers. Yi Ŭi-hyŏn visited this town in 1720, and reported that a descendant of Cao Bing, a prominent official of Northern Song (906 – 1127), came up to him with an album of portraits of the Cao family members. But Yi regretted that the descendant would sell this family treasure. ④Hong Tae-yong 洪大容 (1731 – 1783), joining a 1765 envoy, recorded that whenever Korean envoys entered the city, art dealers would approach them selling calligraphy, paintings, and antiques. ⑤Most of them were local literati (xiucai). Pak Chi-wŏn once visited two art dealers, Mr. Hu and Mr. Lin, both of which offered Pak a gift, one painting of an "Immortal under the Moon," and one painted fan, and Pak returned each a fan and a heart-soothing pill 清心丸, a highly prized Korean medicine in China. Pak, however, was not prepared to buy anything, and Mr. Lin looked sad at the time of parting. ⑥Kim Kyŏng-sŏn received two persons carrying about ten pieces of calligraphy and painting works. He caught sight of a calligraphy piece of Su Shi, a privileged literati artist of North Song (916 – 1127). ⑦

Artistic Activities in Beijing

The trips were usually hasty, and artistic activities of Korean envoys on

---

① YS2, p. 585.
② YS1, p. 1124.
③ YS1, p. 844.
④ YS2, p. 483.
⑤ YS1, p. 290.
⑥ Pak, Chi-wŏn, *Yŏrha Ilgi*, Sŏul T'ŭkpyŏl-si: Taeyang Sŏjŏk, 1973, p. 594.
⑦ YS1, p. 1005.

route were sporadic. But once the envoys arrived at the capital city Beijing, such activities became remarkably vigorous in the capital Beijing. Generally speaking, Beijing was an art ocean. During the long period of stay, the Koreans could relax their mood, and have relatively sufficient time to pursue their artistic interests. When circumstances allowed, they visited historical monuments, literati's residences, drinking shops, churches, and markets to see paintings; they sought out Chinese literati, officials, and artists to exchange art works; they bought art works either from markets or from art dealers coming to them. It is really a matter of individual aesthetic desire that determined how much one could get from it.

We should keep in mind that one of the functions of Korean envoys was selling Korean goods and purchasing Chinese products. The commerce took place at the hostel; an official group Xuban 序班 manipulated prices and they in fact significantly increased the costs of both Korean and Chinese traders. The members of Xuban were poorly paid minor officials in the Ministry of Rites, and they were given this chance to promote their economy. Valuable and therefore profitable items were under their firm control, and we learn that books, paintings, brush and inks were among them. ①Chinese books, basically of Confucian classics, history, philosophy, and literature, stood out as the staple purchase. Sŏ Mun-jung 徐文重 (1634 – 1709), vice-ambassador in 1690, and Yi Ŭi-hyŏn, explicitly made lists of books to be purchased in Beijing. ②By 1765, the Xuban officials even followed envoy members to markets to prevent them from personal trading. ③Despite the annoying profession, some Xuban officials with artistic skill earned some friendship from the Koreans. Kim Yuk 金堉 (1580 – 1658) recorded in his two poems to have received a painting fan and a landscape from a Xuban with the surnam Mao. ④

More often Korean envoys could sit in their hostels receiving streams of art

---

① YS1, p. 1015.
② YS2, p. 281; YS2, p. 511.
③ YS1, p. 331.
④ *Hangguk Misulsa Charyo Chipsong*, IV, p. 166.

dealers and officials. The works they brought were mixed of genuines and fakes, and the connoisseuring certainly tested the Koreans eyes. Yi Ŭi-hyŏn, during his stay at the hostel in 1720, this time in the monastery Beijisi 北极寺, because a Russian envoy had taken the hostel Yuheguan, saw two silk paintings. One depicted a willow tree, and two pairs of birds underneath, while another showed some flowers including a lotus, and two birds underneath. Yi commented that the paintings had the spirit of awkward spontaneity. The works bore the two characters of "Wanli 万历," the title of Emperor Shenzong (1573 – 1619), and a seal "treasure of emperor's brush 御笔之宝." Although fake works often carried these sorts of inscription and seals, he denied the possibility based on the faded color of the seal and minor wears on the silks. ①He also encountered a personal work of Emperor Shenzong. Although the price was high, he managed to negotiate through the Xuban to trade in the work. He also purchased some European works. But he regretted that he could not get the personal brushwork of Emperor Yingzong (1436 – 1449) due to prohibitive price. ②Thus in his account of purchases, he listed all these three paintings. But he also mentioned calligraphy works (rubbing) of Mi Fu 米芾, Yan Zhenqing 颜真卿, Zhao Mengfu, and Dong Qichang. ③Kim Yuk, who came to China in 1636, reported that the imperial physician Lu Guoxiang 陆国祥, who visited when he was ill, brought a scroll of silk painting. ④

The 1720s probably mark a milestone in the history of Korean envoy. Earlier ones could only be envious of those later ones. As noted above, the restriction rules of foreigners' movement in Beijing were relaxed since then, and Korean envoys had chance to engage with Chinese officials and literati. Over time, they could explore the capital city, visit art traders, European Jesuits, and establish personal friendship with top officials in the Qing government. Koreans with keen artistic zeal would find themselves quite busy with all these

---

① YS2, pp. 490 – 491.
② YS2, p. 495.
③ YS2, p. 511.
④ YS1, p. 218.

varieties of contacts.

Chinese officials and people of the gentry class, needless to say, constituted the mainstream themes. In 1720, Yi Ŭi-hyǒn's envoy did not seem to be freed from the rules. Only one officer of his envoy entered the residence of Nian Xiyao 年希尧, a brother of Nian Gengyao, and witnessed lavish display of antiques and paintings. ①The situation changed dramatically in 1765. The limitation rules remained in full force, but Hong Tae-yong sent valuable gifts to a responsible official Xu Zongmeng 徐宗孟,② and obtained freedom of movement. Therefore Hong could communicate with two members of the Imperial Secretariat Hanlin 翰林, Mr. Wu and Mr. Peng. He visited Peng's house, and saw some rolled scrolls and a displayed one on a wall. ③Although they conversed mostly on history, education, and other subjects, they did discuss paintings. According to Hong's brief description, Peng once asked: "Do you love calligraphy and painting?" Hong answered: "I do like to view them, but have no distinction." Then Peng had his servants bring out two scrolls, one of Dong Qichang, and the other of Wen Zhengming 文征明. Peng further showed a calligraphy work of Wen Tianxiang 文天祥, a heroic Confucianist official of Southern Song (1127 – 1279).④

Over time the Koreans, especially the high-rank figures, could conduct personal interaction with Chinese high officials. Sǒ Ho-su 徐浩修（1736 – 1799）, vice ambassador of a 1790 envoy, received an ink bamboo painting along with ink-stone from Ji Yun 纪昀, the Minister of Rites as well as an accomplished calligrapher and painter. ⑤Sǒ was an expert on calendar calculation, and he held a discourse with a Chinese calendar specialist Weng Fanggang 翁方纲.⑥ Another high official, Tie Bao 铁保, a renowned calligrapher, granted Sǒ three scrolls of doublets, one box of Anhui ink-stick,

---

① YS2, pp. 492 – 493.
② YS1, p. 246.
③ YS1, p. 234.
④ YS1, p. 236.
⑤ YS1, p. 502.
⑥ YS1, p. 507.

and one ink-stone.①

Yu Tǔk-kong 柳得恭（1749-after 1801）, a brilliant poet, connoisseur, and painter, had many discourses with Chinese privileged literati and officials on art works. These activities are evident in their poems he collected in his memoirs. Cheng Jinfang 程晋芳 extolled the "Spring Morning at the Han Palace 汉宫春晓图" by Qiu Ying 仇英, which Cheng, Ji Yun and other renowned literati appreciated together.②Another piece came from Weng Fanggang commenting the "Snow Goose on Weedy Island 芦洲雪雁", said to be done by a Yuan dynasty artist.③Wu Shingqin 吴省钦, also a member of the circle consisting of Cheng and Weng, wrote many pieces on a number of works, including Qiu Ying, Xu Wei 徐渭, Zha Shibiao 查士标. Yu himself composed a poem in honor of a bamboo painting he received from Luo Ping 罗聘, a popular painter in Liulichang 琉璃厂, the prominent art market in Beijing.④

The memorial document of Yu Tǔk-kong provided a remarkably long list of names of officials, scholars, and artists within his contact during his stay in Beijing in 1801. On the next day of his arrival, Yu Tǔk-kong visited Ji Yun, and asked about a few rare books of Zhu Xi. Ji then used his connections in Southern China to search for them. He then held a few conferences with another scholar official Li Mozhuang 李墨庄.⑤An art collector Huang Pilie 黄丕烈 brought a painting of "Worshipping Books 祭书图," which depicts the historical city Gusu 姑苏, and asked for his inscriptions.⑥Yu also received two paintings, one ink bamboo, and one orchid, from two artist friends. He learned from the painter of the ink bamboo that in painting bamboo, a few branches are superior to the other.⑦Pak Sa-ho, accompanying an 1828 envoy, also connected a few powerful officials, among whom were Chen Jichang, a high military official and

---

① YS1, p. 514.
② YS1, p. 629.
③ YS1, p. 639.
④ YS1, p. 637.
⑤ YS1, p. 656.
⑥ YS1, p. 661.
⑦ YS1, pp. 662–663.

a renowned calligrapher, as well as Ji Yun, Weng Fanggang, and Tie Bao. ①

Apart from the conduit of Chinese officials and scholars, the Koreans could see art works under various circumstances. Pak Sa-ho once entered a liquor shop located close to the city gate Zhengyangmen. To his astonishment, the shop was exquisitely decorated with fine furniture, rare plants, calligraphy works and paintings of renowned artists. He found that the customers, of the gentry class, had the habit of drinking while commenting on the art works. Therefore a work could become famous later on, and the shopkeeper could also sell it at a high price. ②Pak heard news about a grandson of Dong Qichang. This man did not have the fortune of the grandfather; he bought a mule and traveled in Sichuan, and when he returned, he gave himself to liquor. He happened to meet a Korean, to whom he cried out his hard life. ③

Another important theme of the Koreans' artistic activities was visiting art markets. One major market that caught the attention of Koreans was the temple Longfusi 隆福寺. At the time of Hong Tae-yong's visit in 1765, the market was opened regularly for certain days per month, and it featured a diversity of daily life necessities. It also included bookstores and art shops. But when he probed the price, the sellers, who downplayed Koreans' affordability, spoke out prohibitive prices. ④

Liulichang, as a well-established art market, received far more attention from the Koreans. In fact many Koreans had intimate relation with art dealers, and there they were further exposed to broader circles of literati and artists. Hong Tae-yong, for example, was introduced to two Imperial University students Zhou and Jiang, and they met in the bookshop Weijingzhai 味经斋. He had a short conversation with the owner of the bookshop, who was an uncle of Zhou, and learned about the printing technique in China. ⑤Kim Chŏng-jung 金正中 (18th century) seemed to have visited the market rather frequently in 1791. He

---

① YS1, pp. 884–885.
② YS1, p. 881.
③ YS1, p. 883.
④ YS1, p. 318.
⑤ YS1, pp. 238–240.

was asked to buy a book for a relative, but he went there mostly for satisfying his own literati appetite. Once he accompanied another envoy member pen-named Song Wôn 松园 (real name unknown) to an art dealer Zhang Shuiwu 张水屋, and saw the "Old Vine Book Studio 古藤书屋图" But he had a more intimate connection with another dealer Cheng Shaobo 程少伯, the owner of the shop Juhaozhai 聚好斋. He often spent days conversing and exchanging poems with Cheng, and students from the Imperial University, and many attendees of Imperial Examinations. He was particularly excited to meet a descendant of Zhu Xi. ①He certainly was happy to produce some calligraphy work as gifts, as well as to receive art works from them. Kim presented to Cheng one painting and four heart-soothing pills,② and the latter offered a scroll peony painting by a recent master, which he originally intended to sell to Kim. ③

Song Wôn instead had an intimate relationship with Zhang Shuiwu. He visited Zhang's shop frequently, and unlike Kim Chŏng-jung, he often purchased art works from his shop. At one time, one painted fan, one scroll of "Eight Scenes of Three Wu 三吴八景图" and one piece of "Riverside Village and Mountainous Temple（江村山寺图）" but he did not give the names of the artists, presumably some less-known ones. Zhang himself was skilled in poetry and calligraphy, and he left a poem on the last painting. ④He also engaged in communication with members of the Imperial University in Zhang's shop, and consequently he received gifts such as calligraphy works and seals from them. ⑤When the time of departure arrived, both Kim and Song Wôn had a melancholy farewell party with the two dealers; again they exchanged calligraphy works and paintings.

Such contact with merchants and artists was not necessarily limited to the lower-class members of Korean envoys. Yu Tŭk-kong, the chief ambassador of an 1801 envoy, also had many associates at Liulichang. He already knew Mr.

---

① YS1, p. 575.
② YS1, p. 574.
③ YS1, p. 585.
④ YS1, p. 577.
⑤ YS1, p. 579.

Tao in the course of buying books, but this time he ran into Mr. Cui. Cui had a comfortable patio where Yu could read books in his shop in summer. As their friendship grew, they started to exchange gifts; Yu offered Korean brush, ink, ink-stone, and knife, whereas Cui responded with a painted fan. Cui then introduced a famous portrait painter, Chen Sen 陈森, to Yu. Chen asked Yu whether he had done any portrait of himself at home. Yu said no; he explained that Korean painters said that people with distinctive marks, beard, and cheekbones are easy to portray, while the plain face of Yu is difficult to depict. Chen replied that the skill of a painter did not depend on the feature of the face. Chen then offered to make one portrait of Yu. He finished it in one time, and afterwards added a setting of old plum tree. At seeing this work, the vice ambassador of Yu's envoy were so impressed that they also asked to be portrayed by Chen.[①]

The third important contact that the Koreans would make was with the Europeans, primarily the Jesuits. The Koreans, according to Ledyard, began to hear of the Europeans and Jesuits since the early sixteenth century. They had also known of European scientific achievement and Catholic doctrines. Crown Prince Sohyŏn, who was held hostage in Beijing in 1644, became acquainted with Father Adam Schall von Bell (汤若望, 1591 – 1666), and received many religious and scientific books and artifacts from him. Since 1720, when Yi Ŭi-hyŏn personally visited one Jesuit church, regular direct contact was channeled between the Koreans and Jesuits.[②] Yi likewise received from Father Xavier Fridelli (1673 – 1743), known as Fei Yin 费隐 in Chinese, two Catholic treatises, *Sanshan Lunxueji* 三山论学记 (by Jules Aleni) and *Zhuzhi Qunzheng* 主制群征 (by Adam Schall), as well as fifteen paintings of various sizes, which Yi returned with some Korean products.[③] From this time on, either Koreans or Fathers sought out the other party and the communication continued.

---

① YS1, p. 664.
② Ledyard, Gari, Korean Travelers in China over Four Hundred Years, 1488 – 1887, in James B. Palais ed., *Occasional Papers on Korea*, Number two, The Joint Committee on Korean Studies, 1974, p. 16.
③ YS2, p. 517.

Such condensed encounters were bound to foster the growth of the Catholic religion and Practical Study (Sirhak 实学) in Korea. ①The subject, however, runs out of the scope of this paper, and will not be elaborated here.

  I shall return to the artistic activities of the envoys. After Yi Ŭi-hyŏn Koreans often visited Catholic churches in Beijing, and their thrilling experience of the exotic fresco paintings drove subsequent envoys to visit them. The Catholic, nevertheless, was not the only order of the Christian religion in Beijing. There was a period in the early nineteenth century when the Koreans stopped visiting the Catholic churches because of several brutal persecutions of the Catholics in Korea since 1801,② and they turned to the Russians and visited their Eastern Orthodox chapel. ③In spite of these divergences, the mainstream of contacts remained with the Catholic order. Records describing fresco paintings in the Catholic churches often appeared in the diaries of Yi and subsequent envoys. Pak Chi-wŏn had the most sensitive mind to the realistic paintings:

  "Now in the Catholic church between the walls and ceiling, the painted clouds and figures cannot be conceived with our wisdom and mind; neither could they be described with our language and words. When I am about to look at them, (they) glare like lightening and seem to grab my eyes; and I hate that they would perceive my mind; when I am about to hear them, they seem to bend down and turn around eyes and speak to my ears, and I regret that they would penetrate my hidden inside; when I am about to talk to them, they break silence, making thundering sound. Looking closer at them, I find wild brushwork, but in their ears, eyes, mouth, and nose, and in their hair and texture, there are differentiation of shading, and fine touches. And they seem to breathe and move, and the reason is that there is differentiation of dark and bright, front and back (towards the light), which create the voluminous effect. 今天主堂中墙壁藻井之间，所画云气人物，有非心智思虑所可测度，亦

---

  ① Ledyard, Gari, Korean Travelers in China over Four Hundred Years, 1488 – 1887, in James B. Palais ed., *Occasional Papers on Korea*, Number two, The Joint Committee on Korean Studies, 1974, p. 16.
  ② Lee, Ki-baik, *A New History of Korea*, Seoul: Ilchokak, 1984, p. 240.
  ③ YS2, p. 842.

非言语文字所可形容，吾目将视之而有赫赫如电先夺吾目者，吾恶其将洞吾之胸臆也，吾耳将听之而有府仰转眄先属吾耳者，吾惭其将贯吾之隐蔽也，吾口将言之则彼亦将渊默而有雷声，逼而视之笔墨麤疎，但其耳目口鼻之际，毛发腠理之间，晕而界之，较其毫分，有若呼吸转动，盖阴阳向背而自生显晦耳。"[1]

The contacts with the Catholic order did not proceed without trouble. By the year of 1765, the Jesuits felt discontented with Korean envoys, and tried to avoid them. Hong Tae-yong explained that the reason lies in imprudent behaviors of previous Korean visitors in the churches. As an expert in astrology, Hong was most interested in the accurate measuring techniques that the Europeans mastered. But like other Koreans, he could not neglect the realistic depiction of figures and architectures in the fresco paintings of the churches. He also had keen eyes for them. Hong paid more attention to subject and skill, and his observations were rather incisive:

"Inside the gate there is an eastern wall of about two zhang high. A door penetrates the wall. The door is half-opened, and outside it are buildings after buildings, which gives a spectacular view. I ask Sep'al (Hong's servant), who says in smile: "it is painting." I walk closer up and see it; it is truly painting…In the north there is a guest hall…on the eastern wall is painted a celestial scene, whereas on the western wall a cartographic map of the realm…Further into a guest hall…in the north there is an even higher hall. The painting is not so spectacular, but rather delicate and lifelike…on the two walls are architectures and figures in realistic colors. The architectures are rendered in the contrast of concave and convex, and the figures move like real persons. The painting is even good at depicting distance, with river valleys emerging out of and disappearing in mist. The distant sky is pasted with positive colors. When looking around, (I) do not feel that it is false. I hear that the western painting is distinguished not only by unrivaled smart composition, but also by the method of calculating proportion, which is derived from arithmetic. The figures in the

---

[1] Pak, Chi-wǒn, *Yǒrha Ilgi*, Sǒul Tǔkpyǒl-si: Taeyang Sǒjǒk, 1973, p. 643.

paintings all let their hair loose, and wear (garb) with large sleeves, and their eyes are glaring. None of the objects in the halls are ever seen in China, and are probably made in the Western Ocean. 入门，东有砖墙，高可二丈。穿墙而为门。门半启，望其外楼阁栏桷重重，意其有异观也。招世八问之，世八笑曰：'画也。'前数步察之，果画也。……北有客堂……东壁画盖天象，西画天下舆地。……又請入从堂……北有堂益高。妆饰不甚眩耀，惟精巧如神。……见两壁画楼阁人物皆设真彩。楼阁中虚凹凸相参人物浮动如生。尤工于远势，若川谷显晦，烟云明灭。至于远天空界，皆施正色。环顾然不觉其非真也。盖闻洋画之妙，不惟巧思过人，有裁割比例之法，专出於算术也。画中人皆披发衣大袖，眼光炯然。宫室器用俱中国所未见，意皆西洋之制也。"[1]

Impact of Artistic Activities on the Korean Art

The artistic activities surveyed above necessarily constitutes an image that Korean envoys might have brought back home a great number of Chinese paintings. Unfortunately little effort has been taken to collect Chinese works extant today in Korea; it would be impossible to comb through the holdings in Korean museums here. It suffices to glean records of works that contemporary Koreans had witnessed. This could be a daunting task if it were not for the *Hanguk Misulsa Charyo Chipsong*. The piecemeal information that sparsely scatters in the received texts of the Chosŏn Dynasty comes to our disposal in handy seven volumes. The fourth and sixth volumes, specifically covering the middle and late periods (since 1724), reveal an astonishing quantity of Chinese paintings in various collections in contemporaneous Korea.

The quantity of Chinese paintings, not including those not explicitly identified, in Korean documents is amazing. Many of them came out of earlier first-order artists, whose works became extinct in market in late Chosŏn. Kim

---

[1] YS1, p. 241.

Ryu 金鎏 (1571 – 1648) recorded that Mr. Sin accidentally obtained the work "Shanglin Ode 上林赋" of Qiu Ying in Shenyang. ①Cho Yông-sôk 赵荣祏 (1686 – 1761) acquired a landscape scroll of Dong Qichang from his neighbor, who obtained it during his trip to Beijing. ②There were even several references to works of more remote figures such as Wang Wei 王维, a Tang dynasty artist,③ and Emperor Huizong 徽宗. ④One essayist (date unknown) relates that Kim Tae-myông 金大鸣 received eight ink paintings from Emperor Shizong (1522 – 1566). He then posted the works on a screen. The screen later went as dowry to a Yi family and became a treasure piece of this family. ⑤ In fact, in Korea there were many large albums containing dozens of masterpieces. We learn from a middle-Chosŏn commentator's poems that an album of four volumes, altogether 107 pieces, existed in a collection, and it even held works of Gu Kaizhi 顾恺之, an eastern Jin master, Wang Wei, Tang Yin 唐寅, to mention a few. ⑥Since Gu and Wang's works had already been extinct by this time, the album was more likely a printed catalogue rather than a collection of real paintings. Another lesser album contained works of Wen Zhengming 文征明, Zhu Zhishan 祝枝山, and Zhao Mengfu. ⑦

The significance of the presence of Chinese paintings in Korean society cannot be over-evaluated. The numerous poems and essays collected in the two volumes of the *Hanguk Misulsa Charyo Chipsong* suggest that these works inspired an ever-growing discourse among Korean literati. In fact these paintings became the objects to be transformed in the use of the Koreans, and thus made a powerful force shaping Korean cultural climate. Korean literati collectors frequently created exalting poems and essays in honor of their holdings; they also invited friends to share the exhilarating moments of appreciating these

---

① *Hangguk Misulsa Charyo Chipsong*, IV, p. 18.
② *Hangguk Misulsa Charyo Chipsong*, IV, p. 92.
③ *Hangguk Misulsa Charyo Chipsong*, IV, p. 507.
④ *Hangguk Misulsa Charyo Chipsong*, IV, p. 403.
⑤ *Hangguk Misulsa Charyo Chipsong*, VI, pp. 162 – 163.
⑥ *Hangguk Misulsa Charyo Chipsong*, IV, pp. 158 – 162.
⑦ *Hangguk Misulsa Charyo Chipsong*, VI, pp. 152 – 153.

works. Ch'oe Han-kyông 崔汉卿 kept three paintings of Wen Zhengming, and he showed them to Ho Mok 许穆, a highly-esteemed scholar. Ho had an ineffable time:

"I once viewed the *Gushi Huapu*, and for the first time saw the sublime brushwork of Hengshan (Wen's pen name). His poetry, calligraphy, and painting are all unrivaled and worth eschewing. Later on because of war, it has been lost for dozens of years, and Hengshan's painting is overall rare in the East (Korea). I regret having no means to see them again. Today in Mr. Choe's place I saw them. I knew Mr. Choe had discerning eyes for calligraphy and paintings, and he would not keep a work unless it is a supreme one. Now I am old and ill-stricken, and secluded from people and events, not to mention calligraphy and painting. If it were not for Mr. Choe, how could I have had this chance? 余尝得顾氏画谱，始见衡山笔妙，其诗书画，皆奇绝可玩。其后经乱，失之已数十年。衡山之画，盖不多传于东方，恨无由得复见也。今于崔子处见之。崔子知书画，非绝笔不留之。今吾老多病，于人事且疏绝，况求书画乎？不见崔子，其何以得此？"①

In another case, Yi Sôn 李愃 acquired Zhao Mengfu's "Eight Great Horses 八骏图" during his trip to Shenyang. He then showed it to other Korean literati, such as Ch'oe Myông-gil 崔鸣吉, Kim Sang-son, Yi Sik 李植, who left their commentaries on the work. He finally submitted it to the court where King Sukjong 肃宗, who then created an extolling poem:

"Songxue (Zhao's pen name) is conversant in arts, and the eight horses are even more accomplished. While at rest, they seem to shake their hair, and while tethered, they seem to blow breath. It was obtained in a Liaoyang market, and by accidence it came to the forbidden palace. Whenever I read the inscriptions, endless sentiment and consonance come to my mind…松雪多才艺，八驹画愈工。闘时疑动鬣，牵处若嘶风。初得辽阳市，偶来紫禁中。每看题卷里，感慨意无穷……"②

The constant and substantial influx of artistic experience and actual art

---

① *Hangguk Misulsa Charyo Chipsong*, IV, p. 872.
② *Hangguk Misulsa Charyo Chipsong*, IV, p. 239.

works certainly had significant impact on the Koreans' conception of artistic creation. This is especially the case in the late Chosŏn dynasty (after 1725), when Korean literati left a rich wealth of documents of their contemplation on painting. Hong Yang-ho 洪良浩 (1724 – 1802), who visited China twice, expressed his dissatisfaction with the status of painting in Korea. While Chinese literati could enjoy both calligraphy and painting, Korean literati debased painting as marginal art, and even when some talented persons became skilled in painting, they derided these masters. ①His complaint reveals that he was anxious to promote the career of painters.

Chinese artistic theories and ideals, especially those of the Southern School advocated by Dong Qichang, also entered the discourse of Korean art critics. The treatise *Songch'ŏn P'ildam* 松泉笔谈 commented that Sim Sa-Jŏng particularly adored Chinese (works), and his works particularly bore wildness and power like poems and essays of Su Shi. The anonymous author also noted that another artist, Yi Wŏl-lyŏng 李元灵 depicted a simplified landscape of one tree and one rock with minimal brushwork and reduced taste, so much so that he identified his work with literati paintings. But he also pointed out Yi's works lacked the play of ink, and did not reach the effect of dark wet. In his view, Pyŏn Sang-byŏk 卞尚璧 and Kim Hong-do capture the shape of object, but lack spontaneous quality. He thus concluded that Korean arts, although imitating Chinese works and not lacking distinguished masters, could not compare with Chinese masters. ②

Kim Chŏng-hui 金正喜, a zealous collector of Chinese works and vigorous adherent of Chinese theories, highly appraised Huang Gongwang 黄公望's skill in creating the brilliant spirit of antiquity. Kim accounted that the effect resulted from the technique of ink piling 积墨, and Huang could vary the distance of landscape, depth of valley by applying layers of dry brush. ③In another essay, Kim condemned Korean artists that they did not understand the secret of painting

---

① *Hangguk Misulsa Charyo Chipsong*, VI, p. 804.
② *Hangguk Misulsa Charyo Chipsong*, VI, p. 801.
③ *Hangguk Misulsa Charyo Chipsong*, VI, p. 803.

orchid. He claimed that orchid is the most difficult thing to depict, and there had been only a few masters, such as Wen Zhengming, Shi Tao 石涛, and Zheng Xie 郑燮, who could achieve excellence because of their lofty virtue. The key of painting orchid does not lie in the resemblance to the shape. One can obtain it neither by gradual study of manual, nor by instant enlightenment. Therefore one may attain the nine thousand nine hundred and ninety-nine points, but one cannot attain the last one point. This one point can lie neither within the reach of human ability, nor beyond the reach of human ability. [1]The emphasis on the virtue and enlightenment of a painter spells out the ideals of the Chinese Southern School.

The same mentality turns up in the essay of Cho Yông-sôk when he discussed an album of Chŏng Sŏn. Chŏng's works show no trace of brushwork, but skill of ink splash, so that they look dark and wet, and thus remind of the school of Dong Qichang. He commented that such skill had never been achieved in the past three hundred years. He criticized that Korean landscape painters did not know the method of composition, the sixteen types of texturing, and the ideal of giving clear clues to every rivulet. Although they worked out multiple mountains, they failed to differentiate sides of front and back, distance, height, depth, and they handled water surface simply by cross brushes, regardless of whether it is slow flowing river or turbulent sea waves. He happily remembered that Chŏng accepted his view. Afterward Chŏng went out visiting Mountain Kŭmgang and other scenic places, and he worked so hard that the amount of brushes he had used could bury him. Thus he could initiate a new artistic tradition of landscape painting in Korea. [2]

In the meantime a few critics began to be dissatisfied with Chinese idealistic paradigms, and they cried out for realistic paintings. The main proponent of this idealism, Su Shi (1037 – 1101), condemned faithful depiction of objects that "one who discusses a painting by formal resemblance, he is as naïve as a child; one who thinks a poem must address one object, he

---

[1] *Hangguk Misulsa Charyo Chipsong*, VI, p. 805.
[2] *Hangguk Misulsa Charyo Chipsong*, VI, pp. 816 – 817.

must not understand poetry. 论画以形似，见与儿童邻；赋诗必此诗，定非知诗人。" This antagonism sped up an already-existing tendency in China of pursuing the spirit of objects in painting instead of formal resemblance. This idea even became a dominant paradigm because of the advocacy of the forceful theorist Dong Qichang in the sixteenth century.[1] Yi Ik 李瀷（1681－1763）challenged this paradigm that the spirit of objects lies in the form. If one does not evaluate a painting by formal resemblance, the poem he composed does not address the right object. [2] The author of Hônchaejip 瓛斋集, followed the view of Gu Yanwu 顾炎武, a renowned advocate of practical study of the Qing dynasty, that painting is very relevant to academic matters, and this person criticized current people who would not bother to study the real forms of objects, and only attempted to capture the spirit of subjects. This type of works can satisfy aesthetic view, but it does not help practical matters, such as topographical maps. One victim of such paradigm he brought up is the classical encyclopedia of herbal medicine, *Bencao gangmu* 本草纲目 by Li Shizhen 李时珍. Li spent much of his life in collating the materials in this work, but the work created plenty of problems because he did not have capable artist to illustrate the book. [3]

Another line of impact came with the influx of western paintings. The experience that the Koreans had with fresco paintings and actual paintings they brought back home certainly entered the discourse of a broader audience. Yi Ik saw one such work bought from China, and he found that the architecture protrudes like real ones. He was quick to notice the technique of perspective that create realistic architecture and landscape. He then recalled the preface of Matteo Ricci for the Chinese version of the *Principles of Geometry* 几何原本. He knew that the perspective technique allows one to capture the distance and height so that the sizes of objects and the volume of objects were borne out. [4]

---

[1] Bush, Susan, *The Chinese Literati on Painting: Su Shih* (1037－1101) *to Tung Ch'i-ch'ang* (1555－1636), Cambridge: Harvard University Press, 1971.
[2] *Hangguk Misulsa Charyo Chipsong*, Ⅵ, p. 822.
[3] *Hangguk Misulsa Charyo Chipsong*, Ⅵ, pp. 812－813.
[4] *Hangguk Misulsa Charyo Chipsong*, Ⅵ, p. 831.

第四部分 东亚艺术史

With these high esteems of Chinese paintings and the discourse of painting theories, it is not surprising that Korean painters were often encouraged to copy Chinese works. In East Asia, copying was not only a process of training, but also a process of creating art works. The legendary painting "Wangchuan Villa 辋川图" of Wang Wei appeared to be the most popular subject in Korea. Chŏng Sŏn was reported to have produced such work,① although his prototype was unknown. Yi Ching was another imitator of the subject. The Ming envoy Zhu Zhifan left twenty leaves of paintings reproducing the scenes described in famous poems including the Wangchuan Villa, and Yi was asked to copy all of them.② Another case occurred to Qiu Ying's "Peach Blossom Land 桃源图." Sin Chông-ha 申靖夏（1680 – 1715）owned an appealing piece by Meng Rongguang, but he preferred Qiu's work owned by another person. He borrowed it, and asked the court painter Yi Chi to copy it to a screen. The entire project took fifty days, and Yi's rendition was said to have captured seven out of ten of delicacy of the original. Sin cherished it as his family treasure, and he was delighted to be the most ardent admirer of the subject.③ Huang Gongwang, because of Dong Qichang's glamorization, became another preferential target of imitation in Korea. Kim Chông-hui expressed his opinion:

"(Masters) from Dong Xiangguang (Dong Qichang), down to Wang Yanke (Wang Meng 王蒙), Lutai, Shigu (Shi Tao), all followed the suit of Daci (Huang Gongwang), and fathomed the secrets (of paintings). But they developed their own variations, made small modifications, and formulated their own styles. The work (of Yun Congshan) faithfully imitates Daci, and denies his own idea. It matches (Huang's work) to the hair…I do not mean that this work surpasses those of Xuanzai (Dong Qichang) and other masters…The Eastern people do not have chance to see real works of Daci, but the beginners can start with this work. 自董香光以来，至于王烟客，麓台，石谷诸人，皆于大痴门径，深入秘奥，然各以自家风致，稍变面目，成就一家。此画直从大

---

① *Hangguk Misulsa Charyo Chipsong*, IV, p. 146.
② *Hangguk Misulsa Charyo Chipsong*, IV, p. 146.
③ *Hangguk Misulsa Charyo Chipsong*, IV, p. 69.

痴，不用己意，毛发毕肖……非以此画为过于玄宰诸人也……东人不得见大痴真本，初学如从此画入，可以下手。"[1]

Conclusion

The currently available diaries provide sufficient records of artistic activities, i. e. viewing, exchanging, and trading paintings, of Korean envoys in China. Such events took place on route at many towns where the Koreans could encounter officials of some artistic distinction, historical monuments, literati families, and art dealers. Shenyang, as a capital city of the Qing Empire, was an outstanding location. It witnessed two major events, the meetings of the Korean princes and five high officials with Meng Rongguang in early Qing, and the communications between Pak Nae-gyŏm and Chinese artist officials in 1829. The Shanhaiguan Pass registered an artistic conference between Yi An'nul and Wang Yinglin. Cultural resorts like Guzhucheng, and towns with prominent literati family like Funing supplied numerous paintings for Koreans to see. Art dealers at stations like Fengrun further offered another channel to see and purchase art works.

Such activities could only be intensified once Korean envoys arrived in Beijing. In general they found themselves in an art world, and they had sufficient free time to explore it. Therefore practically nothing could prevent them from satisfying their artistic appetite if they had. Even in the entire Ming and early Qing when the Koreans were largely confined to their hostel, they could conduct communication with streams of artist literati, and art dealers coming to visit them. There were even occasions that they received gift paintings from Chinese emperors when they attended imperial audience. They could also extend their antenna through the intermediate agents Xuban members. When the limitation of movement loosened in the 1720s, Koreans with acute artistic zest were busy visiting cultural monuments in the capital, and communicating with Chinese literati and officials. Such events very often involved viewing and

---

[1] *Hangguk Misulsa Charyo Chipsong*, VI, p. 105.

exchanging art works. They also frequently visited art markets such as Liulichang and Longfusi, and the diaries documented quite a number of trading activities with bonus communications with Chinese gentry people. Furthermore, few Koreans would miss the Christian churches in Beijing. There they held discourse with the Jesuits, experienced the thrilling realistic fresco paintings, and received gift works of art.

It should not go without stating that these records primarily came from a few diaries out of the total thirty-one. The authors of these diaries, like Hong Tae-yong, Pak Chi-wŏn and Yi Ŭi-hyŏn, were exceptional in their refined aesthetic eyes, and their expressive brushes. Such figures were certainly not rare in Korean envoys. Given that the thirty-one copies only represents a tiny portion of the enormous amount of diaries that might have come out of the intensive and persistent Korean envoys, we shall allow ourselves to envision that there were a great number of such members in Korean envoys, and accordingly enormous artistic activities were experienced.

As a consequence of this survey, we are well prepared to predict that Chinese paintings flowed to Korea in a steady pace and in large quantities. Indeed the received records reveal that there were a considerable number of works in the private and royal collections. The pieces recorded in these documents, although not always genuine, were works of major masters of Chinese art history, including Gu Kaizhi, Wang Wei, Liu Songnian, Zhao Mengfu, Wen Zhengming and Dong Qichang. One large-scale album even held one hundred and seven masterpieces altogether, although they were most likely printed copies. It follows that Korean society in the Chosŏn dynasty, not to mention earlier periods, was not short of Chinese works at all.

The presence of a large number of Chinese paintings is bound to cast an expansive impact on Korean art circles. First of all, these works entered the discourse of Korean literati, and became a powerful force in shaping the artistic climate in Korea. The large quantity of literature recorded in the two volumes of the *Hanguk Misulsa Charyo Chipsong* under this study exposes that Korean people highly appreciated Chinese paintings. In fact these volumes recorded many cases that poets often composed poems after Chinese paintings piece by piece. These works, as well as the accumulative experience of Korean envoys, brought Chinese artistic theories to Korea. The records brought above indicate that ink effect and virtuous plants, derived from Chinese southern school, became the paramount ideals of artistic critics in Korea. We should not ignore new movement of realism in the eighteenth-Century, but they also disclosed the fact that the ideals of the idealistic paradigms of Chinese southern school had solidified as the tenacious norm in Korea. Under such artistic environment, copying of Chinese works became a regular practice of Korean artists who attempted to attain some status in the artistic world.

Chinese Lacquerwares from Begram: Date and Provenance*

The Begram site is located some 60 km to the north of Kabul, capital of Afghanistan, lying at the confluence of the Gorband and Panjshir rivers to the north and the intersection of two trade routes—an east-west route between the Mediterranean Sea and India, and a north-south route between Pakistan and China. Undoubtedly a strategic spot in ancient times, it first caught the attention of the two European adventurers Charles Masson and Claude-Auguste Court in the early nineteenth century. ①The thousands of ancient coins they gathered there immediately aroused interest from the western world, and in 1936 the French Archaeological Delegation began to undertake systematic excavations, which brought to light a fortified town 550 meters across, consisting of a main street and two residential areas (Fig. 4 – 2 – 1). The most exciting discoveries come from the eastern area, especially Rooms No. 10 and No. 13 (Fig. 4 – 2 – 2), which have yielded an extraordinary wealth of Roman glassware and bronze sculptures, Indian ivory and Bone Carvings, as well as Chinese lacquerwares. ②

Ever since its discovery, generations of scholars have pondered over the identity of this ruined city. Nineteenth-century scholars associated Begram with the Macedonian Alexandria of the Caucasus or the Hellenistic Nikæa erected in the

---

* The article was originally published in *International Journal of Asian Studies* 8. 1; It is reprinted in this anthology with minor changes, 2011, pp. 1 – 24.

① Ghirshman, R. , *Bégram: Recherches Archéologiques et Historiques sur les Kouchans*, avec la collaboration de T. Girschman, Le Caire: Imprimerie de l'Institut français d'archaeologie orientale, 1946, p. 6.

② The finds in the two rooms were subsequently published in two reports, Hackin, J. , *Recherches Archéologiques à Begram*, chantier no. 2 (1937) par J. Hackin, avec la collaboration de madame J. R. Hackin, Paris: Les Éditions d'art et d'histoire, 1939, Hackin, J. , *Nouvelles Recherches Archéologiques à Begram, Ancienne Kâpicî*, 1939 – 1940, *Rencontre de Trois Civilisations, Inde, Grece, Chine*, Avec la collaboration de J. – R. Hackin, J. Carl et P. Hamelin, Études comparatives par J. Auboyer [et al], Paris: Imprimerie nationale, 1954.

fourth century BC. ① A. Foucher, director of the French Archaeological Delegation, delved into Chinese texts and matched it with Kapisa, the summer capital of the Kushan Empire, which ruled the region about three centuries later. ② This identification laid the foundation for his fellow archaeologists, principally J. Hackin and R. Ghirshman, to designate the eastern residential area as a palace of the empire, and Rooms No. 10 and No. 13 as the royal treasury. Later studies, however, have raised other possibilities. Sanjyot Mehendale considers Begram to be a trading city of the Kushan Empire, and the two rooms "merchant storehouses." ③ Pierre Cambon opines that

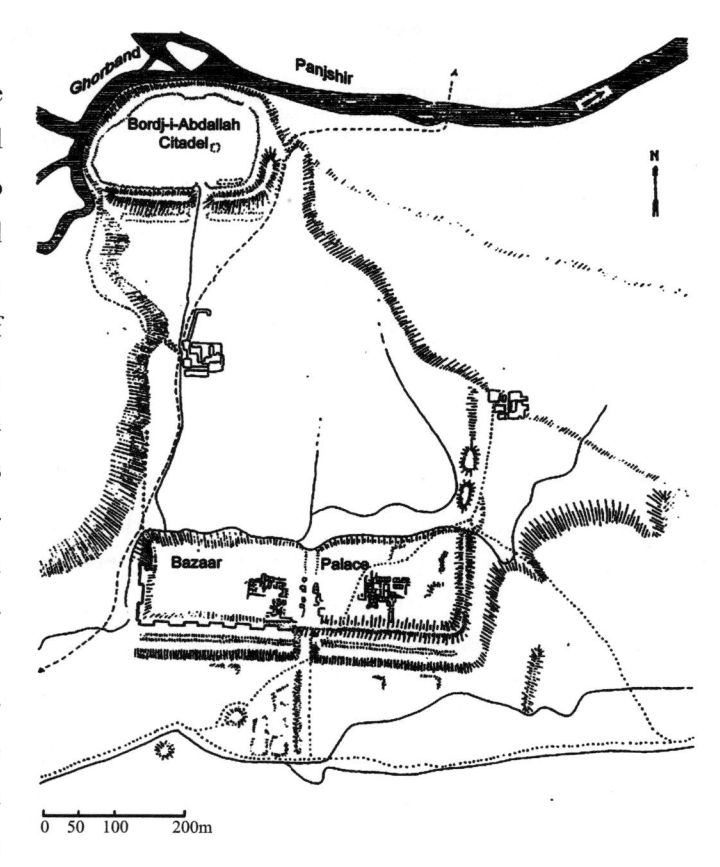

Fig. 4 – 2 – 1 Plan of Begram

(Reproduced from Ghirshman, R., 1946, *Bégram: Recherches Archéologiques et Historiques sur les Kouchans*, avec la collaboration de T. Girschman, p. 6, Le Caire: Imprimerie de l'Institut français d'archaeologie orientale, pl. XXIV)

---

① For a survey of these early propositions, see Mehendale, Sanjyot, *Begram: New Perspectives on the Ivory and Bone Carvings*, PhD dissertation, University of California, Berkeley, 1997, pp. 24 – 26.

② Mani, Buddha Rashmi, *The Kushan Civilization*, Delhi: B. R. Publishing Corporation, 1987, p. 1.

③ Mehendale, Sanjyot, Begram: at the heart of the silk roads, in Fredrik Hiebert and Pierre Cambon eds., *Afghanistan: Hidden Treasures from the National Museum, Kabul*, Washington, D. C.: National Geographic, 2008, p. 143.

第四部分 东亚艺术史

Kapisa was the capital of an earlier Greek kingdom. ①

The discussion of the identity of Begram, to a great extent, is entangled with the early history of Afghanistan in general and the chronology of Begram in particular. In his study of the Roman glassware, together with the Indian ivory and bone carvings from Room No. 10, Hackin delineates a wide span of Begram's history from the first to early fourth century. ②His later report on the treasures from Room No. 13 lays out a more detailed story. The first and second centuries were the most prosperous period in Begram, when it profited from the transcontinental trade between Rome and China. In the third century, it began to decline as this trade activity slackened. In the fifth century, it fell to the rule of the Huns, which is reflected in the citadel with four towers in the palace area. ③

On the basis of stratigraphic evidence, Ghirshman discerns three levels of construction in the western residential area. The earliest level corresponds to the time of the Greek kingdoms in the second century BC, whereas the third level terminates

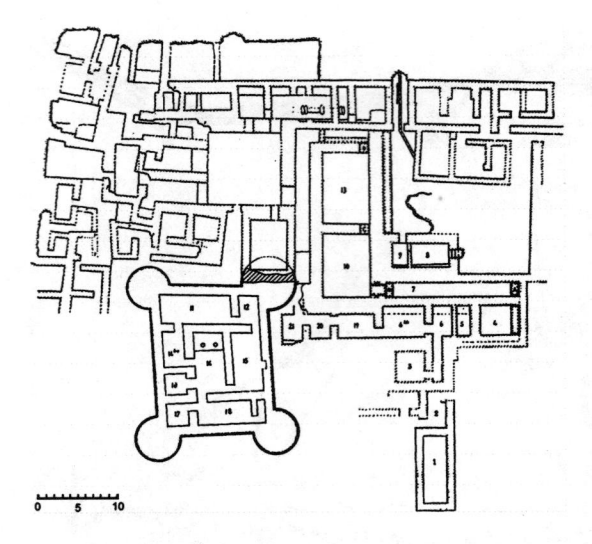

Fig. 4 - 2 - 2　The palace area of Begram

(Reproduced from Hackin, J., 1954, *Nouvelles Recherches Archéologiques à Begram, ancienne Kapici, 1939 - 1940; Rencontre de Trois Civilisations, Inde, Grece, Chine*, p. 9, Avec la collaboration de J. - R. Hackin, J. Carl et P. Hamelin, Études comparatives par J. Auboyer [et al], Paris: Imprimerie nationale)

---

① Cambon, Pierre, Begram: Alexandria of the Caucasus, Capital of the Kushan Empire, in Fredrik Hiebert and Pierre Cambon eds., *Afghanistan: Hidden Treasures from the National Museum, Kabul*, Washington, D. C.: National Geographic, 2008, pp. 160 - 161.

② Hackin, J., *Recherches Archéologiques à Begram*, chantier no. 2 (1937) par J. Hackin, avec la collaboration de madame J. R. Hackin, Paris: Les Éditions d'art et d'histoire, 1939, p. 10.

③ Hackin, J., *Nouvelles Recherches Archéologiques à Begram, ancienne Kâpicî, 1939 - 1940; Rencontre de Trois Civilisations, Inde, Grece, Chine*, Avec la collaboration de J. - R. Hackin, J. Carl et P. Hamelin, etudes comparatives par J. Auboyer [et al], Paris: Imprimerie nationale, 1954, p. 15.

in the fourth century AD. He believes the occupational period of the eastern residential area roughly parallels the second level, the era of the Kushan Empire,① and attributes the destruction of the "palace" to the Sassanian king Shapur I, who presumably occupied Begram between AD 241 and AD 250. ②David Whitehouse, however, does not accept this date. Examining Roman objects from Rooms No. 10 and No. 13, including bronze sculptures, glassware, and plaster casts, he comes up with a much earlier date of about AD 50 – AD 125. ③Yet more recently, Beat Rütti redates a Pharos beaker, which had been customarily assigned to the first century AD, to the late third-early fourth century AD, and the closure of the two treasure rooms to AD 356 – AD 357, when the Sassanian king Shapur II invaded Afghanistan. ④

Apart from these studies centering on Roman goods, specialists have also paid much attention to the Indian ivories and bone carvings from Begram. Comparing motifs on these carvings, Hackin delineates a range of dates from the mid-first century BC till the turn of the third and fourth centuries. ⑤But other scholars reject this broad chronology. Philippe Stern argues that the carvings should all be dated to the first and second centuries AD. ⑥J. L. Davidson narrows the chronology to the first century BC, whereas Mehendale assigns it to

---

① Ghirshman, R. , *Bégram: Recherches Archéologiques et Historiques sur les Kouchans*, avec la collaboration de T. Girschman, p. 6, Le Caire: Imprimerie de l'Institut français d'archaeologie orientale, 1946, pp. 26 – 28.

② Ghirshman, R. , *Bégram: Recherches Archéologiques et Historiques sur les Kouchans*, avec la collaboration de T. Girschman, p. 6, Le Caire: Imprimerie de l'Institut français d'archaeologie orientale, 1946, pp. 99 – 100.

③ Whitehouse, David, Begram reconsidered, *Kölner Jahrbuch für Vor- und Frühgeschichte* 22, 1989, p. 154.

④ Rütti, Beat, Der Pharosbecher von Begram—ein spätantikes Figurendiatret, in *Antike Glastöpferei: Ein vergessenes kapitel der glasgeschichte*, Mainz and Rhein: Verlag Philipp von Zabern, 1999, pp. 132 – 133.

⑤ Hackin, J. , *Nouvelles Recherches Archéologiques à Begram, Ancienne Kapici*, 1939 – 1940; *Rencontre de Trois Civilisations, Inde, Grece, Chine*, Avec la collaboration de J. -R. Hackin, J. Carl et P. Hamelin, etudes comparatives par J. Auboyer [et al], Paris: Imprimerie nationale, 1954, p. 14.

⑥ Stern, Philippe, Les ivories et os découverts à Begram leur place dans l'évolution de l'art de l'inde, in J. Hackin, *Nouvelles Recherches Archéologiques à Begram, Ancienne Kapici*, 1939 – 1940; *Rencontre de Trois Civilisations, Inde, Grece, Chine*, Avec la collaboration de J. – R. Hackin, J. Carl et P. Hamelin. etudes comparatives par J. Auboyer [et al] . Paris: Imprimerie nationale, 1954, p. 20.

the first century AD. ①In fact, Mehendale and Cambon believe that all the artifacts from Rooms No. 10 and No. 13 are synchronic and date from the first century AD. ②

In comparison with Roman and Indian goods, the Chinese lacquerware fragments, which were uncovered from Room No. 13, have received less attention. ③The reason possibly lies in the poor condition of these objects. Due to soil humidity, the organic (wooden and/or hemp) frames of the original wares have rotted away, and what the excavators retrieved are merely fragments of lacquer coating. Eighteen pieces were uncovered, but only a few of them were published in the excavation report. ④Three black and white photos show several caskets *in situ*, and another the décor of a platter. Six fragments are reproduced in four sketches, and they furnish us with a modest amount of information, which is supplemented to some extent by the description in the report. ⑤The one photo and the four sketches thus comprise the entire dataset. Hackin generally

---

① Davidson, J. L., Begram ivories and early Indian sculpture: A reconsideration of dates, in Pratapaditya Pal ed., *Aspects of Indian Art*, Leiden: E. J. Brill, 1972, p. 14; Mehendale, Sanjyot, *Begram: New Perspectives on the Ivory and Bone Carvings*, PhD dissertation, University of California, Berkeley, 1997, p. 213.

② Mehendale, Sanjyot, Begram: at the heart of the silk roads, in Fredrik Hiebert and Pierre Cambon eds., *Afghanistan: Hidden Treasures from the National Museum, Kabul*, Washington, D. C.: National Geographic, 2008, p. 143; Cambon, Pierre, Begram: Alexandria of the Caucasus, Capital of the Kushan Empire, in Fredrik Hiebert and Pierre Cambon eds., *Afghanistan: Hidden Treasures from the National Museum, Kabul*, Washington, D. C.: National Geographic, p. 160.

③ Hackin, J., *Nouvelles Recherches Archéologiques à Begram*, Ancienne Kapici, 1939 – 1940; *Rencontre de Trois Civilisations, Inde, Grece, Chine*, Avec la collaboration de J. -R. Hackin, J. Carl et P. Hamelin, Etudes comparatives par J. Auboyer [et al], Paris: Imprimerie nationale, 1954, p. 11. A few pieces entered the museum of Kabul, but the majority were taken to the Musée Guimet in Paris. See Pirazzoli-t'Serstevens, Michèle, Les laques Chinois de Begram: Un reexamen de leur identification et de leur datation, *Topoi* 11/1, 2003, p. 473.

④ Hackin, J., *Nouvelles Recherches Archéologiques à Begram, ancienne Kapici*, 1939 – 1940; *Rencontre de Trois Civilisations, Inde, Grece, Chine*, Avec la collaboration de J. -R. Hackin, J. Carl et P. Hamelin, Etudes comparatives par J. Auboyer [et al], Paris: Imprimerie nationale, 1954, Figs. 243 – 249.

⑤ Hackin, J., *Nouvelles Recherches Archéologiques à Begram, ancienne Kapici*, 1939 – 1940; *Rencontre de Trois Civilisations, Inde, Grece, Chine*, Avec la collaboration de J. -R. Hackin, J. Carl et P. Hamelin, etudes comparatives par J. Auboyer [et al], Paris: Imprimerie nationale, 1954, pp. 295 – 297.

links them with the Han dynasty. ①V. Elisséeff later made a special study of these finds. ②Citing several datable lacquerwares from Pyŏngyang, the seat of the Han-dynasty Lelang (Nangnang in Korean) Commandery 樂浪郡 in North Korea, Elisséeff is able to narrow the date of the Begram lacquerwares to the first half of the first century AD, and specifically to AD40 – AD50.

At the time Hackin and Elisséeff were wrestling with the Begram lacquerwares, the majority of comparable items had come from Pyŏngyang. Dozens of tombs of ruling aristocrats there were opened by Japanese archaeologists during the first half of the twentieth century. ③The tomb of Wang Xu 王盱 is particularly significant as point of reference, because it yields several pieces datable to AD 45 – AD 69 and others comparable to the Begram finds. A few more datable items came from Xiongnu aristocrats' tombs at Noin-Ula (Noyon uul in Mongolian) in Northern Mongolia, which were excavated by Soviet archaeologists in the first half of the twentieth century also. ④

Recently, Michèle Pirazzoli-t'Serstevens re-examines two items—Nos. 215 and 229 in the original numbering of Hackin's report. Quoting two newly discovered items, she confirms Elisséeff's dating. ⑤However, this study fails to take into account the full current database of Han dynasty tombs and accompanying lacquerwares. From the 1950s, North Korean archaeologists continued to excavate tombs in the precinct of Pyŏngyang, even though no datable

---

① "Han dynasty" in this article refers to the three consecutive dynasties of Western Han (206BC – AD8), Xin (AD9 – AD23) and Eastern Han (AD25 – AD220).

② Elisséeff, V., Les laques chinois de Begram, in J. Hackin, *Nouvelles Recherches Archéologiques à Begram, ancienne Kapici, 1939 – 1940, Rencontre de Trois Civilisations, Inde, Grece, Chine*, Avec la collaboration de J.-R. Hackin, J. Carl et P. Hamelin, Etudes comparatives par J. Auboyer [et al], Paris: Imprimerie nationale, 1954, pp. 151 – 155.

③ Umehara, Sueji, *Chōsen kobunka sōkan*, Tamba-shi: Yōtokusha, 1948, Vol. 2, pp. 3 – 4.

④ Umehara, Sueji, *Studies of Noin-Ula Finds in North Mongolia* 蒙古ノイン・ウラ發見の遺物, Tokyo: The Toyo Bunko, 1969, p. ix; Trever, Camilla, *Excavations in Northern Mongolia (1924 – 1925)*, Leningrad, 1932, description pp. 47 – 49, illustrations pls. 29 – 31.

⑤ Pirazzoli-t'Serstevens, Michèle, Les laques Chinois de Begram: Un reexamen de leur identification et de leur datation, *Topoi* 11/1, 2003, p. 479. In her Ph. D. dissertation, Sanjyot Mehendale simply accepts Elisséeff's conclusions without critical examination, see Mehendale, Sanjyot, *Begram: New Perspectives on the Ivory and Bone Carvings*, PhD dissertation, University of California, Berkeley, 1997, pp. 54 – 55.

lacquerware was found.[1] And, international archaeologists have opened more Xiongnu tombs in Mongolia and Trans-Baikal and sometimes collected sizable caches of Han dynasty lacquerwares, for instance, at the Tamir-1 and Tsaraam cemeteries.[2] An informative report of these findings is yet to come out; the pieces published so far are too fragmentary to offer a basis for comparison. In China proper, discoveries of Han dynasty lacquerwares, which started in the 1940s, grew rapidly after 1949, the founding year of the People's Republic of China, as a result of extensive construction projects. To date, many discoveries have been made in China, mostly in wet southern provinces such as Hubei, Hunan, Jiangsu, Anhui, and Sichuan, but sometimes in dry northern provinces such as Gansu, Hebei, and Shandong, among others.[3] A few of the excavated lacquerwares, including the two cited by Pirazzoli-t'Serstevens, can be dated to specific years of production by inscriptions; most of the un-inscribed pieces can be assigned to broad temporal frames by accompanying ceramics. Beyond that, we may further consider the question of the production sites of the Begram lacquerwares, which may throw new light on the nature of the international contacts that brought Chinese goods to Begram. Pirazzoli-t'Serstevens attributes the two items she cites to two state workshops located in Sichuan,[4] but with the given database, we may re-attribute

---

[1] Personal communication from Wang Peixin, a specialist in the study of Lelang commandery. Also see Wang, Peixin, *Lelang Wenhua: Yi Muzang wei Zhongxin de Kaoguxue Yanjiu*, Beijing: Kexue, 2007, Table 3.

[2] Purcell, David E., and Kimberly C. Spurr, Archaeological Investigations of Xiongnu Sites in the Tamir River Valley, *The Silk Road* 4/1, 2006, pp. 24 – 27. For a preliminary report of the Tsaraam cemetery, see Miniaev, Sergei S., and L. M. Sakharovskaia, Investigation of a Xiongnu Royal Tomb Complex in the Tsaraam Valley, *The Silk Road* 5/1, 2007, pp. 44 – 56; for a report of the lacquerware fragments, see Waugh, Daniel C., The Challenges of Preserving Evidence of Chinese Lacquerware in Xiongnu Graves, *The Silk Road* 4/1, 2006, pp. 32 – 36; for a reading of the inscription, see Pirazzoli-t'Serstevens, Michèle, A Chinese Inscription from a Xiongnu Elite Barrow in the Tsaraam Cemetery, *The Silk Road* 5/1, 2007, pp. 56 – 58.

[3] A comprehensive list of the excavation reports would be many pages long and will not be included here. Readers may instead consult two monographs: Prüch, Margarete, *Die Lacke der Westlichen Han-Zeit*, Frankfurt am Main, Berlin, Bern, New York, Paris, and Wein: Peter Lang, 1997, pp. 536 – 575; Hong, Shi, *Zhanguo Qin Han Qiqi Yanjiu*, Beijing: Wenwu, 2006, pp. 255 – 271. This article will cite some of these in the upcoming pages as necessary. A selection of restorable lacquerwares is published in a catalogue: Fu, Juyou, *Zhongguo Qiqi Quanji*, Fuzhou: Fujian Meishu, 1998, Vol. 3. Some items in this catalogue, however, do not appear in excavation reports.

[4] Pirazzoli-t'Serstevens, Michèle, Les laques Chinois de Begram: Un reexamen de leur identification et de leur datation, *Topoi* 11/1, 2003, p. 476.

Chinese Lacquerwares from Begram: Date and Provenance

them as well as the other pieces from Begram.

In demarcating the chronology of the Begram lacquerwares, one must take into consideration not only datable pieces, but undatable ones as well, and in addition one must have some sense of the stylistic development of Han lacquerwares. A thorough study on this subject, however, has not been done. For the purpose of this article, I would mention a few trends. To begin with, one must bear in mind that lacquerwares are luxury goods, and as the current database shows, they are concentrated in aristocratic tombs. They are also delicate, and their chance of surviving the ravages of time is contingent upon the burial environment. In this context, the early Western Han (206BC – 118BC) boasts a remarkably large quantity of lacquerwares,[1] the major share of which is made up of ear-cups and toilet-boxes for domestic use. [2]Decorative motifs include clouds, dragons, and phoenixes that depict the immortal world. Mostly painted in red on black ground or black on red ground, they are exquisite, colorful, and energetic (Fig. 4 – 2 – 3) (彩图1). As inscriptions on these wares indicate, numerous workshops sponsored by imperial and princely houses were scattered across the empire. A prominent one was "Cheng Shi 成市" or Cheng Workshop located at the city of Chengdu in Sichuan province,[3] whose products have been found in Hunan and Hubei provinces. [4]

A series of changes occur in lacquerwares from the middle Western Han (118BC – 75BC). In general, the multiple-color palette of the previous period gives way to the two-color (black and red) one during this period. Strokes

---

[1] Chinese archaeologists have customarily divided the Western Han dynasty into three phases, the first roughly 206BC – 118BC (to the fifth year of the Yuanshou reign of Emperor Wu), the second 117BC – 75BC (to the last year of Emperor Zhao's reign), and the third 74BC – AD 8 (to the fall of the Western Han dynasty). See Gao, Wei, Qin Han shidai, in Zhongguo Shehui Kexueyuan Kaogu Yanjiusuo ed., *Xinzhongguo de Kaogu Faxian he Yanjiu*, Beijing: Wenwu, 1984, pp. 412 – 414.

[2] Gao, Wei, Qin Han shidai, in Zhongguo Shehui Kexueyuan Kaogu Yanjiusuo ed., *Xinzhongguo de Kaogu Faxian he Yanjiu*, Beijing: Wenwu, 1984, p. 474.

[3] Gao (Gao, Wei, Qin Han shidai, in Zhongguo Shehui Kexueyuan Kaogu Yanjiusuo ed., *Xinzhongguo de Kaogu Faxian he Yanjiu*, Beijing: Wenwu, 1984, pp. 473 – 476) and Hong (Hong, Shi, *Zhanguo Qin Han Qiqi Yanjiu*, Beijing: Wenwu, 2006, pp. 207 – 212) further envisions private workshops in the Qin and Western Han Dynasties.

[4] Wang, Zhongshu, *Handai Kaoguxue Gaishuo*, Beijing: Zhonghua Shuju, 1984, p. 47; Hong, Shi, *Zhanguo Qin Han Qiqi Yanjiu*, Beijing: Wenwu, 2006, pp. 198 – 207.

◇❖◇ 第四部分 东亚艺术史

Fig. 4 – 2 – 3 **A toilet-box from Tomb No. 3 at Mawangdui in Changsha city, Hunan province, early Western Han, diameter 24.1 cm, height 16.9 cm, in the Hunan Provincial Museum**

(Extracted from Fu, Juyou, *Zhongguo Qiqi Quanji*, Fuzhou: Fujian Meishu, 1998, Vol. 3 pl. 78; reproduced with permission from the Fujian Meishu Chubanshe)

become finer and individual motifs smaller in size; compositions become more sophisticated and compact. In the meantime, the workshop marks found on earlier pieces largely disappear. Moreover, a number of innovations come about. First, precious metals like silver and gold are often used in decorating and reinforcing lacquerwares. Two toilet-boxes from Tianchang city in Anhui province, for instance, are equipped with silver quatrefoils on the cover and many gold-foil animals on the cover and wall. [1]Here we find another innovation: animals stand out from the clouds to become focal motifs (Fig. 4 – 2 – 4) (彩图 2). Albeit obscure in both lacquerware inscriptions and historical texts, several excavation reports identify a major production center in the Yangzhou region of Jiangsu province. [2]

This trend of stylistic development continues in the late Western Han (74BC – AD8) and succeeding Xin dynasty (AD9 – AD23). Décor is executed with even filaments and composition becomes even more intricate. In the meantime, the clouds and animals turn simple, monochromic, and static (Fig. 4 – 2 – 6: 2, Fig. 4 – 2 – 7: 2, Fig. 4 – 2 – 8: 3). Gold, silver, as well as jewels are more often employed, and lacquerwares are ever more extravagant. Animals and

---

[1] Fu, Juyou, *Zhongguo Qiqi Quanji*, Fuzhou: Fujian Meishu, Vol. 3, 1998, Pls. 194 and 195. Excavation materials are published in Anhuisheng Wenwu Kaogu Yanjiusuo and Tianchangxian Wenwu Guanlisuo, Anhui Tianchangxian Sanjiaoxu Zhanguo Xihanmu chutu wenwu, *Wenwu* 9, 1993, pp. 1 – 31.

[2] Several excavation reports advocate this view. See Yangzhou Bowuguan, and Hanjiangxian Wuhuaguan, Yangzhou Hanjiangxian Huchang Hanmu, *Wenwu* 3, 1980, p. 8; Yangzhou Bowuguan Jiangsu Hanjiang Yaozhuang 101 hao Xi Han mu, *Wenwu* 2, 1988, pp. 42 – 43; Yangzhou Bowuguan, and Hanjiangxian Tushuguan, Jiangsu Hanjiangxian Yangshouxiang Baonüdun Xinmang Mu, *Wenwu* 10, 1991, p. 60.

figural motifs made of precious metals eclipse the cloud design on the ground. Bands of figural stories also appear on three toilet-boxes from Tomb No. 101, the tomb of a middle-rank official of the Guangling Princedom, at Yaozhuang in Hanjiang county, Jiangsu province. ①

An outstanding characteristic of this period is the appearance of long inscriptions, which provide dates and places of production, on dozens of lacquerwares from Pyŏngyang, Noin-Ula, and China proper. Of these, the earliest goes back to 85BC, and the latest AD102. During these 187 years, the most enduring workshops are the Western Workshop of Shu Commandery 蜀郡工官, and the State Workshop of Guanghan Commandery, both of which are located in present-day Sichuan province—the former may even have been the direct successor of the early Western Han "Cheng Shi", Other known workshops are less stable or ephemeral establishments such as "Kaogong 考工", ② and "Gonggong 供工", ③ and "Changle Daguan 长乐大官", ④ which were operated at the capital of the

Fig. 4 – 2 – 4 A toilet-box from Tomb No. 1 at Sanjiaoxu in Tianchang county, Anhui province, middle Western Han, diameter 9.9 cm, height 9.5 cm, in the Tianchang Museum

(Extracted from Fu, Juyou, 1998, *Zhongguo Qiqi Quanji*, Vol. 3, Fuzhou: Fujian Meishu, pl. 194; reproduced with permission from the Fujian Meishu Chubanshe)

---

① Fu, Juyou, *Zhongguo Qiqi Quanji*, Fuzhou: Fujian Meishu, 1998, Vol. 3, pls. 254 – 256. A preliminary excavation report of this tomb is published in Yangzhou Bowuguan Jiangsu Hanjiang Yaozhuang 101 hao Xi Han mu, *Wenwu* 2, 1988, pp. 19 – 43.

② Gansusheng Bowuguan, Wuwei Mozuizi sanzuo Hanmu fajue jianbao, *Wenwu* 12, 1972, p. 15; Umehara, Sueji, *Shina Kandai Kinenmei Shikki Zusetsu*, Kyoto: Kuwana Bunseido, pl. XXVI.

③ Umehara, Sueji, *Shina Kandai Kinenmei Shikki Zusetsu*, Kyoto: Kuwana Bunseido, 1943, pls. X and XXXI.

④ Umehara, Sueji, *Shina Kandai Kinenmei Shikki Zusetsu*, Kyoto: Kuwana Bunseido, 1943, pl. XXXV.

第四部分 东亚艺术史

Western Han and Xin dynasties, Chang'an. ①These workshops often imitated the products of the Western Workshop of Shu Commandery and the State Workshop of Guanghan Commandery and produced lesser items. ②Within this period, we find the intriguing phenomenon that two types of wares and two types of motifs prevail. ③Ear-cups are decorated with the motif of two confronting phoenixes (Fig. 4-2-7: 2), whereas platters are decorated with the motif of three bears (Fig. 4-2-6: 2). The decorative schemes of Han dynasty lacquerwares are in general modular creations, drawing upon a stable repertoire of motifs-cloud, dragon, phoenix, and geometric designs. ④But the confronting-phoenix and three-bear motifs, although varying in style and technique of execution, are the commonest ones in the decoration repertoires of the state workshops. ⑤

Most products of these state workshops were evidently intended for the imperial house. This is manifested by the two characters *cheng yu* 乘舆, which refer first of all to imperial chariots but also to overall supplies for the imperial house, that appear most often in the above-mentioned inscriptions. These inscriptions, which also enumerate long lists of working artisans and administrative staff, suggest that these workshops were highly industrialized. As one typical piece tells us, the staff engaged on a permanent basis included core-makers *su gong* 素工, base-lacquerers *xiu gong* 髹工, topcoat lacquerers *shang gong* 上工, gilders *tong'er huang tu gong* 铜耳黄涂工, design painters *hua gong* 画工, cinnabar painters *dan gong* 丹工, cleaners *qing gong* 清工, and touch-up artisans *zao gong* 造工. It also included a team of administrative staff, like the commandery clerk for workshop inspection *hu gong zushi* 护工卒

---

① Umehara (Umehara, Sueji, *Shina Kandai Kinenmei Shikki Zusetsu*, Kyoto: Kuwana Bunseido, 1943) further lists the following workshops: "Workshop of the Right 右工" "State Workshop of Zitong Commandery 子同郡工官 (the later name of Guanghan Commandery 广汉郡工官)" and "State Workshop of Chengdu Commandery 成都郡工官 (the later name of Shu Commandery 蜀郡工官)".

② Hong, Shi, *Zhanguo Qin Han Qiqi Yanjiu*, Beijing: Wenwu, 2006, pp. 193-194.

③ Umehara, Sueji, *Shina Kandai Kinenmei Shikki Zusetsu*, Kyoto: Kuwana Bunseido, 1943.

④ Prüch, Margarete, *Die Lacke der Westlichen Han-Zeit*, Frankfurt am Main, Berlin, Bern, New York, Paris, and Wein: Peter Lang, 1997, pp. 220-326.

⑤ Barbieri-Low, Anthony J., *Artisans in Early Imperial China*, Seattle and London: University of Washington Press, 2007, p. 80; Gao, Wei, Qin Han shidai, in Zhongguo Shehui Kexueyuan Kaogu Yanjiusuo ed., *Xinzhongguo de Kaogu Faxian he Yanjiu*, Beijing: Wenwu, 1984, p. 476.

史, factory chief *zhang* 长, assistant factory chief *cheng* 丞, bureau head *yuan* 掾, and foreman clerk *lingshi* 令史. ①With such specialized and organized production, these workshops manufactured the most exquisite and extravagant items of their times.

Lacquerwares of the Eastern Han dynasty are rather modest in quantity. This is partly due to the widespread use of the spacious and airy brick tomb chamber, which is hostile to organic objects such as lacquerwares, instead of the earlier air- and water-tight wooden chamber, which is favorable for the preservation of lacquerwares. ②But more importantly, extravagant lacquerwares gradually fell out of favor with Eastern Han rulers, who began to impose frugal spending on luxury goods; in AD105, the court altogether dismissed products from the aforementioned state workshops. ③Apart from those from Pyŏngyang, only a few dozens of intact wares and well-preserved fragments have been uncovered in China proper. It is striking to note that the two types of motifs described above disappear and that almost all the extant items inscribed with the names of the state workshops from Pyŏngyang are plain. ④Other products manufactured by these workshops are sometimes undecorated too (Fig. 4 – 2 – 5)（彩图3）. ⑤ When decoration occurs, it carries on the stylistic development of the preceding period, composed of large focal motifs of animals and birds on exquisite grounds. ⑥While the ground designs are static, the focal motifs are

---

① Umehara, Sueji, *Shina Kandai Kinenmei Shikki Zusetsu*, Kyoto: Kuwana Bunseido, 1943, pl. XIV. The translation of this inscription given here combines the reading of Hong Shi and the translation of Anthony J. Barbieri-Low. See Hong, Shi, *Zhanguo Qin Han Qiqi Yanjiu*, Beijing: Wenwu, 2006, pp. 175 – 187; Barbieri-Low, Anthony J., *Artisans in Early Imperial China*, Seattle and London: University of Washington Press, 2007, p. 79.

② Gao, Wei, Qin Han shidai, in Zhongguo Shehui Kexueyuan Kaogu Yanjiusuo ed., *Xinzhongguo de Kaogu Faxian he Yanjiu*, Beijing: Wenwu, 1984, p. 477; Fu, Juyou, *Zhongguo Qiqi Quanji*, Fuzhou: Fujian Meishu, 1998, Vol. 3, p. 3.

③ Fan, Ye, *Hou Han Shu*, Zhonghua Shuju, 1965, Vol. 1, p. 422.

④ Umehara, Sueji, *Shina Kandai Kinenmei Shikki Zusetsu*, Kyoto: Kuwana Bunseido, 1943, pls. XXXIX, XL, and XLI.

⑤ Fu, Juyou, *Zhongguo Qiqi Quanji*, Fuzhou: Fujian Meishu, Vol. 3, 1998, pl. 298.

⑥ Guangzhoushi Wenwu Guanli Weiyuanhui, and Guangzhoushi Bowuguan, *Guangzhou Hanmu*, Beijing: Wenwu, Vol. II, 1981, pls. CXVI – CXIX; Umehara, Sueji, *Shina Kandai Kinenmei Shikki Zusetsu*, Kyoto: Kuwana Bunseido, 1943, pls. XLII – XLIII; Fu, Juyou, *Zhongguo Qiqi Quanji*, Fuzhou: Fujian Meishu, Vol. 3, 1998, pl. 297.

rather animated. It appears that the aristocratic tastes of this period changed significantly.

Among the Begram lacquerwares, the bowl of No. 92 (in Hackin's numbering) is visually vague. Severely damaged, it supplies little information about its décor. But Elisséeff proposes that it is a three-register composition like No. 186, and assigns it to the first century AD. Actually, the description only mentions four bands on the exterior, and a certain motif between the second and third bands. Our database shows that such composition already appears on a bowl-like toilet-box of the late Western Han (74BC – AD8). ①The color combination, saturn red on the interior and red décor on a brown-black ground, is a prevalent pattern in Han dynasty lacquerwares. Due to the lack of more details, little can be said beyond that.

No. 215 (Fig. 4 – 2 – 6: 1) contains four fragments of a platter. The bottom piece (Fig. 4 – 2 – 6: 1a) exhibits a roundel consisting of three spirals at the center, three units of identical motif alternating with three clusters of beads, and a ring of beads on the border outside. The motif is rather abstract; Hackin believes that it is a stylized version of the "three bears" motif. ②As related above, the three bears is the standard motif on

Fig. 4 – 2 – 5 A case from Longshenggang in Guangzhou City, Guangdong province, Eastern Han, diameter 8.2 cm, height 12.5 cm, in the Guangzhou Museum

(Extracted from Fu, Juyou, *Zhongguo Qiqi Quanji*, Fuzhou: Fujian Meishu, Vol.3, 1998, pl. 298; reproduced with permission from the Fujian Meishu Chubanshe)

---

① Fu, Juyou, *Zhongguo Qiqi Quanji*, Fuzhou: Fujian Meishu, Vol. 3, 1998, p. 3, pl. 229.
② "Laque", in Hackin, J., *Nouvelles Recherches Archéologiques à Begram, Ancienne Kapici*, 1939 – 1940: *Rencontre de Trois Civilisations, Inde, Grece, Chine*, Avec la collaboration de J.-R. Hackin, J. Carl et P. Hamelin, Études comparatives par J. Auboyer [et al], Paris: Imprimerie nationale, 1954, p. 296.

platters from the state workshops of the late Western Han and Xin dynasties. To date thirteen datable pieces with the three-bear motif from Pyŏngyang and Noin-Ula and two additional pieces from China proper are known, the earliest of which dates to 28BC and the latest to AD14. Throughout this temporal span, the three-bear motif is relatively realistic, and the heads, bodies, and limbs of the bears are recognizable. Moreover, the motif is surrounded by a cloud band. It is so strikingly different from the Begram fragment in that it bears no recognizable resemblance to the latter. One piece that may fill the gap comes from Wang Xu's tomb. ① In terms of both the three-bear motif and the cloud band, it is a transitional piece. This platter, however, does not bear a datable inscription, and one is left unsure if Elisséeff is right in assigning the bowl to AD20 – AD50. ②

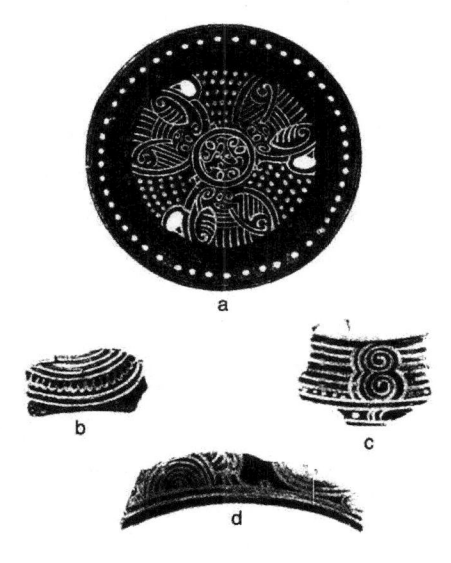

Fig. 4 – 2 – 6: 1 **Lacquerware No. 215 from Begram, from Hackin** 1954

Fig. 4 – 2 – 6: 2 **A platter from a tomb at Xinqiao in Qingzhen county, Guizhou province, Yuanshi year 4 （AD 4）, diameter 27.2 cm, height 4.1 cm, in the Guizhou Provincial Museum**

(From Fu, Juyou, *Zhongguo Qiqi Quanji*, Fuzhou: Fujian Meishu, 1998, Vol. 3, pl. 293; reproduced with permission from the Fujian Meishu Chubanshe)

---

① This platter is published only in Li, Zhengguang, *Handai Qiqi Tu'anji*, Beijing: Wenwu, Appendices, 2002, pl. 1.

② Elisséeff, V., Les laques chinois de Begram, in J. Hackin, *Nouvelles Recherches Archéologiques à Begram, Ancienne Kapici, 1939 – 1940; Rencontre de Trois Civilisations, Inde, Grece, Chine*, Avec la collaboration de J. -R. Hackin, J. Carl et P. Hamelin, Études comparatives par J. Auboyer [et al], Paris: Imprimerie nationale, 1954, p. 153.

◇❖◇　第四部分　东亚艺术史

The other three fragments of No. 215, which escaped the attention of Elisséeff and Pirazzoli-t'Serstevens, may offer us some clue. One fragment (Fig. 4 – 2 – 6: 1b) exhibits a composition of parallel lines and a jigsaw pattern, and another (Fig. 4 – 2 – 6: 1c) a composition of parallel lines, coils shaped like the numeral "8," and dots. The former fragment may have bordered the bottom, to which the latter belongs. No such composition, however, occurs among the datable pieces known to us. The third fragment (Fig. 4 – 2 – 6: 1d) displays a composition of a coil and a cloud, and as frequently attested to by the known samples, constitutes the exterior of the wall of the original ware. The even and stout strokes used to execute the exquisite designs on all the four fragments are found on a number of datable pieces of 16BC – AD14, among which the one from Xinqiao in Qingzhen county, Guizhou province, is the closest comparable (Fig. 4 – 2 – 6: 2) （彩图4）.[1] Based on this comparison, we may assign No. 215 to this temporal range.

No. 229 (Fig. 4 – 2 – 7: 1) is easily recognizable as an ear-cup. Its exterior bears elements of coils, triangles, and what Hackin calls "felt shoe" and "comb" ornaments. Elisséeff immediately recognizes this composition as two confronting phoenixes, a familiar motif on lacquer-wares from Pyŏngyang. By the stylized rendering of the motif, he dates this fragment to AD5 – AD13, but after considering the evolution of this motif, he gives a later span of AD13 – AD50. He perceives that the diagrams inside the X frame change from semicircle to rectangle and finally to triangle.[2] The current database allows us to trace the origin of the confronting phoenixes back to the early Western Han. One sample is an ear-cup from a tomb at Gufenyuan in the city of Changsha, Hunan province, which shows two confronting phoenixes,[3] Their beaks and eyes are realistic, but other parts are sketchy—the two legs and the tail are in the form of

---

[1] Umehara, Sueji, *Shina Kandai Kinenmei Shikki Zusetsu*, Kyoto: Kuwana Bunseido, 1943, pls. XI, XVIII, XXXI, XXXIII, XXXV and XXXVII; Fu, Juyou, *Zhongguo Qiqi Quanji*, Fuzhou: Fujian Meishu, 1998, Vol. 3, p. 3, pl. 293. The report on the tomb from which the Xinqiao platter comes has not been published.

[2] Elisséeff, V., Les laques chinois de Begram, in J. Hackin, *Nouvelles Recherches Archéologiques à Begram*, *Ancienne Kapici*, 1939 – 1940; *Rencontre de Trois Civilisations*, *Inde*, *Grece*, *Chine*, Avec la collaboration de J.-R. Hackin, J. Carl et P. Hamelin, Études comparatives par J. Auboyer [et al], Paris: Imprimerie nationale, 1954, p. 154.

[3] Fu, Juyou, *Zhongguo Qiqi Quanji*, Fuzhou: Fujian Meishu, 1998, Vol. 3, pl. 15. The excavation materials are unpublished.

Chinese Lacquerwares from Begram: Date and Provenance

lines. Between the two slender birds, there are two large semicircles tangent to each other, with two small ovals inside. The felt-shoe-like wings are not found here. For the middle Western Han, Tomb No. 17 in Hanjiang county provides an ear-cup bearing the same motif. The phoenixes on this ware have lengthy necks and felt-shoe-like wings but without legs. ①An 8BC piece from Pyŏngyang continues this type of bird image, but shows a short tail ending in coils and semicircles with hooks inside the X frame. ②It is in AD3 that the square frame begins to replace the semicircular one, as shown in a piece from a tomb at Yalongba in Qingzhen county, Guizhou province (Fig. 4 – 2 – 7: 2) (彩图 5). The painting strokes are bolder and the motif becomes more compact. No. 229, which unmistakably exhibits the square frame in the lower half of the X frame and the coils, does not resemble the earlier two samples, but looks like a close copy of the Yalongba piece. This is

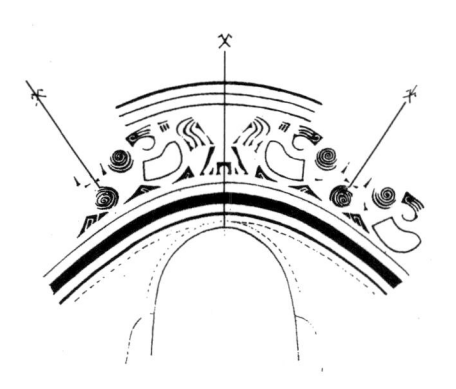

Fig. 4 – 2 – 7: 1 **Lacquerware No. 229 from Begram, from Hackin** 1954

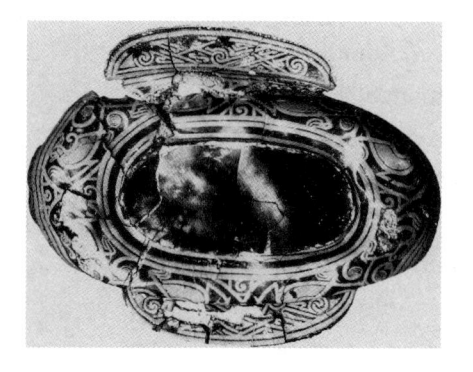

Fig. 4 – 2 – 7: 2 **An ear-cup from a tomb at Yalongba in Qingzhen County, Guizhou Province, Yuanshi year** 3 (**AD** 3), **diameter** 16.6 **cm, height** 3.8 **cm, in the Guizhou Provincial Museum.**

(From Fu 1998a, pl. 292; reproduced with permission from the Fujian Meishu Chubanshe) (A color version of this figure is available at journals.cambridge.org/ASI)

---

① Fu, Juyou, *Zhongguo Qiqi Quanji*, Fuzhou: Fujian Meishu, 1998, Vol. 3, pl. 202. The excavation materials are unpublished.

② Umehara, Sueji, *Shina Kandai Kinenmei Shikki Zusetsu*, Kyoto: Kuwana Bunseido, 1943, pl. X.

the type of bird motif that adorns ear-cups from 2BC – AD13. [1] By contrast, the few Eastern Han pieces known to us are all plain. [2] No actual example of the triangular frame, the final stage of Elisséeff's evolutionary chart, has ever been found. On these grounds, I am inclined to place No. 229 in the temporal scope of 2BC – AD13.

The motifs of the three bears on No. 215 and the confronting phoenixes on No. 229, as commented on above, occur exclusively on products of the state workshops. Pirazzoli-t'serstevens attributes them to the Western Workshop of Shu Commandery and the State Workshop of Guanghan Commandery. This is not necessarily so. As noted earlier, the state workshops at Chang'an also produced the two types of wares within the given temporal frame. The original wares of the Begram fragments could have been produced at any of these state workshops.

The designs of No. 216 (Fig. 4 – 2 – 8: 1) and No. 219 (Fig. 4 – 2 – 8: 2) are similar in many ways. No. 219 shows the exterior of a toilet-box. No. 216 is thought by Elisséeff to be a fragment of an ear-cup; but because the design never occurs on any known ear-cup, the original ware is more likely an oval toilet-box with a straight end, like the item from Wang Xu's tomb (Fig. 4 – 2 – 9: 2). The décor on No. 216 consists of two registers, one composed of interlacing wavy filaments and the other of interlacing angular filaments, which constitute polygon-like shapes. That of No. 219 is composed of interlacing pentagonal filaments. In both cases, the décor contains C-shaped clouds in the angles and parallel lines crosscutting the filaments. By contrast, the bottoms of the two wares are decorated with worm-like curves. The entire ensemble of motifs finds no analogy among known samples. Elisséeff generally comments that the interlacing filaments are current in the first half of the first century AD. But with the aid of the currently available database, we may delineate with greater precision the dates of individual components.

---

[1] Nine examples are known to date. See Umehara, Sueji, *Shina Kandai Kinenmei Shikki Zusetsu*, Kyoto: Kuwana Bunseido, Frontispiece, 1943, pls. XIII: 2, XIV – XV, XX, XXII, XXIII: 2, XXXIV; Fu, Juyou, *Zhongguo Qiqi Quanji*, Fuzhou: Fujian Meishu, 1998, Vol. 3, pl. 292.

[2] Four examples are known. See Umehara, Sueji, *Shina Kandai Kinenmei Shikki Zusetsu*, Kyoto: Kuwana Bunseido, 1943, pls. XXXIX – XLI, XLVII: 3.

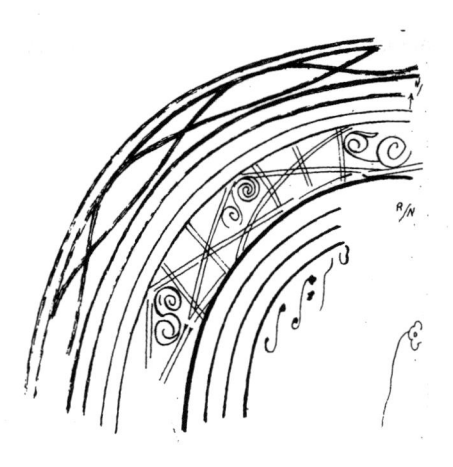

Chinese Lacquerwares from Begram: Date and Provenance

Fig. 4 – 2 – 8：1　Lacquerware No. 216 from Begram
［from Hackin, J., *Nouvelles Recherches Archéologiques à Begram, ancienne Kapici, 1939 – 1940, Rencontre de Trois Civilisations, Inde, Grece, Chine*, Avec la collaboration de J. -R. Hackin, J. Carl et P. Hamelin, Études comparatives par J. Auboyer (et al), Paris：Imprimerie nationale, 1954, p. 9, Fig. 248.］

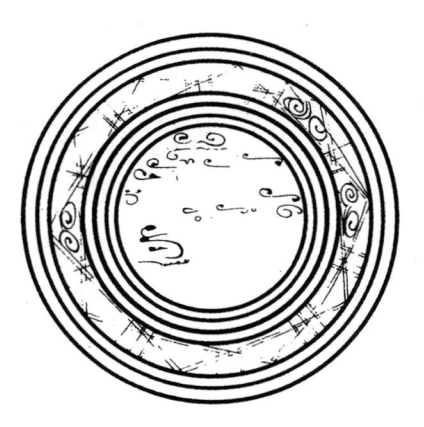

Fig. 4 – 2 – 8：2　Lacquerware No. 219 from Begram
［from Hackin, J., *Nouvelles Recherches Archéologiques à Begram, ancienne Kapici, 1939 – 1940, Rencontre de Trois Civilisations, Inde, Grece, Chine*, Avec la collaboration de J. -R. Hackin, J. Carl et P. Hamelin, Études comparatives par J. Auboyer (et al), Paris：Imprimerie nationale, 1954, p. 9, Fig. 248 bis.］

The motif of interlacing polygonal filaments first deserves our attention. It can be traced back to two items found in a case from Tomb No. 5, dating to the middle Western Han, at Wuzuofen in Guanghua city, Hubei province, which bear two

· 399 ·

interlacing pentagons.① However, in many cases the number of angles varies. The most similar design is found on the bottom and cover of a toilet-box from Tomb No. 101 of the late Western Han at Yaozhuang (Fig. 4 - 2 - 8: 3, Fig. 4 - 2 - 8: 4)(彩图 6). ②The encircling border is executed with double filaments and a single filament; C-like clouds and parallel lines are profusely interposed along the filaments. The bottom shows a band of interlacing polygonal filaments. With this comparison, we may assign Begram No. 216 and No. 219 to the late Western Han. ③

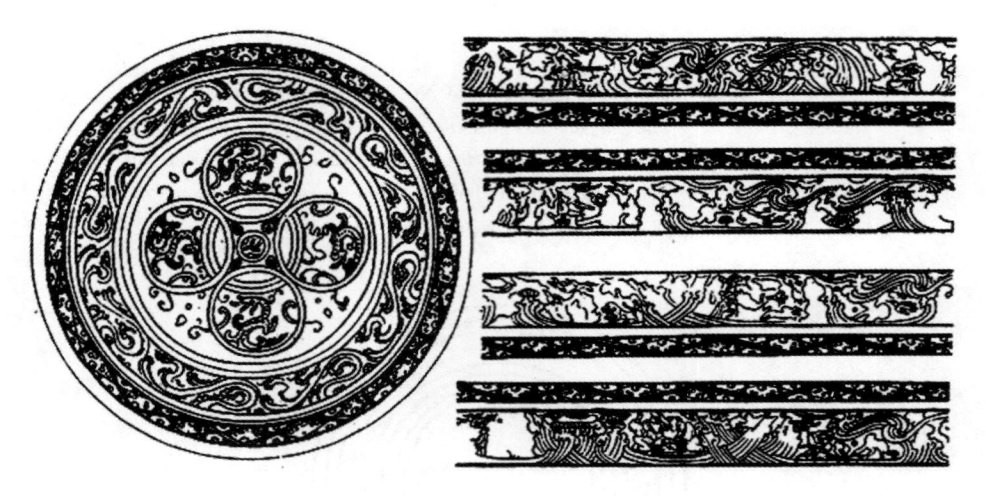

Fig. 4 - 2 - 8: 3 **A toilet-box from Tomb No. 101 at Yaozhuang, Hanjiang county, Jiangsu province, late Western Han, diameter 22.5 cm, height 14.5 cm, in the Yangzhou Museum**

(Extracted from Yangzhou Bowuguan, Jiangsu Hanjiang Yaozhuang 101 hao Xi Han mu, *Wenwu* 2, 1988, Fig. 30: 5, 4, reproduced with permission from the Yangzhou Museum)

---

① Hubeisheng Bowuguan, Guanghua wuzuofen Xi Han mu, *Kaoguxuebao* 2, 1976, Fig. 18: II. 1 - 6.

② For the excavation materials, see Yangzhou Bowuguan, Jiangsu Hanjiang Yaozhuang 101 hao Xi Han mu, *Wenwu* 2, 1988, Fig. 30: 5, 4. For a color image of the item itself, see Fu, Juyou, *Zhongguo Qiqi Quanji*, Fuzhou: Fujian Meishu, Vol. 3, 1998, pl. 254.

③ Margarete Prüch categorizes the interlacing filaments as "lianxu jihewen," to which she assigns the décor of a *zun*-box from Yangjiashan in Changsha, Hunan province, a case from Haizhou in Lianyungang, Jiangsu province, and a toilet-box from Tomb No. 101 at Yaozhuang in Hanjiang county (Prüch, Margarete, *Die Lacke der Westlichen Han-Zeit*, Frankfurt am Main, Berlin, Bern, New York, Paris, and Wein: Peter Lang, 1997, pp. 315 - 316). From a stylistic perspective, the décor of the former two is different from that of the latter.

Fig. 4 - 2 - 8 : 4 A jar from Tomb No. 101 at Yaozhuang, Hanjiang county, Jiangsu province, late Western Han, diameter 7.8 cm, height 6.9 cm, in the Yangzhou Museum

(Extracted from Fu, Juyou, *Zhongguo Qiqi Quanji*, Fuzhou: Fujian Meishu, Vol. 3, 1998, pl. 260; reproduced with permission from the Fujian Meishu Chubanshe)

Like the above interlacing filaments, the worm-like motif on No. 216 and No. 219 results from a long-term stylization of clouds. An early example is found on a platter from Tomb No. 1 of the early Western Han at Dafentou, in Yunmeng county, Hubei province.①There the large clouds are executed with modulated lines, and the bold ones take the shape of large worms. A simpler version is found on a rectangular box of the middle Western Han from Sanjiaoxu in Tianchang county, Anhui province.②The closest parallel appears on a jar from the late Western Han Tomb No. 101 at Yaozhuang (Fig. 4 - 2 - 8 : 4) .③The belly of the jar is inscribed with S- and O-like strokes, which are the extreme stylization of the clouds of previous periods.

Although the compounding of the above two types of motifs on the fragments never recurs on any known samples, it most likely took place during the late Western Han. Due to the lack of inscriptional materials, a narrower chronology cannot be delineated at present.

The production site of No. 216 and No. 219 is not easy to determine, because boxes bearing long inscriptions are few. So far only two items of this kind have been discovered in Tomb No. 2 of the consort of the prince of

---

① Fu, Juyou, *Zhongguo Qiqi Quanji*, Fuzhou: Fujian Meishu, Vol. 3, 1998, pl. 7; Hubeisheng Bowuguan, Yunmeng Dafentou yihao Hanmu, *Wenwu Ziliao Congkan* 4, 1981, pp. 1 - 28.

② Fu, Juyou, *Zhongguo Qiqi Quanji*, Fuzhou: Fujian Meishu, Vol. 3, 1998, p. 193. For the excavation report, see Anhuisheng Wenwu Kaogu Yanjiusuo, and Tianchangxian Wenwu Guanlisuo, Anhui Tianchangxian Sanjiaoxu Zhanguo Xihanmu chutu wenwu, *Wenwu* 9, 1993, pl. 4 : 2.

③ Fu, Juyou, *Zhongguo Qiqi Quanji*, Fuzhou: Fujian Meishu, Vol. 3, 1998, pl. 260; Yangzhou Bowuguan, Jiangsu Hanjiang Yaozhuang 101 hao Xi Han mu, *Wenwu* 2, 1988, Fig. 6 : 16.

Quanling at Yaoziling in Yongzhou city, Hunan province.[1] The inscription on one *zhi*-goblet indicates that the cover and body were produced, in 8BC and 16BC respectively, at the workshop "*Gonggong.*" The other was produced at the workshop "*Kaogong*" in 8BC. The former is painted with interlacing wavy filaments only, and the latter *zhi*-goblet the incised diamonds and parallel lines, a conventional motif of the Western Han. Neither of them exhibits the polygonal filaments that adorn No. 216 and No. 219, which implies that the motif does not belong to the decoration repertoires of state workshops.

The comparison of Begram No. 216 and No. 219 with the toilet-box from Tomb No. 101 at Yaozhuang nevertheless enlightens us as to the issue of provenance. Unlike the décor of the state workshops that is executed in bold strokes, the interlacing filaments on these wares are meticulously rendered. These complementary motifs, however, appear to be the stylized derivative of the bands of consecutive rhombi often seen, with variation, on toilet-boxes, *an*-tables, *he*-boxes, and *si*-boxes from tombs found at Huchang,[2] Ligangcun,[3] Laoshan,[4] in Hanjiang county, and Sanjiaoxu in Tianchang county.[5] Dating from the middle Western Han through the Xin dynasty, these bands have their individual units filled with C-like clouds, circles, and feathers. All these sites, like Yaozhuang, fall within the territory of the Guangling Princedom during the late Western Han and Xin dynasties.[6] The concentration of this distinctive motif, over a protracted length of time, indicates a local artistic tradition in this territory. Indeed, during this time the Guangling Princedom had a prominent

---

[1] Hunansheng Wenwu Kaogu Yanjiusuo, and Yongzhoushi Zhishanqu Wenwu Guanlisuo, Hunan Yongzhoushi Yaoziling erhao Xi Han mu, *Kaogu* 4, 2001, Fig. 21: 1-2.

[2] Yangzhou Bowuguan, and Hanjiangxian Wuhuaguan, Yangzhou Hanjiangxian Huchang Hanmu, *Wenwu* 3, 1980, pl. 1, toilet-box.

[3] Yangzhou Bowuguan, and Hanjiangxian Tushuguan, Jiangsu Hanjiangxian Yangshouxiang Baonüdun Xinmang Mu, *Wenwu* 10, 1991, Fig. 35: 5-6, Fig. 38: 1-2, all *an*-tables.

[4] Yangzhou Bowuguan, Yangzhou Xi Han 'Qiemoshu' muguo mu, *Wenwu* 12, 1980, Figs. 10: 12.

[5] Anhuisheng Wenwu Kaogu Yanjiusuo, and Tianchangxian Wenwu Guanlisuo, Anhui Tianchangxian Sanjiaoxu Zhanguo Xihanmu chutu wenwu, *Wenwu* 9, 1993, Figs. 42-44.

[6] Fu, Juyou, *Zhongguo Qiqi Quanji*, Fuzhou: Fujian Meishu, Vol. 3, 1998, p. 39.

lacquerware production center,[①] to which we may attribute Begram No. 216 and No. 219.

No. 186 (Fig. 4 – 2 – 9: 1) comprises three fragments, possibly from one small box. One fragment shows a band of three double-ovals. Such motifs occur rarely, and the only known examples are seen on five toilet-boxes, all of which are placed in one case, from Wang Xu's tomb (Fig. 4 – 2 – 9: 2). The other two fragments of No. 186 display the identical design that consists of a band of coiling clouds executed with fine lines. Despite being in the form of a sketch, the clouds resemble those that adorn the covers of these five wares and the wall of the containing case. Neither of the two motifs helps us with the task of dating. The double-oval does not repeat itself beyond this tomb and the clouds are not confined to any particular time period. What helps us is the designs on the wall of the containing case. The top and bottom registers, the same in composition, are made up of a band of interlacing filaments which form rhombi traced with beads. Inside and outside, the diamonds are painted with C-like clouds. The ensemble of interlacing filaments and C-like clouds and the extravagant décor align the case with the previously mentioned group of lacquerwares, particularly an *an*-table from the Baonüdun tomb of the Xin dynasty,[②] and appear to be from the same group from which No. 186 probably originated.

Fig. 4 – 2 – 9: 1 Lacquerware No. 186 from Begram

[Extracted from Hackin, J., *Nouvelles Recherches Archéologiques à Begram, ancienne Kapici*, 1939 – 1940, *Rencontre de Trois Civilisations, Inde, Grece, Chine*, Avec la collaboration de J. -R. Hackin, J. Carl et P. Hamelin, Études comparatives par J. Auboyer (et al), Paris: Imprimerie nationale, 1954, p. 9, Fig. 246.]

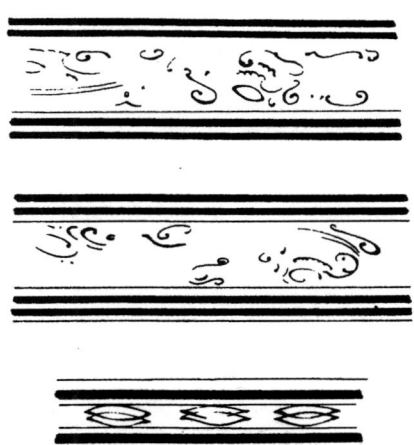

---

① Fu, Juyou, *Zhongguo Qiqi Quanji*, Fuzhou: Fujian Meishu, Vol. 3, 1998, p. 39.
② Yangzhou Bowuguan, and Hanjiangxian Tushuguan, Jiangsu Hanjiangxian Yangshouxiang Baonüdun Xinmang Mu, *Wenwu* 10, 1991, Fig. 35: 5 – 6.

◇❖◇ 第四部分 东亚艺术史

Fig. 4-2-9: 2 **A case from Wang Xu's tomb at Pyŏngyang, Eastern Han, diameter** 26.2 **cm, height** 8.6 **cm, in the National Museum of Korea**

(Extracted from Umehara, Sueji, *Shina Kandai Kinenmei Shikki Zusetsu*, Kyoto: Kuwana Bunseido, 1943, pl. XVIII)

The example from Wang Xu's tomb also gives us a clue regarding the provenance of No. 186. The design, consisting of a section of interlacing filaments filled with parallel lines alternating with a section of C-like clouds, falls into line with that of the abovementioned group of lacquerwares that were probably products of local workshops of the Guangling Princedom, to which I am inclined to assign No. 186.

The foregoing analysis offers no dramatic changes but some slight adjustments to Elisséeff and Pirazzoli-t'serstevens's dating. The present database allows us to ascribe the Begram lacquerware fragments to the late Western Han and Xin dynasties, or 74BC – AD23. This chronology, however, coincides with a misty period in the history of Central Asia. P. Bernard tells us that the last Greek kingdom at Begram succumbed around 70BC to some unnamed nomadic tribes.[①] The next known power in this region is the Kushan Empire, but the actual date of its emergence is still uncertain. A crucial point in the chronology of Kushan is the era of Kanishka, the fourth king of this empire. To date there have been widely differing opinions on the time when he lived, varying from AD78 to AD278; weighing the available evidence, B. N. Puri insists on his earlier opinion that this era starts around AD142. If so, the Kushan Empire

---

① Bernard, P., The Greek kingdoms of Central Asia, in János Harmatta, B. N. Puri and G. F. Etemadi ed., *History of Civilizations of Central Asia*, UNESCO Publishing, Vol. II, 1994, p. 103.

might have arisen around the turn of the second century AD.①The Yuezhi nomads, as Chinese written records tell us, conquered Bactria to the north of the Hindu Kush between 139BC and 128BC.②But it is not sure whether or not they ruled Begram to the south between 74BC and AD23.

As Chinese historical texts inform us, Central Asia came to the attention of the Western Han empire from the late second century BC. In the course of dealing with the Xiongnu nomads, Emperor Wu (r. 140BC – 87BC) obtained the intelligence that the Xiongnu had driven away the Yuezhi people. In 138BC, he sent Zhang Qian to them in the hope of forging an alliance against the Xiongnu. The mission did not succeed, but it brought the Western Han regime to the attention of the Western world. In 120BC, the Western Regions (roughly the present-day Tarim Basin and parts of Central Asia to the west of it), the intermediary area lying between China and Afghanistan, came under the control of the Western Han empire. In the same year, Zhang Qian set out on another mission to Wusun and other Central Asian states. The mission again failed, but it attracted diplomatic missions from various states to China. In 108 and 101BC, two Han military expeditions were dispatched to Central Asia and the second one conquered Ferghana. Thereafter, by appointing officers and founding colonies, China maintained, with some brief interruptions, direct control over the Western Regions—the gateway to Central Asia.③These actions induced most of the Central Asian states to send tribute and hostages to China as a symbol of submission, although Yingshih Yu points out that such contact was not just political—many missions were actually merchants seeking profitable transactions with the Chinese court.④The Western Han empire, for the sake of its own political interests, often dispatched missions to these states with

---

① Puri, B. N., The Kushans, in János Harmatta, B. N. Puri and G. F. Etemadi ed., *History of Civilizations of Central Asia*, UNESCO Publishing, Vol. II, 1994, pp. 249 – 252.

② Enoki, K. G. A. Koshelenko, and Z. Haidary, The Yüeh-chih and their migrations, in Janos Harmatta, B. N. Puri and G. F. Etemadi ed., *History of Civilizations of Central Asia*, UNESCO Publishing, Vol. II, 1994, p. 175.

③ Hulsewé, A. F. P., *China in Central Asia*, Leiden: E. J. Brill, 1979, pp. 46 – 49.

④ Yu, Yingshih, Han foreign relations, in Denis Twitchett and Michael Loewe ed., *The Cambridge History of China*, Cambridge: Cambridge University Press, Vol. 1, 1986, pp. 377 – 462.

enormous gifts. With the downfall of the Xin dynasty, however, Chinese power dwindled and the Western Regions reverted to the sway of the Xiongnu nomads; it was not until AD73 that the Eastern Han empire reestablished dominance in this region.①In this context, it is no coincidence that lacquerwares of the late Western Han and Xin dynasties made their way to Begram.

The question of how the Chinese lacquerwares arrived at Begram cannot be answered with certainty. They might have traveled along the sea route, landed in India and continued their journey to Begram. The available evidence, however, favors the possibility that they reached there via the Silk Road. For one thing, a number of lacquerwares of the Western Han and later dynasties, some of which might have been produced at state workshops of the Guanghan and Shu Commanderies, have been found at many sites along the northern and southern routes girding the Tarim Basin.②For another thing, a wooden slip of 63BC – 13BC found at the postal station Xuanquanzhi near Dunhuang records that a Western Han officer provided food to Yuezhi envoys. Another slip from around 65BC, originally found by Aurel Stein at Niya, another site along the Silk Road, tells that a Kushan envoy delivered a memorial to the Western Han empire requesting an envoy.③Given the intimate connection of politics and trade, the Chinese lacquerwares might have been brought to Begram by these envoys.

The Begram lacquerwares further enlighten us as to the nature of contact between China and Central Asia. According to the analysis given above, nos. 215 and 229 were probably produced at state workshops, whereas nos. 186, 216 and 219 possibly came from local workshops of the Guangling Princedom. While products from the local workshops were meant for aristocratic families, those from the state workshops were for the imperial house. Data from

---

① Hulsewé, A. F. P., *China in Central Asia*, Leiden: E. J. Brill, 1979, pp. 26, 49.

② Gong, Guoqiang, Lun Xinjiang Tianshan yinan diqu de Han Jin shiqi de qiqi, in Zhongguo Shehui Kexueyuan Kaogu Yanjiusuo ed., *Ershiyi Shiji de Zhongguo Kaoguxue: Qingzhu Tong Zhuchen Xiansheng Bashiwu Huadan Xueshu Wenji*, Beijing: Wenwu, 2006, pp. 734, 743 – 748.

③ Lin, Meicun, Niya Hanjian zhong youguan Xi Han yu Dayuezhi guanxi de zhongyao shi liao, in Lin Meicun, *Han Tang Xiyu yu Zhongguo Wenming*, Beijing: Wenwu, 1998, pp. 256, 260.

mortuary remains cited above demonstrate that both types of products were included in the lists of gifts that the imperial house bestowed upon domestic aristocrats (i. e. of Guangling Princedom, Lelang Commandery) as well as foreign aristocrats (i. e. of the Xiongnu) .[①]In this context Begram could be a princely residence—although we do not know which polity it belonged to. Given Yingshih Yu's caution, one could also consider it to be a residence of merchants, who went to China in the disguise of princely delegates. But the concentration of luxury goods from various sources, i. e. lacquerwares from China, ivory and Bone Carvings from India, and glass vessels and bronze sculptures from Rome, identifies Rooms No. 10 and No. 13 more likely with the residence of a local ruler, which had some politico-economic contact with China between 74BC to AD23.

Acknowledgements

I owe a great debt of gratitude to the anonymous reviewers for their critical comments. Without them this article would have been marred with errors and infelicities. All remaining defects are my own responsibility. I am also grateful to the Fujian Meishu Chubanshe and the Yangzhou Museum for generously granting permission to reproduce images in this article.

---

① Michèle Pirazzoli-t'Serstevens recently offers the idea that the state workshop products found at Qingzhen and Lelang were given by the imperial house to local "barbarian chieftains" rather than domestic aristocrats as part of her diplomatic maneuver, which is obviously applicable to the Begram lacquerwares. Pirazzoli-t'Serstevens, Michèle, Chinese Lacquerware from Noyon uul: Some Problems of Manufacturing and Distribution, *The Silk Road* 7, 2009, pp. 38 – 39.

关于洛杉矶县立博物馆收藏的一件唐卡的几个问题

洛杉矶县立艺术博物馆（Los Angeles County Museum of Art）收藏有一幅奇特的罗汉唐卡（图4-3-1，以下简称为洛杉矶唐卡）（彩图7）。唐卡中央是一个坐姿罗汉。罗汉身穿一件镶金边袈裟，耳戴硕大的耳珰；右手持长杖，左手作说法印。在罗汉的左侧是一个持梵荚的僧人。同罗汉一样，僧人也有头光，头光周围有飞舞的蝴蝶。罗汉右侧的僧人没有头光，似乎注视着一只飞向花朵的蝴蝶。这两个僧人应该是罗汉的胁侍。在罗汉前面，是一个跪着的供养人。从他的面部特征来看，应该是一个中亚人。他的手里捧着一只装满宝石的碗准备献给罗汉。在罗汉周围，错落有致地分布了一些岩石和植物；在他前面有一小片草地，上面有几只鹿在吃草。这些细节描绘的大概是罗汉修行所在的自然环境。

以西藏唐卡的形式表现汉式的罗汉像是洛杉矶唐卡的一个特别之处。本文下面会讲到，这幅唐卡还有许多独特的细节，使得它的图像显得十分神秘，让人琢磨不透。所以这幅唐卡以前经过几次展览，学者们也作过一些分析，但是专门的研究还没有。在藏传佛教艺术的研究史上，也曾出现过一些类似的"神秘"唐卡。1973年，J. 楼芮（Lowry）看到了四件西藏唐卡，让他大惑不解。上面的题记说它们是明朝皇帝在1477—1513年间赠给藏人的，可是这些唐卡无论是图像还是风格都是藏式的。中文题记和西藏图像放在一起，他就弄不清楚它们是哪里生产的了。[①] 两

---

* 本文原刊于《艺术史研究》第11卷，第379—390页。收入本书时略有改动。

① Lowry, J., Tibet, Nepal or China? An early group of dated tangkas, *Oriental Art* 19/3, 1973, p. 314.

年以后，D. 基德（Kidd）明确地告诉他这些唐卡是汉地生产的。他在 G. 图奇（Tucci）的《西藏画轴》（*Tibetan Painted Scrolls*）发表的一件唐卡上认出了一行题记并认出了它的内容："大庆法王领占班丹（Rin-chen-dPal-ldam）大护国保安寺信造。"这里的"大庆法王领占班丹"实际上就是明正德帝（1506—1521 年在位）。汉文题记后面还有一段藏文题记。不过这段题记实际上是中文题记的藏文音译，只有"领占班丹"完全译成藏文。基德推测，这段题记不是藏人写的；撰写者可能只是粗通几个藏字，而并不懂得藏文。①

楼芮所见的融合汉藏元素的唐卡对今天的学者而言已经不再神秘。由于近几十年来国内外学者的共同努力，我们已经对元明两朝汉藏之间密切的交往活动有了详细的了解，学者们也辨识出了不少两朝宫廷专门定制的、作为礼物送给藏人的藏式艺术品。西藏成为元朝的行省后，统治西藏的萨迦派上师经常向元朝中央朝贡，同时他们也经常收到来自大都的丰厚的银锭和绸缎礼物。萨迦上师也被任命为国师，管理整个元朝的宗教事务，八思巴（1235—1280 年）即是最著名的一个例子。在这些来往于藏地与中央的政治和宗教使团里还常常有艺术家的身影，来自尼泊尔的阿尼哥（Anige，1245—1306 年）是其中最出名的一个。从 1260 年起，阿尼哥开始在元朝供职，在宫廷作坊督造佛教（包括藏传和其他派别）寺庙和法器。② 因此，元朝的宫廷作坊在制作藏式艺术品时，恐怕少不了藏人艺术家的帮忙。

明朝在推翻元朝以后也努力推广治藏政策。1373 年，洪武帝设立两个指挥使司来管理卫藏和多康，归属位于河州（今甘肃临夏）的西安都指挥使司统辖。③ 洪武帝和后来的几代明代皇帝经常授予西藏喇嘛和贵族

---

① Kidd, David, Tibetan Painting in China, *Oriental Art* 21/1, 1975, pp. 56 - 60; Kidd, David, Tibetan Painting in China Author's Postscript, *Oriental Art* 21/2, 1975, pp. 158 - 160.
② Jing, Anning, The Portraits of Khubilai Khan and Chabi by Anige (1245 - 1306): a Nepalese Artist at the Yuan Court, *Artibus Asiae* LIV1/2, 1994, pp. 56 - 71.
③ 张廷玉：《明史》第 331 卷"西域志三"，中华书局 1974 年版。

封号和厚礼；一些礼单上明确提到了皇家作坊制造的绸缎、唐卡和佛像。① 三大法王——噶玛派的哈立麻（De-bzhin-gshegs-pa）、萨迦派的昆泽思巴（Kun-bkras-pa）和格鲁派的释迦也失（Sakya Ye-shes）——受永乐帝的邀请，相继来到明朝宫廷，并且获得了"法王"和帝师的封号。② 以后西藏有名的喇嘛和贵族定期带着使团来到明廷。尽管学者们对于明代皇帝的意图看法不一，③ 但藏传佛教在明朝宫廷的深度影响却是事实，甚至于正德帝自封为"大庆法王"，并给自己取了藏名"领占班丹"，④ 停留在北京的西藏喇嘛也帮助建造了法海寺等汉藏合流式寺院。⑤ 因此，和元代大都的情形一样，藏人曾经帮助明朝的宫廷作坊制造藏式艺术品，应该是情理中事。

一　罗汉崇拜

在了解了元明两朝汉藏之间的政治文化交往以后，笔者现在来讨论有关洛杉矶唐卡的几个问题。第一个问题自然是唐卡中罗汉的身份。不过

---

① Robinson, David M., The Ming Court and the Legacy of the Yuan Mongols, in David M. Robinson ed. *Culture, Courtiers, and Competition: The Ming Court (1368 - 1644)*, Harvard University Asia Center, 2008, p. 372. 1975 年，卡梅（Heather Karmay）发现了一批青铜造像，上面有"明代永乐年裂"题记。这些造像的浇铸使用了"失腊法"技术，做工相当精细。它们显然是明代宫廷作坊或它们的地方分支机构制造的。很多唐卡也是这样制作的。在笔者收集的 25 幅有纪年的唐卡（包括本文提到的四幅）中，三幅是 1907 年从北京流失出去的，两幅仍然保存在大昭寺和罗布林卡寺里。这些唐卡都有汉文题记，说明它们是明代永乐、景泰（1450—1456）、成化（1465—1487）和正德（1506—1521）皇帝的赠品。他们都是明代宫廷定制用作赠送西藏喇嘛的礼物。参 Karmay, Heather, *Early Sino Tibetan Art*, Warminster: Aris and Phillips Ltd, 1975, pp. 83 - 84.

② Karmay, Heather, *Early Sino Tibetan Art*, Warminster: Aris and Phillips Ltd, 1975, pp. 72 - 73.

③ 国内外学者争论的焦点是明代皇帝是否采取了"分而治之"的政策，是否控制了西藏的政治和宗教事务。一些学者（如 Sperling, Elliot, *Early Ming Policy Toward Tibet*, PhD dissertation, Indiana University, 1983）坚决否认，而另一些学者（陈楠：《明代大慈法王研究》，中央民族大学出版社 2005 年版）坚决支持。

④ Richardson, H. E., Tibetan Painting in China: A Postscript, *Oriental Art* 21/2, 1975, pp. 161 - 162.

⑤ Debreczeny, Karl P., *Ethnicity and Esoteric Power: Negotiating Sino-Tibetan Synthesis in Ming Buddhist Painting*, PhD dissertation, University of Chicago, 2007, pp. 139 - 147.

关于洛杉矶县立博物馆收藏的一件唐卡的几个问题

这个问题恐怕没法回答了。我们知道,藏传佛教中的罗汉题材来自汉传佛教。很多学者已经告诉我们,藏传佛教中的罗汉图像的一个主要来源是汉传佛教。[①] 现在所知最早的一部描述罗汉的经典是645年玄奘翻译的印度佛经《大阿罗汉难提蜜多罗所说法住记》(简称《法住记》)。其中描述的十六罗汉在汉传佛教艺术中相当流行,洛杉矶唐卡中的罗汉应是其中的一个。但是这部经典除了罗汉的法力和住所以外,没有提供什么有用的信息来帮助我们区分各个罗汉的图像特征。我们在唐卡上见到的供养人、长杖和其他图像成分显然是汉传佛教创造的,但是这些图像成分也帮不上什么忙。因为汉地艺术家经常任意地改变这些图像成分的搭配,所以张冠李戴的现象相当普遍。[②] 此举一例,元代的颜辉(活动年代在1300年左右)画了好几幅十六罗汉像。日本龙光院收藏的一幅中的第六个罗汉(跋陀罗),同洛杉矶唐卡中的罗汉一

图4-3-1 罗汉像,藏于 Los Angeles County Museum of Art。画家不详,15 世纪上半叶。唐卡,纸质上施矿物颜料和金粉。尺寸为 64.77 × 53.98 厘米

(Los Angeles County Museum of Art, Photo ⓒ Museum Associates/ LACMA)

[①] Tucci, Giuseppe, *Tibetan Painted Scrolls*, SDI Publications, Vol. II, 1999, p. 556; Pal, Pratapaditya, The Arhats and Mahasiddhas in Himalayan Art, *Arts of Asia* 20/1, 1990, p. 71.

[②] 1101年,苏东坡在广州附近的一座寺院里看到了贯休(832—912)的十八罗汉。除掉增加的两个,其他罗汉的顺序同《法住记》记载的一样。参 De Visser, M. W., *The Arhats in China and Japan*, Berlin: Oesterheld, 1923, pp. 115 – 116.

第四部分　东亚艺术史

样，目光平视，同时一个"番夷"向他供奉一碗珠宝。[①] 同样的构图出现在日本永源寺收藏的一幅中的第十三个罗汉（因揭陀）。[②] 要不是这两幅罗汉的顺序可以同《法住记》的记载相对照，我们是无法知道每个罗汉的名字的。因此尽管学者们提出了伐阇罗弗多罗、迦诺迦伐蹉、注荼半托迦等说法，但是洛杉矶唐卡画的是哪个罗汉还是无从判断。[③]

我们再来看洛杉矶唐卡的其他细节（图4-3-1）。罗汉的上面为背景。同华丽的前景不同，背景画成暗淡的深蓝色。在右上角是一个独立的单元，中间是一个人物，两旁各有一个胁侍。中间的人物坐在一把装饰龙头的宝座上，后面有一个蓝色的头光。同前景中的罗汉一样，他脸色从容，目光平视。除了手里拿的净瓶，他跟前景中的罗汉几乎没有差别。因此我们推测他是罗汉的一个化身。在左上角，一个僧人坐在榻上，脚踩着莲花。僧人的周围彩云环绕，后面有金色头冠，头顶有华盖。看起来这个僧人可能是一个已经觉悟的王子。罗汉的头上是一堆岩石，上面站着四个人和三只鹿。这个画面表现的可能是罗汉的住所。据《法住记》（第9，12，13，14，15，16个），六个罗汉是住在山里

图4-3-2　"弥勒在兜率天"壁画，江孜菩提塔。画家不详，1427—1440年

［引自 Ricca, Franco, and Erberto Lo Bue, *The Great Stupa of Gyantse*: *A Complete Tibetan Pantheon of the fifteenth Century*, London: Serindia Publications, 1993, pl. 37（Ricca Franco 教授提供图片使用权）］

---

① Suzuki, Kei, *Comprehensive Illustrated Catalog of Chinese Paintings*, Japanese Collections: Monasteries and Individuals, University of Tokyo Press, 1983, Vol. 4, No. JT93-001.

② Suzuki, Kei, *Comprehensive Illustrated Catalog of Chinese Paintings*, University of Tokyo Press, 1983, Vol. 4, No. JT108-006.

③ Pal, Pratapaditya, *The Art of Tibet*, The Asia Society, Inc., 1969, p. 132; Pal, Pratapaditya, *Art of Tibet*, Los Angeles County Museum of Art, 1990, pp. 136-138; Béguin, Gilles, *Dieux et Demons De L. Himilaya*, Paris: Editions des musees nationaux, 1977, pl. 84.

的。但是这个情况并不能帮助我们断定罗汉的身份。

这种前景和背景相结合的构图很少见于罗汉像。在汉传佛教的传统里，罗汉无论成组的还是单个的都表现为在一个地理环境从事世俗的活动。不过这种构图往往见于佛像。如俄勒冈大学艺术博物馆（University of Oregon Museum of Art）收藏的年代为1477年的一幅轴画，上面画的是药师佛坐在一个绿色的宝座上，背景属蓝天，彩云充满了整个画面。[1] 同样的构图见于白居寺（建于1418年）的"转法轮"壁画和寺内菩提塔（建于1427—1440年）内的"弥勒在兜率天"壁画（图4-3-2）（彩图8）。[2] 在后一幅壁画中我们看到了若干山水画因素如岩石和植物，而不是一幅完整的山水画。这样看来，洛杉矶唐卡并不是要表现罗汉在一个地方活动，而是表现他代替佛在说法。因此背景中的三组人物表现的可能是罗汉的"本生"故事：左上角的王子脱胎为中间居住在山里的罗汉，然后又脱胎为右上角的罗汉。

在现有的佛教艺术中，以佛礼事罗汉的例子现在知道的恐怕只有洛杉矶唐卡一个。因为缺乏对比材料，我们就很难深入理解这幅唐卡的含义。不过，这幅唐卡的一个细节，给我们揭开了它的另外一面。这就是右上角罗汉宝座上的绣花靠垫。它的红色底子上绣了一些花朵和飞鸟。飞鸟的种类看不清楚。不过前景中罗汉座下的垫子也绣了一些花朵和飞鸟，上面的飞鸟可以看得清楚，肯定是凤凰（图4-3-1）。这样的坐垫和靠垫很少出现在西藏的绘画中。我们知道的唯一的例子是白居寺菩提塔内的"觉密"壁画（图4-3-3）（彩图9）。[3] 在明代，凤凰是一品文官的象征，所以这些垫子代表了拥有者高贵的身份。[4] 历史文献告诉我们，在永乐帝赠予哈立麻的礼物中就有裀褥和

---

[1] Weidner, Marsha, *Latter Days of the Law*, Spencer Museum of Art, the University of Kansas in association with University of Hawai Press, 1994, pl. 3.

[2] Ricca, Franco, and Erberto Lo Bue, *The Great Stupa of Gyantse: A Complete Tibetan Pantheon of the fifteenth Century*, London: Serindia Publications, 1993, pl. 37.

[3] 壁画见 Ricca, Franco, and Erberto Lo Bue, *The Great Stupa of Gyantse: A Complete Tibetan Pantheon of the fifteenth Century*, London: Serindia Publications, 1993, pl. 105; for the date, pp. 27-28.

[4] 申时行：《明会典》卷61，中华书局1989年版，第386页。

织金袈裟,① 其中裀褥可能包括坐垫。我们知道明朝在赠送礼物时,是根据西藏高僧和贵族的地位区别对待的。② 虽然我们不知道永乐帝送给哈立麻的坐垫的图案,但是可以肯定洛杉矶唐卡中的坐垫是明朝送给西藏的一位高僧或贵族的礼物。加上罗汉华丽的袈裟,我们不能不认为唐卡中的罗汉实际上是西藏中部的一个高僧或贵族的化身。在我国佛教艺术史上,这并不奇怪。在北京的法海寺(建于 1439—1443 年)里,明代的皇室人物常常被画成神的形象。③ 因此,笔者推测,洛杉矶唐卡表现的不仅仅是对一位罗汉的崇拜,而且是对一位高僧或贵族的崇拜。

二 年代

由于上述的重新认识,我们恐怕需要重新考虑洛杉矶唐卡的年代问题。关于这个问题,G. 贝衮(Béguin)认为它是 15 世纪的绘画,是一幅模仿元代绘画的作品。④ P. 帕尔(Pal)、M. M. 芮(Rhie)和 R. A. F. 泽曼(Thurman)一致把它定为一

图 4-3-3 "觉密"壁画,江孜菩提塔东北四号龛。画家不详,1427—1440 年

(引自 Ricca, Franco, and Erberto Lo Bue, *The Great Stupa of Gyantse: A Complete Tibetan Pantheon of the fifteenth Century*, London: Serindia Publications, 1993, pl. 105, Ricca Franco 教授提供图片使用权)

---

① 壁画见 Ricca, Franco, and Erberto Lo Bue, *The Great Stupa of Gyantse: A Complete Tibetan Pantheon of the fifteenth Century*, London: Serindia Publications, 1993, pl. 105; for the date, pp. 27-28.
② Rinpothe, Robert N., *Paradise and Plumage: Chinese Connections in Tibetan Arhat Painting*, New York: Rubin Museum of Art, Chicago: Serindia Publications, 2006, p. 30.
③ Weidner, Marsha, Imperial Engagement with Buddhist Art and Architecture: Ming Variations on an Old Theme, in Marsha Weidner ed, *Cultural Intersections in Later Chinese Buddhism*, Honolulu: University of Hawaii Press, 2001, p. 125.
④ Béguin, Gilles, *Dieux et Demons De L. Himilaya*, Paris: Editions des musees nationaux, 1977, p. 112.

幅14世纪的作品。[1] 他们认为，洛杉矶唐卡的主题是一个住在某个地方的罗汉，唐卡上面的山水画因素只是机械地与罗汉形象拼凑在一起，因此整幅作品并不是一幅完整可信的山水画。他们因此推断，创作这幅唐卡的画家应该还没有掌握汉地山水书和西藏图像相结合起来的方法，所以它的年代要早一些。[2] 这三个学者还引用了其他一些证据——尤其是宋元人物画——来为唐卡断代。P. 帕尔注意到了元代绘画中类似的圆脸和络腮胡子等特征。[3] M. M. 芮和 R. A. F. 泽曼则指出了洛杉矶罗汉的风格、姿势和袈裟款式与元代颜辉作品的一些类似特征。[4] 但是需要指出的是，所有这些特征并不限于元代的作品。洛杉矶罗汉的绘画风格和姿势的许多特征也见于 15 世纪的寺院壁画和唐卡中。华丽的罗汉袈裟就见于现藏吉美博物馆（Musée Guimet）的一件年代为1454年的罗汉画。[5] 因此，洛杉矶唐卡的制作时间就有可能下延到 15 世纪——事实上，更多的证据表明这幅作品很可能制作于 15 世纪上半叶。

看到洛杉矶唐卡，我们首先会注意到罗汉的脸部特征。J. 斯图亚特（Stuart）认为，这样的人物画法糅合了汉地的两个肖像艺术手法：写实主义和平视的姿势。对于眼球、眼睛、鼻子、嘴唇和胡须部位的细致描绘是

---

[1] Pal, Pratapaditya, *The Art of Tibet*, The Asia Society, Inc., 1969, p. 132; Pal, Pratapaditya, *Art of Tibet*, Los Angeles County Museum of Art, 1990, pp. 137–138; Rhie, Marylin M., and Robert A. F. Thurman, *Wisdom and Compassion: The Sacred Art of Tibet*, Tibet House New York in association with Abradale Press, Harry N. Abrams, Inc., Publishers, 1996, pp. 105–106.

[2] Pal, Pratapaditya, *Tibetan Paintings: A Study of Tibetan Thankas Eleventh to Nineteenth Centuries*, Ravi Kumar: Sotheby Publications, 1984, pp. 123–124; Rhie, Marylin M., and Robert A. F. Thurman, *Wisdom and Compassion: The Sacred Art of Tibet*, Tibet House New York in association with Abradale Press, Harry N. Abrams, Inc., Publishers, 1996, p. 106.

[3] Pal, Pratapaditya, *Art of Tibet*, Los Angeles County Museum of Art, 1990, p. 138.

[4] Rhie, Marylin M., and Robert A. F. Thurman, *Wisdom and Compassion: The Sacred Art of Tibet*, Tibet House New York in association with Abradale Press, Harry N. Abrams, Inc., Publishers, 1996, p. 106.

[5] 这幅罗汉画原来属于一套水陆画，系明代皇家出资为北京的一座寺院所绘。其中的 34 件流失到吉美博物馆，这幅是其中之一。见 Weidner, Marsha ed., *Latter Days of the Law: Images of Chinese Buddhism 850–1850*, Spencer Museum of Art, The University of Kansas in association with University of Hawaii Press, 1994, p. 57.

◇❖◇ 第四部分　东亚艺术史

图4-3-4　杨洪（1381—1451）像，藏于 Freer Gallery of Art and Arthur M. Sackler Gallery, Smithsonian Institution, Washington, D. C.。画家不详，作于1451年前后。立轴，丝质，施墨和色。尺寸为220.8×127.5厘米

（Freer Gallery of Art and Arthur M. Sackler Gallery 提供照片和使用权）

人物画长期发展的结果。在汉地，对人物脸部的写实描写最早出现在北宋的佛教长老与僧人的肖像画中。[1] 这种追求形似的画风，虽然受到了文人画家的压制，但仍然延续到了南宋和元代。在元代，这些手法甚至被写进人物画手册。王绎（活动时间大约为1333—1368年）的《写像秘诀》就说到，人物画应该从鼻子开始，然后是眼睛和其他部位，最后是脸的轮廓。[2] 17世纪出版的《芥子园画传》（编于1669年）更是收录了一些描绘脸部特征的模本。[3] 罗汉的画法应该受了更早的一部类似的手册的启发。罗汉的平视姿势最早出现于东汉。不过在大多数情况下佛像的眼睛是朝下的。但是宋元以后，罗汉和佛陀的画像中开始有平视的例子，如日本东海庵、龙光院和永源寺所藏的作品。[4] 在汉地，写实与平视两个艺术手法的完美结合大概发生在明代中期，其代表作就是1451年左右的杨洪将军（1381—1451年）像（图4-3-4）（彩图10）。

其次，我们会注意到罗汉的双脚的表现。

---

[1] Stuart, Jan, *Worshipping the Ancestors: Chinese Commemorative Portraits*, The Freer Gallery of Art and the Arthur M. Sackler Gallery, Smithsonian Institution, Washington DC, in association with Stanford University Press, 2001, pp. 77-82.

[2] Stuart, Jan, *Worshipping the Ancestors: Chinese Commemorative Portraits*, The Freer Gallery of Art and the Arthur M. Sackler Gallery, Smithsonian Institution, Washington DC, in association with Stanford University Press, 2001, pp. 80-81.

[3] Stuart, Jan, *Worshipping the Ancestors: Chinese Commemorative Portraits*, The Freer Gallery of Art and the Arthur M. Sackler Gallery, Smithsonian Institution, Washington DC, in association with Stanford University Press, 2001, p. 82, Fig. 3:6.

[4] Suzuki, Kei, *Comprehensive Illustrated Catalog of Chinese Paintings*, Japanese Collections: Monasteries and Individuals, No. JT93-001, University of Tokyo Press, Vol. 4, 1983, NoJT1-002, JT93-001, JT108-006.

关于洛杉矶县立博物馆收藏的一件唐卡的几个问题

他们伸出袈裟，一只脚底朝上，一只脚底侧向。这种奇特的姿势无论在汉传还是在藏传佛教的罗汉像中都很少见到。一个可资对比的例子是上述的吉美1454年罗汉像，其罗汉的一只脚也伸出袈裟。当然，双脚暴露这一形式特点在藏传佛教艺术中经常出现，尤其见于12世纪或13世纪的佛陀、大黑天和高僧像中，[①] 或许是对佛陀、祖师脚印崇拜的反映。根据吉美罗汉像，我们有理由认为，对罗汉脚印的崇拜出现在15世纪的上半叶，而洛杉矶唐卡或许与此崇拜有关。

图4-3-5 "转法轮"壁画，白居寺。画家不详，15世纪上半叶
［引自金维诺主编《中国壁画全集》第34卷，《藏传寺院壁画》第4册，彩页84（金维诺教授提供图片使用权）］

  上述的两个证据都将洛杉矶唐卡的年代指向1450年左右。事实上，这一年代还可以从第三个证据——即唐卡的颜色搭配——得到支持。虽然罗汉左侧的胁侍的圆形头光属于汉传佛教传统，但主尊罗汉、右上角的罗汉和左上角的王子的水滴形头光则属于藏传佛教传统。这四个头光都是以深蓝色或褐色分层平涂而成的。无论在颜色的选择还是在技法方面，它们都接近于建于1418年的白居寺里的"转法轮"壁画（图4-3-5）（彩图11）。[②] 洛杉矶唐卡的颜色组合即朱砂、金、蓝、绿、褐和紫也见于白居寺的壁画。我们知道，西藏壁画的颜色组合不仅因时间和地区而不同，而且因寺院的不同而不同。例如，哲蚌寺（建于1416年）的壁画就不同于白居寺，它所采用的颜色是蓝绿色、深褐色、

[①] Pal, Pratapaditya, *Tibetan Paintings: A Study of Tibetan Thankas Eleventh to Nineteenth Centuries*, Ravi Kumar: Sotheby Publications, 1984, pl. 8, pl. 14, pl. 6.

[②] 金维诺主编：《中国壁画全集》第34卷，《藏传寺院壁画》第4册，天津人民美术出版社1993年版，彩版84。

巧克力色、乳白色和玫瑰色。① 有鉴于白居寺壁画和洛杉矶唐卡在颜色组合上的相似性，我们或许可以推测：洛杉矶唐卡和白居寺壁画是一个画派的画家所为。如果这个推测成立，那么此唐卡的年代便可定为15世纪上半叶。

三 产地

关于洛杉矶唐卡的产地，P. 帕尔、M. M. 芮和 R. A. F. 泽曼都认为是藏人画家作于藏地。② 笔者认为洛杉矶唐卡的制作者不能排除汉人画家的可能性。前面我们已经指出，在元明两代，汉藏两地的画家频繁往来，互相交流学习，以至于尼泊尔绘画和汉式绘画在1430—1450年间很自然地融合起来，形成了一种新的藏式绘画。③

上面我们已经触及了洛杉矶唐卡中的来自汉藏两个方面的因素。一方面，前景的罗汉和胁侍、右上角的罗汉和胁侍、供养人、各人物服饰、岩石和植物的绘画技法均为汉式。另一方面，罗汉崇拜的主题、罗汉的"本生故事"的题材、袒露双脚的形式和朴拙的山水构图都可能是藏地艺术的因素。此外，罗汉眼里的红色、唐卡形式、颜色组合以及僧人和华盖的绘画技法也应该是藏式。根据这些汉式和藏式因素的糅合情况，理论上讲，这幅唐卡的作者既可能是汉人，也可能是藏人，当然也可能是汉人和藏人组成的团队。

不过，考虑到洛杉矶唐卡中罗汉的肖像式描绘，笔者倾向于认为洛杉矶唐卡中主尊罗汉的作者是汉人画家。我们需要特别注意两个地方：

---

① 金维诺主编：《中国壁画全集》第31卷，《藏传寺院壁画》第1册，天津人民美术出版社1989年版，彩版136—145；Jackson, David, *A History of Tibetan Painting*: *The Great Tibetan Painters and Their Traditions*, Wien: Verlag der Osterreichischen Akademie der Wissenschaften, 1996, pp. 19–42.

② Pal, Pratapaditya, *The Art of Tibet*, The Asia Society, Inc., 1969, p. 132; Rhie, Marylin M., and Robert A. F. Thurman, *Wisdom and Compassion*: *The Sacred Art of Tibet*, Tibet House New York in association with Abradale Press, Harry N. Abrams, Inc., Publishers, 1996, p. 106.

③ Jackson, David, *A History of Tibetan Painting*: *The Great Tibetan Painters and Their Traditions*, Wien: Verlag der Osterreichischen Akademie der Wissenschaften, 1996, pp. 82–83。瞿昙寺、夏鲁寺、白居寺、哲蚌寺和色拉寺的壁画也可以证明。

关于洛杉矶县立博物馆收藏的一件唐卡的几个问题

唐卡中人物的脸部特征和脸部造型。除了王子和他的侍从外，这些人物都有圆鼓的脸庞、轮廓分明的鼻梁、眼睑、眼球、皱纹和嘴巴，所表现的是个真实而立体的人物脸庞。这样的脸部描绘，如上所述，最早出现于宋代。在西藏，11—15 世纪的藏式绘画有自己的一套人物画传统。例如，白居寺菩提塔里的弥勒像（图 4-3-2）的脸部是以鼻梁中央的一条竖线为中心的，虽然画出了鼻孔，但是鼻子的轮廓并没有画出来。眼睑画成弯曲的豆荚形，所以弥勒看起来好像是在俯视。除了眼睛和嘴，画家在脸部没有投入多少精力；脸部表面系平涂而成。[①] 在西藏和青海，这种绘画风格非常普遍，甚至出现在相当汉化的瞿昙寺壁画中。[②] 该寺在 18 世纪曾经重建，但是现存的大部分壁画都是明代的。其中瞿昙殿、宝光殿和隆国殿的壁画都是藏式形象，而走廊内的佛陀的本生故事都是汉式人物、建筑和山水。[③] 但是值得我们特别注意的是，所有人物的脸部都是按照藏式传统画的。[④]

这样看来，西藏的画家，无论他们是否已经掌握汉式绘画的题材和技法，都必须遵守一些藏地的艺术传统。洛杉矶唐卡的汉式人物形象在众多已知的西藏壁画中是个孤例，所以罗汉的作者应该包括汉地的汉人。但是考虑到唐卡中的西藏因素，我们认为藏人艺术家可能也参与了唐卡的制作，负责唐卡以及王子和侍从的绘画，并可能绘制了人物的头

---

① 扎塘寺（1081 年始建，1093 完工）的壁画是一个例外。平涂法被用来表现坑凹不平的地方。不过人物的脸部描绘仍然属于这个传统。见金维诺主编《中国壁画全集》第 33 卷，《藏传寺院壁画》第 3 册，天津人民美术出版社 1992 年版，彩版 5—39。

② 瞿昙寺位于明代的陕西省今青海省乐都县境内。因为协助明朝平定动乱和处理西藏事务有功，从洪武到宣德的历代皇帝都提供了优厚的资金用于该寺的建造和扩建。所以它虽然是一座藏传寺院，但是它的建筑和绘画都深受汉文化的影响。参 Sperling, Elliot, Tibetan Buddhism, Perceived and Imagined, along the Ming-Era Sino-Tibetan Frontier, in Matthew T. Kapstein ed., *Buddhism between Tibet and China*, Boston: Wisdom Publications, 2009, p. 156; Debreczeny, Karl P., *Ethnicity and Esoteric Power: Negotiating Sino-Tibetan Synthesis in Ming Buddhist Painting*, PhD dissertation, University of Chicago, 2007, pp. 154 – 155.

③ Debreczeny, Karl P., *Ethnicity and Esoteric Power: Negotiating Sino-Tibetan Synthesis in Ming Buddhist Painting*, PhD dissertation, University of Chicago, 2007, pp. 192 – 195.

④ 金维诺主编：《中国壁画全集》第 31 卷，《藏传寺院壁画》第 1 册，天津人民美术出版社 1989 年版，彩版 113—123；金维诺主编：《中国壁画全集》第 34 卷，《藏传寺院壁画》第 4 册，天津人民美术出版社 1993 年版，彩版 133—140。

光以及设定了蓝绿的色调——他们甚至还可能监督了唐卡的整个制作过程。像前面提到的明朝宫廷唐卡一样，洛杉矶唐卡可能是15世纪上半叶明朝宫廷为一位西藏高僧或贵族定制的。

四　结论

根据前面的分析，我们现在对洛杉矶唐卡有了一个全新的认识。这幅唐卡是一幅有关罗汉崇拜的作品。在这里，画家把罗汉当作佛陀对待，给予他大部分画面，并描绘了他的"本生"故事。罗汉的坐垫上所绣的凤凰图案，说明他是一位曾经受到明朝宫廷礼遇的藏地高僧或贵族的化身。他的脸部描绘手法是汉地肖像画长期发展的结果，其年代接近于1451年的杨洪将军像。罗汉的坐垫所绣的凤凰图案与江孜菩提塔内的"觉密"壁画相似，而他的袒露的双脚可以同1454年的吉美罗汉像相类比。所有这些线索表明，此唐卡的年代为15世纪上半叶。此外，唐卡所用的颜色组合与白居寺壁画的相同，说明两者出自同一个画派的画家之手。至于唐卡的产地，虽然许多题材和技法因素都是藏式，但是罗汉脸部的肖像式描绘属于汉画风格，完全不符合藏式绘画传统。因此很有可能汉人和藏人艺术家共同参与了这幅唐卡的制作，而制作地点可能就在明代的宫廷作坊。

五　鸣谢

本文是作者在加州大学洛杉矶分校留学期间受Sonya Quintanilla和Robert L. Brown教授主持的"西藏的艺术和建筑"讨论课的启发而写成的。Sonya Quintanilla教授和她的母亲Marilyn M. Rhie教授以及王玉冬博士曾审阅了本文的初稿并给予了建设性的意见。在此谨向他们致以最诚挚的感谢。文中所有错误都由作者承担。

Kang Sehwang's Scenes of Puan Prefecture-Describing Actual Landscape Through Literati Ideals*

In the earlyeighteenth-Century *chin'gyŏng* 真景, "true scenery" or "true view," painting emerged in Chosŏn Korea as a dominating landscape genre. [1] While earlier artists were preoccupied with legendary or historical landscapes rooted in Chinese tradition, *chin'gyŏng* painters turned their eyes to real landscapes in their own country. Earlier artists had mainly been inspired by Chinese models, but *chin'gyŏng* painters traveled to scenic sites on the Korean peninsula and produced works based on their empirical observations. It is thus no coincidence that the term *chin'gyŏng* appeared in the writings of artists who actually painted this genre of landscapes, starting

---

* The article was originally published in *Arts Asiatiques* 65, 2011, pp. 75 – 94. It was jointly authored by Burglind Jungmann and Liangren Zhang, is so reprinted in this anthology with minor changes. The article is based on a research paper by Liangren Zhang for a seminar at UCLA on Korean true scenery painting in 2001 conducted by Burglind Jungmann. The two authors were then able to identify the handscroll as a work by Kang Sehwang. Thanks to financial support of the Friends of Art History of UCLA Liangren Zhang was able to visit the sites recorded in the handscroll in the summer of 2004 and discuss his findings with leading Korean scholars Byun Young-sup and Hong Sŏnp'yo. The completed article was made available to Byun Young-sup in the summer of 2009 before the publication of her own article on the handscroll: Pyoam Kang Sehwang ŭi "Ugŭmam to" wa "Yu Ugŭmam ki", *Misul charyo* 78, 2009, pp. 23 - 60. 作者为 Burglind Jungmann, Liangren Zhang。

① Since the term "true view" implies that the representation of the landscape is "true," it can lead to the misunderstanding that the painter aimed at a faithful ("realistic") depiction of the landscape. However, the way *chin'gyŏng* is used in contemporaneous sources (and in earlier Chinese texts) implies that the landscape itself exists. Because "true scenery" shifts the emphasis from subject to object, it is preferred here. For further explanation, see Jungmann, Burglind, *Painters as Envoys: Korean Inspiration in Eighteenth-Century Japanese Nanga*, Princeton University Press, 2004, pp. 190 - 194.

in the early eighteenth Century. ①Although variations can be found in Chinese texts as early as the tenth and eleventh centuries, it was never an established term in China. ②In Chosŏn Korea, however, it emerged from a climate of self-searching and newly surfacing self-confidence, sparked by Reform Confucianism (sirhak "实学, practical learning"). Rather than emphasizing "realism" in the representation of a landscape, however, it came to differentiate native real scenery from foreign ideal landscape.

Korean art historians started to investigate the chin'gyŏng genre in the 1970s, seeking to uncover the greater significance of this artistic movement. Yi Sŏngmi proposes that the term chin'gyŏng does not simply mean real landscape, but real landscape of Chosŏn Korea. In her view, the character "chin 真" has the connotation of being native and of high quality. She also emphasizes the change of intellectual milieu in Korea since the seventeenth century. ③Ever since the "barbarian" Manchus, brought down the Ming dynasty in 1644, Chosŏn intellectuals shifted their attention to a growing appreciation of their own land and culture. According to Yi Sŏngmi, technical innovations, Western literature, and paintings were also a source of inspiration for the chin'gyŏng movement. The preeminent scholar, Yi Ik (李瀷, 1681 – 1763), a leading figure of Reform Confucianism and friend of the painters Yun Tusŏ (尹斗緒, 1668 – 1715) and Kang Sehwang (姜世晃, 1713 – 1791), had seen Western paintings and was aware of the

---

① According to recent research, Yun Tŏkhŭi (1685 – 1766), the son of Yun Tusŏ, was the first to mention the term. We also know from records that he painted true sceneries, however, although none is extant today. See Cha, Miae, Kŭn'gi Namin sŏhwaga kŭrup ŭi Kŭmgangsan kihaeng yesul kwa Naksŏ Yun Tŏkhŭi ŭi 'Kŭmgang yusangnok,' *Misulsa Nondan* 27, 2008, pp. 173 – 221.

② Jungmann, Burglind, *Painters as Envoys: Korean Inspiration in Eighteenth-Century Japanese Nanga*, Princeton University Press, 2004, pp. 188 – 190.

③ Yi, Sŏngmi, Artistic Tradition and the Depiction of Reality: True-view Landscape Painting of the Chosŏn Dynasty, in *Arts of Korea*, New York: The Metropolitan Museum, 1998, pp. 332 – 335, 340 – 343; Yi, Sŏngmi, *Korean Landscape Painting: Continuity and Innovation Through the Ages*, Elizabeth, New Jersey, and Seoul: Hollym, 2006, pp. 93 – 97.

principles of linear perspective. ①Although Yi Ik was not entirely convinced of the value of Western devices, Kang Sehwang experimented with linear perspective and chiaroscuro effects in his landscape paintings, most prominently in his album *Journey to Songdo* (Fig. 4 – 4 – 14, Fig. 4 – 4 – 15). ②In addition, Kang Sehwang was probably the most important propagator of the term *chin'gyŏng*. He used it frequently in his writings. Moreover, as his comments and colophons on works by famous contemporary painters suggest, he occupied a prominent position in artistic circles, a position that undoubtedly helped to disseminate the term. ③

This paper will focus on a handscroll by Kang Sehwang, *Scenes of Puan Prefecture*, purchased for the collection of the Los Angeles County Museum of

---

① He, however, did not find Western devices entirely appropriate for Korean painting; see Ko, Yŏnhŭi, *Chosŏn Hugi Sansu Kihaeng Yesul Yŏn'gu: Chŏng Sŏn Kwa Nongyŏn Kŭrubŭl Chungsimŭro*, Seoul: Ilchisa, 2001, p. 275, note 31, Yi Ik was indeed highly aware of the Christian faith and the new sciences the Jesuit priests had brought to China, but he was selective in his acceptance of such novelties and particularly critical of Matteo Ricci's proselytism. See Lee, Peter H. ed., *Sourcebook of Korean Civilization: From the Seventeenth Century to the Modern Period*, New York: Columbia University Press, Vol. 2, 1996, pp. 132 – 136.

② The album was first introduced to a Western audience by Susan Cox: An Unusual Album by a Korean Painter, Kang Se-hwang, *Oriental Art* 19/2, 1973, pp. 157 – 168. Further research was done by Byun Young-sup [Pyŏn Yŏngsŏp], *P'yoam Kang Sehwang Hoehwa Yŏn'gu*, Seoul: Ilchisa, 1988, pp. 96 – 110, and by Kim Kŏnni, P'yoam Kang Sehwang ŭi Songdo kihaeng ch'ŏp yŏn'gu, *Misulsahak Yŏn'gu* 238/239, 2003, pp. 183 – 211. For color illustrations of the whole album, see *P'urŭn Sorŭn Nŭkchi Annŭnda-Ch'ang Song Pul no-P'yoam Kang Sehwang*, exhibition catalogue, Seoul: Yesul ŭi chŏndang, 2003, no. 72. See also Yi, Sŏngmi, Artistic Tradition and the Depiction of Reality: True-view Landscape Painting of the Chosŏn Dynasty, in *Arts of Korea*, New York: The Metropolitan Museum, 1998, pp. 354 – 356; and Jungmann, Burglind, *Painters as Envoys: Korean Inspiration in Eighteenth-Century Japanese Nanga*, Princeton University Press, 2004, pp. 202 – 203.

③ For more information on Kang Sehwang's life and work, see Byun Young-sup, *P'yoam Kang Sehwang Hoehwa Yŏn'gu*, Seoul: Ilchisa, 1988, pp. 96 – 110 and Byun Young-sup, On Kang Sehwang: the Lofty Ideals of a Literati Artist, in *The Fragrance of Ink: Korean Literati Paintings of the Chosŏn Dynasty (1392 – 1910) from Korea University Museum*, Seoul: Korean Studies Institute, Korea University, 1996, pp. 192 – 215. The circle included such prominent painters as Sim Sajŏng (1707 – 1769), Ch'oe Puk (1718 – 1786), Hŏ P'il (1709 – 1768), Kang Hŭiŏn (1710 – 1764), Kim Hongdo (1745-ca. 1806), and Sin Wi (1769 – 1845).

Art in 2000.① It is not only a major work of the artist in a Western collection but it uniquely combines "Three Treasures" (*samjŏl*, Chinese: *sanjue*) 三绝: calligraphy, literature, and painting, and is thus a superb example of Chosŏn literati art. We will investigate the relationship between Kang Sehwang's travelogue and his paintings, trying to shed light on his ideas about traveling itself, about writing travelogues, and about rendering actual scenery. A careful analysis of the handscroll and of related texts, published in his anthology *P'yoam Yugo* 豹庵遗稿, will help us to understand the process of the creation of the scroll and the painter's intention, that is, to understand its position within the context of his life and times.②

The Handscroll *Scenes of Puan Prefecture*

The handscroll, *Scenes of Puan Prefecture* (Fig. 4 – 4 – 1) (彩图 12), consists of a travelogue that narrates a tour in the Pyŏn Mountains 边山 in North Chŏlla province and five paintings that depict scenic sites the painter saw during this tour. Although it bears neither a signature nor a date, it can be attributed to Kang Sehwang on the basis of available evidence. First, the travelogue can be found almost unchanged in Kang's *P'yoam Yugo*. Moreover, the calligraphy can be attributed to Kang on stylistic grounds. Its accomplished and spontaneous writing style leaves little doubt that it is in fact the original from which the published text was transcribed and not a copy from the publication.③

---

① The scroll was first published in *Miguk Pangmulgwan Sojang Han'guk Munhwajae*, 1989, p. 194, Fig. 23 – 24, as part of the collection of Robert Moore and then, after being acquired by the Los Angeles County Museum of Art by Keith J. Wilson [Korean Art at the Los Angeles County Museum of Art, *Orientations* 31/2, February 2000, p. 29].

② Kang, Sehwang, *P'yoam Yugo*, Songnam: Han'guk chŏngshin munhwa yŏn'guwŏn. P'yoam is one of the artist's pen names, 1979.

③ A detailed discussion of the calligraphy would go beyond the scope of this article. For comparable examples, see *P'urŭn Sorŭn Nŭkchi Annŭnda-Ch'ang Song Pul no-P'yoam Kang Sehwang*, nos. 28 – 32. *P'yoam Yugo*, compiled by Kang Sehwang's fourth son, Pin, in 1792, was published as late as 1979 by the Academy of Korean Studies. A forger would only have been able to use the travelogue's text if he either had access to the family collection or if he had copied it after its publication. Both possibilities are highly unlikely.

Kang Sehwang's Scenes of Puan Prefecture

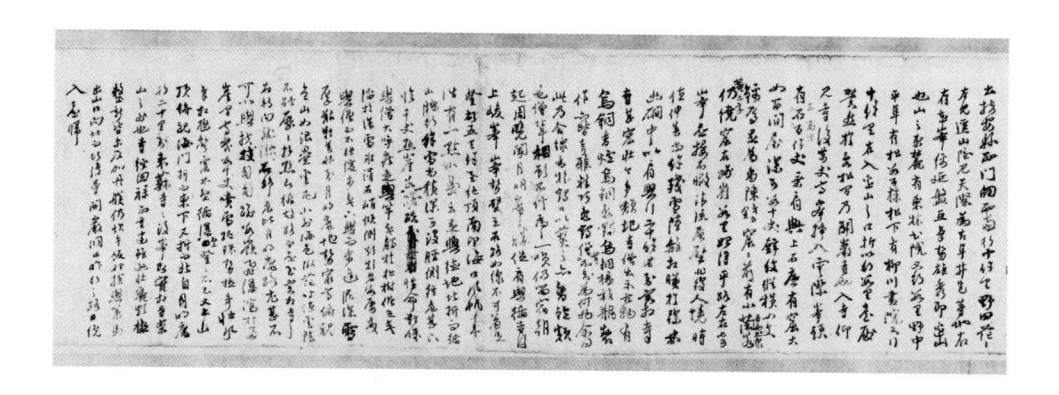

Fig. 4-4-1　Kang Sehwang, *Scenes of Puan Prefecture*, handscroll, ca. 1770, **ink on paper**, 25.4 × 267.3 厘米

(Los Angeles County Museum of Art, Los Angeles. Photo ⓒ Museum Associates/ LACMA)

The *Scenes of Puan Prefecture* handscroll is pasted together from six rectangular sheets of paper, each approximately forty-five centimeters long. Viewed from right to left, it starts with an extended ink landscape, followed by the travelogue, and four smaller sketches. All landscapes bear inscriptions declaring the name of the scenic site. In the order of their appearance on the scroll, these are "Ugŭm Rocks 禹金巘", "Munjo Screen 门照", "Silsang Monastery 实相寺", "Yongch'u Pond 龙湫" and "Kŭngnak Hermitage 极乐庵". In contrast to most handscrolls which contain text and images in a more systematic manner, the artist paid scant attention to the overall layout here. ① He obviously heeded the height but not the width of the paintings and the travelogue. Therefore, the width of the five paintings varies greatly. For instance, the first painting, "Ugŭm Rocks," is about three times wider than the last one, "Kŭngnak Hermitage." The composition thus adds to the impression of spontaneous work that the calligraphy style already implies. Its "disorderly" impulsive character sets it apart from Kang Sehwang's other works. Such spontaneity and the fact that it is unsigned make the handscroll unique. Judging from his other works and his inscriptions on the paintings of contemporaries, Kang Sehwang was never shy to acknowledge his authorship. He often added modest phrases that emphasize—in contrast to their literal meaning—how proud he was of his creations. We will therefore have to ask why, in this case, he chose to create such an "unpolished" work and why he chose to remain anonymous.

In order to further investigate the unique character of the scroll, it is worthwhile to reconstruct the process of its creation. On closer inspection, the first scene, consisting of, according to the painter's inscription, "Ugŭm Rocks," and an unnamed mountain peak, occupies the first two sheets. The unnamed peak extends beyond the joint between the second and the third sheets and finishes close to the travelogue (Fig. 4-4-2). The sequence

---

① Usually East Asian painters, when dealing with a series of single sites, either integrated them all into one composition along a travel route or depicted them on separate album leaves. Kang Sehwang's own series of paintings of his travels to Kaesŏng (Songdo) and Beijing, to be discussed later, are good examples of the second kind. In his landscape handscrolls, for instance, of the Tosan Academy and of two landscapes after Dong Qichang and Shen Zhou, text and images are also more evenly arranged. For illustrations, see *P'urŭn Sorŭn Nŭkchi Annŭnda-Ch'ang Song Pul no-P'yoam Kang Sehwang*, nos. 61 and 69.

Fig. 4 − 4 − 2 Mountain peak next to Ugŭm Rocks, detail of Fig. 4 − 4 − 1

of the first three sheets suggests two possibilities. Kang either painted the landscape first and then started to write, or he wrote the travelogue first and then added the two sheets to the right and painted Ugŭm Rocks and the single peak. The fact that the travelogue starts at the beginning of a sheet of paper, leaving about as much space to the right as on the top, suggests the second possibility. In this case, Kang Sehwang would have extended the space to the right after writing the travelogue, painted Ugŭm Rocks, and placed the unnamed mountain close to the first line of the travelogue in order to join the second and third sheets, in much the same way as seals are often placed over the joints of two sheets to ensure that they are kept in place. The paper containing the travelogue was not long enough, so Kang added another one to the left. There is some space left on the fourth sheet when the text ends, and he filled it with half of the second scene, "Munjo Screen" (Fig. 4 − 4 − 3), with the joint between the fourth and the fifth sheet cutting through the composition to the left of the inscription. The next two scenes,

第四部分　东亚艺术史

Fig. 4 – 4 – 3　**Munjo Screen, detail of Fig**. 4 – 4 – 1

"Silsang Monastery" and "Yongch'u Pond" (Fig. 4 – 4 – 4) are so close together that they almost appear as one landscape. In his travelogue, Kang narrates that he went directly from the monastery to the impressive waterfall of Yongch'u Pond, thus implying that the sites were close to each other. However, he may have had a formal reason to integrate them into one composition, namely to cover the next and final joint, which can be found to the right of the waterfall. Finally, the artist added the small "Kŭngnak Hermitage" painting (Fig. 4 – 4 – 5) filling the remaining space on the sixth sheet of paper.

　　The unevenness of the space between the paintings and their varying sizes gives the impression that the landscape scenes were arranged around the travelogue, as illustrations or visual reminders, rather than conceived in their own right. Thus, the travelogue is the centerpiece of the composition. The fact that the text and the images are not well integrated gives the handscroll

Fig. 4-4-4　Silsang Monastery and Yongch'u Pond, detail of Fig. 4-4-1

its somewhat raw, unfinished character. This suggests that the handscroll was the first attempt to record the impression of the journey, both visually and verbally. It thus stands in contrast to a finished work, created after the artist had digested his impressions and honed them into a presentable form.

The travelogue is executed in cursive style with elegance and ease; it attests to the artist's accomplished skills in calligraphy (Fig. 4-4-6).[①] Kang picked up a saturated brush, kept writing until it dried, and then dipped it into the ink again. The manner of writing indicates that he let his brush go at its own will. While his handwriting is legible at the beginning, it becomes increasingly cursive and more difficult to read. In addition, he casually added or crossed out characters. For instance, in the eleventh line, after describing a cave he remarks on the name of the site and adds to the character *jin* 陈 " or said to be—*gŭm* 金", noting that it is known as Ugŭm or Ujin Rock. In the transcription for the published text it was eventually determined as gŭm. Later, at the end of the same line and the beginning of the next one, he added seven characters to further describe a small Buddhist Hall in front of the cave which

---

① For a complete translation of the text, see Appendix.

◇❖◇　第四部分　东亚艺术史

Fig. 4 – 4 – 5　**Kǔngnak Hermitage, detail of Fig**. 4 – 4 – 1

had "a plaque on the lintel [inscribed with] the three characters of *Okch'ŏnam* 玉泉庵 (*Jade Spring Hermitage*)." ① On other occasions, he was apparently not satisfied with the words and crossed out several characters. Erasing one character in line thirty-six, for instance, he substituted it with "*isang* 而上 (upwards)" to edit the sentence "I climbed upwards alongside the waterfall." ② In these cases, the ink tone of the correction does not differ from that of the line he adjusted, suggesting that he amended and edited them immediately. Because the text is written with certainty and

---

① See end of section 2 in Appendix.
② See end of section 6 in Appendix.

fluency, we may suppose that the artist initially constructed the entire travelogue in his mind and then wrote it down without pausing—in one breath, so to speak. Yet, it is striking that the essay appears to be perfect in composition and wording. Apparently, he did not regard "defects" as a problem, but cherished the "spontaneity" of the writing.

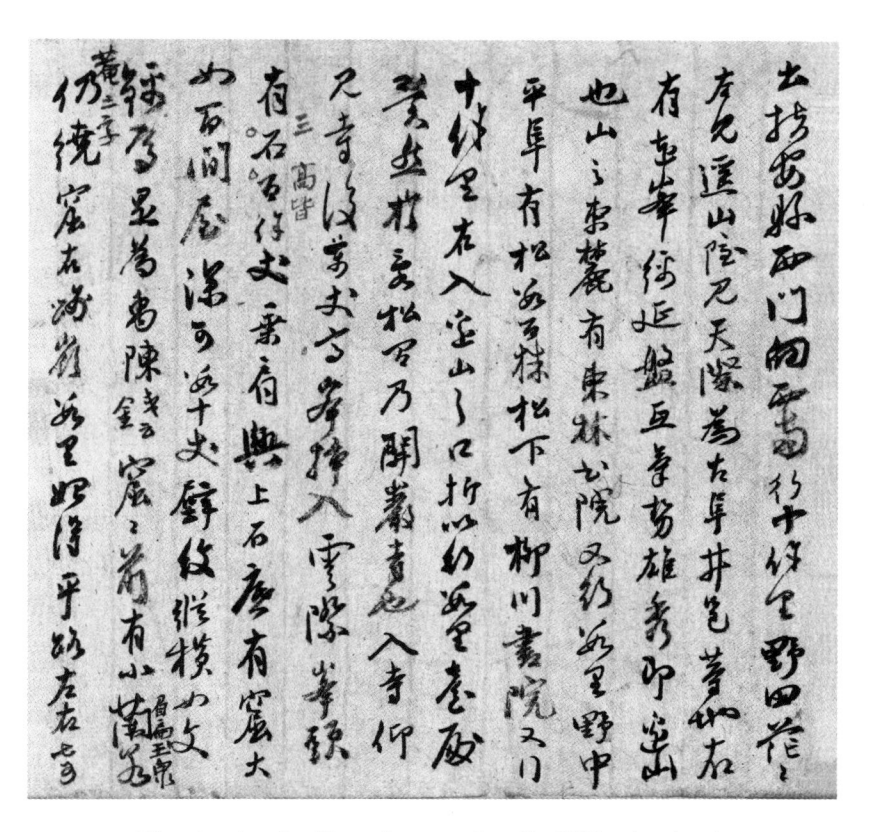

Fig. 4-4-6　Travelogue, detail of Fig. 4-4-1

The date when Kang Sehwang created *Scenes of Puan Prefecture* can be deduced from another travelogue included in *P'yoam Yugo*. It records an excursion in 1770 to a coastal area around Kyŏkp'o 格浦, a town located within the vicinity of Mt. Pyŏn (Fig. 4-4-7) (彩图 13). [①]Kang

---

① Kang, Sehwang, Travel to Kyŏkp'o Port, in *P'yoam Yugo*, Songnam: Han'guk chŏngshin munhwa yŏn'guwŏn, 1979, pp. 245-248.

Sehwang visited his second son, Wan 俒, who had been appointed usŭng 邮丞 (postal clerk) in Puan Prefecture 扶安县 in 1763, and possibly held this position until his early death in 1775. We have good reason to suppose that the journey to Puan also took place in 1770, in connection with the Kyŏkp'o excursion.

Kang Sehwang, whose family was poor due to the early death of his father, lived for almost thirty years, between 1744 and 1773, in Ansan 安山, an economically flourishing town not far from Seoul. Ansan was also a cultural center, as a number of eminent scholars, artists, and collectors resided there or were in active contact with its residents, including Yi Ik, Hŏ P'il 许佖 (1709—1768), Ch'oe Puk 崔北 (1712—1786), Sim Sajŏng 沈师正 (1707—1769), and Kang Sehwang's brother-in-law, Yu Kyŏngjong 柳庆种 (1714—1784), an important member of the Namin 南人 (Southerner) faction. Kang was a central figure in this intellectual circle.[1] When he took the opportunity to travel, it was usually on invitation or to visit one of his sons. Over a decade earlier, in 1757, he had visited Kaesŏng 开城, the capital of the previous Koryŏ dynasty, at the invitation of the governor of the city, O Such'ae 吴遂采 (1692—1759), and had painted the album *Journey to Songdo* on O's request.[2] In 1788, Kang went to visit his first son, In 偩, who held office in Hoeyang 淮阳 in present-day Kangwŏn province, and from there he made a trip to the famous Diamond Mountains 金刚山 (Kŭmgangsan) and produced the *Journey to the Diamond Mountains* album.[3] It is therefore plausible that he made the excursion to Mt. Pyŏn during his stay with Wan.

---

[1] Hong, Sŏnp'yo, Chosŏn sidae Kyŏnggi chiyŏk yŏn'go munin hwagadŭl ŭi hoehwa hwaltong, in *Yet Kurim sok ŭi Kyŏnggido*, Seoul: Kyŏnggi munhwa chaedan, 2005, pp. 25 – 32; Kim, Kŏnni, P'yoam Kang Sehwang ŭi Songdo kihaeng ch'ŏp yŏn'gu, *Misulsahak Yŏn'gu* 238/239, 2003, pp. 185 – 188.

[2] Kim, Kŏnni, P'yoam Kang Sehwang ŭi Songdo kihaeng ch'ŏp yŏn'gu, *Misulsahak Yŏn'gu* 238/239, 2003, p. 194.

[3] Kang, Sehwang, Travel to the Kŭmganyang Mountains, in *P'yoam Yugo*, Songnam: Han'guk chŏngsin munhwa yŏn'guwŏn, 1979, pp. 254 – 256.

Verbal and Visual Representation of True Scenery

The five sites depicted in the *Scenes of Puan Prefecture* handscroll are located in the area of the Pyŏn Mountains in North Chŏlla province. ①The inscriptions written to the right of each painting readily identify the sites. The subjects of the five paintings and the travelogue do not completely overlap but rather complement each other. As already mentioned, the paintings document "Ugŭm Rocks," "Munjo Screen," "Silsang Monastery," "Yongch'u Pond," and "Kŭngnak Hermitage." Except for "Munjo Screen" and "Kŭngnak Hermitage," they are marked in a contemporaneous map (Fig. 4-4-7). So are a number of other sites which the travelogue mentions and describes, such as Tongnim Academy 东林书院, Kaeam Monastery 开巖寺, Naeso Monastery 来苏寺, and Wŏlmyŏng Hermitage 月明庵. There is little doubt that the handscroll was produced from a real tour. ②

In the following, we will analyze, in the order of the travelogue, the verbal description of each site in comparison to the pictorial representation of the scenes in the five paintings. For this purpose, we will frequently refer to the travelogue, a complete translation of which can be found in the Appendix. We will further compare both visual and verbal descriptions with photographs taken during field research in June 2004. Although Kang Sehwang traveled in the early spring rather than in summer, and roads and trails have been modernized in recent decades to boost tourism, the general landscape does not seem to have changed drastically in the past two hundred years. We are therefore able to catch a glimpse of the travel experiences Kang Sehwang had.

At the beginning of his travelogue, Kang Sehwang writes that he saw a

---

① Today, a national park has been established in the vicinity of Mt. Pyŏn.

② Yang, Pogyŏng, Kunhyŏn chido ŭi paldal kwa 'Haedong Chido', in *Haedong Chido*, Seoul: Seoul University, Kyujanggak, Vol. 3, 1995, p. 72. Byun Young-sup traced Kang's tour which, according to her estimation, would have taken two days, see Byun, Young-sup, Pyoam Kang Sehwang ŭi "Ugŭmam to" wa "Yu Ugŭmam ki", *Misul charyo* 78, 2009, pp. 29-31.

· 433 ·

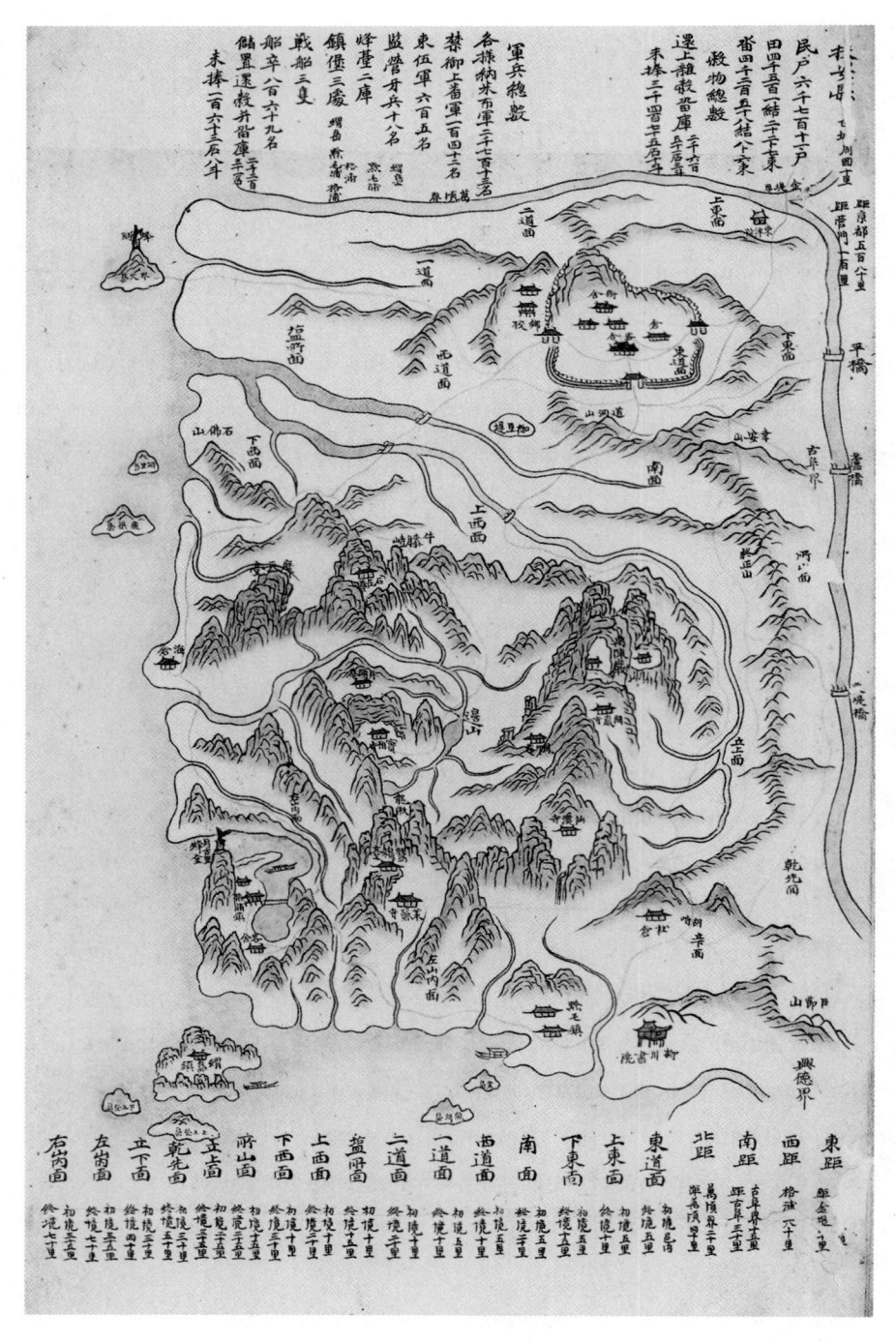

Fig. 4 – 4 – 7 **Map of Puan Prefecture** 1747 – 1750
(*Haedong Chido*, Seoul: Seoul National University, Kyujanggak, Vol. 2, 1995, p. 22)

mountain silhouette emerging in the far distance above the horizon on his left and undulating, intertwining chains of mountains on his right, all of which constituted a magnificent view (Appendix, Section 1). "Munjo Screen" (Fig. 4-4-3) may be regarded as the first site Kang Sehwang encountered after he left the seat of Puan Prefecture. Yet, in the handscroll this scene is placed behind "Ugŭm Rocks" and the travelogue. While "Munjo" appears as a label written beside the scene, the name does not appear in the text. It can, however, also be translated as "picture of the gate (to the mountains)" and the small figures, one of them riding a sedan chair, ascending a narrow path leading into a valley between high rocks, are undoubtedly meant to represent Kang's travel party. In the painting, the recession of peaks on the right suggests distance, and the rising formations on the left highlight the grandeur of the rocks in the foreground. In the far distance, towering peaks arise, embodying the distant mountains looming on the horizon. The tiny figures of the travelers ascending the mountain path on the lower right accentuate the imposing height of the mountains.

Neither the textual nor the pictorial descriptions of the site hold true to reality. The vicinity of Mt. Pyŏn consists of low, gently rolling hills. The highest point is the peak on which Wŏlmyŏng Hermitage stands, 459m above sea level. The hills are neither as rocky nor as cozy as Kang rendered them. The downward movements of the brush describing the texture of the rocks, at times resembling "axe-cut" strokes, reveal his intention to create awe-inspiring mountains by employing conventional elements of Namjonghwa 南宗画, the literati painting style that flourished during Kang Sehwang's times and provided the basis of true scenery landscape painting. [1]In addition, Kang combines several perspectives.

---

[1] The true scenery genre may be regarded as a part of literati or Namjonghwa ("Southern school") landscape painting. The depiction of actual scenery before the Namjonghwa movement emerged in the seventeenth century was often regarded as documentary painting. Namjonghwa elements in true scenery painting were thus crucial to the recognition of the genre as an art form. For further information on Namjonghwa, see Yi, Sŏngmi, Southern School Literati Painting of the Late Chosŏn Period, *The Fragrance of Ink: Korean Literati Paintings of the Chosŏn Dynasty* (1392-1910) *from Korea University Museum*, Korean Studies Institute, Korea University, 1996, pp. 174-191; Yi, Sŏngmi, Korean Landscape Painting: Continuity and Innovation through the Ages, Elizabeth, New Jersey, and Seoul: Hollym, 2006, pp. 80-92; and Jungmann, Burglind, *Painters as Envoys: Korean Inspiration in Eighteenth-Century Japanese Nanga*, Princeton University Press, 2004, pp. 47-71.

The peaks to the right of the path are seen from an equal height, whereas those on the left rise from foreground to background in a curve as if perceived from a bird's eye perspective. The towering peaks in the background belittle all the rocks in the foreground. The trees in the middle ground are extremely high, reaching more than half the height of the mountains.

Continuing his journey, Kang Sehwang approached Kaeam Monastery (Appendix, Section 2). He saw peaks "tens of thousands of *chang* 丈 high," piercing into the clouds; they were crowned with three rocks another "hundreds of *chang* high."[①] After ascending the mountain, he caught sight of a cave as big as "one hundred *kan* 间" and probably "dozens of chang" deep underneath the three rocks.[②] These were Ugŭm Rocks, which Kang beautifully describes as bearing criss-crossing veins like a brocade design. In front, he found Okch'ŏn Hermitage. This section of the travelogue, again replete with exciting details and a lively description of the overwhelming impact the rocks had on the traveler, reveals Kang Sehwang's intention to enhance the experience of the journey.

The visual representation of "Ugŭm Rocks" is the first painting one encounters when opening the scroll (Fig. 4-4-1). Since, in *P'yoam Yugo*, the text is titled "Record of a Journey to Ugŭm Rocks," this scene may have been meant to introduce the actual theme of the journey, and can be compared to more formal titles written in large characters at the beginning of other handscrolls. As the photography of the site illustrates, the rockface of the three rocks, mentioned by Kang Sehwang in his travelogue, consists of basalt layers that indeed resemble a brocade pattern (Fig. 4-4-8). The painting, however, depicts the three peaks as if they dominated numerous mountains that cluster around them. In reality, from Kaeam Monastery one can only see the three rocks joined together on one hill (Fig. 4-4-9). Additionally, the

---

① Chang was a traditional measurement in both Korea and China. A *chang* literally equals 10 chi, which equals about 12.5 inches. See Wilkinson, Endymion, *Chinese History: A Manual*, Revised and enlarged edition, Cambridge and London: The Harvard University Asia Center for the Harvard-Yenching Institute, 2000, Table 17.

② *Kan* describes the space between two columns ("inter-columnium") in East Asian architecture and measures approximately 2.4 × 2.4 meters.

angle from which the three rocks are depicted in the painting supposes a horizontal view from another mountain of about the same height. It is unlikely that Kang climbed any other mountain. Moreover, the cave below the rocks is difficult to see from Kaeam Monastery due to the dense forest on the hill. Thus, rather than showing the site from a single perspective, Kang Sehwang again integrated his experience during the climb and the imagined view from an equal height into one composition. It is obvious that he aimed to create a majestic vision of the three rocks. The single mountain painted to the left of "Ugŭm Rocks" (Fig. 4-4-2), which is not further identified by the painter, appears to be a rather generic scene. It might represent a site Kang Sehwang had seen somewhere on his way, but could equally just be inserted as an indicator of the ongoing journey. As already mentioned, it secures the joint between the two sheets of paper.

Fig. 4-4-8 **Rockface of Ugŭm Rocks, photo by Liangren Zhang, 2004**

On the next step of his journey, Kang Sehwang wrote that his eyes were restlessly occupied by fantastic peaks, streams, and layered cliffs; he felt as if it were far from the mundane world (Appendix, Section 3). It was already the

◇❖◇　第四部分　东亚艺术史

middle of spring, but snow shimmered amidst deep trees and hidden creeks. Kang traveled through this fantastic land for twenty miles before arriving at Silsang Monastery. Upon arriving at the monastery, Kang finds little to say, except that the monks here were unexpectedly ignorant of antiques (Appendix,

Fig. 4 - 4 - 9　View of Ugŭm Rocks from Kaeam Monastery, photo by Liangren Zhang, 2004

Section 4). In his painting, the monastery complex occupies most of the space, and the open arrangement of the buildings denotes a sense of peace (Fig. 4 - 4 - 4). Kang depicts the halls and trees in a conventional, fairly schematized manner, like elements taken from a manual, and he again employs a bird's eye view, as if looking at the monastery from a distance. The mountains behind the complex reach beyond the upper edge of the scroll so that only their lower part can be seen, suggesting that they are overwhelmingly high. They are roughly sketched with broad brush strokes. These bold, fibrous strokes together with the thick black vertical and horizontal lines of the tall trees create a pleasant contrast with the two images on either side. It becomes obvious that

· 438 ·

Kang Sehwang's Scenes of Puan Prefecture ◇❖◇

Kang was far more interested in the visual effect of the painting than in rendering the actual site. The monastery was burnt down in the 1950s during the Korean War, and by 2004, only two isolated halls had been restored. The site indeed appeared to be spacious. In contrast to the painting, however, the hill directly behind the monastery is densely forested (Fig. 4 – 4 – 10). There is a rocky ridge to its left (Fig. 4 – 4 – 11), which looks impressive and could have inspired Kang's sketchy background cliff. Kang thus altered the topography by moving the barren rocks to the center.

Fig. 4 – 4 – 10 **Partial view of Silsang Monastery, photo by Liangren Zhang, 2004**

Kang Sehwang stayed overnight at Silsang Monastery and the next morning headed for Wŏlmyŏng Hermitage, the highest point in the area of Mt. Pyŏn (Appendix, Section 5). The trail, Kang Sehwang narrates, was as narrow as a thread so that one could barely find a foothold. After being tossed in the sedan chair for some miles, he reached the summit. From here, he saw the sea and some tiny islands. The view, however, did not deeply impress him; his narration

· 439 ·

reads like a factual statement. What thrilled him was the climb to Wŏlmyŏng Hermitage and the way to Yongch'u Pond, which he describes elaborately and animatedly. The snow on the trail was still thick enough to bury one's shin. The trip was highly precarious, because the hanging cliffs along the trail dropped to a depth of thousands of *chang*—a casual tumble would have cost his life. In spite of the danger, the monks who carried the sedan chair were running fast; sometimes the poles of the sedan chair hit the pine trees, and sometimes the monks' feet were stuck in the deep snow. On the icy, slippery trail, they came close to falling over several times. Although he repeatedly cautioned the monks, they could not slow their pace. At times, he had to descend from the sedan chair and creep along with a staff. The actual trails to the two spots are still perilously steep and slippery when the weather is wet (Fig. 4 – 4 – 12). Yet, they seem less dramatic than Kang Sehwang's description; it appears that his main concern was to create an exciting travel story.

Fig. 4 – 4 – 11 Rocks to the left side of Silsang Monastery, photo taken by Liangren Zhang, 2004

Fig. 4-4-12 Precarious trail to Yongch'u Pond, photo by Liangren Zhang, 2004

At Yongch'u Pond, Kang Sehwang encountered a "flying waterfall" between cliffs, which poured down to a depth of "dozens of *chang*," and generated "spraying snowflakes and bouncing pearls." (Appendix, Section 6). He describes the waterfall as sensational: winds and vapors clashed, and thundering sounds sent tremors over forest and valley. In the painting, the waterfall occupies the center of the painting, and the downpour strikes the pond forcefully (Fig. 4-4-4). The waterfall stirs up bubbles to the effect that we hear the thundering sound. Kang Sehwang's goal here is to convey the compelling visual, acoustic, and psychological power of the waterfall. During the early summer visit in 2004, the waterfall carried little water and therefore appeared less impressive than it would in early spring when melting snow would increase its water mass (Fig. 4-4-13). Again, the bird's eye view makes it seem even more dramatic.

After leaving Yongch'u Pond, Kang Sehwang visited Naeso Monastery, and

第四部分 东亚艺术史

Fig. 4-4-13　Yongch'u Pond, photo by Liangren Zhang, 2004

found little of notice there again (Appendix 1, Section 7). Having had lunch at the monastery, he returned to Puan City. The narration in this conclusion flows faster without the elaborate descriptions Kang presented earlier. The last painting on the scroll depicts Kŭngnak Hermitage (Fig. 4-4-5), a place that is neither mentioned in the travelogue nor marked in contemporaneous or modern tourist maps. It shows a building nestled in a deep cave. The high trees surrounding it create a serene environment, but the towering rocks are overwhelmingly precipitous. The dark, wet axe-cut strokes are freely applied, and they augment the sweeping force of the rocks. All these devices work together to create a secluded and undisturbed scene.

Artistic Ideals

Our analysis of travelogue and paintings revealed that Kang Sehwang, in his *Scenes of Puan Prefecture*, takes a somewhat subjective approach to actual scenery. His masterful prose captures all the wonderful scenes and thrilling moments. It reads like an adventure novel: episodes of unexpected sights, sounds, and precarious roads unfold one after another, leaving the reader breathless. The paintings, although imaginative in their perspective of the various sites from a distance, rather than the closeup view that Kang must have had during his journey, are sketchy, often use conventional Namjonghwa 南宗画 elements, and thus function as illustrations or visual support for the text.

It is interesting to note that Kang Sehwang was quite indifferent to local history. Several sites he visited witnessed important political events. Ugŭm Rocks, for instance, was part of a fortress of the Paekche Kingdom (18BC – AD 660). ①Silsang Monastery was built by Monk Choŭi 草衣 in 689, and renovated by Prince Hyonyŏng 孝宁, son of King Taejong 太宗 (1400 – 1418) of the Chosŏn dynasty. A historically minded literatus would have attempted to

---

① According to the information on the sign that the local administration posted at the site, a Paekche general named Poksin attempted to resist the united army of Silla (led by General Kim Yushin) and Tang (led by General Su Dingfang) but failed.

inquire about such events. Kang Sehwang, however, seems to have been preoccupied with experiencing the landscape.

The concentration on travel and the description of nature echoes a literary trend of the late Ming supported by the Gong'an School 公安派. Gong'an thinkers promoted the expression of personal genuine emotion to be the goal of literature as opposed to the orthodox archaism prevalent at the time that sought to revive the classical poetry and prose through wholesale imitation. Thus, in place of the universal truth, they stressed personal feelings; in place of refinement, they valued spontaneity and simplicity; and in place of classical formal structure and technique, they fostered an individualistic and style of writing. [1]Yuan Hongdao 袁宏道（Zhonglang 中郎, 1568 – 1610）, the leading figure of the Gong'an School, contributed most to these self-expressionist ideas and perpetuated them in his own writings. [2]Yuan was well known in Chosŏn Korea and particularly admired by the Nongyŏn group 农渊派, a circle of poets around the brothers Kim Ch'anghyŏp 金昌协（Nongam 农岩, 1651 – 1708）and Kim Ch'anghŭp 金昌翕（Samyŏn 三渊, 1653 – 1722）. They are also known as the Paegak Group 白岳派 after the area in Seoul beneath Paegak（now Pugak 北岳）Mountain where they lived. [3]These scholars belonged to the Noron 老论（Old Doctrine）faction that dominated politically at the Chosŏn court for most of the

---

[1] Ren, Fangqiu, *Yuan Zhonglang Yanjiu*, Shanghai: Shanghai Guji Press, 1983, pp. 57 – 66; Chou, Chih-p'ing, *Yüan Hung-tao and the Kung-an School*, Cambridge and New York: Cambridge University Press, 1988, pp. 35 – 52.

[2] His travelogues are masterpieces of "prose miniature," in which he appeared "as an observant tourist and as a connoisseur of elegant, aesthetic scenes." See Strassberg, Richard E., *Inscribed Landscapes: Travel Writing form Imperial China*, Berkeley: University of California Press, 1994, p. 305. Taking every scene as an autonomous image, Yuan described not only the visual and acoustic sensations of each scene, but also his personal emotional response to it. Ni, Qixin, ed., *Zhongguo Gudai Youjixuan*, Beijing: Zhongguo lüyou, 1985, p. 24.

[3] The name, Nongyŏn, is a combination of the first character of Kim Ch'anghyŏp's pen name and the second of Kim Ch'anghŭp's; see Ko Yŏnhŭi, *Chosŏn Hugi Sansu Kihaeng Yesul Yŏn'gu: Chŏng Sŏn Kwa Nongyŏn Kŭrubŭl Chungsimŭro*, Seoul: Ilchisa, 2001, pp. 66 – 68; and Ko Yŏnhŭi, Chosŏn ŭi chin'gyŏng sansuhwa wa Myŏng-Ch'ŏng-dae sansu p'anhwa, *Misulsa Nondan*, 1999, pp. 137 – 162. Paegak group is the term Ch'oe Wansu uses in his *Korean True-View Landscape Paintings by Chŏng Sŏn* (1676 – 1759), edited and translated by Youngsook Pak and Roderick Whitfield, London: Saffron Books, 2005.

eighteenth-Century. It is thought that their strong interest in Korean landscape is partly due to their opposition to recognizing the "barbarian" Manchu regime that had established the Qing Empire in China in 1644. They were also patrons of Chŏng Sŏn 郑敾 (1676 – 1759), the famous painter of true scenery, and especially favored the Diamond Mountains as a travel destination. Members of the Nongyŏn group were particularly fond of traveling and created a new genre of travel literature that fitted with the new approach to nature championed in Chŏng Sŏn's landscapes. Politically, Kang Sehwang had more in common with their opponents, the relatively powerless Namin (Southerner) faction, whose central figure was Yi Ik, Kang's close friend. A piece in his *P'yoam Yugo* fiercely condemning the tourism-like craze of traveling to the Diamond Mountains can be read as a critique of the Nongyŏn group and their followers:

"Traveling the mountains is the most cultivated thing in the world, then why is traveling the Diamond Mountains the most vulgar thing? This is not to say that the Diamond Mountains are not worth traveling. However, just because they feature mountains by the sea and immortal realms with caves and residences of spirits and divinities they claim great fame throughout the country. Whether children or womenfolk, no one has not, since shedding their milk teeth, had [the name] echo in their ears and rolled on their tongues. … This means that since ancient times these mountains were used by monks to seduce people to flock to them and recently [this tendency] has become extreme. Of those peddlers, beggars, wild women, and village hags who nowadays follow on each others' heels to the gorges in the East, who can understand what mountains are about? 游山是人间第一雅事，而游金刚为第一俗恶事，何也？非谓金刚之不足游也。而金刚独以海山仙区灵真窟宅大擅一邦之名。童儿妇女莫不自龆龀而惯于耳而腾于舌。……意者昔之此山为僧辈诳诱，人皆辐凑，殆有加于近日也。今之贩夫庸丐野婆村妪踵相蹑于东峡者，彼恶知山之为何物？"[1]

In contrast to the Nongyŏn Group, Yi Ik and other Namin scholars,

---

[1] Kang, Sehwang, Travel to the Kŭmganyang Mountains, in *P'yoam Yugo*, Songnam: Han'guk chŏngshin munhwa yŏn'guwŏn, 1979, pp. 254 – 255.

including the painter Yun Tusŏ, concentrated on new trends from Qing China and Europe. However, they took a critical approach, opposing Sinocentrism, and regarding themselves as equals. When writing about their travel experiences, they were more interested in human conditions than natural phenomena. ①Kang Sehwang's travelogue displays a different approach. He was able to free himself from factional preferences when it came to literature. His uncompromising pursuit of spontaneity and freedom at the expense of refinement and convention in the travelogue of *Scenes of Puan Prefecture* and his vivid description of his travel experiences are closer to Yuan Hongdao's and the Nongyŏn group's spirit than to that of his Namin friends. While he rejected the Nongyŏn Group's extensive travel activities—a criticism that could also have a socio-economic background, since many members of the circle were undoubtedly among the most affluent citizens of Seoul—he did not hesitate to employ a similar writing style that reflects his own passion for traveling and viewing scenery. ②

From another passage in *P'yoam Yugo*, we learn that Kang Sehwang was, in fact, aware of Yuan Hongdao's writings. However, in his own special way, appearing modest on the surface yet revealing his pride underneath, he lets a friend say that his (Kang Sehwang's) work surpasses Yuan Hongdao's travel literature. ③In the same passage, he claims that Yuan, like himself, valued common scenery over "celestial mountains," describing how simple fences and small dwellings with vegetable gardens provide a delightful leisurely experience that outshines the "myriads of white jade peaks" of the Diamond

---

① Ko, Yŏnhŭi, *Chosŏn Hugi Sansu Kihaeng Yesul Yŏn'gu*: *Chŏng Sŏn Kwa Nongyŏn Kŭrubŭl Chungsimŭro*, Seoul: Ilchisa, 2001, pp. 275–276.

② Moreover, as Marion Eggert explains, poetic, emotional responses to native scenery had been a strong element of Korean travel literature before the eighteenth-century, see Eggert, Marion, Das 'Aufsuchen von Landschaften (kugyông)': Elemente einer Poetik des vormodernen koreanischen Reiseberichts, in Xenia v. Ertzdorff-Kupffer, Gerhard Giesemann, Hg., *Erkundung und Beschreibung der Welt. Zur Poetik der Reise- und Länderberichte*, Amsterdam: Rodopi, 2003, pp. 541–556.

③ Kang, Sehwang, Seeing off Sŏkkajae Yi Ch'idae T'aegil to the Diamond Mountains, in *P'yoam Yugo*, Songnam: Han'guk chŏngsin munhwa yŏn'guwŏn, 1979, pp. 233–234.

Mountains. ①Yuan Hongdao, however, did not particularly distinguish between "celestial mountains" and "common scenery." It seems, rather, that Kang used the famous model here to emphasize his own priorities.

The Painter's Intent

Kang Sehwang produced three other important series of paintings recording his travels, *Journey to Songdo*, *Journey to China*, and *Journey to the Diamond Mountains*, all in album format. ②Like the *Scenes of Puan Prefecture* handscroll, all three albums contain paintings of actual scenery along his travel route. However, it is important to notice the difference in representational techniques between these four works.

Journey to Songdo contains his most famous work in the true scenery genre and is undoubtedly his most elaborately painted album (Fig. 4 - 4 - 14, Fig. 4 - 4 - 15) (彩图14、彩图15). It consists of sixteen paintings of scenic sites around the former Koryŏ capital Songdo 松都, present-day Kaesŏng. Although it is undated, recent research has revealed that Kang visited the area in 1757 on the invitation of governor O Such'ae 吴遂采 (1692 - 1759) and did the paintings at his request. ③In "Yŏngt'ong-dong 灵通洞" (Fig. 4 - 4 - 14), a tiny figure—probably referring to Kang Sehwang himself—moves on horseback on a narrow, steep path into the mountains, followed by a servant.

---

① Kang, Sehwang, Seeing off Sŏkkajae Yi Ch'idae T'aegil to the Diamond Mountains, in *P'yoam Yugo*, Songnam: Han'guk chŏngshin munhwa yŏn'guwŏn, 1979, pp. 233 - 234.

② The original name of the last album is *Journey to Mt. P'ungak*. As Yi Sŏngmi has explained, the Diamond Mountains were given different names according to the season. P'ungak, referring to the color of maple leaves, is their autumn name. See Yi, Sŏngmi, Artistic Tradition and the Depiction of Reality: True-view Landscape Painting of the Chosŏn Dynasty, in *Arts of Korea*, New York: The Metropolitan Museum, 1998, p. 345. For illustrations, see Byun, Young-sup, *P'yoam Kang Sehwang Hoehwa Yŏn'gu*, Seoul: Ilchisa, 1988, Figs. 54 - 1 to 54 - 10, and *P'urŭn Sorŭn Nŭkchi Annŭnda-Ch'ang Song Pul no-P'yoam Kang Sehwang*, exhibition catalogue, Seoul: Yesul ŭi chŏndang, no. 82.

③ See Kim, Kŏnni, P'yoam Kang Sehwang ŭi Songdo kihaeng ch'ŏp yŏn'gu, *Misulsahak Yŏn'gu* 238/239, 2003, p. 194. Byun Young-sup already referred to an inscription of 1757 by a close friend, Hŏ P'il, on another painting mentioning that Kang went to Kaesong in the 1750s; see Byun Byun, Young-sup, *P'yoam Kang Sehwang Hoehwa Yŏn'gu*, Seoul: Ilchisa, 1988, Figs. 46 - 1 to 46 - 18.

第四部分　东亚艺术史

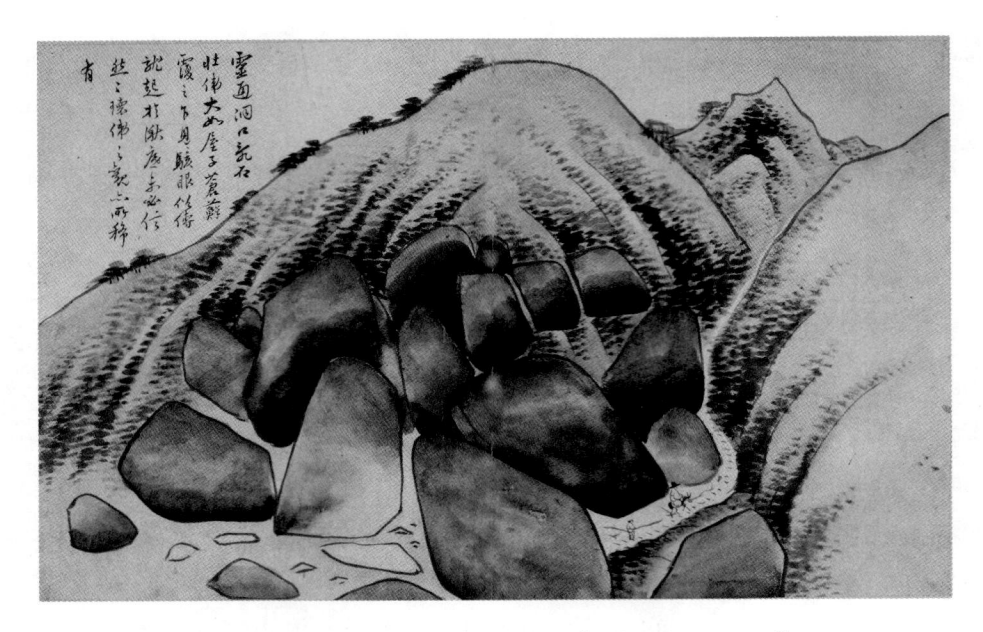

Fig. 4-4-14　Kang Sehwang, "Yŏngt'ong-dong"
(From *Journey to Songdo*, ca. 1757, ink and light color on paper, 32.8 × 53.4 cm, photo©The National Museum of Korea, Seoul)

The miniature scale of the figures emphasizes the enormous size of the rocks in the center of the painting. The rocks are carefully outlined and shaded in light and dark ink tones and hues of green that recall Western water color technique and convincingly describe the volume of the stones, their wet spots, and mossy surfaces. [1]How much Kang Sehwang departed from the traditional way of depicting stones becomes apparent when this leaf is compared to another painting from the same album, "Paeksŏk-dam 白石潭" (Fig. 4-4-15). Here, the contours of the flat stones are more conventionally drawn: the width and tonality of the strokes do little to describe the surface. It is rather an exercise in brushwork, displaying hooks at the turns and small axe-cut strokes on the narrow vertical sides. Both leaves, however, have similar backgrounds, consisting of hills covered with Mi dots—which undoubtedly derive from Chŏng

---

[1]　For a translation of the inscription, see Yi, Sŏngmi, Artistic Tradition and the Depiction of Reality: True-view Landscape Painting of the Chosŏn Dynasty, in *Arts of Korea*, New York: The Metropolitan Museum, 1998, p. 120.

Fig. 4-4-15   Kang Sehwang, "Paeksŏk-dam"
(From *Journey to Songdo*, ca. 1757, ink and light color on paper, 32.8 × 53.4 cm, photo©The National Museum of Korea, Seoul)

Sŏn's true scenery formula. "Yŏngt'ong-dong" thus stands as a highly successful experiment in combining traditional and newly introduced Western painting techniques. Other leaves of the Songdo album attest to the same sense of experimentation. The first leaf, for instance, shows the entrance to Kaesŏng in a receding perspective, "Taesŭng-dang 大乘堂—Hall of the Great Vehicle" uses different perspectives on the temple hall, while "Southern Gate-Tower of a Mountain Fortress" portrays a view over high mountains towards the far horizon, again in a Western manner. ①The whole album presents itself, not only as a visual narrative of Kang Sehwang's journey, but also as a testing ground for the technical and conceptual potential of landscape painting. Compared with the album leaves of *Journey to Songdo*, the paintings of *Scenes of Puan Prefecture* are sketchier; they were produced in a short time in a hasty

---

① For a comparison of "Southern Gate-Tower" with Ike Taiga's *True Scenery of Kojima Bay*, see Jungmann, Burglind, *Painters as Envoys: Korean Inspiration in Eighteenth-Century Japanese Nanga*, Princeton University Press, 2004, pp. 201-203.

manner. Yet, although they employ conventional brush techniques and compositional elements they are skillfully done and spark the viewer's imagination.

In 1784, Kang Sehwang was sent to Yanjing 燕京, the capital of Qing China, as an envoy. There, he visited a Christian church (most likely the South Cathedral which had already attracted the interest of earlier Chosŏn envoys), viewed Western style paintings, and met Jesuit painters. ①Although he had been exposed to Western paintings and ideas several decades earlier, as can be seen in *Journey to Songdo*, these new unmediated experiences with European visual concepts must have left a profound impression. While Kang Sehwang, in his paintings of his *Journey to China*, did not give much attention to rendering the volume of mountains, stones, and rocks, he was clearly interested in giving a comprehensive picture of the scenery. Assuming a bird's eye view, he took note of the position of buildings, figures, and landscape elements, and of their spatial relationships within the layout (Fig. 4-4-16) (彩图 16). ② This may not be as convincing to an eye used to such illusory images as his "Yŏngt'ong-dong" leaf, but it would give a person unfamiliar with the site a clear impression of its spatial structure. The album would have served the purpose of being shown around after Kang's return from China to give some information about his experiences on the road. In comparison, the paintings of *Scenes of Puan Prefecture* are again too sketchy, carefree in their brushwork, and conventional in their choice of pictorial elements to fulfill such a purpose.

---

① Kang, Sehwang, *P'yoam Yugo*, Songnam: Han'guk chŏngshin munhwa yŏn'guwŏn, 1979, p. 163. For information on earlier envoys' encounters with the Jesuits in Beijing, see Ledyard, Gari, Korean Travelers in China over Four Hundred Years, 1488-1887, in James B. Palais ed., *Occasional Papers on Korea*, Number two, The Joint Committee on Korean Studies, 1974, pp. 1-42.

② An album consisting of seven leaves that was published by Byun, Young-sup, *P'yoam Kang Sehwang Hoehwa Yŏn'gu* (Seoul: Ilchisa, 1988, Figs. 53-1 to 53-7) appears to be a copy of *Journey to Beijing*. The leaf owned by Tongdosa, published here (Fig. 16), is undoubtedly from the original album. It is accompanied by a leaf of Kang's calligraphy (see *P'urŭn sorŭn nŭkchi annŭnda-ch'ang song pul no-P'yoam Kang Sehwang*, exhibition catalogue, Seoul: Yesul ŭi chŏndang, no. 107). If compared with Figs. 53-3 and 53-6 in Byun, Young-sup, *P'yoam Kang Sehwang Hoehwa Yŏn'gu*, Seoul: Ilchisa, 1988, differences in brushwork and composition of both painting and calligraphy become apparent.

Kang Sehwang's Scenes of Puan Prefecture

Fig. 4 – 4 – 16   Kang Sehwang, "Yizhaimiao"
(Album leaf from *Journey to China*, 1784, ink on paper, 26.5 x 22.5 cm, photo ⓒSŏngbo Museum, Tongdosa)

As already mentioned, Kang Sehwang was not particularly fond of the Diamond Mountains. However, he took the opportunity to travel there in 1788 while visiting his first son, In, who held a government post close to the mountains in Hoeyang at the time. He also met Kim Hongdo 金弘道 (1745- before 1818) and Kim Ǔnghwan 金应焕 (1742 – 1789) who traveled and painted the mountains by order of King Chǒngjo 正祖, (r. 1776 – 1800).[①]

[①]   According to Kang's own record, two more sons and two friends joined the party. Kang, Sehwang, *P'yoam Yugo*, Songnam: Han'guk chǒngshin munhwa yǒn'guwǒn, 1979, pp. 254 – 262. For a partial translation, see Oh, Ju-seok, *The Art of Kim Hong-do. A Great Court Painter of 18th Century Korea*, Chicago: Art Media Resources, 2005, pp. 154 – 155.

During the journey, he was impressed by spectacular rock formations and mushroom-like peaks, but he chose to rest in a monastery for two days rather than to continue the tour. Even when his companions returned to tell him about extraordinary places, he did not regret his rest. He felt content with having spent only one or two days on sightseeing and producing only a few sketches. ①Kim Hongdo had produced more than a hundred. Sixty extant album leaves thought to be done by Kim Hongdo at the time probably come closest to Western ideas of "realistic" representation, an idea Kang advocated in his later years. ②It appears that he also sought to put his ideas into practice in this album, albeit not as carefully and elaborately as Kim Hongdo. In general, *Journey to the Diamond Mountains* shows a similar approach to his *Journey to China*, providing comprehensive overviews of each site. ③

Byun Youngsup has divided Kang Sehwang's long artistic career into three periods. Until the age of forty-four (1756), he focused on landscapes in the Namjonghwa style, which, inspired by Ming literati paintings and painting manuals, aimed to imitate masterpieces of Chinese ancient masters. From the age of forty-four to fifty (1762), he began to paint true sceneries; he attained maturity in this genre after the age of fifty. *Scenes of Puan Prefecture* thus belongs to the third period. But if we look at his earlier works such as the *Journey to Songdo* album (1757), and later works such as the *Journey to*

---

① Kang, Sehwang, *P'yoam Yugo*, Songnam: Han'guk chŏngshin munhwa yŏn'guwŏn, 1979, pp. 261 – 262.

② Oh Juseok identified sixty album leaves as works done by Kim Hongdo on this journey, see Oh, Ju-seok, *The Art of Kim Hong-do. A Great Court Painter of 18th Century Korea*, Chicago: Art Media Resources, 2005, pp. 141 – 150. For illustrations of the entire album, see *Tanwŏn Kim Hongdo, T'ansin 250 Chunyŏn Kinyŏm T'ŭkpyŏlchŏn*, exhibition catalogue, Seoul: The National Museum of Korea, 1995, pls. 1 – 60. Their authenticity is contested by Yi Sŏngmi, see Yi, Sŏngmi Artistic Tradition and the Depiction of Reality: True-view Landscape Painting of the Chosŏn Dynasty, in *Arts of Korea*, New York: The Metropolitan Museum, 1998, pp. 123 and 146 – 151.

③ Chŏng Sŏn's and Kang Hŭiŏn's different renderings of Mt. Inwang represent the shift in the conception of true scenery painting in the later half of the eighteenth-Century. Kang Sehwang's colophon on Kang Hŭiŏn's painting also conveys his new "Westernized" approach to the representation of actual sites; see Yi, Sŏngmi, Artistic Tradition and the Depiction of Reality: True-view Landscape Painting of the Chosŏn Dynasty, in *Arts of Korea*, New York: The Metropolitan Museum, 1998, pp. 115 – 117.

China (1784) and *Journey to the Diamond Mountains* albums (1788), we can see a marked public/ private distinction, as well as a process of technical refinement in Kang Sehwang's art.

Conclusion

The travelogue and five paintings of the handscroll *Scenes of Puan Prefecture* provide us with the rare opportunity to analyze the integration of literature, calligraphy, and painting in the work of a major Chosŏn artist. They also allow us to reflect on true scenery paintings done for different purposes, on different occasions, and for a different audience. Moreover, we catch a glimpse of Kang Sehwang's approach to nature, observation, and travel, and his ideas about literati painting. The travelogue is central to the whole work; it covers most of the middle two sheets of paper, while the paintings frame it on two more sheets on either side. Given the spontaneity of the writing and the carefree style of the calligraphy, it appears that Kang Sehwang wrote the text shortly after completing the journey. The continuous, accomplished narration suggests that it was done in one sitting, from memory, and without reference to any notes taken during the expedition. Similarly, the sketches appear to have been created from memory to illustrate the travelogue without referring to sketches done onsite. This is revealed by comparisons with the photographs and with other true scenery paintings which Kang painted during his travels to Kaesŏng, Beijing, and the Diamond Mountains, which show a far greater effort to convey a faithful image of the actual site.

The elaborate and lively description of his travel experiences bears some resemblance to the ideals of the travel literature of Yuan Hongdao and of the Nongyŏn group, around the brothers Kim Ch'anghyŏp and Kim Ch'anghŭp, who were political opponents of his own circle of friends. Kang thus shows an independent attitude in his choice of literary inspiration, an attitude that, in fact, further manifests itself in his preference for ordinary sites over famous attractions. While he criticized travelers to the famous Diamond Mountains, he obviously took pleasure in visiting Mt. Pyŏn, a landscape that nobody else seems to have explored. ①

The main difference between the handscroll and Kang's travel albums is the contrast between public and private art. We know that *Journey to Songdo* was produced for O Such'ae, the governor of Kaesŏng. It is not surprising that it contains the most elaborate and careful true scenery paintings Kang Sehwang ever created. The album was obviously meant to reciprocate the governor's special favor. In the cases of the *Journey to China* and *Journey to the Diamond Mountains* albums, we do not know of any patron for whom they might have been created. However, they are both drawn in a way that ensures they could easily be shown to somebody to give information on specific sites and narrate the trip. The *Scenes of Puan Prefecture* cannot serve either purpose.

We have to again take into consideration that the artist did not indicate his name anywhere in the handscroll. Only the fact that the travelogue itself is transcribed in Kang Sehwang's anthology *P'yoam Yugo* and the stylistic comparison of his calligraphy connects this handscroll with his oeuvre. Usually, Kang Sehwang did not shy away from drawing attention to his presence. He is conspicuous as the premodern Korean artist of whom the most portraits and self-portraits are extant. ②Moreover, he not only signed his major works but obviously also enjoyed commenting on them, and the phrases of modesty he often added at the end of his colophons are meant to show how much his work

---

① In addition to the Diamond Mountains, a great number of other places were favored in true scenery paintings and travel literature, such as the Eight Scenic Spots of Kwandong. Again, Chŏng Sŏn's are most representative; see Ch'oe, Wansu, *Korean True-View Landscape Paintings by Chŏng Sŏn (1676 - 1759)*, edited and translated by Youngsook Pak and Roderick Whitfield, London: Saffron Books, 2005. In contrast, Kang Sehwang's paintings of Mt. Pyŏn are the only known representations of this landscape to date.

② According to Yi T'aeho, ten portraits of him are extant, of which four are self-portraits. See "Chosŏn hugi ch'osanghwa ŭi chejak kongjŏng kwa kŭ piyong," in *P'urŭn Sorŭn Nŭkchi Annŭnda-Ch'ang Song Pul no-P'yoam Kang Sehwang*, exhibition catalogue, Seoul: Yesul ŭi chŏndang, 2003, p. 403 and pls. 1 - 7, and Byun, Young-sup, *P'yoam Kang Sehwang Hoehwa Yŏn'gu*, Seoul: Ilchisa Byun, 1988, pp. 30 - 36 and Figs. 1 - 4, 6 - 9.

was appreciated. ①In order to understand why this self-confident artist chose to hide his authorship in the case of *Journey to Mt Pyŏn* we will have to reconsider the date when it was created. Kang was fifty-eight years old in 1770 when he painted *Scenes of Puan Prefecture*. This date falls within a period when Kang Sehwang is said to have given up painting because King Yŏngjo 英祖（r. 1724 – 1776）had warned him not to risk his reputation as a scholar by becoming a famous painter. According to Kang's own account, the event occurred on the occasion of his second son, Wan's success in the national exams in 1763. Kang allegedly cried until his eyes were swollen, broke and burnt his brushes, and did not start painting again until the King died in 1776. ②The hiatus lasted almost twenty years until the King's death. Yet, Kang Sehwang does not appear to have abandoned his cherished art entirely. ③While it is likely that he continued to produce paintings during this period, he may not have shown them as publicly as he did before and after. This also explains the free, easy-going manner that characterizes both his calligraphy and paintings: he made *Scenes of Puan Prefecture* for his private memory and entertainment. The confidential nature of the work accounts for the somewhat eccentric characteristics of the handscroll, i.e. the casualness in producing the five paintings and the spontaneity in writing the travelogue. On the other hand, the uncompromising pursuit of freedom in calligraphy, literature, and painting

---

① For instance, in his colophon on his landscape after Dong Qichang he says, "… the paper was thick and hard, so that I could not reach his (Dong Qichang's) wonderful ink technique, how could [this painting] satisfy a close view? In the next days, I would have found better paper and copied it again, but Suji (Yi Pogwŏn, 1719 – 1792) took this scroll to store it." A similar attitude shines through the last phrase of Kang's inscription on Kim Hongdo's screen of the *Elegant Gathering in the Western Garden*: "I feel ashamed of my scattered and coarse brushwork, which has nothing to be compared with Yuanzhang's (Mi Fu's) and only spoils the beautiful painting [by Kim Hongdo]. How can I escape from the blame of those looking at this work?" For illustrations, see Byun, Young-sup, *P'yoam Kang Sehwang Hoehwa Yŏn'gu*, Seoul: Ilchisa, 1988, Figs. 19 and 120.

② When Wan passed the civil exam in 1763, someone mentioned that Kang Sehwang was famous for his painting and literature, see Kang, Sehwang, *P'yoam Yugo*, Songnam: Han'guk chŏngshin munhwa yŏn'guwŏn, 1979, pp. 494 – 495.

③ Byun Young-sup assigns several other works to this period; see Byun, Young-sup, *P'yoam Kang Sehwang Hoehwa Yŏn'gu*, Seoul: Ilchisa, 1988, p. 218, Table 3.

reveals how much Kang Sehwang espoused literati ideals, making *Journey to Mt Pyŏn* a truly exceptional work of art.

Appendix

Translation of the Travelogue

游禹金巃记

Record of a Journey to Ugŭm Rocks

Section 1

出扶安县西门向西南行十余里，野田茫茫。左见遥山隐见天际，为古阜井邑等地；右有连峰延绵盘互，气势雄秀，即边山也。

Leaving Puan county [seat] through the West Gate and heading southwest, I traveled for over ten miles, [entering] boundless fields. I saw, on my left, distant mountain silhouettes on the horizon, where Kobu and Chŏngŭp Counties are located; on my right, there was a row of mountain ridges spreading and intertwining, [creating] a powerful and splendid view. These were the Pyŏn Mountains.

Section 2

山之东麓有东林书院。又行数里，野中平阜有松数百株；松下有柳川书院。又行十余里，右入边山之口。折以行数里，台殿翼然于乱松间，乃开巃寺也。入寺仰见寺后万丈高峰插入云际。峰头有三石，高皆百余丈。乘肩舆上石，底有窟大如百间屋，深可数十丈；壁纹纵横，如纹锦焉。是为禹陈或云金窟。窟前有小兰若眉扁玉泉庵三字。

At the eastern foot of the mountains, there stood Tongnim Academy. Traveling several miles further, I found on flat knolls in the fields hundreds of pine trees; beneath the pines, there was Yuch'ŏn Academy. Some ten miles further ahead, on the right, I entered the pass into the Pyŏn Mountains. Turning [into the mountains] and traveling for several miles, [I found] terraces with halls [aligned symmetrically] like wings amidst disheveled pine trees. This was Kaeam Monastery. Upon entering the monastery, I looked up and saw a ten-thousand-*chang* high peak behind it piercing into the clouds. On the summit, there were three rocks, each [again] over one hundred *chang* high. Riding a sedan chair, I ascended [the peak] towards the rocks, and at their base, found a cave as large as a room of one hundred *kan* and probably dozens of *chang* deep; the rock face had vertical and horizontal veins like patterned brocade. This was Ujin (also called Ugŭm) Cave. In front of the cave, there was a small Buddhist hall with a plaque on the lintel [inscribed with] the three characters of Okch'ŏn (Jade Spring Hermitage).

Section 3

仍绕窟右，逾岭数里始得平路。左右奇峰，应接不暇；清流层壁，非复人境。时值仲春，尚余残雪，陆离相映于深林幽涧中。以肩舆行二十余里，到实相寺。

Veering then to the right of the cave, I crossed mountain ridges for several miles before reaching a flat trail. To the left and right of the road, fantastic mountain peaks kept capturing my eyes leaving no leisure; [together with] clear streams and layered walls, it was no longer a mundane world. It was [already] mid-spring, yet some snow remained shimmering here and there amidst deep forest and hidden creeks. After traveling by sedan chair for over twenty miles, I arrived at Silsang Monastery.

Section 4

寺甚宏壮，今多颓圮。寺僧出示古物；有乌铜香炉，乌铜龟鹤，乌铜杨枝瓶。制作亦皆奇雅精巧。龟鹤，僧辈不知为何物。余曰："此乃含线香于鹤口以爇之，亦香炉类也。"僧辈相顾不信，为之一笑。仍留宿，朝起周览。

The monastery, [once] of rather splendid scale, was now largely dilapidated. The monks brought out some antiques to show to me: a black bronze incense-burner, a black bronze turtle and crane, and a bronze vase [decorated] with willow branches. The artisanship of all this was elegant and exquisite. As for the turtle-crane, the group of monks did not know what object it was. I said: "This is used for holding stick incense in the mouth of the crane and burning it, also a kind of incense-burner." The group of monks glanced at each other in disbelief, to which I responded with a smile. Still, I stayed overnight and on the next morning started to explore the surroundings.

Section 5

闻月明庵之胜，促肩舆循寺后上峻峰。峰势壁立，石路如线，不可着足。登顿五里余，至绝顶。南望海口，风帆来往。有一点小岛，云是兴德地。北折而循山腰行。余雪尚积，深可没胫侧。径危甚，下临千丈悬崖；若一磋跌，性命难保。舆僧大呼疾走；舆竿或触于松树，僧足或陷于深雪。冰滑石峭，倾侧欲颠者数。屡戒舆僧而不能缓步。或下舆而步，逢泥深雪厚，艰难万状。

Having heard of the scenic beauty of Wŏlmyŏng Hermitage, I urged the sedan chair [carriers] to follow the path behind the monastery ascending the precipitous peak. The peak stands upright like a wall, and the rocky path resembles a thread hardly allowing any foothold. After climbing and pausing [for breath] for over five miles, I reached the highest point. [From there] to the south, I saw the seaport in the distance with sailboats coming and going. There was an island as tiny as a dot, said to be the land of Hŭngdŏk county. I turned northward and went along the waist of the mountain. The remaining snow was still deep enough to bury one's shin. The slanting footpath was very precarious facing an overhanging cliff that dropped a thousand *chang* deep. A casual stumble would have cost our lives. The sedan chair-carrying monks shouted out loud and walked swiftly; sometimes the pole of the sedan hit the pine trees, and sometimes the monks' feet sank deep into the snow. The icy path was slippery and rocks were steep, and we lost balance and almost fell over several times. I frequently warned the sedan chair-carrying monks but they could not slow down. From time to time, I descended from the sedan chair and walked, and when there was deep mud and thick snow, it was extremely difficult [to move forward].

Section 6

到月明庵，地势最高，俯视全山如浪叠云屯；山外海色微茫。时值云阴，不能历历指点。即循故路而还。至实相寺之右，转向龙湫。石路之危，比月明庵路尤甚。不可以舆，扶杖匍匐。逾数岭，飞瀑泻于两崖间，高几数十丈。喷雪跳珠，势极奇壮；风气相逐，声震林壑。循瀑而上登。登不已，又上山顶，俯视海门。

Arriving at Wŏlmyŏngŏng Hermitage, the highest topographical point, I looked down upon the whole mountain range, which resembled undulating waves and gathering clouds; beyond the mountains, the color of the sea was vaguely visible. It was cloudy at the time so I could not clearly point out every spot. I returned, following the previous route, and to the right of Silsang Monastery took a turn towards Yongch'u, the Dragon Pond. The rocky path was even more dangerous than that to Wŏlmyŏng Hermitage. It was impossible to ride the sedan chair, and I crept along leaning on a staff. I crossed several mountain ridges and [came to] a flying waterfall that poured down between two cliffs several dozens of *chang* high. The force of [its water creating] spraying snow and bouncing pearls was absolutely miraculous. Wind and vapor clashed, and the thundering sound sent tremors through woods and ravines. I climbed upwards alongside the waterfall. Climbing without stop, I reached the summit again and overlooked the gate to the sea.

Section 7

折而东下，又折而北，自月明庵行二十里，到来苏寺。寺后峰即实相寺案山之外也。寺经回禄而重建。虽逊壮丽，颇极整新，皆未及加丹雘。仍炊午饭。始舍舆策马，出山口向北而行。复寻开巘洞口昨行之路，日才入还归。

Descending eastward and then turning north, I traveled from Wŏlmyŏng Hermitage for twenty miles and reached Naeso Monastery. The peak behind the monastery is actually the outer side of the mountain facing Silsang Monastery. The monastery was destroyed by fire but had been rebuilt. Although it was not as magnificent [as before], it was quite neat and new, [though] all of it still needs to be painted. Yet, I had lunch cooked there. Starting out [on the home journey], I abandoned the sedan chair and spurred a horse, exited the mountains, and headed north. Following the path to the entrance of Kaeam Cave that we had traveled yesterday, I returned home just at the time of sunset.

第五部分
欧亚考古见闻

俄罗斯考古见闻[*]

学考古的好处之一就是可以开眼界。乌拉尔山脉以东的阿卡依木（Arkaim）就是一处让人兴奋的青铜时代城堡。遗址发现于1987年，此后经过大规模的发掘，揭露了一半。城堡保存完好，大体呈圆形，由内而外为方形广场、内城圈和外城圈（图5-1-1）。结构有点像我国福建客家人的承启楼，只是规模要大一些。外城墙的直径为150米，基础宽4—5米；内城墙直径85米，基础宽3—4米。据推测，城墙的高度不低于3.5米。两圈城墙内房屋呈放射状分布，背靠

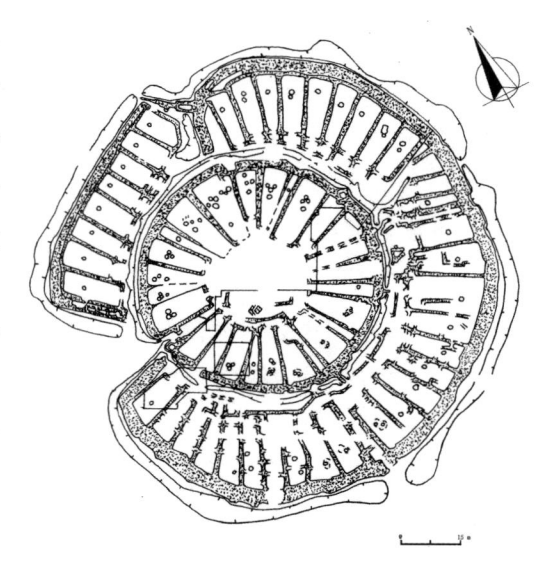

图5-1-1 阿卡依木城堡平面图

（Maliutina, T. S., G. B. Zdanovich, Keramika Arkaima: Opyt tipologii, *Rossiĭskaia Arkheologiia* 4, 2004, Fig. 1）

城墙，前临环形街道。两城内部的房屋总共40座，规模都在100—140平方米上下。里面有小院和建筑，小院中还有水井和火炉。它们不仅可以汲水取暖，还可以冶炼金属（图5-1-2）。可见青铜器生产曾经是古代居民的一项主要的经济活动。城堡内普遍出土的木炭、矿石、铜渣便是充分的证明。中心广场经过平整，夯实，并可能铺有一层石灰面，可以聚会和举行仪式。外城圈之外还有壕沟。通道可知有四个，已发掘的一个位于西北方向，发现有复杂的垛墙和城门设施。城墙与壕沟在此

---

[*] 本文原刊于《中国文化遗产》2005年第10期，第88—93页。收入本书时略有改动。

◆❖◇ 第五部分 欧亚考古见闻

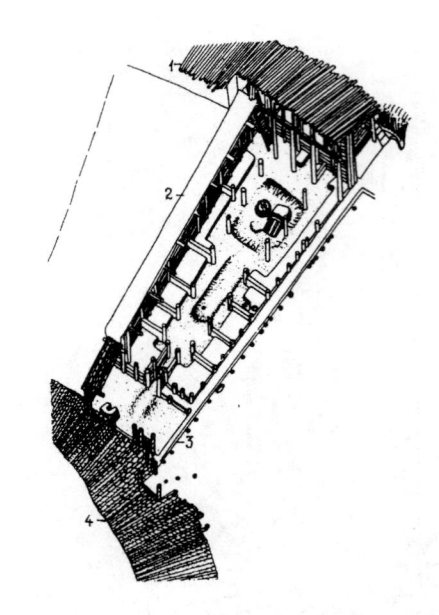

图 5-1-2 阿卡依木城堡的外城圈房屋及城墙复原图

（Zdanovich, G. B., Arkaim: arii na Urale ili nesostoiavshaiasia tsivilizatsiia, in G. B. Zdanovich ed., *Arkaim: Postranitsam drevnei istorii Iuzhnogo Urala: Issledovaniia, Poiski, Otkrytiia*, Cheliabinsk: Kamennyi Poias, 1996, p. 28）

猛拐进入城内达7—8米。不过这是一个假门，不熟悉这些防御设施的敌人将会陷入三面的围攻。真正的城门位于南侧，也是三面围攻的结构。两个入口均为狭窄的廊道，便于防守。[1] 如此严密的防御设施，在广袤的欧亚大草原上并不多见。

像这样的城堡在乌拉尔以东地区不只阿卡依木一处。类似的遗址总共发现有21处，相互之间距离在40—70千米上下，因此有"城堡之国"之称（图5-1-3）。因为是草原地区，在飞机上可以清楚地看到这些城堡的轮廓。事实上，它们就是借助于航片发现的。不过它们的形状不光是圆形，还有正方形、椭圆形。其中的辛塔什塔城堡发现于70年代，位于阿卡依木以西50千米，只是遗址已被经过的河流冲刷去一半。年代与阿卡依木相同，为公元前18—前16世纪。布局与阿卡依木相同，也是中心广场加两个圆形城圈。城圈内的房屋中也普遍发现有冶炼遗迹。更为引人注目的是，城堡以北发现有同时期的两片土坑墓地以及三个圆形冢墓。其中最大的一座高为4.5米，底部直径为72米，周围环绕一道围墙和壕沟。中央为四根大圆木（桦木）圈起的椁室，长4米，宽3.8米。可惜墓葬已经被盗掘一空。不过周围保存有一些人骨、牛头骨片和碎陶器。椁室上面以圆木覆盖，其上再以土坯堆砌而成穹隆顶。椁室周围分布有放射状的圆木建筑。整个布局很像城堡。

---

[1] Zdanovich, G. B., Arkaim: arii na Urale ili nesostoiavshaiasia tsivilizatsiia, in G. B. Zdanovich ed., *Arkaim: Postranitsam drevnei istorii Iuzhnogo Urala: Issledovaniia, Poiski, Otkrytiia*, Cheliabinsk: Kamennyi Poias, 1996, pp. 21–42.

辛塔什塔墓葬出土有相当丰富的青铜工具、武器和装饰品（图5-1-4），说明古代居民因为经营青铜冶炼积累了不同寻常的财富。设施严密的城堡，可能就是为了防备觊觎财富的外敌。墓室中经常还随葬完整的马匹、双轮马车、马镰。墓地SM的12号墓里，就发现了四匹马的骨架。在墓室的东南角还有山羊的腿骨和头骨。在棺室西部两侧发现两个埋放车轮的小坑，一个保存两根车辐的痕迹，另一个四根，车轮间距为120厘米。人骨已经腐朽，但不同于其他墓葬的是，人骨架都放在车厢里，周围发现有马骨架，两个骨制的马嚼，六个石制和骨制的箭头。据推测，该马车的轮径为90厘米，轮宽4厘米，车厢最长为105厘米，最宽为90—100厘米，高度为90厘米。车辕长度160—180厘米，靠在东西向中轴线上但略微偏移的两根木柱上。辛塔什塔墓葬出土的马车比最早的西亚马车（公元前4000年）要晚，但比我国安阳的商代马车要早。看来马车在中国的出现与欧亚大草原恐怕不无关系。

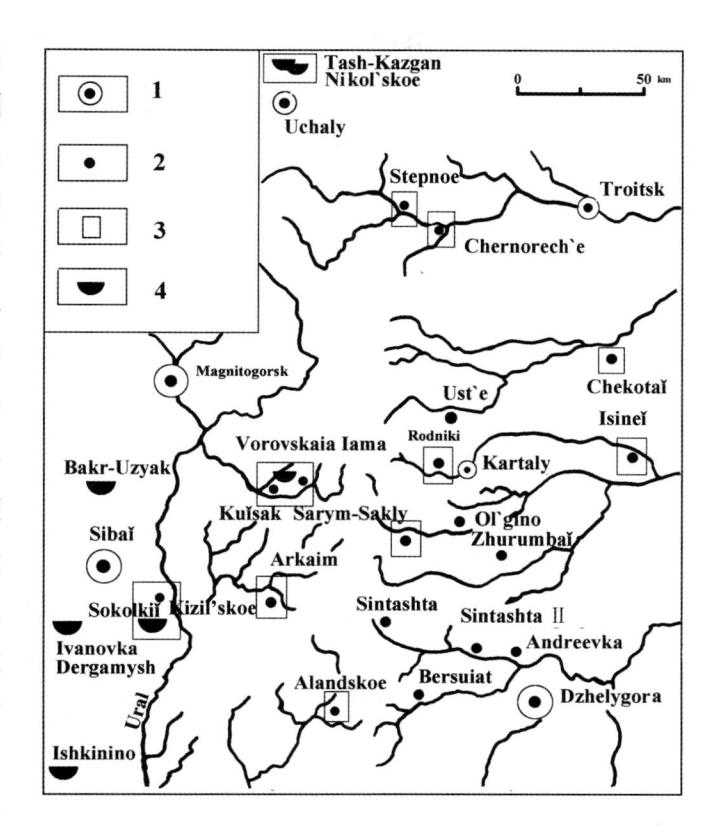

图5-1-3 城堡之国，公元前18—前16世纪

（Zaykov, V. V., A. M. Yuminov, A. P. Bushmakin, E. V. Zaykova, A. D. Tairov, G. B. Zdanovich, Ancient copper mines and products from base and noble metals in the Southern Urals, in Karlene Jones-Bley and D. G. Zdanovich eds., *Complex Societies of Central Eurasia from the 3rd to the 1st Millennium BC*, Washington D. C.: Institute for the Study of Man, 2002, p. 418）

阿卡依木—辛塔什塔遗址的发现正是印欧语系发源地研究升温的时

第五部分 欧亚考古见闻

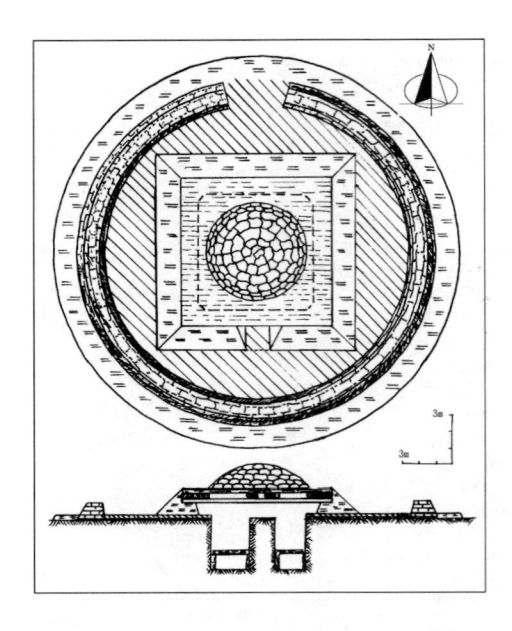

图 5-1-4 辛塔什塔城堡附近的大型土冢复原图

(Gening, V. F., G. B. Zdanovich, and V. V. Gening, *Sintashta—Arkheologicheskie Pamiatniki Ariĭskikh Plemen Uralo-Kazakhstanskikh Stepe*? Cheliabinsk: South-Ural Book Publisher, 1992, p. 275)

候。阿卡依木城堡内的水井底部发现有马和牛的趾骨、肩胛骨和下颚骨。斯达诺维奇认为这些牺牲反映了印欧语系广泛流传的火神生于水的神话。库兹米娜明确指出代表印度—雅利安语支的文献《阿维斯陀》与《梨俱吠陀》中的许多细节在两个遗址中都得到了验证：手制陶器、马的崇拜、马车。而且两座城堡的同心圆结构和辐辏式的房屋布局都反映了《阿维斯陀》记载的始祖依玛王在雅利安的发源地所建造的城堡的形象。美国学者琼斯—布雷（Karlene Jones-Bley）注意到这两个遗址的其他特征：单个人葬、冢墓、祭庙一类的建筑，墓葬随葬品和建筑规格所反映的阶级分化，中央为男性墓周围为妇幼墓的格局，人殉与动物殉，屈肢葬也都与两部文献所反映的社会状况相吻合。雅利安人在这里兴起之后就带着他们的安德罗诺沃文化向东扩散到西伯利亚、阿尔泰地区，向南经哈萨克斯坦扩散到印度（图 5-1-5 和图 5-1-6）。

印欧语系的起源是一个学术之谜。问题最早是由 19 世纪两位出访印度的英国学者派森（James Parson）和琼斯（Sir William Jones）爵士提出的。他们发现在亚洲的伊朗语、梵语与欧洲的希腊语之间存在许多相似的地方，因此设想它们发源于同一个语言，即原始印欧语。此后希腊的线性文字 B、赫梯文书、安那托利亚的卢文象形文字和中国的吐火罗文书的发现为这一假说增添了许多新的材料。线性文字 B 可以确定在公元前 1300 年，而最早的赫梯文书可以确定在公元前 2200—前 1800 年。根据斯瓦德什（Morris Swadesh）发明的衰变率（一种语言的 100

个核心词汇在 1000 年后保存 86%，这样到 8% 的时候就是 11700 年前了），俄罗斯语言学家干姆克雷利泽（Thomas Gamkrelidze）和依万诺夫（Vyacheslav Ivanov），英国语言学家马罗里（James P. Mallory）将原始印欧语的年代推算到公元前 4000 年。

关于原始印欧语，学术界有很多争议。有些学者根本不承认原始印欧语系的存在：所谓的印欧语系各语言之间的相似无非是文化交流的产物。更多的争议发生在相信它存在的学者们中间。关于原始印欧语的分化过程，就有三种假说：第一，树状分支式，它假设两个近似的语言来源于同一个祖先，近似特征越少，两种语言的亲缘关系就越疏远，分化的时间就越早；第二，波状流动式，它假设原始印欧语像波浪一样一步一步地向前推进；第三，

图 5-1-5　辛塔什塔墓地出土的铜器（部分）

［Gening, V. F., G. B. Zdanovich, and V. V. Gening, *Sintashta—Arkheologicheskie Pamiatniki Ariĭskikh Plemen Uralo-Kazakhstanskikh Stepe*?（in Russian）, Cheliabinsk: South-Ural Book Publisher, 1992, p.195］

干姆克雷利泽和依万诺夫结合了前两种模式，提出原始印欧语经过了若干次分化的假说。最早是安那托利亚语支的分离，然后是吐火罗与意大利—哥特语支的分化，再后就是雅利安—希腊—亚美尼亚，波罗的海—斯拉夫—日耳曼，意大利—哥特，吐火罗与安那托利亚的分化。学者们大多通过原始印欧语词汇来复原原始印欧人的生态环境（地理、动物、植物）和文化成就（埋葬习俗、宗教、冶金技术、骑马、双轮或四轮车）。干姆克雷利泽和依万诺夫采用的就是这种方法。但是英国考古学

家伦福儒（Colin Renfrew）持反对意见。他认为，一、有关技术的词汇，如"轮""车"，很容易传播。二、语言学的证据不可以字面解释，否则原始印欧语就只知道黄油而不知奶，只知道雪和脚而不知雨和手。三、以现存语言来复原历史上的某种早期语言是困难的。比方说，所有的拉丁支的语言中都有"神甫"一词。伦福儒问道：是不是所有的拉丁人都是基督徒呢？

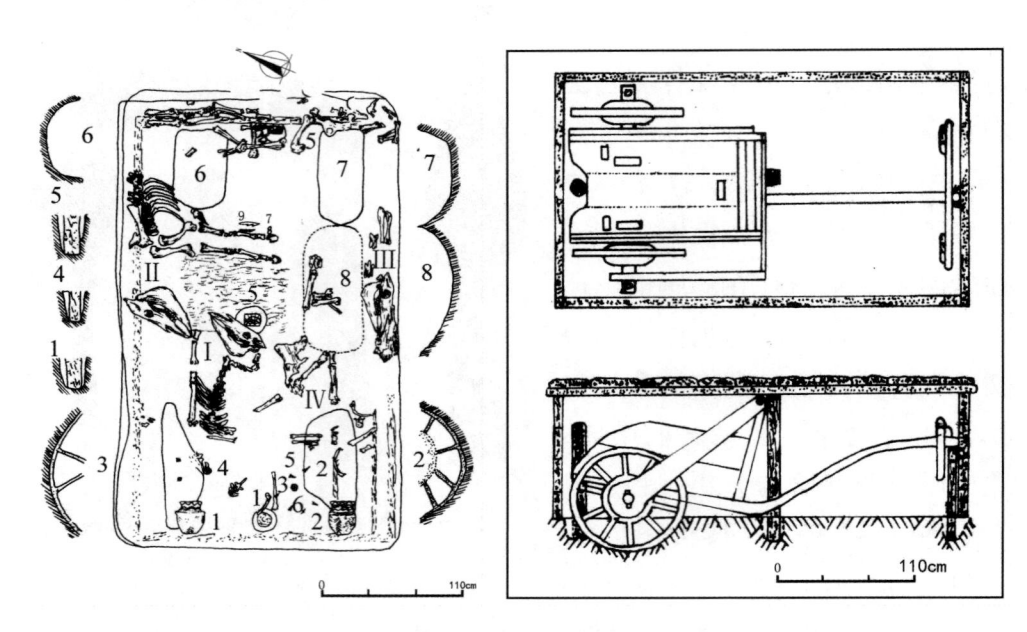

图 5-1-6　辛塔什塔墓地 SM12 号墓出土的四匹马和马车复原图

[Gening, V. F., G. B. Zdanovich, and V. V. Gening, *Sintashta—Arkheologicheskie Pamiatniki Ariĭskikh Plemen Uralo-Kazakhstanskikh Stepeĭ* (in Russian), Cheliabinsk: South-Ural Book Publisher, 1992, pp. 162, 166]

　　由于语言学本身还不能解决原始印欧语的老家问题，考古学家开始介入。最早的假说是德国学者柯斯纳（Gustaf Kossinna）的德国北部绳纹陶器文化说，然后是英国考古学家柴尔德（Gordon V. Childe）的俄罗斯南部说。因为两种假说在 20 世纪 30 年代都不幸地成了政治宣传的工具，所以考古学家在以后的几十年里都避讳印欧语系的起源问题。只是到了 20 世纪 70 年代，美国学者金布塔斯（Marija Gimbutas）旧题重温，接受了柴尔德的假说，并指认环黑海地区的铜石并用和青铜时代的冢墓文化为原始印欧人的文化。需要说明的是，这些考古学家都抱有这样的假设，即原始印欧语人带着他们的文化扩散到现在的欧亚语系分布地域。柯斯纳提出绳纹陶器文化说就是因为该文化广泛分布于中欧与北欧。而金布塔斯认为冢墓文化的许多因素从南俄罗斯传播到欧洲和欧亚大陆。这种假说为很多考古学家采用，因为它描述的吐火罗、伊朗语和印度—雅利安语支的扩散过程更为可信。库兹米娜进一步提出俄罗斯境内东欧的土坑墓文化是印度—雅利安的始祖。该文化向东传播，形成安德罗诺沃文化，即伊朗与雅利安人的共同祖先。雅利安人发明了骑马术和战车，所以能够横扫中亚，侵入印度。该理论确有很强的说服力，因为安德罗诺沃文化的畜牧经济与生态环境，同《阿维斯陀》与《梨俱吠陀》的记载很相符合。问题是上述文化因素在印度都没有出现，尤其是马和车，所以它还不能自圆其说。

　　实际上，以考古学方法探索原始印欧语的起源也存在不少困难。一方面，一种物质文化不一定代表一个特定的语言群体，因为文化交流也可以解释文化因素的扩散。另一方面，我们看不到绳纹陶器文化和冢墓文化在欧洲与西伯利亚的广泛分布，更不要提伊朗与印度地区。而且，语言人群的迁徙不一定会导致目的地文化的变化。迄今为止，还没有人说原始印欧人迁徙到的地方是无人区。因此研究者还要考虑外来文化如何与本地文化相处的问题。

　　笔者是2003年春季第一次听说阿卡依木遗址的，所以这次来俄的目标之一就是要看看这个遗址。凑巧八月份那儿举行学术会议，去的愿望就更强烈了。辛塔什塔和阿卡依木遗址的发现在学术界颇为轰动，近几年来发掘者频频举行学术会议，广邀欧美学者，知名度提升得很快。不过今年的会议没有邀请国外的人来，只限于俄罗斯本国，但从莫斯科、圣彼得堡、新西伯利亚、鄂木斯克、阿尔泰来了不少有分量的人物。我们先在车寥宾斯克国立大学（Cheliabinsk State University）集中，然后乘会议包租的汽车前往阿卡依木。行程近400千米，在笔者的地理概念里是相当远了。可是俄罗斯人颇不以为然，在西伯利亚出门都是几百千米，这400千米根本不算什么。沿途经过横亘欧亚大陆的森林—草原和草原两条地带，地形平缓起伏，状如微风拂动的水面。所谓的乌拉尔山，不过是略微隆起的山包而已。

　　我们到达的第二天，会议的组织者斯达诺维奇（G. Zdanovich，辛塔什塔和阿卡依木的主要发掘者之一）就带我们去参观阿卡依木遗址。

◇❖◇ 第五部分　欧亚考古见闻

图 5-1-7　冶金技术的模拟表演，当时下了一场雨，观众都淋湿了，但兴致仍旧盎然（张良仁摄）

遗址表面为草地，与周围没有什么差别。只有标牌上的遗址平面图和房屋、城墙的复原模型提醒我们脚下面就是遗址。斯达诺维奇说阿卡依木的发掘是因为当时正在建一个水库，将在遗址上建立水坝。工程眼看就要完成，只剩下水坝了。但是遗址挖开以后，学者们都觉得特别重要，所以就四处呼吁，要求保护。整个过程颇为艰难，但最后原定的坝址还是挪了位置。看完遗址后，开始会议发言。会议的主题是"人类与古代文化传播"，下面列了许多专题，如神话、宗教仪式、密室、埋葬习俗、古代艺术、考古学方法和材料。民族学、神话学、天文学及考古学的结合，反映出俄罗斯学者宽阔的视野和深厚的功底。发言顺序虽然按资历排列，但是每次发言之后，大家都可以自由提问，没有资历之分。需要指出的是，本次会议不仅有研究生，还有一个本科生的发言，讲的是他搞的实验考古。在俄罗斯学术会议很多，不仅有教授级的，还有专门的研究生和高年级本科生的学术会议。俄罗斯学术之所以发达，部分得益于他们注重不同层次的均衡发展。

会议期间饱眼福的机会很多。来自克美罗瓦国立大学（Kemerovo State University）的人在会场布置了一个岩画拓片的展览。其中有很多表现帐篷生活、狩猎场面和野兽，题材出人意料的丰富多彩。该校的考古系在岩画上很有优势，收藏有大量的来自阿尔泰、哈萨克斯坦山区的岩画。令人叫绝的是，有些岩画本身就出土在墓葬中，所以可以断代。阿卡依木遗址附近还发现了一些斯基泰时期的冢墓，以大原木搭建而成，然后用土覆盖。还有一座形状特别的胡须墓。之所以如此称谓，是因为墓葬的两侧各延伸出一条石头堆砌的矮墙，像人的胡须。哈萨克斯坦和我国的新疆都有很多这样的墓葬，但它出现在乌拉尔山以东是笔者没有想到的。搞古代冶金的卢萨诺夫（I. A. Rusanov）还展示了他们复原的青铜时代冶炼技术。他先在地面上挖一个直径约50厘米，深50厘米的小坑，然后把铜矿石砸成小碎块，放入陶碗中。他把陶碗放入小坑内，上面放木炭和木柴，再用泥封住坑口，只留一个小口。一侧皮囊不停地向坑里鼓风，同时他把准备好的动物脂肪和烧好粉碎的动物骨骼放入坑内，以提高温度（图5-1-7）。整个过程看起来很简单。他说大约12个小时以后就可以得到铜块。

图5-1-8 斯基泰冢墓模型（张良仁摄）

阿卡依木遗址本身实际上已经成立了一个研究中心和一个旅游中心。苏联解体以后，为了增加收入，俄罗斯的考古机构都想办法搞旅游项目。阿卡依木城堡形状独特，再加上旅游中心的着意宣传（他们专门制作了一个电视片），吸引了不少人来此度假。他们还特别搞了几个小型博物馆，复原了两个斯基泰时期的冢墓（图5-1-8）。游客大多自己开车来，只需付不多的钱，就可以使用旅游中心的地方，或租用简易房或搭建帐篷。对大多数人而言，主要目的是休息，考古一类的东西是顺带看看的。不过旅游中心禁止销售白酒（伏特加），对嗜酒的俄罗斯人来说无疑是一项残酷的政策，他们这样做是为了防止游客酗酒生事。来自旅游的创收，则用于考古发掘和学术会议上。本次会议所需的经费，就有一部分来自旅游收入。与会者只需交微薄的资料费（论文提要），而中心负责四天的食宿费用。1991年苏联解体以后的几年中，俄罗斯经济崩溃，科研经费极度匮乏，但学术机构还是想办法支撑了下来。

　　坐在返回新西伯利亚的火车里，窗外的桦木林时而合拢，时而豁然大开，像魔术师一样不停地撩拨着我们的好奇心。让人不禁遐想：这个地广人稀的地方，还隐藏着多少像辛塔什塔和阿卡依木这样的秘密呢？

　　［鸣谢：2003年我赴新西伯利亚做学术访问，期间参观了阿卡依木研究中心。此次旅行得到了加州大学洛杉矶分校（UCLA）的中国研究中心（Center of Chinese Studies）、艺术史系友会（Friends of Art History）的资助］

在中哈萨克斯坦考古[*]

大地像微风拂过的海面，时不时地涌起一波一波的峰峦，然后又舒缓地平铺开来。落日越过峰峦洒下一片片金色。人烟很少，除了几座冶金小城外，沿途看不到什么村庄。在这广袤而沉寂的草原上，我们的汽车就像在亘古的时空隧道中蠕动着。

同行的是一位来自意大利巴罗那大学（Bologna University）的教授莫利兹奥（Maurizio Cattani）和他的学生盖伯利尔（Gabriel Gattucci）。这位教授以前在土库曼斯坦工作。他们大学的几位考古学家在那里已经发掘多年。青铜时代那里是绿洲农业文明繁盛的地方，他们的一项很有意思的发现就是在一座城市的周围发现了安德罗文化（Andronovo culture）的小型居址。安德罗文化是广泛分布于西伯利亚大草原的一支经营畜牧经济的文化。它在中亚地区的出现显然反映了畜牧文化与农业文明的接触，学术前景不可限量。可惜几年前土库曼斯坦的外交政策突然改变，使他们无法继续在这里的合作项目。莫利兹奥对游牧业的起源有兴趣，所以他就转到哈萨克斯坦开展工作。

我们要去的地方是一个青铜时代的冶金遗址，名为塔迪萨依（Taldysai）。遗址近旁就是同名的村子。苏联时代为了把原本游牧的哈萨克人定居下来，建立了许多这样的村子。盖房子，建图书馆，搭蒸汽浴澡堂，拉电线，生活条件还是蛮不错的。我们三个"外宾"住在一家条件较好的人家里。我们共用一个大房间，打地铺，支起三只桌子，开始了我们在哈萨克斯坦的田野生活。

房东是一位五十多岁的妇女，上过大学，还去过当时的东德。苏联时代，大学教育普及率相当高，所以在这样一个小村庄见到一个中年的大学生并不稀奇。她的性格非常爽朗，总喜欢跟我们聊天，开玩笑，打

---

[*] 本文原刊于《中国文化遗产》2005 年第 3 期，第 90—97 页。收入本书时略有改动。

◇❖◇　第五部分　欧亚考古见闻

听各国的风俗习惯。尽管我们三人的俄语都不流利，但是她往往能够激发我们谈话的兴致。同这样的人在一起，生活中总是充满阳光的。

图5-2-1　塔迪萨依遗址全景（张良仁摄）

　　塔迪萨依遗址坐落在一条小河的河岸上（图5-2-1）。中哈萨克斯坦没有高山，河水的来源全仰赖于降雪。所以河流少而且小，只有春天雪融的时候会发生洪水。在古代，铜矿采掘以后，有水源的地方就近冶炼，没有水源的地方则要送往有水源的地方。遗址保存完好，自青铜时代废弃以后就一直掩藏在草地下面。如果不是12年前的一次洪水冲开一个口子，那么今天它还不会被人发现。哈萨克斯坦的考古学家还不知道中国的洛阳铲，所以他们在平坦的草原上寻找居住遗址并不容易。不过他们也不是毫无头绪。这里的居址和墓地往往挨得很近。墓葬因为暴露的石板或者隆起的坟堆很容易发现，所以他们就可以顺藤摸瓜找到居址。

图5-2-2　杰兹卡兹干地质博物馆收藏的天然铜矿（张良仁摄）

　　中哈萨克斯坦指的是卡拉干达（Karaganda）省所管辖的地理区域。境内铜矿极为丰富，矿脉多，储量大，现在是当地的经济支柱。新石器时代的人们即已认识铜矿，并于青铜时代的早期（公元前2000—前1500年）开始制造铜器（图5-2-2）。但是大规模的冶炼活动却肇始于青铜时代的中期（公元前1500—前1200年）和晚期（公元前1200—前800年）。迄今发现的矿坑与冶炼遗址已经遍布于东部的巴尔喀什湖（Balkhash）以北，阿塔苏（Atasu）、杰兹卡兹干（Zhezkazgan）以及乌垒塔乌（Ulytau）地区。青铜合金所需的锡，以前人们推测来自东哈萨克斯坦和阿尔泰的山区，但现在阿塔苏和乌垒塔乌（Ulytau）地区都已

· 474 ·

经发现锡矿，显示了本地锡源的存在。塔迪萨依就属于乌垒塔乌地区。

塔迪萨依遗址本身似乎没有铜矿。但是12千米以外就有一座矿冶城市，名为杰兹迪（Zhezdy）。城市很小，是苏联时代为开采这里的铜矿而建的。现在铜矿已经耗竭，所以很多人离开了这座城市，留下一排排空荡的居民楼。据说这里也曾发现过青铜时代的采矿遗址。再往南60千米，就是杰兹卡兹干市。这一带方圆100平方千米以内都是铜矿。20世纪30—50年代，考古学家与地质学家发现了密集的古代矿坑和冶炼遗址，可惜大多被现代的工厂摧毁了。经过3000年的开采，先民们仍然把大部分矿藏留给了现代人。但是在当今的技术条件下，要不了多少年，这里也要挖掘一空了。

在阿塔苏地区，遗址保存得相当完好。这里发现有四个冶铜遗址以及与它们相邻的墓地。这些遗址本身并无铜矿，其矿源可能是往东南100千米以外的一个叫作卡拉扎耳（Karazhal）的地方。因此之故，自青铜时代末期废弃以后没有经过后人的扰动。实际上，许多房址和冶铜遗迹在地面上就可以看得清楚。20世纪50—80年代中哈萨克斯坦考古队发掘了这四处遗址。其中的阿塔苏Ⅰ号揭露面积最大，将近4000

图5-2-3　鬼斧神工的石山（张良仁摄）

（前面二人分别为塔迪萨依遗址的发掘领队柔达斯别克和工地负责人、考古学家安塔尼娜，后面二人分别为一起参加发掘的莫利兹奥和盖伯利尔）

平方米。发现有15座房址，7座冶铜作坊。这里的熔炉一般就地挖一个直径1.5—3米，深约1.7米的大坑。坑壁贴上4—5厘米的泥层。冶金学家们认为坑壁上还预设有空气管将外面的空气吸入坑内以提升温度。从熔炉还往外延伸出一条长4.5米的烟道，用途也在于此。这样的熔炉周围往往散落一些熔渣、木炭、碎铜矿石。他们所复原的熔炉，由地下的坑以及地上的石砌的塔形柱构成一个密封的空间。据说这样的熔炉需要人不停地鼓风达十几个小时，才能得到一些粗铜。粗铜含有很多的杂质，需要经过提炼才能用于铸造器物。

笔者来中哈萨克斯坦是要参加这里的发掘工作,当然也希望看看以后合作的前景。理论上说,哈萨克斯坦的学术潜力是很大的。一方面是因为考古工作一直做得少,其中以中哈萨克斯坦做得最多,但即以这里而言,到今天也还遗留很多空白。新石器时代、铜石并用时代和早期青铜时代的遗址发掘得很少,而且青铜时代的绝对年代序列没有建立起来。另一方面是遗址和地域的特殊性。如上所述,这里已经发现有许多保存完好的青铜时代的采矿和冶炼遗址,对于研究古代冶铜技术是一批不可多得的材料。如果加上早期铁器时代的墓葬,那么还可以探索其他金属(铁、金、银)冶炼技术的起源。这里也是探索游牧经济起源的一个重要地区。历史上,游牧民族曾数次冲击乃至摧毁了东亚、中亚、西亚、欧洲和非洲的农业文明,所以它的起源让不少人(特别是欧洲、日本学者)着迷。中哈萨克斯坦,以及北哈萨克斯坦都是草原地区,这里已经积累了不少青铜时代和早期铁器的遗址和墓葬材料,为将来解开游牧经济起源之谜铺垫了坚实的基础。

图5-2-4 石山上的岩画,上面表现了马、骆驼和其他动物的形象(张良仁摄)

中哈萨克斯坦也将为探索我国青铜冶炼技术起源提供重要线索。迄今为止,国内外学术界对这个问题仍然有两种假说。一种是本土起源说,另一种是外来说。持后面一种假说的Robert W. Bagley(1987年)曾指西亚为发源地。大家都知道,西亚的两河流域兴起的是锤打技术,与我国二里头时期兴起的铸造技术迥然不同。他提出的证据是我国龙山文化的薄胎陶器以及部分此类陶器的泥钉仿自锤打技术。但是这种技术在龙山时期、二里头和商周时期的青铜器上看不到一点痕迹,所以该说还缺乏支持。在这种情况下,我们应该考虑与我国西北部比邻的西伯利亚、阿尔泰和哈萨克斯坦。这些地区的青铜时代的起始年代与我国的二里头文化一期相近,所采用的是铸造技术以及铜锡合金，与我国大体接近。而它们的铸造技术则来源于俄罗斯境内的起始年代更早的东欧（公元前4000年内进入青铜时代）。所不同的是，这些地区生产的青铜器为兵器、工具和小装饰品，而我国则主要为容器。但是深入地比较研究这些地区的青铜器和我国新疆、青海、甘肃乃至中原地区龙山时代的同类产品，将会在这个问题上有所突破。梅建军和Colin Shell已经为我们揭示了一些前景。他们的研究表明，新疆地区的青铜器不仅形制而且铸造技术都源于西伯利亚和阿尔泰地区的阿凡纳谢沃文化（Afanas'eva culture，铜石并用时代）以及后来的安德罗诺沃文化（Andronovo culture，约公元前1500—前1200年）。

塔迪萨依遗址的发掘工作已经开展了八年，揭露面积只有700平方米。迄今发现的有十几个像是熔炉的竖穴坑和几口可能与冶炼有关的水井。已经揭开的还有好几个没有清理到底。实际上他们开的探方为2米×2米，留20厘米的隔梁。笔者在国内发掘多年，习惯了大面积揭露的做法，所以感觉他们的发掘很慢。过了些时间就觉得这种挖法很有道理：一是表土很薄，只有15厘米厚，可以开这么小的探方；二是这样的探方便于控制地层和测绘遗迹，这样拼合起来的遗址平面图错位很小。哈萨克斯坦的考古学家，沿袭了苏联时代的优良的学术作风。无论是谁，发掘一律使用手铲，细细地抠，慢慢地剔，所以遗迹做得到位而不过火。发掘中许多复杂的问题，尤其是像这样的冶铜遗址，可以有充裕的时间去琢磨。他们的绘图、照相、记录也非常详细、精确。这样速度是慢了，但是质量很高。所谓发掘即是破坏，在这里降低到了最大程度。

这个工地的领队是柔达斯别克（Zholdasbek Kurmankulov），哈萨克人，大高个，经验丰富，办事干练，是一位称职的领导。他从20世纪70年代开始就一直在中哈萨克斯坦工作，所以对这个地域的遗址、岩画非常熟悉（图5-2-3、图5-2-4）。现在他除了接待来宾和联络地方文博机构之外，有空时经常开车出去跑调查。工地的负责人则是另外一位资深的考古学家安塔尼娜（Antonina S. Ermolaeva），俄罗斯人，非常热爱考古，很少看到她闲着。上工时向大家交代完一天的工作后，她就去看各个探方的发掘情况，解决问题，整理出土遗物，

◇❖◇ 第五部分 欧亚考古见闻

作记录，检查绘图。下工后往往是大家都走了，她还在那里写记录，晚上她还要整理遗迹图和出土遗物。就这样日复一日，丝毫没有倦怠的样子。

哈萨克斯坦搞考古的人很少，整个国家加在一起才有二十来个，经费也很紧张。1991年从苏联独立出来以后，工厂倒闭，农场解散，经济几近崩溃。有几年时间连生计都成问题，科研就更谈不上了。所以搞科研的人转行做生意的为数不少。因为经费吃紧，本工地的发掘在前些年是断断续续的。近几年因为该国大力开发油田，经济开始复苏，政府也开始向科研增加投资，学术才得以重新回到轨道。但是工地上用钱很节省。研究生也当作在编人员一人多用，开车，绘图，整理器物，接待客人，管理财务，真是麻雀虽小，五脏俱全。

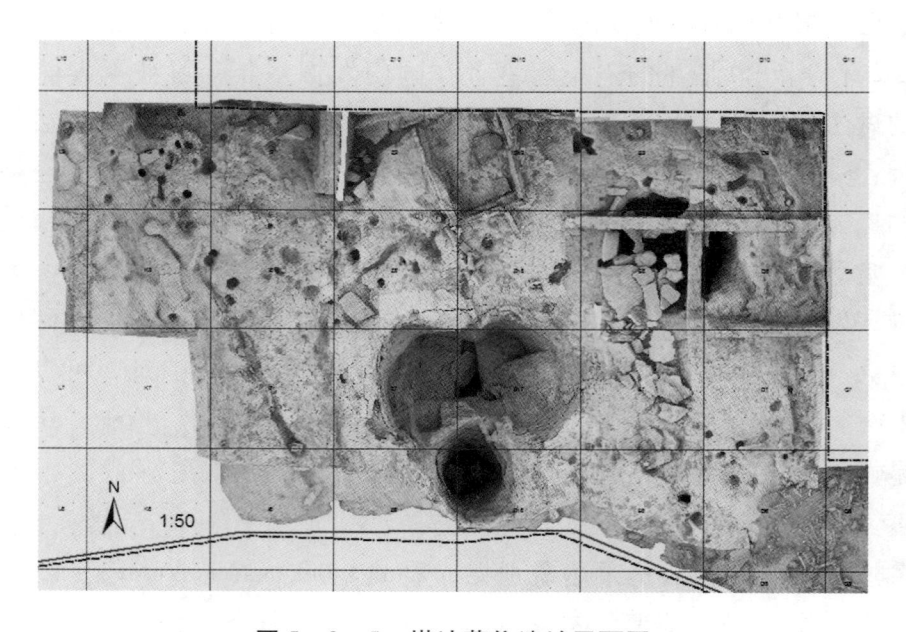

图5-2-5 塔迪萨依遗址平面图

[局部，表现遗址的探方网格与数字照片的重叠。上面可以看到四个熔坑、一条石板铺成的烟道和许多小柱洞。莫利兹奥（Maurizio Cattani）制作并提供]

安塔尼娜安排笔者清理一个像是熔炉的竖穴坑。坑口直径大约为1.2米，完全被9块大小不一的石板所覆盖。石板下发现有两层锅底状的烧结面。上层烧透达5厘米，表面漆黑油亮，看样子当时曾使用动物骨头和油脂作为燃料。填土中充满草木灰,其中还残留几块烧过的骨头和一块铜矿石。其下面为垫土,再往下,是另一层烧土。可以看得出,每层工作面使用时间都不长,好像是一次性的;一个竖穴坑可以使用两次以上。这样的土坑,如果是熔炉的话,技术含量并不高。古代的工匠可以

图 5-2-6 墓地所在谷地景观(张良仁摄)

轻易地挖一个,用上一两次,然后轻易地放弃它,再挖一个新的。同样的情形发生在另外一个竖穴坑里。这里一个燃烧面被塌落的生土完全覆盖,但后来的人并没有费力把生土弄走,只是在生土堆上重新做了一个燃烧面。

莫利兹奥和盖伯利尔忙着测绘遗址平面图。莫利兹奥对地理信息系统(GIS)和全站仪(Total Station)很在行。这些年他与柔达斯别克合作的内容就是制作数字平面图。同往年一样,今年他们不辞辛苦从意大利扛了一整套全站仪到这个工地。首先他们用全站仪测得各个遗迹的数据,然后用 GIS 或者 ARCVIEW 程序处理。这样做出的遗址图既能反映平面位置,又能反映等高线,是立体的。当然,还可以随意添加、更改颜色、标识。他做出的一个遗址图是一个三维模型,可以任意转变角度,就好像放在手上看一样。更为绝妙的是,莫利兹奥把数字照片也搬上了平面图(图 5-2-5)。尽管高空照片是凹形的,但他使用一个程序可以对它们进行矫正。这样遗址里发现的任何遗迹、遗物,无论大小,都可以在他的平面图上表现出来。当代科技的潜能在这里发挥得淋漓尽致。

在杰兹迪有一家很有特色的冶金博物馆,里面收藏了很多 19 世纪和 20 世纪初的采矿机械。其中的英国人(当时他们在哈萨克斯坦有矿场)引进的美国造大熔炉有几个立方米的容量,真让笔者这个外行看得目瞪口呆。在这里还看到了根据阿塔苏 I 号遗址发现的熔炉复原的模型(图 5-2-8)。时任总统那扎尔巴耶夫(Nazalbaev)曾在这里亲自点火

第五部分 欧亚考古见闻

试验了一次。展室内当然陈列有不少来自各个遗址的冶炼工具以及各种各样的铜矿石。该馆馆长是一个很有能量的人物。"二战"时拿了很多勋章，战后任杰兹卡兹干市政府秘书长。卸任后就倾注其所有的精力组建了这个博物馆。上面所说的展品大部分是他利用个人关系要来的，没花一分钱。

图 5-2-7 乌垒塔乌镇附近的青铜时代晚期（公元前 2000 年末）墓地

（墓群四周用大石块砌成矮墙，形成一个完美的四方形。中央是一个大墓。墓地在 20 世纪 50 年代已经发掘，只留下墓坑让参观者观看。张良仁摄）

由塔迪萨依往北 50 千米是乌垒塔乌镇。说是镇，其实比国内的很多村子还要小。只是环绕一个小湖错落着几十家住户。50 年代调查时曾发现冶金聚落，现在压在村子底下。遗址很重要，因为附近的河床里发现有锡矿石。可惜当时没有发掘。我们要去参观的地方是柔达斯别克主持的另外一个发掘工地，离此镇有 40 千米。这里是一个墓地，大部分墓葬都没有堆高，但是地面上可以看到碎石砌成的石圈。有一个墓葬群看起来很特别（图 5-2-7）。它的中央是一个大墓，用巨型石板砌成墓室。石材很方便，几十米外就是山，但是要搬运这些沉重的石板还得费点劲。大墓周围是十几座略小一些的墓葬。墓葬群四周用大石块砌成矮墙，形成一个完美的四方形。这个青铜时代末期（公元前 2000 年末）的墓葬群 20 世纪 50 年代就已经发掘，只留下了墓坑让我们观看。

墓地位于一个小山谷（图 5-2-6）。山谷非常开阔，大约有 12 平方千米。偌大的地方，在国内相当于五六个村子的面积，却只住了三户人家，一家小农场。因为人烟少，远离公路，环境宁静而优美，仿佛是一个世外桃源。不过在这里发掘就没那么浪漫了。晚上天气寒冷，住在帐篷里毫无舒适可言。柔达斯别克带我们去看谷内的几个墓葬和居址。

首先是三个排成一行的大石堆墓,直径二十余米,顶部高约3米,有塌陷的凹坑。柔达斯别克说是塞克人的,其规模与东哈萨克斯坦发现的非常轰动的金人墓接近,弄不好这里也出个金人(图5-2-9)(彩图17)。但是要挖掘这样一个大墓,按照他们的做法,要耗资3万美金。不远处还有两个没有隆起的石堆,只有一个高出地表20厘米的石砌的小台子。柔达斯别克说是匈奴人的墓葬。离这里大约3千米处,还有一片5世纪的村落遗址。房屋的墙体全为自然的石块砌成,没用任何石灰,所以谈不上规整。最高处也只有1.5米的样子,上面还得用毛毡覆盖。总共有14座左右,最大的大概是9平方米。

图5-2-8 阿塔苏Ⅰ号遗址发现的熔炉模型,杰兹迪冶金博物馆陈列(盖伯利尔摄)

随着时间的推移,笔者所发掘的"熔坑"越来越小。揭去石板后,笔者留下一半,挖一半,所以坑内变得窄小,难以腾挪身体。过不了半个小时,就腰酸背疼。这时候,笔者就坐在探方边上休息,看着村子里的活动。村民们正忙着过冬的草料。村子周围草很浅,冬草要到30千米以外去割。在乌垒塔乌的山谷里,笔者就看到割倒

图5-2-9 阿拉木图附近的伊塞克(Issyk)塞克人墓地出土的金人,哈萨克斯坦的中央历史博物馆大厅展出(盖伯利尔摄)

的草料。因为劳动力并不多,村民们要依靠拖拉机、大长车收割和运输。每户人家都堆起山一样的草垛,但实际上畜群最大的人家一年也只能养二百多头羊(图5-2-10)。这里没有冬天的草场。中哈萨克斯坦没有高山,西伯利亚冷空气长驱直入,带来寒冷多雪的天气。在没有现

◇❖◇ 第五部分 欧亚考古见闻

代机械的古代,不知牧民们是如何让牲畜过冬的。即使只保留几只种畜,需要的草料也还是不少。他们大概需要花更多的时间准备草料。

夜晚的时间大部分是在工作中度过的。莫利兹奥和盖伯利尔忙着处理白天测量的数据,加工遗址平面图。而笔者要学俄文,看资料。不过,时不时地就有年轻人组织跳舞。打开汽车的音响,大家在露天就可以跳起来。哈萨克斯坦人男女老少都能跳舞,活得轻松潇洒。我们的女房东和队里的一位老司机兴致来了也会加入行列。不过,男孩子们大多比较腼腆。这时候柔达斯别克和安塔尼娜也会在场。他们的动作跟广播体操差不多,但是他们的出现让气氛一下子活跃起来。

草原上的天气说冷就冷,进入9月后不久就开始大幅度降温。当年的发掘季节也该结束了。柔达斯别克、安塔尼娜带领队里的年轻人做收尾的工作。他们首先要用塑料布盖住所有已经揭开的熔炉和其他遗迹,然后搬运发掘出来的浮土把它们压住。既可以防寒,也可以防初春的洪水。全是繁重的体力活,但柔达斯别克、安塔尼娜都是身先士卒。晚上他们还要结账,整理记录,收拾出土器物。整个考古队加速运转,但是井然有序,像一台磨合好的发动机。最后整个考古队乘坐三辆车离开了。村民们还在堆草,牛羊还在慢悠悠地走着。大草原依旧那么宁静,好像我们没有来过一样。

图5-2-10 塔迪萨依村庄的草垛（张良仁摄）

[鸣谢:此次参加中哈萨克斯坦的发掘得到加州大学洛杉矶分校（University of California, Los Angeles）科臣考古研究所（Cotsen Institute of Archaeology）的考古朋友会（Friends of Archaeology）的资助]

俄罗斯考古访问纪行[*]

2012年7月24日，我们一行五人抵达新西伯利亚，到俄罗斯开展为期15天的学术考察。因为新疆的古代金属器与西伯利亚息息相关，所以我们此次访俄的一个核心目的就是认识西伯利亚的古代文化和金属器。

一 新西伯利亚

新西伯利亚是我们访俄行程的第一站。因为是夏季，俄罗斯的考古学家们都在田野，新西伯利亚考古与民族研究所的大楼空空荡荡。我们参观了该所的露天博物馆。博物馆从前任所长奥科拉德尼科夫院士（A. P. Okladnikov，1908—1981年）开始建设，起先是整体搬运了雅库特的一座建于16世纪末17世纪初的教堂到这里，后来又从米努辛斯克盆地收集来一些石雕，其中有奥库涅沃文化的巫师像。斯基泰—塔加尔时期的鹿石、突厥石人和近代的藏传佛教遗物。这里还陈列了一些西伯利亚西北部鄂毕河下游的曼西人的祖先木雕像（图5-3-1）。

图5-3-1 新西伯利亚考古与民族研究所露天博物馆陈列的曼西人在树上搭建的小木屋，里面放祖先灵魂的象征物，旁边摆了一些木雕，象征祖先。子孙们定期到这些祭祀场所来祭祀祖先，杀羊敬祖，然后大家分享（郭物摄）

---

[*] 本文原刊于《中国文化遗产》2013年第2期，第96—105页。收入本书时略有改动。

第五部分 欧亚考古见闻

该所的室内博物馆已经扩大，现在有了旧石器、新石器、青铜时代、早期铁器时代和中世纪展室。因为面积不够，每个时期、每个文化只能做简要性的介绍。展品都重新布置过了，放了以前没有见过的发掘成果，有远东的，有索普卡—II墓地的，有伊尔敏文化的，有巴泽雷克文化的卡尔金冢的。值得注意的是，博物馆非常注重社会教育，一是专门开发了遥控动画，观众可以随意观看一些石器的制作和使用方法。二是强调动手，现场展示纺织品的编织方法，并让观众自己尝试（图5-3-2）（彩图18）。

二 图瓦

图5-3-2 新西伯利亚考古与民族研究所陈列的卡尔金冢复原像（张良仁摄）

25日清晨，我们登上火车。前往阿巴坎市。火车一直在森林与草原间行驶，在山麓与河谷之间盘旋。速度不快，但是摇摆得很厉害。这是彼得大帝时代铺的西伯利亚大铁路，已经跟不上时代的步伐了。一路上草甸很多，郁郁葱葱，显然雨水非常充足。村庄和城市很少，城市也都是一些稀稀拉拉的低矮的房屋。火车走了22个小时，于26日早上5点到达阿巴坎市。当地的考古学家安德烈（Andrey I. Gotlib）接上我们继续前往图瓦。从阿巴坎出发，经米努辛斯克市，大约走了一个小时进入萨彦岭。翻过萨彦岭就到了图瓦境内，这里也是河谷草原和山峰森林，只不过比米努辛斯克盆地要干燥得多。

第二天，我们就到图瓦博物馆参观。这是一栋新建筑，宽敞明亮。二、三层为展厅部分，有自然地理、民族学和历史展厅。考古部分只有两个展厅，陈列的主要是阿尔赞一号和二号冢出土的文物。阿尔赞一号冢发掘于20世纪70年代，发掘前已经被盗，出土遗物很少。但是该冢的木构建筑非常引人注目。它在地面上用规格、材质统一的原木搭建椁室，以两个大椁室为中心，周围搭建三圈小椁室。中央的两个木椁墓室埋了17人，周围的椁室埋了不少马，也有人。但是大部分椁室都是空的。埋葬完后，上面再用石块封盖，高5米，直径不清楚了（图5-3-3）。二号冢是2000—2003年艾米塔什博物馆和德国考古研究所共同发掘的。其形制与一号冢不同，中央为一个土坑木椁墓，夫妇合葬，随葬了大量的金器，属于衣服坠饰、首饰、武器。值得注意的是，男女头上的前额都贴了一个野猪像，头冠上各自带了 4 个和 2 个马像。二人颈部挂了一个精致的项圈，衣服上贴了 2000 多枚野猪像，腰上系了一条腰带，

图 5-3-3 图瓦博物馆陈列的阿尔赞一号冢模型（郭物摄）

上面挂了许多动物牌饰和包金铁剑、箭囊和弓。女人的衣服上点缀火焰形的金饰，头上还戴了一个尖髻高冠。该冢出土的金器，一部分留在图瓦博物馆，大部分拿到艾米塔什博物馆去了。除了这些大冢，图瓦还发现了其他同时期的墓葬，出土有铜镞、铜斧，陶器很少（5-3-4）。

因为当地要修建克孜勒—阿巴坎的铁路，沿线需要进行考古调查和发掘。俄罗斯科学院考古研究所的伊莉娜（Irina V. Rukavishnikova）就负责其中的一个地点，离克孜勒大约 30 千米。考古工地就在艾贝克河谷中。两侧的二层台地上就是低

图 5-3-4 图瓦博物馆陈列的阿尔赞二号冢出土器物（郭物摄）

矮的草原，上面有一些小冢。他们正在发掘一座石堆冢，椭圆形，长 26 米，属于图瓦本地的蒙衮—泰加文化（青铜时代晚期）或艾德堡文化（早期铁器时代）。封堆刚刚揭开，表面盖满了石块。伊莉娜的丈夫也在这里工作，负责拍照，然后用照片绘图，以节省时间。封堆上可以看到三个墓葬，表面略微塌陷。她的挖法是将冢分为六个探方，留隔梁，以便观察剖面（图 5-3-5）。

吃过中午饭，来自圣彼得堡的物质文化史研究所的女考古学家玛丽娜（Marina E. Kilunovskaia）带我们继续前行。玛丽娜负责整个艾贝克河谷的考古工作（图 5-3-6）。翻过山梁，就到了一个谷地，是一

◇◆◇ 第五部分 欧亚考古见闻

图5-3-5 参观伊莉娜负责的考古工地（郭物摄）

图5-3-6 艾贝克河谷的一个墓地（陈建立摄）

个施工营地，旁边就是一个小水库。在营地，她给我们介绍了河谷的聚落和墓地分布图。然后我们继续前行，一路上看了四个地点。在第一个地点，她说有蒙衮—泰加文化和艾德堡文化。前者的墓葬中央为石砌墓室，周围一圈石板围墙，然后覆盖一层石块，后者的形状有所不同，中心的墓葬为石板，周围三圈石板围墙。这些墓葬都没有出土陶器，其他器物也很少，玛丽娜开玩笑说这是"干净的考古学"。玛丽娜还给我们讲了图瓦考古，从旧石器、新石器，一直讲到青铜时代和早期铁器时代。20世纪80年代他们在托拉—达什（位于阿尔赞国王谷）居址，发现了阿凡纳谢沃和奥库涅沃文化的地层。可惜当时的发掘面积很小，出土的东西不多。

28日早上，我们出发离开克孜勒，前往图兰镇，去参观阿尔赞国王谷。我们来的时候就经过这个小镇，距离克孜勒约1个小时车程。在这里与圣彼得堡的艾米塔什博物馆来的康斯坦丁（Konstantin V. Chugunov）会合，一起前往阿尔赞国王谷。2000—2004年发掘阿尔赞二号冢的时候，康斯坦丁就是俄方负责人。

阿尔赞国王谷是一个非常开阔的河谷，中间为乌尤克河，草地比周围其他河谷要高一些。从图兰出发，开车约20分钟到达阿尔赞二号冢（图5-3-7）。康斯坦丁介绍说，国王谷中一共有四座大冢，这是其中最小的一座（公元607年），年代比一号冢（公元前9—前8世纪）要晚。他现在觉得这座冢挖得快了些，一些问题没有解决，比如建造程序。冢墓直径为50米，高2米，周围有一圈列石。中央

· 486 ·

为石块封堆。列石与封堆之间分布几座墓葬。封堆下又有几座墓葬，东侧的为男性，西侧的为女性，中心墓葬在东北侧，里面埋放一对男女。封堆内的东南侧埋有一个马坑，封堆向南有一条黄土道路。冢的外围有许多圆形祭祀坑，里面埋有焚烧过的动物骨架，可以

图5-3-7 阿尔赞二号冢（郭物摄）

辨认出是羊。在东南侧，是石块堆砌的祭坛。该冢出土的器物十分丰富，部分陈列在图瓦博物馆。二号冢已经改造成露天博物馆，东北的3段墙没有发掘，冢的旁边用发掘出土的土和石块搭建了一个2米高的台子，便于游客参观。墙里面的一些石块上面发现有岩画，康斯坦丁推测它们是从周围的山上搬来的。可惜周围的山上没有发现岩画。中心墓葬的北侧立了鹿石。在封堆中央有两个大长方形坑，可是什么也没有发现。他认为是盗洞，而德国人认为是空墓。

往北走大约1千米，为阿尔赞三号冢。康斯坦丁说它与没有发掘之前的二号冢相近，规模更大，直径达90米。周围为斜坡，已经看不到列石，只看见封堆，高约3米。上面有若干下陷的大坑，可能是墓葬所在，也可能是取土造成的。它的北侧还有一座，编号为四

图5-3-8 青吉台大冢

号冢。离开三号冢，前往阿尔赞一号冢。这座冢位于阿尔赞村旁边的农场（已经废弃）里。一号冢发掘于1971—1974年，修建木椁的木头部分留了下来。去年为了测年，重新挖开，取了些炭样。现在表面已经看不见什么，只是一块平坦的台地。

我们接着奔向更北的青吉台墓地（图5-3-8）。一路上可以看

第五部分 欧亚考古见闻

到很多冢，成一条线排列。今年康斯坦丁挖的是最北的一座，直径90米，高3米左右。冢的结构与阿尔赞二号冢相似，有鹿石（向北）、列石和封堆，但是也有一些独特之处。一是在原始地面上堆了若干层湖泊的淤土。二是周围挖一圈壕沟，在沟底也堆了一层湖泊淤土。康斯坦丁这次挖得很小心，在壕沟、列石、封堆开了若干处探沟，来解决冢的结构问题。从剖面上可以看到，封堆由两层沙土和两侧石块交叉堆成。封堆边缘用石板横砌，外围堆淤泥。列石两侧通过堆石块来加固。看完工地，康斯坦丁带我们到营地看他们的阿尔赞二号冢发掘课件。他们复原了四个阶段的建造过程：第一，最早修建两周列石和围墙，里面用黄土铺垫一个圆形和一个梯形，对着圆形还有两道弧线，中间埋一些墓葬，外围东南侧修了两圈祭坛，东侧16个牺牲坑。第二，中央石堆、中央和南侧立石碑，东北侧增加牺牲坑。第三，东西两侧修建墓葬，东南角两周列石之间填石块。增加牺牲坑。第四，列石以内全部填石块，增加牺牲坑至整个一周。康斯坦丁也介绍了有关该冢出土器物的研究。他将一些金器和武器与哈萨克斯坦的别列伊和中国的玉皇庙、洋海的材料做了对比。

离开康斯坦丁的营地后我们返回阿巴坎市。一路森林茂密，山花烂漫，空气清新，让人陶醉（图5-3-9）。

图5-3-9 萨彦岭山上森林茂密，山间花草繁盛。在森林中间穿行，幽静而清澈（郭物摄）

三 阿巴坎

第二天早上，我们在阿巴坎与安德烈再次见面。我们先到米努辛斯克市看博物馆，然后回到阿巴坎再看博物馆。米努辛斯克市离阿巴坎25千米，一路草原、河流，风景秀丽，不多会儿就到了博物馆。米努辛斯克博物馆是1877年建造的老建筑，起初是一家私人博物馆，后来改为国立博物馆。一个大厅里面摆了许多奥库涅沃文化的石人。石人在阿凡纳谢沃和卡拉苏克时代都有，但是都没有奥库涅沃文化发达。其特征为上、中、下三段，上段的圆脸上有三个眼睛，头上竖起几缕头发，像太阳的光芒，侧面有耳环。中段为腰部，挂着短剑。奥库涅沃石人经常为塔加尔和突厥时期移走重新使用。突厥人在上面刻了突厥文。这样的突厥时期奥库涅沃石人数量不少。米努辛斯克市曾经是俄罗斯考古的中心，许多著名的老一辈考古学家，如捷普洛霍夫（S. A. Teploukhov）、吉谢列夫（S. V. Kiselev）、瓦捷茨卡娅（È. B. Vadetskaia）、克兹拉索夫（L. R. Kyzlasov）和格寥兹诺夫（M. P. Griaznov）都在这里工作过，所以博物馆的墙上也挂了他们的照片。不过博物馆内发掘品很少，大部分为征集品。

另一个展厅为考古厅。从旧石器时代开始，安德烈说哈卡斯共和国的旧石器最早为6万年。里面有漂亮的标枪。新石器时代，人们仍然从事采集狩猎，并且开始制作陶器。但是没有细石器时代。从阿凡纳谢沃文化开始，欧罗巴人种来到米努辛斯克盆地，带来了畜牧、冶金和农业。后起的奥库涅沃文化的居民则多为蒙古人种，生产平底陶器和金属器，与洞穴墓文化有联系。安德罗诺沃文化，以前人们认为发源于米努辛斯克盆地，现在大家认为发源于南乌拉尔。陶器和青铜器都很发达，居民也为欧罗巴人种。在安德罗诺沃文化之后，就是卡拉苏克文化和塔加尔文化。二者都具有独特的青铜器（图5-3-10），后者还有巨大的冢墓。塔加

图5-3-10 米努辛斯克博物馆陈列的塔加尔文化的金属器（郭物摄）

尔文化可能中国学者不太熟悉，它分布于哈卡斯、阿尔泰和图瓦，比卡拉苏克的范围要小。在塔加尔文化（公元前7—前2世纪）之后兴起了捷辛文化（公元前2—前1世纪），时代相当于匈奴。再往后就是匈奴、塔什特克（2—5世纪）和吉尔吉斯帝国时期。在匈奴时代，这里出现了许多汉代的瓦当和铜镜。

下午我们到阿巴坎博物馆参观。这里也有一个奥库涅沃石人展厅，里面陈列了一些巨大的石人（图5-3-11）。考古厅很小，同样摆了一些阿凡纳谢沃、奥库涅沃、卡拉苏克和塔加尔文化的陶器和铜器，但是没有匈奴、塔什特克文化的东西。不过这里的东西不少是发掘出土的，跟米努辛斯克博物馆的征集品有很大差别。

图5-3-11 阿巴坎博物馆陈列的奥库涅沃文化石人（郭物摄）

次日我们到阿巴坎周围看塔加尔大冢。一路上都是茫茫草原，高低起伏，只有汽车碾压出来的道路，人很容易迷失。安德烈说他在这里挖了三年，也还是会迷路。沿途可以看到很多塔加尔家墓，三五成组。大约走了1个小时，我们到了一座大冢，名为巴列茨基劳格（图5-3-12）。这是一座方形冢，周围用石块砌起围墙，外侧每隔1米左右用石块横向放置以便支撑围墙。不少石块上面有塔加尔时期的岩画，还有个别的青铜时代晚期的岩画，每边长53—54米，墙高11米。门道在东侧，高1.5米，两侧立巨石。墓葬在中轴线的西侧，墓道也在西侧。因为被盗，所以没有发现什么东西。这座墓葬现在成了旅游点，局部做了修复。安德烈说塔加尔墓葬规模与阿尔赞冢相当，但是形制不同，出土器物也不同。这座大冢只有一座墓葬，周围也没有牺牲坑。

图5-3-12 巴列茨基劳格大冢（郭物摄）

看完这座大冢，我们又去看国

王谷的大冢。穿过大草原，大小不一的冢墓星罗棋布。安德烈说国王谷内大型冢墓20座，中型的有100多座。走了大约20分钟，到了一个冢墓，名为小萨贝克。该冢没有发掘。四边立巨石，共20块，每块重约30—40吨。边长50米左右，高7米。东侧也有门道，但是已经完全覆盖，整个冢墓呈金字塔形。这样的冢墓目前只挖了两个，即巴列茨基劳格和大萨贝克，其余的俄罗斯政府已经不让发掘。

图5-3-13 萨贝克大冢（郭物摄）

走了大约10分钟，我们就到了萨贝克大冢（图5-3-13）。冢墓确实很大，大致呈正方形，边长70米，原高14米左右，为西伯利亚最大的冢墓。四边里竖立一圈巨大的大石板，均为东向，大石板之间有横立大石板。在东墙内的横向石板还垒了木头，其他三面墙都没有，原因不明。门向东，两侧各立两个大石板。石板比其余的冢墓都大。墓葬已经被盗，只出土了若干金片和铜剑。这座冢墓发掘于20世纪30年代，发掘者就是吉谢列夫，因为出土东西少，所以没有发表报告，只出版了一些小册子。冢墓已经圈起来，成了一座博物馆，旁边有展室，展示了一些复制品。

离开萨贝克大冢，下午我们继续向西沿着铁路线行走，一路人烟稀少，走五六十千米才能见到一座村庄，到了维巴克河的河谷，又看了一座塔加尔墓葬。规模不大。墓葬旁边立着奥库涅沃文化的石人，上面刻有单把豆和牛（图5-3-14）。该遗址附近还有阿凡纳谢沃和奥库涅沃文化的墓葬。继续前行，走了一段土路，然后又翻了两个山丘，到了一片广阔的草原。这里名叫恰—塔斯，哈卡斯语为"战争"。这里密密麻麻地分布着塔加尔、捷辛、塔什特克和吉尔吉斯时期的冢墓，形制各不相同。捷辛时期的为圆形冢墓，没有巨石作为边界。塔什特克有巨石，但是冢为圆形，没有石墙，墓葬为土坑木椁墓。吉尔吉斯时期的冢为土冢，没有巨石，但有列石。

图5-3-14　维巴克河谷的奥库涅沃文化石人

四　圣彼得堡

第二天（31日）早晨，我们乘飞机前往圣彼得堡。当天我们参观了圣彼得堡老城。老城在彼得堡岛上，是彼得大帝为了便于防守有意选择的。城堡不大，外围有一圈城墙，只有三座桥通往大陆和其他两个岛。老城是彼得大帝从意大利请来建筑师设计建造的，城市的建筑呈现出巴洛克风格。城堡里的喀山大教堂存放着历代沙皇和皇后的棺材，其中就有彼得大帝和凯瑟琳皇后的。1992年，人们找到了末代沙皇尼古拉二世的遗骨，并于1998年接回喀山大教堂。喀山大教堂的旁边就是造币厂，彼得大帝时代开始使用，至今仍在开工。我们绕了一圈，到了老城的监狱。据介绍，这是沙俄时代审讯重要犯人的地方。监狱本身有一道城墙，而且防守严密，所以没有发生过越狱事件。在这里关押过的有十二月党人，包括列宁的大哥，但是没有关过列宁和其他布尔什维克领导人。城堡厚20米，高12米，上面摆设大炮，用于防守。

8月1日早上，我们去艾米塔什博物馆参观。艾米塔什博物馆收藏了很多名画，有一个大展厅展出的都是伦布朗的画。文艺复兴时期的名家画作也有不少，如达·芬奇的，米开朗琪罗的。因为凯瑟琳皇后非常热衷于收藏绘画，其后历代沙皇也都购买艺术品。因为时间不多，我们主要参观的是考古展厅。考古展厅分五个部分。一部分为旧石器至斯基泰时期,包括东欧的特利波里、土坑墓、波尔塔夫卡、木椁墓和斯基泰文化,也有西伯利亚的阿凡纳谢沃、奥库涅沃、安德罗诺沃、卡拉苏克、塔加尔、巴泽雷克、斯基泰、塔什特克、突厥和蒙古,以及中亚和北高加索各个时期的器物,展品极其丰富。其中一个展厅专门陈列了巴泽雷克大冢出土的马车、毛织品和马具(图5-3-16)。

图5-3-15　圣彼得堡物质文化史研究所图书馆(陈建立摄)

图5-3-16　艾米塔什博物馆陈列的巴泽雷克马车（郭物摄）

下午我们去拜访了圣彼得堡物质文化史研究所。该所的大楼原为沙皇的房产,现在看上去有些破旧,但是原来很是气派豪华。研究所从19世纪成立到现在,已经经历了几次更名。现在拥有若干考古研究室,也有冶金、碳十四实验室。中亚和高加索研究室的工作地域为西伯利亚(包括图瓦和米努辛斯克盆地)、中亚和高加索。该所的图书馆非常好,收藏了19世纪以来的俄罗斯和国外的考古文献,藏书丰富而完整(图5-3-15)。东方文献研究所主要从事亚洲国家(阿拉伯、中国、日本)的古代文献的研究,同时也有不少珍贵的收藏。在这里我们见到了东方文献研究所所长波波娃(I. F. Popova),她是研究我国西夏文书的,中文很好,在学术界名气很大,也经常来中国访问。之后我们又去拜访克雷恩(L.S. Klejn)教授。克雷恩是俄罗斯著名的考古学家,精通英文,喜欢琢磨考古理论,与世界上有名的考古学家,如张光直和伦福儒,都有书信来往。他坐过牢,写过很多书,包括类型学和考古学方法,最近刚刚完

成了英文版的《俄罗斯考古学史》。虽已有80岁高龄，但是精神很好，思维非常敏锐。今年他曾经委托笔者寻找俄罗斯人类学家史禄国的照片。史禄国是沙皇后裔，也是现代人类学先驱之一，通晓通古斯语言，发表了《北方通古斯的社会组织》和《满族的社会组织：满族氏族组织研究》。十月革命后他逃到中国，在清华大学和"中央研究院"工作过，曾经是费孝通的研究生导师。可惜他不懂汉语，在我国不为人所知，他的照片也因为这些机构历经劫难，没有保存下来。

2日早上我们参观了研究所库房收藏的文物。在这里不同类型的文物由研究人员自己负责保管、研究和陈列。我们看到19世纪和20世纪初出土的米努辛斯克盆地铜器和铁器。这里保存了许多卡拉苏克和塔加尔的铜器，包括刀、短剑、斧和耳环等（图5-3-17）。下午我们去看著名的金器展厅。

图5-3-17　卡拉苏克文化和塔加尔文化金属器（陈建立摄）

这个展厅需要预约，并且不能拍照。展厅陈列了彼得大帝从西伯利亚收集来的大量金器，其中很多都是斯基泰和塔加尔时期的东西。

五　莫斯科

离开圣彼得堡，我们乘火车于4日早上到达莫斯科。这次来莫斯科主要是与我们《新疆史前金属器研究》课题的俄方合作伙伴切尔内赫（E. N. Chernykh）教授见面（图5-3-18）。切尔内赫教授是举世闻名的欧亚大陆冶金考古专家，出版了18本著作，包括那本剑桥出版的《苏联的古代冶金》。我们已经翻译了他的《欧亚大陆北部的古代冶金》一书。此次合作，就是希望结合新疆和南西伯利亚的考古材料和金属器材料。当天下午，切尔内赫教授在他的实验室，为我们准备了欢迎晚餐。

第二天，我们先去了普希金艺术博物馆的现代艺术馆。展厅分为三层，这里陈列着不少塞尚、高更、毕加索的画。短暂停留后我们就去参观东方艺术博物馆。该博物馆的米老虎副馆长前几年发掘了突厥时期的布尔巴仁城址，可惜这次没有见上。博物馆收藏了亚洲很多国家的民族艺术，如中国、韩国、日本、西藏、东南亚、印度、伊朗、中亚和高加索、布里亚特、蒙古的服装和绘画。博物馆的工作人员常去图瓦和远东各地收集民族文物，也从事发掘，在图瓦、中亚和高加索都有项目，只可惜该馆现在没有发掘文物的展览。据说正在筹划中，准备两年以后开放。

图 5-3-18　会见切尔内赫教授（郭物摄）

下午笔者参观了普希金博物馆。里面陈列了埃及、叙利亚、伊朗、希腊、罗马的精美文物，其中埃及的木乃伊彩棺、特洛伊的金器、叙利亚的雕刻和希腊的彩陶最引人注目（图 5-3-19）。

图 5-3-19　普希金博物馆陈列的埃及木乃伊彩棺（张良仁摄）

第五部分 欧亚考古见闻

8月6日是我们回程的日子。抓紧最后的时间，我们去参观了红场的历史博物馆（图5-3-20）。博物馆内有旧石器、新石器、铜石并用（特利波里文化）、土坑墓、辛塔什塔、阿巴舍沃、安德罗诺沃、木椁墓、塔加尔、斯基泰和塔什特克各时代的文物。其中的辛塔什塔和阿巴舍沃的出土物是我们在别的地方所看不到的。此外还有斯拉夫、早期俄罗斯和蒙古时期前后的俄罗斯历史文物。展品大多为陶器、铜器和骨器，聚落和墓葬模型很少。陈列还是十年前的样子，变化不大。博物馆大楼是19世纪的建筑，保留着那个时期的装修。

图5-3-20 红场的历史博物馆（郭物摄）

离开前，我们回到实验室，与切尔内赫教授告辞。我们的俄罗斯考古访问至此结束。

英国访问纪行*

2016年4月，应英国谢菲尔德大学都楠（Roger Doonan）教授的邀请，水涛教授和笔者到英国访问了14天。由于都楠教授的精心安排和全程陪同，我们得以参观了一些遗址，访问了谢菲尔德大学、李约瑟研究所和牛津大学，欣赏了大英博物馆和伦敦博物馆的展览，见闻不少，收获良多。

一　大英博物馆

因为笔者计划在南京大学开设《世界考古》课程，所以要收集资料，此次访英自然不会错过大英博物馆。我们到达英国的第二天，就去参观了该馆。该馆成立于1753年，最早的一批藏品来自于医生思诺安爵士（Sir Hans Sloane）。此人收集了71000件希腊、罗马、埃及、近东、远东和美洲文物，因为不想死后这些文物流散，就卖给了国王乔治二世。议会和国王协商建立大英博物馆，但是该馆既不属于国王，也不属于教会，而属于国家，向公众开放；而且它从一开始就胃口很大，从全世界收藏各种文物。1778—1800年，库克（James Cook）船长在全世界收集的文物引起了英国人对异域土著社会的兴趣。1801年，英国打败了法国，此后埃及的大型石雕源源不断地涌入该馆。1840年起，大英博物馆开始派人到小亚细亚和近东发掘亚述都城尼姆鲁德和尼尼微，将出土的大型浮雕和楔形文书收入囊中。斯坦因和伍雷（Leonard Woolley）又带来新疆和乌尔王陵的部分文物。与此同时，大英博物馆

---

* 本文原刊于《大众考古》第9期，上篇，83—90页；第10期，下篇，81—88页。收入本书时略有改动。

第五部分 欧亚考古见闻

本身也在不断扩建,以容纳迅猛增长的藏品。

我们由南门进入博物馆,穿过柱廊和安检,直接来到 4 号展厅看古埃及雕刻。一进门就看到很多人在围观罗塞塔碑。该碑是 1802 年乔治三世捐给大英博物馆的,上面同时镌刻了古希腊和埃及象形文字,为释读后者提供了钥匙。由于不懂文字,我们就没有停留,径直看雕像去了。这里收藏的古埃及国王头像、半身像、狮身人面像、石碑和神庙壁画让人叹为观止,其中就有拉美西斯二世坐像。该像不完整,现存部分只是原像的上部分,但是看上去非常高大。坐像原有一对,均由整块石材雕刻而成,而石材采自尼罗河中游的阿斯旺,大约 20 吨。如此之重的石材采好以后,要装上特制的船,运到拉美西斯二世的神庙门口两侧,立起来,再由工匠仔细地雕刻。然后还要上色,今天还能看到残存的颜料:眼珠黑色,皮肤红色,头巾蓝黄色条纹相间。拉美西斯二世脸庞圆润,嘴巴微闭,眼睛炯炯有神,看上去是个年轻英俊的青年。其写实的造型、唯美的风格和高超的技艺,堪与米开朗琪罗的大卫像相媲美。在这尊坐像的背后,就是雄伟的神庙。神庙前面是一排圆柱,其中一根呈莎草形,高达 4.5 米。神庙内精致地刻着死者形象、祭拜死亡之神的场面和死亡之书。如此看来,一位国王的神庙工程非常浩大,加上金字塔本身,所需的人力和物力就更匪夷所思了。过去觉得商代国王的王陵规模大,随葬的青铜器多,已经过于奢华,但是埃及古代国王的王陵毫不逊色。

大英博物馆的文字说明做得非常详细而又不啰唆,值得称道。正因为如此,观众不仅可以了解古埃及的历史,而且可以了解古埃及人为什么要耗费大量的人力物力用于建造金字塔和神庙。关于这一点他们已经用雕刻、绘画和文字告诉了我们。古埃及人相信人死后有灵魂,可以效仿死亡之神 Osiris 可以再生。他们不仅要活着崇拜他,死后也要崇拜他。因此我们在神庙内会看到死者向他供奉食物和啤酒的场景。墓室墙壁、棺材和莎草纸上的咒语和死亡之书保佑死者获得永生。有时候灵魂会以死者的形象出现在墓室的假门上,等候子孙的供奉。这种对永生的追求也体现在棺材和木乃伊的制作上。三楼的 59 号展厅陈列了许多木棺和木乃伊。在古埃及人看来,死亡并非人生的终点，而是向一个新的人生转变的过程。人由若干关键部分组成，也就是人体和心脏以及灵魂卡（ka）和巴（ba）。卡可以让人在死后继续生活，但是他需要后代提供酒食；巴可以离开人体，自由活动，但是如果人体不存在，它就无法回到人体，自己也会灭亡。这种观念类似于我国古代的魂魄观念，人死后灵魂就分为魂和魄，魄要留在墓葬里，生者要提供各种衣服、酒食、歌舞，让它过得舒服，否则它会跑到人间，祸害子孙后代。魂要上天，生者要打点好各路鬼怪，以求它可以进入神仙世界。只不过在古中国，没有像古埃及那样用建筑、绘画、雕刻和文字将这种观念表现得淋漓尽致。为了死者的灵魂，古埃及人修建墓室，供奉酒食，并且制作木乃伊。为了保护尸体，人们要把内脏和脑髓取出来，然后用麻布包裹，放入木棺。木棺绘画死者供奉死亡之神和死亡之书。死亡之神可以保证死者得以重生，而死亡之书保证巴可以自由地离开和回到尸体。

大英博物馆现在拥有1300万件文物，97个展厅。我们前后只有两天的时间，无法走遍各个展厅。该馆的中国藏品非常丰富，其中斯坦因从新疆和甘肃带回去的文书和文物就有不少，可惜时间不够，只好割爱。笔者想把重点放在近东，因此除了埃及，只能选择西亚。在4号展厅旁边的5号，陈列着亚述的大型圆雕。1845—1861年，大英博物馆的考古学家拉雅德（Austen H. Layard）发掘了尼姆鲁德，带回了不少雕刻。其中有守卫宫殿门口的人首狮身像，有歌颂国王功德的方尖碑，以及表现国王军功和帝国威严的巨幅浮雕。这些东西笔者在美国的大都会博物馆看过不少，但是在大英博物馆看到布满三个展厅墙壁的巨幅浮雕，仍

图5-4-1 拉奇什浮雕（张良仁摄）

然震撼不小（图5-4-1）。看完亚述浮雕，就前往52号厅看伊朗部分。此部分主要展出了波斯帝国的浮雕和器物，而帕提亚和萨珊时期的东西不多。其中波斯波利斯王宫的巨幅浮雕复制品，再现了属国进贡、

波斯王猎狮的景象（图5-4-2）。各地统治者都喜欢展现自己的文治武功，但是没有像近东的古代国王们这么露骨，把它刻在宫殿的浮雕里，写在碑铭中。大英博物馆在西亚发掘的另一处遗址是闻名遐迩的乌尔王陵（Ur）。这是1922—1934年与美国宾夕法尼亚大学合作的项目，所得的文物对半分。我们看到了两顶金冠，其中一顶的死者是一位18—20岁的女性。该墓的许多器物都被倒塌的填土压扁，发掘者伍雷采用填注蜡液的办法加以固定，将死者的头骨和金冠取回。这些墓葬埋的是否为国王和王后，其实是没有确切证据的。伍雷只是根据墓葬的规格推测的，后人也就这样跟着说了。这些墓葬均为竖穴土坑，一边有斜坡供人出入。在墓室的旁边还有陪葬者，其中包括乐师和士兵，他们有时随葬有车辆和丰厚的随葬品。可惜黎凡特地区的史前时代的文物并不多，勉强能凑个年代框架。本来笔者想看看有关农业起源、文字起源和城市起源的文物，恐怕不能如愿了。

图5-4-2　波斯波利斯浮雕（张良仁摄）

二　伦敦

来伦敦之前，本来想端个学者的架子，不去一般游客爱去的地方，但是终究未能免俗，因为不去，还真是无法了解伦敦的历史和文化。在伦敦的第三天，陪同我们的谢菲尔德大学博士生钱多多就带着我们在伦敦街上飞奔，穿过中国城，然后与都楠教授会合。就这两天的见闻而言，伦敦完全是个大都市了。在宾馆、在商店、在大街、在酒吧（pub），我们听不到几个正宗的伦敦腔，听到的是来自世界各地的各种口音的英语；见不到扎堆的白人，见到的是各种肤色混合的人群，说明在伦敦各种肤色和宗教的人群已经很好地融合到一起了。

不过，沿路看到的一些建筑，让笔者想起了英国辉煌的帝国时代。

在特拉法加广场（Trafalgar Square），我们的目光立刻就凝固在那根高耸入云的纳尔逊石柱（实高44.27米）上了。基座上四只巨大的铜狮守护着这根石柱，柱头上纳尔逊（Horatio Nelson）元帅持剑站立，仿佛在指挥他的舰队（图5-4-3）。这根石柱骄傲地告诉我们，他率领的舰队在西班牙的特拉法加战胜了法国和西班牙联合舰队，英国从此成了海上霸主。此广场和附近的滑铁卢地铁站，时刻在提醒法国游客，让他们回想起法国屈辱的历史。不过这个广场在过去的一百多年里发生了多次游行示威。1887年11月13日，3万多抗议者在此聚集反对失业，与警察发生了大规模冲突，示威人群焚烧了周围的几栋楼，打伤了一些骑警，而骑警也撞伤了不少示威者，踩死了一个人，史称"流血星期天"。虽然如此，英国政府采取了比较温和的处置手段，没有下令让警察开枪动刺刀，只是让他们用木棍和马匹予以镇压。

继续往前走，经过唐宁街，就看到了风格独特的大本钟和旁边的国会大厦。大本钟原名钟塔或史蒂芬塔，2012年改名为伊丽莎白塔，以纪念伊丽莎白二世登基60年。这座塔建成于1858年，属于新哥特风格。其挺拔峭立的塔身与国会大厦的密集的尖顶塔柱相互辉映，浑然一体。其时正是大英帝国的巅峰时期，英国开始吸收世界各地的文化和艺术为自己所用。1941年，德国空军对伦敦实施了大轰炸，但是大本钟运转如故，分秒不差，可见当初设计的精准。不过在20世纪，它发生了若干次停摆，也发生了走快和走慢的情况，有些是因为维修，有些是因为天气。在过去的150多年里，也换过一些部件。都楠教授说，主钟早在1859年被钟摆撞裂，当时工程师只是把钟体转了几度，继续使用。近些年有人提议把钟拆下来重铸或者另铸一钟，但是文物界

图5-4-3 纳尔逊石柱（张良仁摄）

并不赞成，因为该钟已经成了文物，成了英国的标志；而且本身已经裂了一百多年，还非常准确，所以就不要换了。

大本钟的旁边就是中国游客耳熟能详的威斯敏斯特大教堂（Westminster Abbey）。这是各国游客都爱去的地方，本来想脱俗不看，不曾想都楠教授非要拽我们进去，说不看我们会后悔的。他说得没错，这座教堂积淀的东西太深厚了。根据可靠的史料，这座教堂建于10世纪后半叶，1042—1052年忏悔者爱德华（Edward the Confessor）重建这座教堂，给自己死后准备一个埋葬之所。现在的建筑是亨利八世于1245年开始建造的，以尊奉忏悔者爱德华，同时把它当作自己的埋葬之所。今天整个大厅高大敞亮，不见华丽的雕塑和壁画，只见彩色玻璃画。在1760年以前这里也是大多数英王加冕、结婚和葬身之处。有意思的是，棺材表面的死者雕像仰面朝天，双手合十，在死亡世界继续崇拜上帝，让人想起中国商周时期的贵族在死后继续崇拜祖先的情形。从克伦威尔时代开始，这里成了许多名人的葬身之所，以褒扬他们的贡献。我们看到了克伦威尔（Oliver Cromwell，国会革命的领导者，只有名牌，其尸骨后来为保王党斩首，散落他处）、达尔文、牛顿和韦伯佛司（William Wilberforce，废奴运动的领导者）的长眠地，也看到了乔叟、拜伦和莎士比亚等诗人和作家的名字。此外，一位"一战"时期阵亡的无名士兵也埋在这里。在一个尊重人才又不怎么折腾的国度里，就不奇怪科学和教育很发达了。

除了这些中学课本略有涉及的中世纪以后的历史时期之外，伦敦其实还拥有很多史前和罗马时期的遗址。我们在伦敦博物馆看到，人类早在45万年前就已经出现在伦敦，6万年前尼安德特人来到这里。公元前4000年，这里进入新石器时代，虽然这里仍然森林密布，但是居民已经开始生产陶器、种植农作物和饲养家畜。不过定居房屋还没有出现，说明他们仍然过着迁徙的生活。大约公元前2300年，冶金技术来到这里，不过主要用于制作奢侈品。都楠教授告诉笔者，泰晤士河和两岸经常出土铜器，但是没有发现当时的聚落，所以不能排除它们是古人故意扔在河里，献给水神的。其中武器多出自河中，而工具多出自陆地上的窖藏。小伍德寇特（Little Woodcote）窖藏就出土了43件竖銎斧，

13件有翼斧，2件剑刃和69件铜锭。其中有些竖銎斧很像塞伊玛—图尔宾诺现象的器物，都楠说把它们丢进后者的器物堆里，英国的考古学家不一定能分辨出来。在公元前1000至罗马人到来之前，这里的居民不少，只有少量的铜器。不过在罗马人到来之前，一些本地部落已经与罗马接触，说拉丁语，而不说凯特语。因此罗马人的到来，不完全是征服，因为部分部落已经罗马化了。不过罗马人来了以后，就建了伦敦城（Londonium），修了道路。罗马殖民者带来了新的建筑、道路、文字、雕刻、钱币、陶器和金属器，而本地的习俗和陶器工艺也延续下来。不过，真正从意大利来的殖民者很少，大部分士兵和商人可能来自德国、法国和英格兰本土。笔者问都楠，为什么罗马帝国要在这里建立殖民地？是因为受到了英格兰部落的威胁？还是为了英格兰的资源？都楠说这个问题不好回答。不过伦敦博物馆告诉我们，英格兰出产的羊毛、奴隶、铅和猎狗都是罗马帝国需要的商品。可惜时间仓促，没有看到盎格鲁—撒克逊时期和更晚的陈列。

三　大奥莫铜矿

离开伦敦博物馆，都楠就开车带我们直奔谢菲尔德市。第二天就前往威尔士，参观那里的一个青铜时代（2400BC—800BC）的采矿遗址大奥莫铜矿（Great Orme Mine）。向西出了谢菲尔德市，就进入匹克区国家公园（Peak District National Park）。这里属于英国的高地，实际上海拔只有300米。里面丘陵起伏，草原绵延，美不胜收。都楠一面开车，一面介绍。公园一部分为沙砾，只能长草；另一部分为石灰岩，可以耕种。这里有罗马时期的城堡和马路，与当时开采的巴斯通（Buxton）铅矿相连。公园内还有其他矿产资源，现在开发的有矿泉水和石灰岩，用于生产水泥。1951年国家公园成立，虽然土地并非属于国家，而是属于民间组织国家信托（National Trust，负责保护自然和文化遗产）、农场和公司，但是法律限制公园内的开发和建设。近几年，一些公司在协议到期后，因为没有续签，只好关门。公园内还有一些城镇和乡村，主要依靠养羊、矿泉水和旅游。14—18世纪，这里还曾

◇❖◇ 第五部分 欧亚考古见闻

经是羊毛纺织的中心，外地羊毛送到这里的小作坊加工；后来由于工业化，纺织中心转移到别处，但是小作坊延续了下来。此外，中国读者熟悉的名著《傲慢与偏见》中的许多场景就来自于德比郡境内部分。还有很多作家曾经在这里生活，在这里创作。有了美景和名人古迹，匹克区国家公园自然就成了一个旅游胜地。

　　离开了匹克区国家公园，过了曼彻斯特，我们不久就进入了威尔士。在国内一直不明白英国的政治体制，到了这里才知道。威尔士是个独立的国家，与苏格兰和英格兰一样，拥有自己的国会，但同属于英联邦。在13世纪，英格兰征服了威尔士；16世纪，英格兰吞并了威尔士，并将其纳入自己的法律体系。不过它仍然保持了自己的民族身份，自认为是五个凯尔特国家之一。虽然大多数人讲英语，但是威尔士拥有自己的语言和文字，与英语差别极大。都楠是爱尔兰人，不懂威尔士文，因为妻子懂，所以认得几个单词。威尔士词汇有一些很长的，为此都楠带我们在一个小镇的火车站停留了一下，让我们见识了这个小镇的名字："LLANFAIRPWLLGWYNGYLLGOGERYCHWYRNDROBWLLLLLANTYSILIOGOGOGOCH"。其长度堪比一个句子，事实上，它是一个带有很长定语的名词："The Church of Mary in the hollow of the White Hazel near the Fierce Whirlpool and the Church of Tysilio by the Red Cave"（图5-4-4）。

图5-4-4　威尔士的一个小镇（张良仁摄）

英国访问纪行

威尔士靠近大西洋，所以属于典型的海洋性气候。其特征就是一天之内天气变化多端，刚刚还是晴天，一会儿来了一片云，下起了雨，常年如此。所以一路上少见农田，而多见草场。威尔士多山，矿产资源（煤、铁和铜等）丰富。18世纪工业革命以后，威尔士一度成为采矿和重工业基地，但是1970年以后这些产业衰落，其经济开始转型。我们要去的大奥莫铜矿位于威尔士西北的兰迪德诺（Llandudno）半岛上。此处在维多利亚时代就修成了一个度假胜地，修了很多海湾宾馆和一条登山有轨电车。从山下到山上是一条陡坡，笔者从来没有想过电车还有如此之强的爬坡能力。大奥莫铜矿遗址就在山上，维多利亚时代曾大规模开采，废石填满了青铜时代的矿坑（图5-4-5）。遗址于1987年开始发掘，但是政府一直不愿出钱，所以当地人自己投资。铜矿在青铜时代开采到地下75米，可能到了水位就停止了。后来维多利亚时代继续下挖，到了100多米深，进入水位以下，直到抽水速度赶不上渗水速度为止。现在考古发掘还在继续，为了方便游客他们在里面打通了巷道，修了道路。矿脉很多，有的很窄，显然只有儿童才能进去；有的很大，成了一个巨大的山洞。在矿坑内他们发现了大量的石锤、兽骨和少量陶器。还有一些奇特的现象：第一，发现了成堆的石锤，没有用过，都楠认为它们不是实用的，而是礼仪用的；第二，在巷道内发现不少粉碎矿石的石砧；因为巷道内空间狭窄，光线昏暗，所以古代矿工一般把矿石运出去，在地面上粉碎矿石。从巷道的数量和体积来看，古代开采的矿石数量不小，保守估计达205—270吨。但是这些铜矿石去了哪里？遗址周围没有发现冶炼遗址。事实上，英国的古代铜矿很多，但是没有发现任何冶炼聚落。都楠说他们做

图5-4-5 Roger Doonan、水涛和作者在大奥莫铜矿巷道内（钱多多摄）

了很多地面调查，没有发现炉渣。不过，最新的一项同位素研究表明，来自大奥莫铜矿的铜料所生产的铜斧广泛见于不列颠和丹麦。

四　约克

第二天我们前往约克（York）。由谢菲尔德市往北，开车1个小时就到了。这个区域属于低地，一路都是平坦的平原，可见一片片油菜花地。这里的天气似乎也更为稳定，一天都是晴天，所以日照和热量更为充足，适合农业。谈到土地，都楠说过去每户人家都有一块大小不等的土地，并用篱笆圈起来，里面放羊或者种地，已经有一千多年的传统。但是近年来开始有公司收购土地，为了规模生产，它们拔掉了地块之间的篱笆。这样做虽然提高了生产效率，但是破坏了生态环境。

英国的许多城市以钢铁出名，但约克是个例外。它的经济以农业为主，但是让人想不到的是，它以巧克力著称。其生产历史已经有300多年，并且拥有不少世界名牌。本市也以丰富的历史古迹闻名，因此成了一个旅游胜地。考古学资料表明，人类在细石器时期，也就是公元前8000—前7000年开始在这里生活。在罗马人到来之前，这里活跃着罗马人所说的布里甘特（Brigantes）部落。公元71年，罗马人建造了第九军团军营，一开始是木构，后来改为石砌，位置在奥斯（Ouse）河和佛斯（Foss）河之间地势较高、视野开阔的三角形台地，时称艾伯拉肯（Eboracum）。此军营面积20万平方米，曾经居住6000名士兵。罗马皇帝哈德良（Hadrian，76—138年）、塞维鲁（Septimius Severus，145—211年）和康斯坦丁一世（Constantius I，250—306年）都曾在这里处理朝政，因此此城就是当时小不列颠的都城。康斯坦丁一世死于约克，其子康斯坦丁大帝（272—337年）就在这里登基。但是当时的宫殿一直没有发现，现在只见一根粗壮的石柱。在公元400前，连续不断的洪水把约克摧毁了。

约克的景点很多。现存的约克大教堂（York Minster）建成于1480年，属于哥特式建筑。建筑用精密切割的砂岩方块垒砌而成，展现了精美的尖锥体的角柱和门窗。这座教堂颇有来头，它不只是约克郡最重要的教堂，还是中世纪欧洲北部最大的教堂，地位仅次于坎特伯雷大教堂。离此不远就是约克郡博物馆。博物馆是新修的，侧重儿童教育，为此减少了展品。里面只有少量旧石器、新石器和青铜时代的石器，而且不少是私人捐赠品，没有出土背景。但是罗马时期的石雕、墓碑和陶器不少。在博物馆旁边有一段城墙，一端有十四角塔楼，基础为罗马时期的，所用红色的薄砖是该时期的特征。从博物馆走不远可见克里福德塔（Clifford's Tower）。塔也在两河交汇处，底部为圆形土丘，类似于冢墓。都楠说它可能是盎格鲁—萨克森时期修的。塔身最早是征服者威廉（William the Conqueror，1028—1087年）修建的，后来亨利八世于13世纪重修。我们拾阶而上，又从门道两侧的螺旋台阶爬到顶部的走道。在这里我们可以居高临下，看到周围的建筑。在这些建筑周围还围着一段老城墙，长约7.2千米。城墙也是方石垒砌的，本身不高，5米左右，但是下面垫土，高度有所提升。外侧有射击口，具有防御功能，样子与我国西安的明代城墙相似，但是规模无法相比。

五　谢菲尔德大学

回到谢菲尔德大学，开始我们的访问。说是访问，其实就是互相认识。说起来很巧，谢菲尔德大学几年前就和南京大学签了合作协议，合建了电子工程实验室，教师和学生开始合作研究和教学互换。巧的是，这两年一位南京去的学生钱多多进入该校学习，然后就极力撺掇他的导师都楠与南大合作。正好都楠在俄罗斯乌拉尔山的田野项目要收尾，正在寻找新的项目，于是就答应了。这样都楠和同事代（Peter Day）于前年来华访问，今年1月访问南大，然后约好4月我们回访。都楠说校长本涅特（Keith Burnett）是个中国通，认识副总理刘延东和南大校长陈骏，习近平主席访英时曾经参与会见。对于我们的考古合作，他非常支持。此次很遗憾他在美国访问，没有见面。

没来英国之前，笔者还真不了解谢菲尔德大学的情况。这是一所1897年由三所学校合并而成的大学，时称谢菲尔德大学学院，1905年改为现名。在英国和世界都享有盛誉，拥有五名诺贝尔奖奖金获得者。

◇❖◇　第五部分　欧亚考古见闻

全球排名 80（QS 世界大学排名 2015—2016 年），英国排名 16；2011 年因学生体验优秀获得泰晤士高等教育"年度大学"称号。该校考古系成立于 1964 年，科林·伦福儒（Colin Renfrew）曾经在这里工作过七年，后来从这里去了剑桥大学。后来又有一些教师流失；前几年伦敦大学学院（UCL）花重金挖走了四名教师，其中就有发掘巨石阵遗址的皮特森教授（Mike Peterson）。历年来该系毕业的博士生到剑桥、牛津和其他高校工作，成为各机构的骨干力量。

　　考古系在谢菲尔德大学是个大系，原来拥有两栋楼，这几年因为经济危机，失去了一栋楼。但就是这样，在一所大学能够拥有一栋楼并不多见。我们参观了整个楼，才知道它为什么需要一栋楼。在本楼内，除了教室，还有众多标本室。该系从一开始，就注重收集标本，现有人骨、动物骨骼、鱼类、植物标本室，占据了本楼的大部分空间（图 5-4-6）。动物骨骼标本室有马、牛和羊等各类动物的各个部位的骨骼。这些标本室就是该系的宝贝，吸引了英国和欧洲的考古学家前来访问和研究。该系还有许多实验室，除了上述标本室附带的实验室，还有都楠和代教授的岩相、金相和扫描电镜实验室；实验室没有专门的实验员，研究生们经过导师的训练后，自己动手做实验，自己分析数据。此外，都楠还搞了一些实验考古学，让学生自己冶炼与铸造和烧陶器；在访问

图 5-4-6　谢菲尔德大学的动物标本室（张良仁摄）

期间，我们就看到学生们在制作铜斧的木柄。教师们为此做出了巨大的牺牲，他们或者合用一间办公室，或者只有一间小办公室。

由于可以接触标本和充分的动手机会，该系很受世界各国学生的欢迎。其中有四个中国学生，一个在南京见过。随便聊了几句，他们在国内学的是财会、化学、艺术史，很喜欢这里的实验教学。在今年公布的QS排名中，该系为全球13强，在英国排名第二，仅次于UCL（别忘了UCL挖走了谢菲尔德大学的师资）。所以系里搞了简单的庆祝活动，因此我们见到了搞动物考古的阿尔巴雷拉（Umberto Albarella）教授，也见到了搞植物考古的琼斯（Glynis Jones）教授。琼斯教授在土耳其的查塔尔土丘（Chatal Hoyuk）工作过，但是主要在欧洲工作，研究农作物的传播。她有个学生可能对我们的伊朗项目感兴趣。笔者原来担心英伊关系，都楠为此询问过别人，老太太也证实，英国在伊朗有个研究所，只不过伊斯兰革命以后人员收缩，但是还在运作。

谢菲尔德始建于罗马时期，是个历史名城，也是个钢铁城市，还是不锈钢的发源地。现在钢铁生产已经衰落了，不过文化遗产还是不少。离开谢菲尔德的早上，都楠特意带我们去了一家传统的制剑作坊。谢菲尔德过去有很多铸剑作坊，现在只剩下一家，成了一家博物馆。在这里我们首先看到了打剑房，由水轮驱动巨大的齿轮，带动硕大的铁锤将铁剑锤打成形（图5-4-7）。旁边是炼铁炉，坩埚用本地特有的土壤制作，用一次就废，所以积攒了很多新坩埚。其形状为炮弹形，类似于炼锌的坩埚。不过做坩埚时他们用铁质模子，塞进浆土后，用铁杵一次挤压成形。旁边还有加工铁剑和磨剑的作坊。都楠说这里的手工剑是礼仪用剑，客户大多是各国的国家元首和将军。他们有时会亲自来这里看加工过程，所以成了本地的一景。一大早只有一个人上班，伺候炉子，加工剑的配件。于

图5-4-7 谢菲尔德市传统铸剑作坊的打剑房（张良仁摄）

是与他寒暄了几句，正要转身离去，都楠揭开了桌上的一张纸，原来是两把精美的小刀，是送给我们的礼物。这是他事先安排好的，目的是为了给我们一个惊喜。谁说英国男人只会打个雨伞戴个礼帽扮绅士，没有情调和幽默？

六　剑桥

　　虽然剑桥大学的名气如雷贯耳，但是实际上并不了解。都楠一路介绍了一些情况，回国后笔者自己又上维基百科补课。当年一部分牛津大学的学者不满当时的国王，跑到了剑桥这个平坦潮湿的沼泽地，于1209年成立了剑桥大学，2009年是该校建校800周年。1231年，国王亨利三世给予自主管理权力，并给予它和牛津以垄断地位。因此一直到19世纪，英国只有这两所大学。15世纪，人文主义思想传播到剑桥，带来了希腊和希伯来语言学和文学。从此剑桥不仅培养牧师，而且培养学者。17世纪，剑桥已经成为一个思想活跃、辩论盛行的地方。还是学生的克伦威尔接触到了加尔文教，于1640年以一票的优势被选进议会，后来改变了英国的历史，因此这"一票既毁了教会也毁了国王"。王室复辟以后，不改成命，让剑桥继续拥有自主管理权力。同时，笛卡尔思想来到剑桥，带来了自然科学，也带来了牛顿这颗明星。1870年，当时的校长资助了一所实验室，就是卡文迪什实验室（Cavendish Laboratory）；此时哲学、经济和自然科学发达，涌现出了达尔文（Charles Darwin）、培根（Francis Bacon）、罗素（Bertrand Russel）、凯恩斯（John Maynard Keynes）和维特根斯坦（Ludwig Wittgenstein）等学者。

　　剑桥大学的体制非常独特。它拥有31所学院，学院高度自治，但是遵守统一的章程，因此它是一个松散的学院联合体。大学经费来自国家拨款，而学院则为国王、王后和公爵捐资建立，拥有地产或者其他资产，募集捐款，自负盈亏。在英国有个说法，在剑桥和牛津之间，一个人是走不出两校的土地的。大学负责研究生招生，而学院负责本科生招生。大学负责所有学生的教学、考试和学位，而学院负责学生的生活。一个学院拥有许多学科的学者，而大学的各个专业、系或学院可以见到不同学院的学者。剑桥大学拥有114个图书馆，分布在各个学院、系和研究所。最大的是大学图书馆，拥有800万册图书；它也是一座"版权图书馆"，全英国的出版社，都要寄一本新出的书给它，所以该图书馆的藏书非常丰富（图5-4-8）。剑桥大学出版社，也是世界第二大大学出版社，每年出版5万册图书、学术期刊和教材，每年向大学上缴为数不少的收益。只是图书定价太高，很让学者们诟病。

徜徉在剑桥大学校园，让人觉得处在仙境（fairyland）之中。移步易景，处处是古老而精致的哥特式建筑，在在为大片而整齐的草坪，让人流连忘返。都楠说剑桥不似人间，笔者很赞同。我

图5-4-8 剑桥大学图书馆（张良仁摄）

们这次没有矫情，直接奔往国王学院前面的康河和草坪。那里是徐志摩写《再别康桥》的地方，也是林徽因驻足的地方。我们没有找到林徽因的脚印，但是看到了一块纪念碑，上面刻着徐志摩的诗句"轻轻地我走了，正如我轻轻地来，我挥一挥衣袖，不带走一片云彩。"在李约瑟研究所所长梅建军的带领下，我们参观了国王学院的教堂（图5-4-9）。此教堂是亨利七世以后经历三代国王，前后90年修成的教堂。屋顶高敞，线条精细，两侧窗户装了很多色彩斑斓的玻璃画。这些都是原来的天主教留下来的。剑桥是基督教改革的中心，教堂原先的雕像也都拆掉了。这里的唱诗班很有名，每年英国广播公司（BBC）都会来直播。

我们本来想参观麦当劳考古研究所，结果那天学校还在放假，没有见到伦福儒和琼斯教授（Martin Jones），也没有看成实验室。剑桥大学还有许多博物馆和独立的研究所。中国人民大学的一位老师现在这里访问，说她所在的古代印度和伊朗信托（Ancient India and Iran Trust）有

第五部分 欧亚考古见闻

图 5-4-9 剑桥大学国王学院的教堂（张良仁摄）

许多中亚和伊朗的藏书，所以约了她去参观。路上经过菲兹威廉博物馆（Fitzwilliam Museum），由于时间有限，迅速进去看了一眼，里面的近东和埃及文物不少。然后到古代印度和伊朗信托。这是一栋住宅小楼，里面陈放着五个学者收藏的图书，覆盖印度、中亚和伊朗。1978年，他们觉得英国学术界忽略了这些区域，既缺少研究机构，也缺少教席，所以就买了这栋楼，成立这个信托，借以推动这些领域的发展。他们把自己的图书集中放在这里，举办学术会议和讲座，接待访问学者，甚至资助了几个研究项目，如巴基斯坦考古发掘、《摩尼教字典》和《大夏年代学》的出版。图书馆的书很多，放了好几间屋子，还有不少重本、抽印本、手稿等。由于缺乏经费，他们把后面的一套房屋出租了，这位老师就住在那里，方便用图书馆。她整天泡在图书馆，研究国内发现的粟特文书。来国外访问的国内学者中不少忙着生孩子逛风景，让外国同行非常厌恶，而她的出现让他们看到了另一类中国学者。

在剑桥访问，当然不能错过蜚声中国的李约瑟研究所。研究所坐落在一个小花园内，里面樱花正烂漫地开着。李约瑟（Joseph Needham）原本学化学，早年因出版《化学胚胎学》当选为英国皇家学会会员。1937年认识鲁桂珍，一见钟情，也对中国科学史发生了兴趣；他当时已经娶了一个老婆，但是两人没有离婚；老婆死后，李约瑟把情人转正；最后三人的骨灰都埋在了一起，这样三人的爱情都修成了正果。

1943—1946 年，李约瑟以外交官的身份来华，长途旅行，收集资料，并结识了郭沫若和竺可桢。在中国助手王铃的帮助下，出版了15卷《中国科学和文明》（后面几卷由其他学者完成），得到了中外学术界的赞誉。1971 年当选为人文科学院院士，1992 年获得女王颁发的荣誉同伴者勋衔，集三个荣誉于一身，在英国学术界罕见。梅建军教授带我们参观了整个研究所。他说《中国科技和文明》已经出了 27 本，现在他在编写有色金属卷（图 5-4-10）。李约瑟时代的陈设和鲁桂珍的办公室都还在。办公楼后面是一个花园，走廊曲折，小桥流水，竹木扶疏，深得中国花园的精髓。梅建军说该研究所也是个独立的单位，自负盈亏。其成立就是有人捐款买了地，又修了楼，捐款者大多为华人。现在的运转就是基金在支撑，当然，研究所还要继续募捐，以求发展。该所现在每年都会邀请一些博士后和学者来访问，今年邀请的大多数是搞中国建筑史的。

图 5-4-10　27 本已出版的《中国科技和文明》（张良仁摄）

七　牛津

离开剑桥，我们就前往牛津。和剑桥一样，牛津是个大学城；但是和剑桥不一样，它更像人间，绿地不多，街道拥挤。因为拥挤，学生宿舍和实验室都在步行或者自行车可达范围。其创立年代不明，但是有证据表明 1096 年就有人在此教书，因此它是世界上第二古老的大学。1167 年，由于国王亨利二世禁止英格兰学生去巴黎大学上学，他们别无选择，牛津因此发展迅速。1209 年，由于前述原因，部分学者跑到剑桥成立了剑桥大学；这两所英国最古老的大学因此合称为"牛桥（Oxbridge）"。与

◇❖◇ 第五部分 欧亚考古见闻

剑桥一样，它起初是个教会大学，许多教派在这里生根发展；同时，一些贵族捐资建立学院来满足自己的需要。15世纪以后，文艺复兴思想流入，带来了希腊语研究。在英国内战期间（1642—1649年），牛津曾经是保王党的堡垒，但是18世纪以后，它就不卷入政治了。19世纪以后，经过一系列改革，神学要求（信仰和崇拜）逐渐退出，科学和医学研究得到强化。现在它拥有38个独立学院，其运作方式与剑桥相同，这里不再赘述。与剑桥不同的是，该校为研究生提供奖学金。它也拥有世界上最大的大学出版社。

牛津大学的罗森教授（Dame Jessica Rawson）是个举世闻名的汉学家，研究兴趣很广，从西周青铜器到汉代玉器，都曾耕耘，成果颇丰。她原先在大英博物馆工作，1994年到牛津大学，2010年退休。但是退休以后，她继续做研究，而且将自己的研究领域扩展到了欧亚草原。为了接待我们，她专门安排了为期一天的工作坊。原来西北大学的一个学生刘睿良在等候我们。他说留学前曾经咨询我，笔者说了句"要自信"，让他记忆至今。在实验室稍坐一会儿，笔者在美国加州大学洛杉矶分校（UCLA）的师妹安可（Anke Hein）、罗森、台湾来的留学生徐幼刚和其导师帕拉德（Mark Pollard）陆续来到。简单介绍之后，就到楼下报告厅。笔者先讲新疆东部的古代冶金，主要讲分期和人群迁徙问题。罗森和帕拉德（Mark Pollard）不断插话，说对笔者的分期没有意见，但可以用他们的方法来回答我的问题，让人很想知道他们的方法。后来根据都楠的提议，笔者又介绍了我们去年在俄罗斯和伊朗的工作。

下午继续报告。帕拉德讲了他们的火焰（FLAME）计划，目的是要做器物群的历史，意思是要追踪器物的变迁史，即金属器的再利用和重熔（图5-4-11）。做这个项目需要大量的微量元素和铅同位素数据。在这方面他们拥有欧洲的5万个数据，俄罗斯的5000多个，伊朗和阿富汗也有一些。他们的方法是把砷（As）等四种元素的组合为铜器分了16组。其中第二组砷铜在欧洲的分布很有意思，它集中分布在西班牙和希腊，也就是欧洲的东西两端，说明两个区域各有原料来源。在中国，刘睿良收集整理了7000个数据（其中赛克勒博物馆的较多），分别作了商和西周铜器组的分布图，可以看到一些有意思的现象。在欧亚草原，徐幼刚整理了一些数据，得到了一些结果。他们感到遗憾的是，中国取样难，数据少。他承认重熔金属（recycling）很复杂，但是他似乎有了办法。他用了一个案例，说明用锶同位素可以揭示两个来源的铜器重熔混合以后得到了一个新产品。之后笔者讲了卡拉苏克文化冶金技术向中国北方传播的路线问题，罗森大概听了很高兴，还问笔者发表了没有。

图 5-4-11　牛津大学的古代冶金工作坊 从右向左：水涛、罗森、徐幼刚、帕拉德、安可、都楠、张良仁（钱多多摄）

八　巨石阵

巨石阵举世闻名，好奇心驱使我们把它列入我们的参观项目之一。我们访问了牛津大学之后，就前往巨石阵。出了古香古色的牛津，就是一望无际的低山丘陵。随着道路的盘旋起伏，一片片泛绿的草地和一条条篱笆树迎面而来，里面的羊群或者吃草或者休憩，悠闲自得。英国从中世纪开始就把草场分隔成豆腐块，然后种篱笆树或垒砌石墙，至今已有一千多年。不过现在出现了一些大农场，为了方便规模经营，拔掉了篱笆树，拆掉了石墙，形成了大片的农田。巨大的天空像个穹隆盖住了整个大地，一簇簇雪堆絮叠的云团遮挡着蓝天，

第五部分　欧亚考古见闻

一如在西伯利亚大草原。今天天气不好，一大早就乌云密布，时而飘来雨滴，凉风阵阵，让人不胜寒冷。但是在英国待了几天的我们已经习惯了这样的阴阳天气。而阳光和热量不足，恐怕是英国农田和人口稀少的原因。

我们的汽车走了两个小时，就到了威尔特郡的巨石阵（Stonehenge）。Stonehenge 一名见于 11 世纪的英国文献，时称"Stanheng"，意为悬挂的石头，离萨里斯伯里镇（Salisbury）不远。遗址位于萨里斯伯里平原的小岗之上，周围人烟稀少，"in the middle of nowhere"。不过巨石阵举世闻名，引来了一辆又一辆的旅游大巴。现在一家公司经营着这处景点，修了旅游中心，买了中巴，把游客送到巨石阵附近。一下车就看见了高大的巨石阵，众多游客熙熙攘攘，沿着规划好的路线观赏拍照。

巨石阵因其壮观而引人注目。17 世纪，就有一些古物学家发掘这个遗址；20 世纪以后一些考古学家又做了更为仔细的发掘，对它的认识也逐渐深入，发现它是一个埋葬和祭祀遗址。在这里最早出现的是细石器时代的 4 根或 5 根木柱（8000BC），木柱已经腐烂，只留下柱洞。它们位于巨石阵附近，洞径很大，达 75 厘米。这样的遗迹在英国只此一例，但是在斯堪的纳维亚发现若干。3100BC，也就是新石器时代，人们开挖了一圈环壕，直径 110 米；又用挖出的白垩土堆成了一圈土堤，但是留出了南北两个通道。环壕内可见一圈 56 个土坑，直径 1 米。它们原来也许栽了木柱，形成一个柱圈，但是现在没有证据。这些土坑原先埋了 63 具火葬人骨，经过性别和年龄鉴定，里面有成年男女和儿童。发掘者发现土坑底部经过重压，因此推测原来埋过石柱，用于标记墓葬位置。3000BC，由南北通道往里又埋了一排木柱，同时 25 个前期柱洞内又埋入了火葬人骨，此外还有 30 处火葬遗迹，因此环壕内成了火葬墓地。

真正的巨石阵始建于 2600BC；此时人们抛弃了木柱，改用石柱。他们在中央挖了两周柱坑，这些柱坑原来埋了 80 根石柱，但是今天只见到 43 根。所用的石柱为蓝色，每根 2 吨重，2 米高，系从 240 千米以外的威尔士的普蕾瑟利山（Preseli Hills）运来的。2011 年，人们在这里发现了巨大的采石场，证实了巨石阵蓝色石柱的来源地。此时北门得到扩建，以便观察夏至日出和冬至日落时的阳光。此门内外可能还立了别的石柱。同时一条通向阿旺（Avon）河的大道（Stonehenge Avenue）修成。此路由平行的浅沟和土棱构成，长达3千米。原谢菲尔德大学的皮特森教授认为，古人沿着这条道路到巨石阵祭祀祖先。在此后的2600BC—2400BC期间，75根巨型砂岩石材相继运到这里，形成了巨石阵。它们可能来自以北40千米处的马波若山（Marlborough Downs）。石柱经过加工，上面像木柱和木梁那样做出榫和卯，然后立起，顶部再加30根砂岩横梁。每根石柱4.1米高，25吨重；两根石柱的间距是1米。这样的石圈直径是33米。在石圈内，还有5组双石柱+横梁，形成一个马蹄形，开口向东北方向。这些石材更大，重达50吨，高6—7.3米不等（图5-4-12）。在其中一些砂岩石柱上雕刻出了短剑和斧子，其雕刻年代不明，但是器形是青铜时代的。皇家艺术学院（Royal College of Art）的研究者发现，部分石块在敲击之后发出很大的不断变化的回声。

图5-4-12 巨石阵（张良仁摄）

2400BC以后，当地就进入了青铜时代。这一阶段人们把精力集中在巨石阵的蓝石圈上。他们首先在外圈砂岩石柱之间立了一圈蓝石柱，其顶部也加工出榫，说明上面原先也有横梁。后来又在内外圈砂岩石柱之间又立了一圈蓝石柱,在内圈以内立了一圈马蹄形蓝石柱,其上没有经过修整,原来没有横梁。在此圈蓝石柱内移入了一块祭石。但是本期蓝石柱根基不稳,很快就倒了。不过在巨石阵周围出现了很多土冢。再往后(1930BC—1600BC),蓝石柱圈的东北部分移走,形成一个马蹄形,与中心的砂岩石柱圈对应。

九　埃夫伯里

　　巨石阵不是本地区唯一的此类遗址。我们在巨石阵之前,已经看过了北面17千米的埃夫伯里(Avebury)遗址。其年代也是新石器时代,也是世界文化遗产,如今也是一个旅游胜地,但是另有一番味道。遗址周围同样为低山丘陵,如今为成片的草场,但是在细石器时代(9600BC—5800BC)这里长满森林。在此时期,英国与欧洲大陆连为一体,居住着狩猎—采集人群。遗迹和遗物都很少,只是在埃夫伯里以西300米处发现了一些细石器,表明这里原有他们的宿营地。4000BC,农作物和家畜传入英国,人们开始定居,过去的森林带逐渐退缩。这里也出现了石器、动物骨骼和陶器。埃夫伯里遗址的出现表明人们已经拥有农业生产,否则无法投入浩大的人力物力到遗址的建设中。外围挖一圈宽12—15米,深达10米的环壕,挖出的土堆在环壕以外形成土堤,里面有一圈巨石组成的圆圈,直径331米,是英国最大的石圈。有人认为石圈原有98块砂岩石柱,高达6米,重达40吨有余(图5-4-13)。其建造年代可能在2870BC—2200BC之间。人们发现,这些巨石可以发出回声。中央又有两个小石圈,北面的直径98米,但是今天只剩下了四

图5-4-13　埃夫伯里遗址(张良仁摄)

根,其中只有两根是立着的。其内侧还有三根石柱,开口向东北。南面的直径108米,石柱保存得更少。究其原因,就是中世纪的基督教

对本地的异教遗迹深感烦恼，所以搞了大规模的破坏活动。由环壕向两侧延伸出两条胡须般的道路，道路竖立两排巨石。在大石圈以南，还有一个大型土山西尔伯里（Silbury），高达 40 米左右，据 Lonely Planet 说，它是欧洲最大的土方工程。遗址没有出土重要的器物，其用途不得而知。尽管缺乏遗物，与巨石阵一样，人们推测整个遗址群是一个祭祀用的场所。

十　西肯尼特长冢

在大型土堆以南不远处，是一座新石器时代的西肯尼特长冢（West Kennet Long Barrow）。墓葬位于山冈上，公元前 3500 年开始建造，持续使用到 2500BC。整个长冢像一根法式面包，形体很长，达 100 米，是英格兰最大的一座。入口处用巨石搭建墓口，里面有一条通道，两侧对称分布着若干大石块砌筑的石室，放置人骨。19 世纪的古物学家做了发掘，发现了 46 具人骨，其中有婴儿和老年人。这些人骨杂乱无章，部分头骨和肢骨已经遗失，说明古人定期把人骨移出长冢，然后再捡拾部分骨骼放回原处。在青铜时代，人们又在墓口处立了几块巨石，将其封堵，结束了长期的埋葬行为。

十一　结语

看完西肯尼特长冢，我们继续上路，向希斯罗机场方向前进。中途看了一个早期铁器时代的城址和一个新石器时代的长冢（图 5-4-14），晚上在一个斯温顿（Swindon）的小镇过夜，没想到在这里找到了一家中餐厅。第

图 5-4-14　新石器时代长冢（张良仁摄）

◇❖◇ 第五部分 欧亚考古见闻

二天，我们中的一部分去了温莎城堡，笔者则去了大英博物馆，继续使命；都楠也该回谢菲尔德大学上课了。第三天，我们带着满满的英国考古、博物馆、大学和风土人情方面的新知识，踏上了返回南京的飞机，我们历时 14 天的访问也就结束了。

中伊合作考古，续写丝路故事*

为什么到伊朗考古？伊朗不仅是古代文明的起源地之一，而且是文化交流的十字路口，连接了西方的地中海、东方的中国、北方的欧亚草原和南方的印度河流域，在历史时期的"丝绸之路"上扮演着重要角色。

一 伊朗史前文化的待解之谜

伊朗在史前时期所扮演的文化摇篮和通道角色，迄今尚未深入研究。早期作物、驯化动物、冶金、彩陶和土坯建筑的传播路线至今仍是未解之谜，最基础的史前文化序列也未建立，绝对年代数据存在相当多的缺环，而古代陶器、冶金术、建筑技术都存在研究空白。虽然与周边区域的联系，包括戈尔干平原、中央高原、土库曼斯坦西南部已有所涉及，但有关长距离交流，如我国新疆，则成果寥寥。这些工作都需要依赖未来田野发掘工作的进一步开展。

2016年3月，南京大学与伊朗文化遗产和旅游研究所（RICHT）签订了为期五年的合作协议。同年11—12月，南京大学和伊朗文化遗产、手工和旅游组织北呼罗珊省办公室（相当于我国的省文物局）组成的中伊联合考古队发掘了纳德利土丘（Tepe Naderi）（图5-5-1）。这座大型土丘位于科佩达格山脉南麓，靠近土库曼斯坦，所以古代丝绸之路的旅行者要前往近东和罗马，它是必经之路。近年来，当地的文化遗产管理部门计划保护纳德利土丘，但是各种资料都非常匮乏。于是我们决定发掘这座土丘，为该遗址的保护工作铺路。

---

* 本文原刊于《光明日报》2017年2月28日第12版。收入本书时略有改动。作者为：张良仁、水涛。

◇❖◇ 第五部分 欧亚考古见闻

图 5-5-1 纳德利土丘（水涛摄）

　　土丘是近东、伊朗、中亚和南亚特有的聚落形式。一个土丘累积了几个时代的生活遗存，前后跨越几百年，甚至几千年。这种遗址在整个伊朗广泛分布，包括干旱且山洪频发的中央高原、湿润且土壤肥沃的戈尔干平原以及高海拔的山地。但在我国新疆，尽管地貌环境与伊朗极其相似，至今还未发现土丘遗址。

　　为什么伊朗古代居民要把房址建立在之前的废墟上，而不是换一个位置？他们这么做是为了躲避在干旱地区破坏性极强的山洪，还是长久以来形成的文化选择？关于这个问题，前人的研究很少。此外，北呼罗珊省是如何参与长距离文化往来的？历史时期尤其是中世纪，北呼罗珊省的居民在远距离交流中发挥了重要作用，其绿松石和青金石贸易闻名于世。那么在史前，这条交流通道是如何发展起来的？在驯化绵羊、黄牛、小麦、大麦从伊朗到中亚甚至到东亚的东传，以及水稻、小米从中国向伊朗向欧洲的西进中，北呼罗珊省又扮演了怎样的角色？近东起源的冶金技术、彩陶和土坯建筑又如何传播到中亚、南亚和我国西部？

　　这些未解之谜，有待考古发掘的成果来解决。

二　延续六千年的土丘

纳德利土丘规模巨大，历史久远。根据前人的地表调查，它是一圆形土丘，使用年限从铜石并用时代（公元前4500—前3600年）一直延续到伊斯兰时期（公元651年至今），前后延续5000多年。19世纪，土丘顶部还有城堡，周围还有一圈城墙，但是这些城堡已经消失，而城墙坍塌殆尽。

怎样发掘这样一个大型土丘？中伊联合考古队制订了一个长期工作计划，逐步收集资料，研究上述问题。2016年11—12月，中伊联合考古队做了为期24天的田野工作。首先做了全面调查，经测绘，土丘基础的最大直径达185米，土丘现存高度为20米，底部在现存地面以下5米。最后，发掘了一条长29米的探沟，跨越土

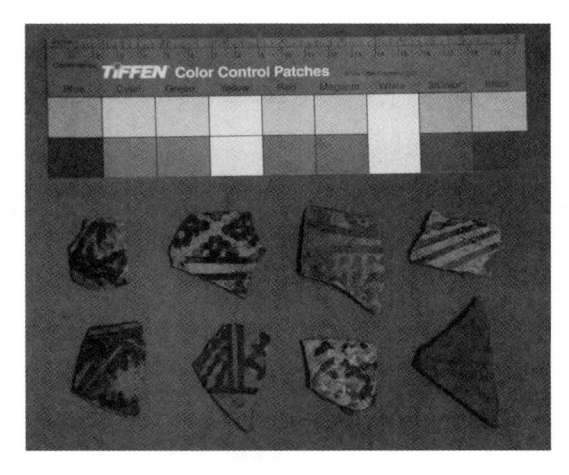

图 5-5-2　中亚纳马兹加风格彩陶
（张良仁摄）

丘内外，由此发现了从铜石并用时代到伊斯兰时期的文化堆积。其中伊斯兰时期的土坯墙和两层淤土非常引人注意，说明这里曾经两次长时间积水，因此留下了很厚的淤土；而在积水离去之后，人们又在这里活动，留下了陶片和兽骨等遗物。在铜石并用时代和青铜时代的文化堆积中，考古队发现了土库曼斯坦纳马兹加风格的彩陶（图5-5-2）和里海南岸戈尔干平原的灰陶，揭示了伊朗北呼罗珊省与中亚和戈尔干平原之间的文化联系。

更有意思的是，我们在一个伊斯兰时期的灰坑发现了一件青花砂胎碗（图5-5-3）。青花瓷是我国元朝创烧的瓷器，一部分青花就是用伊朗进口的钴料烧成的，在明清时代大量出口到欧洲。伊朗曾经属于蒙元时期的伊尔汗国，青花瓷器也自然大行其道。不过，伊朗人

第五部分　欧亚考古见闻

图5-5-3　仿烧青花砂胎器（张良仁摄）

并不满足于从中国进口青花瓷，而是开始仿烧青花砂胎器，15世纪更为普遍。这次发现的青花砂胎碗就是一件仿烧品，碗的造型和花纹都有意模仿中国产品，但是技术没有学到家，花纹简单而且模糊。其实在伊朗历史上，这不是第一次学习中国的陶瓷技术：在11和12世纪，伊朗人就从中国宋代的单色瓷吸收灵感，烧出了光泽油亮的釉陶。

三　接触和交流

图5-5-4　传授钻探技术（马强摄）

这次中伊考古合作，不仅是一次学术合作，而且是一次考古工作方法的交流。我方不仅有发掘人员、测绘人员和科技考古学家，还带去了探沟发掘法和钻探技术。在伊朗，无论本国的还是外国的考古学家，一般采用2米见方的探方，从土丘顶部往下一直挖到生土。这种方法能够获得地层，但是无法解决其他问题。这次采用了大探沟发掘法，发掘了一条长达29米、宽2米的探沟，是一次全新的尝试。这种方法不仅可以获得地层资料，而且可以获得较大范围人类活动的信息。这次合作也引进了中国的钻探技术。钻探是我国考古学家调查遗址的传统方法，在发掘一座遗址以前做全面的钻探，以便了解整个遗址（墓葬、居址）的范围和地层。而过去伊朗考古学家一般采用小探方发掘来了解一座土丘的范围和深度，费时而且费力，无法大规模实施。我方带去了探铲和精通钻探技术的研究人员，手把手将钻探技术传授给伊朗同行（图5-5-4）。在传授过程中，双方完成了一系列工作，既了解了纳德利土丘的范围，也了解了土丘周围的文化层。

　　伊朗介于地中海文明与东亚文明、欧亚草原文明与印度文明之间。19世纪就有欧洲学者前往发掘，但对于丝绸之路国际学术界的研究还非常有限，而有关史前丝绸之路的研究更是微乎其微。纳德利土丘的发掘，由于其优良的地理位置和漫长的历史，将为我们探讨古代丝绸之路、冶金技术、农作物和家畜传播，提供大量的新鲜资料。在伊朗，我国投入的学术力量很少，只有若干研究波斯文学和语言的学者，研究伊朗历史的几乎没有，研究伊朗考古的更是空白。而在历史上，两国曾经发生过密切的文化联系，与现在冷淡的学术研究形成了冰火两重天。现在我国学者到伊朗做考古工作，才迈出了第一步。不过，这次中伊合作，除了研究古代丝绸之路，还交流了发掘方法和钻探技术，因而延续了丝绸之路的精神：接触和交流。

一杯红茶一个馕　一把手铲方中忙
——南京大学赴伊朗考古记（一）*

"一箪疏食一壶浆，一卷诗书树下凉。"这是波斯诗人海亚姆（Omar Khayyam，1048—1122 年）的一句脍炙人口的诗。夏季的伊朗高原炎热干燥，在树荫下纳凉读书，自然是一件惬意的事情。可惜，这不是我们中伊联合考古队能够享受到的。

我们南京大学师生和其他成员于 2016 年 11 月 17 日乘飞机前往伊朗，由北京而阿布扎比而德黑兰而马什哈德，马不停蹄地折腾了二十几个小时，于当地时间凌晨两点到达目的地希尔凡市。希尔凡市位于伊朗的东北部，阿特拉克河上游（Atrek Valley），北侧为科佩特山（Kopet Dagh），翻过山就是土库曼斯坦的首都阿什哈巴德，南侧是阿拉山（Ala Dagh）。阿拉山的南侧是丝绸之路上的一个重要部分——"伟大的呼罗珊之路"。它还有个更为著名的名字——青金石之路。著名的希萨尔土丘（Tepe Hissar）在青铜时代就是一个重要的矿石中转与加工中心，也是一个金属冶炼和奢侈品贸易中心；距希萨尔遗址不远的桑—依—恰克马克（Sang-e-Chakhmaq）是一处新石器遗址，从这个遗址得到的材料来看，伊朗东北部与大麦、小麦的传播以及小麦的二次驯化有着重要联系。

我们来到希尔凡市，是为了发掘这里的纳德利土丘（Tepe Naderi）（图 5 - 6 - 1）（彩图 19）。这是一座大型土丘，是伊朗东北部最大的土丘之一，纳德利在波斯语中意为"与国王有关的"。但是有关这座土丘的历史，文献资料非常匮乏，我们并不知道哪位国王在这里生活

---

* 本文原刊于《中国文物报》2017 年 2 月 24 日第 7 版。收入本书时略有改动。作者为：刘彬彬、张良仁。

一杯红茶一个馕　一把手铲方中忙　◇❖◇

图 5-6-1　纳德利土丘雪景（佚名摄）

过。只是在 19 世纪，恺加王朝的国王纳赛尔丁来过此地，其随从留下了一些文字描述和照片。根据这些资料，我们知道纳德利土丘的顶部曾经存在一座城堡，周围还有一圈带有四十座瞭望塔的围墙。但是现存的只是一座近 20 米高、最大底径达 185 米的孤独土丘，上面的城堡已经无影无踪，而围墙也只剩下了残垣断壁。近几年，当地的文物主管部门计划保护这座土丘，修建遗址博物馆，为此移除了土丘上面的电视塔，并邀请我们前往发掘（图 5-6-2）。

虽然现在只有一座土丘，但是还有许多工作要做。20 世纪 70 年代，意大利的都灵大学曾在阿特拉克上游做过调查与发掘工作，纳德利土丘也是调查对象之一。根据调查结果，该土丘目前已知的史前遗存最早为纳马兹加二期（铜石并用时代）的彩陶，一直延续到铁器时代的

图 5-6-2　伊朗国会议员来访（Ali Sayyed 摄）

· 527 ·

第五部分 欧亚考古见闻

亚兹文化（Yaz）。阿特拉克上游在新石器至早期铁器时代，与中亚绿洲的定居文明有着密切联系，哲通（Djeitun）、安诺（Anau）以及纳马兹加（Namazga）风格的彩陶、阿姆河文明（Oxus Civilization，即BMAC）的墓葬在这一区域都有所发现。目前已知年代最早的定居遗址为亚姆土丘（Tepe Yam），距今约7000年。为什么土库曼斯坦西南阿塔克（Atak）低地地区的因素出现在伊朗高原边缘地区，而且如此之早且又如此频繁？在阿契美尼德（Akhmenid）、帕提亚（Parthian）和萨珊王朝，这个区域又有哪些远距离的文化交流？这些都是学术界困惑已久的问题。

土丘是广泛存在于中亚、近东、南亚甚至地中海地区的一类聚落。中国社会科学院考古研究所近年在乌兹别克斯坦发掘的明铁佩遗址（Ming Tepe）、斯坦福大学在土耳其发掘的恰塔霍裕克遗址（Çatalhöyük）都是这类聚落。它们不同于国内苏皖浙的土墩墓，一般包含多个时期的建筑，而各个时期的建筑由下至上依次叠压，形成了山包的样子。在伊朗，无论是在干旱少雨的伊朗高原，还是在潮湿闷热的戈尔干平原，这种土丘随处可见。而在我国新疆，地貌和气候条件与伊朗高原相近，却没有发现一座土丘。我们不禁好奇：为什么伊朗的古人选择在过去的废墟上修建房屋？要知道，在废墟修建房屋是个费时费力的事情；比起废墟，在原始地面上修建村落要容易得多，伊朗地广人稀，为什么不换个地方？

我们的田野工作自然是围绕着土丘展开。我们与伊朗文化遗产、手工业和旅游组织北呼罗珊省办公室（相当于我国的省文物局）组成了中伊联合考古队。本来今年我们计划在土丘上开一条台阶形探沟，但是土丘过于陡峭，发掘之后探沟保护非常困难，所以我们选在土丘底部的平坦区域发掘探沟。这条探沟长29米，跨越土丘内外，以便了解土丘的形成过程和土丘以外的淤土和文化层。此外，我们钻探和测绘了土丘，了解了土丘的边界和深度。由此我们知道，纳德利土丘顶部呈不规则圆形，直径约74米，底部最大直径约185米，现高20米，深达5米，也就是土丘的最初地面在现存地面5米以下。

为了勘探纳德利土丘，我们带来了洛阳铲。这种工具让伊朗考古研究中心（ICAR）很感兴趣，特意派了一名学生和一位研究人员来学习洛阳铲的使用方法（图5-6-3）。此次我们在土丘坡脚共钻了37个点位以确定土丘原始范围；在土丘以外共钻了30个点位以了解地层情况。根据钻孔土样分析，遗址原始边缘南北约148米，东西约185米；土丘外围西南部、西部地层较深，堆积丰富，常见炭屑、砖块、土坯、陶片；北部、东南部、东部地层较浅，文化堆积单薄。勘探结果表明，现在所能见到的土丘底径要小于原始土丘；土丘以外区域仍有文化堆积和生活遗迹。

图5-6-3 伊朗队员学会了钻探（张良仁摄）

在发掘方面，我们与伊朗同仁的工作方法有着较大差异。以往伊朗大多采用小探方试掘，即发掘2米见方的小探方，向下发掘至生土。这一方面是由于经费有限，另一方面则是发掘目的使然。多数的发掘并不涉及后续的保护与展示，伊朗方面通常希望在短时间内了解到一处土丘遗址的文化序列。而我们这次在土丘南侧开了一条2米宽，29米长的探沟，目的是了解土丘内外的文化堆积。前面的钻探表明土丘外围的生土层大多在3—5米以下，而在我们发掘的这条探沟中，8米以下仍存在青铜时代的生活遗存。我们将探沟内的堆积共分为11层，历史时期除了一段土坯墙，未见清晰的建筑遗存；有意思的是，我们在伊斯兰时期的地层中发现了数量不少的青花器残片，其中绝大部分都是波斯的仿烧品。青花瓷在我国元代创烧，后来产品和烧造技术都传播到了波斯，在15世纪以后仿烧青花砂胎器在波斯盛极一时。史前的彩陶以纳马兹加三期、四期居多，而最早的陶片属于纳马兹加二期，与先前意大利考古队的调查结果一致。同时土丘南部由于雨水冲刷，形成了一个天然断崖。为了了解土丘的建筑形态和人类活动，我们在断面做了清理工作，发现了三大层建筑。此外，我们还在断崖上布探沟，逐层发掘，目前发现

第五部分 欧亚考古见闻

了两个地层和两个疑似馕坑的遗迹。由同出陶片来看,其年代可能为帕提亚时期和亚兹三期。

由于我们是第一次在伊朗发掘遗址,碰到的困难并不少。最让人头疼的就是天气。在我们到来之前,伊方领队阿里·瓦赫达提(Ali Vahdati)就已经告诉我们,希尔凡的冬天雨雪很多,并不适合发掘。果不其然,发掘开始后第四天就下起了大雪。相较于雨水,雪花不算什么;但是真正考验我们的是零下十度的气温。每过一夜,土都冻得坚如磐石,一铲下去都能听到金属的撞击声。我们每天7点上工,下午4点收工,能感受到太阳暖意的只有中午的两个小时。久而久之,大家都形成了"人体生物钟",一感到冷就知道下午两点已过。其次是语言。我们这支国际考古队共有14名成员,中方6人,伊方7人,还有1位塞尔维亚来的女学生。于是最常见的景象就是中方队员聚在一起说汉语,伊方队员聚在一起说波斯语,而塞尔维亚姑娘一脸茫然地窝在角落里。偶尔听到自己的名字,但是又不知道大家说她什么。伊方领队阿里的英语相当好,几乎成为我们交换意见的唯一途径;而他不在的时候,连拷贝测绘数据都能折腾一上午。同当地的民工交流,我们只能连比画带猜,有时一激动,汉语、英语和刚学的几个波斯语单词一股儿脑全出去了。

短短的二十几天时间很快就过去了。虽然两条探沟都没有挖完,但是绘图、洗陶片和挑选样品这些工作一样不能少,所以每天都非常忙碌,自然没有闲暇体验海亚姆的"一箪疏食一壶浆,一卷诗书树下凉"的惬意。但是我们白天在天寒地冻的工地上发掘,晚上坐在温暖的房子里喝茶吃馕,倒是感受到了另外一种诗意:"一杯红茶一个馕,一把手铲方中忙"(图5-6-4)。

图5-6-4 红茶和馕(张良仁摄)

玫瑰花的全部价值，只有夜莺才知道
——南京大学赴伊朗考古记（二）*

"玫瑰花的全部价值，只有夜莺才知道"，这是伊朗诗人哈菲兹的诗句。同样的，伊朗考古的辛苦与愉悦，只有去过才会懂。

2018年7月15日傍晚，南京大学考古文物系师生和其他成员一行10人，从乌鲁木齐的地窝堡国际机场登上飞机，开始了为期40天的伊朗考古。

我们首先到达德黑兰，在这里停留两天，办理一些事务。我们当中的大多数人都是第一次来到伊朗，因此茶余饭后便相约出门逛街。七月的德黑兰十分燥热，整个城市弥漫着一股汽油的味道。街上的出租车有黄色和绿色两种，据说伊朗女性外出时可以乘坐两种出租车，但乘坐绿色的更为安全。伊朗对人们的服饰规定十分严格，在如此炎热的夏季，我们一路见到的女性无一例外都戴着头巾，穿着长过臀部的上衣和盖住脚踝的长裤，个别女性甚至一袭黑纱从头裹到脚；而男性也必须穿着盖过脚踝的长裤。正所谓入乡随俗，我们考古队里的女性在下飞机前便戴上了头巾。我们一群人走在大街上十分引人注目，时不时有人用波斯语问我们是不是中国人。

办完事务后，我们便奔赴北呼罗珊省的希尔凡市，开始我们今年的田野工作。纳德利土丘遗址位于该市的西南郊，状如覆斗，顶部呈不规则

---

* 本文原刊于中国考古网2018年12月17日。收入本书时略有改动。作者为：张佳杨、张良仁。

圆形，直径约74米，底部最大直径达185米，现高20米，是伊朗东北部最大的土丘之一。根据前人的地表调查，它的使用年代从铜石并用时代一直延续至伊斯兰时期，前后延续5000多年，文化堆积丰厚。我们选择发掘这座土丘，目的是研究土丘的起源、了解古代居民的经济形态、完善伊朗北呼罗珊省的考古文化序列，并考察其在文化交流中的角色。

图 5-7-1　中伊考古队合影（佚名摄）

图 5-7-2　伊斯兰时期的仿华青花陶（阿里·瓦赫达提摄）

今年并不是第一次中伊合作发掘纳德利土丘。2016年冬季，我们和北呼罗珊省文化遗产、手工业和旅游办公室组成的联合考古队，曾做了为期二十几天的工作。当时主要是钻探、测绘土丘，了解土丘的边界、深度和土丘内外的堆积情况；并在土丘底部及南侧各开了一条探沟，做了少量的发掘。其中土丘底部探沟（T1）长29米，宽2米，地层主要为淤土。由于时间不足，该探沟只有局部区域发掘到8米以下的生土层。土丘南侧探沟（T2）长约 7 米，宽约 2 米，仅向下发掘了 1 米，发现了两个疑似窖坑的设施。

在 2016 年工作的基础上，今年我们把土丘底部的探沟向上延伸至土丘顶部，形成一条长 55 米、宽 2 米的大探沟（T1），一共分为 8 段（图 5-7-1）。通过发掘，我们在土丘下面的一个灰坑里发现了比 2016 年更多的伊斯兰时期的仿华青花陶，从其断面和纹样来看，应为当地仿烧品（图 5-7-2）（彩图 20）。在淤土层下面，我们发现了早期铁器时代和青铜时代的坡积土。我们在土丘上的探沟中发现了五层青铜时代的土坯砖建筑，其中最早的也是最外围的是一道土坯围墙，可能是早期聚落的围墙（图 5-7-3）。近东是最早出现土坯建筑的地区，大约在公元前 9000 年左右，在黎凡特和安纳托利亚便使用土坯来砌墙和铺地面。大约在公元前 8000 或公元前 7000 年，土坯迅速向外传播到扎格罗斯山脉中部、中亚、南亚，在甘吉达列遗址（Ganj Dareh）及

图 5-7-3 青铜时代的土坯墙
（张良仁摄）

梅尔加赫遗址（Mehrgarh）都留下了单排的土坯建筑。与此同时，模制技术取代了手制技术，由此产生了长方形和方形土坯，极大地提高了土坯的生产和修建效率。到了青铜时代（3400BC—1300BC），随着城市的增多，土坯的使用范围也进一步扩大。此次我们在遗址中发现的土坯多为长方形，砖中可见大小不一的用作羼和料的砂石。我们取了一些砖的样品带回国，用于后续分析。

土丘南部由于受到雨水冲刷和人为破坏，形成了一个天然断崖。2016 年在此布了一条探沟（T2），并做了少量发掘。今年我们继续向下发掘（图 5-7-4），现已发掘到第五层居住面，在此发现了一截土坯墙、大量陶片、少量铜器、石器、骨器及小件雕塑。该探沟今年仍然没有发掘到生土层，目前所发现的遗迹和遗物都属于青铜时代。不过，这里发现的少量铜器值得关注。西亚是冶金技术发生的重要地区，而伊朗占着举足轻重的地位。约在公元前 7000 年，在艾利科什遗址（Ali Kosh）便发现了冷锻加工而成的纯铜珠。到了青铜时代，

◇❖◇ 第五部分 欧亚考古见闻

伊朗冶金已经形成了埃兰、卢里斯坦及伊朗高原三大冶金传统，出现了希萨尔（Tepe Hissar）、伊布里斯（Tal-e Iblis）及雅赫亚（Tepe Yahya）等冶金生产中心。然而与中国青铜时代不同的是，伊朗的青铜器多为青铜工具、装饰品及武器，不见大型礼器。我们此次发现的少量铜锥和箭头均为小型铜器。

图 5-7-4　T2 发掘场景
（张良仁摄）

为了更好地认识纳德利土丘遗址，今年我们继续开展多学科研究。我们邀请了中国科学院遥感中心的郭子祺、乔彦超和秦静欣。他们在土丘顶部布了 18 条探地雷达测线，在土丘顶部及外围区域分别布了 12 条和 3 条电法测线，以此来了解土丘及其周边的地层堆积（图 5-7-5）。通过探查和反演，他们在纳德利土丘顶部发现了两层建筑，第一层在地表以下 0.8—2.2 米，第二层在地表以下 3.2 米。两层存在着不同电阻率的土坯，第一层存在两种类型的土坯，而第二层则只有高电阻率的土坯。土丘周边的地层几乎全为淤土，地表以下 6 米左右即为地下基岩。我们还邀请了南京大学地理与海洋科学学院的马春梅、贾鑫在土丘下面的探沟（T1）内分层采集土样、炭屑和骨头样品，用于研究沉积年代与环境。此外，中国科学院地质与地球物理研究所的唐自华也应邀采集了遗址内发掘出土的动物牙齿，用于锶同位素分析，以此来研究当地动物的活动情况。

图 5-7-5　探地雷达工作场景
（郭子祺摄）

玫瑰花的全部价值，只有夜莺才知道

在伊朗7、8两个月不是发掘的好季节，近四十天的时间里，只下过一次雨。酷热、烈日、风沙，无一不在考验着我们对考古的热情。对于这一点，感受最为深刻的要数在土丘南侧断崖的探沟（T2）中发掘的刘彬彬和张亦弛两位同学了。这条探沟一侧为土丘，一侧为几米高的断崖，稍有不慎，便会摔下来。在此发掘，白日里阳光直射，毫无遮蔽之处；土丘上部时不时有土和碎石块滚落下来，他们还要小心提防。这里倒土不方便，只能往断崖下面倒，但是扬起大量灰尘，因此每天下工他俩都是灰头土脸。遇上大风的日子，漫天飞沙，眼睛根本无法睁开。发掘之初他俩是有伊朗工人的，但是过了一段时间后，工人们都嫌太热走了，最终只留下他们两人在那里发掘。

纳德利土丘附近有许多住户，这些住户们对我们的工作十分好奇。发掘时，时常有人过来围观，我们考古队也吸收了一位对考古感兴趣的女生，让她参与了一段时间的发掘。村子里还有一个叫阿扎尔（Azar）的男孩，约莫七八岁的样子，眼睛大大的，睫毛长长的，十分好看（图5-7-6）。

图5-7-6　小小考古学家——阿扎尔
（刘彬彬摄）

他几乎每天都要跑来工地玩耍，帮我们拿锄头、拿刷子，给我们带来一种豌豆粒大小、有些酸的小果子。我们考古队里的刘彬彬十分喜爱这个男孩，总是带着他。到了最后，阿扎尔就成了他的小小助手，算是公共考古的一个小成果了。

我们聘请的民工是附近村庄的，他们当中会英语的人并不多。每当需要交流时，我们往往是连比带划，有时还夹杂着一些现学的波斯语，可谓"话到说时方恨少"。当地人有时会指着一些物品，问我们用中文怎么讲。就这样，我们学波斯语，他们学中文，倒也是互有长益。值得一提的是，这些民工十分守时，每到早上十点的茶歇时间，他们会自动停下干活；茶歇结束时，他们也会准点回到各自岗位，完全不需要我们催促。

除了自然环境外，这里的住宿对我们也是极大的挑战。今年我们住在

第五部分 欧亚考古见闻

离遗址不远的一所技校的宿舍楼。宿舍楼有上下两层，伊朗人住在一楼，中国人住在二楼；男性、女性分住楼的两侧。宿舍里为普通的上下铺，与中国宿舍不同的是，由于伊朗人喜爱地毯，每一间宿舍里均铺有厚厚的地毯；为了便于打扫，进屋时需要脱鞋

图 5-7-7　为我们表演的当地民间艺术家（张佳杨摄）

（图 5-7-7）。一楼有厕所和洗澡间，不过都是男女共用的。洗澡水只有冷水，好在是 7、8 月，下工之后冲个凉水澡也未尝不好。

我们的一日三餐都很简单（图 5-7-8），主食为馕和米饭，配着烤牛肉、烤鱼肉、烤鸡肉、烤西红柿一起吃。伊朗的馕和新疆的馕不同，长椭圆形，偏薄，由于不是现做的，所以口感略有些绵软，咬起来稍稍费力。米饭有两种，一种是普通的白米饭，一种是用藏红花泡水煮过的米饭，呈黄色，我们吃饭时往往是一份白米饭配上一点藏红花米饭。蔬菜很少，有时候好几天才能吃到一次。受伊斯兰教教义的影响，伊朗人不饮酒，喜欢

图 5-7-8　日常饮食（张佳杨摄）

喝红茶和一种名为"Doogh"的饮料。这种饮料由酸奶和薄荷混制而成，初尝时仿佛吞了一大口怪味牙膏，习惯之后，倒也觉得清爽，是下工后消热解暑的好东西。

玫瑰花的全部价值，只有夜莺才知道

我们实行八小时工作制，一周工作六天，周五休息。每逢周五，我们便可以去附近的农场转转。由于伊朗地广人稀，当地有很多农场。人们在自己的农场里种植黄瓜、葡萄、苹果、向日葵，也在这里纳凉消遣。我们每次去参观，总会受到热情的招待。炎炎夏日，主人们在树荫下铺上毯子，摆上瓜果，大家一同坐下来喝一杯红茶，配上几块方糖，好不惬意（图5-7-9）。虽然彼此交流起来并不顺畅，但总是能在欢笑中度过时间。

图5-7-9　农场里的欢乐时光（刘彬彬摄）

希尔凡的夏天似乎格外的短暂，近四十天的发掘工作很快就结束了。但是烈日炎炎的伊朗之夏、独具风味的伊朗之食、热情好客的伊朗之人，都会留在我们的记忆里，不会随着发掘的结束而消失。伊朗诗人哈菲兹说："玫瑰花的全部价值，只有夜莺才知道"；而伊朗考古的辛苦与愉悦，只有亲自去过才会品味到。

（鸣谢：此文写作过程中，得到了中国科学院遥感中心郭子祺、乔彦超和秦静欣、南京大学地理与海洋科学学院马春梅的帮助，特此致谢！）

认识伊朗文化遗产
——苏西亚纳平原[*]

前　言

2018年8月25日，我们结束了在北呼罗珊省纳德利土丘的一个半月的发掘，辗转来到苏西亚纳平原，开始了憧憬已久的伊朗文化遗产考察之旅。这次的考察主要有两个目的：其一，让三名硕士研究生亲眼看看考古文献提到的一些重要遗址，增加感性认识；其二，进一步了解伊朗的历史和文化。由于时间有限，这次考察集中在舒什周围的几个遗址上。

在夜幕中，我们乘坐的飞机降落在阿瓦士。阿瓦士是伊朗胡齐斯坦省的首府，坐落在札格罗斯山以西，波斯湾以北的苏西亚纳平原上。在充满高原、山脉和盐漠的伊朗，苏西亚纳是一片平坦的平原，也是两河流域的一部分，水源充足，土壤肥沃。凭借其与生俱来的地理优势，这里一直是波斯帝国的粮仓。文化上，它是两河流域文明向东传播的通道；而在政治上，它是波斯帝国向西扩张的跳板。

刚走出机场，一股热风扑面而来。当时已经是8月底，在我们发掘的伊朗东北部，白天的气温已经降到了30度左右。在那里，我们度过了一个炎热的夏季，在高达38度的气温中发掘了40多天，感觉已经到了自己承受能力的极限。但是伊朗领队瓦赫达提告诉我们，苏西亚纳平原是伊朗最热的地方，今年最高温度达55度，现在虽然降了不少，但是仍然有四十七八度。我们虽然生活在号称"火炉"的南京，但是只

---

[*] 本文原刊于《大众考古》2019年第7期，第31—43页。收入本书时略有改动。作者为：张亦弛、张良仁。

经历过 40 度的天气，而且大多数时间躲在有空调的房子里，听到苏西亚纳这样的高温，心里不免忐忑起来，真想换个凉爽的时间来。但是那样的机会不容易有，于是我们索性横下心来，体验一下炎热的生活，感悟古人的生存智慧，理解伊朗的文化遗产。

一

我们看的第一个世界文化遗产就是距离阿瓦士最近的乔加·赞比尔（Chogha Zanbil）（图 5-8-1）。我们首先看到的是一座阶梯式的金字塔形建筑，矗立在一马平川的黄土台地上。这就是举世闻名的神塔（ziqqurrat），它的核心用土坯筑成，表面用烧砖垒砌，原来是五层，边长 105 米，高约 53 米。虽然现在只剩两层阶梯，高度已不到原来的一半，但是依旧气势恢弘。神塔四面各有一个门道可以通向第一层顶部，但是只有西南门可以通往第二层，或许也是可以到达顶部神庙的唯一通道。神庙中供奉着埃兰文化最重要的神——尹苏辛纳克（Inshushinak）。门道附近还有一些很有意思的设施。东南门前两边各有一排七个覆斗形的小台子，底宽约 80 厘米，可能与某种在日出时举行的宗教活动有关。神塔的东北、西北和西南面曾经各有一个圆形的圣坛，但是目前只剩下西北和西南两个，应该也是举行宗教活动的设施。在埃兰帝国的首都苏萨，曾经发现过一个青铜模型，根据模型上的铭文，它展现的是一个与日出有关的宗教仪式——两个男人在两座宗教建筑之间举行净礼，其中一个把水浇到另一个人手上，周围有水槽、大罐子，还有几棵树。模型中的宗教建筑就是阶梯式的，很容易让人联想到乔加·赞比尔的神塔；而三阶的建筑两侧各有四个排成一列的小台子，看起来有点像乔加·赞比尔神塔门前的覆斗形台子。神塔门道前还曾经有用于守卫的瘤牛雕像，其中一个现在保存在德黑兰的伊朗国家博物馆。

这座神塔不是这里唯一的建筑，实际上它是一座城市——杜尔·温达什（Dur Untash）的核心，在它的周围有三道围墙，也就是保护神塔的三道屏障。紧邻神塔的是近圆形的内墙。除了神塔，内墙的西北部还有三座神庙，分别供奉着纳彼里萨（Napirisha）、吉里利莎（Kiririsha）

· 539 ·

和伊什尼卡拉布（Ishniqarab）。这些神庙要比神塔卑微许多，但是从位置来看，它们的地位比内墙以外的神庙更为崇高。再向外是一道近方形的围墙，也就是外墙，它与内墙之间的空间是古城的中间区域。中间区域也有一些神庙和其他建筑。例如东边的角落里分布着四座并排的神庙，供奉着一组神，其中三座神庙的结构相似，只有最北侧的与众不同。中间区域偏北侧也有一座横长方形的神庙，它的院子里还有一处陶窑。中间区还有一些道路，把外墙的大门和主要建筑连接起来。但是这些路是碎砖块铺成的，等级比神塔四周的整齐的方砖铺成的道路要低得多。外墙以外，大城墙以内是古城的外部区域。这片区域空间很大，但是只有东部聚集在一起的三座宫殿和一座神庙，其中一座宫殿的地下室里发现了五座拱顶砖墓，里面埋葬的有可能是王室随从。在其他区域没有发现建筑，无法容纳大批人口，也就是说，这座城市并不是统治者居住的地方——他们可能居住在不远的苏萨，而是供他们崇拜诸神的地方。平时只有一些祭司和仆人居住，所以这座城市是一座"神庙城市"。

图 5-8-1 乔加·赞比尔（张亦弛摄）

认识伊朗文化遗产

神塔是两河流域苏美尔文明的神庙建筑，在两河流域以外并不多见，而乔加·赞比尔就是其中之一。这个遗址原来是石油勘探公司在飞机航拍时发现的，法国考古队的吉尔什曼得知后花了 11 年（1951—1961 年）发掘了这座土丘，把整个土丘揭露出来。他在神塔内发现了

1. 神塔
2. 伊什尼卡拉布神庙
3. 吉里利莎神庙
4. 纳彼里萨神庙
5. 希什米提克和鲁胡拉提尔神庙
6. 纳普拉泰普众神庙
7. 施穆特和贝莱特-阿里神庙
8. 阿达德和萨拉神庙
9. 频尼吉尔神庙
10. 二号宫殿
11. 三号宫殿
12. 一号宫殿（有砖墓）
13. 努斯库神庙

图 5-8-2 杜尔·温达什城址平面图

（采自乔加·赞比尔遗址宣传册）

数千块带有楔形文字的砖，根据这些铭文，我们知道了它的一些历史情况（图 5-8-3）。公元前 1250 年，埃兰帝国的国王温达什·纳彼里萨（Untash-Napirisha）建起了这座城市（图 5-8-3）。公元前 640 年，亚述王阿舒尔巴尼帕尔（Ashurbanipal）在最后一次征讨埃兰帝国时摧毁了它，洗劫了城

图 5-8-3 有楔形文字的墙砖

（张良仁摄）

中的神庙。在这次战争中，附近的其他神庙也惨遭劫掠。此时已经处于埃兰王国的末期，随着波斯和米底的兴起，埃兰帝国的神庙也逐步衰落。实际上，杜尔·温达什的建设并未完成。在国王温达什·纳彼里萨（Untash-Napirisha）死后，此城的建设便搁置下来，直至被亚述摧毁。它终究没能等到万人朝拜的那一天。

二

在乔加·赞比尔参观时才10点，气温就已经升到了40度以上，我们一边走，一边忙着擦汗，脑袋开始微微作痛。由于天气炎热，现在是旅游淡季，整个遗址里冒着酷暑参观的就我们几个人。而遗址的保安坐在屋檐下，一边喝茶，一边聊天，倒也舒适自在。我们也赶紧坐到屋檐下休息片刻，然后奔赴著名的古城苏萨。到了苏萨已经是中午12点，此时温度更高，但是当地的考古学家说，最热的时候还不是现在，而是下午4点以后，过了6点才会好些。这里的游客同样只有我们几个。实际上，为了防暑，当地政府规定的工作时间是上午5：00—8：00，下午5：30—11：30，所以博物馆此时还关着门，只是因为同行的伊朗考古学家打了招呼，才专门为我们开放了。

苏萨也是一座大型土丘，虽然现在地面高度并不大，但是拥有8000多年的历史。公元前7000年，一个小村子出现在这个遗址。公元前4700—前4400年，这里出现了彩陶，人们将这段时期命名为苏西亚纳I期，此后一直有人居住。在埃兰帝国（2700BC—540BC）、阿契美尼德帝国（550BC—330BC）和帕提亚帝国（247BC—224AD）时，苏萨是首都，在之后的萨珊和伊斯兰时期，它不再是首都，但是继续有人居住。

苏萨的一个重要发现是有关楔形文字起源的证据。苏萨出土了大量公元前3500—前3200年的陶筹，此后的埃兰时期地层里出土了早期的楔形文字。这些材料构成了一个完整的证据链，为美国学者史蔓特—白瑟拉特（Denis Schmandt-Besserat）的陶筹说奠定了基础。1969—1971年，她得到了一笔奖学金，去研究近东前陶时期（公元前8000—前6000年）的泥质器物，但是意外地发现了各种小陶器：锥形、球形、饼形、四边形和柱形。这种器物经过精心制作，是最早入窑烧造的陶器，而且分布广泛，这让她觉得它们一定有某种用途。后来她发现陶筹的形状与最早的刻划符号相同。经过几年的思考，她提出了一个新观点，即楔形文字并非起源于图画，而是从三维的陶筹逐步演变而来。这就是学术界有名的文字起源陶筹说，而苏萨提供了一条关键的证据链。

1946年起，法国考古学家吉尔什曼（Roman Ghirshman）在苏萨王城（Royal City）区的东北部做了大规模的深度发掘，发现了从埃兰时期到伊斯兰时期共15个地层。现在我们看到的是一个巨大的15米深的坑，下面是埃兰早期的城市，街道、房屋、大型建筑等城市要素都清晰可见（图5-8-4）。埃兰早期的建筑布局很紧密，不同建筑共用一面墙，相互紧贴，街道也很窄，这样可以尽可能地减少暴露在阳光下的区域。较小的房屋和贵族的大型建筑结合在一起，房屋有砖铺的庭院和大厅。与此同时，西边的神庙区有尹苏辛纳克（Inshushinak）和伊什尼卡拉布（Ishnikarab）的神庙，前者是地狱的领主，决定死者的命运，后者负责护送死者到地狱。埃兰中期，王城区域除了住房之外，也有神庙和墓葬。这一阶段的大型建筑和神庙多数经过翻新，也建了不少新的礼仪性建筑，宗教气息愈发浓厚。在神庙区的宁胡尔萨克（Nin-Hursag）神庙中曾出土过一尊高约130厘米的青铜塑像。塑像表现的是埃兰王温达什·纳彼里萨的妻子纳彼尔阿苏（Napirasu），它最初放在乔加·赞比尔的一个神庙里，王死后被转移到苏萨。这一时期，用浮雕砖装饰墙面的做法流行起来。它们类似于南朝墓葬中的砖画，许多砖拼成一幅完整的图像，但是砖块要大得多。这种砖不是一般的黏土砖，而是带釉的。阿帕达纳土丘上的尹苏辛纳克神庙的一面墙是用浮雕砖装饰的，上面有人、半人半牛和椰枣树的形象，不过图像和制作都显得比较粗放。随后的新埃兰时期，苏萨可能逐渐失去了政治和军事的中心地位，但仍然是重要的宗教和文化中心，神庙区的神庙依旧繁荣富足。

阿契美尼德时期是苏萨的全盛期。公元前540年，居鲁士大帝打败

◇❖◇ 第五部分 欧亚考古见闻

图 5-8-4 吉尔什曼在王城区发掘的最早期城市（张良仁摄）

了米底人，占领了苏萨。在冈比西斯二世统治期间，苏萨成为首都。后来大流士大帝开始了大规模的建设。在阿帕达纳土丘的顶部仍然可以看到一个宏大的宫殿建筑群，即大流士宫。它有六个庭院，大小房间加起来足有110个。墙体是土坯垒砌的，今天看到的只有草拌泥保护层，但是在阿契美尼德时期，墙面富丽堂皇，上有壁画或者灰泥装饰，还有用彩色釉砖拼成的翼兽、狮子、人物等图像。这时的釉砖装饰明显要成熟许多，图像设计和砖的制作都更加精细，色彩丰富。阿帕达纳宫是大流士宫的主殿，包括一个中央柱厅、四周的回廊和四角的塔楼。中央柱厅里均匀排布着6排6列共36根立柱，高约23米，柱顶有典型的公牛柱头。它与波斯波利斯的阿帕达纳宫极为相似，因此被看作是波斯波利斯宫殿的原型。在这里还发现了刻有楔形文字的泥版，记载了当时修建宫殿的情况。由于土丘表面凹凸不平，所以在建造宫殿之前需要先平整这片土地。工人们先在土丘周围筑了20米宽的高墙，然后在土丘上挖掘直到生土层，形成一个平台，这样可以保证建筑基础稳固。挖出的碎石和土就转移到墙外。原材料和工人来自各个地区，比如木材来自亚述、卡尔马尼亚（Carmania，大概是现在的克尔曼地区），黄金来自萨迪斯（Sardis）和巴克特里亚，青金石、玛瑙、绿松石来自粟特和花剌子模，银和乌木来自埃及，石工来自爱奥尼亚（Ionia）和萨迪斯，金匠来自米底和埃及，烧砖匠来自巴比伦……阿契美尼德帝国的控制力和影响力由此可见一斑。从正门进入宫殿的路旁原来立着一尊巨大的大流士

图 5-8-5　大流士宫（张亦弛摄）

雕像，但是遗憾的是头部遗失了，原来应该有 3 米高。他穿着传统的波斯长袍，但是左臂弯曲置于胸前，左脚前伸的姿势又和埃及的形象如出一辙。从衣褶里的埃及文、埃兰文和古波斯文题记得知，这个雕像就是大流士下令在埃及制作的，为了让后人记得他曾经征服过埃及。看来大流士大帝比较明智，并不指望波斯人能一直控制埃及这片土地，千世万世传之无穷（图 5-8-5）。

在随后的塞琉古和帕提亚时期，苏萨不可避免地经历了一个希腊化时期。后来，阿尔达希尔一世攻占苏萨时，将这座城市付之一炬。重建之后，苏萨成了两河和波斯湾地区的一个经贸中心。王城（Royal City）区是萨珊时期的一片住宅区。萨珊前期，

图 5-8-6　阿帕达纳宫的柱头（张良仁摄）

密集而整齐的土坯房屋分布在道路两侧。中心有一座大型土坯建筑，三条回廊围绕在方形的大厅外侧。它的几个柱础是阿契美尼德时期的，来自大流士宫。发掘者还发现了一些墙块上残留的壁画，上面有月亮、

◇❖◇　第五部分　欧亚考古见闻

星星、云朵，还有两个骑手追逐着瞪羚、野猪、水牛的狩猎场景，色彩仍清晰可见。除了倒塌的建筑外，还有大量墓葬散布在房屋内、庭院里、街道上，有成年人的也有孩子的。死去的人们被埋在有十字标记的罐子里，他们是基督教徒。萨珊帝国的官方宗教是琐罗亚斯德教，但是帝国境内还有基督教、摩尼教、犹太教等各种宗教。随着政治军事环境的变化，宗教冲突此起彼伏。在沙普尔二世时期，由于基督教在罗马的地位上升，政府对基督教徒的迫害达到了顶峰。发掘者吉尔什曼认为，坍圮的墙体和大量墓葬就是沙普尔二世迫害基督徒，用300头大象摧毁了城市的证据。到了萨珊后期，房屋的质量明显下降，极少使用土坯，而是直接用压实黏土替代，同时陶器的质量也大不如前，看来沙普尔二世的这次打击让苏萨元气大伤，但直至伊斯兰时期，它仍然在创伤中挣扎着。

图 5-8-7　法国考古城堡（张良仁摄）

天色渐晚，我们沿着沙石路往回走，此时法国城堡已经沐浴在夕阳的余晖里。这是19世纪法国考古队发掘苏萨时的工作站（图 5-8-7）。1834 年，狄拉福（Marcel Dieulafoy）最早来苏萨发掘时，附近没有地方可以居住，只有一些供朝圣者休憩的帐篷，而当地人和当地政府又不接受他们，所以他们不得不住在自己建造的简易土屋里。即便如此，麻烦依旧不断，当地人认为这些外国人带来了疾病、洪水、飓风和不祥的日食，所以考察队备受袭扰，只好配枪来自卫。由于这种恶劣的工作环境，1897 年，当德·摩尔根（de Morgan）再次来到苏萨时，他通过与伊朗政府的协商获得了一笔资金，建造了这样一座欧式城堡，既保障了人和遗物的安全，又大大改善了工作环境。城堡的主体是两层楼，有工作室、车库、餐厅、厨房、卧室、会议室、浴室、读书室，甚至还有图书馆和画室，围出了一高一低两个院子。现在院子里放着发掘时使用的工具，让我们见识了当时的"机械化发

认识伊朗文化遗产

掘"——运土的"小火车"、各种滑轮、吊钩、小型起重机，还有铁链做的软梯、木制三脚架……城堡外墙并不都是直上直下的，一条车道盘桓而上，进入城堡一楼；在二楼还有几座瞭望塔，所以整座建筑看起来不仅高大而且很有层次。最值得一提的是，建造城堡的材料都是来自苏萨遗址各个时期的砖和土坯，有些甚至还有刻写的埃兰文字。壮观的城堡背后是开拓者的一段艰辛往事，他们受过的苦为一批批后继者换来了安全舒适的环境和一份独有的体验——与古城相伴，与古砖同眠。

图 5-8-8　苏萨考古队使用过的工具（张良仁摄）

三

第二天一早，我们就驱车前往舒什塔尔，参观这里庞大的古代水利工程（图 5-8-9）。波斯诗人菲尔多西在《列王传》中描述道："在舒什塔尔有一条宽阔的大河，河宽不见对岸，连鱼也难于横游而过。"他所说的大河就是卡伦河（Karun River）。卡伦河是伊朗的第一大河，发源于扎格罗斯山脉，从北向南流至舒什塔尔；在这里分成两条支流——舒泰特河（Shoteit）与加加河（Gargar），在班德吉尔（Band-e Ghir）汇合成一条河后继续向南流。两条支流之间的广阔区域是宜居宜农的米亚纳布（Mianab）平原（波斯语的意思是"水中间的平原"），而舒什塔尔城就坐落在三角洲平原的最北端。在这座老城的周边，分布着十余处桥、坝、暗渠、磨坊区等遗迹，它们共同组成了舒什塔尔的水利系统。

只要提到古代水利设施，我国读者都会自然而然地想到成都的都江堰。整个成都平原由岷江出山口向东南倾斜，所以岷江一发洪水，成都

· 547 ·

◇◆◇ 第五部分 欧亚考古见闻

平原就成了一片汪洋。因此在古代，成都平原饱受水患之苦；与此同时，在天热少雨之时，成都平原又得不到岷江之利，成了一片干旱之地。战国末期李冰在岷江出山口开凿的都江堰，就很好地解决了这两个问题。其鱼嘴把岷江水分为两股，一股继续顺岷江南流，一股沿人工开凿的宝瓶口流入内江，既可以防洪，也可以灌溉；而鱼嘴和宝瓶口之间的飞沙堰又可以调节水量，由鱼嘴分流到此的洪水可以回到岷江，从而保障内江不受影响。这样，都江堰既免除了成都平原的水患，又为它提供了稳定的灌溉水源，因此创造了一个"天府之国"，自己也成了世界文化遗产。

相比之下，舒什塔尔水利工程还要更复杂，更庞大。工程开始于米赞（Mizan）分水坝，在这个地方，卡伦河分为两股，其中2/6的水量进入人工开凿的加加河，其余4/6水量进入舒泰特河。所以舒泰特河和加加河还有两个名字，Chahar Dangeh 和 Do Dangeh，意思是"四部分"和"两部分"。米赞水坝长约390米，高4.5米，是一座用砂岩和砂浆筑成的堤坝，现在出于加固和保护的目的在上面覆盖了一层混凝土。水坝中段是一片平台，东段不均匀地开了九个口，西段也开了一个口，河水就从这些开口向南进入加加河渠。这些水口的底部高低不同，可以保证河水在枯水期同样得到合理的分配。水坝东侧角落里有几段残留的矮墙，表明这里曾经有一个水磨，但其原貌不得而知。站在坝上向东北方向望去，可以看到河对岸的舒什塔尔新城与河滩上悠闲地吃着草的牛群。离开米赞水坝继续向西，就到了八角形的科拉法兰吉塔（Kolah Farangi Tower）。关于这座小塔的作用众说纷纭。据说在建设米赞水坝时会有人在塔上监督工人们劳作，也有人说它是用来监测河流水位的，还有人认为这是一座导引塔，或许与它西边约500米处的一座城堡有关。

虽然才10点左右，但是天气已经酷热难耐。在附近的小公园稍事休整后，我们继续步行前往水磨和瀑布区。这是舒什塔尔为数不多的需要门票的景点。买了门票之后，我们进入了这片占地5公顷的区域。虽然天气炎热，但是映入眼帘的汩汩水流和震耳欲聋的瀑布声似乎带来了一丝凉意，水里悠哉的鸭子们也给一片土黄色的建筑增添了些许生机。

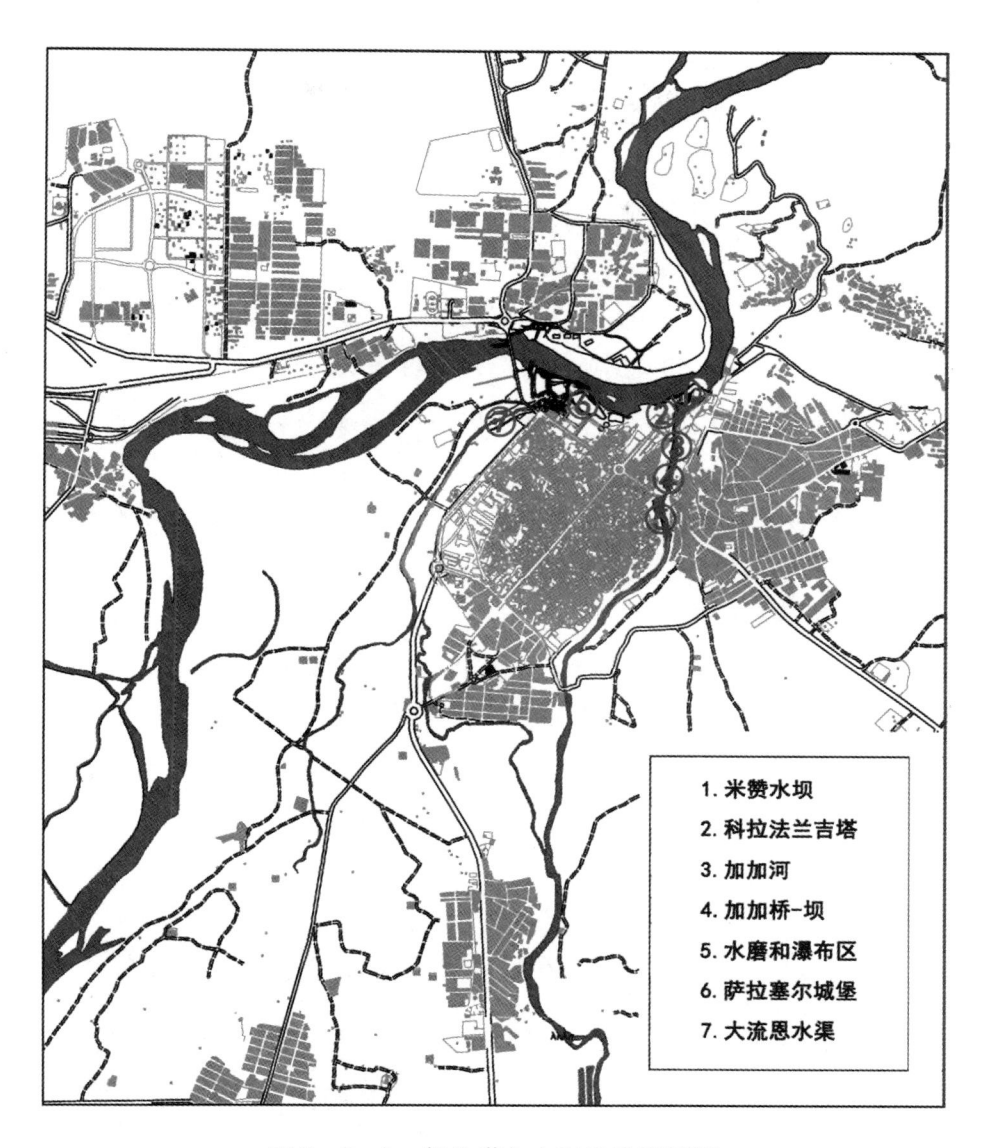

图 5-8-9 舒什塔尔水利设施平面图

（图片来源：http://whc.unesco.org/）

这个磨坊和瀑布区是整个舒什塔尔水利系统的精华所在。一条大坝把加加河拦截起来，形成了20多米的落差。在大坝南侧的河道中央，有一个宽阔的大平台，高出河面10米左右；这一大平台北侧的大坝下方和东侧的河岸边也各有一个平台。人们在这些平台上建了磨坊，在平台的岩体内部开凿了斜坡水道。同时，古人在大坝内开凿了多个涵洞，将上游

第五部分　欧亚考古见闻

的河水分成了三股。其中西侧和中间的两股通过一些小水口流入下游的磨坊区，再进入平台内的水道，多余的水则直接进入东侧的河道。在这个区域一共有46个磨坊，每个磨坊一般有一个或两个房间，有穹顶或者拱形入口。磨坊中的水磨分为上下两部分，上部是一块木板承托着相叠的两块石磨盘——下面一块固定，上面一块通过一根轴与下部的动力装置相连。而每个磨坊下方都有一条在岩石中开凿的水道。由于大坝形成的高差，水流在离开大坝的涵洞时就已经有了一股冲劲；而当水流至磨坊附近时，又会遇到一个竖井，从井口可以看到水流从竖井倾泻而下，这一落差再次增加了水的流速和力量，足以推动竖井出口处的轮片，继而带动上方的石磨盘转动。每条水道上都有一个水闸，需要使用石磨时就打开水闸，工作结束时把水闸关上，湍急的水流就变成了涓涓细流。除了巧妙地利用高差之外，古人也对这些水道的高差和宽度做了精密的计算，使水量得到了很好的控制，不多也不少，正好满足水磨的需要。舒什塔尔的这些磨坊可以用来加工粮食。这些粮食除了满足当地人生活的需要，还很有可能供应着帝国其他地区，进入千家万户。除了粮食加工之外，制作玻璃等手工业生产活动也离不开磨坊（图5-8-10）。

图5-8-10　水磨和瀑布区（张良仁摄）

在舒什塔尔，还有一处令人印象深刻的遗迹。这就是位于城北舒泰特河岸边的山冈上的萨拉塞尔（Salasel）城堡，建于萨珊时期。这里地势高，视野宽，是一处具有防御和监控功能的建筑，曾经由庭院、宫殿、军营、公共浴室、水池、围墙、城垛等部分组成。其中最值得一提的是五座凉房（shavadun）。这是一种人工开凿的地下建筑，每座凉房有两个类似竖井的"Si-sara"通向地面，用于通风换气。舒什塔尔的夏季气温可以达到50度，但是凉房内部却可以保持在20几度，为人们提供了一个避暑纳凉的场所。萨拉塞尔城堡是另一条阿契美尼德时期的人工水渠——大流恩（Dariun）水渠的起点（图5-8-11）。它的开口就在城堡下方河岸的岩壁上，一共有八个集水口。八股水流经过一段距离后汇集，之后在哈克（Khak）水坝分成两支，最后分别注入卡伦河的两条支流。大流恩是米亚纳布平原最重要的水利设施之一，曾经灌溉了约33000公顷的耕地。现在这条水渠已经停止使用，人们在它的下方重新开凿了一条。水渠虽然保证了水的供给，但也给了侵入者可乘之机，所以水渠顶部有一些砖砌的拱窗，这是士兵站岗的地方，以提防敌人通过水渠进入城堡。离开大流恩水渠，沿着山脚的道路往前走，可以看到一些挖在岩体上的小屋，据说是古代的贵族出资开凿的凉房，可以用来避暑。

图5-8-11 大流恩水渠（张良仁摄）

苏西亚纳平原实际上是两河平原的延伸。这里炎热干燥，虽然幼发拉底河、底格里斯河和其他河流泛滥带来了肥沃的土壤，但是如果没有水源，就是一片荒漠。因此修建水利设施是统治者扩疆辟土、发展农业的重要措施。舒什塔尔水利工程大部分是在萨珊时期，尤其是沙普尔一世时修建的。沙普尔一世雄才大略，是第一个把自己称为"伊朗与非伊朗的众王之王"的萨珊统治者。他曾经三次打败罗马军队，分别杀死、俘虏、降服一个罗马皇帝，为此他到处让人刻浮雕写题记，纪念自己的功勋。在一次战争中，他抓了 7000 名罗马战俘，把这些俘虏用在修建比沙普尔（Bishapur）和衮德沙普尔（Gundeshapur）城以及舒什塔尔水利设施上。在舒什塔尔水利设施的帮助下，卡伦河不仅哺育着舒什塔尔的居民，也滋养着整个米亚纳布平原的辽阔土地。据调查，萨珊时期米亚纳布平原上有 50 余处聚落，占地面积 700 余公顷，这样的聚落密度与水资源的充分利用是密不可分的。直至今日，这一令人惊叹的水利设施依然在发挥着它的作用。"这河唇的青青春草，我们在枕之而眠"，伊朗诗人海亚姆笔下的生活自然而平和。舒什塔尔的人们每夜伴着卡伦河的波涛声入眠，他们的梦里，应该也有河唇的青青春草在随风飘摇吧。

四

我们一行的最后一站是衮德沙普尔（Gundeshapur）。我们先去了城址旁边的博物馆。该城是沙普尔一世打败罗马皇帝瓦莱里安后建立的。他把许多战俘转移到这里，让他们按照罗马城市安条克的样子建设这座城市。之后，沙普尔二世在这里建立了最早的大学，修建了图书馆；5 世纪时，被罗马驱逐的聂斯托里派教（景教）徒带来了希腊科学；呼斯鲁（Khosrow）在位时，十分重视科学和艺术，从希腊引进了哲学，使衮德沙普尔成为一个哲学中心；而后音乐家也来到这里；9 世纪时，因为地震，阿巴斯哈里发（Abbasid Caliphate）把所有的图书器物转移到了巴格达。城址在博物馆以西 1 千米有余，地面上到处都是砖块和陶片，几个小土包零散地分布在田野上。早在 20 世纪 60 年代，考古学家就在这里开过几条探沟，虽然发现了一批陶片，但基本没有碰到萨珊的建筑遗迹。两年以前的发掘也只发现了伊斯兰时期的建筑，而萨珊时期的建筑还在 8—10 米以下。看样子这个城址还是一片处女地，等待考古学家来开垦。

衮德沙普尔迄今为止的一项重大发现是一条过河涵洞。这座长方形城址的西侧有一条小河——思亚曼殊儿（Siah Mansur），但它是一条季节性河流，枯水期干涸，丰水期又可能有洪涝的危险，不能作为供应城市用水的稳定水源。因此当时的人们就建设了一条引水渠，从20千米以外的德兹河引水。这条水渠修在地下，每隔一段距离就有一个天井，布局类似于坎儿井。水渠到了思亚曼殊儿西岸后，就面临着如何穿越它的问题。人们选择了涵洞。涵洞从西岸开始，穿过河床，从东岸回到地下水渠，进入城内。它是用烧砖砌筑成的一条券顶式管道，最宽处有3.3米，末端虽然有所收窄，但也有2.3米宽，1.8米高。涵洞上面用鹅卵石和石灰浆铺成，掩埋在河床的层层卵石下面。要不是前几年涵洞坍塌，人们还不知道它的存在。我国遗址中也见到过不少涵洞设施，比如高句丽国内城的排水涵洞、西安隋唐皇城的过水涵洞等，但是它们都是城市的排水涵洞，基本没有过河的问题。在前几年的南水北调工程中，也多次利用

图5-8-12 衮德沙普尔的过河涵洞（张良仁摄）

了过河涵洞，但是使用的是现代科技和混凝土。河底涵洞不光要考虑洞内水压，还要考虑洞外水流的压力和冲刷、河底构造、防渗水、防侵蚀等多种问题，所以这条涵洞在当时也是一项高科技工程（图5-8-12）。

短短的两天很快就过去了，没有尽兴但是不得不返回。这次我们饱尝了苏西亚纳平原的酷热，也见识了古人的生存智慧，看到了不少精彩绝伦的文化遗产。当我们坐上从阿瓦士回德黑兰的飞机时，已经入夜。从舷窗向外望去，下方的城市一片明亮，而文化遗产们早已消失在黑暗中。它们不与现代的灯火争辉，却在历史长河中闪耀了几千年，成为苏西亚纳平原上最璀璨的繁星。

· 553 ·

学者相聚大不里士　共话古代丝绸之路
——第三届丝绸之路考古与文保国际学术讨论会纪要[*]

2018年11月14—15日，由南京大学、维也纳应用艺术大学和伊朗文化遗产与旅游研究所主办，伊朗文化遗产与旅游研究所和大不里士伊斯兰艺术大学承办的第三届丝绸之路考古与文保国际学术讨论会在伊朗东阿塞拜疆省大不里士市召开。大不里士曾经是伊尔汗国（1256—1335年）的首都，也是古代丝绸之路的一个重要站点。它也是一座旅游城市，尽管历史上饱受地震摧残，但仍然保留了一些历史建筑，该市的大巴扎是世界文化遗产。会议承办方还特意选择了由古代驿站修缮而成的雅姆驿站宾馆（Yaam Caravanserai）作为会议地点。84名伊朗、中国、奥地利、德国和俄罗斯的考古学家和文物保护专家参加了本次会议。

丝绸之路考古与文保国际学术讨论会是一个系列会议，两年一次，在丝绸之路沿线国家举办。第一次是2014年在西北大学召开的。在奥地利欧亚—太平洋大学联盟（Eurasia-Pacific Uni-Net）前主席温克尔娜（Brigitte Winklehner）的支持下，笔者（当时在西北大学任教）和维也纳应用艺术大学克里斯特（Gabriela Krist）教授联合在西北大学举办了第一届"丝绸之路考古与文物保护"国际学术讨论会。本次会议邀请了中国、奥地利、德国、俄罗斯、印度等国从事丝绸之路沿线考古和文物保护工作的60多名考古学家和文物保护专家参加，目的在于打破地域和学科壁垒，进一步拓宽学术合作的空间。2016年，笔者和克里斯特教授继续合作，以同样的模式在南京大学举办了第二届"丝绸之路考古与文物保护"国际学术讨论会，来自奥地利、俄罗斯、伊朗、德国、

---

[*] 本文原刊于《中国文物报》2018年12月14日第6版。收入本书时略有改动。

英国、意大利、瑞士、美国、澳大利亚及国内多个高校和研究机构的考古和文物保护方向的 70 多名学者和学生参与了此次会议。会后在奥地利出版了论文集（英文）。

在第二届会议上，伊朗考古研究中心（简称 ICAR）主任丘别克（Choubak）博士表示，希望在伊朗举办第三届"丝绸之路考古与文物保护"国际学术讨论会。伊朗与中国的文化交流由来已久，笔者和克里斯特教授想借此机会增进和伊朗学术机构的联系，就愉快地接受了她的请求。并且商定，张良仁教授和克里斯特教授担任会议的学术顾问（图 5-9-1），为会议的筹备工作提供指导，而会议需要的经费和人力由伊朗方面解决。

图 5-9-1　大不里士会议的学术顾问（佚名摄）

11 月 13 日下午 6 点多，伊朗各级领导到达，开幕式开始。原定伊朗副总统（兼伊朗文化遗产、手工业和旅游组织主席）出席开幕式，因故缺席。东阿塞拜疆省文化遗产、手工业和旅游办公室主任和省长发表讲话，简要回顾了该省的旅游事业、文化遗产和考古工作。接着克里斯特教授和笔者上台讲话。笔者在讲话中说，伊朗因为介于东亚和地中海、欧亚草原和印度次大陆之间，是古代丝绸之路的重要部分，在古代丝绸之路上曾经扮演着重要的角色。但是在国际学术界，其重要性没有得到重视，此类会议伊朗学者参加的少，此类论文伊朗学者发表的少。笔者的讲话得到了与会学者的共鸣。

会议为期两天，于 11 月 14—15 日举行，一位专业同传译员负责英语和波斯语的翻译。会议收到了 52 篇论文，但是限于时间，只有其中 26 篇论文可

图 5-9-2　参加会议的中国学者和学生

第五部分 欧亚考古见闻

以宣读（图5-9-2）。来自各个国家的学者分享了他们的研究成果，极大地丰富了我们对丝绸之路的认识。过去人们认为中国南方出现的外来因素是海上丝绸之路来的，中国人民大学的李梅田搜集了湖北襄阳地区墓砖和湖南铜官窑瓷器上的中世纪胡旋舞形象，为我们揭示了粟特人曾经沿汉江向长江中游迁徙的史实，因而修正了我们的看法（图5-9-3）。有关西汉时期中国与伊朗的文化交往的直接证据过去知道得并不多，南京大学的殷洁展示了云南石寨山滇墓、广州南越王墓和扬州江都王墓出土的花瓣纹银盒和铜盒，在阿契美尼德王朝的银器中发现了类似器物，但是她认为是在帕提亚时期传入中国的。商周时期中原地区的玉器加工非常发达，一般认为其原料来自中国西部的和田。甘肃省文物考古研究所的陈国科近几年发掘了河西走廊的几处马鬃山玉矿，这次介绍了罕峡遗址的发掘成果。根据其陶器特征，开采

图 5-9-3 李梅田教授在做报告

者属于骟马文化，并可能属于印度—斯基泰人，其玉料也输送到了中原地区。

来自欧洲的学者也分享了自己的研究成果。阿尔泰国立大学的提什金（A. A. Tishkin）和谢列金（N. N. Seregin）长年在阿尔泰地区发掘。阿尔泰地区是古代草原丝绸之路的一部分，其中额尔齐斯河是一条重要的文化通道。不过，在各个时期里，阿尔泰地区都是游牧帝国的边缘。提什金报告了各个时期的外来产品。在巴泽雷克文化墓葬中，出现了中国产品（铜镜、丝绸和漆器）和伊朗产品（挂毯），可能还有伊朗的马匹。在匈奴时期和柔然时期，匈奴人和鲜卑人扩展到这里，带来了皮带、金牌饰和衣服。谢列金接着报告了突厥和蒙古时期的外来产品，其中既有中国来的钱币和铜镜，也有西方来的物品。奥地利考古研究所的斯特斯卡（Martin Steskal）长年在土耳其西南侧的城址以弗所

(Ephesos)工作。以弗所是希腊化和罗马时期的一座港口城市，也是古代丝绸之路上的一个重要中转站。这次他介绍了城址发现的土葬和火葬，提出这两种葬式是个人选择，而不是统治阶级或宗教的选择。德国亚洲艺术博物馆的施密特（Birgit A. Schmidt）则致力于20世纪初德国探险家切割下来的克孜尔石窟壁画的保护和展示。这些壁画和当时的记录在"二战"中损失了一部分，剩余部分存放在柏林的亚洲艺术博物馆。这次她报告了森木塞姆窟壁画的虚拟复原工作。这些壁画块现在脱离了洞窟，她要做的就是虚拟重建洞窟，以便让观众身临其境地欣赏这些古代艺术。

在有关丝绸之路的国际学术会议中，伊朗一直没有得到应有的重视。这次我们把会议放在大不里士这座丝绸之路上的古城，就是想改变这种现状。而这次会议的确提供了很多以往外界不知道的情况。近几年笔者和伊朗合作伙伴瓦赫达提（Ali Vahdati）在北呼罗珊省联合发掘纳德利土丘，发现了中亚的青铜时代彩陶和伊斯兰时期的仿华青花砂胎器，体现了北呼罗珊省与中亚和中国的长途联系。德黑兰大学的拉雷（Haeede Laleh）教授讲了以内沙普尔为中心的手工业生产和贸易网络。内沙普尔是呼罗珊的一个重要城市，其贸易网络覆盖阿富汗的赫拉特，科佩达克山脉和中央高原的盐漠。粮食和手工业产品在这个区域内流通，并通过这个区域向伊朗内陆流通。伊朗文化遗产与旅游研究所的欧姆拉尼（Behruz Omrani）讲述了伊朗的王家之路（The Royal Road）。连接苏萨和萨迪斯（Sardis）的王家之路是大流士一世修建的，在丝绸之路开通以前300年就修好了，后来波斯人延伸了这条路，把美索不达米亚、印度和北非连接起来。亚历山大大帝就是沿着这条道路进入波斯的。后来随着这条王家之路的延伸，伊朗最终连接起了东亚和罗马。

其他一些学者讨论了丝绸之路上的建筑。伊朗文化遗产与旅游研究所的莫拉迪（Amin Moradi）讨论了伊朗西北部的塞尔柱时期（1037—1194）的大型建筑（塔形清真寺和塔形墓葬），它们继承了伊尔汗时期的大型建筑，同时做了一些改变。该所的阿施拉菲（Mahnaz Ashrafi）研究了加兹温—基兰线的萨法维—喀伽时期的安埠（Anbooh）和曼吉尔（Manjil）桥。加兹温—基兰线是丝绸之路的一部分，但是地貌比较崎

◇❖◇ 第五部分 欧亚考古见闻

岖，所以桥梁是道路必不可少的部分。但是两座桥梁还增加了驿站的功能。由于商业贸易的增长，桥的周围逐渐出现了仓库和马厩，成为商人过夜的地方。拉巴夫—哈尼基（Meysam Labbaf-Khaniki）介绍了伊朗东北部丝绸之路上的城堡。萨拉赫（Sarakhs）平原介于土库曼斯坦和伊朗之间，是呼罗珊的门户；它不仅是商人和僧侣的通道，也是草原游牧民族入侵伊朗的通道。为了保护这个门户，人们在一些山口修建了城墙和城堡。不过现存遗迹，根据附近的陶片来看，可能是9—10世纪修建的。在萨珊时期（224—651年），中央穹隆顶加四个券顶的四方建筑（Chahartaq）往往是拜火庙，但是它们有时与城堡一起出现在丝绸之路沿线的隘口上。沙默罕默德普尔（Alireza Shahmohammadpour）介绍了呼罗珊的"巴泽胡尔（Baze Hur）"例子。这个隘口扼守一条由北而南的道路，在一侧的山头上有一座城堡，在另一侧则有一座四方建筑。

在这次会议上，伊朗收藏的中国青花瓷也是一个引人注目的话题。元明时期，中国瓷器受到伊斯兰世界的热捧，这是我们知道的；我们不知道的是，各个国家的君主曾经修建中国屋，展示自己的藏品。海德堡大学的博士生俞雨申告诉我们，中国屋（Chini-khana）见于撒马尔罕、赫拉特和伊斯法罕等城市，但是现存最早的中国屋是阿达比尔勒宫。伊朗汉学家帕尔瓦尔（Fakhri Daneshpour Parvar）来华留过学，见过夏鼐先生。这次她介绍了阿达比尔勒宫收藏的中国瓷器（图5-9-4）。在伊尔汗、帖木儿（1370—1507年）和萨法维（1501—1736年）时期，该宫前后收藏了1161件青瓷、五彩和青花瓷。后来在战争和外族入侵时，一部分遭到损坏。剩下的中国瓷器放在中国屋墙上的成排成列的小龛里，供人欣赏。后来因为地震，许多瓷器又遭到毁坏。其中一部分移到了伊朗的国家博物馆，现在留在阿达比尔勒宫的只有71件，其中几件为"大明万历年制"

图5-9-4 伊朗汉学家Fakhri Daneshpour Parvar（张良仁摄）

"大明弘治年制""大明正德年制"和"康熙年制"。另一位伊朗汉学家拉希米法尔（Mahnaz Rahimifar）介绍了伊朗若干青花瓷收藏的历史。

16日主办方安排了参观，会议代表前往承办方之一大不里士伊斯兰艺术大学。该校原为1931年德国人建的一座皮革厂。后来废弃，最后改为现在的大学。该校规模不大，只有六个系，其中考古和文物保护系拥有六个实验室，从事壁画、油画的分析和保护。伊朗土丘遗址众多，文物丰富，保护是一个大问题。像这样的保护实验室仍然不多，将来我国文保工作者可以在这个方面与伊朗开展合作。在一个展厅，我们看到了学生们的艺术作品，里面有木镶嵌画、细密画、玻璃器、陶器、刺绣地毯，在此领略了伊朗人细致入微的手工技术。伊朗是手工业大国，通过这样的实际创作来教授传统工艺，保持了它们的活力。在另一个展厅，是伊斯兰艺术国际展览的作品，里面有来自孟加拉国等伊斯兰国家的地毯、细密画。原来他们学校还举办过国际工艺作品展览。

参观结束后，校方安排了五场报告，介绍了他们的考古与文物保护工作。大不里士是伊尔汗国的首都，也是丝绸之路上的一个重要中转站。德国考古研究所的富赫思（Christian H. Fuchs）与该校合作，发掘和保护伊尔汗时期的拉什迪亚（Rashidiyya）城址。该城址位于大不里士的东北部，是1340年伊尔汗国丞相修建的一座学术中心。伊朗和德国联合考古队采用多种科技方法重点调查了南部的大塔。在伊尔汗国的夏都乌姜（Ojan），现在的博斯坦阿巴德，该校韦拉亚提（Rahim Velayati）率领的考古队做了系统的调查，发现了一座驿站和一段丝绸之路。在这个时期，釉砖技术得到了发展，一些新技术如镶嵌、釉下砖得到了应用。随着工匠的迁徙，这些技术传播到了伊朗的各个地方，而他们的名字出现在了呼罗珊、小亚细亚和中亚的建筑上。

总体而言，伊朗方面对这次会议非常重视。在受到美国经济制裁的情况下，他们依然举办本次会议，说明伊朗希望融入国际学术大家庭。在会议上，各个国家的学者分享了丝绸之路沿线的考古研究和文物保护成果，实现了本系列会议的宗旨。需要强调的是，因为经费和时间限制，很多想来的后来没有参加。现在伊朗的考古和文保力量仍然薄弱，我国可以开展更多的合作项目。

第六部分
书　　评

评韩建业《中国北方地区新石器时代文化研究》[*]

《中国北方地区新石器时代文化研究》的作者韩建业从大学时代起就全身心地钻研我国考古学。攻读硕士和博士学位期间，大量阅读国内外考古学研究成果和理论探索的文献，得以开阔视野并打下功底。多年的勤奋耕耘结出了丰硕的果实，先后有《王湾三期文化研究》（《考古学报》1997年第1期）、《殷墟墓地分区研究》（《考古》1997年第1期）、《试论豫东南地区龙山时代的考古学文化》［《考古学研究》（三）］等重磅文章发表。他主笔的发掘报告有三部：《驻马店杨庄》，《岱海考古》第一、三卷，其他散见于各种学术刊物的论文多达20余篇。其研究时代跨新石器到夏商，其研究地域跨长江到长城。年纪不到40岁而有如此成就，他无疑是我国青年学者中的佼佼者。本书为作者2000年完成的同名博士论文修改后出版的（文物出版社2003年版），系北京大学中国考古学研究中心2000年重大项目"聚落演变与早期文明"阶段性成果之一。全书正文273页，序5页，插图257幅，表8个。

一

这是一部锐意创新的著作。不仅因为它开辟了一个新领域，而且因为它提出了许多新问题，迸发出了许多新思想。而这些新问题和新思想猛烈地冲击了我国考古学上一些根深蒂固的观念。这也是一部厚积薄发

---

[*] 本文原刊于《边疆考古研究》第三辑，2005年，第339—347页。收入本书时略有改动。

的著作。读者不难发现，这些新问题和新思想，正是作者近十年孜孜不倦的钻研所凝聚的结晶。

本书是最早关注北方地区的著作之一。这片包括陕北、晋中北、冀西北在内的地区，在历史上，除内蒙古中南部以外，考古发掘与研究都比较薄弱，尤其是史前时代。由于地缘的关系，北方有考古专业或考古系的大学大多忽略了这一地区。作者就读的北京大学考古系就偏重于黄河和长江流域。然而本书的意义不仅仅是开拓了一个新领域，扩展了我们的认识范围：它叩开了一个学术宝藏。北方地区介于中原的农业文化区与北亚的草原文化区之间，对于研究古代文化交流、人群迁徙、游牧业（nomadism）的起源具有特别的意义。狄宇宙[①]曾经指出，北方地区（该文所指的范围还包括新疆、甘肃、内蒙古东部）在青铜时代和早期铁器时代（相当于商代与两周时期），不仅是畜牧经济为主的草原地区文化与农业经济为主的中原地区文化交往的中间地带，而且是许多独立于商周文明的农业经济文化和畜牧经济文化的发源地。而本书进一步为我们勾勒出了一幅新石器时代（公元前5000—前1900年）高清晰度的北方地区文化与中原地区文化交流的画面。更为重要的是，本书为我们揭示了一个全新的社会复杂化的模式即"北方模式"（第203页）。中原地区在仰韶三期（距今5500年）即已出现阶级分化，到龙山后期（公元前2200—前1900年）则已迈入早期国家的门槛；与此相反，北方地区从兴隆洼期（公元前5700年）到龙山后期一直停留在平等社会的阶段。本书所揭示的这种滞后现象有力地打破了潜移默化于我们头脑中的单一的人类社会稳步前进的中原模式，明确地向我们揭示了社会发展的多样性。

本书的一部重头戏是为北方地区建立了一个系统的年代序列和区系类型。这项工作的分量不轻。一是本地区的遗址存在的年代都很短，大多不超过本书所划分的一个时期。要建立本书的七个时期（兴隆洼时

---

① Di Cosmo, Nicola, The Northern Frontier in Pre-Imperial China, in Michael Loewe and Edwurd L. Shaughessy ed., *Cambridge History of Ancient China*, Cambridge University Press, 1999, pp. 885 – 966.

期、仰韶文化的四期、龙山文化的两期），作者需要收集一大批遗址的材料。然而现有的资料不仅分散，而且发表的质量也良莠不齐。所以资料的爬梳梳理本身就是一项艰巨而棘手的任务。二是本书的年代序列和区系类型跨越兴隆洼、仰韶和龙山三个时代，要完成这样的工作非要具备全面而深厚的中原以及内蒙古东部新石器考古的研究功底不可。由作者来做这项工作是再合适不过，正所谓机遇只降临有准备的人。他一方面得益于对中原地区仰韶时代与龙山时代文化都有精深造诣的导师严文明，另一方面得益于他大学毕业以后勤勤恳恳的研究，对这两个时代的文化分期和区系类型已经打下坚实的基础。

在这一部分，作者向我们展现了一套颇为独特的研究方法。建立如此大规模的年代序列，全书毫无那种烦琐的型式分析，给读者省去了许多"鸡肋式"的烦恼。他采用的方法是先将整个北方地区划分为内蒙古中南部、晋中北与冀西北、陕北三个小区。每个小区内他选择一系列典型遗址、典型单位以及典型器物，建立起各小区的年代序列，然后再整合整个北方地区的年代序列。这样既利用了地层，又把握住典型单位中典型器物的整体变化。整个分期做得干脆利落。即使各期的陶器特征描述也很简洁，读起来很流畅。本书还配有翔实、精美的分期图，读者可以自己去检验，相当客观。在划分区系类型时，他又抓住典型器物来归纳各期的文化特征，只不过这里他区别开两个层次的陶器组合。第一层次代表某期内整个北方地区的文化，而第二层次则反映各个地方类型的特征。

这里我们发现本书的一个新动向：它描绘了一幅动态的地区之间文化交流的画面。他所划分的类型、分布地域是随时期变化的。如仰韶一期（公元前4800年起），作者分出冀西北、岱海、鄂尔多斯—晋中三个小区（类型）；但其后的仰韶二期（公元前4200—前3500年），他只分了内蒙古—晋中（白泥窑子类型）和晋北—冀西北两个小区（马家小村类型）。各期内各类型的来源各不相同，因为同时期中原地区的文化类型也在不断变化。这里充分展现了作者的学术功底：他可以对比七个时期中两个地理区域各类型的陶器群而游刃有余。如仰韶一期里，冀西北和岱海来源于后冈类型，鄂尔多斯—晋中则可能是半坡与后冈两个类

◇❖◇ 第六部分 书评

型融合的产物。在仰韶二期，中原地区仰韶文化分化为四类遗存：史家类型（渭河流域和汉水上游）、东庄类型（晋南豫西）、河南中部（没有命名类型）、后冈类型（豫北冀南）。白泥窑子类型和马家小村类型都是受东庄类型影响产生的，虽然也继承了本地仰韶一期的一些因素。在这两期以及后面的仰韶三期（公元前 3500—前 3000 年）、四期（公元前 3000—前 2500 年）里，中原地区一直是北方地区文化的输送方。但本书特别指出，进入龙山时代后，北方地区就开始向中原地区传播本地创造的文化因素（鬲、卜骨、细石器镞）。因此，呈现在我们面前的北方地区的文化，就像大海一样吞纳百川，然后又像波浪一样冲击到晋南乃至整个中原地区。这种画面实质上是我国考古学观念上的一次飞跃。一方面，它突破了一种僵化的切蛋糕式的或者是分省地图式的区系类型学：一个地区或一个省的文化是本地起源，本地发展，是一脉相承到如今。另一方面，它冲击了根深蒂固的一个中心说——中原地区不再是创造新文化的永不熄火的发动机，也不再是"野蛮海洋里的文明孤岛"。①

聚落形态是一个前沿课题。本书从房屋形制、内部结构、聚落分布和层次分化四个方面系统地追溯了聚落形态在七个时期内的变化，但它特别关注聚落内部与聚落之间的等级分化，是其独到之处。在兴隆洼期，本书推测这样的聚落"是一个以氏族为基础的"，包括大约"单体房屋、排和整个聚落"三级社会组织的公社。进入仰韶一期以后，聚落中出现了区别于其他房屋的"可能为村落集会、议事"的大型房屋；这时"有着向心结构的房屋布局，反映出一种利益与共、血缘凝聚、颇有秩序的平等社会状态"。仰韶三期，这种平等社会仍然延续下来，但是家庭的地位开始凸显出来。本书发现的"北方模式"在聚落形态上表现为北方地区在仰韶三期以后，陆续出现"中心聚落和一般聚落的差别，以及一定程度的贫富分化现象"和聚落群。这实际上也是思想上的一个突破。一种至今仍然盛行的研究方法是把遗址纯粹当作无机的文化载体，视之为房屋、墓葬、器物等成分的组合体。而本书把遗址当作具

---

① 张光直：《商文明》，张良仁、岳红彬、丁晓雷译，辽宁教育出版社 2002 年版。

评韩建业《中国北方地区新石器时代文化研究》

有生命力的行为个体,还原了它作为从事政治、经济、文化活动的社会组织的本色。这对传统观念也是一个有力的冲击。

人地关系是本书提出的另一个前沿课题。这里作者吸收了地质学、地理学、气候学的研究成果,以此来检验各期文化的经济形态、房屋结构、人群移动。比起以往只满足于琢磨坛坛罐罐或者附上几个分析报告(孢粉、动物骨骼、金属成分等)的做法来,这种结合自然科学来解释考古学现象的方法是一个很大的进步。难能可贵的是,作者运用这些学科的术语时,一点也不显得生涩。这一部分讲的是仰韶一、二期为气候暖湿时期,适宜农耕,来自东部的镇江营一期和西部的半坡类型的农民迁徙到北方地区。仰韶三期以后,气温下降,降水减少。这一时期农业虽然继续存在,但是来自东北和东部的狩猎人群进入北方地区;同时节约木材的窑洞式房屋在晋中开始使用。仰韶四期,温度与降水降到一个临界点,与此相应的变化是标志着原始战争的石围墙和石墙房屋出现。龙山后期温度下降,北方地区由于人口压力的增长,大量人群开始南迁。过去人们大多将类似的文化变化归因于政治事件(如夏商更替),而本书的自然环境说则为我们解释古代的人群流动提供了一个新的视角。

二

由上所述,本书为我们以后的研究提供了许多新思路和新观念。同时,它们对我们以后的研究提出了挑战。这主要表现在:一是本书发现的一些考古学现象的学术价值,还可以进一步挖掘;二是本书的考古学材料表明,我国考古学亟须填补和完善一些理论;三是本书所提出的一些新问题,需要有力的论证手段的支持。而迎接这些挑战将会推动我国考古学的前进。在此本人提出一些粗浅的想法,供读者参考。

如前所述,本书观察到北方地区在社会复杂化进程上的滞后性,是它的一个新发现。鉴于目前我们对于古代社会发展的认识是以中原地区为背景建立起来的,本人设想:如果对中原地区和北方地区的社会发

◇❖◇　第六部分　书评

展、经济形态、自然环境作进一步的比较研究，是否可以发现气候、地理等自然条件对政治、经济、社会形态的制约作用，乃至摸索出一些新的决定社会复杂化进程的自然与社会因素来呢？不论答案如何，这种研究所得到的社会发展规律将会更加客观，其适用范围也会更为广阔。

　　本书以若干种普遍分布的陶器来归纳各期的仰韶文化与龙山文化的方法，再次引发出考古学文化的划分问题。夏鼐的定义已经成为我国考古学界公认的标准。他所提出的三个条件："一群特征、多处遗址、充分认识"，[①] 现在看来，很容易满足，仰韶文化也是完全符合的。不过，迄今所命名的文化中，大部分在陶器群上，虽然不完全一致，但相当接近，像大家常提的"商文化"、"二里头文化"、一些原先认定的大文化如龙山。本书表明，该文化各期的典型遗址的陶器群是千差万别的。如仰韶一期代表冀西北类遗存的四十里坡遗址，"主要器类为红顶钵、锥足鼎、直口球腹双耳壶、圆唇盆、盆形甑、彩陶罐等"，而代表岱海小区类遗存的石虎山Ⅰ和Ⅱ遗存，"器类主要有红顶钵、红顶盆、釜、釜形鼎、壶等……外还有直腹罐、圈足碗、圈足纽式器盖、小勺"。实际上，它们之间的共同器物仅限于作者归纳的"钵、壶、盆"。此外，且不说中原地区，北方地区的地理环境就很复杂多样，包括"中部黄土丘陵梁峁区、东部山地盆地区、西部沙地丘陵区和西北河套平原区"。虽然同属农耕文化区，但生态、经济和聚落形态差异都不小。在这样的共性和特性面前，仰韶文化是否需要予以拆分，实质上是一个界定考古学文化的标准问题。[②] 夏鼐提出的三个条件没有回答这一问题；它需要我们做进一步的探索。

　　在谱系研究中，作者采用了我国考古学界常见的套路，即比较中原地区和北方地区各类型共同存在的某种陶器纹饰和其他文化因素，由此

[①] 夏鼐：《关于考古学上文化的定名问题》，《夏鼐文集》第二编，社会科学文献出版社2017年版，第354—358页。

[②] 类似的标准问题发生在分布于西伯利亚和哈萨克斯坦的大文化安德罗诺沃文化（Andronovo）上。该文化在墓葬形制、尸体的摆放姿势和随葬品上相当一致。它命名于20世纪20年代，但50年代以后俄罗斯和哈萨克斯坦的学者依据一些看起来很细微的差别（陶器的花纹、形制、棺椁的材料和建造方法）将它分解开来（Aakul'文化、Fedorov文化和Nura、Atasu类型）。

评韩建业《中国北方地区新石器时代文化研究》

追寻两个地区之间的文化交流。在解释文化交流时，这种套路隐含一个假设，即如果类似的东西在两个地方出现，那是因为一个地方的人群迁徙到另一个地方去了。这种方法有的时候是可行的，比方说中原地区仰韶文化第一期遗存在北方地区的出现。因为严文明在序言中说，北方地区仰韶文化以前的"遗存至今只有极个别而难以确定的发现"，也就是说，"那里的居民一定是非常稀少的"。但是在其他时候就有些牵强。按照这个思路，本书提出的龙山前期北方地区的老虎山文化（的居民）大规模南迁，向中原地区带去了鬲、卜骨和细石器镞的假说，就面临两个难题：一是这些南迁的北方人怎么就带去了鬲、卜骨和细石器镞。二是他们怎么带去了中原地区诸文化所呈现的那么多种鬲形器（按作者的描述，北方地区流行斝式鬲，而客省庄二期文化和齐家文化均为斝式鬲和单把袋足鬲，后冈二期文化则无鬲有鬹，第127—145页）。看起来，这种假设在解释文化交流上还有盲区，我们还需要寻找更多的解释模式。

　　文化传播的方式，我国还没有专门的理论研究。实际上这是一个复杂的问题，值得引起学术界的重视。本人学过艺术史，这里不妨举一个例子。虽然本例属于历史时期，有文献记载的优势，与新石器时代的情形大不相同，但是它可以拓宽我们的思路。17世纪、18世纪的朝鲜画家很推崇我国明清时代的文人山水画，那么他们是如何学习中国画的呢？我国的画家很少到朝鲜去，一般的朝鲜画家也难得有机会到我国来。他们中只有少数几个人可以随同每年几次的政府使团到北京来，与我国的有艺术修养的官员（晚明的文人画泰斗董其昌作为政府官员曾接待过朝鲜画家，属于例外）和民间画家（集中于琉璃厂）交流。但是他们还是见不到当时代表中国最高水平的南方画派（杭州、松江、扬州）的艺术家和作品，当然谈不上与他们直接切磋了。不过，使团中的成员（不限于画家）往往通过交换和购买得到一些作品（包括赝品）、画册、画谱，回国后送给或者卖给他们认识的画家和收藏家。这样，朝鲜画家顶多可以接触到中国二三流的作品，印刷粗糙（较当代技术而言）的画册、画谱和"微言大义"的理论著作，至于中国画具体的技术细节和思想内涵，大多靠自己去揣摩领会了。不过，他们并不只是简

◇❖◇ 第六部分 书评

单地模仿，而是形成了自己的以郑敾（1676—1759年）为首的山水画派，体现出朝鲜本土的文化氛围和艺术追求。① 由此看来，不仅文化传播的方式复杂多样，有予也有取，而且接受方并非全盘照搬，而是根据自己的需要予以吸收转化。在此，我们可能需要有一点"以人为本"的思想，需要考虑人类自身在文化行为中的主观能动性，从而避免把一个人群视为不加选择地接受外来文化的简单的容器。

在聚落形态部分，本书为我们讲述了一个大家庭的兴起和聚落间原始战争出现的故事。两个视角都很新颖，值得我们借鉴。遗憾的是，目前有关聚落的考古资料参差不齐。仰韶一期的石虎山Ⅰ、Ⅱ聚落，二期的王墓山坡下、龙山前期的园子沟、老虎山算是全貌清楚的，仰韶三、四期以及龙山后期就缺乏这样的遗址。即使前面所说的三期也只有一两处，没有多少统计价值。资料的不完备，自然降低了故事的可信度。如果说仰韶四期的寨子圪旦的石围墙（本身宽度作者没说）是原始战争出现的迹象，那么仰韶一期的石虎山Ⅰ的环壕（口部残存宽度为1.3—3米）作为防御设施也未尝不可。由此本人设想，将来如果有人选择两三个具有不同时期聚落的区域作全面的调查和测绘工作，结合现有的发掘资料，那么他或她就有可能缕出聚落形态变化（居址地貌类型的转换、房屋布局与经济形态的变化、祭祀遗迹的出现、聚落的扩大）的规律来。其实岱海地区，如本书图二、图三所示，就是一个很理想的研究区域，因为这里已经发现有16处属于不同时期的聚落。即使就岱海一个地区而言，前景也是相当不错的。

人地关系是本书最富挑战的部分。归根结底，我国对古代气候的研究至今还很薄弱。我们高兴地看到，现在已经有一些气象学家如史培军等开始到考古工地取样。但不容置疑的是，这仅仅是个起步。本书所能收集到的与北方地区相关的五张曲线图（图三、四、五、七、八）大多是整千年（如1000BP、2000BP）取一个测点，只有表一有两个500年的测点（1500BP、3500BP）。这样画出来的曲线图显然过于粗放，难以切合精确到几百年的考古学文化的需要。本书将距今5500年（仰韶

---

① Artistic Activities of Korean Envoys in China，见本书。

三期）的干冷期里窑洞式房屋在晋中的出现以及距今 5000 年（仰韶四期）的持续干冷期里人口压力的增加和争夺资源的战争的爆发与气候变化相联系也是它所能期待的最好的结论。这里本人热切希望有更多的气象学与考古学相结合的研究，那么将来得到的气候波动曲线图就有可能变得精密可靠，那时再来做人地关系这个课题也许能得出更为准确的结论来。[①] 同时，以现有的材料而言，如果从另一个角度来看，也有可能得出一个粗略的但是相对可信的结论来。本人注意到，虽然图三（鄂尔多斯地区 1000 年冷暖变化过程）的温度没有显示波动现象，但是图四（鄂尔多斯地区 10000 年干湿变化过程）、图五（1000 年来黄旗海湖面水位变化曲线）和图六（岱海距今 11000—1000 年湖面变化数据表）反映的距今 5000—2000 年之间的降水值起伏很有规律。其中图四的最高值与最低值与今天和公元 1000 年差不多。将来如果有人对这两个时期的气候变化以及它们对生态、经济、社会的影响作一番深入研究的话，他或她说不定能建立起一个不错的参照标准来推演新石器时代的情形。那时我们再去衡量气候变化给社会带来的后果就更有根据了。

三

本书在研究和行文方面还有一些有待完善的地方。这些细节在目前的学术著作中并不少见，在此指出来以引起注意，不妥之处请读者批评。本书对一些考古学现象的解释带有一些主观臆测的成分。为了抵抗敌人的进攻而建造石围墙，是一种很容易想象得到的说法。但是如果换个角度，说石围墙的建造是为了防御野兽和山洪似乎也可以。野兽自不必说。至于防洪，本书提到的冲沟和水土流失已经显示了这种可能性。

---

① 这里简要介绍一下俄罗斯的古气候研究，以资参考。相对来说，该国在这方面的研究力量较为雄厚，历史较长，而且是多学科相结合，但各学科得到的结论有时会发生冲突。比方说，乌拉尔山以东地区青铜时代的气候，孢粉分析说距今 4300—3500 年之间为干旱期，古地理学说距今 3800—3400 年之间出现湿润气候和针叶林，古土壤学说与当代气候接近，但最后向干旱和大陆性气候转变，考古学和古动物学资料则说是湿润气候，并且冬天较为温暖（见 Zdanovich, G. B., 1997, Arkaim kul'turnyi kompleks èpokhi srednei bronzy Iuzhnogo Zaural'ia, *Rossiĭskaia Arkheologiia* 2, 1997, pp. 47–62）。

◇❖◇ 第六部分 书评

这再次说明，系统的区域调查与测绘是有必要的。那样做就可以排除一些可能性，从而得出一个可靠的结论来。本书提出单座房屋代表核心家庭，自成一区的房屋代表大家庭，若干区组成家族公社。这作为一种假说当然可以，不过本书没有提供遗址以外的辅助的证据。这里本人指的是民族学以及社会结构方面的研究，但迄今为止，我国仍然缺乏这样的研究。将来如果有人对社会结构和聚落形态做一番系统的梳理，那么他或她就填补了我国考古学上的一个空白。官地房址 F5 内 H61 的五具成年男性尸体的身份也是以前难得碰到的现象，所以作者在"英雄"与"罪犯"之间拿捏不定一点也不奇怪。面对这样的难题，本人也想不出一个更好的解释来。但是如果从有人已经提出的居室葬入手，[①] 那么本书就有了一个坚实的出发点。本书所揭示的文化面貌相似、地域接近的岱海聚落群是一个有趣的细节。但是目前我国还没有一个现成的解释模式，所以本书推测这样的聚落群（如岱海北岸）为友好相处、共同对外的军事联盟，也是可以理解的。不过从立论的角度讲，如果作者能够参照历史和自己的社会观察先衡量推测的合理性，那么所做的推测会更加可靠。据本人所知，春秋时期邻国之间的战争此起彼伏，可是并没有多少邻国的文化存在显著的差别。[②]

在行文上，本书还不够规范。作为学术论文，不仅文字讲究平实、简洁，讲究准确地表述论证的过程和观点，而且引用书目讲究完备。本书中的口语词汇"公家"，文学语言"站在山头望，欣然有澄清天下之志；后看，则高峰仰止，气为之折"，哲学词汇"天人合一"都是不宜使用的。书中还有不少似乎无助于论证的描述文字。如介绍仰韶四期内蒙古中南部和陕北遗存时，作者好像忘了他的典型遗址、典型陶器方

[①] 陈星灿：《史前居室葬俗的研究》，《华夏考古》1989 年第 2 期，第 93—99 页；杨虎、刘国祥：《兴隆洼文化居室葬俗及相关问题探讨》，《考古》1997 年第 1 期，第 27—36 页。

[②] 此处可能有争议。部分学者认为，进入春秋时期以后周文化分裂，形成各具特色的诸侯国文化（如齐文化、晋文化、楚文化之类）。但是罗泰（von Falkenhausen, Lothar, The Waning of the Bronze Age: Material Culture and Social Developments, 770BC – 481BC, in Michael Loewe and Edward L. Shaughnesey ed., *Cambridge History of Ancient China*, Cambridge University Press, 1999, pp. 450 – 544）指出，春秋时期中原地区各诸侯国延续了西周时期的周文化，面貌相当一致。

法，结果陶质、陶色、石器、骨器一股儿脑全搬到了书上，好像典型遗址能代表同类遗址所有的文化特征似的。书中模糊词汇"影响"随处可见。这个词汇包含的意思有很多；比方说，人群 A 卖或送陶器给人群 B 是影响，人群 A 教人群 B 做陶器是影响，人群 A 做陶器给人群 B 看也是影响。因为本书旨在通过陶器来追寻人类的行为，所以选择更为准确的词汇是有必要的。这不仅仅是用词的问题，而且是研究方法的问题。如果作者考虑到这些具体而复杂的行为方式的话，他也许会考虑"人群迁徙"以外的解释模式。此外，本书关于"典型遗址、典型单位、典型器物"三个概念的叙述，让本人回忆起了苏秉琦、殷玮璋的《地层学与器物类型学》一文（《文物》1982 年第 4 期）。可是本章的文献目录中只收入了严文明的《考古资料整理中的标型学研究》（《走向 21 世纪的考古学》，三秦出版社 1997 年版）。两篇文章内容有相似的地方，作为学术论文都应当收入，而且说明有关理论的传承变化，以求公允。

精烹细调　可以咀嚼
——读许宏《最早的中国》*

去年 8 月,《最早的中国》样书刚出来,作者就送了我一本。作为多年的同事,我欣然收下,把书搁在案头,隔三岔五地读上几段,所以到现在才读完。但是正是因为读得慢,所以能够细细品味作者的文字,体察作者的细腻。毫不夸张地说,这是一本精烹细调的,很有嚼头的科普著作。

本书讲的二里头遗址位于河南省偃师市二里头村,是我国青铜时代的一个最重要的遗址,一直受到国内外学术界的瞩目。1959 年中国社会科学院考古研究所著名的历史学家徐旭生在伊洛河流域调查"夏墟"时发现了这个遗址。进入 20 世纪 60 年代,考古工作者在这里发现了一个大规模的夯土建筑基址(Ⅰ号宫殿),因而认定这个遗址是我国早期的一个都邑,其年代早于安阳,也早于郑州商城。20 世纪七八十年代,发现了另一座大型夯土基址(Ⅱ号宫殿)和我国最早的青铜礼器,进一步肯定了该遗址的都邑地位。作为我国青铜时代早期的一个都邑级别的遗址,它一直是国内外学术界探讨我国文明起源和国家起源的焦点。

本书是一本科普著作。写科普,当然首先要"有科可普"。在这方面,作者不仅掌握 1959 年以来的许多重要发现资料,而且更重要的是,他还拥有自 1999 年他本人担任二里头工作队队长以来取得的许多突破性成果。比较重要的,一是宫城和周围的道路网在过去的发现中,只有几座零星的宫殿台基,现在发现它们是一个宫城的组成部分,同时作者

---

* 本文原刊于《中国文物报》2010 年 4 月 30 日第 8 版。收入本书时略有改动。

精烹细调　可以咀嚼

和他的工作队又发现了几座新的宫殿台基。这样宫城就展现出一个全新的面貌——后来的宫城中轴对称、南北延伸的布局之源就在这里。二是伊洛河流域的同时期聚落。作者和他的工作队在二里头遗址所在的伊洛河流域开展聚落调查，发现了一个等级分明的聚落遗址群。这样，二里头遗址不再是一个孤立的都邑，而是坐落在一个金字塔形聚落体系的塔尖上。

　　读者不要以为老天特别关照作者，让他在不长的十年内能有如此目不暇接的发现。这是作者敏锐的眼光和细致的工作的结果。正如作者自己所说，他梳理了过去的发掘记录，从中发现了宫城城墙的蛛丝马迹，然后在田野工作中追踪线索，最后才找到整个围墙。所以宫城的发现并不是天上掉下的馅饼，而是作者心血的结晶。同时，读者们不要以为发掘宫城就像刨土豆一样，翻开土它就出来了。我国的古代建筑不比希腊罗马的建筑，都是土木结构，发掘起来极其困难。经过历史长河的洗刷，墙体以上一般都已经消失了，剩下的只是基础部分。但是因为建造基础所用的土取自本地，所以基础和周围的地面非常不易区分。在二里头遗址尤其如此。这是因为二里头遗址经过后世的居住和生产已经被破坏得七零八碎了，在坑坑洼洼的地面上寻找宫城城墙需要过硬的发掘技术和过人的耐心才行。作者有长期的城址发掘工作经验，在1996—1998年河南偃师商城宫城的发掘过程中本人也见识了他精湛的发掘技术，所以作者说的"机遇属于有准备者"是一点没错啊。

　　然而，作者并没有满足于介绍二里头遗址的发现，他还广泛吸纳了国内外学术界的研究成果。在这里我们见识了作者开阔的视野和勤勉的学风。长期以来，不少学者只满足于阅读国内出版的研究文献，谈论一些传统问题如城市布局、文明起源、文化性质和文化交往。在本书中，除了上述问题，作者还吸收了他本人关于我国古代礼制和城市发展的研究成果，同时吸收了国内外关于二里头遗址的"人口构成"和"城市民生"的最新的研究成果。其中谈到了古代居民所赖以生存的粮食和家畜问题，以及古代奢侈品（如玉器、青铜器、漆器）的生产问题。因此本书不仅对一般读者有用，对考古工作者也非常有用。像我这样对二里头遗址已经相当熟悉的人来说，也能从本书得到不少收获。

当然,有关二里头遗址,还有一些问题需要解决。书中谈到的"人口构成"和"城市民生"都是当代考古学提出的新问题,有关这些问题的研究才刚刚开始。这是因为以往的注意力多集中在宫殿区,宫殿区以外虽然有过一些发掘,但是情况还远远不太清楚。我们或许可以想象,在宫殿区的周围生活着贵族和平民。就像我国首都北京不仅有中央和北京市政府,还有许多科研单位、企业和居民区,这样才是一个完整的都城。因此发掘古代贵族和平民的居住区,将有助于我们了解他们的历史面貌和整个都邑的社会形态。他们是否聚族而居?他们是否从事农业、手工业(纺织品、装饰品、工具、日用器皿)的生产?他们是否能够自给自足,还是存在某种程度上的产业分工?我们期待作者和他的同事在这些方面取得新的进展。

同时,我们还要提醒读者本书存在的一些问题。尽管作者时时小心,但还是掉进了传统思维的陷阱。他说:"中国史前文化及早期文明基本上是在相对封闭的地理条件下起源和独自发展的。"他写这句话的时候,大概是拿着现代中国版图的眼光来看问题的。然而,我们知道,中原的夏商王朝所统辖的土地很小,大体相当于今天的河南省和周围省份的部分地域。但是它们并不封闭,而是同周围乃至遥远的文化之间保持着活跃的交流活动。比方说,二里头文化的玉璋出现在越南和广东等地,同时欧亚大陆的青铜技术也可能传到了二里头,所以才有了后来商周时期大规模的青铜器生产。这些事实都是本书已经向我们揭示了的。

在大多数问题上,作者非常严谨,让人肃然起敬。在二里头文化属夏属商的定性问题上,学术界的分歧很大。作为二里头队的队长,作者常常有表态的压力。但是他没有跟随目前学术界的"主流观点",即二里头遗址为夏代晚期都城。他说:"目前的考古学与文献史学研究的进展,尚不足以支持以夏王朝的史迹为核心内容的'夏文化'以及'夏代'的最终确立。"在现有的资料条件下,这是一个客观的看法。因为有关夏代和商代早期历史的可靠的文献记载只有区区几条,它们并不能为我们准确地指认其都邑所在,也不能提供准确的年代范围。同时,考古学材料本身并不能告诉我们二里头遗址是属于夏族还是属于商族。这个问题,恐怕只有等文字材料的出现才能得到最终的解决。

精烹细调　可以咀嚼　◇❖◇

但是作者的有些说法是值得商榷的。在谈到夏商周断代工程时，他说："夏商周断代工程公布的年表，将夏、商、周王朝建立的年代分别定为公元前2070年、前1600年和前1046年，也只能看作是一种说法而已"。这句话似乎带有一点藐视权威的味道。夏商周断代工程集若干学科的力量经过若干年的攻关，它所得到的年代框架，虽然不一定是正确的，但应该说是现有的年代方案中最为可靠的。

书中数次提到良渚文化。但是学术界对这个文化的认识还很肤浅，长期以来，考古学家们只发现了它的一些墓葬和祭坛，获得了它得以出名的大量的玉器，但是它的城址和聚落发现得很少。因此，有关良渚文化的衰落在学术界是一个有待解开的谜团。所以，作者把它的灭亡视为该文明的经济方式纯洁的结果（第62页）有些草率。因为考古资料还少，我们还不能说良渚文化的经济活动是纯洁还是混合的。根据我们的经验，良渚文化应当不只是依赖于水稻，应当还从事其他农作物的耕作和家畜的饲养。虽然它可能不种北方的农作物粟，但是如果气候没有发生突变，它的各种经济活动应当能够满足它的生存需要。

本人指出上述的一些问题，并不是说本人能写得更好。老实说，本人没有作者这样的学识来写这本书。作者在二里头遗址精心耕耘多年，对该遗址的发掘和研究情况谙熟于胸，因而能够取舍自如，无所拘碍。更为难能可贵的是，作者能够放下自己的研究工作，来写这样的利人不利己的科普著作。在国外，考古学家们不仅经常搞"Open House（开放日）"和"Public Lecture（公共讲座）"，而且还有人专门写科普著作，以便回馈社会，吸引社会关注并支持考古。在我国，尹达先生1954年就曾号召考古学家"向广大人民进行关于古代文物的宣传教育工作"（《关于开展考古工作的建议》，《文物参考资料》1954年第3期）。他呼吁博物馆和文化馆举办经常性的或定期的展览会、考古工作者举办现场展览会或讲演会、编制幻灯片和录制电影。他认为，这是"动员和组织群众性的保护历史文物的重要环节；同时，也是进行爱国主义教育中的重要组成部分"。但是，过去由于发掘工作繁重，考古学家没有时间写科普读物。今天考古学家们有时间了，但仍然不愿写，要不就大写特写墓葬里出土的宝贝，好像考古工作者只是在挖宝。至于考古工作者究竟是干什么的，社会仍然不清楚。

由于对科普的忽视，考古学家越来越与社会脱节。他们越来越满足于摆弄自己的坛坛罐罐，越来越局限于几个传统问题，如文化性质和文化联系。他们写的考古报告和论文连我们的兄弟学科历史学的学者们都看不懂，更不要说社会公众了。如果我们的考古科普工作做得更好一些，社会不仅会支持我们的工作，而且会给我们提出许多新鲜的问题，大大开阔我们的视野。我记得，十几年前我在偃师商城宫城发掘的时候，一位德国的考古学家曾经问我宫城的厕所在哪里，把我问得目瞪口呆。吃喝拉撒睡乃是人类的正常需要，但是我们过去更多的是盯着宫殿基址，而忽略了其他遗迹。

当然，科普著作固然要有人愿意写，还要有人善于写。写科普本身也是一门学问。它不仅要有料，还要有"技"。这样写出来的东西读者才能看懂，而且愿意看。在这方面，作者是用足了心思的。全书不厚，233页，便于携带。各个章节也都短小精悍，可以几分钟读完。这样读者可以利用零散的时间而不用抽出大块的时间来读它。各个章节的题目不仅简洁，而且俏皮，给人以阅读的冲动。此外，本书还特别讲究细节，对一些考古学术语做了详细的说明，并且对一些生僻字做了拼音。一般读者无需借助字典就可以读完本书。此外，除了本书的正文，遍及全书的边注、脚注、图注都为读者们提供了丰富的信息。正如前面所说，无论是社会公众还是考古学家都能从中得到收益。这是一本难得的科普著作，一本"精烹细调，可以咀嚼"的著作。

建德垂风　维城之基

——读罗泰教授《宗子维城》*

我是罗泰教授（Lothar von Falkhausen）的学生，以自己的学养来评论老师的著作，实在是不够格的。我虽然从大学时代就学习中国考古，而且工作后从事过一段时间的商周考古，但其实没有什么功底，历史文献和古文字都不曾入门。到美国留学后，又换了方向从事俄罗斯考古，就连早年积累的一点家底也丢光了。不过因为跟随罗泰教授读书，课上课下，耳濡目染，所以对他的学问多少有些了解。后来又因为参与《宗子维城》中文版的审校，将《宗子维城》原版和译稿仔细阅读过几遍，对其内容有些了解，所以在此写下一点个人感想。

在国际汉学界，罗泰教授是一位非常特别的学者。他先后在波恩大学学习汉语，在北京大学学习中国考古学，又在哈佛大学学习人类学，在京都大学学习中国考古学，所以通晓欧洲、中国、美国和日本有关中国考古学的研究范式和研究成果。他熟谙西方人类学理论，但是他不像其他一些美国学者，不喜欢摆弄理论，而喜欢做实证研究。他喜欢广交朋友，只要来到中国，即马不停蹄地到处拜访考古学家，探访考古工地，会晤旧雨新知；有人来到洛杉矶，只要他在，无论多忙，他都会抽出时间来接待。他自己出身德国贵族，谈吐优雅，举止从容，上自年长的学者，下到年轻的学生，无不愿意与他交谈。因而他对于我国考古学界的人和事、学术动态，比我们中国大多数学者（包括我）还了解且每每有深刻的见解，是位名正言顺的汉学家。他尊于师长，友于同学，

---

* 本文原刊于《文汇学人》2019 年 6 月 14 日和 6 月 21 日。收入本书时略有改动。

◇❖◇ 第六部分 书评

尊于专业，曾为夏鼐、苏秉琦、俞伟超和邹衡等先生撰写评传，自谓非"使徒行传"，而是尝试梳理近百年中国考古学史。他和俞伟超先生交往尤多，对俞先生的感情也极深，所以《宗子维城》题献给俞伟超先生。而对于学术，罗泰先生喜欢较真，经常撰写书评，充当学术界的"啄木鸟"；虽然不免得罪人，但是乐此不疲。所谓"文如斯人"，读者在咀嚼《宗子维城》时，当会体会到他的这些品质。

《宗子维城》英文版和日文版出版于2006年，韩文版出版于2009年，中文版从翻译到出版迁延时日，前后耗时近十年。我因参与本书审校，所以知晓其中之艰难。细推敲起来，原因有四：第一，作者当年赴美留学虽没有参加GRE考试，但是喜欢用GRE词汇，这些词汇翻译起来非常困难；第二，他饱读《春秋》《左传》等历史文献，深谙微言大义之道，然对于翻译者而言，言外之意最难传达；第三，他将人类学理论和概念融会贯通，渗透到字里行间，而我国人类学基础薄弱，翻译者不太熟悉那一套语言，所以翻译起来非常吃力；第四，他自己非常爱惜羽毛，译稿出来后，找了三位学者（包括我）审校三遍，自己又最后审校一遍，才把书稿交付出版社。在今天追求经济效益的潮流中，一般的出版社，早就放弃了，好在上海古籍出版社，有眼光，有定力，舍得耐心，耗得时间，始终不离不弃。好在本书一面世，就得到了我国读者的追捧，总算没有辜负出版社的一番执着和投入。

关于本书，夏含夷（Edward L. Shaughnessy）、杜朴（Robert L. Thorp）、马思忠（Magnus Fiskesjö）、杜德兰（Alain Thote）和汪涛等西方汉学家都前后写过书评。除了一些客套性的溢美之词，他们提出了一些批评意见，归纳言之，有如下几点：第一，本书把史墙盘放在西周晚期，因而提出礼制改革突然开始于西周晚期，是一家之言；大多数学者则认同李学勤的看法，把史墙盘的年代定为共王之世，从而将礼制改革的起始时间放在西周中期，即懿、孝和夷王之世。第二，东周时期族群和文化多样，不存在一个称为"中国"的社会。第三，本书只利用考古资料，而本书所勾勒的时代是《诗经》诸诗兴起的时代，但是由于未使用历史文献，本书没有讲述当时人们的爱情生活。第四，本书过于注重青铜器，而忽略了陶器；而由陶器来看，楚文化不一定属于周文化。以上这些意见，实际并不专针对本书，而是在西方汉学界由来已久，至于《宗子维城》中的回答是否令学界及读者满意，还需请读者自行判断。

一

《宗子维城》凡分九章，没有涉及政治、军事，也没有涉及经济和精神层面，只探讨周代的社会问题。应当说，周代社会因为有历史文献和古文字材料的便利，过去已有很多学者做过研究，成果可以说汗牛充栋，进一步研究的空间似乎"山重水复疑无路"。本书故意舍弃历史文献和古文字材料而不用，只利用考古资料，不曾想"柳暗花明又一村"，新发现和新见解层出不穷，大幅度地修正或丰富了我们对于周代社会原有的认识。

（一）氏族制度

氏族（一般称"宗族"，本文采用书中所用的"氏族"）制度是西方人类学关注的一个问题，也是研究社会复杂化的一个方向。马克思和恩格斯讲的私有制起源就与它有关，只不过当时民族学刚刚起步，材料并不丰富，他们依赖的是摩尔根（Lewis Henry Morgan，1818—1881年）收集的印第安人的社会调查资料和希腊罗马时代的历史文献。20世纪西方学者在美洲、太平洋岛屿、大洋洲和非洲做了大量的民族学调查；当时苏联和中国学者也做了大量的民族学调查，因此民族学资料可谓汗牛充栋，可惜大家没有利用这些材料调整观点。西方人类学家也没有利用这些资料进一步研究氏族制度与社会复杂化的关系。我的《村落与社会进化》（《考古》2017年第2期）做了一些尝试。我提出，平等的部落社会实际上就是一个个氏族，土地为氏族所共有，作为成员的家庭拥有土地；而到了酋邦和国家，一个氏族或氏族联盟征服另一些氏族或氏族联盟，掌握了土地所有权，于是征服者成了统治阶层和剥削阶层，而被征服者成了被统治阶层和被剥削阶层。国家级社会本身也经历了长期的发展，由王国向帝国的转变就是一个重要的发展阶段。按照上述理论的推演，在这个阶段，由于国家权力的强大，氏族制度逐渐遭到破坏。

《宗子维城》一书研究的时间段为西周到战国时期，正是商周王国向秦汉帝国转变的阶段。在人类学上，这是一个以往研究不太充分的阶段。罗泰教授此书充分利用了陕西扶风庄白一号窖藏微氏氏族青铜器群的器物形态，分析研究，提出问题。这批铜器因为器物较多，历时较长，铭文内容丰富，一向受到研究者的重视。其中杰西卡·罗森（Jessica Rawson）等人采用西方的艺术史方法分析了这批铜器的纹饰，从而将它们分为三期。而罗泰教授则利用铜器上的铭文，探讨西周的氏族制度和祖先崇拜。铭文中既有献器者（donor）的名字，也有受祭祖先（dedicatee）的名讳，本书利用这些人名重建了微氏氏族史墙支族的祖先谱系，并且依据《仪礼》记载，提出古代氏族每五代分裂一次，各个支族的地位依兄弟的排行伯仲季叔而定。这样每个氏族就像原子裂变，随着年代的推移，生长出众多高低不等的支族来。而且随着时间的推移，一个支族的祖先逐渐增多，各个支族的成员，为了节约人力物力，只能选择重要节点上的祖先（氏族创始人、支族创始人）和近祖（曾祖父、祖父、父亲）来祭祀。

这是《宗子维城》的一个重要贡献，它把我们对于西周氏族制度的认识提高到一个新的水平。摆在我们面前的是一个经典形态的氏族制度，至于它的后续变化，本书则着力不多。而实际上，本书所谈到的春秋战国时期的一些变化，如赋税制、郡县制、常备军和军功制都与此相关。有关西周和东周的井田制，因为文献记载零星且多语焉不详，长期以来争议不断，不绝于耳。周天子拥有名义上的全国土地所有权，他将土地和土地上的人口分配给王室、诸侯和卿大夫等各级氏族（支族）；至于氏族或支族内部土地如何分配，如何耕种，如何纳贡，我们则多不得而知。施行赋税制后，诸侯国国君直接向本国百姓征收赋税，因而财力大为增强，国力日臻强盛；而相应的，各级贵族的财力则大为削弱。土地可能在这一过程中由氏族所有渐变为个人私有。郡县制实行以后，一个国家不再由大大小小的氏族管理，而是由君主和各级官府直接管理。军队在西周时期由大大小小的贵族自备武器、战车组成，规模甚小；后来改由农户出兵，脱离土地，成为职业军人，国家供给衣食和武器，于是出现了几十万人的庞大军队。同样，相应的，此时各级贵族的军事力量也急剧缩小。这样以土地改革为核心，财力和兵力都向国家集中，为后来中央集权国家的出现奠定了基础。可惜其中的诸多细节，今天我们均无从了解。但是所有这些变化都像一只只重锤，砸向了氏族制度。

（二）列鼎制度

等级制度的物化表现也是西方人类学关心的一个问题。在"过程主义考古学"（processual archaeology）风头正盛的 20 世纪 60 和 70 年代，学者们努力寻找一套客观而普遍适用的标准来衡量，于是有了萨克思（A. A. Saxe）等人的"能量消耗指标"。但是到了 80 年代，"后过程主义"（post-processual archaeology）兴起，这种物化标准遭到了怀疑。罗泰教授无疑吸取了"后过程主义"的一些思想，因而为读者特别指出了两点：墓葬首先是丧葬礼仪遗留下来的产物，所以它并不直接或只是反映死者的社会地位；墓葬行为主要体现的不是墓主本人的意志，而是在世的后嗣维护自身社会地位的需要。当然，作者没有放弃物化标准，相反做了精彩的分析。在商周时期，这种物化标准显然是存在的。唐际根和韩建业先后分析了殷墟西区墓葬所展现的社会分化，发现在墓道数量、墓室规模、棺椁数量、青铜器和车马数量等诸多方面都有相应展现。这一物化标准在本书研究的西周晚期和春秋时期墓葬，也有充分的体现。这一现象在人类学上非常重要，需要我们思考：为什么在商周王朝有如此显著的物化表现？而在世界其他地方则不那么明显呢？

到了西周晚期和春秋时期，这种物化表现又有了新的变化，即出现了现代意义上的严格的量化标准。简而言之，此即国内外学者耳熟能详的"列鼎制度"。但是这一制度并没有完整地记载在历史文献中，是高明和俞伟超两位先生拼合了散见于各处文献的片言只语而复原起来的，然后与考古资料对应。然而对应的情况并不是很好，一些诸侯墓（如中山王墓）里出土了周天子级别的"九鼎八簋"，而周天子墓当时还没有发现，随葬情况不得而知；近年来虽然在周公庙发现了周天子级别的大墓葬，但是盗损严重，器物组合不明。所以李学勤先生提出了一个修正方案，即周天子的规格可能更高一些，是"十二鼎十簋"，而诸侯是"九鼎八簋"。现在无法确定哪个方案是对的，但是"列鼎制度"的存在则是没有疑问的。作者于书中所分析的三门峡虢国墓地，为我们提供了九鼎、七鼎、五鼎和三鼎等各种规格的样例，就是一个很好的证明。

《宗子维城》的一个重要论点就是东周时期的众多诸侯国大多接受了"列鼎制度"（包括配套的棺椁、车马、编钟诸方面的等级制度），因而都属于"周文化圈"。这一论点是"反潮流"、"反传统"的，是罗泰教授的创见。以往国内外学者注重各诸侯国随葬陶器上的差别，从而命名了众多的"齐文化"、"晋文化"、"秦文化"、"燕文化"、"吴文化"。徐良高和王巍在20世纪90年代就曾经呼吁重视礼仪制度，可惜并没有引起大家的普遍重视；东周各诸侯国在"列鼎制度"上的一致性，研究者过去多熟视无察。书中作者先后以晋国、虢国等姬姓诸侯，以及中山国和楚国等异姓诸侯的墓葬材料证明，西周晚期形成的"列鼎制度"已为当时的大多数诸侯国（除了吴国和越国）所接受。这种对于"列鼎制度"的认同表明，"周文化圈"在东周时期不是在缩小，而是在扩大。

在此基础上，作者又利用"列鼎制度"来观察诸侯间和性别间的等级、地位差别，大大丰富了我们对周代社会的认识。书中着重比较了虢国墓地和山西北赵晋侯墓地，发现虢国墓地有"七鼎六簋"，而晋侯墓地的六座春秋时期"晋侯"墓中四处随葬了"五鼎"，只有一或两座随葬了"七鼎"。作者认为，虽然两个氏族均属于姬姓，但是它们的始祖在亲疏关系上或有所差异：虢国氏族的首领是周文王胞弟的后裔，而晋国的首位国君唐叔虞只是周武王的小儿子（叔）。性别差异则是人类社会的普遍现象，但是女性的地位到底如何呢？历史文献中并没有现成的答案。夫妇合葬在东周时期较为常见，本书得以比较了两者之间的差异，发现一对夫妇墓中，女性享用的列鼎规格比男性低一级；而同级的男女墓葬中，女性的随葬品则要多于男性。为什么会这样呢？这恐怕是我们将来需要回答的问题。

《宗子维城》利用列鼎制度作为"手术刀"，仔细剖析了侯马上马墓地的社会形态。迄今为止，我国已经发掘的周代墓地不少，但是要么被盗掘，要么发表材料不完整，无法观察一个聚落的整体社会形态。上马墓地是一个例外，它是唯一一个全面发掘、完整发表的墓地。从1960年到1987年，考古工作者在该墓地共发掘了1387座墓葬，占全部墓葬的95%，其中只有一座被盗掘。该墓地分六个区域，按照通常的假设，一座墓地代表一个氏族，那么一个分区就代表一个支族。其中V区可能属于排行最老的支族，年代最早的四座墓葬（西周晚期）就位于此分区。其他分区在春秋时代早期同时投入使用，后在春秋晚期逐渐废弃。作者从葬具和随葬品两个方面入手，发现代表社会地位的一椁两棺墓和青铜礼器墓在I区多，在V区少，而在III区和VI区则完全不见，说明各个支族地位的不平等。并且，在辈分最高的V区，随葬品总体上朴素无华；而在辈分较低的I区，葬具和随葬品规格反而较高。因此，在上马墓地，决定一个分支的地位，其辈分的高低至多起到了部分作用。

（三）礼制重组

杰西卡·罗森在分析庄白一号窖藏的铜器时，提出了"礼制改革"的看法。"礼制改革"不见于文献记载，是她通过细致的艺术史分析所发现、体察出来的，其内容的核心即是"列鼎制度"的形成。而在列鼎组合中，商代延续下来的、种类繁多、数量客观的酒器消失不见，取而代之的是成套的鼎和簋以及编钟。一般认为酒器用于萨满仪式，酒器的消失意味着萨满教退出了历史舞台。与此同时，个体庞大的对壶、形制和纹饰整齐划一的列鼎和列簋的出现，说明此时贵族更加注重展示其社会地位。杰西卡·罗森认为"礼制改革"开始于西周中后期，但罗泰教授认为开始于西周晚期，具体来说，是墙活着的年代，也就是厉王世。夏含夷和杜朴不接受这一说法，认为墙的年代是共王世，其儿子的年代是懿、孝、夷三世。本书似乎预见了这样的批评，提出了两条辩护意见：一是根据纹饰风格，史墙盘属于西周晚期；二是根据从文王到共王的跨度，史墙盘铭文应该省略了高祖和折之间的几代族长。所言有一定道理，不过本书仍然没有解决一个矛盾：在讨论庄白一号窖藏铜器的风格时（书中表2），本书将折器归入西周早期（约公元前1050—前

950年），而在讨论微氏族长世系时（书中表7），则把折放到了西周中期（约前950—前850年）。这样看来，"礼制改革"始于何时，还是一个待解之谜。

《宗子维城》的另一项重要贡献，是关于春秋中期的"礼制重组"。这也是一次不见于历史文献的"礼仪改革"，是作者从考古资料和铜器铭文中发掘出来的。此时礼仪的中心不再是祖先，通过王孙诰甬钟可以看到，铭文强调的是献器者对宗主即楚王的忠诚，而不是赞颂祖先的功绩；且墓葬随葬的编钟是为了款待宾客（诸侯嘉宾、父兄诸士），而不是为了愉悦祖先。与此同时，在一般的贵族墓葬中，多见明器而少见真器，其原因可能是在世的后代不愿意或无力花费资源，为死者提供完整而珍贵的礼器组合。劣等材料制作的，或规格缩小的"明器组合"，越来越多地用于墓葬，到战国时已蔚然成风。而与此同时，墓葬的结构和随葬品也开始模仿世俗建筑和宇宙空间。和巫鸿教授一样，作者也认为著名的曾侯乙墓复原了统治者活着时的宫殿，"东室"和"南室"殉葬了21名年轻女子；中室摆放了成套的礼器和乐器，象征君主听政、接待来使、举办宴会、进行国礼和祭祀祖先之所需；而北室则是存放马车和兵器的府库。

与此相对应，死亡世界开始日渐"官僚化"，战国墓葬出土的遣册就是给地府官员核对随葬品之用的。而在高等级贵族的墓葬中，除了与时俱进地体现地方风格和时代特征的"常规"礼器之外，还随葬了一套恢复西周晚期礼制改革的"特殊"青铜礼器（九鼎八簋）。也即是说，高等级贵族以"复古礼器"与一般贵族区分开来。此两种礼器都有可能是明器，但是二者普遍出现在周文化圈的国君墓和高等贵族墓葬中，如淅川下寺、荆门宝山2号墓、南阳长台关1号墓、新郑李家楼郑国国君墓、辉县琉璃阁魏国国君墓、寿县西门内蔡侯申墓、随州刘家崖曾国国君墓。与此同时，低级贵族和平民的差异逐步缩小。通过比较春秋和战国时期的楚墓，作者发现，春秋时期墓葬的棺椁和随葬品依然按照等级配置，而战国时期下层贵族和平民的差别则在消失，青铜礼器消失不见，为明器所替代。而不再使用陶器，也没有殉人。随葬武器的大批出现，表明军人由过去的贵族扩大到了平民阶层。

（四）民族差别

在西方，将考古学文化与民族研究等同起来的历史文化范式，在20世纪60年代就逐渐退出学术舞台。在苏联时期，这种范式在斯大林"民族学说（Ethnos）"的驱动下延续了下来。我国学者学习、接受了斯大林"民族学说"，由此催生出"区系类型学"，成为我国考古学的一个"支柱理论"。民族起源问题也成了学者们热衷探讨的问题，而陶器成了解决问题的钥匙。20世纪80年代和90年代，大家忙着争论夏文化、先商文化和先周文化。"先周文化之争"就纠缠在瘪裆鬲和袋足鬲上。即使到了春秋时期，大家仍然以诸侯国为单位，命名了"楚文化"、"晋文化"、"齐文化"和"鲁文化"等，并且试图证明这些文化彼此各有源流，上承新石器时代文化，以为它们都是本地起源、本地发展，一脉相承到秦始皇统一中国方截止。

《宗子维城》打破了这种观念。作者着重分析了商人和秦人的墓葬习俗。根据历史文献，周人在征服商人之后，将商人迁徙到了洛阳和曲阜。考古学家一般认为，商人依然保持了自己的文化习惯，其中最为突出的就是延续了腰坑和陶器组合。在陕西的西周墓葬中，腰坑极少，而在安阳的商代墓葬里则相当普遍。郭宝钧和林寿晋两位先生1955年就指出了腰坑是洛阳地区商人特有的文化因素。但是在东方，比如山东，腰坑频繁出现，一直持续到东周中期。而在曲阜，墓葬腰坑只是在西周晚期方才出现。相反在洛阳，所发现的腰坑不晚于西周中期。与此同时，腰坑还出现在没有安置"商遗民"的侯马天马—曲村晋国墓地、上村岭虢国墓地和琉璃河燕国墓地，因此已很难说腰坑即是商人特有的丧葬习俗。

陶器是我国考古学家探讨民族起源的一把钥匙。一些洛阳和曲阜的发掘者认为，周人墓随葬的陶器为鬲或罐或鬲＋罐，而商人墓随葬的陶器为鬲＋簋＋豆。但是作者一再强调，它们只是墓葬大小、随葬品多少之别，此外无他。大墓随葬的陶器少、铜器多，而小墓则随葬的陶器多、铜器少。这种差别不仅见于洛阳和曲阜，而且见于不曾安置商人的天马—曲村、上村岭和上马墓地。上述发掘者还认为，商人墓随葬分裆鬲和平裆鬲，而周人墓随葬联裆鬲和瘪裆鬲。它们的确发源于不同的区域，但是它们只是代表了不同的制陶传统，通过陶工代代相传。在洛阳，西周早期"商式鬲"居多，而"周式鬲"较少，这与我们期望的征服者带来新器类的情况不相符；到了西周中期和晚期，"商式鬲"则为"周式鬲"所同化。在曲阜，"周式鬲"不仅不见于"商人墓"，且不见于居址；当地作坊生产的大部分鬲为"商式鬲"。历史文献将秦人视为起源于西北的"异族"，其特有的埋葬习俗就是屈肢葬和东西向。但是《宗子维城》指出两个特征也同时出现在秦国以外，如西周时期的天马—曲村墓地，那里42.8%的墓葬人骨向东或向西，而屈肢葬占16.1%。在当时的历史背景下，这些特征并不意味着秦人大量出现在天马—曲村。作者提出，东西墓向和屈肢葬应该是特殊的宗教习俗，在西北地区尤为流行。相反，秦墓的随葬品与周文化其他地区的情况一致，其中青铜器尤为特别。作者指出，它们的形制非常保守，公元前600年以后，周文化其他地区的青铜礼器的形制和纹饰变化很大，只有秦国铜器仍然保留着西周晚期的形制和组合，陶器也仍旧模仿西周晚期的铜器。而在秦文化起源地的天水毛家坪遗址，发掘者发现了屈肢葬和腰坑，但是腰坑流行于东方，而屈肢葬流行于西北，因而学者们提出了完全相反的"秦人东来说"和"西来说"。这里出土的陶器以周式为主，但是还有寺洼文化的。显然这是秦人与"异族"文化共存的地方。但是作者认为，这些陶器的使用者仍然可能是"异族"，也就是秦人，而不是周人。总而言之，仅靠陶器是不能解决族别问题的。

当然，罗泰教授并没有完全反对在考古学资料中寻找异族的做法。一个案例就是宝鸡益门村2号墓。此墓位于渭河南岸，秦国都城雍城（公元前677—前384年）西南20千米处。其周围发现了"主流"秦人的墓地，但是这座墓葬属于哪个墓地还不得而知。由随葬品的纹饰风格可知，2号墓的年代当为公元前6世纪晚期。发掘者认为墓主人是秦人，因为该墓为竖穴土坑墓，使用棺椁，而且东西向。但是作者认为墓主人为外来的游牧人群，因为该墓没有随葬成套陶器或成套青铜器，而随葬了大量的金器和铁器，此外还随葬了一套青铜马具和短剑。这些器物少见于秦国墓地，而多见于欧亚草原的游牧人群的墓葬中。之所以这样考虑，是因为此墓与秦文化不同，所属的文化分布在"秦文化"之外。作者认为，只有像益门村2号墓这样出土成套的非周器物才能算是判断"异族人"的证据。

（五）"周文化圈"的扩张

我在南加州大学做博士后研究的时候，听历史系从事中国史研究的约翰·威尔斯教授（John Wills，1936—2017年）提出一个问题：中国为什么这么大？很简单，似乎很容易回答，但实际上相当复杂。这不仅仅因为现在的中国版图很大，而且因为"汉文化圈"覆盖范围也很大。"汉文化圈"逐渐扩大的过程，实质上是一个"汉文化认同"扩大的过程。可惜关心此问题的国内外学者并不多，而《宗子维城》的作者则给了我们清晰的答案。

《宗子维城》讨论的是"周文化圈"的扩张，为此作者归纳出了两个途径。一个是非周民族的融入。山东半岛的东部在西周以及春秋早期，通过铜器铭文或者历史地理，可知属于东夷氏族。但是到了春秋中期，莒国、郳国和纪国的文化面貌已经与齐鲁等周文化相差无几了。其器物组合、铜器形制与铭文表明，莒国已经完全接纳了"周文化圈"的礼制；《春秋》和《左传》记载，莒国这样东夷政治体的代表，经常参加诸侯国的会盟。中山国的统治者出身于狄人，但是该国的都城布局，中山王的竖穴土坑墓、两条墓道和"九鼎八簋"表明，他们接受了周人的礼仪制度。该墓出土的三件铜器上的长篇铭文，记载了中山王参加的联合伐燕，同时使用了周代青铜铭文典型的仪式语言。楚人和秦人起初也是非周族群，但是在春秋战国时期都接受了周人的"列鼎制度"。与之相反，长江下游的吴、越两国没有吸收"列鼎制度"，墓葬随葬原始瓷器，铜器构成无规律可循，墓主埋在土墩墓（屯溪）里。

另一个途径是扩张。在西周初期，周王朝通过封建，将王子、功臣和先王后裔分封到原来商王朝的地盘。随着时间推移，各个诸侯国逐步扩张领土。在战国时期，秦国将农民迁徙到黄土高原，到达大荔、耀县

· 589 ·

和铜川,甚至到了更北的清涧。在同时期,燕国将移民迁徙到原来的夏家店上层文化区域,到了西拉木伦河流域。在南方,楚国最早控制了湖北和河南南部的大片区域,后来又扩展到了湖南和安徽。在湖南境内,楚人势力渗透进入湘江流域,将原住民驱赶到广东和广西。在重庆,战国时期的楚国墓葬出现在楚国西界以西 500 千米的忠县崖脚墓地,与本地的"巴人墓"共存。此墓地距离甘井河河谷的盐场极近,来到此地的楚人很可能是为了贩运食盐到食盐匮乏的楚国腹地。

二

由上可知,作者挑战了许多传统看法,颠覆了许多传统观念。读者未必都会赞同作者的观点,但是读了本书之后自会获益匪浅。我以为,本书的价值不仅仅在于提出了诸多新观点,而且在于提供了一些新视角和新方法,提出了一些新问题,值得读者关注。

(一) 古 DNA 研究

本书经常涉及的一个重要问题就是每个墓地的墓主人的血缘关系。前文一再提到一个假说,即一个墓地的男性墓主同属于一个氏族。这个假说在我国历史文献中是有线索的,《周礼春官》记载了专门掌管墓地的"冢人"。虢国墓地的材料似乎也支持这种假说。从 20 世纪 50 年代到 90 年代,这里一共发掘了 252 座墓葬。这些墓葬分为几组,每组以成对的大墓为中心分布了大小不一的墓葬,这些墓葬组由北向南排列。每组似乎代表一代人,而中心的大墓似乎代表族长和夫人。这一布局似乎在天马—曲村墓地得到了印证。但是这一假说一直没有得到证实。现在古 DNA 研究技术已经成熟,通过分析男性人骨的 Y 染色体,我们就可以梳理男性墓主之间的血缘关系。与此同时,关于女性,也存在另一个假说。本书提到,女性一般来自于外氏族。通过分析线粒体,建立数据库,我们可以发现其女性的来源。令人高兴的是,吉林大学古 DNA 实验室已经开始行动,分析了新疆哈密地区泉儿沟等若干墓地的墓主人的基因,发现一部分人之间确实存在着血缘关系。

（二）外语

本书研究的是汉学问题，但是引用了大量的日文、英文、德文和法文学术文献。作者自己很谦逊，称："有些中文读者或许也会发现，熟悉一下西方以及日本学者的著作不无益处。"不过客观地说，学术发展到了今天，阅读外国考古文献已经是一项基本功了。不读外国文献，就不知道外国汉学家做了什么工作，怎么思考，就不能掌握学术前沿。而在这方面，外国汉学家尽管人数不多，但是大多通晓多门语言，掌握中国、日本和西方国家的学术成果，因此在学术研究上要优于我国学者。如前面提到的"礼制重构"，即是罗泰教授发现的。如果说我国老一辈学者还有资格嘲笑西方汉学家，因为当时有些汉学家欠缺汉语功底，那么现在我们恐怕没有什么优势了，要说有，就只有考古发掘权了。20世纪80年代以后成长起来的汉学家，功底深厚，在古文献（如《周礼》、《春秋》、《左传》）、古文字和考古方面接受了全面的训练，研究水平飞速提升。现在打开西方考古学著作，可以发现我国学者能够贡献的主要是发掘资料，而不是研究成果；即使是提供发掘资料，也不尽如人意，总是缺东少西。现在我们要培养中国考古学人才，还要仰仗日本和西方国家的汉学家。归根结底，就是我们的研究生培养方式存在问题：一则过于专业化（古文字、考古和历史成为三个学科，相互分离）；二则忽略外语，无法跟踪国际学界的前沿动态；三则缺乏人类学和考古学理论训练。我国考古学科要创世界一流，现有的研究生培养方式恐怕需要改变了。

（三）历史文献

我国考古学的一个突出特征，就是带有浓厚的历史主义和金石学倾向。从过去的夏都（二里头）热到最近的尧都（陶寺）热就是其表现。一个学者要研究周代，就有诸子百家、金石文字和简牍文书可供利用。罗泰教授告诉我们，这些文字材料存在着各种问题，需要慎重对待，不能拿来就用。诸子百家为了说服统治者，在描述社会现实时往往夸大其辞；金文和简牍文书为宗教文字，带有各种偏见。这些材料和考古材料一样，需要经过分析才能利用。可惜我国学者往往不仅拿来就用，而且迷信历史文献和铜器铭文，跟着它们走，而忘了考古学的独立性。作者主张，历史文献和考古资料需要"分进"，也就是分别研究，然后"合击"，也就是整合两种资料开始研究。作者是这么想的，也是这么做的。实际上，本书还纠正了一个流传几千年，历史文献灌输给我们的观念，就是孔子眼中的"人民在秩序井然的等级社会里各安其位"的理想社会，并非形成于西周初期，而是西周晚期。

（四）类型学

蒙特留斯（Gustav O. Montelius，1843—1921年）的"类型学"从1930年引入中国以后，至今仍为考古学家广为使用。在特定的社会环境里，从50年代到80年代，类型学逐渐受到推崇，成了"中国考古学派"的一个标签。作者指出，虽然"类型学"行之有效，但是它不是一门真正的科学，而只是一个工匠的习惯而已。国家文物局颁布的新版《田野考古工作规程》（2008年）已开始纠正这种"类型学"崇拜，但是历史惯性仍然不小。而与此同时，我国学者在描述器物的形态特征时往往比较主观，不同报告的类型无法对照比较。实际上作者随手就抓到了一个纰漏。在对照晋国北赵与天马—曲村墓地的陶鬲分期序列时，他发现北赵的陶鬲属于天马—曲村的两个类型，但是发掘者把北赵的两类陶鬲放在了一个分期序列中。不过，作者仍然利用了一些发掘报告的分期成果，但是用的是在经过碳十四年代和地层学验证以后的成果。

（五）人类学

人类学在美国是个优势学科，分支繁多，有文化人类学、经济人类学、社会人类学和城市人类学，为考古学、历史学和艺术史研究源源不断地输入新鲜血液，同时又从上述学科得到滋养，彼此相长，持续发展。但是在我国，人类学极其薄弱，不仅人类学系少，而且教师少，培养的学生也少，因而对于我国考古和历史学界的贡献微乎其微。本书作者深受西方人类学熏陶，本书所用的"氏族""姓族"概念就是例子。氏族（lineage）实际上就是我们过去常用的宗族，姓族（clan）实际上就是我们过去常用的氏族。氏族和姓族是西方人类学的老问题，研究成果较多，本书引用的 Roger M. Keesing 就是一位。但是作者没用宗族和氏族这两个我国学术界熟悉的术语，而选用了氏族和姓族，就是为了更好地陈述人类学的理念。氏族是能够追溯真实祖先的血缘集团，而姓族是能够追溯到一个虚构的祖先的"几十个甚至数百个"氏族。由于姓族可以吸纳没有血缘关系的氏族，所以它成了统治集团笼络同盟的一种手段。在本书中，二者成了打开周代社会的钥匙。这样姬姓（周）、姜姓（齐）和子姓（商）都是姓族，而不是过去认为的氏族。姬姓和子姓的差别是姓族之间的差别，而不是过去认为的商周民族之间的差别。姓族之间互相通婚，从而实现了文化融合，形成内部文化统一的"周文化圈"，从而与其他民族区别开来。

（六）统计学

本书经常使用统计学来观察社会分化和男女差别，表明统计学是个强大的工具。可惜在我国考古学研究中，统计学一直没有得到重视，因此失去了研究一些重要问题的机会。也因为少了统计学这根弦，考古工作者在整理发掘报告时就不太注意资料的统计价值。因此迄今公布的大部分考古学材料，既不全面，也不具有统计需要的代表性。作者说，这个问题并非仅仅在中国才有，但是在中国这种问题格外严重。实际上，陈铁梅编写的《定量考古学》已于 2005 年出版，教材有了，现在要做的就是在我国大学的考古学科普及这门课程，把统计学的理念和方法传授给学生。

（七）人口

我国现在已经发现了不少东周时期的城址和村落，但是里面的居民一直无人关注。实际上，现已发现了不少大型墓地，可以用来研究人口问题。作者利用上马墓地的发掘资料做了精彩的分析。在这座墓地，只有 19 座儿童墓，占总数的 1.8%，远远低于前现代社会 50% 以上的婴儿死亡率。这种情况表明，上马聚落的绝大多数夭折儿童没有埋入墓地。同时，女性比例（与男性 100∶112）偏低，低于正常的 100∶96，因此少数女性没有进入墓地。这些没有进入墓地的人口埋到哪里去了呢？这也是人们不太关注的问题。作者推测他们埋在了聚落里，而这种墓葬容易为人忽略。发掘者将上马墓地分为九段，将墓葬分到各段以后，可以看到第二到第五猛增，之后持续减少。经过统计，这块区域在公元前7世纪中叶，人口数在250—350之间，如果算上儿童、底层女性和外来人口，还要翻上一倍；这样估算下来，上马村落的人口数量当在500—700之间。人口是社会学的一部分，也是一个富有潜力的研究领域。我们希望，我国考古工作者在以后的工作中关注人口问题。

三

前面发表了一些个人感想。评论一本书，既要看到它的新见解，也要看到它的新启发。有关周代社会的论著不在少数，但是本书独辟蹊径，利用考古资料来研究周代社会，分析了一系列新问题，得出了一系列新看法，让人耳目一新。作者虽然没有专门提出理论，但是人类学理论像地下水一样流淌于全书，滋润着全书的各个章节；其中氏族制度、列鼎制度、礼制重组、民族差别和周文化圈扩张，突破了过去的研究视野，改变了我们对于周代社会的认识。除此之外，本书提到的古DNA研究、驾轻就熟的中文、日文和西文文献、统计学和人口学方法，为我国读者打开了窗户，拓宽了研究视野。因此，我国读者可以从此书受益的地方很多。其价值，或许可以借用《资治通鉴》魏明帝景初三年的一句话"建德垂风，维城之基"来形容。

（鸣谢：曹兵武、罗泰和孟繁之先后审阅了本文初稿，指出了文中的一些错误和不足，在此向他们表示感谢。至于本文仍然存在的错误，则由笔者承担）

第七部分
研究生培养

研究生怎样做研究？*

自从改革开放以来，我国研究生（含硕士和博士）招生数量从1978—1979年的1.1万迅速增长到了2011年的56万。这些研究生毕业以后很多进入高校和研究所工作，成为我国科研力量的新鲜血液。因此，他们的培养水平直接决定了我国科研力量的强弱。对硕士研究生的要求，《中华人民共和国学位条例》规定："具有从事科学研究工作或担负专门技术工作的初步能力"；而对博士研究生，条例要求更高，规定"在科学或专门技术上做出创造性的成果"。《关于国务院学位委员会第一次（扩大）会议的报告》要求硕士和博士研究生"在学术上应相当于国外相应的学位水平"。而近年教育部、国家发展改革委、财政部发布的《关于深化研究生教育改革的意见》（教研〔2013〕1号）进一步要求学术学位研究生以提高创新能力为目标。

创新不是一件容易的事情，达芬奇和爱迪生的时代已经远去，容易摘的苹果前人都已经摘完。现在要创新，就不能不做艰苦的研究。那种不愿坐冷板凳，十年磨一剑地做研究，而靠欺骗和抄袭，是做不出创新的。同时，做研究不能光靠吃苦，还需要遵循学术规范，接受充分的学术训练；否则，也是做不出有价值的创新的。本人在高校从事教育若干年，发现理科研究生与国际接轨较好，问题并不严重；而文科研究生存在的问题较多，不知如何选题、如何论证和如何处理数据，其根本原因在于缺乏研究方法和研究能力的训练。在此本人将分享一些个人看法，试图为文科研究生提供一些建议。为了方便读者理解，本人还以自己指

---

* 本文原刊于《壹学者》2017年12月13日。收入本书时略有改动。

导的研究生为例，介绍几个关键步骤的操作方法。本人主要从事考古学，举的例子也是考古学的，不过读者可以依理类推，将上述方法用于自己的研究中。

做研究的第一步就是发现新问题。这一步本身并不容易，发现了新问题就完成了研究的一半；当然，这并不等于完成了研究，只有解决了这个新问题才算结束。一个研究生刚进入一个研究领域，从发现新问题到解决新问题，既需要知识的积累，也需要能力的培养。发现新问题需要批判分析已有的研究文献和资料，而解决新问题需要研究方法的训练。

因此一个研究生需要经历一个漫长而艰难的过程：第一，选择一个领域；第二，搜集文献目录；第三，阅读文献并归纳前人研究成果；第四，发现新问题；第五，设计研究方案；第六，获取和分析资料（含数据）；第七，得出结论。结论来自于论证，而论证来自于资料（含数据），这些原则都不言而喻，无需多说。但是1—6项过程，现在许多研究生并不清楚，需要说得详细一些。在实施这些步骤的同时，一个研究生还要接受必要的学术训练，这样加起来一般需要两年的时间，第三年正好可以完成学位论文。这样说来一个研究生在三年时间里是没有时间浪费的，一入学就需要开始上述步骤。有些研究生在一、二年级仅仅上些课程，指望在第三年完成一篇学位论文，是不切实际的。

一 怎样选领域？

一般来说，一个研究生要么自己寻找选择论文题目，要么导师指定题目。但是如果事先没有做过充分的阅读文献，这样做往往带有很大的盲目性：这个题目要么有人做过，要么过于超前，要么是个死胡同。其成功的概率与拍脑袋做决定是一样的：有成功的案例，但是概率很小。要想找到成功的选题，也就是既有新意，又可行的，就要充分阅读文献。一个能力较强的研究生也可以通过跟踪国际学术前沿来寻找论文题目，但是这样做也有弊端。他/她将来往往只能跟着国际知名学者做些补丁式的创新，而无法在一个领域做出开拓性的创新。

由于学术发展迅速，一个学科拥有越来越多的领域；一个人穷其一生已经无法通晓一个学科，遑论若干学科了。作为一个成熟的研究者，因为兴趣的指引，一生可以跨越若干领域乃至若干学科，是应有之义。但是作为一个新人，研究生首先要选择一个领域。这个领域不能大，也不能小。因为后续要阅读文献，领域大小视文献量而定。有的领域历史悠久，从事的研究者多，那么文献就多；反过来说，不能太小，太小了视野狭窄，而且缺乏拓展空间。比如说有人想研究中国陶瓷，那么中国陶瓷史作为一个领域就太大了，因为中国地域广，历史长，一个研究生想研究整个中国的古代陶瓷就是痴人说梦了。当然，也不能选择一个遗址的陶瓷作为领域，因为这样太窄，无法发掘该遗址出土陶器的科学价值。一般而言，需要选择某个时段、某个区域，如环太湖地区的新石器时代或者黄河下游地区的魏晋南北朝时期。

有时候，由于课题需要，导师为研究生指定选题（如上海广富林遗址出土的陶器）。这种时候也需要选个合适的领域，如环太湖地区的新石器时代，以便在较大的时空范围内研究这个选题。有时候导师为研究生提供一批新资料，如江西南昌海昏侯汉墓的发掘资料。但是由于我国汉代墓葬资料丰富，重复性强，如何发掘这批资料的学术价值，是个值得琢磨的问题。这个时候，研究生同样需要选个合适的领域（秦代和汉代考古），以便把它放在合适的时空范围内去研究。

二 搜集文献目录

这里所谓的文献，包括原始资料（如发掘简报和发掘报告、《史记》、《资治通鉴》和历史档案）、研究论文和著作、考古发现新闻和图录。为什么要阅读文献？这是因为学术发展到了今天，我们只有寻找精准的新问题并予以解决，才能有效地推进学术发展。在军事上，这就是精确打击，只打击需要打击的目标，而不必伤及无辜；在医学上，这就是靶标研究，寻找癌变基因，并予以根除。那么要寻找精准的新问题，就需要熟读文献。纵观学术史，我们可以看到学术研究和资料积累都是一个接力过程。在一个研究领域，前人取得了一些成果，积累了一些资料（除了历史文献，还包括发掘资料、科学分析资料），后人要接过前人没有完成的任务，发现新问题，继续前进。这就像接力赛，一个人跑完了一段，另一个人接过棒跑下一段，就是找到了自己的位置，就可以完成自己的使命。

就本人的经历而言，我国的文科研究生几乎没有阅读文献的概念。所以许多研究生要么重复研究同一个问题，得到了大同小异的结论，要么单打独斗，与他人的研究工作缺少关联。这两种情况都是研究资源（人力、时间和经费）的浪费。而阅读文献就是入门的基本功。一方面，一个研究者，无论资历深浅，刚进入一个新领域都是"所见无非牛者"，不知如何下手；阅读文献后，对本领域烂熟于胸，发现了前人没有研究的问题或者没有解决的问题，就达到了"未尝见全牛也"的境界。另一方面，研究生可以了解该领域的资料储备。资料就像厨师的食材，厨师做饭需要知道有什么食材，所谓巧妇难为无米之炊；研究生也需要知道自己拥有什么方法和什么资料，否则选题再好，如果没有方法或者资料不足也是白费力气。实际上，有些新问题前人已经意识到，他们没有研究是因为缺乏资料，或者因为缺乏技术手段。

那么如何阅读文献呢？迄今为止，我国考古学文献已经汗牛充栋，全部阅读完全不可能，也无必要。这就需要选择，搜集自己需要的文献的目录。那么怎么搜集文献目录？这要围绕选题来定，要看选题牵涉哪些方面，然后按方面收集文献目录。本人指导的一名研究生想研究原始瓷，起初整理的是全国的原始瓷文献，结果发现太多，于是缩小到原始瓷比较集中的环太湖地区。

为此他收集了以下几个方面的文献：第一，环太湖地区的所有原始瓷著作和论文，锁定选题为苏南地区原始瓷的产地问题；第二，苏南地区出土原始瓷的墓葬和聚落的发掘资料，了解发现原始瓷的遗址、出土数量、发掘单位、领队和现在存放机构，以便联系，索取样品；第三，现在国内陶瓷分析实验室、仪器、价格和数据处理方法。因为产地问题需要成分分析，需要用X荧光光谱（XRF）、中子活化（NAA）或电感耦合等离子（ICP）等仪器，需要设计研究方案，这些资料都是必不可少的；第四，国外研究陶瓷产地的新技术和新方法，以保证分析方法不落后于国际水平；第五，类型学方法，除了成分分析，该生还需要比较分析浙北和苏南的原始瓷的器形，为产地研究打下基础；第六，中国陶瓷史，了解中国陶瓷发展的大趋势，看原始瓷与前后的陶器和瓷器的发展关系；第七，环太湖地区的史前考古学文化，了解广富林、马桥文化和吴越文化的概况；第八，太湖的古地貌以及航运史，因为太湖周围的古地貌与今天不同，不同时期也有变化，所以需要收集商周时期的地貌资料。除了发掘简报、发掘报告、上述各个方面的论文和著作，还要搜集考古发现报道、学术会议消息，以了解最新考古发现；还要收集原始瓷图录，为论文提供插图。

在搜集文献目录时，要尽量彻底收集，不要遗漏。很多研究生一拿到选题就到知网搜文章，到校图书馆找书，以为这样就穷尽了所需文献。殊不知现在还有不少中文期刊没有进入知网，而我国高校图书馆的中文图书收藏也多不完整，西文图书期刊更是寥寥无几，有的连西方电子期刊论文库JSTOR都没有。好在现在我国考古学有些现成的综合目录。1900—1990年有四本《中国考古学文献目录》，里面收录了简报、报告、论文、著作和图录。从1984年起有《中国考古学年鉴》，每年一本，里面除了上述几个方面的目录，还有会议、考古新发现、展览和学术访问。当然，最近几年的还没有出来，这就需要去翻阅相关的刊物，如《考古》《东南文化》等可能刊登有关原始瓷的期刊；最新图书目录则可以向北京的考古书店写信索取书单。外文期刊文献则通过JSTOR来搜索，外文图书则可以利用西方主要大学（如哈佛大学、芝加哥大学和加州大学洛杉矶分校）图书馆的书目检索。这样收集下来的文献目录会有几十页，研究者就对自己需要看的文献有个全面的概念了。

三 阅读文献

做完文献目录，就要有计划、有步骤地阅读文献了。在阅读之前，当然要收集文献本身。现在知网提供了大部分中文期刊文章的电子版，图书馆也有部分图书；没有的就要想办法收集，或者购买或者托人扫描复印，然后一个接一个专题阅读。

在学生搜集目录和阅读文献的时候，不能仅仅自己做。他（她）需要做笔记，向导师汇报。由于搜集文献目录本身需要几周时间，汇报时导师就可以点评，指出哪些不足，然后研究生可以在后面予以补充。在阅读文献时，学生也要做笔记，记录所看文献的主要内容；而且要予以分析，指出其长处和短处，然后向导师汇报。如果学生以前没有这种阅读文献的经历，缺乏批判性思维，在操作过程中会存在各种问题，需要导师帮助解决。在听完汇报后，导师提问题，指出其没有注意的一些重要细节；帮助他归纳整理，认识前人的研究成果，发现其存在的问题。

四 设计研究方案

在阅读文献之后，一个领域在研究生面前就是一个筛子了：到处都是问题。但是研究生需要明白的是，这些问题前人不一定没有发现，只是他们顾不上或者条件不具备。这时候研究生需要做的就是找一个自己有能力，价值又比较高的新问题做自己的选题。有了选题，就要设计研究方案，这在理工科已经比较普遍，但是在文科还没有这样的意识，遑论实施了。研究方案包括研究思路、需要资料（数据）、获得资料（数据）的方法和处理资料（数据）的方法。因为考古学跨学科较多，考古学选题多种多样，研究生需要根据不同选题采取不同方法。

上述研究生选择了苏南地区的原始瓷产地问题作为自己的选题。这是一个前人做过，但是做得不多；分析技术已经成熟，但是做得不够的选题，空间很大。根据选题，其研究方案为：

第一，由于浙北原始瓷窑址出土的原始瓷已经做了不少成分分析，其数据可以拿来使用，他只需要再做少量分析即可；他需要做的主要是分析苏南地区出土的原始瓷，因为这项工作前人做得很少。他需要从已发掘遗址中选择原始瓷样品；当然，在选择时还要考虑区域和时代的均衡，使样品具有代表性。

第二，到各考古机构采集样品。过去出土的原始瓷大多数进了博物馆，而文物一旦进了博物馆，取样就非常困难。所以取样要尽量找考古机构，与发掘项目负责人协商，请他们提供样品。

第三，联系实验室分析样品。现在我国实验室较多，仪器比较多样，价格不一，导师可以根据自己的经费情况（现在研究生一般没有研究经费）选择。本人为上述研究生选择了上海博物馆和南京大学的实验室。

第四，比较分析苏南地区和浙北的原始瓷器形。由于成分数据指向两种可能：首先，原料即瓷土贸易；其次，产品即原始瓷贸易。要确定产品贸易，就需要比较器形。这样器形和成分就构成了两重证据，这样得到的结论就比较可信了。

五　搜集和分析资料

考古学论文一般需要用到四类资料：发掘简报或报告、历史文献、科技分析数据和图像。我国学术界没有经过西方后现代主义的洗礼，对各类资料的缺陷认识不足，所有资料一般拿来就用。但是事实上，我国的考古发掘简报或报告良莠不齐，往往带上了各种烙印。有的遗址干燥，有机物保存好，而有的遗址水分较多，没有有机物，但是并不意味着古代不用有机物。有的发掘者认真，各种资料交代得清楚，而有的发掘者马虎，资料发表得少，遗漏得多。它们还往往带有浓厚的物质文化史烙印，发表资料侧重于文化属性和年代框架，而忽略了其他学术问题。历史文献也是如此，带有撰写者的局限。它们叙事侧重于政治，而淡化了经济、技术和日常生活。在使用这些历史文献的时候，需要排除各种局限的干扰。

由于考古学的发展，与其他学科结合的选题越来越多，因此除了传统研究需要的发掘资料，现在还增加了科学分析数据。各种分析仪器都有自己的功能，也有自己的局限，研究生要根据自己的选题，了解并加以利用。上述研究生在采集了原始瓷样品之后，就利用上海博物馆和南京大学的台式XRF分析胎的成分，以便与浙江北部窑址出土的原始瓷样品比较。

六　学术训练

　　有了选题，学生要根据自己的情况接受训练。现在许多研究生成天无所事事，以为上课修学分写篇毕业论文就行了。在导师的帮助下，研究生勉强凑成一篇论文，凑合毕业；但是毕业后不知道怎样做研究了。这是缺乏学术训练的典型症状。其实研究生真正要学的是研究能力；要掌握研究能力，就需要接受学术训练。一般来说，一个考古学专业的研究生需要接受以下训练：

　　第一，专业课程。做研究需要功底，也就是需要掌握一个学科的基础知识。现在很多研究生本科不是学考古学的，这就需要补修中国考古学概论和断代考古课程，以了解考古学的时空框架、学术界关心的学术问题、已有的考古发现和研究成果。

　　第二，科技考古。考古学论文除了发掘资料，还经常利用其他手段获得资料和数据。这就需要学习各种科技分析仪器，了解它们的功能。能够掌握仪器的操作方法当然最好；如果不能，则需要学会分析数据。

　　第三，考古学理论。理论是我国考古学科的弱项。人们往往以为类型学和地层学就是考古学理论，其实二者不过是考古学的基本方法。西方考古学理论非常多，涉及社会复杂化、经济人类学、景观考古等各个方面，可以打开研究生的思路。我们经常盼望一双"慧眼"，能够敏锐地捕捉学术问题，其实考古学理论就可以给我们这双"慧眼"。实际上，考古学理论是西方许多大学研究生的核心课程。只是这些理论往往用英文发表，读起来比较费力，广泛阅读不太现实；那么起码根据自己的选题，选择阅读相关的理论著作和论文。

　　第四，外语。《关于国务院学位委员会第一次（扩大）会议的报告》"对硕士学位要求一门外语。对博士学位，大多数专业要求两门外语"。在我国大部分高校，在研究生阶段，只要求学习英语，不要求学习第二门外语；当然也没有设置二外课程。实际上，在我国很多研究生的论文中，连英语文献都没有，更别提其他语言的文献了。其实光有英文还是不够的，应该学习二外。为什么要学习外文，而且还要学二外？

就是因为外国有许多汉学家在研究中国考古学，除了英语，还用本国语言发表。本人知道日本、德国和法国学者发表了不少关于中国考古学的文章。举例而言，日本有个大家林巳奈夫，其著作《殷周青铜器综览》是经典著作，是研究中国青铜器必读之物。我们要做世界一流的学问，就需要知道世界各国汉学家的研究成果，这样才能做出实实在在的创新。当然，学习外语需要投入大量的精力，往往需要两年时间才能达到阅读水平；所以学生不能茫无目的地学习二外，而要根据选题的需要学习二外。

一般而言，上述几个方面的训练，尤其是二外，需要研究生一入学就开始安排，通过两年的学习，大概在三年级掌握了研究能力，就有可能写出一篇像样的论文来。

结　　语

综上所述，创新就是要发现和解决新问题，这就需要经过一个长期而艰苦的过程。学生首先要选择一个领域，然后收集该领域的文献目录；再阅读文献，以便了解前人的成果，发现新问题；有了新问题，还要设计研究方案并实施方案，以便获取需要的资料（数据），以便完成论证，解决新问题。当然，完成这个过程，一个研究生还需要经过相应的学术训练，包括专业课程、科技分析方法、考古学理论和外语。只有这样，他（她）才具备了研究能力，才能成为一个合格的研究者。

研究生怎样写论文？*

本文之所以专门写论文写作，而没有涉及研究，是因为研究和论文写作是两项工作，各有各的要求。做研究是要发现和解决新问题，而写论文是要把研究过程和成果公之于众。不过，不是所有研究成果都写成论文公之于众，有很多政府部门和公司也做研究，但是并不发表其成果。只是在一般情况下，人们一边做研究一边写论文，没有意识到它们是两项工作而已。本人把论文剥离出来，是为了强调论文写作方面的要求和规范。

为什么写论文？首先这是现实的需要，因为现在读学位、评职称都要求写论文发论文。而对于一个以研究为职业的人，写论文是安身立命的事情。当然，写论文本身有很多好处：第一，有助于整理思维；写论文是个讲逻辑，重证据的事情，也是个需要灵感的事情，随时写下头脑中的念头和想法，可以随时思考完善。第二，有助于记忆；一篇论文，尤其是人文学科的论文，往往含有大量的信息和细节，靠头脑硬记已经相当困难；随着一个人记忆力的衰退，他/她只有把研究过程写下来，才能随时翻阅审核。第三，有助于传播；一个人的研究成果仅靠口头传播，范围毕竟有限；写成论文发表在期刊上，就可以传播到世界各地和后世读者手中。第四，有助于检验和认可，让别人检验你的想法；一个人的研究成果，尤其是重大成果，需要经过其他学者的检验才能定论，也才能得到学术界的认可。

在论文写作方面，我国高校的研究生同样存在各种问题：第一，怕

---

* 本文原刊于《壹学者》2017年11月29日。收入本书时略有改动。

写论文，一写论文，不知如何下手；第二，不知如何论证，往往机械地堆砌材料，论点和证据两层皮；第三，逻辑混乱，关键术语的定义经常发生漂移，一个术语在前文是一个含义，在后文是另一个含义；第四，文字表达能力低下，语句不通，错别字、语法错误随处可见；第五，不知何为抄袭，不仅抄别人论文，而且抄自己论文。现在社会期望研究生能发表高水平论文，而这些情况不免让这种期望落空。一个重要原因就是我国研究生在高中和本科阶段缺乏论文写作方面的训练。

一　原则

科学研究发展到了今天，已经形成了一整套严密的规范。总体而言，论文写作需要遵循以下几个原则：

第一，可阅读。论文写出来是为了让人读的，所以论文应该结构完整、文字流畅、插图充分，让人读得懂，愿意读。

第二，可验证。一篇论文解决了一个新问题，其结论需要接受读者的检验。所以论文应该是问题、方法、思路和观点表述清晰，资料和数据真实充分。读者可以顺着论文的思路，可以检验观点是否可以成立。

第三，可追溯。现在论文都要求有注释，这是为了说明资料来源。一个严谨的审稿者和编辑会查阅这些注释，看作者是否准确地转达了所引论文的原意。而作者也通过充分、准确的注释，避免剽窃之嫌。

第四，可检索。写论文是为了让同行读的，但是现在每年发表的论文成千上万，大多数读者需要通过文献检索来寻找自己需要的论文。一位研究者要让读者发现自己的论文，就要在内容提要和关键词上下功夫。

二　论文要素

做研究写论文很辛苦，研究者当然希望有更多的读者看到它，引用它。现在各高校也多用引用率来评估论文，所以研究者需要在这个方面下功夫。而一篇论文能否被读者阅读和引用取决于许多因素。其中一个

第七部分 研究生培养

重要的因素就是结构是否完整，内容是否充实。现在的论文很像八股文，一般由内容提要、关键词、前言、正文、结语、插图和参考文献几个部分组成。这是学术界约定俗成的结构，缺一不可。各个部分各司其职，各有各的要求。

第一，内容提要。我们生活在一个信息爆炸的时代，学术论文汗牛充栋，一个人终其一生往往都无法阅读一个学科所有的论文。读者只能根据自己的需要筛选了，在筛选论文时他们首先看内容提要，以便了解以下信息：其一，作者要解决什么问题；其二，为什么选这个题目；其三，用什么方法（或用什么资料）；其四，得到了什么结论；其五，如果有争议，作者怎么看。读者在得到这些信息后，决定要不要看全文。所以研究者在撰写内容提要时，需要体现以上几项内容。篇幅不能太短，短了不能写足上述要素；当然也不能太长，长了就啰唆。

第二，关键词。在信息爆炸的时代，我国读者一般使用知网和JSTOR这样的电子数据库搜索论文时，往往输入关键词。所以，研究者在写关键词时需要斟酌，以便让读者找到自己的论文。可惜的是，很多人选择关键词往往很随意，选择了一些无关紧要的词。我们需要以己度人，了解读者喜欢用什么关键词检索。一般来说，关键词要能体现选题的重要方面。就本人所在的考古学科而言，关键词一般包括对象（如器物、遗址、遗迹）、时代（如青铜时代、商周时期、南北朝）、地域范围（长江下游、河西走廊、太行山）、领域（原始瓷、城市、盐业考古）、理论（世界体系、景观考古、经济人类学）和技术（锶同位素、DNA分析、岩相分析）。

第三，前言。此部分为正文的前奏，其目的就是回顾研究文献，提出新问题和研究方案。这一部分的主要任务是介绍一个选题的研究史，点评前人的论著，既指出他们的成果，又剖析他们的不足。实际上，这就是把文献阅读部分的工作成果收入其中。在前人的遗留问题之中，挑选一个重要的，又可行的问题作为自己的选题。锁定了研究对象还不够，在此部分还要提出一个研究方案来。

写前言时研究者需要注意若干事项。首先，研究者要意识到，前言的最终目的是提出新问题，而前面的文献回顾起铺垫作用。所以，虽然新问题在前言中最后出现，但是在写作时，是最先要搞清楚的。因此研究者不需要把读过的所有文献都纳入前言，只需要反映研究进展的论文就行。其次，研究者需要抱持客观公正的态度评论前人的工作。现在有些研究者为了避免得罪人，故意不提前人的研究工作；而有些研究者出于个人或派系恩怨，刻意抬高或贬低一些学者。这些都不是研究者应有的态度；一个研究者应该客观地肯定前人取得的成就，同时找到前人的不足，这样才能准确地锁定问题，推动一个选题向前迈进。

第四，正文。此部分要展现论证过程。选题不同论证过程也不同，需要分别对待。文史方面的选题可以分解成若干子问题，然后提供证据，形成子观点；最后由子观点构成大观点。科技考古方面的选题，则需要利用研究方法或技术手段，讨论辨析由此获得的数据，然后得到结论。

在此部分，研究者需要注意两件事情。一是确保观点与证据链吻合，这就要求观点要有证据支撑，而证据要为观点服务。现在很多研究生不懂论证，喜欢堆砌证据，然后抛出一个或几个毫无关联的观点，其结果就是证据和观点两层皮。二是公平对待不同意见。有些问题前人研究过，提出了一些观点。现在很多研究者要么无视，要么轻率地否定他们的观点。公正的做法是，分析这些观点，检验其逻辑、证据链，看看是否有问题；如果有问题，就指出问题，如果没有问题，就要检验自己的证据链，看看是否有问题。如果不能推翻前人的观点，就承认分歧。

第五，结语。结语的要害在于简要重复论文的主要部分，也就是新问题、研究方法、证掘和结论。结语不能太短，短了不能充分呈现论证过程；也不宜太长，长了就有啰唆之嫌。在这个部分不能出现新资料和新观点；任何新资料和新观点（想法）只能出现在正文中，结语只是归纳复述正文的重要内容。

第六，插图。插图样式多样，可以是照片、线图和表格，现在还可以是视频。它是重要的支撑资料，一方面可以说明研究对象，一方面可以提供物证。它们既可以展示比较抽象的理论、概念和研究对象，帮助读者理解它们，也可以展示物证和数据，支撑论文。它们既不能太多，也不能太少，关键是能够说明论文中的关键概念、对象，或者呈现数据。在此部分，插图要与正文结合；也就是说，正文的重要理论、概念和器物需要插图来说明，观点需要物证和数据来支撑；同时插图不能漫无目的，要为论文服务，否则就不要使用。插图需要添加文字，说明插图名称、图例、比例。当然，如果插图涉及知识产权，还要注明来源。

第七，注释。研究者在写作论文时，少不了引用以往的研究成果，或者观点，或者数据（资料），或者方法。为了尊重以往成果，研究者需要做注释，以避免剽窃之嫌。需要注意的是，这里所说的以往成果，既有他人的，也有作者自己的。我国不少学者往往在意他人成果，而忽略了自己的成果。做注释还有另外用途，就是方便读者查阅出处，检验论文是否严谨扎实。因为如果研究者在做注时，没有看过所引论文，或者一知半解，容易出错。实际上，注释是一个研究者的信誉晴雨表，如果在注释上不认真，读者会认为研究者是个马虎的人，靠不住的人。至于注释的格式，现在各个大学发布的学位论文规范都有说明。发表时，各个出版社和期刊也有自己的规定，这里就不赘述了。

第八，文献目录。现在学位论文一般要求在论文末尾放文献目录。但是文献目录一定要与脚注相一致，脚注里面出现的目录要有，同时目录有的脚注也得有。

三　几个要点

除了上述八个要素，作者还需要注意以下几点：

第一，术语。写学术论文免不了用到术语。术语是学术界约定俗成的，也是一个学科的基石，其创造和废弃都要慎重；一般来说，研究者要尽量延续传统，使用已有的术语。当然，学术要发展，术语也要更新。在这种情况下，作者需要说明已有术语的不足，以及新术语的优点，以求其他学者接受。过去有些学者喜欢标新立异，随意创造术语，致使术语满天飞，让人无所适从，是不可取的。

第二，为读者的需要而写作。人们在写作学位论文时，为了满足学校制定的论文规范，力求完整。但是在发表时，则需要根据期刊和读者的要求，做些调整。我们知道不同期刊的读者群是不同的，他们对于论文各个方面的熟悉程度有所差异。文科读者对于科技考古所用的方法和仪器不太熟悉，作者需要浓墨重彩地介绍它们；而对于历史背景比较熟悉，作者在这方面需要淡化。理科读者对于实验仪器和实验程序比较熟悉，作者无需详细描述；而对于他们不熟悉的历史背景和考古学背景，则需要充分说明。

第三，抄袭。现在知识产权已经为人们所熟悉，抄袭也成了学者们的禁忌。所谓"抄袭"，就是使用了他人的文字或想法（概念、观点）却没有注明出处，并且导致读者认为这些文字或想法是作者自己的时候，就是抄袭。但是在实践中，仍然存在各式各样的问题。一是忽略了自己，在引用自己以前的论文时，没有做注释；但是抄袭自己也是抄袭。二是喜欢大段抄录他人文字。实际上引用有三种方式：概述、转述、直接引用。在简要引用若干学者的观点时，可以归纳他们的共同之处和相异之处，这就是概述。在较为详细地介绍一个学者的论证过程时，用自己的话复述一遍，这就是转述。两种方式都是学术界常用的引用方法。直接引用就是直接摘录他人文字，需要谨慎使用，一般只能用于以下几种情况：（1）引用他人论述作为原始资料，如《史记》等历史文献的史料；（2）引用权威学者的论述作为论据；（3）引用他人的论述作为自己的批评对象，直接引用以保证不会歪曲原意。

第四，语言。论文之美不在于辞藻，而在于新问题和新发现。所以论文语言要平实而准确，避免使用文学修辞方法如排比、比喻和夸张等。现在一些学者动辄引诗摘赋，抒情释怀，都不是论文应有的。论文也要避免使用口语。

第五，发掘论文价值。写论文的首要目标当时是介绍研究成果；除此之外，学者还要善于发掘此成果的学术价值，讨论学术界关心的大问题或理论。这是因为学术研究也有很多层次，有微观的个案研究，也有宏观的整体研究，还有理论研究。而整体研究和理论研究既能指导个案研究，也需要个案研究做支撑。如果用个案研究来支撑或修正一个大问题或一个理论，那么它就发挥了应有的作用。

四　论文训练

上文可见研究是论文的源头，没有研究，就没有论文。但是有了研究，不一定有论文。这是因为论文写作是一门技能，一位学生需要时常练习才能掌握。在美国，一个学生从高中就开始写论文，进入大学后就经常写论文，因此掌握了查阅文献、收集证据、整理思路和推敲文字的能力；而进入研究生阶段后，一个学期就要写三、四篇论文了。因此，一个研究生到了毕业的时候，就已经是一个写作论文的老手了。但是在我国，一个学生难得写一篇论文，只是在本科和硕士毕业时才有机会写一篇，练习机会少，写作能力自然就不高。因此，研究生需要在三年中多次反复写作论文，以培养自己的写作能力。

五　结语

综上所述，写论文是一个非常复杂的工程。写作一篇论文需要遵循可阅读、可检验、可追溯和可检索四条原则。作者需要明白论文的结构，清楚各个要素即内容提要、关键词、前言、正文、结语、插图和参考文献的功能，写好每个要素。此外，论文还要注意术语的延续性、体悟读者的需要、避免抄袭、使用平实语言和发掘论文价值。所有这些都需要一个研究者接受长期的、反复的论文写作训练。